ISBN 978-0-265-04322-6
PIBN 11034690

1 MONTH OF
FREE
READING

at

www.ForgottenBooks.com

By purchasing this book you are eligible for one month membership to ForgottenBooks.com, giving you unlimited access to our entire collection of over 1,000,000 titles via our web site and mobile apps.

To claim your free month visit:
www.forgottenbooks.com/free1034690

English
Français
Deutsche
Italiano
Español
Português

www.forgottenbooks.com

Mythology Photography **Fiction**
Fishing Christianity **Art** Cooking
Essays Buddhism Freemasonry
Medicine **Biology** Music **Ancient
Egypt** Evolution Carpentry Physics
Dance Geology **Mathematics** Fitness
Shakespeare **Folklore** Yoga Marketing
Confidence Immortality Biographies
Poetry **Psychology** Witchcraft
Electronics Chemistry History **Law**
Accounting **Philosophy** Anthropology
Alchemy Drama Quantum Mechanics
Atheism Sexual Health **Ancient History**
Entrepreneurship Languages Sport
Paleontology Needlework Islam
Metaphysics Investment Archaeology
Parenting Statistics Criminology
Motivational

REPORTS

OF

CASES DECIDED

IN THE

APPELLATE COURT

OF THE

STATE OF INDIANA,

WITH TABLES OF CASES REPORTED AND CITED, TEXT-BOOKS
CITED, STATUTES CITED AND CONSTRUED, AN INDEX
AND NOTES TO THE REPORTED CASES

PHILIP ZOERCHER,
OFFICIAL REPORTER

NORMAN E. PATRICK, Assistant Reporter

VOL. 52

CONTAINING CASES DECIDED AT THE NOVEMBER TERM, 1912,
NOT REPORTED IN VOLUME 51.

INDIANAPOLIS:
WM. B. BURFORD, PRINTER TO THE STATE
1914

CASES REPORTED

A

Adams Brick Co., Osborn v..175
Adams, Southern R. Co. v...322
Ailes v. Miller..............280
Angola R., etc., Co. v. Butz..420
Antioch Baptist Church v.
   Morton..................546

B

Baltimore, etc., R. Co. v. Cin-
   cinnati, etc., R. Co........639
Bank of Advance v. Miller..706
Barber Asphalt Pav. Co. v.
   City of Indianapolis......587
Barnett, Gaskill v..........654
Barton v. Barton...........319
——— v. ———................537
Beach, Knapp v.............573
Beard, Cleveland, etc., R. Co.
   v........................105
———, Columbia Creosoting Co.
   v........................260
Brendel, Grubb v...........531
Brotherhood, etc., v. Corder..214
Bryant, Davis v............343
Butz, Angola R., etc., Co. v...420

C

Camp v. Camp...............250
Campbell v. Maryland Casual-
   ty Co....................228
Carpenter, Northern Assur-
   ance Co. v................432
Caswell-Runyan Co., Mitten
   v........................521
Cheyne Electric Co., Indian-
   apolis Outfitting Co. v.....153
Chicago, etc., R. Co., City of
   Bloomington v............510
———, Newsom v.............577
Cincinnati, etc., R. Co., Balti-
   more, etc., R. Co. v........639
City of Bloomington v. Chi-
   cago, etc., R. Co..........510
City of Indianapolis, Barber
   Asphalt Pav. Co. v.......587
——— v. Ray.................388
Clark, Cleveland, etc., R. Co.
   v........................646

Claycomb, Marion, etc., Con-
   struction Co. v...........681
Cleveland, etc., R. Co. v.
   Beard....................105
——— v. Clark..............646
——— v. Nichols...........349
——— v. Rumsey............371
——— v. Wheeler...........704
——— v. Van Laningham.....156
Cline v. Strong............286
Columbia Creosoting Co. v.
   Beard....................260
Cooley v. Kelley...........687
Corder, Brotherhood, etc., v...214
Corydon Can. Co., Ladoga
   Can. Co. v............... 23
Cottman, Pittsburgh, etc., R.
   Co. v....................661
Craig v. Zent.............. 19
Croan v. Myers............143
Cropper v. Glidewell....... 52

D

Daub, Mortimer v.......... 30
Davis v. Bryant...........343
Dixon v. Thompson.........560
Dougan, Heston v.......... 40
Downey v. National Exchange
   Bank....................672

E

Emmerson, Indianapolis
   Southern R. Co. v........403
Empire State Surety Co., Ma-
   rion, etc., Bed Co. v......480
Espenlaub v. Hedderick.....139

F

Farmers State Bank, Miller
   v........................ 5
Farrell, Michigan, etc., R. Co.
   v........................603
Faylor, Studabaker v.......171
Felts, Griffith v...........268
Ferger, Kreitlein v........199
Fife v. Ohio Investment Co...108
Friedley, Southern R. Co. v..192
Fuller v. Fuller...........488

G

Gaskill v. Barnett...........654
General Convention, etc., v.
Smith....................136
German, etc., Trust Co. v. La-
fayette Box, etc., Co......211
Glidewell, Cropper v........ 52
Great Council, etc., Red Men
v. Green..................198
Green, Great Council, etc.,
Red Men v................198
Griffith v. Felts.............268
Grubb v. Brendel...........531

H

Harmon, Koehler v.........315
Haverkamp, Vandalia Coal
Co. v.....................397
Hedderick, Espenlaub v.....139
Heritage v. Heritage........ 76
Hert, Mascari v.............345
Heston v. Dougan........... 40
Hisey, I. F. Force Handle Co.
v.........................235
Hogshire, Miller v..........706
Holthouse v. Poling.........568
Hubbard v. Ranje...........611
Hunt, Swain v..............628

I

I. F. Force Handle Co. v.
Hisey....................235
Indianapolis Coal Co., Jordan
v.........................542
Indianapolis Outfitting Co. v.
Cheyne Electric Co........153
Indianapolis Southern R. Co.
v. Emmerson..............408

J

Jackson, State, ex rel., v.....254
Johnson, Pittsburgh, etc., R.
Co. v....................457
Jones, Modern Woodmen v...149
Jordan v. Indianapolis Coal
Co........................542

K

Kelley, Cooley v.............687
Knapp v. Beach.............573
Koehler v. Harmon.........315
Kreitlein v. Ferger.........199

L

Ladoga Can. Co. v. Corydon
Can. Co................... 23
Lafayette Box, etc., Co., Ger-
man, etc., Trust Co. v.....211
Lake Erie, etc., R. Co. v. Ma-
rott......................332
——, Town of Cicero v......298
Lake Shore, etc., R. Co. v.
Myers 59
——, Rossiter v............. 88

M

McAdams, Weidenhammer v. 98
McCool, Wagner v..........124
McKinney, Sanitary Can Co.
v.........................379
Maberry, Terre Haute, etc.,
Traction Co. v............114
Manning v. Wilson.......... 1
Marion, etc., Bed Co. v. Em-
pire State Surety Co......480
Marion, etc., Construction Co.
v. Claycomb..............681
Marion, etc., Traction Co.,
Moore-Mansfield, etc., Co.
v.........................548
Marott, Lake Erie, etc., R.
Co. v....................332
Maryland Casualty Co., Camp-
bell v....................228
Mascari v. Hert.............345
Mellette, Miller v..........707
Michigan, etc., R. Co. v. Far-
rell......................603
Miller, Ailes v.............280
—— v. Bank of Advance....706
—— v. Farmers State Bank. 5
—— v. Hogshire............706
—— v. Mellette............707
Miller v. Sharp............. 11
Mitten v. Caswell-Runyan Co.521
Modern Woodmen v. Jones..149
Moore-Mansfield, etc., Co. v.
Marion, etc., Traction Co...548
Morgan, Park v............478
Mortimer v. Daub.......... 30
Morton, Antioch Baptist
Church v................546
Myers, Croan v.............143
——, Lake Shore, etc., R. Co.
v......................... 59

N

National Biscuit Co. v. Wilson......................630

CASES REPORTED.

National Exchange Bank, Downey v..................672
Nave v. Powell.............496
Newsom v. Chicago, etc., R. Co.......................577
——, Thompson v..........444
Nichols, Cleveland, etc., R. Co. v.....................349
Northern Assurance Co. v. Carpenter...................432

O

Ohio Investment Co., Fife v..108
Ohlwine v. Pfaffman........357
Osborn v. Adams Brick Co...175

P

Paine, Tishbein v..........441
Park v. Morgan.............478
Patterson v. Southern R. Co.618
Paul v. Snyder..............291
Penn, etc., Plate Glass Co. v. Poling 492
Pfaffman, Ohlwine v.......357
Pittsburgh, etc., R. Co. v. Cottman.....................661
—— v. Johnson.............457
Poling, Holthouse v..........568
——, Penn, etc., Plate Glass Co. v.....................492
Powell, Nave v.............496

R

Ranje, Hubbard v..........611
Ray, City of Indianapolis v..388
Rossiter v. Lake Shore, etc., R. Co.....................88
Rumsey, Cleveland, etc., R. Co. v.....................371

S

Sanitary Can Co. v. McKinney......................379
Seigmund v. Tyner.........581
Sharp, Miller v............ 11

Smith, General Convention, etc., v....................136
Snyder, Paul v.............291
Southern R. Co. v. Adams...322
—— v. Friedley............192
——, Patterson v............618
—— v. Town of French Lick.447
—— v. Utz.................270
State, ex rel., v. Jackson.....254
Strong, Cline v............286
Studabaker v. Faylor........171
Swain v. Hunt.............626

T

Terre Haute, etc., Traction Co. v. Maberry...............114
Thompson, Dixon v.........560
—— v. Newsom............444
Tishbein v. Paine..........441
Town of Cicero v. Lake Erie, etc., R. Co...............298
Town of French Lick, Southern R. Co. v.............447
Tyner, Seigmund v.........581

U

Utz, Southern R. Co. v.....270

V

Vandalia Coal Co. v. Haverkamp....................397
Van Laningham, Cleveland, etc., R. Co. v.............156

W

Wagner v. McCool..........124
Weidenhammer v. McAdams. 98
Wheeler, Cleveland, etc., R. Co. v.....................704
Wilson, Manning v.......... 1
——, National Biscuit Co. v.630

Z

Zent, Craig v.............. 19

CASES CITED

Abshire v. Williamson, 149
Ind. 248.............348, 445
Adams v. Williams, 125 Ga.
430......................560
Aetna Life Ins. Co. v. Bock-
ting, 39 Ind. App. 586.....439
—— v. McNeely. 166 Ill. 540.104
Ahlendorf v. Barkous, 20 Ind.
App. 657..................344
Alabama, etc., R. Co. v. An-
derson, 109 Ala. 299.......670
Alameda Macadamizing Co.
v. Pringle, 130 Cal. 226....596
Albaugh Bros., etc., Co. v. Ly-
nas, 47 Ind. App. 30...107, 269
Alcorn v. Morgan, 77 Ind. 184.576
Alexander v. Spaulding, 160
Ind. 176..................139
Allen v. Aetna Life Ins. Co.,
145 Fed. 881..........231, 232
—— v. Studebaker Bros.
Mfg. Co., 152 Ind. 406.....209
American Bonding Co. v.
State, ex rel., 40 Ind. App.
569.......................259
American Car, etc., Co. v.
Clark, 32 Ind. App. 644....
...............318, 425, 429
American Cent. Life Ins. Co.
v. Rosenstein, 46 Ind. App.
537.......................152
American Fidelity Co. v. In-
dianapolis, etc., Fuel Co.,
178 Ind. 133..............269
American Mut. Life Ins. Co.
v. Mason, 159 Ind. 15......695
American Trust, etc., Bank v.
Gueder & Paeschke Mfg.
Co., 150 Ill. 336..........678
Anderson v. Anderson, 128
Ind. 254..................651
—— v. Leonard, 51 Ind. App.
14........................150
—— v. Mitchell, 58 Ind. 592..468
Anoka Lumber Co. v. Fidelity,
etc., Co., 63 Minn. 286.....231
Arthur v. Gordon, 37 Fed.
558.......................18
Ashley v. Henderson, 32 Ind.
App. 242..................494
Aspy v. Botkins, 160 Ind. 170.430
Atchinson, etc., R. Co. v. Wad-
dell Bros., 38 Tex. Civ. App.
434.......................560

Atlas Engine Works v. Ran-
dall, 100 Ind. 293.........183
Avery v. Akins, 74 Ind. 283.. 80
Avery Planter Co. v. Peck, 86
Minn. 40..................506
Ayres v. Farmers', etc., Bank,
79 Mo. 421................678

Baddeley v. Patterson, 78 Ind.
157.......................443
Bailey v. Leishman, 32 Utah
123.......................576
Baillie v. Augusta Sav. Bank,
95 Ga. 277................677
Balbach v. Frelingheysen, 15
Fed. 675..................678
Baltimore, etc., R. Co. v.
Board, etc., 156 Ind. 260...311
—— v. Cavanaugh, 35 Ind.
App. 32...................317
—— v. City of Seymour, 154
Ind. 17..............704, 705
—— v. Dickey, 43 Ind. App.
509.......................607
—— v. Freeze, 169 Ind. 370..696
—— v. Hickman, 40 Ind. App.
315.......................414
—— v. North, 103 Ind. 486..
.....................311, 312
—— v. Reed, 50 Ind. App.
220....................... 39
—— v. Rosborough, 40 Ind.
App. 14...............63, 354
Bamberger v. Geiser, 24 Or.
203.......................134
Barber Asphalt Pav. Co. v.
City of Louisville, 123 Ky.
687.......................597
Barfield v. Gleason, 111 Ky.
491.......................596
Barrett v. Cleveland, etc., R.
Co., 48 Ind. App. 668......684
Barry v. Wachosky, 57 Neb.
534.......................560
Bartholomew v. Grimes, 51
Ind. App. 614.........107, 345
Bartlett v. British America
Assur. Co., 35 Wash. 525..
.....................487, 488
Bascom v. Toner, 5 Ind. App.
229.......................206
Bass v. Citizens Trust Co., 32
Ind. App. 583.............693

Bates v. State, ex rel., 75 Ind. 463......................344

Bates Mach. Co. v. Trenton, etc., R. Co., 70 N. J. L. 684.425

Baum v. Palmer, 165 Ind. 513 331

Beaning v. South Bend Electric Co., 45 Ind. App. 261..401

Beard v. Becker, 69 Ind. 498.554

—— v. Lofton, 102 Ind. 408..508

Beardsley v. Knight, 10 Vt. 185...................... 87

Beasley v. Phillips, 20 Ind. App. 182...................466

Beatson v. Bowers, 174 Ind. 601......................151

Beatty v. Miller, 47 Ind. App. 494...................... 7

—— v. O'Connor, 106 Ind. 81 109

Beaver v. Fulp, 136 Ind. 595.644

—— v. Irwin, 6 Ind. App. 285......................528

Bedford, etc., R. Co. v. Rainbolt, 99 Ind. 551.........409

Begein v. Brehm, 123 Ind. 160 203

Beggs v. Edison Electric, etc., Co., 96 Ala. 295...........425

Beitman v. Hopkins, 109 Ind. 177.....................466

Belt R., etc., Co. v. Mann, 107 Ind. 80...................120

Bemis v. Wilder, 100 Mass. 446......................341

Bennett v. Preston, 17 Ind. 291......................321

Benthall v. Seifert, 77 Ind. 302......................659

Bierhaus v. Western Union Tel. Co., 8 Ind. App. 246...697

Bingham v. Kimball, 17 Ind. 396......................282

Bivens v. Newcomb, 2 Ind. *98......................205

Blair-Baker Horse Co. v. First Nat. Bank. 164 Ind. 77....430

Bloomington Mut. Ben. Assn. v. Blue, 120 Ill. 121......225

Blume v. State, 154 Ind. 343.653

Board, etc., v. Gibson, 158 Ind. 471..................580

—— v. Lods, 9 Ind. App. 369 259

—— v. Redifer, 32 Ind. App. 93......................329

—— v. Shipley, 77 Ind. 553, ...13, 443

Bolton v. Richard, 6 Term 139......................679

Bomberger, Wright & Co. v. Griener, 18 Iowa 477......505

Bonesteel v. Van Etten, 20 Hun (N. Y.) 468..........296

Boord v. Boord, 163 Ind. 307. 4

Boseker v. Chamberlain, 160 Ind. 114..................453

Bottles v. Miller, 112 Ind. 584 101

Bottorff v. Wise, 53 Ind. 32.. ....527, 529

Bowen v. Thwing, 56 Minn. 177......................284

Bower v. Thomas, 22 Ind. App. 505..................259

Bowman v. Olrick, 165 Ind. 478...................... 4

Boyd v. City of Milwaukee, 92 Wis. 456.................506

Bozeman v. Cole, 139 Ind. 187 446

Brackney v. Fogle, 156 Ind. 535...................... 39

Bradshaw v. City of Jamestown, 109 N. Y. Supp. 618..597

Brant v. Barnett, 10 Ind. App. 653..................282

Brickley v. Weghorn, 71 Ind. 497......................109

Briggs v. Fleming, 112 Ind. 313......................113

Briscoe v. Brett, 2 Ves. & B. 377......................554

Broadstreet v. Hall, 32 Ind. App. 122..................386

—— v. McKamey, 41 Ind. App. 272..................135

Brooklyn, etc., R. Co. v. Brooklyn City R. Co., 33 Barb. (N. Y.) 420.........644

Brooks v. Pittsburgh, etc., R. Co., 158 Ind. 62...........684

Brotherhood, etc., v. Barton, 46 Ind. App. 160...........366

Brown v. Grepe. 135 Ind. 4.. 79

—— v. Jenks, 98 Cal. 10....596

—— v. Ohio, etc., R. Co., 138 Ind. 648..................190

—— v. Piper, 91 U. S. 37....424

—— v. Russell & Co., 105 Ind. 46...................505, 506

—— v. Underhill, 4 Ind. App. 77......................557

Bryan v. Uland, 101 Ind. 477. 55

Bruner v. Brotherhood, etc., 136 Iowa 612............225

Brunson v. Henry, 140 Ind. 455......................146
Buchanan v. Hubbard, 119 Ind. 187..................697
Buckeye Mfg. Co. v. Woolley, etc., Works, 26 Ind. App. 7......................146
Buehner Chair Co. v. Feulner, 28 Ind. App. 479......425
Bundy v. Cunningham, 107 Ind. 360..................615
Burke v. Mead, 159 Ind. 252. ....287, 425
Burns v. Reigelsberger, 70 Ind. 522..................555
Butler University v. Conard, 94 Ind. 353..............534
Byrum v. Henderson, 151 Ind. 102...................... 55

Cagliostro v. Indelli, 102 N. Y. Supp. 918..............208
Calahan v. Dunker, 51 Ind. App. 436..............366, 536
Caldwell v. Fire Assn., etc., 177 Pa. St. 492..........441
Cal Hirsch & Sons, etc., Co. v. Peru Steel, etc., Co., 50 Ind. App. 59.............. 16
Capital Fire Ins. Co. v. Shearwood, 87 Ark. 326........487
Carder v. Primm, 52 Mo. App. 102......................571
Carger v. Fee, 140 Ind. 572..443
Carr v. Duval, 14 Pet. *77... 16
—— v. Kolb, 99 Ind. 53.....309
Carter v. Aetna Life Ins. Co., 76 Kan. 275..........231, 232
Cartmel v. Newton, 79 Ind. 1 ....16, 18
Case v. Ellis, 9 Ind. App. 274........................694
Catterlin v. City of Frankfort, 87 Ind. 45..................468
—— v. ——, 79 Ind. 547.... ....517, 519
Cavanaugh v. Smith, 84 Ind. 380......................628
Chamberlain v. Waymire, 32 Ind. App. 442.............425
Chamness v. Chamness, 53 Ind. 301..................544
Channon v. Sanford Co., 70 Conn. 573.................634
Chapell v. Shuee, 117 Ind. 481 308
Chapman v. Smith, 16 How. 114......................530

Chesapeake, etc., R. Co. v. Steele, 84 Fed. 93.........166
Chicago City v. Robbins, 2 Black (U. S.) 418.........519
Chicago, etc., R. Co. v. Barnes, 164 Ind. 143.............. 62
—— v. Brannegan, 5 Ind. App. 540...................607
—— v. Derkes, 103 Ind. 520.576
—— v. Dinius, 170 Ind. 222..267
—— v. Fretz, 173 Ind. 519...262
—— v. Hamerick, 50 Ind. App. 425..................426
—— v. Marshall, 38 Ind. App. 217..................629
—— v. Newkirk, 48 Ind. App. 349..................269
—— v. Stephenson, 33 Ind. App. 95..................376
—— v. Stepp, 44 Ind. App. 353......................607
—— v. Turner, 33 Ind. App. 264......................354
—— v. Union Rolling-Mill Co., 109 U. S. 702.........553
—— v. Walton, 165 Ind. 253.150
—— v. Wysor Land Co., 163 Ind. 288..................107
Chicago, etc., Terminal R. Co. v. Whiting, etc., St. R. Co., 139 Ind. 297..............644
Childs v. Wyman, 44 Me. 433.285
Cincinnati, etc., R. Co. v. City of Anderson, 139 Ind. 490..310
—— v. City of Connersville, 170 Ind. 316..............518
—— v. Claire, 6 Ind. App. 390......................518
—— v. Gaines, 104 Ind. 526..119
—— v. Grames, 136 Ind. 39 ....163, 354
—— v. Madden, 134 Ind. 462 184
—— v. Revalee, 17 Ind. App. 657......................410
—— v. Worthington, 30 Ind. App. 663............410, 411
Citizens St. R. Co. v. Lowe, 12 Ind. App. 47.........122
—— v. Reed, 28 Ind. App. 629......................191
City Council, etc., v. Barnett, 149 Ala. 119.............596
City Nat. Bank, etc., v. Burns, 68 Ala. 267.................679
City of Anderson v. Fleming, 160 Ind. 597.........517, 530
City of Chicago v. Keefe, 114 Ill. 222..................414

City of Columbus v. Allen, 40 Ind. App. 257..............124

City of Crawfordsville v. Braden, 130 Ind. 149......424

City of Delphi v. Lowery, 74 Ind. 520............386, 491

City of Elkhart v. Wickwire, 87 Ind. 77.............516

City of Fort Wayne v. Lake Shore, etc., R. Co., 132 Ind. 558................811

City of Franklin v. Harter, 127 Ind. 446.............376

City of Kansas City v. Hanson, 8 Kan. App. 290......597

City of Lafayette v. Wabash R. Co., 28 Ind. App. 497...309

City of Lebanon v. Twiford, 13 Ind. App. 384.........585

City of Logansport v. Jordan, 171 Ind. 121.............270

— v. Kihm, 159 Ind. 68....250

City of Louisville v. Selvage, 106 Ky. 730............596

City of New Albany v. Ray, 3 Ind. App. 321..........152

City of Peru v. Cox, 173 Ind. 241................452

City of Portland v. Atlantic, etc., R. Co., 66 Me. 485....517

City of Seymour v. Jeffersonville, etc., R. Co., 126 Ind. 466.....................311

City of South Bend v. Turner, 156 Ind. 418.........106, 383

City of Terre Haute v. Evansville, etc., R. Co., 149 Ind. 174...............310

City of Valparaiso v. Chicago, etc., R. Co., 123 Ind. 467...
...................310, 311

City of Vincennes v. Spees, 35 Ind. App. 389.........520

— v. Thuis, 28 Ind. App. 523.....................520

City of Warsaw v. Fisher, 24 Ind. App. 46.............39

Clarke v. Pennsylvania Co., 132 Ind. 199.............66

Clear Creek Stone Co. v. Dearmin, 160 Ind. 162........431

Cleveland, etc., R. Co. v. Beard, 52 Ind. App. 105...372

— v. Carey, 33 Ind. App. 275...............71, 267, 652

— v. Clark, 51 Ind. App. 392..............142, 648, 665

— v. Foland, 174 Ind. 411.624

Cleveland, etc., R. Co. v. Hadley, 170 Ind. 204......410, 412

— v. Harrington, 131 Ind. 426................163, 376

— v. Heineman, 46 Ind. App. 388.............241

— v. Huddleston, 21 Ind. App. 621.............585, 658

— v. Ketcham, 133 Ind. 346
.........................277

— v. Lynn, 171 Ind. 589...376

— v. Miles, 162 Ind. 646...
...........63, 64, 66, 69, 414

— v. Miller, 165 Ind. 381..517

— v. Morrey, 172 Ind. 513.241

— v. Newell, 104 Ind. 264. 74

— v. Powers, 173 Ind. 105.580

— v. Starks, 174 Ind. 345..120

— v. Van Laningham, 52 Ind. App. 156............. 66

— v. Van Natta, 44 Ind. App. 608.................607

— v. Wynant, 134 Ind. 681
.........................173

Cline v. Lindsey, 110 Ind. 337
.... 74

Clodfelter v. Hulett, 72 Ind. 137......................282

Close v. Crossland, 47 Minn. 500.....................504

— v. Pittsburgh, etc., R. Co., 150 Ind. 560.........580

Cluggish v. Koons, 15 Ind. App. 599.................173

Clupper v. Clupper, 163 Ind. 418......................338

Clute v. Clute, 197 N. Y. 439.103

Coddington v. Canaday, 157 Ind. 243...............119

Colchen v. Ninde, 120 Ind. 88.469

Cole v. Searfoss, 49 Ind. App. 334..............142, 388, 665

— v. Wade, 16 Ves., Jr., *27.....................702

Coleman v. Floyd, 131 Ind. 330.....................321

Collier v. Rutledge, 136 N. Y. 621.....................297

Collins v. Williams, 21 Ind. App. 227.................430

Colson v. Thompson, 2 Wheat. *336.....................287

Columbia Bank v. Birkett, 174 N. Y. 112.........206, 207

Columbia Creosoting Co. v. Beard, 52 Ind. App. 260....191

Commercial Union Assur. Co. v. State, ex rel., 113 Ind. 331......................219

Conant v. National St. Bank, 121 Ind. 323..........146, 506

Connolly v. Bolster, 187 Mass. 266......................231

Connor v. Woodfill, 126 Ind. 85.....................585, 600

Consolidated Stone Co. v. Summit, 152 Ind. 297......
............262, 280, 417, 683

—— v. Williams, 26 Ind. App. 131..................419

Consolidated Traction Co. v. Scott, 58 N. J. L. 682......414

—— v. Thalheimer, 59 N. J. L. 474................410, 412

Continental Life Ins. Co. v. Houser, 89 Ind. 258......485

—— v. ——, 111 Ind. 266....485

Cooper v. Helsaback, 5 Blackf. 14.................571

County of Macon v. Shores, 97 U. S. 272.............135

County of Northampton v. Geisinger, 1 Lehigh Val. Law Rep. (Pa.) 113.......555

Cowan v. Henika, 19 Ind. App. 40...................253

Crafton v. Mitchell, 134 Ind. 320......................555

Cragle v. Hadley, 99 N. Y. 131......................679

Crane v. Kimmer, 77 Ind. 215 ....79, 80

Crawford v. Lawrence, 154 Ind. 288................545

Creighton v. Hoppis, 99 Ind. 369....................615

Crist v. Wayne, etc., Loan Assn., 151 Ind. 245......348

Crossan v. May, 68 Ind. 242..282

Cummins v. City of Seymour, 79 Ind. 491............309

Custard v. Wigderson, 130 Wis. 412................206

Dantzer v. Indianapolis Union R. Co., 141 Ind. 604......456

Daugherty v. Herzog, 145 Ind. 255..................685

—— v. Payne, 173 Ind. 603..495

—— v. Wheeler, 125 Ind. 421 211

Davidson v. Coon, 125 Ind. 497...................... 87

Davis v. Chicago, etc., R. Co., 159 Fed. 10.............. 69

—— v. Cleveland, etc., R. Co., 140 Ind. 468............585

Davis v. Iverson, 5 S. Dak. 295..................507, 508

—— v. Mercer Lumber Co., 164 Ind. 413.....425, 429, 620

—— v. Reamer, 105 Ind. 318 279

Davison v. Brown, 93 Wis. 85 469

Dawson v. Lawrence, 13 Ohio 543........................ 87

Deadman v. Yanthis, 230 Ill. 243........................536

Delaware, etc., Tel. Co. v. Fiske, 40 Ind. App. 348.30, 580

De Maries v. Jameson, 98 Minn. 453................634

Denney v. State, ex rel., 144 Ind. 503.................173

Dennis Simmons Lumber Co. v. Corey, 140 N. C. 462....575

Deposit Bank, etc., v. Peak, 110 Ky. 579.............284

Diamond Block Coal Co. v. Cuthbertson, 166 Ind. 290.402

Dickerson v. Turner, 12 Ind. 223......................101

Dieckman v. Louisville, etc., Traction Co., 46 Ind. App. 11..................65, 66

Diezi v. G. H. Hammond Co., 156 Ind. 583.............620

Dill v. Marmon, 164 Ind. 507 ....623, 625

Dillard v. Dillard, 97 Va. 434 701

Diven v. Johnson, 117 Ind. 512.....................146

Dobbins v. McNamara, 113 Ind. 54.................628

Doble v. Brown, 20 Ind. App. 12..................446, 447

Doe v. Bevan, 3 M. & S. 353.340

—— v. Carter, 8 T. R. 57.... ....340, 341

—— v. Smith, 1 Ind. *451... 79

Domestic Block Coal Co. v. De Armey, 179 Ind. ——... ....321, 328, 599

Donald v. Kell, 111 Ind. 1...205

Dougherty v. Missouri R. Co., 81 Mo. 325.............410

Douglass v. Keehn, 71 Ind. 97......................544

Douglass Axe Mfg. Co. v. Gardner, 10 Cush. (Mass.) 88......................505

Dugan v. Hollins, 4 Md. Ch. 139....................... 86

Du Souchet v. Dutcher, 113 Ind. 249.................307

Eames v. Home Ins. Co., 4 Otto 621.................218
Eel River R. Co. v. State, ex rel., 143 Ind. 231.........629
Effinger v. Fort Wayne, etc., Traction Co., 175 Ind. 175. ....36, 38
Eggleston v. Wagner, 46 Mich. 610....................... 17
Electrical Accumulator Co. v. Brush Electric Co., 44 Fed. 602.......................553
Eller v. Evans, 128 Ind. 156.. 79
Elliott v. Kansas City, 198 Mo. 593.................173
—— v. ——, 8 Ann. Cas. 658, note.......................173
Ellis v. City of Hammond, 157 Ind. 267............... 74
—— v. Snyder, 83 Kan. 638.103
Ellison v. Branstrator, 45 Ind. App. 307.............365
—— v. Ganiard, 167 Ind. 471 137
Elwood v. McDill, 105 Iowa 437.......................505
Elwood State Bank v. Mock, 40 Ind. App. 685..........383
Emerick v. Miller, 159 Ind. 317........................554
Equitable Trust Co. v. Torphy, 37 Ind. App. 220.......... 28
Eureka Vinegar Co. v. Gazette Printing Co., 35 Fed. 570..424
Evans v. Evans, 105 Ind. 204.453
Evansville, etc., R. Co. v. Berndt, 172 Ind. 697...... ....70, 645, 665
—— v. Griffin, 100 Ind. 221..685
—— v. Marohn, 6 Ind. App. 646..................:.......279, 684
—— v. State, 149 Ind. 276...516
Evansville, etc., Traction Co. v. Evansville Belt R. Co., 44 Ind. App. 155..........645
—— v. Johnson, — Ind. App. —....................168
—— v. Spiegel, 49 Ind. App. 412.......................633
Everett-Ridley-Ragan Co. v. Traders Ins. Co., 121 Ga. 228.................487, 488
Excelsior Pav. Co. v. Leach, 34 Pac. (Cal.) 116........596

Faris v. Hoberg, 134 Ind. 289 685
Farmers Ins. Assn. v. Reavis, 163 Ind. 321.............439
Farnum v. Hefner, 79 Cal. 575.......................341
Faught v. Faught, 98 Ind. 470 526
Faust v. City of Huntington, 91 Ind. 493.............309
Favorite v. Stidham, 84 Ind. 423.......................282
F. C. Austin Mfg. Co. v. Clendenning, 21 Ind. App. 459..505
Federal Cement Tile Co. v. Korff, 50 Ind. App. 608....623
Fehler v. Gosnell, 99 Ky. 380.597
Fenton v. Fidelity, etc., Co., 36 Or. 283...............231
Ferdinand R. Co. v. Bretz, 47 Ind. App. 642.............269
Ferris v. State, 156 Ind. 224.608
Field v. Brown, 146 Ind. 293..556
Finley v. Cathcart, 149 Ind. 470.................83, 84, 525
First Nat. Bank v. Dickson, 6 Dak. 301................678
—— v. Greenville Nat. Bank, 84 Tex. 40................677
—— v. Henry, 156 Ind. 1...617
—— v. First Nat. Bank, 76 Ind. 561..................676
Fischli v. Fischli, 1 Blackf. *360.......................525
Fitzmaurice v. Puterbaugh, 17 Ind. App. 318.............279
Fitzpatrick v. D. M. Osborne & Co., 50 Minn. 261.......505
Fleener v. Driscoll, 97 Ind. 27....................... 82
Flowers v. Poorman, 43 Ind. App. 528.................182
Flutter v. New York, etc., R. Co., 27 Ind. App. 511.....417
Ford v. Postal Tel. Cable Co., 124 Ala. 400.............616
Fort Wayne, etc., Traction Co. v. Miller, 48 Ind. App. 633. ....36, 38
—— v. Roudebush, 173 Ind. 57.......................402
Fort Wayne, etc., R. Co. v. Woodward, 112 Ind. 118...607
Fourth Nat. Bank v. Mayer, 89 Ga. 108................678
Fowler v. Fort Wayne, etc., Traction Co., 45 Ind. App. 441.......................580

Franklin v. Lee, 30 Ind. App. 31......................257
Franklin Nat. Bank v. Whitehead, 149 Ind. 560........112
Frolich v. Cranker, 21 Ohio C. C. 615....,......635, 638
Fromlet v. Poor, 3 Ind. App. 425......................528
Fry v. Hare, 166 Ind. 415....308
Furry v. O'Connor, 1 Ind. App. 573............528, 571

Gaar, Scott & Co. v. Shaffer, 139 Ind. 191..............615
Gascho v. Lennert, 176 Ind. 677......................660
Gavin v. Shuman, 23 Ind. 32 563
Gazlay v. Williams, 147 Fed. 678......................341
Gentry v. Purcell, 84 Ind. 83.528
George v. Robinson, 36 Ind. App. 310..................344
Georgia Home Ins. Co. v. Rosenfield, 95 Fed. 358...486, 488
German Mut. Ins. Co. v. Neiwedde, 11 Ind. App. 624...439
Germania Fire Ins. Co. v. Pitcher, 160 Ind. 392......270
Gibson Electric Co. v. Liverpool, etc., Ins. Co., 159 N. Y. 418...................488
Gilliland v. Jones, 144 Ind. 662......................466
Gilman v. Fultz, 37 Ind. App. 609......................443
Glens Falls Ins. Co. v. Michael, 167 Ind. 659.436, 437, 439
Globe Accident Ins. Co. v. Reid, 19 Ind. App. 203....629
Goble v. Dillon, 86 Ind. 327.. ....527, 529
Goddin v. Neal, 99 Ind. 334..205
Gold v. Pittsburgh, etc., R. Co., 153 Ind. 232.........311
Good v. Elwood Lodge, etc., 160 Ind. 251..............231
Gordon v. Gordon, 96 Ind. 134 13
Gosnell v. City of Louisville, 104 Ky. 201...............596
Gowdy Gas Well, etc., Co. v. Patterson, 29 Ind. App. 261......................321
Graber v. Gault, 103 App. Div. 511................203
Grand Rapids, etc., R. Co. v. Ellison, 117 Ind. 234.....409

Granger v. Adams, 90 Ind. 87 112
Grau v. Grau, 37 Ind. App. 635...................... 28
Green v. American Car, etc., Co., 163 Ind. 135.....317, 385
—— v. Brown, 146 Ind. 1... 81
—— v. Glynn, 71 Ind. 336... ....527, 528
—— v. McGrew, 35 Ind. App. 104.............563, 564
Greenawaldt v. Lake Shore, etc., R. Co., 165 Ind. 219... ....163, 354, 376
Gregory v. Cleveland, etc., R. Co., 112 Ind. 385......120, 620
—— v. Smith, 139 Ind. 48...348
Griffin v. Wallace, 66 Ind. 410..................526, 527
Griffis v. First Nat. Bank, 168 Ind. 546.............. 55
Griffith v. State, 36 Ind. 406.468
Grimes' Execs. v. Harmon, 35 Ind. 198.................137
Grover v. Cavanagh, 40 Ind. App. 340................364
Guenther v. State, 141 Ind. 593......................199

Haack v. Theise, 99 N. Y. Supp. 905.............206, 208
Habig v. Dodge, 127 Ind. 31.. 55
Hadley v. Hadley, 147 Ind. 423..................699, 703
Haines v. Haines, 69 N. J. L. 39........................104
Hall v. City of Lebanon, 31 Ind. App. 265.............455
Hamilton v. DuPre, 111 Ga. 819......................560
Hancock v. Diamond Plate Glass Co., 37 Ind. App. 351.173
Hanover Fire Ins. Co. v. Dole, 20 Ind. App. 333.........439
Harding v. Railway Transfer Co., 80 Minn. 504........635
Harmon v. Foran, 48 Ind. App. 262....166, 242, 375, 383
Harness v. Steel, 159 Ind. 286 430
Harris v. Curtis, 34 Ind. App. 438.......................211
Hartlep v. Cole, 120 Ind. 247.494
Hartwig v. Schiefer, 147 Ind. 64.......................148
Haskell & Barker Car Co. v. Przezdziankowski, 170 Ind. 1..........................625

Haskett v. Maxey, 134 Ind. 182...................... 55

Haughton v. Aetna Life Ins. Co., 165 Ind. 32...........152

Hawkes v. Phillips, 7 Gray (Mass.) 284...............285

Hawley v. Smith, 45 Ind. 183 540

Hay v. Bash, 87 Ind. App. 167........................499

Haymaker v. Schneck, 160 Ind. 443..................347

Haynes, Spencer & Co. v. Erk, 6 Ind. App. 332...........199

Hays v. Carr, 83 Ind. 275....536
—— v. Ford, 55 Ind. 52.....203

Heap v. Parrish, 104 Ind. 36.615

Heaston v. Krieg, 167 Ind. 101 172

Hedrick v. Robbins, 30 Ind. App. 595..................270

Helney v. Lontz, 147 Ind. 417 112

Hembling v. City of Grand Rapids, 99 Mich. 292......395

Hendricks v. Commercial Ins. Co., 8 Johns. (N. Y.) *1...487

Hendrix v. Sampson, 70 Ind. 350........................ 54

Henry v. Frazier, 53 Ind. App. —...................534
—— v. Rowell, 64 N. Y. Supp. 488......................296

Herrick v. Flinn, 146 Ind. 258 344

Heyde v. Sult, 22 Ind. App. 83........................307

Highland Ave., etc., R. Co. v. Birmingham Union R. Co., 93 Ala. 505..............644

Hinshaw v. Security Trust Co., 48 Ind. App. 351......693

Hoadley v. House, 82 Vt. 179.504

Hoard v. Bradbury, 156 Ind. 30........................697

Hoffman v. First Nat. Bank, 46 N. J. L. 604...........678

Hoffman v. Isler, 49 Ind. App. 284................. 29

Hoffmeyer v. State, 37 Ind. App. 526...........318, 425

Holliday v. Anheier, 174 Ind. 729......................150

Holloran v. Midland R. Co., 129 Ind. 274.............494

Hoover v. Sidener, 98 Ind. 290........................505
—— v. Weesner, 147 Ind. 510......................257

Horton v. Erie R. Co., 72 N. Y. Supp. 1018.............644

Hotmire v. O'Brien, 44 Ind. App. 694..................580

Houpt v. Dutton, 170 Ind. 69.499

House v. City of Greensburg, 93 Ind. 533..............455

Houston, etc., R. Co. v. O'Donnell, 90 S. W. (Tex. Civ. App.) 886................. 95
—— v. O'Donnell, 99 Tex. 636 95

Howe v. Lewis, 121 Ind. 110. ....526, 527

Hudelson v. Hudelson, 164 Ind. 694..................490

Hull v. Thoms, 82 Conn. 647.205

Hunt v. Rousmanier, 8 Wheat. *174..............608

Huntley v. Cline, 93 N. C. 458...................... 87

Hurley v. McIver, 119 Ind. 53...................... 4

Hymera Coal Mining Co. v. Mahan, 44 Ind. App. 583...402

Hynds v. Hays, 25 Ind. 31...152

Illinois Cent. R. Co. v. Slater, 129 Ill. 91...............414

Indiana Car Co. v. Parker, 100 Ind. 181..............623

Indiana, etc., Oil Co. v. Grainger, 33 Ind. App. 559.508

Indiana, etc., R. Co. v. Barnhart, 115 Ind. 399......... 35
—— v. Snyder, 140 Ind. 647.623

Indiana Mfg. Co. v. Wells, 31 Ind. App. 460...........425

Indiana R. Co. v. Maurer, 160 Ind. 25.................. 66

Indiana Rolling-Mill Co. v. Livezey, 47 Ind. App. 396..250

Indiana Trust Co. v. International, etc., Assn., 36 Ind. App. 685..................541

Indiana Union Traction Co. v. Benadum, 42 Ind. App. 121 ....365, 366
—— v. Keiter, 175 Ind. 268.. 7
—— v. Myers, 47 Ind. App. 646..................38, 168
—— v. Scribner, 47 Ind. App. 621......................182

Indianapolis, etc., R. Co. v. Hamilton, 44 Ind. 76...... 64

Indianapolis, etc., R. Co. v.
Indianapolis, etc., Transit
Co., 33 Ind. App. 337......312
—— v. Ragan, 171 Ind. 569..580
Indianapolis, etc., Traction
Co. v. Arlington Tel. Co.,
47 Ind. App. 657..........257
—— v. Brennen, 174 Ind. 1..552
—— v. Newby, 45 Ind. App.
540......................119
Indianapolis St. R. Co. v. Bolin, 39 Ind. App. 169......103
—— v. Haverstick, 35 Ind.
App. 281..................652
—— v. Hoffman, 40 Ind. App.
508......................376
—— v. James, 35 Ind. App.
543......................684
—— v. Kane, 169 Ind. 25....625
—— v. Marschke, 166 Ind.
490...................... 38
—— v. Ray, 167 Ind. 236...
.....................424, 607
—— v. Schmidt, 163 Ind. 360
.................267, 607, 652
—— v. Schomberg, 164 Ind.
111......................122
Indianapolis Traction, etc.,
Co. v. Croly, — Ind. App.
—.......................168
—— v. Kidd, 167 Ind. 402.38, 122
—— v. Kinney. 171 Ind. 612.624
—— v. Menze, 173 Ind. 31... 37
—— v. Miller, 40 Ind. App.
403......................383
—— v. Smith, 38 Ind. App.
160..............106, 122, 123
Indianapolis Union R. Co. v.
Neubacher, 16 Ind. App. 21
.....................280, 684
—— v. Ott. 11 Ind. App. 564.383
—— v. Waddington, 169 Ind.
448......................607
Inhabitants of Lowell v. Boston, etc., R. Corp., 23 Pick.
(Mass.) 24................517
Inland Steel Co. v. Smith, 168
Ind. 245..................580
In re Griffin, 33 Ind. App. 153
.........................453
In re Monroe, 114 Fed. 398...207
In re Smith, 73 L. J. 74......702
In re State Bank, 56 Minn.
119......................678
In re Wilkin, 183 N. Y. 104..699
Irvin v. Buckles, 148 Ind. 389
.................79, 81, 84, 85
Isbell v. Stewart, 125 Ind. 112
.... 79

Ittenbach v. Thomas, 48 Ind.
App. 420.................383

Jackson v. Corliss, 7 Johns.
*531.....................341
—— v. Jackson, 149 Ind. 289
.........................259
—— v. Silvernail, 15 Johns.
*278.....................341
—— v. Smith, 120 Ind. 520..309
Jaqua v. Harkins, 40 Ind.
App. 639.................468
Jarboe v. Brown, 39 Ind. 549.209
Jas. H. Love & Co. v. Ross,
Crawford & Graham, 89
Iowa 400.................505
Jeffersonville R. Co. v. Hen-
dricks, 26 Ind. 228.......410
Jenny Electric Mfg. Co. v.
Flannery, 53 Ind. App. —
.................318, 425, 429
Jessup v. Jessup, 7 Ind. App.
573......................321
Johnson v. Culver, 116 Ind.
278.................361, 362
—— v. Johnson, 153 Ind. 60. 55
—— v. Prine, 55 Ind. 351...209
—— v. Tyler, 1 Ind. App. 387
.........................370
—— v. Zimmerman, 42 Ind.
App. 165.................155
Johnston v. Stephenson, 26
Mich. 63................. 18
Joseph v. Wild, 146 Ind. 249..585
Judy v. Jester, 53 Ind. App.
—.......................364
Justice v. Pennsylvania Co.,
130 Ind. 321.............624

Kansas Cent. R. Co. v. Allen,
22 Kan. 285...........94, 95
Karges Furniture Co. v.
Amalgamated, etc., Union,
165 Ind. 421.............490
Kasson v. Noltner, 43 Wis.
646......................134
Keller v. Reynolds, 12 Ind.
App. 383.................666
Kelley v. Houts, 30 Ind. App.
474......................209
Kelly v. Pittsburgh, etc., R.
Co., 28 Ind. App. 457.....584
Kent v. Fullenlove, 38 Ind.
522.................465, 466
Kentucky, etc., Bridge Co. v.
Quinkert, 2 Ind. App. 244
.................409, 410, 412

Keys v. McDowell, 54 Ind.
App. —...................670
King v. State, ex rel., 47 Ind.
App. 595..................269
Klein v. Ninde, 45 Ind. App.
672.......................490
Kleyla v. State, ex rel., 112
Ind. 146..................109
Knauss v. Lake Erie, etc., R.
Co., 29 Ind. App. 216.....409
Knickerbocker Ice Co. v.
Gray, 165 Ind. 140........150
Knight v. McDonald, 37 Ind.
463....................... 80
Knoefel v. Atkins, 40 Ind.
App. 428..............294, 386
Koontz v. Hammond, 21 Ind.
App. 76...................101
Kramer v. Williamson, 135
Ind. 655..................364
Kraus v. Lehman, 170 Ind.
408.......................471
Kreuter v. English Lake Land
Co., 159 Ind. 372.........446
Krum v. Chamberlain, 57 Neb.
220.......................288
Kurtz v. Carr, 105 Ind. 574..526
Kyle v. Kavanagh, 103 Mass.
356....................... 16

Lake Erie, etc., R. Co. v.
Charman, 161 Ind. 95......402
—— v. Fike, 35 Ind. App.
554...................119, 670
—— v. Juday, 19 Ind. App.
436.......................122
—— v. McHenry, 10 Ind.
App. 525.................. 66
—— v. Oland, 49 Ind. App.
494....................... 66
Lake Shore, etc., R. Co. v.
Boyts, 16 Ind. App. 640.... 64
—— v. Myers, 52 Ind. App.
59........................378
Lamborn v. Bell, 18 Colo. 346
.........................425
Lane v. State, ex rel., 27 Ind.
108.......................443
Langley v. Mayhew, 107 Ind.
198......................3, 4
Larrance v. Lewis, 51 Ind.
App. 1....................534
Lathan v. Staten Island R.
Co., 150 Fed. 235.......... 72
Leak v. Thorn, 13 Ind. App.
335.......................443
Lengelsen v. McGregor, 162
Ind. 258.................. 29

Leo Austrain & Co. v. Spring-
er, 94 Mich. 343..........135
Levi v. Hare, 8 Ind. App. 571.321
Lewis v. Albertson, 23 Ind.
App. 147..................545
—— v. Edwards, 44 Ind. 333.209
Lewis Tp. Improv. Co. v.
Royer, 38 Ind. App. 151...
.......................106, 544
Lillie v. Trentman, 130 Ind.
16........................545
Lindsey v. Brawner, 29 Ky.
Law Rep. 1236............597
Lock v. Moulton, 108 Cal. 49. 48
Lockwood v. Lockwood, 56
Conn. 106.................173
Loeb v. Tinkler, 124 Ind. 331.308
Lorings v. Marsh, 6 Wall. 337
.........................608
Louden v. Walpole, 1 Ind.
*319..................206, 208
Louisville, etc., R. Co. v.
Ader, 110 Ind. 376........120
—— v. Argenbright, 98 Ind.
254.......................148
—— v. Berkey, 136 Ind. 181.623
—— v. Bryan, 107 Ind. 51.120
—— v. Creek, 130 Ind. 139.. 27
—— v. Crunk, 119 Ind. 542..410
—— v. Hendricks, 128 Ind.
462.......................608
—— v. Jones, 108 Ind. 551..119
—— v. Kelly, 92 Ind. 371...409
—— v. Krinning, 87 Ind. 351.119
—— v. Lucas, 119 Ind. 583..409
—— v. Miller, 141 Ind. 533..477
—— v. Reynolds, 118 Ind. 170
.... 13
—— v. Snyder, 117 Ind. 435.412
.... 99.
—— v. Summers, 131 Ind. 241
......................27, 684
—— v. Thompson, 107 Ind.
412...................409, 412
—— v. Whitesell, 68 Ind. 297
.........................607
—— v. Williams, 20 Ind.
App. 583..................165
Lowden v. Pennsylvania Co.,
41 Ind. App. 614.......69, 376
Lynch v. Curfman, 65 Minn.
170.......................504

McAfee v. Montgomery, 21
Ind. App. 196.............666
—— v. Reynolds, 130 Ind. 33.211

McAllister v. City of Tacoma, 9 Wash. 272..............596
—— v. Henderson, 134 Ind. 453..................585, 661
McAlpin v. Cassidy, 17 Tex. 449......................616
McCardle v. Barricklow, 68 Ind. 356..................585
McCollum v. Huntington, 51 Ind. 229.................. 28
McCoy v. Kokomo R., etc., Co., 158 Ind. 662..242, 376, 384, 417
McCullough v. Davis, 108 Ind. 292......................615
McFadden v. Schroeder, 9 Ind. App. 49............... 74
McGlynn v. City of Toledo, 22 Ohio C. C. 34..............597
McIntosh v. State, 151 Ind. 251...................... 87
McIntyre v. Orner, 166 Ind. 57......................65, 69
McKee v. Root, 153 Ind. 314..348
McKinney v. Hartman, 143 Ind. 224..................494
McLeod v. Despain, 49 Or. 536 134
McMaster v. New York Life Ins. Co., 183 U. S. 25......436
McNaught v. McClaughry, 42 N. Y. 22..................285
McNaughton v. City of Elkhart, 85 Ind. 384..........515
Madison Tp. v. Dunkle, 114 Ind. 262..................205
Magnuson v. Billings, 152 Ind. 177......................269
Main v. Griffin, 141 N. C. 43..506
Maitland v. Reed, 87 Ind. App. 469.................490
Malott v. Central Trust Co., 168 Ind. 428.........277, 653
Malott v. Hawkins, 159 Ind. 127......................579
Mankin v. Pennsylvania Co., 160 Ind. 447.............608
Manning v. Ancient Order, etc., 86 Ky. 136...........225
Market St. R. Co. v. Central R. Co., 51 Cal. 583.........644
Marsh v. Low, 55 Ind. 271...505
Marshall v. English-American Loan, etc., Co., 127 Ga. 376.206
Martin v. Martin, 118 Ind. 227...................... 47
—— v. Motsinger, 130 Ind. 555......................344
—— v. Wright's Admrs., 13 Wend. *460..............296

Marvin v. Brooks, 94 N. Y. 71 571
Masterson v. Southern R. Co., 170 Ind. 296.............190
Mattox v. Stevens, 140 Ind. 282......................563
Mayor v. Grottendick, 68 Ind. 1......................617
Mayer v. Haggerty, 138 Ind. 628..................466, 470
Medley v. German Alliance Ins. Co., 55 W. Va. 342....486
Memphis, etc., Packet Co. v. McCool, 83 Ind. 392......412
Merom Gravel Road Co. v. Pearson, 33 Ind. App. 174..211
Mershon v. National Ins. Co., 34 Iowa 87.............440
Mesker v. Leonard, 48 Ind. App. 642.............386, 387
Metropolitan Life Ins. Co. v. Johnson, 49 Ind. App. 233..226
—— v. McCormick, 19 Ind. App. 49..................485
Metropolitan Nat. Bank v. Loyd, 90 N. Y. 530....678, 679
Metzger v. Huntington, 139 Ind. 501..............102, 104
Michigan Cent. R. Co. v. Hammond, etc., Electric R. Co., 42 Ind. App. 66......645
Michigan Mut. Life Ins. Co. v. Frankel, 151 Ind. 534..348, 493
Migatz v. Stieglitz, 166 Ind. 361..............210, 290, 344
Miller v. Coulter, 156 Ind. 290......................139
—— v. Farmers State Bank, 52 Ind. App. 5........706, 707
—— v. Fuller, 21 Ind. App. 254......................199
—— v. Noble, 86 Ind. 527... 80
—— v. Powers, 119 Ind. 79..258
Mitchell v. Bain, 142 Ind. 604 659
—— v. Colglazier, 106 Ind. 464......................615
—— v. Friedley, 126 Ind. 545 555
Mississinewa Min. Co. v. Andrews, 28 Ind. App. 496....174
Mize v. Rocky Mountain Bell Tel. Co., 38 Mont. 521...... 94
Modern Woodmen, etc., v. Vincent, 40 Ind. App. 711..439
Moles v. Bird, 11 Mass. *436.285
Monongahela River, etc., Co. v. Hardsaw, 169 Ind. 147..386

Monteith v. Kokomo, etc., Co., 159 Ind. 149..............425

Moore v. Slack, 140 Ind. 38..446

Morehead v. Murray, 31 Ind. 418......................135

Morgan v. Squier, 8 Ind. 511.252

Morgantown Mfg. Co. v. Hicks, 46 Ind. App. 623... 37

Morrice's Case, 6 Coke 12.... 87

Morris v. Ellis, 16 Ind. App. 679......................112

—— v. Harris, 9 Gill (Md.) 19......................... 86

—— v. Morris, 119 Ind. 341.172

Morrison v. Wisconsin, etc., Ins. Co., 59 Wis. 162......225

Moss v. Witness Printing Co., 64 Ind. 125..............152

Mossie v. Cyrus, 61 Or. 17...288

Mozingo v. Ross, 150 Ind. 688 ....102, 103, 104

Mug v. Ostendorf, 49 Ind. App. 71...................309

Muncie Pulp Co. v. Hacker, 37 Ind. App. 194.......... 75

Muncie St. R. Co. v. Maynard, 5 Ind. App. 372.........36, 38

Munson v. Wray, 7 Blackf. 403......................576

Murdock v. Waterman, 145 N. Y. 55......................104

Murphy v. Williamson, 5 Cent. L. J. 116................. 80

National Biscuit Co. v. Wilson, 169 Ind. 442..........631

National Commercial Bank v. Miller & Co., 77 Ala. 168..678

National Gold Bank, etc., Co. v. McDonald, 51 Cal. 64...678

National Surety Co. v. Schneiderman, 49 Ind. App. 139......................487

Needham v. Wright, 140 Ind. 190......................557

Newby v. Rogers, 40 Ind. 9..576

Newcastle Bridge Co. v. Doty, 168 Ind. 259..........184, 660

New England Fire, etc., Ins. Co. v. Robinson, 25 Ind. 536..................218, 219

New v. Jackson, 50 Ind. App. 120......................364

New Jersey, etc., R. Co. v. Tutt, 168 Ind. 205.....658, 659

Newman v. Perrill, 73 Ind. 153......................693

New York, etc., R. Co. v. Callahan, 40 Ind. App. 223.... 63

New York, etc., R. Co. v. Doane, 105 Ind. 92.......469

—— v. Flynn, 41 Ind. App. 501...................... 39

—— v. Forty-Second Street, etc., R. Co., 50 Barb. 309...644

—— v. Leaman, 54 N. J. L. 202...................... 72

Nichols-Shepard Co. v. Rhoadman, 112 Mo. App. 299....506

Nitche v. Earle, 117 Ind. 270.477

Noblesville Foundry, etc., Co. v. Yeaman, 3 Ind. App. 521.307

Noftsger v. Smith, 6 Ind. App. 54......................148

Northcutt v. Buckles, 60 Ind. 577......................693

Northern Assur. Co. v. Grand View Bldg. Assn., 183 U. S. 308......................488

Northwestern, etc., Assn. v. Bodurtha, 23 Ind. App. 121.485

Nowlin v. Whipple, 120 Ind. 596......................660

Null v. Williamson, 166 Ind. 537......................660

Nutter v. Hendricks, 150 Ind. 605......................534

Nysewander v. Lowman, 124 Ind. 584..............362

O'Brien v. Central Iron, etc., Co., 158 Ind. 218......455, 456

O'Connell v. New York, etc., R. Co., 187 Mass. 272......232

Oddie v. National City Bank, 45 N. Y. 735..............679

Oglebay v. Tippecanoe Loan, etc., Co., 41 Ind. App. 481..580

Ohio, etc., R. Co. v. Smith, 5 Ind. App. 36..............199

—— v. Trowbridge, 126 Ind. 391................279, 684

Ohio Farmers Ins. Co. v. Vogel, 166 Ind. 239......438, 439

Oil-Well Supply Co. v. Priddy, 41 Ind. App. 200.......... 39

Old v. Mohler, 122 Ind. 594..338

Old Wayne, etc., Assn. v. McDonough, 164 Ind. 321......695

Olive Sternenberg & Co. v. Sabine, etc., R. Co., 11 Tex. Civ. App. 208............. 93

Oölitic Stone Co. v. Ridge, 169 Ind. 639.........182, 195

Orth v. Orth, 145 Ind. 184...139

Over v. Dehne, 38 Ind. App. 427......................695

—— v. Schiffling, 102 Ind. 191..135

Owen v. Dresback, 154 Ind.
392....................348
Owen School Tp. v. Hay, 107
Ind. 351................443
Owens v. Tague, 3 Ind. App.
245....................282
Owensboro City R. Co. v. Bar-
ber Asphalt Pav. Co., 107
S. W. (Ky.) 244.........597

Palmer v. Chicago, etc., R.
Co., 112 Ind. 250.........120
—— v. Logansport, etc., Grav-
el Road Co., 108 Ind. 137..308
Parish v. Kaspare, 109 Ind.
586...................585, 660
Parry Mfg. Co. v. Eaton, 41
Ind. App. 81.............197
Patterson v. Lanning, 10
Watts (Pa.) 135........86, 87
—— v. Patterson, 13 Johns
*379....................296
Pearcy v. Michigan Mut. Life
Ins. Co., 111 Ind. 59.......370
Peirce v. Oliver, 18 Ind. App.
87.....................624
Pence v. Waugh, 135 Ind. 143
......................22
Penney v. Bryant, 70 Neb. 127
......................500
Pennsylvania Co. v. Ebaugh,
152 Ind. 531.............580
—— v. Frund, 4 Ind. App.
469....................518
—— v. Horton, 132 Ind. 189. 35
—— v. Krick, 47 Ind. 368.... 64
—— v. McCaffrey, 139 Ind.
430.....................69
—— v. Smith, 98 Ind. 42....120
—— v. Witte, 15 Ind. App.
583.....................22
People v. Bloom, 193 N. Y. 1..173
People, ex rel., v. Campbell,
88 Hun 527.............425
—— v. Featherstonhaugh, 172
N. Y. 112..............597
—— v. Maher, 9 N. Y. Supp.
94....................597
—— v. Wemple, 129 N. Y.
543...................425
People's Sav., etc., Assn. v.
Spears, 115 Ind. 297.......527
Peoria, etc., R. Co. v. Attica,
etc., R. Co., 154 Ind. 218..
......................106, 307
Pere Marquette R. Co. v.
Strange, 171 Ind. 160..410, 413
Perkins v. Hayward, 124 Ind.
445...................259, 477

Perry v. Pernet, 165 Ind. 67..545
Peru Heating Co. v. Lenhart,
48 Ind. App. 319.........417
Peter v. Beverly, 10 Pet. *532
......................698
Petree v. Fielder, 3 Ind. App.
127....................199
Petrie v. Ludwig, 41 Ind. App.
310....................579
Philip Zorn Brewing Co. v.
Malott, 151 Ind. 371......808
Pickett v. Toledo, etc., R. Co.,
131 Ind. 562.............585
Pickrell v. Jerauld, 1 Ind.
App. 10.................528
Picot v. Page, 26 Mo. 398.... 87
Pierse v. Bronnenberg, 40 Ind.
App. 662................146
Pigg v. State, 145 Ind. 560..329
Pittsburgh, etc., R. Co. v. Adams, 105 Ind. 151.....184, 266
—— v. Browning, 34 Ind.
App. 90................645
—— v. Burton, 139 Ind. 357. 64
—— v. Carlson, 24 Ind. App.
559...................651
—— v. Collins, 168 Ind. 467.666
—— v. Cozatt, 39 Ind. App.
682....................267
—— v. German Ins. Co., 44
Ind. App. 268............ 63
—— v. Higgs, 165 Ind. 694
....................37, 331
—— v. Johnson, 49 Ind. App.
126..............468, 469, 471
—— v. Lightheiser, 163 Ind.
247....................241
—— v. ——, 168 Ind. 438...417
—— v. Lynch, 43 Ind. App.
177....................354
—— v. Martin, 82 Ind. 476..165
—— v. Moore, 110 Ill. App.
304....................414
—— v. Muncie, etc., Traction
Co., 174 Ind. 167.........645
—— v. Noftsger, 21 Ind. App.
599....................526
—— v. ——, 148 Ind. 101...456
—— v. O'Connor, 171 Ind.
686....................173
—— v. Reed, 44 Ind. App.
635....................386
—— v. Richardson, 40 Ind.
App. 503................411
—— v. Rogers, 45 Ind. App.
230....................241
—— v. Terrell, 177 Ind. 447
....................64, 71

Pittsburgh, etc., R. Co. v. Town of Crown Point, 150 Ind. 536........704, 705, 706
—— v. Wright, 80 Ind. 236..354
Poffenberger v. Blackstone, 57 Ind. 288............... 46
Polley v. Pogue, 38 Ind. App. 678......................209
Porter v. Midland R. Co., 125 Ind. 476...................585
—— v. Millard, 18 Ind. 502..152
—— v. Waltz, 108 Ind. 40...615
Portland v. Bituminous Pav. Co., 33 Or. 307............596
Posey County Fire Assn. v. Hogan, 37 Ind. App. 573...219
Post v. Aetna Ins. Co., 43 Barb. 351·.................218
Postal Tel., etc., Co. v. Chicago, etc., R. Co., 30 Ind. App. 654..................312
Potts v. Whitehead, 23 N. J. Eq. 512.................16, 18
Pyott v. State, 170 Ind. 118..585
Price v. Huddleston, 36 Ind. App. 450.............494, 495
Princeton Coal, etc., Co. v. Lawrence, 176 Ind. 469....402
Princeton Coal, etc., Co. v. Roll, 162 Ind. 115........119
Pritchett v. Sheridan, 29 Ind. App. 81.................. 10
Protection Life Ins. Co. v. Foote, 79 Ill. 361..........226
Prothero v. Citizens St. R. Co., 134 Ind. 431..........409
Pullman's Palace-Car Co. v. Central Transp. Co., 49 Fed. 261......................553
Pulse v. Miller, 81 Ind. 190.. 13
Purviance v. Purviance, 14 Ind. App. 269.............295

Ransdel v. Moore, 153 Ind. 393..................137, 138
Redpath v. Nottingham, 5 Blackf. 267...............148
Reed v. Browning, 130 Ind. 575......................308
Reeves & Co. v. Byers, 155 Ind. 535..................506
Republic Iron, etc., Co. v. Berkes, 162 Ind. 517...35, 403
—— v. Ohler, 161 Ind. 393.. ....183, 184
Reynolds v. Nugent, 25 Ind. 328......................644
—— v. Robinson, 64 N. Y. 589 297

Rhodius v. Johnson, 24 Ind. App. 401..................344
Richardson v. Pate, 93 Ind. 423......................446
Riddle v. Backus, 38 Iowa 81.295
Riggs v. Purcell, 66 N. Y. 193.339
Rink v. Lowry, 38 Ind. App. 132...................... 75
Rittenhouse v. Knoop, 9 Ind. App. 126.................571
Roberts v. Fort Wayne Gas Co., 40 Ind. App. 528.....499
Robertson v. Ford, 164 Ind. 538......................266
—— v. Van Cleave, 129 Ind. 17......................696
Robinson v. Aetna Fire Ins. Co., 135 Ala. 650.........487
—— v. Bank of Winslow, 42 Ind. App. 350.............616
—— v. Skipworth, 23 Ind. 311......................344
Robinson & Co. v. Nipp, 20 Ind. App. 156.............616
Roeder v. Keller, 135 Ind. 692 534
Rogers v. Beach, 115 Ind. 413 536
—— v. Turley, 4 Bibb (Ky.) 355...................... 87
Romona Oölitic Stone Co. v. Shields, 173 Ind. 68......402
Rooker v. Rooker, 75 Ind. 571 139
Rose v. Owen, 37 Ind. App. 125......................446
Ross v. Menefee, 125 Ind. 432.113
—— v. Thompson, 78 Ind. 90.585
—— v. Van Natta, 164 Ind. 557......................308
Rowe v. Beckett, 30 Ind. 154.698
—— v. Rand, 111 Ind. 206..540
Runner v. Scott, 150 Ind. 441 308
Rush v. Foose Mfg. Co., 20 Ind. App. 515.............557
Russ v. Russ, 142 Ind. 471...580
Russell v. Branham, 8 Blackf. 277......................491
—— v. Place, 94 U. S. 606..529
Ryan v. Rhodes, 167 Ind. 121 525

St. John v. Hendrickson, 81 Ind. 350..................361
Salem-Bedford Stone Co. v. O'Brien, 12 Ind. App. 217..608
Sanders v. Frankfort Marine, etc., Co., 72 N. H. 485....232

Sawyers v. Cator, 8 Humph. (Tenn.) *255.............. 87

Saylor v. Union Traction Co., 40 Ind. App. 381..........122

Schmidt v. German Mut. Ins. Co., 4 Ind. App. 340.......224

—— v. Zahrndt, 148 Ind. 447 490

Schrader v. Meyer, 48 Ind. App. 36...............107, 269

Scott v. Cleveland, etc., R. Co., 144 Ind. 125...............321

—— v. Collier, 166 Ind. 644..314

—— v. Smith, 171 Ind. 453..174

Scranton City v. Sturges, 202 Pa. St. 182................597

Seig v. Long, 72 Ind. 18.....199

Seisler v. Smith, 150 Ind. 88..534

Sell v. Keiser, 49 Ind. App. 101.......................308

Sells v. Delgado, 186 Mass. 25 699

Shafer v. Shafer, 129 Ind. 394 4

Shank v. Smith, 157 Ind. 401 ....596, 597

Sharkey v. Evans, 46 Ind. 472 ....527, 528

Shearer v. R. S. Peale & Co., 9 Ind. App. 282...........206

Shelbyville, etc., Turnpike Co. v. Green, 99 Ind. 205.....659

Shepardson v. Gillette, 133 Ind. 125.................321

Sherlock v. Alling, 44 Ind. 184 409

—— v. Louisville, etc., R. Co., 115 Ind. 22...............584

Sherman v. Sherman, 3 Ind. *337......................147

Shields v. State, 149 Ind. 395 37

Shipman v. Keys, 127 Ind. 353 4

Shirk v. Mitchell, 137 Ind. 185 ....506, 595

—— v. Wabash R. Co., 14 Ind. App. 126............. 35

Shoner v. Pennsylvania Co., 130 Ind. 170.............. ....27, 190, 280, 417, 684

Short v. Home Ins. Co., 90 N. Y. 16....................439

Shortle v. Terre Haute, etc., R. Co., 131 Ind. 338.......644

Shoultz v. McPheeters, 79 Ind. 373.......................555

Shroyer v. Pittenger, 31 Ind. App. 158..................443

Shuck v. State, ex rel., 136 Ind. 63....................279

Sidener v. Bible, 43 Ind. 230..112

Siebe v. Heilman, 38 Ind. App. 37.......................294

Singer v. Tormoehlen, 150 Ind. 287.................344

Slaughter v. Detiney, 10 Ind. 103.......................205

Slusser v. Palin, 35 Ind. App. 335.......................446

Smith v. Holloway, 124 Ind. 329....................... 95

—— v. Kidd, 68 N. Y. 130..135

—— v. Miller, 44 Ind. App. 168.......................480

—— v. Molleson, 148 N. Y. 241.......................284

—— v. Pedigo, 145 Ind. 361..558

—— v. Pinnell, 143 Ind. 485. 46

—— v. Pittsburgh, etc., R. Co., 26 Ohio C. C. 44...... 95

—— v. Putnam, 3 Pick. (Mass.) 221................341

—— v. Smith, 8 Blackf. 208 576

Snodgrass v. Meeks, 12 Ind. App. 70................. 4

Souders v. Jeffries, 98 Ind. 31 28

Sorden v. Gatewood, 1 Ind. *107......................205

South Bend, etc., Plow Co. v. Cissne, 35 Ind. App. 373... ....242, 249, 250

—— v. Geidie, 24 Ind. App. 673.......................608

South East, etc., R. Co. v. Evansville, etc., R. Co., 169 Ind. 339.................645

Southern Ind. R. Co. v. Brown, 30 Ind. App. 684..585

—— v. Davis, 32 Ind. App. 569.................329, 652

—— v. Fine, 163 Ind. 617..653

—— v. Harrell, 161 Ind. 689.625

—— v. Martin, 160 Ind. 280.625

—— v. Peyton, 157 Ind. 690.166

Southern R. Co. v. Bullett, 40 Ind. App. 457............329

—— v. De Pauw, 174 Ind. 608.......................182

—— v. Elliott, 170 Ind. 273..607

—— v. Roach, 38 Ind. App. 211.......................106

—— v. Utz, 52 Ind. App. 270 ....27, 417, 684

Speeder Cycle Co. v. Teeter, 18 Ind. App. 474.........250

Spitzmesser v. Spitzmesser, 26 Ind. App. 532.............308
Splawn v. Chew, 60 Tex. 532.225
Stagg v. Compton, 81 Ind. 171 13
Stalcup v. Dixon, 136 Ind. 9..209
Standard Forgings Co. v. Saffel, 176 Ind. 417...........411
Standard Oil Co. v. Bowker, 141 Ind. 12............62, 623
Standley v. Miles & Adams, 36 Miss. 434..............285
—— v. Northwestern, etc., Ins. Co., 95 Ind. 254......485
Stanley's Estate v. Pence, 160 Ind. 636.............253, 254
Stanwood v. Stanwood, 179 Mass. 223.................699
State v. Comer, 157 Ind. 611..557
—— v. Hindman, 159 Ind. 586.......................231
State Bank v. Backus, 160 Ind. 682.................260
State, ex rel., v. Adams, 15 Ind. App. 310.............338
—— v. Central States Bridge Co., 49 Ind. App. 544......155
—— v. District Court, etc., 80 Minn. 293.................597
—— v. Griffin, 16 Ind. App. 555......................112
—— v. Scott, 171 Ind. 349..182
Stauffer v. Linenthal, 29 Ind. App. 305.............218, 443
Steele v. Empson, 142 Ind. 397..................310, 312
—— v. Thalheimer, 74 Ark. 516..........................206
Steers v. Holmes, 79 Mich. 430.......................285
Stenbom v. Brown-Corliss Engine Co., 137 Wis. 564.....232
Stengel v. Boyce, 143 Ind. 642 112
Stephens v. Smith, 27 Ind. App. 507.................344
Stephenson v. Boody, 139 Ind. 60..................... 55
Stevens v. Hays, 8 Ind. 277..536
—— v. Howerton, 49 Ind. App. 151.................307
—— v. Stewart, 28 Ind. App. 378......................151
Stewart v. Terre Haute, etc., R. Co., 103 Ind. 44........693
Stockwell v. Whitehead, 47 Ind. App. 423............. 7
Stone v. Brown, 116 Ind. 78..258
—— v. Stone, 158 Ind. 628..694

Stoy v. Louisville, etc., R. Co., 160 Ind. 144........65, 69, 354
Strohecker v. Housel, 3 Clark (Pa.) *327................ 87
Strong v. Ross, 36 Ind. App. 174.......................580
Strunk v. Pritchett, 27 Ind. App. 582..................456
Stubblefield v. McAuliff, 20 Wash. 442..................104
Stuckman v. Roose, 147 Ind. 402.......................112
Studabaker v. Faylor, 170 Ind. 498.......................173
Studebaker v. Alexander, 179 Ind. ——....................534
Sullivan Mach. Co. v. Breeden, 40 Ind. App. 631.....506
Sun Life Ins. Co. v. United States Fidelity, etc., Co., 130 N. C. 129.............488
Supreme Lodge v. Hutchinson, 6 Ind. App. 399...........224
Supreme Lodge, etc., v. Johnson, 81 Ark. 512...........225
—— v. Schmidt, 98 Ind. 374.224
Supreme Tent, etc., v. Ethridge, 43 Ind. App. 475....580
Swain v. Hardin, 64 Ind. 85..148

Taber v. Zehner, 47 Ind. App. 165.......................253
Tabor v. Missouri Valley R. Co., 46 Mo. 353...........165
Taggart v. Tevanny, 1 Ind. App. 339...................296
Tate v. Hamlin, 149 Ind. 94 ....445, 548
Tayloe v. Merchants' Fire Ins. Co., 9 How. 390......218
Taylor v. Canaday, 155 Ind. 671.......................260
—— v. Williams, 45 Mo. 80..288
Teele v. Bishop of Derry, 168 Mass. 341.................139
Tell City Canning Co. v. Wilbur, 46 Ind. App. 550......580
Temster v. Warner, 137 Ind. 79.......................260
Terre Haute, etc., R. Co. v. Buck, 96 Ind. 346.....410, 412
—— v. Schaefer, 5 Ind. App. 86.......................607
—— v. Sheeks, 155 Ind. 74..326
—— v. State, ex rel., 159 Ind. 438.................554, 555
Teter v. Clayton, 71 Ind. 237. 80
Thacker v. Chicago, etc., R. Co., 159 Ind. 82.......623, 624

Thatcher v. Hayes, 54 Mich. 184...........................571

Thieme & Wagner Brew. Co. v. Kessler, 47 Ind. App. 284 107

Thompson v. Connecticut Mut. Life Ins. Co., 139 Ind. 325..494
—— v. Bowman, 73 U. S. (6 Wall.) 316................102

Thomson-Houston Electric Co. v. Western Electric Co., 65 Fed. 615..................424

Thorp v. Hanes, 107 Ind. 324. 55

Tilly v. Cook County, 103 U. S. 155..................16, 18

Timmonds v. Taylor, 48 Ind. App. 531....................308

Todd v. Crail, 167 Ind. 48...151

Toledo v. McGlynn, 67 Ohio St. 498....................597

Toledo, etc., R. Co. v. Cory, 39 Ind. 218................607
—— v. Pavey, 30 Ind. App. 284........................124

Towles v. McCurdy, 163 Ind. 12....................172, 174

Town of Fredricksburg v. Wilcoxen, 158 Ind. 359....580

Town of Knightstown v. Homer, 36 Ind. App. 139.......544

Town of Rosedale v. Ferguson, 3 Ind. App. 596.......392

Town of Salem v. Walker, 16 Ind. App. 687............. 20

Town of Woodruff Place v. Raschig. 147 Ind. 517......309

Townsend v. Cleveland Fire Proofing Co., 18 Ind. App. 568.......................112

Tracewell v. Farnsley, 104 Ind. 497.................. 74

Traders Ins. Co. v. Cassell, 24 Ind. App. 238............488

Tucker v. Hyatt, 151 Ind. 332.209
—— v. Roach, 139 Ind. 275.. 28

Turner v. City of Indianapolis, 96 Ind. 51.............392

Ullsperger v. Meyer, 217 Ill. 262........................576

Union Mut. Life Ins. Co. v. Buchanan, 100 Ind. 63..... 87

United States Cement Co. v. Cooper, 172 Ind. 599..317, 318

United States Fidelity, etc., Co. v. Ridgley, 70 Neb. 622 ....487, 488

United States Sav., etc., Co. v. Harris, 142 Ind. 226....321

Utterback v. Terhune, 75 Ind. 363....................55, 80

Van Camp v. City of Huntington, 39 Ind. App. 28....526

Vandalia Coal Co. v. Yemm, 175 Ind. 524...387, 398, 401, 408

Van Dyke v. Norfolk, etc., R. Co., 112 Va. 835..........288

Van Natta v. People's St. Railway, etc., 133 Mo. 13..414

Van Sholck v. Niagara Fire Ins. Co., 68 N. Y. 434......440

Venable v. Beauchamp, 3 Dana (Ky.) *321.......... 87

Verdin v. City of St. Louis, 131 Mo. 26................596

Viall v. Genesee Mut. Ins. Co., 19 Barb. (N. Y.) 440......440

Vulcan Iron Works Co. v. Electric, etc., Min. Co., 54 Ind. App. ——......155, 466, 477

Wabash R. Co. v. DeHart, 32 Ind. App. 62..............516

Walling v. Burgess, 122 Ind. 299........................466

Ward v. Pittsburgh, etc., R. Co., 25 Ind. App. 405...... 46

Wasson v. Lamb, 120 Ind. 514 ....678, 679

Watt v. Crawford, 11 Paige 470........................553

Weakley v. Wolf, 148 Ind. 208........................453

Weaver v. Apple, 147 Ind. 304 314

Webster v. Bligh, 50 Ind. App. 56....................107

Wells v. Christian, 165 Ind. 662........................425

Welty v. Indianapolis, etc., R. Co., 105 Ind. 55..........607

Western Assur. Co. v. McAlpin, 23 Ind. App. 220......219

Western, etc., Railroad v. City of Atlanta, 74 Ga. 774.....518

Westfall v. Wait, 165 Ind. 353 174

Wharton v. Stevens, 84 Iowa 107........................586

Whetsel v. Louden, 25 Ind. App. 257.................. 4

Whitcomb v. Whiting, 2 Dougl. *652...............101

White v. Redenbaugh, 41 Ind. App. 580.................536

Wickwire v. Town of Angola, 4 Ind. App. 253..........515

Wilks v. Burns, 60 Md. 64...288
William Laurie Co. v. McCullough, 174 Ind. 477........ 89
Williams v. Cox, 97 Tenn. 555
...........................678
——— v. Frybarger, 9 Ind. App. 558.......................338
——— v. Perkins, 21 Ark. 18..283
Wilson v. Cooper, 95 Fed. 625.508
——— v. Jackson Hill Coal, etc., Co., 48 Ind. App. 150..213
Winder v. Scholey, 83 Ohio St. 204....................138
Winders v. Sperry, 96 Cal. 194.......................283
Wipperman v. Hardy, 17 Ind. App. 142.................282
Wirrick v. Boyles, 45 Ind. App. 698..................150
Wiseman v. Gouldsberry, 45 Ind. App. 677.............580
Wolfe v. McMillan, 117 Ind. 587.......................620
Wood v. Lake Shore, etc., R. Co., 49 Mich. 370..........410

Woodruff v. Imperial Ins. Co., 83 N. Y. 133..............440
Woods v. Matlock, 19 Ind. App. 364...................253
Woolery v. Louisville, etc., R. Co., 107 Ind. 381.......... 75
Wright v. Anderson, 117 Ind. 349.......................526
——— v. Nipple, 92 Ind. 310...
.......................82, 79
Wyatt v. Sweet, 48 Mich. 539.554

Xenia Real Estate Co. v. Macy, 147 Ind. 568........106

Yandes v. Lefavour, 2 Blackf. 371.....................101
Yanthis v. Kemp, 40 Ind. App. 649..................494, 495
Young v. Biehl, 166 Ind. 357. 4
——— v. City of Tacoma, 31 Wash. 153...............596
——— v. Powell, 87 Mo. 128...571

Zink v. Dick, 1 Ind. App. 269.694

STATUTES CITED AND CONSTRUED

Constitution U. S., Art. 4, §1.................................694
1 Fed. Stat. Annot. 559.......................................204
1 Fed. Stat. Annot. 578.......................................204
1 Fed. Stat. Annot. 589.......................................203
1 Fed. Stat. Annot. 679..................................204, 205
Section   249 Burns 1908.....................................554
Section   285 Burns 1908................................212, 213
Section   294 Burns 1908.....................................584
Section   315 Burns 1908.....................................557
Section   338 Burns 1908.....................................554
Section   343 Burns 1908.....................................118
Section   348 Burns 1908.....................................629
Section   368 Burns 1908.....................................337
Section   418 Burns 1908.....................................254
Section   520 Burns 1908.....................................172
Sections 558, 559, 560 Burns 1908............................579
Section   561 Burns 1908.....................................580
Section   573 Burns 1908.....................................683
Section   660 Burns 1908.....................................579
Section   677 Burns 1908.....................................446
Section   679 Burns 1908.....................................493
Section   681 Burns 1908................................446, 547
Section   691 Burns 1908.....................................580
Section   698 Burns 1908.....................................490
Section   1110 Burns 1908.....................................534
Section   1450 Burns 1908................................467, 468
Section   1451 Burns 1908...........................465, 468, 470
Section   1752 Burns 1908..................................... 46
Section   2299 Burns 1908.....................................113
Section   2786 Burns 1908..................................... 2
Section   3017 Burns 1908............................54, 55, 57
Section   4012 Burns 1908.....................................137
Sections 5250-5254 Burns 1908................................515
Section   5431 Burns 1908..................................... 70
Section   7464 Burns 1908.....................................576
Section   7469 Burns 1908.....................................575
Section   7472 Burns 1908................................111, 112
Section   8021 Burns 1908.....................................424
Section   8029 Burns 1908.......................317, 385, 424
Section   8655 Burns 1908................................515, 644
Section   8700 Burns 1908.....................................313
Section   8714 Burns 1908.....................................567
Section   8910 Burns 1908................................450, 452
Section   8911 Burns 1908.....................................452
Section   8916 Burns 1908................................451, 452
Section   8959 Burns 1908.....................................313
Sections 8960-8966 Burns 1908................................515
Section 10233 Burns 1908......................................367
Section 10300 Burns 1908......................................367
Section 10355 Burns 1908......................................563
Section 10380 Burns 1908......................................563
Section 10388 Burns 1908......................................563

Section 10394 Burns 1908.....................................564
Sections 3647-3650 Burns 1901................................454
Section   2644 Burns 1894...........................54, 55, 56, 57
Section   249 R. S. 1881.....................................554
Section   292 R. S. 1881.....................................584
Section   312 R. S. 1881.....................................557
Section   833 R. S. 1881.....................................554
Section   338 R. S. 1881.....................................118
Section   343 R. S. 1881.....................................629
Section   362 R. S. 1881.....................................337
Section   409 R. S. 1881.....................................254
Section   497 R. S. 1881.....................................172
Sections 533, 534, 535 R. S. 1881...........................579
Section   547 R. S. 1881.....................................683
Section   629 R. S. 1881.....................................579
Section   636 R. S. 1881.....................................446
Section   638 R. S. 1881.....................................493
Section   640 R. S. 1881..............................446, 547
Section   650 R. S. 1881.....................................580
Section 1054 R. S. 1881.....................................534
Section 1331 R. S. 1881......................465, 468, 470
Section 1463 R. S. 1881...................................... 46
Section 2269 R. S. 1881...................................... 2
Section 2486 R. S. 1881.............................54, 55, 57
Section 2487 R. S. 1881.........................54, 55, 56, 57
Section 2969 R. S. 1881.....................................137
Sections 3184-3187 R. S. 1881...............................454
Section 4020 R. S. 1881..................................... 70
Section 4905 R. S. 1881.....................................576
Section 4910 R. S. 1881.....................................575
2 R. S. 1876 p. 344... 80
1 R. S. 1852 p. 251.............................54, 55, 56, 57
Acts 1885 p. 124.....................................467, 468
Acts 1889 p. 405.....................................212, 213
Acts 1891 p. 199.....................................563
Acts 1895 p. 74.....................................367
Acts 1895 p. 233.....................................515
Acts 1897 p. 240.....................................111, 112
Acts 1890 p. 131.................................55, 56, 57
Acts 1899 p. 231.........................317, 385, 425
Acts 1901 p. 366.................................563, 564
Acts 1903 p. 49.....................................367
Acts 1903 p. 338.....................................490
Acts 1905 p. 210....................313, 515, 567, 644
Acts 1905 p. 584.....................................113
Acts 1907 p. 617.........................450, 451, 452
Acts 1907 p. 652.....................................580

TEXT-BOOKS CITED

3 Am. and Eng. Ency. Law, 1084..........................225
4 Am. and Eng. Ency. Law 46 ....414, 415
22 Am. and Eng. Ency. Law 1101.........................699
27 Am. and Eng. Ency. Law 205..........................112
7 Am. and Eng. Ency. Law (2d ed.) 131-135........... 16
16 Am. and Eng. Ency. Law (2d ed.) 183..............616
17 Am. and Eng. Ency. Law (2d ed.) 672..............102
19 Am. and Eng. Ency. Law (2d ed.) 300..............101
26 Am. and Eng. Ency. Law (2d ed.) 106..............290
29 Am. and Eng. Ency. Law (2d ed.) 858..............575
30 Am. and Eng. Ency. Law (2d ed.) 197..............505

1 Beach, Contracts §5........643
—— §147...................643
—— §157...................644
2 Black, Judgments §615.....519
1 Brant, Suretyship and Guaranty (3d ed.) §24.........283
Buskirk's Practice 61.......494

1 Clark & Skyles, Agency §92.102
Cooley, Briefs on Ins. 2467..488
9 Cyc. 347..................644
14 Cyc. 421.................555
20 Cyc. 87..................362
23 Cyc. 850.................468
25 Cyc. 1356................101
37 Cyc. 1336................564
38 Cyc. 6...................102
38 Cyc. 101, 102............102
38 Cyc. 104.................103

2 Dillon, Mun. Corp. (2d ed.) §§795, 796................517
2 Dillon, Mun. Corp. (5th ed.) §§789, 790................392

Elliott, App. Proc. §246......494
—— §§345, 346.............209
—— §628...................477
—— §632...................148

Elliott, App. Proc. §§631-652. 74
—— §642................... 74
1 Elliott, Evidence §252......617
Elliott, Insurance (1907 ed.) §177......................488
3 Elliott, Railroads §1092....518
—— §1317.................623
12 Ency. Pl. and Pr. 1033....308
17 Ency. Pl. and Pr. 189.....308
Ewbank's Manual §175......494

Gillett, Indirect and Collat. Ev. §33...................617

Jones, Landlord and Tenant §§464, 466.................339
Joyce, Insurance (1897 ed.) §1397.....................487
—— §1407.................487

1 Labatt, Master and Servant §171......................635
Lewin, Trusts (9th ed.) 689..699
2 Lewis, Eminent Domain (3d ed.) §417.............313

McAdam, Landlord and Tenant (4th ed.) §141.......340
Mechem, Agency §71........102
—— §274.................616
—— §§283, 284............135
Mechem, Sales §1805........504
—— §1807................505
1 Morse, Banks and Banking (3d. ed.) §201...........679

1 Page, Contracts §274.......643
—— §301.................643
1 Page & Jones, Taxation by Assessment §516...........596
2 Perry, Trusts §475........698
—— §505.................699
6 Pomeroy, Eq. Jurisp. §764..288

Sheldon, Subrogation (2d ed.) §§1-3....................112
Story, Agency (9th ed.) §87..616
—— §127...............134, 135

1 Taylor, Landlord and Tenant §408..................341
Thompson, Carriers 200-204...410
1 Thompson, Negligence §10.. 35

2 Thompson, Negligence §1900 35

4 Thompson, Negligence §4065 183

Thornton & Ballard's Practice §639, note 1...............494

Tiedeman, Mun. Corp. §306..517

2 Van Fleet, Former Adjud. §§422-435...................529
—— §572.......................530

2 Washburn, Real Prop. (5th ed.) 553..................699
—— 554................699, 700

Wharton, Negligence (2d ed.) §804.......................165

3 Wigmore, Evidence §1919.. 49
—— §2192..................173
—— §2196..................173

4 Wigmore, Evidence §2320..173
—— §2386..................173
—— §2391..................174

1 Wood, Fire Ins. (2d ed.) §176.......................438

2 Wood, Fire Ins. 1163......440

Wood, Landlord and Tenant (2d ed.) 714..............341

Wood, Limitations (2d ed.) §120.....................296

2 Wood, Railway Law 1178..409
—— 1125..................410

Woollen, Spec. Proc. §1034... 47

2 Works' Practice §1088.....404

JUDGES

OF THE

APPELLATE COURT

OF THE

STATE OF INDIANA,

WHOSE OPINIONS ARE CONTAINED IN THIS VOLUME.

———

Hon. JOSEPH G. IBACH.*¶
Hon. DAVID A. MYERS.‡†
Hon. MILTON B. HOTTEL.¶
Hon. ANDREW A. ADAMS.¶
Hon. EDWARD W. FELT.¶
Hon. MOSES B. LAIRY.¶
Hon. JOSEPH H. SHEA.**
Hon. FRANK S. ROBY.§

*Chief Justice at November Term, 1912.
‡Presiding Judge at November Term, 1912.
§Appointed March 21, 1901; elected in 1902 and 1906.
†Appointed October 18, 1904; elected in 1904 and 1908.
¶Elected in 1910.
**Elected in 1912.

OFFICERS

APPELLATE COURT

ATTORNEY-GENERAL,
THOMAS M. HONAN

REPORTER,
PHILIP ZOERCHER

CLERK,
J. FRED FRANCE

SHERIFF,
HARRY W. PEMBERTON

LIBRARIAN,
W. CARY CARSON

CASES DECIDED

IN THE

APPELLATE COURT

OF THE

STATE OF INDIANA,

AT INDIANAPOLIS, NOVEMBER TERM, 1912, IN THE
NINETY-SEVENTH YEAR OF THE STATE.

MANNING *v.* WILSON, EXECUTOR.

[No. 8,338. Filed December 19, 1912.]

1. WILLS.—*Election by Widow.—Effect.—Right to Statutory Allowance.*—Where a husband has made specific testamentary provision for his widow, more valuable or more acceptable than that which the law gives her, and has disposed of the remainder of his estate in such a manner as to evince a clear intention to limit the interest of his widow to the provision so made for her, and she elects to take under the will, she will be bound by such election and can not claim the $500 allowance provided by §2786 Burns 1908, §2269 R. S. 1881. p. 3.

2. WILLS.—*Election by   idow.—Statutory Allowance.—Intention of Testator.*—The intention of a testator, that a specific testamentary provision for his widow shall be in lieu of her rights under the statute, need not be declared in so many words, but may be deduced or implied, when the enforcement of the widow's claim under the law would be plainly inconsistent with the will. p. 4.

3. WILLS.—*Intention of Testator.—Provision for Widow.—Statutory Allowance.*—Whether a testator intended that a specific testamentary provision for his widow should be in lieu of her rights under the statute, so that an election to take under the will would deprive her of the $500 allowance provided by §2786 Burns 1908, §2269 R. S. 1881, must be gathered from the testament itself, and the fact that the estate is solvent, and that land devised to testator's children had been sold prior to the widow's action to recover such statutory allowance, cannot be considered. p. 5.

From Jay Circuit Court; *James J. Moran*, Judge.

Action by Catherine Manning against David S. Wilson, executor of the last will and testament of William Manning, deceased. From a judgment for defendant, the plaintiff appeals. *Affirmed.*

William A. Thompson and *R. W. Sprague,* for appellant. *S. A. D. Whipple & Son,* for appellee.

ADAMS, J.—Appellant, as the widow of William Manning, brought this action against appellee, as executor of the last will of said Manning, to recover the statutory allowance of $500, provided by §2786 Burns 1908, §2269 R. S. 1881. On request, the court made a special finding of facts, and stated conclusions of law thereon. Judgment in favor of appellee on the conclusion of law.

The facts found by the court, in so far as they affect this appeal, may be summarized as follows: William Manning died testate on August 30, 1910. His last will and testament was duly admitted to probate by the Jay Circuit Court on September 5, 1910, and on said day appellee was appointed executor of said will. William Manning left surviving him, appellant, who was a childless second wife, and four children. He left an estate, consisting of real estate and personal property including certain notes. His real estate was of the probable value of $10,000. By the will of her husband, appellant was given all the household furniture, except certain items specifically bequeathed to the testator's children. She was also given certain real estate in the city of Dunkirk, on which there was a brick building. The balance of the real estate owned by decedent was devised to his four children in equal shares. The real estate so devised was subsequently sold by a commissioner, in an action for partition among said children, for the sum of $6,800. The personal property of decedent, not specifically bequeathed, consisted of twenty-one promissory notes of $10 each, and one check for $10, all of the appraised value of $188, and given for real estate sold by decedent after the execution of the will.

The court also found that $175 will be required to pay and discharge the court costs and attorneys' fees in the settlement of testator's estate. On the facts found, the court stated, as its conclusions of law, that appellant, by electing to take under the will, and declining to take under the law, waived her right to the statutory allowance of $500; that she take nothing by her complaint, and that appellee recover his costs.

It is apparent that but one question is presented for determination: Did appellant, under the facts found by the court, waive her right to the statutory allowance of $500, by electing to take the provision made for her by the will of her deceased husband?

It will be noted from the finding that the testator made a testamentary disposition of his entire estate, except certain notes, appraised at $188, a sum little more than the amount which the court finds will be required to pay the costs of administration. The real estate devised by the will is found to be of the probable value of $10,000. The part devised to testator's children sold for $6,800, and it follows that the part devised to appellant was worth approximately $3,200. This is a larger sum than she would have received by taking under the law the share of a childless second wife.

The general rule of construction prior to the decision in the case of *Langley* v. *Mayhew* (1886), 107 Ind. 198, 6 N. E. 317, 8 N. E. 157, was that a husband had no power to make a testamentary disposition of his property which the 1. law casts upon his widow, or to deprive her of her absolute allowance of $500, given by statute. The later cases, however, have very greatly relaxed this rule, and it is now uniformly held that where the husband has made specific testamentary provision for his widow, more valuable or more acceptable than that which the law gives her, and has disposed of the remainder of his estate in such a manner as to evince a clear intention to limit the interest of his widow to the provision so made for her, and she elects to take under the will, she will be bound by her election, and cannot be heard to claim in addition the $500 allowed by statute, when the allowance of such claim would defeat the manifest purpose of the testator. *Langley* v. *Mayhew, supra; Hurley* v. *McIver* (1889), 119 Ind. 53, 54, 21 N. E. 325; *Shipman* v. *Keys* (1891), 127 Ind. 353, 356, 26 N. E. 896; *Shafer* v. *Shafer* (1892), 129 Ind. 394, 395, 28 N. E. 867; *Boord* v. *Boord* (1904), 163 Ind. 307, 309, 71 N. E. 891; *Bowman* v. *Olrick* (1905), 165 Ind. 478, 482, 75 N. E. 820; *Young* v. *Biehl* (1906), 166 Ind. 357, 359, 77 N. E. 406; *Snodgrass* v. *Meeks* (1895), 12 Ind. App. 70, 73, 38 N. E. 833; *Whetsel* v. *Louden* (1900), 25 Ind. App. 257, 261, 57 N. E. 952.

In *Boord* v. *Boord, supra,* the court said: "While it is true that a testator has no power to deprive his widow of the $500 allowed by statute, or of any other right conferred by law, yet if, in making a testamentary disposition of all his property, he makes for her another provision more valuable, or more acceptable, which is clearly intended to be in lieu of her legal rights, and the widow accepts such provision, such acceptance is held to be a confirmation of such testamentary disposition, and a waiver of her rights under the law."

In *Bowman* v. *Olrick, supra,* the court said: "This intention of the testator need not be declared in so many words, but may be deduced or implied when the en-
2. forcement of the widow's claim under the law would be plainly inconsistent with the will."

In *Hurley* v. *McIver, supra,* the court said: "Where a husband has made specific provision for his widow, and has also disposed of all his other property in such a way as to make it apparent that the assertion by the widow of the right to take both under the law and under the will would defeat the manifest purpose of the testator, she will be confined to the provision made by the will, after she has effectually elected to take the benefits so provided."

As we have seen, appellant in this case elected to take under the will, which made more generous provision for her than that provided by law. The remainder of testator's estate was specifically devised to his children, leaving practically no part of his estate undisposed of, out of which the $500 could be made. The enforcement of appellant's claim,

        under the statute, would require a surrender to her

3.   by testator's children of a part of the estate devised

        to them, thus defeating the clear intent of the will.

The fact that the estate was solvent, and that the land devised to testator's children had been sold prior to the bringing of this action, cannot be considered in determining the intention of the testator. That intention must be gathered from the testament itself.

The trial court did not err in stating its conclusion of law on the facts found.

Judgment affirmed.

NOTE.—Reported in 100 N. E. 106. See, also, under (1) 40 Cyc. 1987; (2) 40 Cyc. 1959, 1963; (3) 40 Cyc. 1959. As to when a widow is by a will required to elect between its benefits and her right to dower, or in the community property, see 92 Am. St. 695. On the question of the election by a widow between provisions of will and other rights, see 18 L. R. A. (N. S.) 272.

MILLER v. FARMERS STATE BANK.

[No. 7,715. Filed December 20, 1912.]

1. PRINCIPAL AND AGENT.—*Execution of Notes.*—*Authority of Agent.* —*Determination.*—In an action against defendant as surety on a promissory note, where it was claimed by plaintiff that defendant's name was signed by defendant's son, pursuant to a general authority, the question of such general authority was a question of fact to be determined from a preponderance of all the evidence. p. 7.

2. APPEAL. — *Review.* — *Findings.* — *Presumptions.* — *Evidence.*— On appeal all presumptions will be indulged in favor of the finding of the trial court, and if there is any evidence in the record to support the judgment, the same must be upheld. p. 7.

3. PRINCIPAL AND AGENT. — *Execution of Notes.* — *Authority of Agent.*—*Evidence.*—*Sufficiency.*—In an action on a note, on the

theory that defendant's name was signed as surety by his son pursuant to a general authority, evidence that defendant and his son transacted business in partnership for many years, that they owned a farm as tenants in common which the son later occupied in the business of buying and selling live stock and in which business he often had use for large sums of money, that the son was a man of standing in the community, that the personal relation of defendant with his son was most cordial, together with positive testimony that eight or nine years before the execution of the note sued on, defendant had given his son authority to use his name as surety on notes, and that notes thus signed by the son at different times thereafter, were, after the son's death, recognized by defendant as binding obligations on himself, was sufficient to show a general authority in the son to sign defendant's name so as to render him liable as surety on the note sued on, notwithstanding defendant's denial of having given authority to sign that particular note. p. 8.

4. EVIDENCE.—*Self-disserving Statements of Party.—Nature.*—Self-disserving statements by defendant admitting his liability on notes to which his name was signed by his son, and his son's authority to thus sign his name, made by defendant when it was incumbent on him to speak the truth, are not in the nature of impeaching evidence, for which a foundation must be laid, but, in addition to being evidence that the admissions were made, constitute evidence of the facts admitted. p. 10.

5. PRINCIPAL AND AGENT.—*Declarations of Agent.—Res Gestae.*—In an action against defendant on a note to which his name had been signed by his son, since deceased, evidence of declarations made by the son at the time of the execution of the note, but in defendant's absence, relative to his authority to sign his father's name, was admissible as part of the *res gestae*, when properly limited in its effect so as not to bind defendant on the question of such authority. p. 10.

6. BILLS AND NOTES.—*Note Executed by Agent.—Evidence.*—In an action on a promissory note to which defendant's name had been signed by his son, where there was evidence that defendant had given his son general authority to use his name on notes, the introduction of the note in evidence was not erroneous. p. 11.

From Boone Circuit Court; *James B. Kent,* Special Judge.

Action by the Farmers State Bank against Matthew G. Miller. From a judgment for plaintiff, the defendant appeals. *Affirmed.*

B. F. Ratcliff and *Higgins & Rogers,* for appellant.
Terhune & Adney, for appellee.

ADAMS, J.—Suit by appellee against appellant alone on a promissory note for $1,300, payable to appellee, bearing the names of Joseph S. Miller and appellant, Matthew G. Miller. Issue of fact was formed on the complaint by plea of *non est factum.* Trial by the court, finding and judgment for appellee.

The error assigned and relied on for reversal is that the court erred in overruling appellant's motion for a new trial. The question presented for determination by the record and briefs relates to the execution of the note. It is not contended by appellee that appellant actually signed his name to the note in suit, or specifically authorized the signing of the same. It is, however, insisted by appellee that, prior to the date of the note, appellant had given to his son, Joseph S. Miller, general authority to sign his (appellant's) name to notes as surety for said son, and that appellant's name to the note in suit was signed by Joseph S. Miller, pursuant to such general authority. If Joseph S. Miller, at the time he executed the note sued on, had general authority to sign his father's name as surety on his paper, then the

1. judgment is clearly right. Whether the son had such general authority was a question of fact for the trial court, to be determined, like any other fact in the case, from a preponderance of all the evidence. On appeal, all presumptions will be indulged in favor of the finding of

2. the trial court. In examining the evidence, we are limited to such evidence as supports or tends to support the judgment; and if there is any evidence in the record supporting the judgment, the same must be upheld. *Stockwell* v. *Whitehead* (1911), 47 Ind. App. 423, 432, 94 N. E. 736; *Beatty* v. *Miller* (1911), 47 Ind. App. 494, 496, 94 N. E. 897; *Indiana Union Traction Co.* v. *Keiter* (1911), 175 Ind. 268, 274, 92 N. E. 982.

It is shown by the testimony that Joseph S. Miller was the only living son of appellant, and for many years, after reaching manhood, both before and after his mar-
3.   riage, he lived with his father, and they were partners in farming, and in buying and selling live stock; that they bought a farm in the neighborhood, and held the same as tenants in common; that subsequently Joseph moved on this farm, at which time he and his father divided their business, Joseph continuing to buy and sell live stock. In the carrying on of this business, from time to time he had use for large sums of money. It is also shown by clear inference that Joseph S. Miller was a man of standing in the community. He was twice the president of the county agricultural society, and at the time of his death was its vice-president. He had been sheriff of Boone county, and was a member of the county council when he died. He is shown to have had his father's entire confidence, and their personal relations were most cordial.

Joseph S. Miller died April 1, 1909, and soon thereafter it developed that many notes were outstanding, which Joseph had given and to which he had signed his father's name as surety. Within a few days after the death of his son, appellant, by agreement, permitted judgment to be taken against him on several of these notes, some of which were not due. To other holders of notes, signed by his son in the same manner, appellant recognized his obligations, and declared his intention to pay, but when it was disclosed that notes aggregating approximately $30,000 were outstanding, appellant "agreed" not to pay. To Samuel W. Ailes, who went to see appellant two days after the funeral of Joseph S. Miller, for the purpose of securing appellant's signature to a note as promised by his son, appellant said: "If Joe had signed my name, it would have been all right. You will remember he used it at the Bank of Advance. Milton Smith came to see me with a note. Milt had a note for a thousand dollars, and I told him it was all right. I told him I gave Joe the privilege to use my name.''

Again, in the examination of the witness, Ailes, the record shows the following question and answer: "Q. I will ask you in that conversation you had with Mr. Miller, what, if anything, Mr. Miller said as to his intention to pay these debts, or what did he say on the subject? A. I think it was when he referred to Smith coming out to see him about his note, and he said 'I thought when Smith was here—I thought after that I would see Joe, and see something about his business'; and he said 'I just neglected it, and did not do it, and I did not know how much he was in debt'. 'But', he said 'I am going to pay it, it haint right that anybody else should pay it, and I am going to see that everybody is paid.' ''

From the evidence of Hiram P. Stephens, the holder of a note executed in the same manner, the record shows the following questions and answers: "Q. What, if anything, did he say about his intention to pay these claims? A. He said 'I had intended to pay these claims, but agreed not to pay them, and I will have to turn you down with the rest.' Q. What, if anything, in that conversation, did he say about his intention to pay this note? A. He said he intended to pay all of them; he said it would break him up, but if he paid the creditors they would get it, and if it went the other way the lawyers would get it, and he would have to be buried in poverty and disgrace. Q. In that conversation, did he say anything about having given Joseph authority to use his name as security? A. Yes, sir. Q. Did he or did he not say he had given Joseph authority to use his name as security? A. Yes, sir, he said about eight or nine years ago.''

At the trial appellant testified in his own behalf. He denied that he had signed the note in suit, or had directed his son to sign it for him. An examination of appellant's evidence, however, fails to disclose that he denied giving his son general authority to use his name on notes for borrowed money. It does not appear that he was asked the question. As the theory of general authority was the one on which appellee predicated its right to recover, the failure of appellant to make any declaration on the subject is at least significant. There was positive testimony before the court that, eight or nine years before, appellant had given his son authority to use his name as surety on notes. Without any denial on his part, this testimony stands uncontradicted, and must be taken as an implied admission.

This court in *Pritchett* v. *Sheridan* (1902), 29 Ind. App. 81, 84, 63 N. E. 865, said: "Such admissions constituted evidence not merely of the making of the admissions themselves, but also of the facts admitted; that is,

4.   that the note represented a valid indebtedness. Such self-disserving statements and conduct of a party to the action, when it was incumbent upon him to speak, and to tell the truth, were not in the nature of impeaching evidence, for which a foundation must be laid, but may properly have been regarded by the trial judge as more truly representing the actual facts in the case than his later testimony to the contrary."

One of the grounds of the motion for a new trial was that the court erred in permitting proof to be made of certain declarations of Joseph S. Miller, in the absence of ap-

5.   pellant, relative to his authority to sign his father's name. The ruling of the court, as shown by the record, was in these words: "The evidence is not competent and will not be considered on the question as to whether or not Joseph Miller had authority from his father, Matthew G. Miller, to sign his name to the note. It is admitted as a verbal fact, and because it may tend to throw light upon the isolated transaction sought to be proved, and to illustrate that transaction. Thus limiting the testimony, the objection will be overruled." The evidence complained of being

offered and received simply as a part of the *res gestae,* and not for the purpose of binding appellant by the declarations of his son, made in his absence, the same was competent, within the limitation fixed by the court.

Further complaint is made that the court erred in permitting the introduction of the note in evidence. This cause

6. for a new trial embraces essentially the determination of the whole case, and what we have already said clearly presages our position on this specification. It may, however, be said, in addition, that there was some evidence before the court, at the time the note was offered, showing that appellant had given his son general authority to use his name on notes.

There was no error in overruling the motion for a new trial. The judgment is affirmed.

NOTE.—Reported in 100 N. E. 119. See, also, under (1) 31 Cyc. 1674; (2) 3 Cyc. 360; (3) 31 Cyc. 1667; (4) 16 Cyc. 1217; (5) 16 Cyc. 1006. As to what is admissible as part of the *res gestae.* see note to *Hinchcliffe* v. *Koontz* (Ind.), 16 Am. St. 407; 95 Am. Dec. 51. As to the admissibility in evidence of the acts and declarations of agents, see 131 Am. St. 306.

MILLER ET AL. *v.* SHARP.

[No. 7,776. Filed December 20, 1912.]

1. CONTRACTS.—*Action.*—*Contract Partly in Writing.*—*Parol Contract.*—Where a written contract is relied on, the entire contract must be in writing, since a contract, partly in writing and partly in parol, is deemed in law a parol contract. p. 13.

2. CONTRACTS.—*Elements.*—*Meeting of Minds.*—To constitute a contract, there must be a meeting of the minds of the parties on one and the same thing. p. 16.

3. SALES.—*Contracts.*—*Offer.*—*Acceptance.*—Where defendant, by letter to plaintiffs, indicated a desire to sell his corn, both old and new, and asked for prices on both, and plaintiffs replied by stating that they understood that he wanted to sell both the new and old corn, stating the prices that they could give for each kind, based on the day's bid, and requesting an acceptance by return mail, and defendant, instead of accepting by return mail,

replied the following day that he would sell the corn on the home farm at the price offered, but that as to the old corn he would like a little more, no valid contract of sale was thereby created, since defendant's acceptance, not being in accordance with the offer, was at most only a partial acceptance of plaintiff's proposition, and not binding upon either party. pp. 16, 18.

4. CONTRACTS.—*Acceptance.*—*Scope.*—The acceptance of a proposal, to constitute a contract, must be as broad as the proposal itself, and exactly meet its terms. p. 17.

From Clinton Circuit Court; *Joseph Combs,* Judge.

Action by Bert Miller and another against Noah B. Sharp. From a judgment for defendant, the plaintiffs appeal. *Affirmed.*

George M. Smith and *Sheridan & Gruber,* for appellants.
Joseph Claybaugh, Thomas M. Ryan and *James V. Kent,* for appellee.

HOTTEL, J.—This is an action for damages alleged to have been sustained by appellants on account of the breach of a contract for the delivery of corn.

The complaint is in two paragraphs a demurrer to each of which was sustained. Appellants refused to plead further and judgment was rendered against them that they take nothing by their suit and that appellee recover his costs. From this judgment appellants appeal.

The errors relied on for reversal are as follows: (1) The court erred in sustaining the demurrer of appellee to the first paragraph of appellants' amended complaint; (2) the court erred in sustaining the demurrer of appellee to the second paragraph of appellants' amended complaint. Each paragraph is based on three separate letters, which taken together are relied on by appellants as forming the contract between them and appellee, for the breach of which this action was brought, and each paragraph avers, in substance, that appellants are copartners, owning and operating a grain elevator in the town of Flora, Indiana, and "engaged in the business of buying grain at said town from farmers and other owners thereof to be delivered at their said elevator at said town of Flora where it was their custom to receive the same.'' The other averments of the complaint and the difference in the theory of the two paragraphs need not be considered or taken into account for the purposes of determining the question here presented. This is so because each paragraph of the complaint is based on the same letters, and must proceed on the theory that the contract is wholly in writing. If verbal it would be void under the statute of frauds, and this fact appearing on the face of each paragraph, it would follow that no cause of action is stated in either. And where a written contract is relied on, the entire contract must be in writing, because if it is partly in writing and partly parol, it will be deemed to be, in law, a parol contract. *Louisville, etc., R. Co.* v. *Reynolds* (1889), 118 Ind. 170, 172, 20 N. E. 711; *Board, etc.,* v. *Shipley* (1881), 77 Ind. 553, 555; *Pulse* v. *Miller* (1881), 81 Ind. 190, 191; *Stagg* v. *Compton* (1881), 81 Ind. 171; *Gordon* v. *Gordon* (1884), 96 Ind. 134.

In fact, as we understand their brief, appellants recognize the law to be as above stated, their contention being that the three letters, made a part of each paragraph of complaint, when taken together, are of themselves sufficient to constitute a written contract between the parties. This being true, the only question to be determined is whether the three letters referred to are sufficient to constitute such contract.

We set out these letters in full. According to the averments of the complaint, the first letter was written by appellee after a conversation held between him and appellant Bert Miller over the telephone, and is as follows:

"Frankfort, Ind. August 3, 1909.
Mr. Burt Miller,
  Flora, Ind.
Dear Sir
  Will write you one cannot talk on phone what they would like always to say what can you engage new corn at delivered in Dec. I may sell mine So if you are not

to buisy drop me a letter this afternoon and Say what
Price you will give for the new and what is the Best
for the old corn 1 want to clean up ever thing this fall
get all the money 1 can and have a good time Spending
it and the Oats if you can See yourself out would like
if you would make it 35 although they are yours at the
Price named on the Phone do the Best for me as you
allways have and I will Stay with you let me know and
I may come over this afternoon

N. B. Sharp."

It is averred that this letter was received by appellants
the day it was written, and Mr. Miller, on behalf of himself and his coappellant, answered it on the day it was received, as follows:

"Flora, Ind. Aug 3, 1909.

Mr. N. B. Sharp,
  Frankfort, Ind.
Sir
    Yours at hand and note you say you want to sell
your corn new and old this market is lower all around
for everything. Could give you 45 cts. pr bu for your
new and 94 cts. pr hundred For Old corn that is on
today bid,
So if you want to sell let me know by return mail
and Oblige Yours truly,

Miller & Walker."

It is then averred that appellee by return mail—namely,
on August 4, 1909—accepted said proposition for the new
corn then growing on the farm, and to be harvested in 1909,
which said letter of acceptance is in the words and figures
following:

"Frankfort, Ind. August 4, 1909.

Mr. Burt Miller Flora Ind
      Dear Sir
did not receive your letter in time to write on morning train Sometimes I think they take mail Past and
then back at any rate I was at the office at 9 a. m. and
your letter was not there as to the corn I will Sell the
corn on the Home Farm at your Price 45 cts. p Bu
their is 48 acres out 24 for me and will be about 800
Bu I think may be my wife will Sell the corn at Coups

I may come over day after morrow if they get done
thrashing here as to the old corn would like a little more
will See you soon

N B Sharp.''

It is insisted by appellee that the judgment of the court
below, holding that these letters were not sufficient to show
a contract between the parties, was correct for the following
reasons: (1) Because the letters themselves do not indicate where the corn was to be delivered, and that in such
case the delivery would be presumed to be at the place where
the corn was situated at the time of the making of the contract, and that the complaint does not aver a demand by
appellants at such place. (2) Because appellants' proposition to pay forty-five cents a bushel for the new corn and
ninety-four cents a hundred for the old was made subject
to the condition that it was on that day's bid, and that the
letter showing the alleged acceptance of the proposition
shows that such acceptance was not had until the following
day. (3) Because appellee's first letter to appellants showed
a desire on his part to sell all of his corn, both old and new,
and that he sought a proposition covering the corn, both old
and new; that appellants' proposition was made fixing a
price on the old corn as well as the new, and that the alleged
acceptance related to the new or growing corn only, and
was not an acceptance of the proposition as made; that for
this reason appellants could have refused to comply with
their proposition, and this being true and appellants not
being bound by an offer accepted in part only, it follows
that appellee was not bound by such acceptance.

As to the first ground of appellee's contention, it is insisted by appellants, in effect, that while the letters in this
case must be sufficient to create the contract, they may be
read and interpreted in the light of a known custom or usage
of the parties to the contract in relation to the place of delivery, and that the averments of each paragraph of the

complaint, with reference to said custom and usage, make them sufficient in this regard.

In view of the conclusions we have reached on the other grounds of appellee's contention, we deem it unnecessary to set out the averments of the paragraphs of the complaint as to said custom and usage, or to determine their sufficiency in this respect.

We think that the complaint is open to the other grounds of objection urged by appellee, and that for this reason the demurrer to each paragraph was properly sustained.

Before there can be said to be an agreement between the parties, there must be a meeting of the minds of such parties on the matter attempted to be agreed on, and no con-

2. tract can be said to have been created between parties where their minds have not agreed on one and the same thing. *Cartmel* v. *Newton* (1881), 79 Ind. 1, 8; 7 Am. and Eng. Ency. Law (2d ed.), 131-135 and notes: *Potts* v. *Whitehead* (1872), 23 N. J. Eq. 512; *Kyle* v. *Kavanagh* (1869), 103 Mass. 356, 359, 360, 4 Am. Rep. 560; *Carr* v. *Duval* (1840), 14 Pet. *77, 10 L. Ed. 361; *Tilly* v. *Cook County* (1880), 103 U. S. 155, 161, 26 L. Ed. 374; *Cal Hirsch & Sons, etc., Co.* v. *Peru Steel, etc., Co.* (1912), 50 Ind. App. 59, 96 N. E. 807, and authorities cited.

Appellee by his first letter indicated a desire to sell his corn, both old and new. He wanted to "clean up everything" that fall, and "get all the money" he could,

3. and with this idea and purpose, expressed in his letter, he asked appellants to drop him a letter, and "say what price" they would "give for the new and what is the best for the old corn."

Appellants understood from the letter received that appellee wanted a price for both old and new corn, as evidenced by the following language in their letter: "You say you want to sell your corn new and old" and they made their proposition accordingly, viz.: "Could give you 45 cts. pr. bu. for your new and 94 cts. pr. hundred for old

corn." Whatever may be said of the acceptance, we think it clear that this proposition was so worded that appellants could rightfully have insisted that they would not be bound by an acceptance of part only, and the mutuality of obligation necessary in all contracts would not permit appellee to be bound by a partial acceptance of a proposition made by appellants, which did not have the effect of binding them also.

The further condition or qualification put into this proposition by the words, "that is on today bid. So if you want to sell let me know by return mail," to us seems important, and, in a measure, controlling. Appellants must have had some reason for putting these words into their proposition. Their evident purpose must have been to advise appellee that the proposition made to him was made on the day's bid, which might be subject to whatever change the next day's bid might make necessary. This is further indicated by the admonition to appellee that if he wanted to sell he must let appellants "known by return mail." We think the entire language and tenor of this proposition indicates an intention to limit it as we have indicated. It will be observed that the language of the proposition is not that we *"will give"* but the language is, "could give * * * on today bid." We think the following language of the court in the case of *Eggleston* v. *Wagner* (1881), 46 Mich. 610, 620, 10 N. W. 37, apt and applicable to the facts of this case: "In order to convert a proposal into a promise the constituents of the acceptance tendered must comply with and conform

4. to the conditions and exigencies of the proposal. The acceptance must be of that which is proposed and nothing else and must be absolute and unconditional. Whatever the proposal requires to fulfill and effectuate acceptance must be accomplished and the acceptance must include and carry with it whatever undertaking, right or interest the proposal calls for, and there must be an entire agreement be-

tween the proposal and acceptance in regard to the subject-matter and extent of interest to be contracted. If the parties do not refer to the same things in the same sense the transaction is simply one of proposals and counter-proposals.''

In *Potts* v. *Whitehead, supra,* at page 514, it is said: ''An acceptance, to be good, must, of course, be such as to conclude an agreement or contract between the parties. And to do this, it must in every respect meet and correspond with the offer, neither falling within nor going beyond the terms proposed, but exactly meeting them at all points and closing with them just as they stand.'' See, also, *Cartmel* v. *Newton, supra; Johnston* v. *Stephenson* (1872), 26 Mich. 63; *Tilly* v. *Cook County, supra; Arthur* v. *Gordon* (1889), 37 Fed. 558.

Appellee, if it can be said from his last letter that he intended any acceptance—a question which we do not decide—could have, at most, intended only an acceptance as 3. to the new corn. The letter of acceptance shows that the acceptance was not until the day following the proposition and that it was not sent by return mail.

For the reasons indicated, we think it appears from the letters relied on as constituting the contract in this case that the minds of the parties to be bound thereby never agreed on the same thing, and therefore, under the authorities, no contract was ever created between them. Neither paragraph of the complaint stated a cause of action, and the demurrers thereto were properly sustained.

Judgment affirmed.

Note.—Reported in 100 N. E. 108. See, also, under (1) 9 Cyc. 753; (2) 9 Cyc. 245; (3) 35 Cyc. 52; (4) 9 Cyc. 265.

CRAIG ET AL. *v.* ZENT.

[No. 7,792. Filed December 20, 1912.]

1. NEGLIGENCE.—*Contributory Negligence.—Jury Question.*—A court is not justified in declaring as a matter of law that a party was guilty of contributory negligence, simply because the facts relating to his conduct are undisputed and seem to indicate a want of due care, but if different inferences may reasonably be drawn from such facts, the question is for the jury. p. 20.

2. WITNESSES. — *Examination.* — *Cross-examination.* — *Evidence.* —While ordinarily a statement against the interest of a party, made in his absence, is not admissible as evidence against him, where, in an action for damages, defendant's attorney elicited from plaintiff on cross-examination part of a conversation had between such attorney and plaintiff, relative to the damage to certain articles, exclusive of plaintiff's horse, it was proper on the redirect examination to show what was further said in relation to the same subject, although it was also thereby shown that defendant's attorney had told plaintiff he ought to have $100 for the damage to his horse. p. 20.

3. TRIAL.—*Reception of Evidence.—Objections.—Time.*—Where a question asked a witness is of such character as to indicate that its answer will divulge matter that is incompetent, an objection to be available, should be interposed before the answer is made. p. 22.

4. APPEAL.—*Review.—Evidence.—Damages.*—Where, in an action for damages, the evidence shows injuries to the person of appellee, which, though slight, are not capable of being definitely ascertained, a verdict for $100 will not be set aside on the ground that the damages are excessive. p. 22.

From Huntington Circuit Court; *Burdge H. Hurd,* Special Judge.

Action by Sylvester Zent against John Craig and another. From a judgment for plaintiff, the defendants appeal. *Affirmed.*

Fred H. Bowers and *Milo N. Feightner,* for appellants. *Watkins & Butler,* for appellee.

LAIRY, J.—Appellants, who are the owners of a machine for drilling wells, left it standing by the side of the highway. This action was brought by appellee to recover damages for personal injuries, and also damages to his horse and buggy occasioned by his horse taking fright at the machine and running away. Appellee recovered a judgment in the sum of $100, from which judgment this appeal is prosecuted.

The action of the trial court in overruling appellants' motion for a new trial is the only one presented by the briefs.

The first question discussed by appellants relates to the sufficiency of the evidence to sustain the verdict. On this question it is asserted that the undisputed evidence

1. shows a state of facts from which the court can say, as a matter of law, that appellee was guilty of contributory negligence in attempting to drive his horse past the machine, after he saw it at the side of the road. A court is not justified in declaring as a matter of law that a party was negligent, simply because the facts relating to his conduct are undisputed and seem to indicate a want of due care. If different inferences may reasonably be drawn from the undisputed facts, it is the province of the jury to draw the inference, and thus to determine whether the party was guilty of negligence. We have carefully examined all of the evidence relating to the conduct of appellee, and we are clearly of the opinion that the question of contributory negligence was one of fact for the jury.

Appellants cite and rely on the case of *Town of Salem* v. *Walker* (1897), 16 Ind. App. 687, 46 N. E. 90, but the facts as disclosed by the evidence in this case do not bring it within the rule announced in that decision.

Appellants next complain of the ruling of the court in permitting the plaintiff to testify to a statement made to

2. him by Mr. Bowers, at the law office of Bowers & Feightner, in the absence of defendants. While plaintiff was testifying as a witness in his own behalf, he stated on reexamination, in response to a question pro-

pounded by his attorney, that Mr. Bowers said in this conversation that plaintiff ought to have $100 damages for
his horse.   Ordinarily a statement of this kind would be
inadmissible as evidence against the defendants.   It is
claimed by counsel for plaintiff that the admission of this
evidence was justified, on the ground that defendants in
cross-examination went into the transaction and developed
a part of what was done and said, and that it was proper
on further examination to show the rest of what was said
on the same subject.   Defendants' attorney on the cross-
examination of this witness did not ask him to relate anything that was said at the time this list was made out.   The
cross-examination shows that some conversation was had
on the subject of damages to the other personal property
mentioned, and that a list was made out which did not include damages to the horse.   It also shows that Mr. Bowers
estimated the damages to the property mentioned in the list,
and that plaintiff, at the time, mentioned the damage to
the horse.   The witness was not asked on cross-examination
to relate any part of the conversation, and he did not state
anything that was said, except that he mentioned to Mr.
Bowers that the horse was damaged, and this statement was
volunteered by the witness, not being responsive to the
question.   Under such a state of the evidence, we do not
think that it was competent on reexamination to show what
was said as to the amount of plaintiff's damages.   But in
this case it appears that Mr. Bowers was appearing at
the trial of the case as one of the attorneys for defendants,
and as such conducted the examination of plaintiff.   In this
examination he elicited the fact that a list of the property
damaged was made out, in which damage to the horse was
not mentioned.   Plaintiff on cross-examination, in response
to a question by Mr. Bowers, testified that Bowers made
out this list and estimated the damages; and that plaintiff
at the time mentioned the damage to the horse.   From this
cross-examination it appears that the damages to various

articles of personal property were discussed, and that Bowers made out a list and estimated the damages to the other articles, but did not include the damage to the horse, although it was mentioned by plaintiff. Defendants having gone into this transaction, and having developed a part of what was done and said there, the court did not err in permitting plaintiff, on reexamination, to show what was further said in relation to the same subject. The

3. error, however, is not available to reverse the judgment, for the reason that a timely objection was not made to the question which elicited the testimony. As shown by the record, defendants made no objection at the time the question was asked, but waited until the answer had been given, and then objected. The question was of such a character as to indicate that its answer would divulge at least a part of the conversation had between plaintiff and Mr. Bowers. If the evidence thus sought to be elicited was incompetent, defendants might object, and have the evidence excluded, or they might waive the objection and permit it to go in; but they cannot wait until after the answer is made, and then permit it to remain if favorable, or, by objecting, have it excluded if unfavorable. *Pence v. Waugh* (1893), 135 Ind. 143, 34 N. E. 860; *Pennsylvania Co. v. Witte* (1896), 15 Ind. App. 583, 43 N. E. 319, 44 N. E. 377.

Appellants also contend that the damages are excessive. On this question we may remark that the evidence shows injuries to the person of appellee, which, though

4. slight, are not capable of being definitely ascertained, and as the damages assessed are only $100, we do not regard them as excessive.

Judgment affirmed.

Note.—Reported in 100 N. E. 94. See, also, under (1) 29 Cyc. 631; (2) 40 Cyc. 2326; (3) 88 Cyc. 1390; (4) 3 Cyc. 381.

LADOGA CANNING COMPANY *v.* CORYDON CANNING COMPANY.

[No. 7,518. Filed June 7, 1912. Rehearing denied December 20, 1912.]

1. TRIAL.—*Verdict.—Answers to Interrogatories.*—A general verdict will stand, as against the jury's answers to interrogatories, where the facts specially found are not inconsistent therewith, or where the verdict and the special findings can be reconciled with each other under any state of facts provable under the issues. p. 26.

2. APPEAL.—*Review.—Presumptions.—Verdict.—Special Findings.* —Every reasonable presumption will be indulged in favor of a general verdict, but nothing will be presumed in aid of the special findings of the jury. p. 27.

3. SALES.—*Breach of Contract.—Measure of Damages.*—The measure of damages for the seller's failure to deliver goods contracted for, is the difference between the market price and the contract price at the place of delivery on the date of the default. p. 27.

4. SALES.—*Breach of Contract.—Verdict.—Answers to Interrogatories.*—In an action against a seller for breach of a contract to deliver 5,000 cases of tomatoes as soon as packed, answers to interrogatories showing that defendant had the 5,000 cases ready for delivery before September 28, that no delivery had been made, except of sample, that on October 10 the market price was higher than the contract price, but failing to show the market price at any other time, are not in conflict with a general verdict awarding plaintiff nominal damages only, since, indulging all presumptions in favor of the general verdict, it means that defendant did not comply with the contract to deliver the tomatoes as soon as packed, and that at the time of the default the market price was no higher than the contract price. p. 27.

5. DAMAGES. — *Breach of Contract. — Nominal Damages.* — Where there has been a breach of a contract by one of the parties, the other is at least entitled to recover nominal damages. p. 28.

6. APPEAL. — *Review. — Harmless Error.—Ruling on Demurrer.* — Error, if any, in overruling appellant's demurrer to a paragraph of answer, was harmless, where the finding was in appellant's favor. p. 28.

7. APPEAL.—*Questions Reviewable.—Evidence.—Bill of Exceptions.* —Where it is not shown that the bill of exceptions containing the longhand transcript of the evidence was presented within time, and the filing thereof, after being signed, does not appear by a

record entry independent of the bill itself, or by the clerk's certificate, the evidence is not in the record and questions arising
thereon cannot be considered. p. 28.

8. APPEAL.—*Bill of Exceptions.—Absence of Judge from State.—
Overruling Motion for Signature Nunc Pro Tunc.—Review.*—
Where judgment was rendered on May 22, and appellant was
given ninety days in which to present and file a bill of exceptions,
and, on August 17, the longhand manuscript was delivered by the
reporter to appellant's attorneys, who, on August 19, left the
same with the clerk to be filed and approved by the judge, the
action of the court in overruling appellant's motion to have the
bill signed *nunc pro tunc*, where the only showing in support of
such motion was that the judge was absent from the State from
July 30 to September 9, was not error. p. 29.

9. APPEAL.—*Bill of Exceptions.—Absence of Judge from State.—
Signature Nunc Pro Tunc.*—The right to have a bill of exceptions
signed *nunc pro tunc*, on the ground that the presentation within
the time allowed was defeated by the absence of the judge from
the State, depends on the diligence shown by the party seeking
such signature, and the question of such diligence is for determination by the sound judgment of the presiding judge from the facts
of the particular case. p. 29.

From Harrison Circuit Court; *C. W. Cook*, Judge.

Action by the Ladoga Canning Company against the
Corydon Canning Company. From a judgment in its favor
for nominal damages, the plaintiff appeals. *Affirmed.*

U. C. Stover and *Wilson & Self*, for appellant.

Evan B. Stotsenburg and *John H. Weathers*, for appellee.

ADAMS, P. J.—Action by appellant against appellee on
the following contract:

"New Albany, Ind. May 19, 1906. Sold to the Ladoga
Canning Company, Ladoga, Indiana, 5000 cases Futures
Standard Indiana Tomatoes, threes, at 80c per dozen,
F. O. B. Factory, Corydon, Indiana; less one and one
half per cent (1½%) for cash in ten days. Goods to
be of 1906 packing and delivery to be made as soon as
packed. Six months guarantee against swell. The seller
hereby agrees to allow buyers the privilege of using
their labels on 2000 cases, with $1.00 per thousand label
allowance. The remaining 3000 to be under seller's

labels. In case of crop failure, we are not liable after we have filled 80% of this contract. In event we are not able to fill 80% we reserve the right to furnish other standard goods instead, or to pay the difference between the contract price and the market price, should there be an advance at the time of delivery.''

This contract was signed by the parties, and it is averred in the complaint that appellee failed and refused to carry out the terms thereof; that appellant has been ready and willing to receive the goods purchased under said contract, and that on appellee's failure to deliver the goods contracted for appellant was obliged to go into the open market and purchase goods of the same quality purchased from appellee, and was obliged to pay the market price of ninety-five cents a dozen cans for such goods; that appellant would have made a profit of fifteen cents a dozen cans, had appellee fulfilled its contract agreement, but on account of its failure so to do appellant was damaged in the sum of $1,500, for which judgment is demanded.

Appellant answered the complaint in fifteen paragraphs, of which the first was in denial and the second a plea of payment. Other paragraphs of answer were challenged by demurrer, and the twelfth, thirteenth and fifteenth were held good. Trial by jury; finding and judgment for appellant in the sum of one cent, and judgment in favor of appellee for costs.

With the general verdict the jury returned answers to sixteen interrogatories. Appellant filed its motion for judgment on the answers to the interrogatories, notwithstanding the general verdict, for $1,500. This motion was overruled, and renewed for the sum of $1,200. Appellant also filed a motion for a new trial, and a motion for a *nunc pro tunc* entry. The overruling of each of these motions, and the overruling of appellant's demurrer to the fifteenth paragraph of answer, constitute the errors relied on for reversal and not waived by failure to argue.

By the answers to the special interrogatories, the jury

found that the parties entered into the contract herein set out, and that appellee did not deliver the tomatoes contracted for, and did not deliver any, in compliance with the terms of sale, except samples; that the packing season at Corydon, Indiana, closed October 10; that appellee notified appellant on October 10 that it would ship appellant 2,000 cases, provided appellant would accept the same in full of said contract; that appellant did not accept said proposition; that the market price of canned tomatoes per dozen cans, of the kind and quality mentioned in the contract, at Corydon, Indiana, "on or about the 10th of October, 1906, and for some days thereafter," was ninety-five cents per dozen; that the market price at Ladoga, Indiana, at the same time was "supposed to be ninety-five cents per dozen"; that appellee has not paid appellant the difference between the contract price and the market price; that appellant refused to accept 2,000 cases under said contract, but not the whole; that appellee has not paid appellant in full for the demand sued on; that no delivery was made, except samples, to Ladoga and St. Louis; that appellee on or about September 28 had 5,000 cases of tomatoes packed, so that the same could have been shipped to appellant; that before September 28, 1906, appellee had 5,000 cases of tomatoes ready to be delivered to appellant.

By the general verdict the jury found in favor of appellant on all the material allegations of its complaint, and against appellee on all the material averments of its affirmative defenses, but found that appellant was entitled to only nominal damages; in other words, the verdict is a general finding that there was a breach by appellee of the contract sued on, but that appellant was not injured thereby.

It is well settled that where a jury with its general verdict returns answers to interrogatories, the general verdict will stand, unless the facts specially found are incon-
1. sistent therewith. It is also the rule that where the general verdict and the special findings can be re-

conciled with each other under any state of facts provable under the issues, the general verdict will stand. *Southern R. Co.* v. *Utz* (1913), 52 Ind. App. 270, 98 N. E. 375, and cases cited. Nothing will be presumed in aid of the

2. special findings of a jury, but every reasonable presumption will be indulged in favor of the general verdict. *Lousiville, etc., R. Co.* v. *Creek* (1892), 130 Ind. 139, 142, 29 N. E. 481, 14 L. R. A. 733; *Shoner* v. *Pennsylvania Co.* (1892), 130 Ind. 170, 181, 28 N. E. 616, 29 N. E. 775; *Louisville, etc., R. Co.* v. *Summers* (1892), 131 Ind. 241, 243, 30 N. E. 873.

The contract sued on provides that the goods sold were to be of 1906 packing, and delivery was to be made as soon as packed, at eighty cents per dozen f. o. b. factory, Corydon, Indiana. The jury found that appellee on or about September 28 had the whole amount of goods contracted for packed and ready for delivery to appellant. The jury also found that before September 28, 1906, appellee had 5,000 cases of tomatoes ready to be delivered to appellant.

The gravamen of this action is the breach of a contract, and to warrant a recovery there must have been a default on the part of appellee, in which event the measure

3. of damages would be the difference between the market price and the contract price on the date of the default at the place of delivery.

By the terms of the contract sued on, it was provided that the tomatoes were to be delivered as soon as packed. While the jury found that appellee had the 5,000

4. cases of tomatoes ready to be delivered to appellant before September 28, 1906, the exact time is not found. By the general verdict, the jury found that delivery had not been made as soon as the tomatoes were packed, and appellee was therefore in default and liable to appellant for at least nominal damages. The answers to interrogatories do not show the market price at any time prior to October 10. The special finding, that the market price

was higher than the contract price on October 10, has no significance, and is not in conflict with the general verdict. The inquiry, to be available, must relate to the market price at the time of default. *McCollum* v. *Huntington* (1875), 51 Ind. 229.

As all presumptions are indulged in favor of the general verdict, the meaning of the verdict must be that appellee did not comply with the contract, wherein it agreed to make delivery of 5,000 cases of tomatoes as soon as packed, and that at the time of default the market price was no higher than the contract price.

It is a well-settled rule that where there has been a breach of a contract by one of the parties, the other is at least entitled to recover nominal damages. *Grau* v. *Grau* (1906), 37 Ind. App. 635, 638, 77 N. E. 816. The answers to interrogatories are not in conflict with the general verdict, and there was no error in overruling the motion for judgment on the interrogatories, notwithstanding the general verdict.

5.

Error predicated on the overruling of the demurrer to the fifteenth paragraph of appellee's answer is not available, for the reason that the finding was in appellant's favor, and the error, if any, was harmless. *Tucker* v. *Roach* (1894), 139 Ind. 275, 278, 38 N. E. 822; *Equitable Trust Co.* v. *Torphy* (1906), 37 Ind. App. 220, 222, 76 N. E. 639; *Souders* v. *Jeffries* (1884), 98 Ind. 31.

6.

Appellee insists that all alleged errors arising on the motion for a new trial are not before us, for the reason that the evidence is not in the record, the bill of exceptions not having been filed after it was signed by the judge. It is now well settled in this State that to bring the evidence into the record, it is necessary to show that the bill of exceptions containing the longhand transcript of the evidence was presented within time, and was filed after being signed; that the filing should be shown by a record entry independent of the bill itself, or shown by

7.

the clerk's certificate. This question was recently passed on by this court in *Hoffman* v. *Isler* (1912), 49 Ind. App. 284, 97 N. E. 188, wherein the rule was clearly announced and the authorities collected and cited. We must, therefore, hold that the evidence is not in the record, and cannot be considered in the determination of this appeal.

The remaining error relied on is that the court
8. erred in overruling appellant's motion for a *nunc pro tunc* entry. This is brought into the record by special bill of exceptions, which shows that the judg-
9. ment was rendered on May 22, 1909, and appellant was given ninety days in which to present and file its bill of exceptions. About August 17, 1909, the reporter delivered the longhand manuscript of the evidence to appellant's attorneys, and on August 19 said transcript was left with the clerk to be filed and approved by the judge. The judge of the court was absent from the State of Indiana from July 30, to September 9, 1909. By the motion, appellant sought to have the judge sign the bill of exceptions as of August 19. The right to have such entry made *nunc pro tunc* depends on the diligence shown by the party seeking it. In this case the only showing was that the judge was absent from the State from July 30 to September 9, 1909. In *Lengelsen* v. *McGregor* (1904), 162 Ind. 258, 268, 67 N. E. 524, 70 N. E. 248, the court said: "The right, however, rests upon diligence, and upon the fact that the exceptor has done all he reasonably could do to secure the prompt approval of his exceptions, and whether he has been diligent or not must be determined by the sound judgment of the presiding judge upon the facts of the particular case." The presiding judge in this case overruled the motion, and we cannot say that he did not exercise sound judgment in so doing.

Judgment affirmed.

NOTE.—Reported in 98 N. E. 849. See, also, under (1, 2, 4) 38 Cyc. 1927; (3) 35 Cyc. 633; (5) 13 Cyc. 17; (6) 31 Cyc. 358; (7) 2 Cyc. 1041; (8, 9) 3 Cyc. 44—New Anno.

MORTIMER, RECEIVER, *v.* DAUB.

[No. 7,579. Filed June 6, 1912. Rehearing denied December 20, 1912.]

1. RAILROADS.—*Interurban.*—*Injury to Persons on Highway.*—*Evidence.*—*Sufficiency.*—In an action for injuries sustained in a collision with an interurban car, where the complaint charged that the car was being operated "at an excessive, negligent and careless rate of speed of about thirty miles an hour," thereby causing unusual, excessive and unnecessary noises which frightened plaintiff's team and caused it to turn upon the track in front of said car, whereby plaintiff was injured, evidence showing that there was at the time a city ordinance in force prohibiting the running of cars at a higher rate of speed than ten miles per hour, and that, as the car approached, it was running at twenty-five or thirty miles an hour and made a loud noise and raised considerable dust, was sufficient to justify the jury in finding that the car was operated in excess of the speed allowed by ordinance, and that the team was frightened by the unusual noise and high rate of speed, and was sufficient to charge defendant with liability although there was some evidence tending to show that at the time of the collision the car had slowed down and was not running to exceed eight or ten miles an hour. p. 34.

2. RAILROADS.—*Operation.*—*Excessive Speed.*—*Negligence Per Se.*—It is negligence *per se* for a railroad company to operate its cars in violation of a statute or municipal ordinance regulating the speed thereof, making the company liable for injury proximately caused thereby to one who is himself without fault. p. 35.

3. APPEAL. — *Review.* — *Evidence.* — *Verdict.* — *Conclusiveness.*—Where the evidence is conflicting, the jury's finding in the general verdict will not 'be disturbed on appeal, if there is any evidence tending to support each material issue. p. 35.

4. RAILROADS.—*Interurban.*—*Injury to Persons on Highway.*—*Duty to Stop Car.*—*Instructions.*—In an action for injuries caused by the collision of an interurban car with plaintiff's team, which had become frightened by the approach of such car, an instruction that while those in charge of a car being operated on and through a public street are not required to immediately stop the car on seeing a team manifesting fright, it is the duty of such person to be constantly on the alert and if he discovers a person so situated that injury must follow unless the car is stopped, it is his duty to make all reasonable efforts to stop such car, and his failure to do so will render the company liable for the resulting

damage, is correct and stated the rule with reference to the duty to stop as favorably to appellant as the authorities warrant. p. 36.

5. APPEAL. — *Review. — Instructions.* — Instructions in an action against a street car company, which attempted only to define certain duties of those in charge of street cars, in the management thereof, for the breach of which there may be a liability against the company, but not purporting to state the entire law of the case, were not objectionable on the ground of ignoring the question of contributory negligence, where other instructions were given which covered that question, since the instructions must be considered as a whole. p. 36.

6. APPEAL.— *Review.— Harmless Error.— Instructions.*— Error, if any, in omitting the element of contributory negligence from instructions, given in an action for damages for personal injuries, was harmless, where it was not contended at the trial that plaintiff was guilty of contributory negligence, and the evidence does not indicate that he was at any time at fault. p. 37.

7. RAILROADS.—*Interurban.—Injury to Persons on Highway.—Instructions.—Issues.—Evidence.*—In an action for injuries in a collision with an interurban car, where the complaint alleged that plaintiff's team became frightened through the negligent operation of the car, and that the car ran against the team, and there was some evidence that the car was running in excess of the speed allowed by ordinance, that as it approached it made unusual and loud noise, frightening the team, that the motorman was signalled to stop the car when 300 feet away, and that the speed was not slackened until the team was struck, an instruction which told the jury that when the operator of the car sees another in danger of peril from which he cannot extricate himself by the exercise of reasonable care and prudence, it is the highest duty of the operator to so act as not to increase such peril, and, if he does so act as to increase the peril, with full knowledge of the facts, it is negligence rendering the company liable for the injuries caused thereby, was not objectionable, as injecting the doctrine of "last clear chance," and was warranted by the issues and evidence. p. 37.

8. APPEAL.—*Review.—Refusal of Instructions.—Burden of Proof.* —An instruction which in substance stated that plaintiff, to recover, must prove each paragraph of his complaint by a preponderance of the evidence, was properly refused. p. 38.

9. APPEAL.—*Review.—Refusal of Instructions.—Inapplicability to Issues.*—A requested instruction, not shown to be applicable to the issues, was properly refused. p. 38.

10. APPEAL.—*Review.—Instructions.—Refusal of Instructions Covered by Others Given.*—The refusal of requested instructions is

not error, where the essential elements of such refused instructions were completely covered and better stated in the instructions that were given. p. 39.

11. TRIAL.—*Instructions.*—*Repetition of Principles.*—It is not
necessary that the rules or principles contained in instructions
should be repeated in different language. p. 39.

12. TRIAL.—*Instructions.*—*Confidential Relation of Physician and
Patient.*—In an action for personal injuries, an instruction is
not objectionable which states that the law recognizes the relation of physician and patient as confidential, and that a physician
is not competent to testify to matters communicated to him by
the patient in the course of his professional services, if the privilege is claimed by the patient, and that plaintiff's failure to
call such physician as a witness should not influence the verdict.
p. 39.

From Superior Court of Allen County; *Owen N. Heaton,*
Judge.

Action by Henry Daub against James D. Mortimer, receiver of the Toledo & Chicago Interurban Railway Company. From a judgment for plaintiff, the defendant appeals. *Affirmed.*

William L. Taylor, James H. Rose and *William A. Campbell,* for appellant.

Sharpless & Atkinson and *Harper & Eggeman,* for appellee.

HOTTEL, C. J.—This is an action for personal injuries.
The complaint was in three paragraphs, a demurrer to each
of which was overruled. After the case proceeded to trial,
the first paragraph was dismissed, and the case was submitted to the jury on a denial to the second and third paragraphs. The jury returned a general verdict for appellee
in the sum of $1,000, with answers to interrogatories.

As no question is raised as to the sufficiency of either
paragraph of the complaint, we set out briefly only enough
of the averments to present the questions raised by the appeal.

These averments, common to both paragraphs, are that
appellant on the day that appellee was injured, was operat-

ing interurban cars over King street in the city of Garrett, which was one of the principal streets of said city, extending in an easterly and westerly direction through a populous part thereof; that such street was much used by the citizens of said city; that it was narrow, and the track of said railway company was in or near the center thereof, and the space between the outer rails and the curbing on either side was narrow, affording barely sufficient room for interurban cars to pass a wagon or other vehicle traveling on said street; that appellee on the day of his injury was driving a team of mules toward the west over said street, and one of appellant's interurban cars was approaching him from the west; that each was approaching the other on a straight and level part of said street, where the view was unobstructed for a distance of a quarter of a mile or more; that said car rapidly approached appellee, and was being operated ''at an excessive, negligent and careless rate of speed of about thirty miles an hour thereby making traffic on said street dangerous, * * * and endangering the lives and limbs of people and * * * frightening horses * * * of ordinary gentleness;'' that ''by reason of said excessive * * * rate of speed of said car the same caused a great deal of unusual, excessive and unnecessary noises calculated to frighten horses or mules of ordinary gentleness, which at said time did frighten plaintiff's mules which fact was seen, or could have been seen by the servant * * * operating said car by the exercise of ordinary care,'' and although such servant knew, or might have known, that said mules were frightened by reason of the approach of said car in said manner, he did not slacken the speed of said car, but continued to approach in the same rapid manner, causing said mules to become more frightened and unmanageable, ''then and thereby causing said mules to turn to the left upon the tracks of said company, and said car being so negligently operated as aforesaid ran against the said span of

mules, knocking one of them down against the wagon tongue
* * * * and on account of the sudden jolt" appellee was
thrown forward, etc., and injured.

The third paragraph contains additional averments to
the effect that said city of Garrett, at the time of appellee's
injury, had in force and effect an ordinance prohibiting the
running of cars within the limits of said city at a higher
rate of speed than ten miles an hour, and that by the
terms of the franchise granted by said city and accepted
by the railway company, under which it obtained the right
to run its cars over said street, said company was prohibited from running its cars faster than ten miles an hour.

In presenting this appeal, appellant presents and relies
exclusively on the following grounds of his motion for a
new trial, viz.:   (1) That the verdict is not sustained by
sufficient evidence, and (2) that the trial court erred in
giving and refusing certain instructions.

The only point which appellant attempts to raise by the
first ground of his motion is that the evidence shows that the
interurban car was not running at a speed of over
1.   eight or ten miles an hour, and that the collision was
purely an accident, caused by a sudden shying of the
mules toward the car. While there is evidence tending to support appellant in his contention, there is also some evidence
supporting the averments of the complaint. There was some
evidence in support of each of the following facts, viz.:
That at the time of said collision there was an ordinance in
full force in said city which prohibited the running of cars
within the limits of the city at a higher rate of speed than
ten miles an hour; that the car in question was traveling
at a high rate of speed; that as it approached appellee's
team it made a loud noise, and raised considerable dust;
that appellee's mules became frightened at the approaching car; that appellee's team was in view of the motorman
when 600 or 650 feet away; that the car was several hundred feet away when the mules commenced to back; that

the motorman saw the team when about 500 feet away, but did not notice them afterwards until just before the collision, when about 25 feet away; that appellee endeavored to control his team, and signalled the motorman in the car when 300 feet away to stop; that the space between the outer rail of the car track and the curb was only about 12 feet; that the speed of the car was not slackened until after it struck appellee's team. Several of the witnesses testified that the car was running at a speed of twenty-five or thirty miles an hour.

Even though it be conceded, as appellant contends, that at the time of the injury to appellee, said car had been slowed down to a speed of three or four miles an hour, there is evidence from which the jury may have found that appellee's mules were frightened by the unusual noise and high rate of speed as it approached them, and that such speed was in excess of that allowed by the city ordinance. This, in connection with the other facts supported by the evidence in the case, was sufficient to charge the railway company with liability, since it is negligence *per se*

2. for a railroad company to operate its cars in violation of a statute or municipal ordinance regulating the speed thereof, and when such negligence is the proximate cause of injury to a person who is himself without fault, the company is liable in damages. 1 Thompson, Negligence §10; 2 Thompson, Negligence §1900; *Pennsylvania Co.* v. *Horton* (1892), 132 Ind. 189, 31 N. E. 45; *Shirk* v. *Wabash R. Co.* (1896), 14 Ind. App. 126, 42 N. E. 656; *Indiana, etc., R. Co.* v. *Barnhart* (1888), 115 Ind. 399, 16 N. E. 121.

It is a well-settled rule that where there is conflict in the evidence the appellate court will not disturb the jury's finding in the general verdict, if there is any evidence

3. tending to support each material issue. *Republic Iron, etc., Co.* v. *Berkes* (1904), 162 Ind. 517, 526, 70

N. E. 815; *Delaware, etc., Tel. Co.* v. *Fiske* (1907), 40 Ind. App. 348, 81 N. E. 1110.

Appellant next complains of instruction No. 4, given by the court at the request of appellee. This instruction told

4. the jury that "while it is true that those in charge of a street car being operated upon a street car track on and through a public street are not required to immediately stop the car upon seeing a horse or team at the side of the street manifesting fright, nevertheless, it is the duty of the person operating such car to be constantly on the alert and if he discovers a person so situated that injury *must follow unless the car is stopped, it is such operator's duty to make all reasonable efforts to stop said car* and if he fails to do so, the company will be liable for any and all damages that may result." Appellant urges that the instruction ignores the true rule that the motorman is not required immediately to stop his car under said conditions, "unless the situation and all the circumstances would cause a reasonable man to see and believe that damage to the property could not otherwise be avoided." The instruction begins by recognizing the rule contended for, and imposes the duty of stopping only when the operator in charge of the car "discovers a person so situated that injury *must follow* unless the car is stopped," in which case it is charged that it is the operator's duty "to make all *reasonable* efforts to stop the car." The instruction was as favorable to appellant in this respect as the authorities warrant. *Muncie St. R. Co.* v. *Maynard* (1892), 5 Ind. App. 372, 381, 32 N. E. 343; *Fort Wayne, etc., Traction Co.* v. *Miller* (1911), 48 Ind. App. 633, 96 N. E. 496; *Effinger* v. *Fort Wayne, etc., Traction Co.* (1911), 175 Ind. 175, 93 N. E. 855, 33 L. R. A. (N. S.) 123, and authorities cited.

It is further complained that this instruction, and the sixth instruction given at the request of appellee,

5. fail to take into account the question of contributory negligence. It is a sufficient answer to this objec-

tion to say that neither instruction purports to state the entire law of the case, or all the elements necessary to a recovery, but each instruction attempts only to define certain duties of those in charge of street cars, in the management thereof, for the breach of which there may be a liability against such street car company.

Other instructions were given to the jury which covered the question of contributory negligence on the part of appellee. The instructions must be considered as a whole, and when so considered no harm could have resulted from the giving of said instructions. *Morgantown Mfg. Co.* v. *Hicks* (1910), 46 Ind. App. 623, 633, 92 N. E. 199; *McIntosh* v. *State* (1898), 151 Ind. 251, 255, 257, 51 N. E. 354; *Union Mut. Life Ins. Co.* v. *Buchanan* (1885), 100 Ind. 63; *Shields* v. *State* (1897), 149 Ind. 395, 406, 49 N. E. 351, and authorities cited.

Furthermore, it does not appear that at any time during the trial of the cause was it contended that appellee was guilty of contributory negligence, nor does the evidence indicate that he was at any time at fault. In such a situation the omission of the element of contributory negligence from the instruction, even if erroneous, would be harmless. *Morgantown Mfg. Co.* v. *Hicks, supra; Indianapolis Traction, etc., Co.* v. *Menze* (1909), 173 Ind. 31, 33, 88 N. E. 929, 89 N. E. 370; *Pittsburgh, etc. R. Co.* v. *Higgs* (1906), 165 Ind. 694, 706, 76 N. E. 299, 4 L. R. A. (N. S.) 1081.

Instruction No. 7, tendered by appellee, is next objected to, and is as follows: "It is a sound doctrine that when one who is operating a street car or interurban car sees another in danger or peril from which such other is unable to extricate himself by the exercise of reasonable care and prudence, it is the highest duty of such person so operating said car to so act as not to increase the peril or danger and if he does act thereafter, in the manner so as to increase the peril or danger with full knowledge of the facts, it is negligence and the company may be made to respond in damages for injury caused by such negligence.'' It is insisted that this instruction ''injects into the case the so-called doctrine of last clear chance,'' and that ''neither the allegations of the complaint nor the evidence in any way give rise to the issue.'' We think that we have above indicated enough of the averments of the complaint and the evidence to show that the issues, and some evidence introduced thereunder, warranted the giving of the instruction.. *Effinger* v. *Fort Wayne, etc., Traction Co., supra; Muncie St. R. Co.* v. *Maynard, supra; Fort Wayne, etc., Traction Co.* v. *Miller, supra,* and authorities cited; *Indianapolis St. R. Co.* v. *Marschke* (1906), 166 Ind. 490, 496, 497, 77 N. E. 945; *Indianapolis Traction, etc., Co.* v. *Kidd* (1906), 167 Ind. 402, 410, 413, 79 N. E. 347, 7 L. R. A. (N. S.) 143, 10 Ann. Cas. 942; *Indiana Union Traction Co.* v. *Myers* (1911), 47 Ind. App. 646, 93 N. E. 888, 892.

The refusal to give instruction No. 3, tendered by appellant, is urged as error. This instruction attempts to tell the jury on whom the burden of proof rested, and tells it

8. that if ''the evidence as to either paragraph of the complaint is equally balanced so that it does not preponderate on either side'' it will be its ''duty to find for the defendant.'' By this instruction appellee would have been required to prove each paragraph of his complaint by a preponderance of the evidence, and for this reason it was properly refused.

Appellant's instruction No. 5, refused, is negative in character, and tells the jury that in view of the allegations of the complaint it has ''nothing to do with the giving

9. of any signal of the approach of the car by way of blowing the whistle or sounding the gong or any omission to give such signal.'' We fail to see wherein this instruction is applicable to the issues, and the page of the record cited by appellant furnishes no evidence which

makes it applicable. Instruction No. 8, tendered by appellant and refused, as applied to the facts of the case
10. at bar, was not a proper instruction, and the rule
of law therein contained was more appropriately
stated, as applied to said facts in appellant's instruction
seven, given by the court. So, as applied to the facts in
this case, instruction No. 12, tendered and refused, is covered by and better stated in instruction No. 13, given at appellant's request. Refusal to give other instructions is alleged as error, but an examination of the instructions refused, and those given, discloses that the essential elements of
the refused instructions were completely covered by others
tendered by appellant and given.

It was not necessary to repeat the same principles or
rules in different language. *Baltimore, etc., R. Co.* v. *Reed*
(1912), 50 Ind. App. 220, 98 N. E. 141; *New York,*
11. *etc., R. Co.* v. *Flynn* (1908), 41 Ind. App. 501, 503,
81 N. E. 741, 82 N. E. 1009; *Oil-Well Supply Co.* v.
Priddy (1908), 41 Ind. App. 200, 204, 83 N. E. 623.

Appellant next contends that the trial court erred in
giving of its own motion instruction No. 1, which told the
jury that the law recognizes the relation of physi-
12. cian and patient as confidential, and that if the confidential privilege is claimed by the patient, the physician is not a competent witness to testify as to matters
communicated to him as such by the patient in the course
of his professional services rendered in such case, and, further, that the fact that such physician is not called by the
plaintiff as a witness should not in any manner influence
the verdict.

It is true that in *City of Warsaw* v. *Fisher* (1900), 24
Ind. App. 46, 55 N. E. 42, this court held a similar instruction bad, but that case has been expressly disapproved by
the Supreme Court in *William Laurie Co.* v. *McCullough*
(1910), 174 Ind. 477, 484, 90 N. E. 1014, 92 N. E. 337. See,
also, *Brackney* v. *Fogle* (1901), 156 Ind. 535, 60 N. E. 303.

No error appearing in the record, the judgment is affirmed.

NOTE.—Reported in 96 N. E. 845. See, also, under (1) 36 Cyc. 1604; (2) 36 Cyc. 1478; (3) 3 Cyc. 348; (4, 7) 36 Cyc. 1632; (5) 38 Cyc. 1778; (6) 3 Cyc. 383; (8) 38 Cyc. 1748; (9) 38 Cyc. 1612; (10) 38 Cyc. 1711; (11) 38 Cyc. 1681; (12) 38 Cyc. 1743. As to the doctrine of remote and proximate cause, see 36 Am. St. 807. As to the relative rights of street car companies and pedestrians and travelers in the street, see note to Western Paving, etc., Co. v. Citizens St. R. Co., (Ind.) 25 Am. St. 475. For a discussion of the operation of street railway cars in violation of a municipal ordinance as negligence *per se,* see 9 Ann. Cas. 840, 8 L. R. A. (N. S.) 1093. As to injuries by street car collisions with vehicles or horses, see 25 L. R. A. 508. As to frightening horse by street car, see 34 L. R. A. 482; 21 L. R. A. (N. S.) 283.

HESTON *v.* DOUGAN.

[No. 7,527. Filed November 15, 1911. Rehearing denied February 16, 1912. Transfer denied December 20, 1912.]

1. LANDLORD AND TENANT.—*Action for Possession.—Denial of Landlord's Title.—Answer.—Sufficiency.*—In an action for the possession of land alleged to be held by defendant as the lessee of plaintiff, an answer alleging title in defendant, denying that the relationship of landlord and tenant existed, and alleging that defendant's signature to the paper relied on by plaintiff as a lease was procured through the misrepresentation and fraud of plaintiff, is not demurrable on the theory that a tenant may not controvert the landlord's title during the existence of the tenancy, since that rule only applies where the relation of landlord and tenant exists and does not control where the existence of such relation is denied. p. 45.

2. APPEAL.—*Review.—Harmless Error.—Ruling on Demurrer.*—Overruling a demurrer to a bad paragraph of answer is harmless, where the matters averred therein are provable under the general denial. p. 45.

3. LANDLORD AND TENANT.—*Action for Possession.—Pleading.—Reply.*—The procedure and pleading in the circuit court, in an action by a landlord against the tenant for possession, follow the procedure in civil cases before justices, and by §1752 Burns 1908, §1463 R. S. 1881, in civil cases before a justice, a replication is unnecessary, so that the action of the circuit court in striking

out plaintiff's reply to a paragraph of answer, in such a proceeding, is not error. p. 46.

4. LANDLORD AND TENANT.—*Action for Possession.—Answer Denying Relation of Landlord and Tenant.—Trial.—Right to Trial by Jury.*—In an action by a landlord against the tenant for possession, the defendant's answer averring that the relation of landlord and tenant never existed, that defendant was the owner of the land, and that the paper relied on by plaintiff as a lease was signed by defendant in reliance on the representations of plaintiff that it was a copy of a lost contract, and in which defendant asked for no affirmative relief, tendered issues provable under the general denial and amounted merely to an argumentative denial, so that the pleadings presented an ordinary action in ejectment, triable by jury. pp. 46, 47.

5. JURY. — *Right to Trial by Jury. — Determination. — Issues.* — Whether an equitable issue is raised so as to prevent the trial of a cause by jury, must be determined from the substantial and material facts averred in the pleadings. p. 47.

6. LANDLORD AND TENANT.—*Action for Possession.—Defenses.—Pleading.—General Denial.*—In an action by a landlord against the tenant for possession, all defenses, legal and equitable, are admissible under the general denial. p. 47.

7. EVIDENCE.—*Conclusion of Witness.*—Where, while testifying as a witness with reference to the execution of a lease, which he claimed he had been induced to sign through the representations of plaintiff, on whom he relied, that the lease was merely a copy of a lost contract, defendant was asked if plaintiff advised him about business affairs, such question was not objectionable as calling for a conclusion, since, under the circumstances, the answer called for was the result of observations and dealings with plaintiff that were peculiarly within the knowledge of the witness. p. 48.

8. APPEAL.—*Objection to Instructions.—Waiver.*—Alleged error in the giving of instructions is waived by appellant's failure to discuss them. p. 50.

9. TRIAL.—*Instructions.—Burden of Proof.*—Instructions informing the jury that the burden is on plaintiff to establish the material allegations of his complaint, and that plaintiff cannot recover if the evidence is evenly balanced on any proposition which he is bound to show by a preponderance of the evidence, telling the jury that the burden is on defendant to prove the material allegations of his affirmative answer, and that if he has not done so he must fail, and stating what is meant by the preponderance of the evidence, correctly state the law. p. 50.

10. LANDLORD AND TENANT.—*Action for Possession.—Instructions.—Issues.*—Where, in a landlord's action for possession, defend-

ant alleged that the relation of landlord and tenant never existed and that he had been induced to sign the lease through the representation of plaintiff that it was merely a copy of a contract relating to a conveyance of the land that defendant had made to plaintiff to secure a debt, an instruction that if defendant and his wife executed a deed to plaintiff solely to secure a debt owing to plaintiff, such deed, though absolute on its face, would be a mortgage and defendant would be entitled to possession of the property mentioned, and that such fact should be considered with all the other evidence relative to that issue in determining whether defendant knowingly executed the lease, was within the issues and a proper instruction on that branch of the case. p. 50.

11. TRIAL.—*Instructions.—Invading Province of Jury.*—Instructions are properly refused, which, if given, would invade the province of the jury. p. 51.

12. APPEAL.—*Review.—Affirmance.*—A judgment will be affirmed. where it appears that the case was fully and fairly presented to the jury and that substantial justice has been accomplished. p. 52.

From Gibson Circuit Court; *Walter S. Jackson*, Special Judge.

Action by Joseph S. Heston against Albert F. Dougan. From a judgment for defendant, the plaintiff appeals. *Affirmed.*

John W. Brady, Oscar M. Welborn, Lucius C. Embree and *Morton C. Embree,* for appellant.

Thomas Duncan, Arthur P. Twineham and *Harvey Harman,* for appellee.

IBACH, J.—This was an action by Heston, appellant, against Dougan, appellee, to recover the possession of certain lands alleged to be owned by appellant and occupied by appellee, as his tenant under a written lease. The issues arose on the complaint, the second paragraph of answer, which is a general denial, the amended third paragraph of answer, and appellant's first paragraph of reply in general denial to the amended third paragraph of answer. Appellee's first paragraph of answer and appellant's second paragraph of reply were stricken out on motion of the opposing parties. The amended third paragraph of answer set out at some length the following alleged facts: Defendant is now and has been for more than twenty years last past continuously the owner in fee simple in possession of the real estate described in the lease set forth in the complaint. He never entered into the possession of said real estate by virtue of the pretended lease, or by any other agreement to rent said real estate from plaintiff, or in any manner whatever except as owner in fee simple. He admits writing his name to the pretended lease, under circumstances as follows: For some time prior to April 3, 1897, he had been indebted to Heston, owing to him $8,805.14, secured by notes and mortgages on the real estate described. On that day, in order to secure a further loan of $700, he executed a warranty deed to said property to Heston, and as a part of said agreement he and Heston entered into a contemporaneous parol agreement, whereby it was agreed that said deed should be executed as a mortgage to secure the debt then owing to Heston, Heston was to carry the indebtedness at the rate of six per cent interest until Dougan should be able to repay him, and was to pay taxes on the real estate, and furnish materials for repair of the buildings. Dougan was to remain in possession of and farm the real estate without hindrance from Heston, and make needed repairs. At any time that Dougan repaid principal and interest, taxes and money spent for repairs, Heston was to reconvey the real estate to him. The deed was executed as security for the loan of $9,504.14, and for no other purpose whatever. About June, 1897, Heston and Dougan reduced to writing the oral contract of defeasance aforesaid. In March, 1903, Heston came to Dougan and pretended that he had lost his written contract and represented to Dougan that he would have another agreement written, similar to the one claimed to have been lost, except as to the time of paying interest. He would have his attorneys prepare such an instrument, and Dougan need not quit work to go to Princeton to sign it, but at his convenience could call at the office of said attorneys and sign the instrument. Dougan has a limited education, reads the English language imperfectly, and for the greater portion of his life has resided near Heston, who is a very intelligent, prosperous and farsighted business man, skilled in the transaction of business. Heston has aided him in conducting his affairs, advised him during his entire lifetime, and largely controlled his 'financial affairs and business transactions. At that time he had the greatest confidence in Heston, and relied on his advice in all business matters, which Heston knew. Heston had his attorneys prepare the pretended lease sued on, and failed, neglected and refused to notify Dougan that the contract was a lease, but fraudulently represented to him that the instrument prepared was an exact copy of the former contract, and not a lease. Dougan relied on these representations, and on March 23, 1903, drove into Princeton with a two-horse load of grain, and went to the office of Heston's attorneys. Finding no place to hitch his horses, he left them unhitched, and went to the office, where he was informed by the attorneys that they had prepared the paper under the direction of Heston. Being anxious about his team, which he had left unhitched, and relying on Heston's representations, he signed the pretended lease set out in the complaint, without attempting to read it, or having it read to him. He did not know until just before this action was brought that the paper he signed was not a copy of the lost contract, but was in terms a lease. He would not have signed it had it not been for his reliance on Heston's representations and his belief that they were true. Heston has never had anything to do with the management of the farm. Dougan has never paid Heston any rent, but has paid him six per cent interest annually on the sum owing him—$9,504.14. The land in question forms a farm of 188 acres in one body, near the city of Princeton, Indiana, and at the time the deed was executed was worth more than $15,000, and its rental value was more than $6 an acre. At the time the pretended lease was executed the land was worth $100 an acre, and Heston knew it. In June, 1902, Dougan went to Heston and told him that he was then ready and willing to repay him all that he owed him, and asked him to reconvey the land to him, and continuously since that day to the present time he has been ready, willing and able to make such repayment. He prays for judgment for his costs.

Trial by jury resulted in judgment for appellee.

The errors relied on for reversal are (1) overruling the demurrer to the amended third paragraph of answer, (2) striking out the second paragraph of the reply to the amended third paragraph of answer, and (3) overruling the motion for a new trial. Appellant contends that the amended third paragraph of appellee's answer is bad because

1. he attempts thereby to controvert his landlord's title to the leased premises, which cannot be done during the existence of the tenancy. This principle, which appellant strongly argues, is well established, and is admitted by appellee. The rule announced, however, is not applicable to the case at bar. The sole purpose of the amended third paragraph of answer is to deny the allegations of the complaint in every particular. Appellee expressly denies in it the existence of the tenancy averred in the complaint, and if the relation of landlord and tenant never did exist between the parties, then appellee would not be controlled by the doctrine that during the existence of the tenancy the tenant is prevented from controverting his landlord's title. Such relation between the parties was absolutely necessary to enable appellant to maintain his action, and it was not improper for appellee to aver such facts as tended to show that no such relationship ever existed between them.

2. It may be said, however, that even if the answer assailed was in fact bad, yet the ruling of the court would not be reversible error, for all matters averred therein were admissible under the general denial. In the case of

Ward v. *Pittsburgh, etc., R. Co.* (1900), 25 Ind. App. 405, 58 N. E. 264, which was an action by a landlord to recover possession of real estate, in which appellant's answer set up facts very similar to those set up by the amended third paragraph of answer in the case at bar, the court said: "Whether or not the appellant's answer contained a sufficient defense, there could be no available error in sustaining the demurrer. If, as contended in argument, the facts pleaded constituted coercion, they could have been made as available on the trial without any pleading on behalf of the appellant as they could have been if the demurrer had been overruled." The decision in the above case is based on the decision in the cases of *Poffenberger* v. *Blackstone* (1887), 57 Ind. 288, and *Smith* v. *Pinnell* (1896), 143 Ind. 485, 40 N. E. 798.

The action of the trial court in striking out appellant's second paragraph of reply to the amended third paragraph of answer was somewhat unusual and irregular, but

3. as appellant was not prejudiced by such ruling, we cannot hold that the court's action in this particular constitutes reversible error. The procedure and pleading in the circuit court in suits begun by a landlord against a tenant to recover lands follow the procedure in civil cases before justices, and by statute in civil cases before justices no replication is necessary, and any matter which might have been replied to any plea may be proved as if so replied. §1752 Burns 1908, §1463 R. S. 1881. *Poffenberger* v. *Blackstone, supra; Smith* v. *Pinnell, supra; Ward* v. *Pittsburgh, etc., R. Co., supra.* Appellant's reply was an unnecessary pleading.

On motion for a new trial, is presented the question whether appellee was entitled to have the case tried by a jury as a matter of right. Appellant contends that

4. the amended third paragraph of answer raises an equitable issue which should have been tried by the court and not by the jury. We must determine this con-

tention from the character of the issues to be decided
5. as they appear from the substantial and material
    facts averred in the pleadings. It will be observed
from appellant's complaint that he claims to hold the fee
simple title to the land, thereby asserting the legal title,
and not merely an equitable interest therein. To this complaint appellee filed a general denial, and in addition thereto a third paragraph of answer, which might be termed
an argumentative denial, wherein he avers facts tending to
show such relations, both business and otherwise, existing
between the parties as to constitute appellant a confidential
adviser of appellee, also that the instrument involved in the
suit was signed by him on account of the faith and confidence which he reposed in appellant, and further averring
that the relation of landlord and tenant never existed between the parties. Appellee did not ask for any affirma-
    tive relief. The cases cited above all hold that in
6. actions of this character all defenses, legal and
    equitable, are admissible under the general denial,
as the statutes are interpreted by them. This being true,
    it will be observed that the substantial averments of
4. the pleadings before us present an ordinary action
    in ejectment, regardless of the special answer filed
by appellee, which we have said amounts simply to an argumentative denial, and the trial court did not err in permitting the cause to be tried by the jury. The Supreme
Court of this State, in the case of *Martin* v. *Martin* (1889),
118 Ind. 227, 237, 20 N. E. 763, lays down the rule as follows: "Whenever the cause of action is one that can only
be enforced by invoking the equitable power of the court,
then the right of trial by jury does not maintain; but if
the cause of action does not depend on the equitable jurisdiction of the court, then a jury trial may be demanded."
Woollen, Spec. Proc. §1034, says: "Our statutory action
for the recovery of real property is intended to substitute for
the old action of ejectment, with its cumbersome machinery

and useless fictions, a simple and more sensible proceeding, that will give a direct road to the merits of the controversy. It clearly contemplates a trial by jury, and the provisions heretofore referred to make the same rule applicable to actions to quiet title. In both actions a jury trial is demandable as a matter of right, upon the request of either party; and this is true where by a cross action the cross-complainant seeks to recover the possession of or to have the title quieted to his real estate.''

The case of *Lock* v. *Moulton* (1895), 108 Cal. 49, 41 Pac. 28, is a case presenting almost exactly the same issues as the present case, being an action in ejectment, in which the defense was that the deed relied on by plaintiff was, though in form an absolute deed, in fact only a mortgage. The court refused a trial by jury of the whole cause, but tried what he called the equitable issue—as to whether the deed was intended to operate as a mortgage—without a jury. For error in refusing to submit the entire case to the jury the case was reversed, on the ground that the allegations in the answer, to the effect that the deed was intended as mere security for a debt, do not constitute an equitable defense, in the proper sense of that term, since they might have been proved under the general denial.

Complaint is made that the court permitted Dougan, testifying in his own behalf, to answer the following questions:

"Well, now, Mr. Dougan, you may state whether
7. or not Mr. Heston had advised you on business affairs? A. He had. * * * Whether he advised you about other business affairs? A. He advised me on all my transactions in business, everything.'' Appellant's contention is that these questions call for the opinion or conclusion of the witness, and not for facts.

The dividing line between what is a fact and what is an opinion does not readily appear in all cases, so that we are not able to give a general rule applicable to all cases requiring the rejection as evidence of what might be termed the opinion or conclusion of the witness. But in this case it was certainly competent for the witness to state that Heston advised him in his business affairs, for this was the statement of an ultimate fact, peculiarly within the knowledge of the witness, and not a mere conclusion. By his answers to the foregoing questions he was simply giving the result of his personal observations and dealings with Heston extending over a number of years, taken collectively, and which he could not in any manner but imperfectly describe if required to give them in detail. The witness might have stated as best he could the number of times he talked with appellant and the subject of each conversation, as nearly as he could remember each separately, and yet he could not have put the jury in his place as to the effect of the several conversations on Heston's part, his conduct, his appearance and various other matters and conditions which may have impressed the witness at each time, and from which he was justified in answering the questions in the manner in which he did answer them. The whole subject of investigation presented by these questions was then open for the defendant to inquire into on cross-examination, and he would have been permitted to carry the investigation as far as he might choose. This is not a relaxation of the well-settled rule that the opinion of a witness who is not a professional person or an expert is not admissible, and the questions were proper under the circumstances of the case before us. 3 Wigmore, Evidence §1919. It is also argued that the alleged relation of appellant as business adviser to appellee was directly involved as an issue made by the pleadings. That such relation existed, was only one of many things which the jury would have to find in order to render a judgment for appellee, and the evidence is not open to the objection that it answers the very question which the jury is to determine.

Appellant also insists that the court erred in refusing to

give to the jury certain instructions tendered, and numbered 9, 13, 15, 16, 20, 21, 23, 24, 30, 31, 32, 35 and 36;
also in giving instructions requested by appellee numbered

8. 1, 3, 13, 14 and 15; and in giving on its own motion
those numbered 1, 2, 3, 4 and 5. Errors as to instructions Nos. 1, 3 and 15, given at the request of
appellee, and Nos. 4 and 5, given on the court's own motion,
have been waived by failure to discuss them.

Instruction No. 1 given on the court's own motion, informed the jury that the burden was on the plaintiff to es-

9. tablish the material allegations of his complaint, and
if on any proposition on which the plaintiff was bound
to show a preponderance of evidence the evidence was
evenly balanced, he could not recover. This instruction was
proper, and shows no favor to appellant or to appellee. By
instruction No. 2 at the court's own motion, the jury was
told that the burden of proof was on defendant to prove the
material allegations of his affirmative answer, and if he
failed so to do he must fail in his suit. Instruction No. 3 informed the jury as to what is meant by the preponderance
of the evidence. Taking these three instructions separately
and together we find that they correctly state the law, and
the jury could not have been misled by any one of them.

Instruction No. 13, given at appellee's request, is as follows: "If you believe from the evidence that on the 5th day

10. of April, 1897, the defendant and his wife executed to
the plaintiff a warranty deed to the lands involved
in this action and that said deed was executed for
the sole purpose of securing an indebtedness of $9,505.14,
then owing from the defendant to the plaintiff, then such
deed, though absolute on its face, would be a mortgage in
fact and under the circumstances, the defendant would be
entitled to the possession of the real estate mentioned in the
lease sued on in this action. If the defendant was entitled
to the possession as hereinbefore explained, then you may
consider that fact with all the other evidence relative to that

issue in determining whether or not the defendant know-ingly executed the lease mentioned in the complaint.'' Ap-pellant insists that this instruction is not within the issues and is not within the evidence. We do not agree with this contention, for it appears throughout the entire proceeding that this was one of the principal controverted questions, and the jury was properly informed by the instruction given, as to the law on this branch of the case.

Again, appellant contends that the trial court erred in giving to the jury instruction No. 14, requested by appellee, the principal objection being that there was no evidence before the jury of any relation of trust and confidence on which it could have excused the negligence of appellee in signing the deed without reading it. It is apparent from the evidence found in the record that it was contended by one party and denied by the other that the signature to the lease was obtained by unfair methods, that confidence of such a high degree was reposed in appellant by appellee, and he was so influenced by reason thereof, as to excuse his failure to read the lease before signing it. The question was one clearly within the issues, and on which much testimony was heard, and it was highly necessary and proper for the court to instruct the jury on this branch of the case, which was correctly done in the instruction given. We also find that this instruction was peculiarly applicable to the case at bar when we read it in connection with instruction No. 2, given of the court's own motion, and instruction No. 19, given at the request of appellant, in which the fraud and deceit re-ferred to in instruction No. 14 are fully explained.

Instruction No. 9 asked by appellant, was fully covered by instructions Nos. 10 and 11, given at his request. Instruction No. 23 was properly refused, because it clearly invaded

11. the province of the jury, and if given would prac-tically have directed what its verdict should be, re-gardless of the fact that there was much conflict in the evidence on the question as to whether or not appellee knew

when he signed the lease that it was such an instrument, or whether he believed that it was a defeasance, and would have instructed the jury to find for plaintiff, notwithstanding there was conflict also in the evidence on the prior relations existing between the parties, and particularly as to whether such relations and conduct on the part of appellant would excuse appellee for signing the instrument without reading it to discover its real character.

Additional objections, some merely technical, are presented because of the refusal to give other instructions requested by appellant. Without discussing those to 12. which we have not already called attention, it is sufficient to say that the case was fully and fairly presented by the court to the jury in what seem to us to be very accurate and intelligent instructions, whereby the attention of the jury was called to every phase of the law applicable to the evidence and issues in the case. It is equally apparent that the case has been fairly tried and substantial justice has been accomplished, therefore the judgment is affirmed.

NOTE.—Reported in 96 N. E. 614. See, also, under (1, 3, 6) 24 Cyc. 1404; (2) 31 Cyc. 385; (7) 17 Cyc. 216; (8) 3 Cyc. 388; (9) 38 Cyc. 1748; (11) 38 Cyc. 1646; (12) 3 Cyc. 418. As to unlawful detainer, see 120 Am. St. 32. As to civil actions for forcible entry and detainer, see 121 Am. St. 369. For a discussion of the estoppel of a tenant to deny the landlord's title in an action by the landlord to recover possession of the premises, see Ann. Cas. 1912 D 101.

CROPPER ET AL. *v.* GLIDEWELL.

[No. 7,650. Filed June 18, 1912. Rehearing denied October 15, 1912. Transfer denied December 20, 1912.]

1. DESCENT AND DISTRIBUTION.—*Surviving Subsequent Wife.— Rights of Children of Intestate.*—Under §2644 Burns 1894, §2487 R. S. 1881, providing that on the death of a husband, leaving a second or subsequent wife by whom he had no children, but leaving children alive by a previous wife, the land which descends to such wife, shall, at her death, descend to his children, the inter-

est of such wife in such lands is a fee simple, which, on her death
is cast upon the children of the intestate as the enforced heirs
of such wife, and the right to take as such enforced heir is one
that cannot be defeated by any act of such wife. p. 54.

2. DESCENT AND DISTRIBUTION.—*Right to Inherit.—Vested Rights.*—
An heir has no vested right to inherit the property of the ancestor. p. 56.

3. DESCENT AND DISTRIBUTION.—*Surviving Subsequent Wife.—
Rights of Children of Intestate.—Statutes.—Repeal.*—Section 3017
Burns 1908, §2486 R. S. 1881, providing that on the death of a
husband, intestate, leaving a widow and one child only, his
real estate descends one-half to each, and §2644 Burns 1894, §2487
R. S. 1881, providing that, if he die leaving a widow who was his
second or subsequent wife, by whom he had no children, but
leaving children alive by a previous wife, the land which descends to such widow shall, at her death, descend to such children, are modified by Acts 1899 p. 131, §2, to the extent of providing that a childless subseqent wife takes only a life estate
in the share descending to her and that the fee vests at once in
the children of the former marriage, but the latter statute is
not in conflict with §2644 Burns 1894, §2487 R. S. 1881, making
the children of a former marriage the enforced heirs of a childless subsequent wife, in so far as such provision applies to an
estate which descended to such childless subsequent wife prior
to the taking effect of said act of 1899. p. 56.

4. DESCENT AND DISTRIBUTION.—*Subsequent Wife.—Lease of Lands.
—Right to Rents Accruing After Death of Subsequent Wife.*—
Where a surviving second wife, whose husband had no children
by her, but who had a child by a former wife, leased for a year
land which descended to her under §3017 Burns 1908 and §2644
Burns 1894, §§2486, 2487 R. S. 1881, and died before the expiration of the term, the rents accruing after her death belonged to
such child, since the wife had no power to incumber the estate
so as to defeat or impair the inheritance vested by law in such
child. p. 57.

From Superior Court of Marion County (76,596) ; *Vinson
Carter,* Judge.

Action by Laura A. Glidewell against Joseph H. Cropper
and another. From a judgment for plaintiff, the defendants appeal. *Affirmed.*

Samuel Ashby, for appellants.

Harding & Hovey and *Smith, Duncan, Hornbrook &
Smith,* for appellee.

LAIRY, J.—On November 1, 1898, Henry T. Hockensmith, a resident of Marion county, Indiana, died intestate, seized of the real estate described in the complaint and cross-complaint, and left as his sole and only heirs at law, his widow, Elizabeth R. Hockensmith, whom he married in 1871, by whom he had no children, and appellee, Laura A. Glidewell, his only child by his first marriage. On March 21, 1908, said Elizabeth R. Hockensmith died testate, and devised all of her real estate to her brother, appellant Joseph H. Cropper.

After the death of Mrs. Hockensmith, a controversy arose as to the title to the real estate which she had inherited as the childless second wife of Henry T. Hockensmith. Mrs. Glidewell claimed title to this land as the enforced heir of her step-mother, and brought this action against appellants to quiet her title thereto. Appellant Joseph H. Cropper, claimed title to said real estate as sole heir of Mrs. Hockensmith, and also as her devisee, and filed a cross-complaint in said action, seeking to quiet his title to the same land.

By §23 of the act of 1852 (1 R. S. 1852 p. 251), on the subject of descent, if a husband died intestate leaving a widow and one child only, his real estate descended

1. one-half to his widow and one-half to his child. §3017 Burns 1908, §2486, R. S. 1881. Section 24 of the same act provides that if a man marry a second or subsequent wife, and has by her no children, but has children alive by his previous wife, the land which descends to such wife shall at her death descend to his children. §2644 Burns 1894, §2487 R. S. 1881.

In construing these statutes the Supreme Court first held that the right of a surviving second or subsequent wife, whose husband had no children by her, but had children by a former wife, was limited to a life estate in the lands descended from her husband. *Hendrix* v. *Sampson* (1880), 70 Ind. 350. It is held, however, by the later decisions that her interest in such lands is a fee simple, and that the children of the husband by his former marriage are her enforced heirs. *Utterbach* v. *Terhune* (1881), 75 Ind. 363; *Bryan* v. *Uland* (1884), 101 Ind. 477; *Thorp* v. *Hanes* (1886), 107 Ind. 324, 6 N. E. 920; *Habig* v. *Dodge* (1891), 127 Ind. 31, 25 N. E. 182; *Haskett* v. *Maxey* (1893), 134 Ind. 182, 33 N. E. 358, 19 L. R. A. 379; *Stephenson* v. *Boody* (1894), 139 Ind. 60, 38 N. E. 331; *Byrum* v. *Henderson* (1898), 151 Ind. 102, 51 N. E. 94; *Johnson* v. *Johnson* (1899), 153 Ind. 60, 54 N. E. 124; *Griffis* v. *First Nat. Bank* (1907), 168 Ind. 546, 81 N. E. 490.

These statutes were in force at the time of the death of Henry T. Hockensmith. By virtue of §23, *supra,* his widow became seized in fee simple of one-half of his real estate, and by virtue of the provision contained in §24, *supra,* his daughter by a former marriage was made the enforced heir of his widow Elizabeth R. Hockensmith. As such heir, this daughter would inherit all of the real estate which descended to her step-mother from Henry T. Hockensmith, and this right could not be defeated by any conveyance, devise or other act of Mrs. Hockensmith.

This much is conceded by appellants, but they contend that this right of inheritance, which was conferred by statute, could be taken away by an act of the legislature, and that this was done by an act approved February 24, 1899 (Acts 1899 p. 131). Section 2 of this act is as follows: "If a man die intestate, leaving surviving him a second or other subsequent wife without children by him, but leaving a child or children or their descendants alive, by a previous wife, such surviving, childless, second or other subsequent wife, shall take only a life estate in the lands of her deceased husband, and the fee thereof shall at the death of such husband vest at once in such child or children, or the descendants of such as may be dead, subject only to the life estate of such widow."

It is conceded by appellants that under the act of 1852, *supra,* Mrs. Glidewell was the enforced heir of Mrs. Hock-

ensmith from the date of her father's death, in the year of
1898, until the taking effect of this act, and that if the step-
mother had died during that time Mrs. Glidewell would
have taken the land in question by inheritance. But appellants insist that the provisions contained in §24, *supra,* by
which she was made such heir, were repealed by the act
quoted, and that after the taking effect of this act she was
no longer the enforced heir of Mrs. Hockensmith.

2.   An heir has no vested right to inherit the property
of the ancestor, and if the law under which Mrs.
Glidewell claims to be the heir of Mrs. Hockensmith
was repealed before the death of the latter, the former
cannot inherit the land in controversy.

Does the act of 1899, *supra,* repeal the provisions contained in §24 of the act of 1852, *supra,* on the subject of
descent?

Section 2 of the act of 1899, *supra,* has the effect to reduce the estate, which a childless subsequent wife takes in
the lands which descend to her from her husband
3.   from a fee simple to a life estate, where such husband dies leaving children by a former marriage or
their descendants surviving him, and §6 of said act repeals
all acts and parts of acts in conflict with any of the provisions of the act of which it is a part. Section 2 of the act applies to all cases where the descent is cast on the childless
subsequent wife by the death of her husband after the taking effect of the act. In such a case she takes a life estate only
in the share which descends to her; but in cases where the
husband had died prior to the passage of the act of 1899,
and the estate had passed to the childless subsequent wife
under the provisions of the act of 1852, §2 of the later act
does not have the effect to reduce the estate which she holds
from a fee to a life estate. Such a construction would render the act unconstitutional.

The act of 1852 is repealed by the act of 1899 only in so
far as the latter act is in conflict with the former. Sections

17 and 23 of the act of 1852 provided what share a widow should take in the real estate of her deceased husband. These sections applied to all widows, and by virtue of their provisions the share which a widow took in her deceased husband's lands vested in her in fee simple. By these sections the childless subsequent wife, whose deceased husband left a child or children by a former marriage, took the same interest and the same estate as any other widow. Section 2 of the act of 1899, *supra,* modifies these two sections to the extent of providing that such childless subsequent wife takes only a life estate in the share of her husband's land which descends to her, and that the fee vests at once in the surviving children by former marriages and the survivors of those who are dead. To this extent it is in conflict with the sections above referred to. The provision which makes the children by a former marriage the enforced heirs of the childless subsequent wife, as to lands descended to her from the father of such children, is contained in §24 of the act of 1852, and the act of 1899 is not in conflict with this provision, in so far as such provision applies to estates, the inheritance of which had been cast on the childless subsequent wife prior to the taking effect of the later act. The provision can, of course, have no application to an estate which descends to such a wife from her deceased husband after the taking effect of the act of 1899, for the reason that no inheritable estate vests in her under this act. We therefore hold that the provision of §24 of the act of 1852, *supra,* is not repealed by implication, but is still in force, and that it regulates the descent of estates of the character under consideration, which vested under the provisions of the act of 1852.

One further question is presented. A short time prior to her death, Mrs. Hockensmith leased the real estate here in controversy to Herman Snyder for the term of

4. one year, at a rental of $170, for which amount she accepted the notes of the tenant. Appellant Joseph

H. Cropper, after the death of his sister, assuming to act as her administrator, took possession of and collected these notes, and had the proceeds thereof in his possession prior to the commencement of this action. The trial court held that appellee was entitled to such part of the proceeds of these notes as represented the rent which fell due after the death of Mrs. Hockensmith. In this we think that the court was clearly right. Mrs. Hockensmith had no right to incumber the estate in such a way as to defeat or impair the right of inheritance vested by law in Mrs. Glidewell. If she could lease for one year beyond her death, she could make a valid lease for ninety-nine years, and take notes for the rent, which, being personal property, on her death would go to her administrator for the benefit of her heirs. The children by the previous marriage of her deceased husband, not being heirs as to her personal estate, would be thus substantially defeated of their rights of inheritance. We think that the rent which accrued after the death of Mrs. Hockensmith belonged to appellee.

In every ruling presented by this appeal, the court consistently held that appellee was the owner in fee simple of the real estate described in her complaint and that appellants had no right, title or interest therein. In this there was no error.

Judgment affirmed.

NOTE.—Reported in 98 N. E. 1012. See, also, under (1, 3) 14 Cyc. 38, 75; (2) 14 Cyc. 25. For a discussion of the right to take property by inheritance or will as a natural right protected by the constitution, see 9 Ann. Cas. 726.

LAKE SHORE AND MICHIGAN SOUTHERN RAILWAY COMPANY *v.* MYERS.

[No. 7,537. Filed May 29, 1912. Rehearing denied December 81, 1912.]

1. NEGLIGENCE.—*Complaint.—Charges of Several Acts of Negligence.*—A complaint for personal injuries is not objectionable for charging several acts of negligence in one paragraph, unless it counts upon the combined effects of two or more of the alleged negligent acts. p. 62.

2. NEGLIGENCE.—*Complaint.—Charges of Several Acts of Negligence.—Proof.*—Where several acts of negligence are charged in the same paragraph of complaint, proof that any one of such acts was the proximate cause of the injury is sufficient to sustain the action. p. 62.

3. RAILROADS.— *Crossing Accident.— Complaint.— Sufficiency.*— In an action against a railroad company for injuries received in a crossing accident, a complaint averring that defendant maintained double tracks across a street that was used by many people, that such crossing was dangerous and was so recognized by defendant, that on the evening of the injury, plaintiff was waiting to cross as soon as defendant's west-bound train had passed, that such train was closely followed by another train on the same track, that plaintiff attempted to cross when said train had passed and was struck by an east-bound train which approached without notice or warning, and charging negligence in failing to light the crossing, in failing to maintain a flagman thereat, in running the west-bound trains in such close proximity to each other as to divert plaintiff's attention from the danger of the east-bound train, in failing to give warning or signal of the approach of the east-bound train, and in running said train at a dangerous rate of speed, sufficiently averred actionable negligence warranting a recovery in the absence of contributory fault on the part of plaintiff. p. 63.

4. NEGLIGENCE.—*Complaint.—Contributory Negligence.—Jury Question.*—Where, in an action for personal injuries, the averments of the complaint do not show contributory negligence as a matter of law, it is for the jury to determine from the evidence whether plaintiff used due care to prevent the injury. p. 63.

5. RAILROADS.—*Crossings.—Signals.—Duty.*—It is the duty of a railroad company, independently of statute or ordinance, to give reasonable and timely warning of the approach of its trains to a public highway crossing. p. 64.

6. RAILROADS. — *Crossing Accident.* — *Contributory Negligence.* — *Verdict.—Answers to Interrogatories.*—Where, in an action for injuries sustained in a railroad crossing accident, the jury's answers to interrogatories show that plaintiff looked and listened before attempting to cross the tracks, that he heard no sound or signal of a train from the west on the north track, but saw a train approaching from the east on the south track, the speed of which he could not determine, that his line of vision was cut off and that as he approached the north track he heard a signal which confused him and caused him to halt, and that his position on the south track was one of danger, it cannot be said that plaintiff was negligent as a matter of law in attempting to cross the north track, since he was not bound to wait until absolutely certain that no train was approaching on the north track, but to use ordinary care in attempting to cross, and such answers are not in irreconcilable conflict with the finding in the general verdict for plaintiff, that he was in the exercise of ordinary care. p. 65.

7. APPEAL.— *Review.*— *Verdict.*— *Answers to Interrogatories.*— A general verdict will not be set aside on appeal on answers to interrogatories that are not in irreconcilable conflict therewith. p. 66.

8. TRIAL.—*Answers to Interrogatories.—Contradictory Answers.—Effect.*—Where the answers to interrogatories returned by the jury are contradictory, they nullify each other and are rendered ineffective. p. 68.

9. RAILROADS.—*Crossing Accident.—Care Required by Person in Perilous Position.—Contributory Negligence.*—The law does not hold a person, who, without fault on his part, is placed in a position of imminent peril, to the same rule of deliberation and care that governs one who is not in such peril and has time and opportunity more accurately to determine his line of conduct, so that where plaintiff, after waiting for a west-bound train to pass on defendant's south track, saw another west-bound train approaching while he was crossing the track, and after he had advanced far enough to see an east-bound train on the north track, was in a position of peril from which there was no escape, except by continuing across the north track or retreating across the south track, it cannot be said as a matter of law that he was guilty of contributory negligence, but the question was one for determination by the jury. p. 69.

10. RAILROADS.—*Highway Crossings.—Rights of Persons on Highway.*—The rights of a person on a public highway are equal to those of a railroad company whose tracks are situate thereon, except as to the latter's right of priority when both need to use the highway at the same time. p. 70.

11. RAILROADS.— *Crossings.— Signals.— Statutory Provision.*— Section 5431 Burns 1908, §4020 R. S. 1881, requiring the sounding of the whistle and the ringing of the bell on the approach of a train to a crossing, applies to crossings in an incorporated town, in the absence of an ordinance of the town prescribing different regulations. pp. 70, 71.

12. RAILROADS.—*Crossing Accident.—Instructions.—Harmless Error.*—An instruction in an action against a railroad company for injuries incurred in a crossing accident, stating that the whistle on defendant's engine should have been sounded when the train was within eighty rods of the crossing, though technically incorrect, was harmless where the jury found that the whistle was not sounded at all. p. 71.

13. APPEAL.—*Review.—Instructions.—Invading Province of Jury.—Refusal.*—An instruction which invades the province of the jury is properly refused. p. 71.

14. RAILROADS.—*Crossing Accident.—Instructions.—Harmless Error.*—In an action against a railroad company for injuries received in a crossing accident, an instruction submitting to the jury the question of whether ordinary care on the part of defendant required the presence of a watchman at the crossing, and an instruction on defendant's liability with reference to lighting the crossing, if erroneous, were harmless, where the jury by its answers to interrogatories, found that defendant's failure to sound the whistle or ring the bell as the train approached the crossing was the proximate cause of plaintiff's injury. p. 73.

15. APPEAL.—*Burden of Showing Error.*—Appellant must show prejudicial error, to obtain relief on appeal, since a judgment will be affirmed where the only errors disclosed by the record were harmless. p. 74.

16. APPEAL.—*Review.—Harmless Error.—Evidence.*—The erroneous admission of evidence which in no way affected the result of the case, was harmless. p. 75.

From DeKalb Circuit Court; *Emmet A. Bratton,* Judge.

Action by Guy Myers, by his next friend, George Myers, against the Lake Shore and Michigan Southern Railway Company. From a judgment for plaintiff, the defendant appeals. *Affirmed.*

Walter Olds and *F. J. Jerome,* for appellant.
P. V. Hoffman and *C. M. Phillips,* for appellee.

FELT, J.—Appellee brought this action, by his next friend, for damages resulting from an injury to appellee alleged to

have been caused by the negligence of appellant. There
was a trial by jury, verdict for appellee in the sum of
$1,000 and judgment thereon.

The first error assigned and relied on by appellant is
that the court erred in overruling the demurrer to the complaint.

The complaint, in substance, avers that appellant's double-
track railroad crosses a street in the business center of
Waterloo; that said crossing was used by many people, both
on foot and in vehicles; that it was a dangerous crossing,
and was so recognized by appellant; that on the evening of
April 4, 1908, appellee was at said crossing, waiting to
cross said railroad as soon as one of appellant's west-bound
freight-trains had passed; that said west-bound freight was
closely followed by another train on the same track; that
when said freight had passed, appellee, without warning
or notice of the approach of another train, attempted to
cross, and was struck by an east-bound train, and injured.

It is then charged that appellant was negligent (1) in not
maintaining a flagman at said crossing during the evening,
(2) in failing to keep said crossing lighted, (3) in running
a second train in such close proximity to said west-bound
freight as to divert appellee's attention from danger on the
other track from a train running in the opposite direction,
(4) in negligently failing to give the statutory or any other
warning of the approach of said east-bound train, and (5)
in running said train over said crossing at night at a dangerous rate of speed of twenty miles an hour.

It is not a valid objection to a complaint for personal injuries that it charges several acts of negligence in the same
paragraph. Proof that any one of such acts was the
1. proximate cause of the alleged injury is sufficient
to sustain the action, unless the complaint counts
upon the combined effects of two or more of such al-
2. leged acts. *Chicago, etc., R. Co. v. Barnes* (1905), 164
Ind. 143, 149, 73 N. E. 91; *Standard Oil Co.* v. *Bow-*

ker (1895), 141 Ind. 12, 16, 40 N. E. 128; *Pittsburgh, etc., R. Co.* v. *German Ins. Co.* (1909), 44 Ind. App. 268, 271, 87 N. E. 995; *New York, etc., R. Co.* v. *Callahan* (1907), 40 Ind. App. 223, 225, 81 N. E. 670.

The averments of the complaint are sufficient to charge appellant with actionable negligence, and to warrant a recovery in the absence of contributory fault on the
3. part of appellee. *Cleveland, etc., R. Co.* v. *Miles* (1904), 162 Ind. 646, 650, 70 N. E. 985. The averments of the complaint do not show appellee to have been guilty of contributory negligence as a matter of law,
4. and it was, therefore, a question for the jury to determine from the evidence whether he used due care to prevent the injury. *Cleveland, etc., R. Co.* v. *Miles, supra,* 654; *Baltimore, etc., R. Co.* v. *Rosborough* (1907), 40 Ind. App. 14, 18, 80 N. E. 869.

The substance of the jury's finding in its answers to interrogatories is as follows: Appellee was injured about 8 o'clock p. m. on April 4, 1908, by being hit by an eastbound freight-train on the north main track of appellant's railroad, at the crossing of said railroad and Wayne street, one of the business streets of the town of Waterloo; that said train was running at a speed of about twenty-five miles an hour; that at said crossing there were two main tracks, and two side-tracks south of the main tracks; that said crossing was much used by the people of the town and surrounding country; that the night of April 4, 1908, was a dark night, and said crossing was not so lighted that the north track could be seen for any considerable distance on such a night while a train was passing over said crossing on the south track; that just prior to the injury, appellee stood on the south side of a west-bound train on the south track waiting for said train to pass so he could cross over to the other side; that he looked and listened for a train from the west, and continued so to do until he started to go across the tracks, which he did as soon as the caboose of the west-

bound train had passed far enough to let him proceed; that
at the time he started to cross said tracks he saw another
train about 240 feet distant, coming from the east on the
south track; that he did not know whether said train was
a freight-train or a passenger-train; that at the time appellee started to cross said tracks he had no knowledge that
a train was approaching on the north track from the west;
that the passing caboose obstructed the angle of his vision so
that he could not see the train approaching from the west,
until near the north track; that if appellee had looked to the
west when he passed across the south main track in the rear
of the caboose of the west-bound train, and before stepping
on the north main track, he could not have seen the east-
bound train in time to have avoided the injury; that as
appellee approached the north track there was a warning
call from the conductor of the west-bound train that a train
was coming, but such call did not say from which direction;
that this call confused appellee, and momentarily halted
him, so that he was caught by the north side of the pilot on
the east-bound train; that but for such delay he would
have gotten safely over; that the bell on the engine of said
east-bound train was not ringing as it approached and
crossed Wayne street, nor was the crossing whistle sounded;
that if the crossing whistle had been sounded appellee could
have heard it and if a flagman had been at the crossing to
signal him back, he would not have been injured.

Independent of statute or ordinance, it is the duty of a
railroad company to give reasonable and timely warning of
the approach of its trains to the crossing of a public
5. highway. *Pittsburgh, etc., R. Co. v. Terrell* (1912),
177 Ind. 447, 95 N. E. 1109, 1113; *Cleveland, etc., R.
Co. v. Miles, supra; Pittsburgh, etc., R. Co. v. Burton* (1894),
139 Ind. 357, 375, 37 N. E. 150, 38 N. E. 594; *Pennsylvania
Co. v. Krick* (1874), 47 Ind. 368, 371; *Indianpolis, etc., R.
Co. v. Hamilton* (1873), 44 Ind. 76, 82; *Lake Shore, etc., R.
Co. v. Boyts* (1897), 16 Ind. App. 640, 646, 45 N. E. 812. In

view of these authorities, it is clear that, under the circumstances, the jury was warranted in finding that appellant
was negligent in the operation of its trains at the
   6.   Wayne street crossing, and that such negligence resulted in appellee's injury. It follows, then, that
the general verdict will stand, unless it appears from the
answers to interrogatories that appellee was, as a matter of
law, guilty of contributory negligence. As already stated,
the answers to interrogatories show that appellee looked and
listened before he attempted to cross appellant's tracks; that
he heard no sound or signal of a train from the west, but
did see a train approaching him from the east on the south
track, the speed of which he could not determine; that his
line of vision was cut off, and as he approached the north
track he heard a signal which confused him and caused him
to halt.

His position on the south track was one of danger, and we
cannot say, as a matter of law, that he was negligent, under
the circumstances, in attempting to cross the north track.
He was not bound to wait until absolutely certain that no
train was approaching the crossing, but to use ordinary care
in attempting to cross. There is nothing in the answers to
interrogatories which is irreconcilable with the jury's finding in the general verdict, that he did use such care. *Stoy* v.
Louisville, etc., R. Co. (1903), 160 Ind. 144, 149, 66 N. E.
615. In the case of *Dieckman* v. *Louisville, etc., Traction
Co.* (1910), 46 Ind. App. 11, 89 N. E. 909, 91 N. E. 179,
speaking of a situation similar to that in the present case,
this court, at page 17, said: "If one acts naturally in a case
of sudden and instant peril, put on him by another, and is
injured, he is not guilty of negligence, although afterwards,
out of the presence of danger, with time to reflect, and in the
light of all known facts, it may appear that another course
of conduct might have led to his escape." To the same
effect are the following cases: *McIntyre* v. *Orner* (1906),

166 Ind. 57, 69, 76 N. E. 750, 4 L. R. A. (N. S.) 1130, 117
Am. St. 359, 8 Ann. Cas. 1087; *Indiana R. Co.* v. *Maurer*
(1903), 160 Ind. 25, 28, 25 N. E. 156; *Clarke* v. *Pennsylvania Co.* (1892), 132 Ind. 199, 31 N. E. 808, 17 L. R. A.
811; *Lake Erie, etc., R. Co.* v. *McHenry* (1894), 10 Ind.
App. 525, 527, 37 N. E. 186.

Dieckman v. *Louisville, etc., Traction Co., supra,* and
Cleveland, etc., R. Co. v. *Miles, supra,* are similar in principle and in their main facts to the case at bar, and the important and controlling questions raised by appellant in this
case are fully answered by those decisions, adversely to appellant's contention. The Dieckman case also distinguishes
the line of cases relied on by appellant from those applicable
in that and in this case, making it unnecessary for us again
to discuss in detail such propositions.

The question of contributory negligence was, under the
averments of the complaint and the evidence, a question for
the jury. The answers to interrogatories are not in
7.   irreconcilable conflict with the general verdict, and
this court cannot on such showing disturb the finding
of the jury. *Lake Erie, etc., R. Co.* v. *Oland* (1912), 49 Ind.
App. 494, 97 N. E. 543; *Cleveland, etc., R. Co.* v. *Van Laningham* (1913), 52 Ind. App. 156, 97 N. E. 573.

Objection is made both to instructions given and to the
refusal of the court to give certain instructions tendered by
appellant. The instructions given were quite as favorable to
appellant as the law will warrant. Those refused all center
around the proposition that the jury should have been told
that appellee was guilty of contributory negligence as a matter of law, and to propositions having to do with the town of
Waterloo and appellant.

We find no error harmful to appellant in relation to the
instructions given or refused. Neither was there any harmful error in the admission or exclusion of evidence as shown
by the record.

The motions for judgment on the answers to the interrogatories and for a new trial were properly overruled.

Judgment affirmed.

ON PETITION FOR REHEARING.

FELT, J.—Appellant, in its petition for a rehearing, insists with much zeal that the court in the original opinion failed to give a sufficiently full and accurate statement of the facts on which to base an opinion and failed to consider in detail some questions presented by the briefs and record.

In view of the character of the questions urged we have with much care reexamined the several questions presented. With reference to the facts found by the jury in answer to interrogatories, in addition to the statement in the original opinion, the finding shows that the crossing where the injury occurred was at the business center of the town, which had a population of about 1,200; that appellant kept a flagman at said crossing from 6 o'clock a. m. to 6 o'clock p. m., but not after that hour; that there was much travel at said crossing after 6 o'clock p. m.; that the train which struck plaintiff was "a pick-up stock train," running on an irregular schedule; that appellee saw the second train approaching on the south track from the east at the time he started to cross the track; that he proceeded across the tracks at the rate of six or eight miles an hour, and it would have required about five seconds for him to cross over; that he did not hear any warning call until he reached and was passing over the north track; that appellee would not have heard the bell ringing in time to avoid the collision had it been ringing; that he could have heard the whistle in time to avoid the collision, had it been sounded a short distance west of the crossing; that the noise of the train on the south track prevented appellee from hearing the approach of the train from the west; that after appellee advanced far enough to have seen the train approaching from the west, to escape a perilous position without crossing over the north track he would have been compelled to retreat across the south track in front of the oncoming train from the east; that appellee was between fifteen and sixteen years of age when injured; that if appellee had looked to the west when at the north rail of the south track, or when four feet south of the south rail of the north main track, he could have seen the train approaching which struck him; that he did not, as he approached and entered on the north main track, look to the west for an approaching train on said track; that the engine which struck him was equipped with an automatic device for ringing the bell, but the bell was not ringing when it approached nor when it passed over the crossing; that the engineer on the east-bound train did not give a crossing whistle of two long and two short blasts; that there was an arc light burning at a crossing, 160 feet away from the place of the accident.

Appellant contends that the answers which show that appellee did not look west after he started across the track, and that if he had looked to the west when at the north rail of the south track, or when four feet south of the south rail of the north main track, he could have seen the train approaching which struck him, show that appellee was negligent in attempting to cross.

The jury in answer to other interrogatories found that if he had looked to the west when he passed across the south main track in the rear of the caboose of the west-bound train, and before stepping on the north track, he could have seen the east-bound train in time to avoid the injury. The foregoing interrogatories are contradictory, and, under a well-established rule, nullify each other and are rendered ineffective. But there are other important facts to be considered in determining whether this court can declare appellee guilty of negligence contributing to his injury.

It is found that when he started to cross he saw the train approaching from the east, following the one that had just passed on the south track; that after he had advanced

9. far enough to see the east-bound train on the north track, to escape a perilous situation, without crossing the north track, he would have been compelled to retreat across the south track in front of the train approaching from the east. These and other findings that need not be repeated show that appellee was in a position of peril from the moment it was first possible for him to see the train that struck him, and in such a situation the law does not hold a person to the same rule of deliberation and care that governs when he is not in such imminent peril and has time and opportunity more accurately to determine his line of conduct. If he is not guilty of negligence in coming into such perilous situation in the first instance, it is a question for the jury to determine whether, under such circumstances and conditions, he used due care or was guilty of negligence contributing to his injury. *Cleveland, etc., R. Co.* v. *Miles* (1904), 162 Ind. 646, 70 N. E. 985; *Stoy* v. *Louisville, etc., R. Co.* (1903), 160 Ind. 144, 149, 66 N. E. 615; *Lowden* v. *Pennsylvania Co.* (1908), 41 Ind. App. 614, 619, 82 N. E. 941; *McIntyre* v. *Orner* (1906), 166 Ind. 57, 69, 76 N. E. 750, 4 L. R. A. (N. S.) 1130, 117 Am. St. 359, 8 Ann. Cas. 108; *Pennsylvania Co.* v. *McCaffrey* (1894), 139 Ind. 430, 436, 38 N. E. 670, 29 L. R. A. 104; *Davis* v. *Chicago, etc., R. Co.* (1907), 159 Fed. 10, 88 C. C. A. 488.

In this case the complaint alleges that as appellee started to cross in the rear of the caboose he saw the second train approaching from the east in such close proximity that his attention was diverted and centered on that train, and he did not see the train approaching from the west. The jury found that the train which struck him was a ''pick-up'' running on irregular time; that the noise of the passing train prevented his hearing the approach of the train on the north track; that he looked and listened for a train from the west before starting to cross; that he could have heard the whistle if it had been sounded for the crossing, and it would have prevented the accident, but the whistle was not so sounded.

Conceding appellant's contention, that it was a useless precaution to look to the west while his view was obstructed by the train on the south track, it was, nevertheless, 10. the exercise of some care to listen for the whistle of a train on the north track. He was on a public highway where his rights were equal to those of appellant, except as to its right of priority when both needed to use the street at the same time. On this state of facts we cannot say as a matter of law that he was guilty of negligence in attempting to cross in the first instance. The question of appellee's negligence was properly submitted to the jury. *Evansville, etc., R. Co.* v. *Berndt* (1909), 172 Ind. 697, 701, 88 N. E. 612.

It is also contended that the court erred in giving instruction No. 3, at the request of appellee, and in refusing to give instruction No. 6, tendered by appellant. The instruction given told the jury, in substance, that appellant was guilty of negligence *per se* if the whistle of the engine that struck him "was not sounded within eighty rods" of the crossing and the bell was not rung continuously from a point eighty rods west of the crossing.

The one refused is as follows:

"The statute of the State of Indiana requiring engines to be equipped with whistle and bell, and the whistle to be sounded and the bell rung on approaching a crossing does not apply to streets in an incorporated town."

The statute (§5431 Burns 1908, § 4020 R. S. 1881) which requires the sounding of the whistle and the ringing of the bell, also provides that it shall not interfere with any 11. ordinance that has been or may be "passed by any city or incorporated town in this state regulating the management or running of such engines or railroads within the limits of such city or incorporated town." There is no showing that the town of Waterloo had, previous to the accident, passed any such ordinance as is contemplated by the statute. In the absence of an ordinance providing regulations differing from those prescribed by the statute, the statute applies to crossings within the limits of such incorporated town. *Pittsburgh, etc., R. Co.* v. *Terrell* (1912), 177 Ind. 447, 95 N. E. 1109, 1112, and cases cited; *Cleveland, etc., R. Co.* v. *Carey* (1904), 33 Ind. App. 275, 282, 71 N. E. 244.

Instruction No. 3 contains a technical error in stating that the whistle should have been sounded within eighty rods of the crossing, while the statute requires it to be

12. sounded when the engine is not less than eighty nor more than one hundred rods from the crossing. If such error could in any case be harmful, it is rendered harmless in this case by the finding of the jury that the bell was not rung nor the whistle sounded. The instruction tendered was erroneous in stating that the statute does not

11. apply to any incorporated towns, whereas it applies to all incorporated towns and cities not having ordinances in force making provisions in conflict with the requirements of the statute.

The first instruction asked for by appellant was a peremptory instruction directing a verdict in its favor, and was properly refused. The third instruction asked and

13. refused was to the effect that appellee was guilty of negligence preventing a recovery if he did not wait, after the west-bound train had passed, long enough, before attempting to cross to enable him to know that there was no train approaching from the west on the north track. On the facts of this case this was an invasion of the province of the jury, and the court did not err in refusing to give it. Appellant also complains of the refusal of the court to give instructions Nos. 7, 28 and 29 tendered by it. These instructions, in effect, told the jury that there could be no actionable negligence against appellant in failing to maintain a watchman at the crossing where appellee was injured unless it was shown that the town had passed an ordinance requiring appellant so to do. The complaint does not charge that

such an ordinance had been passed or was in force at the
time, but, among other acts of negligence, charges, in substance, that under the conditions shown at the crossing at
the time, reasonable and ordinary care on the part of appellant necessitated the keeping of a watchman at the
crossing between the hours of 6 o'clock p. m. and 10 o'clock
p. m.; that it negligently failed so to do, and appellee was
injured because of such failure.

The court in the fourth instruction, given at appellee's
request, in effect, told the jury that if it found the conditions relative to the crossing and the operation of appellant's
trains to be as alleged, and that the sounding of the whistle
and the ringing of the bell, as required by the statute, were
not on its part the exercise of reasonable and ordinary care,
and that such care required the presence of a watchman at
the crossing at the time òf said injury, and appellant failed
so to maintain a flagman at the crossing, and appellee's injury was caused by such failure, he could recover, if himself
free from contributory negligence.   The theory of the instruction seems to be that under certain conditions, to be
determined by the jury from the evidence, compliance with
the statute would not absolve appellant from actionable
negligence, and to free itself from liability it may, under
such peculiar and exceptional conditions, be required to do
something more than comply with the statute, or with an
ordinance duly passed, and authorized by statute.   This
doctrine is recognized in some of the states, but we do not
feel called on to determine the question in this case. *New
York, etc., R. Co.* v. *Leaman* (1891), 54 N. J. L. 202, 23 Atl.
691, 15 L. R. A. 426 and notes; *Lathan* v. *Staten Island R.
Co.* (1907), 150 Fed. 235.

It is not contended by either party that the town had
passed an ordinance requiring appellant to keep a watchman at the crossing where the accident occurred.   The duty
so to do, if it existed, arose because of the conditions at the

crossing and the manner in which appellant operated its trains.

The trial court evidently held the law to be that it was proper to submit to the jury, as a question of fact to be determined from the evidence, whether, under the conditions shown, ordinary care on the part of appellant required the presence of a watchman at the crossing.

Conceding for the purposes of this case, but not deciding, that the court erred in giving instruction No. 4, and in refusing to give those tendered on the subject of a 14. watchman, as above indicated, we think the error, if any, was harmless. One act of negligence charged in the complaint is the failure to sound the whistle and ring the bell on approaching the crossing, as required by statute. Such failure constitutes negligence *per se*. The jury in answer to interrogatories found that the whistle was not sounded and the bell was not rung, also, that appellee could have heard the crossing whistle in time to have avoided the accident if it had been sounded. These facts establish appellant's negligence, and show that it was the proximate cause of appellee's injury. The liability is thus determined, unless defeated by the contributory negligence of appellee.

Instruction No. 4, given by the court, and instructions Nos. 7, 28 and 29 refused, all relate to the question of liability, and since that is shown by the special finding of facts to be fixed by reason of appellant's failure to give the statutory warnings on approaching the crossing, it was not harmed by instructions which relate solely to the question of liability for failure to maintain a watchman at the crossing. They did not add to appellant's burden or make it more liable than was otherwise proven, even if erroneous.

The sixth instruction given by the court and the eighth and ninth requested by appellant and refused were solely on the question of liability with reference to the lighting of the crossing. The error, if any, in the giving and refusing of said instructions was rendered harmless for the same reasons above stated with reference to those on the subject of a watchman.

In Elliott, App. Proc. §642 it is said: "If the answers of the jury to special interrogatories clearly show that the party suffered no substantial injury from a wrong instruction, there is no available error."

In *Cleveland, etc., R. Co.* v. *Newell* (1885), 104 Ind. 264, 272, 3 N. E. 836, 54 Am. Rep. 312, it is said: "Without regard to whether the instruction complained of was in all respects technically and verbally accurate, since it appears from the answers to the special interrogatories that the jury found that the defendant was, in respect of the matters already alluded to, negligent, the error in the instruction, if there was any, was harmless."

It is fundamental that the party appealing must show prejudicial error, to be entitled to any relief on appeal.

15. Here the alleged erroneous instructions all relate to the question of liability. The answers clearly establish facts showing a liability for failure to give statutory warnings. The liability thus established could not be changed by any showing with reference to the lighting of the street or the maintenance of a watchman at the crossing. If the alleged erroneous instructions bore on appellee's alleged contributory negligence, or related to the amount of damages, a different question would be presented.

The principle underlying the doctrine of harmless error has been applied in many ways. Where the record, as in this case, shows clearly that the error, if any, did not harm the complaining party, the judgment will be affirmed, notwithstanding such error. *Elliott, App. Proc.* §§631-652; *Tracewell* v. *Farnsley* (1886), 104 Ind. 497, 4 N. E. 162; *McFadden* v. *Schroeder* (1894), 9 Ind. App. 49, 52, 35 N. E. 131; *Cline* v. *Lindsey* (1887), 110 Ind. 337, 341, 11 N. E. 441; *Ellis* v. *City of Hammond* (1901), 157 Ind. 267, 271,

61 N. E. 565; *Muncie Pulp Co.* v. *Hacker* (1906), 37 Ind. App. 194, 209, 76 N. E. 740; *Rink* v. *Lowry* (1906), 38 Ind. App. 132, 137, 77 N. E. 967; *Woolery* v. *Louisville, etc., R. Co.* (1886), 107 Ind. 381, 384, 8 N. E. 226, 57 Am. Rep. 114.

Furthermore, the record shows clearly that the main controversy in the trial of this case was over appellee's alleged contributory negligence.

Appellant tendered 29 instructions, and the court gave 22 of them, and in all 35 instructions. The instructions, taken as a whole, were favorable to appellant. On the subject of appellee's contributory negligence, those given at appellant's request not only covered every phase of the question applicable to the case, but repeated and reiterated similar and kindred propositions relating to appellee's alleged contributory negligence in such a way as to give undue prominence to the subject and obscure other questions of equal importance.

The special finding of facts on the question of appellant's negligence makes it plain that upon the material and controlling questions of the case the instructions were as favorable to appellant as the law will warrant and were so adroitly presented as to save to appellant every possible advantage.

The alleged error in the admission of evidence is likewise rendered harmless, if error, because its admis-
16. sion could in no way affect the question of appellant's liability, the assessment of damages or appellee's contributory negligence.

The petition for a rehearing is therefore overruled.

Ibach, C. J., Lairy, Adams, Myers and *Hottel, JJ.,* concur.

Note.—Reported in 98 N. E. 654, 100 N. E. 313. · See, also, under (1) 29 Cyc. 565; (2) 29 Cyc. 587; (3) 33 Cyc. 1053; (4) 29 Cyc. 628; (5) 33 Cyc. 956; (6) 33 Cyc. 1142; (7) 38 Cyc. 1927; (8) 38 Cyc. 1926; (9) 33 Cyc. 986, 1111; (10) 33 Cyc. 922; (11) 33 Cyc. 958; (12, 14) 33 Cyc. 1143; (13) 38 Cyc. 1646; (15) 3 Cyc. 887; (16) 38 Cyc. 1411. As to the duty of travelers on highways to use senses to avoid accidents at railroad crossings, see 90 Am. Dec. 780.

As to the care and precaution necessary in crossing a railroad track, see 24 L. Ed. U. S. 403. On the question of the care required of one in sudden emergency, see 37 L. R. A. (N. S.) 43. As to the duty to stop, look and listen after entering on first track see 17 L. R. A. (N. S.) 505. For the duty of a traveler approaching railway crossings as to place and direction of observation, see 37 L. R. A. (N. S.) 136.

HERITAGE *v.* HERITAGE.

[No. 7,823.   Filed October 8, 1912.   Rehearing denied December 31, 1912]

1. PARTITION.—*Judgments.*—*Conclusiveness.*—A judgment in a partition proceeding is conclusive between the parties, and exempt from collateral attack, as to all matters within the issues. p. 79.

2. PARTITION.—*Implied Warranty.*—The law annexes an implied warranty in all compulsory partitions, between tenants in common, of land derived by inheritance, extending to defects which existed in the title of the common ancestor, whereby each partitioner is made the warrantor of every other to the extent of the portion allotted to him, and cannot, therefore, be permitted to assert an adverse interest or title for the purpose of ousting another party to the same partition from his allotted portion. p. 86.

3. PARTITION.—*Adverse Claim.*—*Lease.*—Where the lands of the ancestor were apportioned among his heirs by a proceeding in partition, each heir became the implied warrantor of the title of every other as to the portion allotted to each, so that one of the heirs cannot thereafter assert that he has a right, under a lease executed by the ancestor, but which was not set up in any pleading in the partition proceeding, to hold possession of any of the land allotted to one of the other heirs. p. 88.

From Superior Court of Madison County; *H. Clarence Austill,* Judge.

Action by Albert L. Heritage against Oliver Morton Heritage. From a judgment for plaintiff, the defendant appeals. *Affirmed.*

J. E. Hall and *Chipman, Keltner & Hendee,* for appellant. *Wilkie & Wilkie,* for appellee.

LAIRY, J.—Appellee, who was plaintiff below, brought this action in ejectment against appellant, to recover possession of 51½ acres of land located in Madison county, Indiana. The court made a special finding of facts and pronounced conclusions of law thereon favorable to appellee. Appellant excepted to the conclusions of law at the time, and thereafter the court rendered judgment in favor of appellee. The only error assigned on appeal is that the court erred in its conclusions of law. The facts specially found by the court are, in substance, as follows: that William E. Heritage, the father of plaintiff and defendant, died on the 21st day of October, 1908, the owner of 617 acres of land, of which the land in controversy was a part; that, prior to his death, the father leased to Oliver M. Heritage 151½ acres of said land, which lease was to expire on the first day of March, 1910; that on the 17th day of February, 1909, a granddaughter of said William E. Heritage brought a suit to partition the lands of which her grandfather died seized, making both plaintiff and defendant parties defendant; that both plaintiff and defendant filed answers in general denial to said complaint, and that no averment was contained in the complaint in reference to the lease or tenancy of appellant, and such facts were not presented by any answer filed in the case; that pursuant to the complaint and the issues tendered by the general denials thereto, the court awarded partition, and appointed commissioners to make division of the land, that said commissioners filed their report, setting off to appellant 100 acres of the 151½-acre tract on which he held the lease given him by his father, and setting off to appellee, as a portion of his share in said lands, fifty-one and one-half acres of the tract covered by said lease. On the filing of said report, the court entered judgment confirming the same, which judgment is in part as follows: "That the partition of said real estate so made and reported and as above set out by said commissioners, be and the same is hereby confirmed and made firm, stable and effectual between the several parties therein named and as above shown, and that each of the parties shall hold the real estate above described so set off and partitioned to them in severalty in fee simple and that the rights of the other parties therein severally be forever severed and partitioned, and that the said several tracts be set off as above shown, and shall be and remain the property of each of said parties severally named, divested of any claim or interest of the other parties to this cause.'' The court further finds that appellant went into possession of said tract of 151½ acres under said lease prior to the death of his father, and sowed a part of the land in controversy to wheat, and at the date of said partition suit said appellant was still in possession of said land, claiming under said lease, and the wheat sown by him was growing on the land; that appellee knew at the time of said partition suit that appellant was in possession of said land and claiming the same under said lease, and also knew that one-half of the wheat growing on said land had been inventoried as a part of the estate of his deceased father, and that the commissioners who made the partition knew that appellant was in possession of said 151½-acre tract; that after judgment in said partition suit, appellee demanded possession of said fifty-one and one-half acres, and that appellant at that time refused and still refuses to deliver possession of the same.

On the foregoing facts the court pronounced the following conclusions of law: ''1st. That the plaintiff has been damaged in the sum of $1. 2nd. That the defendant holds possession of said 51½ acres described in the plaintiff's complaint without right. 3rd. That the plaintiff have immediate possession of said 51½ acres described in the complaint herein.''

The position of appellant is that he has a right under the lease from his father to hold possession of the 51½-acre tract, set off to his brother in said partition suit, until the expiration of said lease; while appellee contends that he is entitled to the immediate possession of said land under and by virtue of said decree in partition.

It is very clear that the land of the ancestor, William E. Heritage, descended to his heirs subject to the lease in favor of his son Oliver M. Heritage, and that said lease would have remained in full force and effect as against said heirs until it expired, were it not for the judgment in the partition suit, set out in the special finding of facts. The question to be decided is, Did the decree in the partition suit have the effect to terminate the rights of appellant under his lease so far as it affected land set off to other parties to said partition suit? And, Is appellant estopped by said decree from setting up or asserting any claim under said lease?

The rule that a judgment is conclusive between the parties to it on all the issues determined by it applies as well to judgments in partition as to judgments in any other

1. form of action. *Isbell* v. *Stewart* (1890), 125 Ind. 112, 25 N. E. 160; *Brown* v. *Grepe* (1893), 135 Ind. 4, 34 N. E. 312; *Irvin* v. *Buckles* (1897), 148 Ind. 389, 47 N. E. 822; *Wright* v. *Nipple* (1883), 92 Ind. 310; *Eller* v. *Evans* (1891), 128 Ind. 156, 27 N. E. 418; *Doe* v. *Smith* (1849), 1 Ind. *451. In view of these cases, and many more that might be cited, it must be regarded as settled that a judgment in a partition proceeding is exempt from collateral attack as to all matters within the issues in such proceeding. The difficulty arises in determining, according to the decisions of our Supreme Court, what facts are in issue and what facts are not in issue in such a proceeding. The cases all agree that the title to the land sought to be partitioned may be put in issue by appropriate pleadings directly presenting that question for decision, but the difficulty arises in determining how far title is put in issue by the pleadings ordinarily employed in such proceedings.

In the case of *Crane* v. *Kimmer* (1881), 77 Ind. 215, the court, in discussing the question, said: "In all cases of partition, the rights and titles of the parties are required to be set forth in the petition. 2 R. S. 1876, p. 344, §2. This technically puts in issue the title to the land asked to be divided, and, by an answer in denial or otherwise, the title may be put in issue, and be adjudicated; and it is a general principle of the law, that whatever was or might have been adjudicated, under the pleadings in a case, shall be deemed to have been adjudicated, and the doctrine of *res adjudicata* puts a finality to the question. The decree in a partition suit, however erroneous, if the court had jurisdiction, can not be attacked collaterally in a suit in ejectment. *Murphy* v. *Williamson* [1877], 5 Cent. L. J. 116. This decree not only settles and designates the shares of the owners of the land, but equally settles and fixes their then title to the same.'' This case is expressly disapproved and impliedly overruled on this point in the case of *Miller* v. *Noble* (1882), 86 Ind. 527. In that case the court said: ''It is not shown that the question of title was put in issue. There seem to have been only such pleading as are ordinarily employed in partition proceedings, and only such an assertion of title as was sufficient to entitle appellant to partition. The object of the action, so far as this record shows, was solely to secure a division of the land and an allotment of shares. The decree neither settles nor professes to settle any question of title; it does no more than direct partition. As title was not put in issue, and as the decree does not attempt to settle any question of title, the titles of the respective parties were neither weakened nor strengthened. Ordinarily, proceedings in partition do not settle title; at all events they create no new title—they simply divide into separate shares the land as held under existing titles. *Utterback* v. *Terhune* [1881], 75 Ind. 363; *Avery* v. *Akins* [1881], 74 Ind. 283; *Teter* v. *Clayton* [1880], 71 Ind. 237; *Knight* v. *McDonald* [1871], 37 Ind. 463. * * * The appellant presses upon our consideration the case of *Crane* v. *Kimmer* [1881], 77 Ind. 215, and there are some expressions in the opinion which seem to sustain his theory of the law. In so far as the expressions found in that opinion are in conflict with the cases we have cited, they must be deemed to be incorrect statements of the law.''

In the case of *Green* v. *Brown* (1896), 146 Ind. 1, 44 N. E. 805, it is held that the question of title is not ordinarily in issue in partition proceedings, and that the presumption in such cases is that title is not in issue.

In the later case of *Irvin* v. *Buckles, supra,* it appears that the widow of Wayne Scott, deceased, was the owner of a certain forty-acre tract of land, by reason of the fact that she and her husband held it at the time of his death as tenants by the entireties. She also owned the undivided one-third of 180 acres, of which her husband died seized in his own right. After the death of her husband, the widow brought a suit in partition against the other heirs of her deceased husband, alleging that he died the owner in fee simple of 220 acres of land, described, and in which was included the forty-acre tract owned by said widow. She also alleged that she was the owner in fee simple of the undivided one-third of the lands described, and that her four children were the owners of the undivided two-thirds thereof. Partition was decreed according to the averments of the petition, and sixty acres, including the buildings, were set off to the widow as her full interest in said real estate, and 160 acres were set off to the four children, including the forty-acre tract, which at the time of the death of the ancestor was held by him and his wife as tenants by the entireties. Afterward the 160 acres set off to the four children were partitioned among them, and the forty-acre tract in question was set off in severalty to Jennie Buckles, one of said children. Later, the widow, having intermarried with Hamer Irvin, brought an action in ejectment against Jennie Buckles to recover the forty-acre tract in question, on the theory that she became the owner thereof at the death of her husband,

and that her title was not affected by the proceedings in partition. The trial court held that she could not recover, and this judgment was affirmed on appeal. In the opinion in this case the court reviews the authorities at some length and expresses its conclusions as follows: "From these authorities it is quite clear that while a decree in an ordinary partition proceeding does not conclusively settle any question of title, yet, it is equally clear from them, that some things are conclusively settled and put at rest by the decree. *Wright* v. *Nipple* [1883], 92 Ind. 310; *Fleenor* v. *Driscoll* [1884], 97 Ind. 27. One is, the fact of partition itself, where the court has jurisdiction over the parties and subject. The decree is *res adjudicata* as between such parties and is a bar to another partition proceeding between the same parties for the same land. It is also conclusive as to the proportion owned by each co-tenant. None of them can afterwards say or maintain that he owned a greater proportion, or a greater undivided interest than that which is adjudged by the decree, however true such claim may be; because the decree like all other decrees or judgments imports absolute verity as to every fact essential to its existence. The fact that the parties to such decree were co-tenants, that is either joint tenants or tenants in common in the land according as is alleged in the petition and adjudged in the decree, it would seem is equally essential to the existence of the decree, and if so it is conclusively settled by it. It is observed that none of our cases decide this question. There is no case we have been able to find in our decisions where the petition for partition embraced lands belonging exclusively to one of the parties, or to the petitioner, and as was the case here, alleged to belong to them all as tenants in common, and the decree in partition rendered accordingly. But the above quotations from our cases indicate that this court would have decided that a decree of partition is *res adjudicata* that the parties thereto were co-tenants in the whole of the land involvd in the decree, and estops them from denying such co-tenancy."

The decision in the case of *Finley* v. *Cathcart* (1898), 149 Ind. 470, 48 N. E. 586, 49 N. E. 381, 63 Am. St. 292, was based on the following state of facts: William Cathcart died the owner of fifty acres of land leaving, as his sole heirs seven children, of whom Mrs. Finley, the appellant, was one. In 1892, after the death of her father, Mrs. Finley purchased from two of the children their undivided two-sevenths of said real estate, and had the deeds properly recorded, and the next year she purchased from her brother, Daniel Cathcart, his undivided one-seventh therein, but failed to have his deed recorded. In 1896, Walter Mabry and Stephen S. Mabry, having acquired the interest of William F. Cathcart, another heir of William Cathcart, deceased, filed a petition for partition, making Mrs. Finley, Daniel Cathcart, John M. Cathcart and Minnie Cathcart defendants, alleging that each plaintiff owned the one-twenty-first part in value of said real estate, and that Mrs. Finley owned three-sevenths and each of the other defendants one-seventh, when the truth was that Mrs. Finley owned four-sevenths and that Daniel E. Cathcart owned no interest in the land, having previously conveyed his undivided interest to his sister Mrs. Finley. All the defendants were duly notified of the pendency of said proceedings, and failed to appear and were defaulted. Thereupon the court decreed partition among plaintiffs and defendants in the shares set out in the petition. Commissioners were appointed, who divided the land accordingly, and set off to Daniel E. Cathcart eleven acres, as his share therein. Mrs. Finley brought an action against Daniel E. Cathcart to quiet her title to eleven acres set off to him in such partition proceeding. The trial court gave judgment for the defendant, and on appeal to the Supreme Court this judgment was reversed, and it was held that appellant was entitled to have the title to the real estate, set off to Daniel E. Cathcart in said partition proceeding, quieted in her.

The decision of this case seems to be in direct conflict with the principle announced in the case of *Irvin* v. *Buckles*. *supra,* to the effect that a judgment in partition is conclusive on the parties as to the proportion of the land owned by each co-tenant, and that some of said parties can afterwards maintain that they owned a greater proportion or a greater undivided interest than that which is adjudicated by the decree, however true that may be. This principle announced in the case of *Irvin* v. *Buckles, supra,* is not referred to in the case of *Finley* v. *Cathcart, supra,* and no effort is made to reconcile the two decisions. The learned judge who wrote the later of the two cases calls attention to the fact that both plaintiff and defendant were made defendants to the partition proceeding, and that the only issue tendered to them was tendered by the complaint, and that as no cross-complaint was filed by either defendant against the other, alleging the proportion of said real estate that either defendant owned as against the other, no issue on this question was presented by the pleadings as between said defendants. The only legitimate conclusion that can be reached by this course of argument is that the finding of the court, fixing the proportionate shares of the two defendants in that case, was entirely outside the issues presented, and that a decree based thereon was *coram non judice* and absolutely void. The result of such a conclusion would be, that in every partition proceeding, where there are several defendants, and said defendants default or file answers in general denial, and file no cross-complaint as against each other, the court would have no power to go further than to determine and set off to the plaintiff his interest in the land; and that it would have no power under such issues to partition the land among the defendants; and in every case where the court has assumed so to proceed beyond the issues, its judgment is absolutely void, and subject to collateral attack.

The court in the case we are reviewing did not place its decision on the ground that the decree of the court fixing the proportionate share of each defendant was absolutely void, as being outside the issues, but contented itself with saying on page 481: "Without further extending this opinion, we are constrained to hold that the petition filed by the Mabrys for partition did not put in issue, between appellant and appellee, the title which the former held by the deed from the latter, and therefore, she is not precluded or estopped by the judgment from asserting, as against appellees, her title to the land in dispute through said deed. We must not be understood as holding that, had appellant, under the circumstances, been satisfied with the share assigned to her, and had accepted and acquiesced in such partition, she would not have thereby confirmed the same, and made it effectual between her and the appellee, nor as to what would be her situation were this controversy between her and an innocent purchaser for value from appellee. These questions are not involved, and therefore not decided."

We do not think that these two cases can be distinguished or reconciled on the ground that in the later case the question arose between two parties who were both defendants to the partition suit, while in the earlier case it arose between the person who was plaintiff in the partition suit and one of the defendants. We can hardly think that a different conclusion would have been reached in the case of *Irvin* v. *Buckles, supra,* even though it had appeared that a like decree had been rendered in a partition suit in which Mrs. Irvin and Mrs. Buckles had both been defendants, and wherein neither had filed a cross-complaint.

There is an apparent conflict in the decisions of our courts on the question under consideration, and we are unable to deduce therefrom any rule of uniform application on which all of such decisions can be reconciled, but we believe that this case can be properly decided by the application of the principle of the common law, whereby an implied warranty as between co-tenants was annexed to every involuntary partition of lands.

At common law every partition betwen co-parceners had annexed to it an implied warranty, that if, by any defect of title in the ancestor either of the parceners lost any

2. part of his share by eviction, the party affected might defeat the partition, or, at his election, obtain compensation from his co-parceners for the part so lost. *Dugan* v. *Hollins* (1853), 4 Md. Ch. 139; *Morris* v. *Harris* (1850), 9 Gill (Md.) 19; *Patterson* v. *Lanning* (1840), 10 Watts (Pa.) 135, 36 Am. Dec. 154.

In the case at bar, the title of appellant and appellee and the other heirs of William E. Heritage to the real estate partitioned among them was derived by inheritance from the common ancestor. They took as tenants in common, but the interests which they severally took in such land were acquired by descent or act of law, in the same manner as the estates of co-parceners were acquired in England by the rule of the common law. The right to compel partition of lands in England existed only between parceners, until the statutes of 31 Hen. VIII, by which such right was extended to joint tenants and tenants in common. Prior to the passage of this statute, joint tenants and tenants in common could parcel the land among themselves only by agreement, and there was no reason why the law should annex any implied warranty in such cases, because the parties making such partition were perfectly competent to protect themselves against future losses by liens or paramount titles by the terms of the conveyances; but since the right of compulsory partition has been given to tenants in common by statute, the courts have uniformly held that the law annexes an implied warranty in all compulsory partitions, wherein lands derived by inheritance are parcelled among tenants in common. This implied warranty does not, however, apply to partition among tenants in common who have become such by purchase, or in any other way than by descent from a common ancestor, and the warranty which the law implies extends only to defects which existed in the title of such common ancestor. *Patterson* v. *Lanning, supra; Morrice's Case*(1585), 6 Coke 12; *Venable* v. *Beauchamp* (1835), 3 Dana (Ky.) *321, 28 Am. Dec. 74; *Sawyers* v. *Cator* (1847), 8 Humph. (Tenn.) *225, 47 Am. Dec. 608.

The decisions seem to be in conflict as to whether this implied warranty extends to cases where tenants in common by conveyances voluntarily partition the lands of their ancestor. *Strohecker* v. *Housel* (1872), 3 Clark (Pa.) *327; *Rogers* v. *Turley* (1816), 4 Bibb (Ky.) 355; *Beardsley* v. *Knight* (1838), 10 Vt. 185, 33 Am. Dec. 193; *Huntley* v. *Cline* (1885), 93 N. C. 458; *Venable* v. *Beauchamp, supra; Davidson* v. *Coon* (1890), 125 Ind. 497, 25 N. E. 601, 9 L. R. A. 584; *Dawson* v. *Lawrence* (1844), 13 Ohio 543, 42 Am. Dec. 210; *Picot* v. *Page* (1858), 26 Mo. 398; 30 Cyc. 167, and authorities cited.

As the law makes each partitioner the warrantor of every other, to the extent of the portion allotted to him, and as no principle of law is better settled than that a warrantor cannot assert a claim against his own warranty, it clearly seems to follow that no party to a partition can be permitted to assert an adverse claim or title for the purpose of ousting another party to the same partition from the portion allotted to him.

In the case of *Davidson* v. *Coon,* supra, it was held that an heir who joined in a conveyance by which partition was made of the lands descended from his ancestor, could not afterwards maintain an action to subject the land so partitioned to a lien in his favor for an unpaid legacy, which, by the terms of the will of such ancestor, was made a charge on the land. In that case the court said: "The appellee is in this dilemma: If his deed is to have its usual effect it conveys his interest in the land, and releases his lien; if it is not to have its usual effect, it is because it was executed by him as one of several owners in common, but if it was executed by him as one of several owners he cannot assert his lien since that was buried or merged in his character of an owner.

Rossiter *v.* Lake Shore, etc., R. Co.—52 Ind. App. 88.

We are not unmindful of the doctrine that equity will not suffer a merger to take place where injustice would result, but that doctrine the appellee, after having voluntarily assumed the position of a tenant in common, is in no plight to invoke. Equity almost imperiously demands that this lien shall be merged, for no other course will promote justice. At law where the estate of a lienor meets that of the owner in one person, the lien is merged. The rule must govern here, for there is no equity to break its force.''

The lands of William E. Heritage having been apportioned among his heirs by a proceeding in partition, each heir became the implied warrantor of the title of every other

3. as to the portion allotted to him, and appellant cannot assert, as against the implied warranty which the law imposes, that he has a right under a lease executed by the ancestor to hold possession of any of the lands allotted to appellee.

Judgment affirmed.

NOTE.—Reported in 99 N. E. 442. See, also, under (1) 23 Cyc. 1331; 30 Cyc. 306; (2) 30 Cyc. 311. As to the effect of compulsory partition, see 101 Am. St. 864.

ROSSITER, ADMINISTRATRIX, *v.* LAKE SHORE AND MICHIGAN SOUTHERN RAILWAY COMPANY.

[No. 7,375. Filed December 19. 1911. Rehearing denied February 16, 1912. Transfer denied January 6, 1913.]

1. NEGLIGENCE. — *Complaint.* — *Allegations.* — *Legal Duty.* — In a negligence case, the complaint, to be sufficient, must show that there was a legal duty, owing by defendant to the person injured, which was violated by a want of care on the part of the wrongdoer proportionate to the duty imposed on him by law. p. 92.

2. RAILROADS.—*Injury to Trespassers.*—*Care Required.*—A railroad company owes no duty to a trespasser upon its tracks unless he is observed to be in a perilous position, in which event it at once becomes the duty of those operating the train to do all that persons of ordinary care and caution would do under like circumstances to save him from injury. p. 92.

Rossiter v. Lake Shore, etc., R. Co.—52 Ind. App. 88.

3. RAILROADS.—*Injury to Persons on Tracks.—Negligence.—Violation of Ordinance.*—The violation of a city ordinance regulating the speed of trains, is negligence rendering the railroad company liable for injuries caused thereby to a person who was lawfully upon its tracks. p. 92.

4. RAILROADS.—*Right of Way.—Rights of Owner of Fee.—Injury to Person on Tracks in Service of Owner of Fee.—Liability.*—Where a railroad company holds only an easement, the landowner has certain rights to the use of the right of way which entitle him to enter thereon when such entry is indispensable in the proper use and occupation of the fee in the adjoining land, so that where the complaint, in an action against a railroad company for the death of a surveyor, alleged that it was necessary for the landowner, in the survey of his lands adjoining the right of way, to take measurements along, across, upon and over defendant's right of way, and that while upon defendant's track in the performance of the work of taking such measurements for the landowner, plaintiff's decedent was killed, it cannot be said, as a matter of law that such use of the tracks was an interference with the superior rights of the railroad company so as to render decedent a trespasser, but the question is one of fact to be determined from the circumstances of the case. p. 93.

5. RAILROADS.—*Right of Way.—Trespassers.—Rights of Adjoining Landowner.*—The general rule that between stations and public crossings the track of a railroad company belongs to it exclusively, and that all persons who walk or drive thereon are trespassers, is limited in its operation with respect to the right of the owner of the fee to enter thereon when such entry is indispensable to the proper enjoyment of the adjoining land, and with respect to such owner's statutory right to a private crossing. p. 96.

6. RAILROADS.—*Injury to Persons on Tracks.—Complaint.—Sufficiency.—Allegations as to Place of Injury.*—In an action against a railroad company for the death of plaintiff's decedent caused by the negligent operation of defendant's train in violation of a city ordinance, a complaint charging that defendant was operating trains on its tracks in the city at the time of the injury, that it had four separate railroad tracks on its right of way within the city limits, that it had a railroad bridge within the city limits, that the right of way and the four tracks at such bridge and for a number of rods to the east thereof are curved sharply, that while decedent was necessarily on defendant's right of way, defendant negligently operated its train around said curve and over the curved track through the limits of the city, sufficiently shows that the place where decedent was killed was within the city limits. p. 97.

From Lake Circuit Court; *Willis C. McMahan*, Judge.

Action by Lucy M. Rossiter, administratrix of the estate of Frederick C. Rossiter, deceased, against the Lake Shore and Michigan Southern Railway Company. From a judgment for defendant, the plaintiff appeals. *Reversed.*

Bruce & Bruce, for appellant.
John B. Peterson, for appellee.

IBACH, P. J.—This action was brought by appellant to recover damages for alleged negligence resulting in the death of her husband.

The complaint is in a single paragraph. After averring that appellee is a corporation operating a railway through the city of Hammond, and setting out the location of its tracks, the complaint charges "that on the said September 6, 1905, and for several years prior thereto, by city ordinance, the said city of Hammond had duly enacted an ordinance regulating the speed of trains and cars through its said city limits, that the said ordinance was on September 6 in full force and effect, and one section thereof read as follows: 'That it shall be unlawful for any railroad company, agent or servant or employe of any such company, or other person to permit or cause any locomotive engine, car or train of cars to pass along or upon any railroad within the limits of said city at a greater rate of speed than six miles per hour.' That along the line of the defendant's right of way on September 6, 1905, there was a line of telegraph poles, the poles being placed one hundred feet apart. And along the lines of each of the other railroads both to the north and south of the defendant's line of road were lines of telegraph poles placed one hundred feet apart. That railroads having more than one track upon its right of way generally operate its trains by having the trains run on the right hand tracks; that is to say, on an east and west road, the trains going east will be run on the south track or tracks, and trains going west will be run on the north track or tracks, that being the general custom of the well managed railroads. That the deceased for many years prior to his death was a civil engineer of marked ability and was well known throughout the northern parts of the states of Illinois and Indiana; that he was at all times a man who was careful and methodical. That on the said September 6, 1905, the said Frederick C. Rossiter was engaged in surveying a long, narrow strip of land between the railroad of the defendant and the railroad next nearest to the defendant's road on the north. And the said Frederick C. Rossiter was then and there engaged in surveying the narrow strip of land between the defendant's road and the railroad next nearest the defendant's road on the south. That the said Frederick C. Rossiter was employed to make the said survey by the owner of the fee of the said strips of real estate between the said railroads, and also by the owner of the fee of the real estate upon which the defendant's railroad is situated. That it was necessary in making the said survey to take measurements along, upon and across and over the defendant's right of way. That on the said September 6, 1905, while the said Frederick C. Rossiter was in the line of his employment and duty in making the said survey the said defendant company then and there carelessly and negligently run and operated its train around the said curve upon a left hand track instead of the right hand track, and did then and there run and operate its said train at the dangerous, reckless and unusual rate of speed of seventy-five miles per hour upon and over the said curved track through the limits of the said city of Hammond contrary to the city ordinance in such cases made and provided as heretofore set forth in this complaint, and said defendant did then and there carelessly and negligently fail to blow the whistle or ring the bell or give any warning of the approach of the said train, and said defendant did then and there and thereby carelessly and negligently run the said train of cars against the said Frederick C. Rossiter and did then and there and thereby kill the said Frederick C. Ros-

siter, that the said Frederick C. Rossiter's death was brought
about without any fault or negligence on his part, but solely by reason of the carelessness and negligence of the defendant as aforesaid." The concluding part of the complaint relates to those dependent on the decedent, and the
damages suffered by them. To this complaint a demurrer
for want of facts was sustained. Judgment was rendered
on the demurrer, and plaintiff appeals. She assigns as
error the sustaining of said demurrer.

It is apparent that the theory on which the complaint
proceeds is not one of wilful injury, but rather one of mere
negligence. The rule is that to make a complaint
1. good in an action for negligence, it must appear from
the averments thereof that there was a legal duty
owing to the person injured by the person causing the injury, and that such duty was violated by a want of care on
the part of the wrongdoer proportionate to the duty imposed
on him by law. Appellant contends that her husband
was rightfully upon appellee's tracks, because he was employed by the owner of the fee in the land adjoining and in
the land on which the railroad is situated to go there to
make a survey. Appellee insists that although these facts
may be admitted to be true, and although they account for
decedent's presence upon the tracks, yet such facts are not
sufficient to show that he was rightfully there, but rather
show that he was where he had no right to be. If ap-
2. pellee is correct in this contention, then decedent must
be held to have been a trespasser, and appellee owed
him no duty until he was observed upon the tracks in a
perilous position, when it would at once become the duty
of the agents of appellee operating one of its trains to do all
that persons of ordinary care and caution would do under
like circumstances to save him from injury. If, how-
3. ever, he had a right to be on the tracks of appellee
to make the survey in question, then he was lawfully
there for such purpose, and could not be held to be a tres-

passer, and the failure to comply with the city ordinance regulating the speed of trains would be actionable negligence on the part of appellee.

The determination of the question presented by this appeal is not without difficulty. The identical point has never, we believe, been determined by any of the courts of the land, so that it becomes our duty to decide it, guided largely by the principles of law involved and aided by such decisions as we have been able to find which have been announced by other courts where kindred questions have been involved.

4.

The argument of counsel for appellant is, that where a railroad company exercises for its right of way an easement only, its user is not exclusive, and that the owner of the fee would have the right to a reasonable or necessary use of the railroad right of way, subordinate, of course, to the superior right of the railroad for the use of the easement for railroad purposes, but the railroad company would owe such owner of the fee or his employes the duty not to injure them negligently.

In the case of *Olive Sternenberg & Co.* v. *Sabine, etc., R. Co.* (1895), 11 Tex. Civ. App. 208, 213, 33 S. W. 139, the court said: "Common observation teaches that the owner of the fee may use the land for some purposes without interfering with the operation of the road, and without hindering the company in the exercise of any right. The right to fence the right of way, given by statute, and the duty to keep it free from nuisances, combustible material and the like, as declared by the courts, may not conflict with the use of the land by the owner for some purposes. The track may not be fenced at any place, and cannot be fenced at all places. Combustible material and noxious matter may be kept off the right of way, and still the owner need not necessarily be excluded from all use of it at all times and places. And a particular use of the land by the owner may not obstruct or hinder the exercise of any right or the performance of any duty. But if, in any instance, the right to use the land, claimed by the owner, is, in fact, irreconcilable with the right vested.in the railway company, the latter must prevail. So the question is whether or not the use made of the right of way by the owner of the fee, in this case, is such as is inconsistent with the rights of the railroad company."

In the case .of *Mize* v. *Rocky Mountain Bell Tel. Co.* (1909), 38 Mont. 521, 100 Pac. 971, 129 Am. St. 659, it was held that a laborer who was employed by the owner of the fee to clean out an irrigating ditch which crossed the railroad right of way was not a trespasser on the right of way.

In the case of *Kansas Cent. R. Co.* v. *Allen* (1879), 22 Kan. 285, 293, 31 Am. Rep. 190, the following language is used: "An easement merely gives to a railroad company a right of way in the land; that is, the right to use the land for its purposes. * * * The former proprietor of the soil still retains the fee of the land and his right to the land for every purpose not incompatible with the rights of the railroad company. Upon the discontinuance or abandonment of the right of way, the entire and exclusive property and right of enjoyment revest in the proprietor of the soil. After the condemnation and payment of damages, the soil and freehold belong to the owner of the land, subject to the easement or incumbrance, and such land-owner has the right to the use of the condemned property, provided such use does not interfere with the use of the property for railroad purposes. * * * The paramount right is with the railroad company, and the land-owner can do nothing which will interfere with the safety of its road, appurtenances, trains, passengers, or workmen. * * * In the use of the land, the railroad company had the paramount right, but the defendant in error had also the right to the land for every purpose not incompatible with the rights of the road. If the railroad company required exclusive occupancy of the land taken for the use of its railroad on account of the nature of its operations, or for the security of its trains, its passengers or its employes, it was entitled to such occupancy. * * * It is our opinion that it is a question of fact, not of law, whether the necessities of the railroad demand exclusive occupancy for its purposes, and what use of the property by the owner is a detriment to, or interference with the rights of the road."

The case of *Smith* v. *Pittsburgh, etc., R. Co.* (1904), 26 Ohio C. C. 44, follows the doctrine of *Kansas Cent. R. Co.* v. *Allen, supra,* in holding that it is a question of fact as to what use of the property by the owner of the fee is an interference with the rights of the railroad.

In *Smith* v. *Holloway* (1890), 124 Ind. 329, 24 N. E. 886, the Supreme Court of this State, by Elliott, J., said: "The owner can not interfere with the free use of the right of way, but subject to this use he may make all lawful use of the land." It may be remarked, however, that in all these cases cited, the question was that of the use of some portion of the right of way other than the track, by the owner of the fee. The one reported case which we have been able to find most similar to the present is that of *Houston, etc., R. Co.* v. *O'Donnell* (1905), 90 S. W. (Tex. Civ. App.) 886, and *Houston, etc., R. Co.* v. *O'Donnell* (1906), 99 Tex. 636, 92 S. W. 409. In this case the landowner was struck by a train and injured while on the right of way, returning from an inspection of his stock gates. The supreme court of Texas said: "At the time that he received the injury, O'Donnell was not a trespasser upon the right of way of the plaintiff in error. He owned the fee in the land and having lands on both sides of the right of way with gates for communication between his farms, O'Donnell had the right to enter upon the right of way for the purpose of inspecting and repairing the gates which the law charged him with keeping in repair." We do not consider it necessary, in disposing of this case, to go to the extent of the holding in the O'Donnell case, neither do we consider the right to be on appellee's right of way, at least upon its track, to extend beyond *necessary presence* in the performance of some act necessary to the full possession of the adjoining fee, and in such manner as not to interfere with the uninterupted use of such right of way by the railroad company. But from the cases considered, it will be seen that when the railroad company holds only an easement, the landowner has certain rights to the use of the right of way, and it is readily apparent that it may be at times indispensable for him to enter on the railroad right of way in the proper use and occupation of the fee in the adjoining land. If it appeared from the averments of the complaint before us that his presence on the right of way was merely a matter of convenience, or anything less than an actual necessity, we would not hesitate to hold the complaint insufficient as a matter of law. The complaint alleges that it was necessary for the landowner in the survey of his adjoining lands to take measurements along, across, upon and over the right of way of appellee. We are unable to say that such use of the right of way by the owner of the fee is, as matter of law, an interference with the rights of the railroad company. We must therefore conclude that it is a question of fact, to be determined from the circumstances of the case, whether decedent was necessarily on the right of way and the track in the performance of his employment by the owner of the fee, and whether this was an interference with the superior rights of the railroad company in the operation of its trains.

Appellee argues that between stations and public crossings the track of a railroad company belongs to it exclusively, and all persons who walk, ride or drive thereon 5. are trespassers, and if such persons walk, ride or drive thereon at the sufferance or with the permission of the company, they do so subject to all the risks incident to so hazardous an undertaking. This statement is well supported by authority, but is merely the enunciation of a general rule, which takes cognizance neither of certain rights which the owner of the fee has to the use of the right of way of the railroad, as set forth above, nor of the right of the owner of the fee to a private crossing, as provided by our statute.

Appellee further argues that the complaint charges as negligence the violation of a certain city ordinance of the city of Hammond, but fails to charge that the place 6. where the survey was being made was in the city of Hammond, and that the place where the decedent was killed was in the city of Hammond. We have carefully considered the complaint, and do not find it open to such objection, since it charges that appellee was operating trains on its tracks in Hammond at the time of the injury, that it had four separate railway tracks on its right of way within the city limits, that it had a railroad bridge within the city limits, that the railroad right of way and the four tracks at said bridge and for a number of rods to the east and southeast thereof, are curved sharply, that in making the survey it was necessary to take measurements along, upon and across defendant's right of way, that while decedent was in the line of his employment and duty in making said survey defendant then and there carelessly and negligently and over said curved tracks through the limits of the city of Hammond run and operated its train around said curve, and then and there killed decedent. These allegations sufficiently charge that the place where the survey was being made was in the city of Hammond, and that the place where decedent was killed was within the city limits.

We conclude that the complaint is sufficient to withstand demurrer, and for the error of the trial court in sustaining a demurrer to it the judgment is reversed.

Felt, C. J., Lairy, Myers, Hottel and Adams, JJ., concur.

NOTE.—Reported in 96 N. E. 956. See, also, under (1) 29 Cyc. 565; (2) 33 Cyc. 769; (3) 33 Cyc. 793; (4) 33 Cyc. 899; (5) 33 Cyc.

754; (6) 33 Cyc. 865. As to the duty of railroad companies to trespassers on the track, see 30 Am. St. 53; 36 L. Ed. U. S. 1064. On the question of the duty of a railroad company to keep lookout for trespassers on track, see 8 L. R. A. (N. S.) 1069; 41 L. R. A. (N. S.) 264.

WEIDENHAMMER ET AL. *v.* MCADAMS, EXECUTOR.

[No. 7,596. Filed June 21, 1912. Rehearing denied November 20, 1912. Transfer denied January 7, 1913.]

1. LIMITATION OF ACTIONS.—*Part Payment by One of Several Joint Debtors.—Effect.*—A part payment by one of several joint debtors can serve only to suspend the running of the statute of limitations as against the party making the payment, by himself or duly authorized agent. p. 101.

2. TENANCY IN COMMON.—*Nature of Interests.*—The interests of tenants in common are several, and not joint, and ordinarily neither tenant can bind the estate or person of the other by any act in relation to the common property, not previously authorized or subsequently ratified. p. 102.

3. INFANTS.—*Powers.—Authorization or Ratification of Acts.*—A minor cannot authorize any one to act as his agent, nor can he acquiesce in or ratify the acts of any person so as to make them his own. p. 103.

4. LIMITATION OF ACTIONS.—*Part Payment of Debt.—Implication.— Infants.*—Part payment takes a debt out of the statute of limitations by virtue of the legal implication that such part payment is a new promise to pay the residue of the debt, but such implied promise does not operate to bind an infant, since he cannot toll the statute even by an express promise. p. 103.

5. TENANCY IN COMMON.—*Transactions Concerning Common Property.*—One who deals with a tenant in common, in regard to the common property, does so at his peril. p. 103.

6. INFANTS. — *Capacity to Contract. — Presumptions.* — A person dealing with an infant is bound to know his incapacity to contract. p. 103.

7. LIMITATION OF ACTIONS.—*Mortgage Debt.—Part Payment by Adult Tenant in Common.—Effect on Infant Tenant in Common.* —An adult heir, who is a tenant in common of real estate with a minor heir, is not by virtue of the relation of co-tenancy the implied agent of the minor and cannot, by making part payments on the ancestor's mortgage debt, toll the statute of limitations against such minor. p. 104.

8. TENANCY IN COMMON.—*Incumbrances.*—*Payments.*—*Presumptions.*—Where a mortgage existing on land held by a father and son as tenants in common as heirs of the mother, bound the mortgagors personally to pay the mortgage debt, and the father had joined the mother in the execution of such mortgage, it will be presumed that payments made by him, after the vesting of the tenancy in common, were made in fulfillment of such personal agreement to pay, rather than to relieve the common estate of the burden of the mortgage lien. p. 104.

From Fountain Circuit Court; *J. E. Schoonover,* Judge.

Action by Charles V. McAdams, Executor of the last will and testament of William C. Smith, deceased, against Arthur Weidenhammer and others. From a judgment for plaintiff, the defendants appeal. *Reversed.*

Edwin F. McCabe and *Victor H. Ringer,* for appellants.
William B. Durburow and *Hanly, McAdams & Artman,* for appellee.

IBACH, J.—Action begun by appellee's decedent against Arthur Weidenhammer and others for the foreclosure of three several mortgages, one of which does not affect appellant Weidenhammer's property. The other two mortgages were executed on different days in the year 1892 by said appellant's mother, Nellie Weidenhammer, on property then owned by her, to secure the payment of certain notes which she alone signed. Her husband, Lesher Weidenhammer, who is living, and was made a defendant in this action, joined with her in executing said mortgages. She died on March 26, 1893, three days after said appellant's birth, and he, therefore, is a minor. To the complaint said appellant's guardian *ad litem* answered the statute of limitations. To this answer appellee replied alleging partial payments made by said appellant's father, Lesher Weidenhammer, who at the time of the alleged payments was a tenant in common with said appellant of the real estate affected by said mortgages. Said appellant and appellee agree that the important question is whether after the death of the mother the

father could toll the statute of limitations as to his infant
son by making partial payments on a mortgage on real estate
owned by the father and son as tenants in common as heirs
of the mother. This question is presented by errors assigned in overruling appellants' demurrer to appellee's
second paragraph of reply, and in overruling appellants'
motion for a new trial, and if answered in the negative the
case must be reversed.

Appellee in his brief admits the law to be as follows:
"That an action on a promissory note dated subsequent to
September 19, 1881, is barred in ten years after it accrues;
that, when the debt secured by a mortgage is barred, an
action upon the mortgage is also barred; that the debt
secured is the principal thing and the mortgage only an
incident, and as a necessary corollary to this, that the life
of one is always co-extensive with the life of the other; that
an action upon a mortgage containing a promise to pay the
debt thereby secured is governed by the ten-year statute of
limitations; that the only methods of tolling the statute of
limitations, in actions upon notes or to foreclose mortgages,
are to show an acknowledgement or promise in writing or
a payment, executed or made by a party having authority
to bind the person pleading the statute and who is sought
to be charged in the action; that the law, which attaches to
a payment the effect of tolling the statute of limitations, is
not statutory, but is the common law, being the result of
judicial decisions running throughout English history; that
the principle upon which this doctrine of payment is based,
is that, from the fact of part payment, the law raises an implied promise to pay the residue; that such doctrine of implied promise can not be applied to the appellant, who is a
minor and who made no payments; that the appellant being
in privity with his mother, both in person and estate, has
the right to plead the statute of limitations in this case."
But while conceding these points, appellee argues that since
the lien of appellee continued to exist for the full sum of

his debt, against the interest of each heir and all the land;
since he was under no legal obligation and could not be compelled to accept a part of his debt, less than the whole, or
to release and discharge any part of the land except on full
payment of one of the incumbrances; and since one of the
tenants could not pay a portion of the debt and get a release and discharge of his portion of the security, but was
compelled to pay the entire debt, or in case of his want of
ability or inclination to do that could only pay the interest
and avoid foreclosure; therefore, if the law devolves upon
one the right, privilege or duty to pay an entire debt, although such one may not be the original debtor, a payment
made by such party tolls the statute of limitations as to the
entire debt, and does not suspend it as to the portion of the
debt only in which the party paying is especially and primarily interested; finally, payment of interest on, or a part
of, the ancestor's mortgage debt, by one tenant in common,
effectually tolls the statute of limitations, as to the entire
debt and as to the entire premises included in the mortgage,
in such case the tenant paying acts as the agent of all
the owners of the equity of redemption. As supporting this
last contention he cites several cases, but none from this
State.

In the case of *Whitcomb* v. *Whiting* (1781), 2 Dougl.
*652, the rule was evolved by Lord Mansfield, that a part
payment, acknowledgment or new promise by one of
1.   several joint debtors would start the statute afresh as
to all. But this doctrine has been repudiated by the
great weight of authority in this country, and the better rule
is that such an action binds only the party actually making
it, and does not start the statute afresh as to his co-obligors.
19 Am. and Eng. Ency. Law (2d ed.) 309; 25 Cyc. 1356,
1385. The case of *Whitcomb* v. *Whiting, supra,* has never
been followed in Indiana. See *Yandes* v. *Lefavour* (1830), 2
Blackf. 371; *Dickerson* v. *Turner* (1859), 12 Ind. 223; *Bottles* v. *Miller* (1887), 112 Ind. 584, 14 N. E. 728; *Koons* v.

Hammond (1898), 21 Ind. App. 76, 51 N. E. 506; *Mozingo* v. *Ross* (1898), 150 Ind. 688, 692, 50 N. E. 867, 41 L. R. A. 612, 65 Am. St. 387. In the case last cited the Supreme Court went into the authorities very carefully, and announced as its conclusion that "the correct and better rule is that a partial payment can serve only to suspend the running of the statute of limitations as against the party making the payment, by himself or duly authorized agent." Under this holding, the question before us becomes, Is the co-tenant, by virtue of that relation alone, the authorized agent to bind the other co-tenants by payments on a mortgage debt?

It is a familiar principle of law that the interests of tenants in common are several, and not joint. 38 Cyc. 6, *et seq.* In 1 Clark & Skyles, Agency §92, it is said:

2.   "In order that one tenant in common of real property or co-owner of personal property may bind the other with respect to such property, consent on the part of the other is essential. There is no implied agency, as in the case of a partnership, merely by virtue of their relation." In 38 Cyc. 101, 102, the rule is thus stated: "Under ordinary circumstances neither tenant in common can bind the estate or person of the other by any act in relation to the common property, not previously authorized or subsequently ratified, for co-tenants do not sustain the relation of principal and agent to each other nor are they partners." See, also, 17 Am. and Eng. Ency. Law (2d ed.) 672; Mechem, Agency §71.

In the case of *Metzger* v. *Huntington* (1894), 139 Ind. 501, 37 N. E. 1084, 39 N. E. 235, our Supreme Court said: "It is true that a tenant in common may act as agent for the other owners; but his being a tenant in common and in possession does not of itself make him agent to incumber his co-tenants' interests, still less to impose a personal obligation upon them. There is no such implied agency. Mechem, Agency §71; *Thompson* v. *Bowman* [1867], 73 U. S. (6 Wall.) 316 [18 L. Ed. 736]."

Appellee relies largely on the cases of *Clute* v. *Clute* (1910), 197 N. Y. 439, 90 N. E. 988, 27 L. R. A. (N. S.) 146, 134 Am. St. 891; and *Ellis* v. *Snyder* (1911), 83 Kan. 638, 112 Pac. 594, 32 L. R. A. (N. S.) 253; in which payments on a mortgage by a co-tenant in possession were held to toll the statute as to the other co-tenants. But in each of these cases the facts were such that the court found that the other co-tenants had ratified the acts of the tenant who made the payments, or had acquiesced in them, and thus these cases are no exception to the general rule as above stated.

It is not possible in the present case for us to hold that appellant Weidenhammer acquiesced in the payments made by his father. Said appellant is a minor, and can 3. neither authorize any one to act as his agent, nor acquiesce in or ratify the acts of any person so as to make them his own. Part payment takes a debt out of 4. the statute of limitations because the law implies from that fact a new promise to pay the residue of the debt. *Mozingo* v. *Ross, supra.* But said appellant could not himself have tolled the statute by an express promise, being a minor, and it seems should not be held by an implied promise.

In *Ellis* v. *Snyder, supra,* the Kansas supreme court held minor heirs bound by the payments made by a co-tenant in possession, but in that case the guardian of these heirs was held to have consented. No guardian was appointed for appellant Weidenhammer. It is argued that the equi- 5. ties are with appellee, yet it must be remembered that he who deals with a tenant in common in regard to the common property does so at his peril (38 Cyc. 6. 104 note 76) and one who deals with an infant is bound to know his incapacity to contract. It would have been possible for appellee as an interested party to have gone into court and asked for the appointment of a guardian for said appellant, and thereby the interests of

both the mortgagee and the minor might have been preserved. We have been unable to find a case in this or
7. any other jurisdiction in which the exact point presented has been decided. But from the general rules
applicable, and from an analysis of decisions on analogous
questions, and in view of the holding of the Supreme Court
in the cases of *Mozingo* v. *Ross, supra,* and *Metzger* v. *Huntington, supra,* we feel constrained to hold that an adult heir,
tenant in common of real estate with a minor heir, is not,
by virtue of the relation of co-tenancy, the implied agent of
the minor to toll the statute of limitations against him by
part payments on the ancestor's mortgage debt. In addition
to the cases before cited, we find our holding supported by
the following cases. *Haines* v. *Haines* (1903), 69 N. J. L.
39, 54 Atl. 401; *Murdock* v. *Waterman* (1895), 145 N. Y.
55, 39 N. E. 829, 27 L. R. A. 418; *Aetna Life Ins. Co.* v.
McNeely (1897), 166 Ill. 540, 46 N. E. 1130.

Moreover, appellant Weidenhammer's father had signed
the mortgages, and had expressly bound himself to pay the
debts which the mortgages were given to secure, and
8. it will be presumed that the payments he made were
in fulfillment of such agreement, rather than payments to relieve the burden of a lien against the estate held
in common by him and said appellant as heirs of the mother.
See *Stubblefield* v. *McAuliff* (1898), 20 Wash. 442, 55 Pac.
637.

The court erred in overruling said appellants' demurrer
to appellee's second paragraph of reply, and the decision of
the court is contrary to law. The complaint is sufficient
as against the objections urged. Other alleged errors argued
will not likely occur at a new trial.

Judgment reversed, and cause remanded for new trial.

NOTE.—Reported in 98 N. E. 883. See, also, under (3) 22 Cyc.
514, 539; (4) 25 Cyc. 1392: (5, 7) 38 Cyc. 101. As to acknowledgment of new promise to suspend the running or remove the bar
of the statute of limitations, see 102 Am. St. 751. As to contracts
with infants, and their ratification or disaffirmance, see 18 Am. St.

The Cleveland, Cincinnati, Chicago and St. Louis Railway Company v. Beard.

[No. 7,739. Filed January 7, 1913.]

1. PLEADING.—*Complaint.*—*Sufficiency.*—*Objections on Appeal.*—A complaint, in an action for the wrongful appropriation of a highway, alleging that the ground appropriated was a highway and dedicated to the public for that purpose, and used by the public as a highway for more than thirty years, with the permission, consent; acquiescence and donation of defendant, was, in the absence of a motion to make more specific, sufficient, on the theory of dedication, to bar another action, and is good as against an attack made for the first time on appeal. p. 106.

2. APPEAL. — *Questions Reviewable.* — *Motion for New Trial.* — *Briefs.*—Where appellant's brief contains neither a copy of the motion for a new trial, nor its substance, and does not disclose that such motion was filed, that it was overruled, or that an exception was taken, there is a total failure to comply with the rule requiring appellant's brief to contain a concise statement of so much of the record as fully presents every error and exception relied on, with references to the pages and lines of the transcript, so that an assignment of error in overruling such motion cannot be considered. p. 106.

3. APPEAL.—*Judgment.*—*Presumptions.*—*Burden of Showing Error.* —On appeal every presumption is indulged in favor of the correctness of the judgment of the trial court, and the burden is on appellant to show error, and to point out the same substantially in the manner required by the rules. p. 107.

From Hendricks Circuit Court; *James L. Clark,* Judge.

Action by Lou S. Beard against the Cleveland, Cincinnati, Chicago and St. Louis Railway Company. From a judgment for plaintiff, the defendant appeals. *Affirmed.*

Enloe & Pattison and *Frank L. Littleton,* for appellant.
Doan & Orbison and *Thad S. Adams,* for appellee.

ADAMS, J.—This appeal is taken from a judgment in favor of appellee and against appellant, for the alleged wrongful appropriation of a highway, which provided the only means of going to and from appellee's property. The errors relied on for reversal are (1) that the complaint does

not state facts sufficient to constitute a cause of action, and
(2) that the trial court erred in overruling appellant's
motion for a new trial.

It will be noted that the sufficiency of the complaint is
challenged only by the assignment of errors. The objection urged is that the theory of the complaint,

1. whether that of dedication to the public or of user
by the public for the statutory period, does not appear. The averment in the complaint in this regard is
"that said strip of ground was a highway and dedicated
to the public for that purpose, and used by the public as
a highway for more than thirty years from the 20th day of
October, 1870, with the permission, consent and acquiescence and by the donation of this defendant company."

We do not deem it necessary to determine the theory of
the complaint. No motion was made to make the complaint
more specific, or that appellee be required to separate her
causes of action into paragraphs. The well-settled rule is
that a complaint will be held good when attacked for the
first time on appeal, if sufficient to bar another action. The
complaint before us is clearly sufficient on the theory of
dedication to bar another action. *Southern R. Co.* v. *Roach*
(1906), 38 Ind. App. 211, 215, 78 N. E. 201; *Lewis Tp.
Improv. Co.* v. *Royer* (1906), 38 Ind. App. 151, 154, 76
N. E. 1068; *Indianapolis Traction, etc., Co.* v. *Smith*
(1906), 38 Ind. App. 160, 164, 77 N. E. 1040; *Xenia Real
Estate Co.* v. *Macy* (1897), 147 Ind. 568, 572, 47 N. E. 147;
Peoria, etc., R. Co. v. *Attica, etc., R. Co.* (1900), 154 Ind.
218, 221, 56 N. E. 210; *City of South Bend* v. *Turner*
(1901), 156 Ind. 418, 421, 60 N. E. 271, 54 L. R. A. 396,
83 Am. St. 200.

The further error relied on for reversal is the overruling
of appellant's motion for a new trial. A careful examination of appellant's brief fails to disclose a copy of

2. the motion for a new trial or the substance thereof,
or any reference thereto, except by remote inference.

It is not shown that appellant filed a motion for a new trial, that the same was overruled, or that an exception was taken. The rules of this court require that appellant's brief shall contain a concise statement of so much of the record as fully presents every error and exception relied on, referring to the pages and lines of the transcript. In this respect appellant's brief wholly fails to comply with the rules of this court, and for that reason, under the repeated decisions of the Supreme Court and this court, the second error relied on cannot be considered. *Albaugh Bros., etc., Co.* v. *Lynas* (1911), 47 Ind. App. 30, 93 N. E. 678, 680; *Chicago, etc., R. Co.* v. *Wysor Land Co.* (1904), 163 Ind. 288, 293, 69 N. E. 546, and cases cited; *Thieme & Wagner Brew. Co.* v. *Kessler* (1911), 47 Ind. App. 284, 94 N. E. 338; *Schrader* v. *Meyer* (1911), 48 Ind. App. 36, 95 N. E. 335, and cases cited; *Bartholomew* v. *Grimes* (1912), 51 Ind. App. 614, 100 N. E. 12.

In the recent case of *Webster* v. *Bligh* (1912), 50 Ind. App. 56, 98 N. E. 73, it is said: "When an appeal is taken to this court, every presumption is indulged in favor

3. of the correctness of the judgment of the trial court.

The burden is on appellant to show error in the decision and judgment appealed from, and the error complained of must be specifically pointed out, substantially in the manner provided by the rules. This court will not search the record for errors on which to reverse a judgment."

The judgment is affirmed.

NOTE.—Reported in 100 N. E. 392. See, also, under (1) 31 Cyc. 82; (2) 2 Cyc. 1013; (3) 3 Cyc. 275.

FIFE v. OHIO INVESTMENT COMPANY.

[No. 7,778. Filed January 7, 1918.]

1. CHATTEL MORTGAGES.—*Priority.—Estoppel.*—Where the mortgagor of chattels removed the goods to another county without the consent of the mortgagee, the mere fact that the mortgagee acquiesced in the keeping of the goods in the county to which they had been removed, and made collections from the mortgagor while the property was in such county, and, on failure of the mortgagor to make a payment, suggested that he borrow the money to make such payment, and received part of the money which the mortgagor borrowed, does not estop the mortgagee from questioning the validity of a second mortgage executed for the money borrowed pursuant to such suggestion and recorded in the county to which the property had been removed. p. 111.

2. CHATTEL MORTGAGES.—*Application of Proceeds of Second Mortgage to Payment of Debt Secured by First Mortgage.—Subrogation.*—Where the mortgagor of chattels removed the goods to another county without the consent of the mortgagee, and the mortgagee thereafter acquiesced in such removal and the keeping of the property in the county to which it had been removed, and, on failure of the mortgagor to make a payment, suggested that he borrow the money to make such payment, and the mortgagor thereupon borrowed $84 for which he executed a mortgage on the goods in the county to which they had been removed, and applied $33 of such borrowed money to the payment of the first debt, leaving $80 remaining unpaid, of which the sum of $51.90 was still unpaid when the holder of the second mortgage brought suit to recover the mortgaged property, such facts were insufficient to entitle the second mortgagee to subrogation under the first mortgage. p. 111.

3. CHATTEL MORTGAGES.—*Record.—Failure to Record in County Where Mortgagor Resides.—Effect.*—The failure of the mortgagee of chattels to record the mortgage in the county where the mortgagor resided at the time of its execution, as required by §7472 Burns 1908, Acts 1897 p. 240, renders such mortgage void as against the right of possession of one holding by virtue of a prior valid mortgage. pp. 112, 113.

4. REPLEVIN.—*Proof Essential to Maintain Action.*—To maintain an action in replevin, the plaintiff must show that he has a right to the possession of the property he seeks to recover. p. 113.

5. CHATTEL MORTGAGES.—*Removal of Property.—Consent of Mortgagee.—Effect.*—The removal of mortgaged chattels to another county without the consent of the mortgagee, does not invalidate

the mortgage, since §2299 Burns 1908, Acts 1905 p. 584, §406, making it a penal offense to remove mortgaged property from the county in which the mortgagor resides without the written consent of the mortgagee, in so far as it relates to the personal rights of the parties, is for the protection of the mortgagee, but does not affect the validity of the mortgage. p. 113.

6. CHATTEL MORTGAGES. — *Location of Property.* — *Residence of Mortgagor.*—The presence of chattels in a county other than that of the residence of the mortgagor does not warrant the assumption that the mortgagor resides in such county. p. 113.

From Miami Circuit Court; *Joseph N. Tillett,* Judge.

Action by the Ohio Investment Company against James R. Fife. From a judgment for plaintiff, the defendant appeals. *Reversed.*

Antrim & McClintic and *Blacklidge, Wolf & Barnes,* for appellant.

Jabez T. Cox and *Claude Y. Andrews,* for appellee.

FELT, J.—This is a suit in replevin brought originally by appellee against appellant before a justice of the peace of Peru township, Miami county, Indiana. At the trial of the case in the Miami Circuit Court a special finding of facts was made and the court stated its conclusions of law thereon in favor of appellee. A motion for a new trial was overruled, and judgment rendered on the conclusions of law. The errors relied on question the correctness of each conclusion of law and the overruling of the motion for a new trial.

The finding of facts states, in substance, that on May 9, 1908, A. A. Warnick executed to E. E. Hervert a promissory note calling for $125, and to secure the payment thereof executed a chattel mortgage on two horses, a set of harness and a moving van; that said mortgage was duly recorded on the 18th day of May, 1908, in the recorder's office of Howard county, Indiana, in which county the mortgagor resided; that said mortgagor continued to reside in said Howard county until September 17, 1908, when he moved to and became a resident of

Miami county, Indiana; that on May 17, 1908, said Warnick removed said property from Howard county to Miami county; that on the 17th day of July, 1908, in said Miami county said Warnick, to secure a loan of $84, due in twelve monthly instalments of $7 each, mortgaged to appellee said moving van, harness and one of said horses; that said mortgage was duly recorded in Miami county, that on the 19th day of October, 1909, there was due and unpaid on said note to appellee an instalment of $7; that said mortgage provided that on default of any payment due on said note appellee had the right to take possession of said mortgaged property, and the same should thereupon become the absolute property of appellee; that on or about June 1, 1908, said E. E. Hervert assigned and delivered to Eikenberry Brothers, of Howard county, said first mortgage; that appellant was the agent of said assignees, with full authority to act for them in all matters appertaining to said note and mortgage; that on October 19, 1908, said Warnick notified appellee to take possession of the property covered by its mortgage; that on said day appellant came to Miami county and took possession of said mortgaged property, and while the same was in his possession one Crites, as agent of appellee, before the commencement of this suit, demanded of appellant the possession thereof, and the same was refused; that said property was moved from Howard county to Miami county, without the knowledge or consent of the mortgagee, his said assignees or their said agent, but the same was by them allowed to remain in said county without objection until October 19, 1908, when appellant took possession thereof from the mortgagor for and on behalf of said Eikenberry Brothers; that on said date "there was past due and unpaid on the promissory note" secured by said first mortgage the sum of $51.90; that on and after September 17, 1908, appellant knew said mortgagor was a resident of Miami county. Indiana, and that he kept said property in that county; that

the value of said property is $100; that on the 17th day of
July, 1908, appellant demanded from said mortgagor a payment on the note held by said Eikenberry Brothers, and
suggested that he borrow money with which to make such
payment; that acting on such advice said Warnick negotiated a loan from appellee and executed to it his note for
$84, secured as aforesaid, and on July 18, 1908, paid to ap-
pellant out of the money so obtained, the sum of $33; that
on July 17, 1908, appellee had no knowledge that said property had been mortgaged in Howard county, as aforesaid.

On the foregoing facts the court stated its conclusions of
law, to the effect that appellee was on October 19, 1908, entitled to the possession of said property, and appellant was
not entitled to the possession thereof.

Appellant's first contention is that as against his right of
possession, by virtue of the first mortgage, appellee had no
valid claim to the property, because at the time the second
mortgage was executed the mortgagor was a resident of
Howard county and the mortgage was not recorded in that
county, as required by the statute (Acts 1897 p. 240, §7472
Burns 1908), but was recorded in Miami county.

Appellee contends that because appellant and his
1. principal acquiesced in the keeping of the property
in Miami county and made collections from the mortgagor while the property was in the latter county, and because appellant suggested that the mortgagor borrow
2. money with which to make a payment on said first
mortgage, and actually received a part of the money
so obtained from appellee, he and his principal are estopped
to question the validity of the second mortgage, and appellee
is entitled to be subrogated to the rights of appellant's principal under the first mortgage.

It is not shown that appellant made any representations
to appellee or in any way induced it to make the loan of $84,
or even knew appellee was making such loan until after it

was made. The mere suggestion that Warnick borrow the money and the fact that appellant received a part of the money after the loan was procured, is insufficient to operate as an estoppel. The finding shows that a part of the first mortgage debt had been paid before the second loan was secured, and that only $33 of the $84 borrowed from appellee was paid to appellant; that after such payment was made there remained due on the first debt about $80, and at the time the suit was begun, $51.90. These facts are insufficient to give appellee the right of subrogation under the first mortgage. Had it furnished the money to pay the whole debt secured by the first mortgage and its security failed or proved insufficient, the claim of subrogation would stand upon a better foundation. Sheldon, Subrogation (2d ed.) §§1-3; 27 Am. and Eng. Ency. Law 205; *Stuckman* v. *Roose* (1897), 147 Ind. 402, 406, 46 N. E. 680; *Heiney* v. *Lontz* (1897), 147 Ind. 417, 423, 46 N. E. 665; *Townsend* v. *Cleveland Fire Proofing Co.* (1897), 18 Ind. App. 568, 577, 47 N. E. 707.

This is not a suit between the mortgagor and the mortgagee, but is the same in its legal aspect as a suit by the mortgagee of the second mortgage against the mortgagee of the first mortgage.

Appellee's failure to record its mortgage in the county where the mortgagor resided at the time of its execution, as against appellant's right of possession based on a valid mortgage, rendered the second mortgage void. §7472 Burns 1908, Acts 1897 p. 240; *Sidener* v. *Bible* (1873), 43 Ind. 230, 234; *Granger* v. *Adams* (1883), 90 Ind. 87; *Stengel* v. *Boyce* (1896), 143 Ind. 642, 645, 42 N. E. 905; *Franklin Nat. Bank.* v. *Whitehead* (1898). 149 Ind. 560, 582, 49 N. E. 592, 39 L. R. A. 725, 63 Am. St. 302; *Morris* v. *Ellis* (1896), 16 Ind. App. 679, 683, 46 N. E. 41; *State, ex rel.,* v. *Griffin* (1897), 16 Ind. App. 555, 45 N. E. 935.

To maintain a suit in replevin the plaintiff must
4. show that he has a right to the possession of the property he seeks to recover. *Briggs* v. *Fleming* (1887),
112 Ind. 313, 14 N. E. 86; *Ross* v. *Menefee* (1890), 125 Ind.
432, 439, 25 N. E. 545.

The fact that the mortgagor removed the property from
Howard county without the consent of the mortgagee or his
        assignee, and the further fact that said assignee
5. learned of such removal and acquiesced in the keeping
        of the property in Miami county, did not invalidate
the mortgage recorded in Howard county.   The statute
(Acts 1905 p. 584, §406, §2299 Burns 1908) making it a
penal offense to remove mortgaged property from the county
in which the mortgagor resides without the written consent
of the mortgagee is for the protection of the mortgagee in so
far as it has any relation to the personal rights of the parties, but it in no sense invalidates the mortgage when the
property is so removed.

Appellee's right to the property depended wholly
3. on the validity of its mortgage, and since it was void
        as against the claim of appellant under the first mort-
gage, appellee had no right to the possession of the property.

The provisions of the statute are plain, and the facts
found are insufficient to overcome its positive requirement
        that such a mortgage be recorded in the county where
6. the mortgagor resides. The presence of property in
        a county other than that of the residence of the mort-
gagor does not warrant the assumption that the mortgagor
resides in such county.

The judgment is therefore reversed, with instructions to
the lower court to restate its conclusions of law in favor of
appellant and to render judgment accordingly.

Ibach, C. J., Adams, Hottel, Lairy and *Shea, JJ.,* concur.

NOTE.—Reported in 100 N. E. 392. See, also, under (1) 6 Cyc.
1096—New Anno.; (3) 6 Cyc. 1088; (4) 34 Cyc. 1501. As to the

114   APPELLATE COURT OF INDIANA,

Terre Haute, etc., Traction Co. *v.* Maberry—52 Ind. App. 114.

right of subrogation, see 99 Am. St. 474. As to the registration of chattel mortgages, see 21 Am. St. 282. As to the effect of the defective recording of instruments upon the rights of third persons, see 96 Am. St. 397. As to the effect on the lien of a chattel mortgage of the removal of the property from the place of record to another town or county, see 12 Ann. Cas. 947.

TERRE HAUTE, INDIANAPOLIS AND EASTERN
TRACTION COMPANY *v.* MABERRY.

[No. 7,770. Filed January 8, 1913.]

1. RAILROADS. — *Interurban.* — *Crossing Accident.* — *Complaint.* — *Charge of Negligence.*—*Sufficiency.*—A complaint, in an action against an interurban railroad company for the death of plaintiff's child in a crossing accident, charging that the motorman negligently failed to sound the gong with which the car was equipped, which could have been heard by a person approaching the crossing when the car was a quarter of a mile away, and negligently ran said car against said child, thereby causing the injury, sufficiently charged negligence to withstand a demurrer. p. 118.

2. NEGLIGENCE.—*Complaint.*—*General Charge of Negligence.*—*Sufficiency.*—Objection that the charge of negligence, in a complaint for personal injuries, is not specific, can only be taken by a motion to make the complaint more specific, and, in the absence of such motion, a complaint stating the injury and alleging that it was caused as a consequence and solely by reason of defendant's negligence, sufficiently charges actionable negligence. p. 118.

3. RAILROADS.—*Interurban.*—*Crossing Accident.*—*Wilful Injury.*—*Evidence.*—In an action against an interurban railroad company for the death of plaintiff's child, evidence showing that the motorman saw the child approaching the crossing when the car was about a quarter of a mile away, and watched it continuously until within about fifty or one hundred feet of the place where the injury occurred, before sounding the whistle or making any effort to stop the car, and that he knew the child's attention was diverted from the approaching car, and that the car was going at a speed sufficient to drive it 150 to 200 feet beyond the point where it struck the boy, was, in the absence of any reason for the motorman's failure to sound the whistle or gong in time to attract the child's attention before reaching the point of danger, or for his failure to stop the car sooner, sufficient to justify a finding that the motorman's conduct was wilful. p. 119.

Terre Haute, etc., Traction Co. *v.* Maberry—52 Ind. App. 114.

4. EVIDENCE.— *Wrongful Acts.— Intention.— Presumptions.*— The rule that every person is presumed to intend the natural and probable consequences of his wrongful or unlawful acts applies in civil as well as in criminal cases, and such intent may be shown by direct evidence, or may be inferred from conduct showing a reckless disregard of consequences and a willingness to inflict injury by purposely and voluntarily doing an act with knowledge that some one is unconsciously or unavoidably in a situation to be injured thereby. p. 120.

5. APPEAL.—*Review.—Instructions.—Assumption of Facts.*—An instruction assuming a fact about which the evidence is undisputed is not erroneous. p. 121.

6 RAILROADS.—*Interurban.—Crossing Accident.—Injury to Child.—Instructions.*—In an action for the death of plaintiff's child by being struck by an interurban cár, where the motorman saw the child approaching the track and watched it continuously from the time the car was a quarter of a mile away until within fifty or one hundred feet from the place where the injury occurred, without signalling the approach of the car or attempting to stop it, an instruction that "the presumption that a person seen on an interurban car track or approaching the track will leave it or not enter upon it before the car reaches him, cannot be indulged in where a child of tender years is seen on the track or is seen approaching it apparently unconscious of the approaching car," is not objectionable as being mandatory in telling the jury not to consider any presumption that the child would not come on the track in front of the car. p. 122.

7 RAILROADS.—*Interurban.—Duty Toward Persons on Tracks.—Children.*—Where a person is seen walking on the track, or where there is nothing to prevent the motorman from seeing one in that position, especially a child, and such person is unmindful of the approach of the car, the motorman is bound to use every reasonable care and means at command to warn him, and, if necessary to avoid a collision, to stop the car. p. 122.

8. DEATH.—*Death of Child.—Measure of Damages.—Instructions.*—An instruction, in an action by a father for the wrongful death of his child, that the measure of plaintiff's damages would be the reasonable value of the child's services from the date of its death until it would have become twenty-one years of age less the reasonable expense of providing it with the ordinary necessaries of life during that time, is not objectionable as leading the jury to conclude that the father was obliged to furnish only the bare necessities of life, since the word "ordinary" must have been understood by the jury as synonymous with "usual" or "customary." p. 123.

9. APPEAL.—*Review.—Instructions.—Consideration as a Whole.*— Instructions given in a case should be considered as a whole, and a separate instruction will not be held erroneous for the omission of a point covered by other instructions. p. 123.

10. APPEAL.—*Review.—Objection to Evidence.*—Although appellant saved exceptions to the admission of certain evidence, and to the refusal to admit certain evidence, where no specific objection is pointed out, and none is disclosed by the record, no error can be predicated thereon. p. 123.

11. DEATH.—*Death of Child.—Damages.—Excessive Damages.*—A verdict awarding plaintiff $3,000 for the death of his son, seven and one-half years old, in a collision with an interurban car, is not excessive. p. 123.

12. DAMAGES.—*Excessive Damages.*—Damages assessed by a jury will not be considered excessive unless they are such as to induce the belief that the jury in awarding them acted from prejudice, passion, partiality or corruption. p. 123.

From Hendricks Circuit Court; *James L. Clark*, Judge.

Action by Amos F. Maberry against the Terre Haute, Indianapolis and Eastern Traction Company. From a judgment for plaintiff, the defendant appeals. *Affirmed.*

Brill & Harvey and *W. H. Latta,* for appellant.
Otis E. Gulley and *Thomas W. Perkins,* for appellee.

SHEA, J.—This was an action by appellee against appellant for damages for the death of appellee's minor son, caused by the alleged negligent acts of appellant.

The complaint was in two paragraphs, to each of which appellant's separate demurrer was overruled. Issues were joined by a general denial filed to each paragraph of the complaint. The cause was tried by a jury, and a verdict rendered in favor of appellee. Appellant filed a motion for a new trial, which was overruled, and judgment rendered on the verdict.

The errors assigned are as follows: (1) The overruling of appellant's demurrer to each paragraph of the complaint; (2) the overruling of appellant's motion for a new trial.

The first paragraph of the complaint, in substance, alleges that appellant, on June 24, 1908, owned and operated an interurban railroad through Hendricks county, Indiana, on which cars were operated by electric power; that at the point where the accident happened appellant's road was north of and adjacent to a public highway lying parallel with said railroad, and at that time appellee, with his family, occupied a residence within ten feet of the north line of appellant's right of way, fronting toward said highway and right of way. There was no fence between appellant's road and said highway; but appellant had erected and was maintaining a fence along the north line of its right of way, immediately south of appellee's residence, with an opening therein as a means of ingress to and egress from appellee's residence across said track to a mail-box located on said highway, which mail-box had been so placed by appellee to receive his mail from the rural carrier. On June 24, 1908, at about 10:20 a. m., when a car was approaching from the west on appellant's track, appellee's son, Virgil, seven and one-half years old, went from the residence across the track to the mail-box to get mail. The place where the child crossed the track was in plain, unobstructed view of the motorman operating the car from the time said car came within a quarter of a mile west of said crossing, continuously until it reached said crossing. The car was equipped with a gong and a whistle that could be heard for more than a quarter of a mile when properly operated, and it was the duty of the motorman to keep a close watch ahead as he approached the crossing, and to sound the gong and blow the whistle to warn any one who might be in the act of crossing of the approach of said car; "that said defendant, by its motorman, agents and servants, disregarding its duty and obligations as aforesaid, unlawfully, carelessly and negligently failed, neglected and refused to sound the gong or blow the whistle that was on said car to warn said child of its approach, and of the danger said child was in, but that said defendant, by its motorman, agents and servants, unlawfully carelessly and negligently ran said car upon and

118   APPELLATE COURT OF INDIANA,

Terre Haute, etc., Traction Co. *r.* Maberry—52 Ind. App. 114.

against said child with great force and violence and thereby inflicted upon said child severe, permanent and lasting injuries from which said child died.'' Appellee is the father of said Virgil Maberry, and entitled to his services until he became of age, and by the wrongful acts of appellant he has been deprived of said services.

The second paragraph of complaint is substantially the same as the first, except that it is alleged therein that appellant, by its motorman, agents and servants, wilfully ran its car against said Virgil Maberry, and injured him, from which injuries he died, etc.

Objection is made to the first paragraph of the complaint, because, it is urged, the specific acts of negligence are not sufficiently set out, and that no acts are complained

1. of as the proximate cause of the injury. It would require much discrimination and refinement of expression to say that specific acts of negligence are not alleged, but we may safely say this paragraph contains the general allegation that there was a negligent failure to sound the gong with which the car was equipped, which could have been heard by a person approaching said crossing when said car was a quarter of a mile or more away, and that said motorman negligently and carelessly failed to sound said gong, and negligently ran said car against said child, thereby causing the injury. The general allegation is sufficient to withstand a demurrer.

Section 343 Burns 1908, Subd. 2, §338 R. S. 1381, on the subject of the complaint, says it shall contain ''a statement of the facts constituting the cause of action, in plain and concise language, without repetition, and in such manner as to enable a person of common understanding to know what is intended.''

While the paragraph of complaint cannot be said to be a model pleading, it contains the general allegation of

2. the negligence of appellant, resulting in the injury complained of, and is good as against a demurrer.

It is settled by an unbroken line of decisions that objection for the cause stated can be taken only by a motion to make the complaint more specific. It is decided in *Louisville, etc., R. Co.* v. *Jones* (1886), 108 Ind. 551, 9 N. E. 476, that a complaint to recover for personal injury is sufficient to withstand a demurrer, under the statutes of this State, when it characterizes the act which resulted in the injury as having been negligently or carelessly done, without alleging the specific facts constituting the negligence. See, also, *Lake Erie, etc., R. Co.* v. *Fike* (1905), 35 Ind. App. 554, 74 N. E. 636; *Cincinnati, etc., R. Co.* v. *Gaines* (1886), 104 Ind. 526, 4 N. E. 34, 5 N. E. 746, 54 Am. Rep. 334; *Louisville, etc., R. Co.* v. *Krinning* (1882), 87 Ind. 351. In the absence of a motion to make more specific, a complaint stating decedent's injury and alleging that it was caused as a consequence and solely by reason of defendant's negligence, sufficiently charged actionable negligence. *Indianapolis, etc., Traction Co.* v. *Newby* (1910), 45 Ind. App. 540, 90 N. E. 29, 91 N. E. 36; *Princeton Coal, etc., Co.* v. *Roll* (1904), 162 Ind. 115, 66 N. E. 169; *Coddington* v. *Canaday* (1901), 157 Ind. 243, 61 N. E. 567.

The second paragraph of the complaint is based on the alleged wilful misconduct of appellant's servants, and is sufficient to withstand a demurrer. The demurrers were properly overruled.

In support of the motion for a new trial, appellant insists that the evidence fails utterly to sustain the charge of wilfulness. On this issue, the verdict, it insists, is contrary to law, and therefore appellant's second instruction tendered, and refused by the court, which peremptorily directed the jury to return a verdict for the defendant, should have been sustained.

3. The evidence disclosed that the motorman did see this boy approaching the track, when the motorman was a distance of almost a quarter of a mile away, and that he watched him continuously until within fifty or one

hundred feet of the point where the boy was struck before sounding the whistle or making any effort to stop the car; that he knew the boy's attention was directed to a postal which he received from the mail-carrier, and was conveying to his home. No reason is given by the motorman, or shown by the evidence in any form, for the failure to sound the whistle or the gong at a sufficient distance to attract the boy's attention before he had reached the point of danger. The car was going at a speed sufficient to drive it from 150 to 200 feet beyond the point where it struck the boy. No reason is given for the failure to stop the car sooner. Under numerous authorities, it is the judgment of this court that the jury might very well have concluded that the conduct of the motorman was wilful.

In the case of *Gregory* v. *Cleveland, etc., R. Co.* (1887), 112 Ind. 385, 14 N. E. 228, it is said: "As a rule of evidence, the presumption that every person intends the natural

4. and probable consequences of his wrongful or unlawful acts applies as well in civil as in criminal cases; hence, the unlawful intent may be shown by direct evidence, or it may be inferred from conduct which shows a reckless disregard of consequences, and a willingness to inflict injury, by purposely and voluntarily doing an act, with knowledge that some one is unconsciously or unavoidably in a situation to be injured thereby. An act which in itself might be lawful becomes unlawful when done in a manner or under circumstances which charge the actor with knowledge that it will result in injury to some one. *Palmer* v. *Chicago, etc., R. Co.* [1887], 112 Ind. 250 [14 N. E. 70]; *Louisville, etc., R. Co.* v. *Ader* [1887], 110 Ind. 376 [11 N. E. 437]; *Louisville, etc., R. Co.* v. *Bryan* [1886], 107 Ind. 51 [7 N. E. 807]; *Belt R., etc., Co.* v. *Mann* [1886], 107 Ind. 89 [7 N. E. 893]; *Pennsylvania Co.* v. *Smith* [1884], 98 Ind. 42."

In the case of *Cleveland, etc., R. Co.* v. *Starks* (1910), 174 Ind. 345, 349, 92 N. E. 54, it is said: "It must be made to appear that the act or omission which caused the death was wilful or intentional, and of such a character as that such death must reasonably have been anticipated as the natural and probable consequence of the act; that is, decedent was in a position of imminent peril and unconscious thereof, or unable to extricate himself therefrom, and that the engineer in charge of the train had knowledge of such facts, and power and opportunity to stop the train or avoid the collision, but intentionally omitted to do so, and with such knowledge, power and opportunity wilfully ran such train over the crossing in utter disregard of consequences." (Citing authorities.) The motion for peremptory instruction was properly overruled.

Instruction No. 1, tendered by appellee, is objected to on the ground that it assumes facts which should properly be submitted to the jury. The instruction reads as follows: "I instruct you that if you find by a fair preponderance of the evidence that the motorman who was operating the car that struck Virgil Maberry on the 24th day of June 1908, which inflicted injuries that caused his death saw the said Virgil Maberry on the track (or saw him near or approaching the track with his mind occupied in a way that the said Virgil Maberry was not aware of the approach of the car or if the said motorman had reason to believe that he was not aware of the approach of said car and was not aware of the danger which he was in) it was then the duty of said motorman to exercise ordinary care and it was the duty of said motorman not only to warn said child of the approach of the car by sounding the whistle on the car but it was his duty as soon as he saw that said child was not aware of the danger he was in to place his car under control if he could do so, and if possible and necessary, to stop his car in order to avoid a collision." The portion of this instruction which might be criticised as assuming facts is "that the motorman who was operating the car that struck Virgil Maberry on the 24th day of June 1908, which inflicted injuries that caused his death," etc. The fact that the motorman was operating the car which inflicted the injury which caused the death of Virgil Maberry is wholly undisputed, therefore no error occurred in assuming it in the instruction.

Instruction No. 3 tendered by appellee and given by the court, to which exception was duly saved, reads as follows:

6. "The presumption that a person seen on an interurban car track or approaching the track will leave it or not enter upon it before the car reaches him cannot be indulged in where a child of tender years is seen on the track or is seen approaching it apparently unconscious of the approaching car."

Appellant complains that this instruction is mandatory, namely, in telling the jury it cannot consider any presumption that the child would not come on the track in front of the car. The objection to this instruction is not well taken.

7. The courts everywhere have uniformly held that where a person is seen walking on the track, or where there is nothing to prevent the motorman from seeing one in that position, and such person is unmindful of the approach of the car, it becomes the motorman's duty to exercise every reasonable care and means at his command to warn the person, if possible, and if necessary, he should stop the car to avoid a collision. If the person is a child, he must take that fact into consideration. *Indianapolis, etc., Traction Co.* v. *Smith* (1906), 38 Ind. App. 160, 77 N. E. 1040; *Lake Erie, etc., R. Co.* v. *Juday* (1898), 19 Ind. App. 436, 49 N. E. 843; *Indianapolis, etc., Traction Co.* v. *Kidd* (1906), 167 Ind. 402, 79 N. E. 347, 7 L. R. A. (N. S.) 143, 10 Ann. Cas. 942; *Citizens' St. R. Co.* v. *Lowe* (1895), 12 Ind. App. 47, 39 N. E. 165; *Saylor* v. *Union Traction Co.* (1907), 40 Ind. App. 381, 81 N. E. 94; *Indianapolis St. R. Co.* v. *Schomberg* (1905), 164 Ind. 111, 72 N. E. 1041.

Objection is made to the instruction given by the court on its own motion on the measure of damages. The instruc-

NOVEMBER TERM, 1912.   123

Terre Haute, etc., Traction Co. v. Maberry—52 Ind. App. 114.

tion reads as follows: ''If the plaintiff is entitled to
8. recover the measure of his damages would be the reasonable value of the services of his son Virgil from
the date of his death until he became twenty-one years of
age less the reasonable expense of providing him with the
ordinary necessaries of life during that time.'' This instruction is criticised because the court uses the words ''ordinary
necessaries of life.'' It is urged that the jury might have
concluded that the father was obliged to furnish only the
bare necessities to sustain life. The word ''ordinary'' is
synonymous with ''usual,'' ''customary.'' The jury must
be given credit for knowledge of the usual and ordinary
meaning of words, and therefore it could not have been misled by the instruction, as it is not susceptible of the narrow
construction put on it by appellant's counsel.

The instructions tendered by appellant and given by the
court, taken in connection with all the other instructions in
the case, fairly and fully state the law, as the instruc-
9. tions must be taken as a whole, and separate instructions should not be selected and held to be erroneous,
if an omitted point is covered by other instructions in the
case.

Exceptions were saved by appellant to the admission of
certain evidence tendered by appellee and admitted by the
court. Exceptions were also saved by appellant to
10. the refusal of the court to admit certain evidence tendered, but as no specific objection is pointed out, and
this court finds none in the rulings of the trial court, no
error can be predicated thereon.

The jury returned a verdict for $3,000. Objection
11. is made that the amount is excessive. The court cannot say that the damages awarded by the jury are
excessive. Damages assessed by the jury will not be considered as excessive unless they are such as to induce the
12. belief that the jury in awarding them acted from
prejudice, passion, partiality or corruption. *Indian-*

apolis Traction, etc., Co. v. *Smith, supra; Toledo, etc., R. Co.*
v. *Pavey* (1906), 39 Ind. App. 284, 79 N. E. 529; *City of
Columbus* v. *Allen* (1907), 40 Ind. App. 257, 81 N. E. 114.

The evidence supports the verdict. The motion for a new
trial was properly overruled.

Judgment affirmed.

Note.—Reported in 100 N. E. 401. See, also, under (1) 36 Cyc.
1573; (2) 29 Cyc. 570; (3) 36 Cyc. 1600; (4) 16 Cyc. 1081; (5)
38 Cyc. 1667; (6) 36 Cyc. 1632; (7) 36 Cyc. 1521; (8) 13 Cyc. 385;
(9) 38 Cyc. 1778; (10) 2 Cyc. 1044; (11, 12) 13 Cyc. 375. As to
the negligence in dealing with children, see 49 Am. St. 406. As to
the measure of damages recoverable by a parent for the death of a
minor child by wrongful act, see Ann. Cas. 1912 C 58. On the right
of persons in charge of train to presume that child will get out of
danger, see 6 L. R. A. (N. S.) 283. As to the question of negligent
operation of train at crossing as ground of liability for killing or
injuring child, incapable of contributory negligence, that was
aware of train's approach, see 34 L. R. A. (N. S.) 645.

WAGNER v. McCOOL ET AL.

[No. 7,779. Filed January 9, 1913.]

1. PRINCIPAL AND AGENT.—*Authority of Agent.—Evidence.—Sufficiency.*—In an action to quiet plaintiffs' title to real estate held
by defendant under a deed conveying the land as security for a
loan made to plaintiffs, and to compel a reconveyance, where
plaintiffs had repaid the loan to an attorney by whom such loan
had been made for defendant, evidence showing that interest payments had been made to such attorney and credited on the note
by defendant, that on plaintiffs offering to repay the loan at a
semi-annual interest date such attorney informed them that he
could not accept payment except at an anniversary date, that
shortly before the next anniversary date, defendant, at the request of such attorney and to enable him to "look something
up," left with him the papers connected with such loan, that when
plaintiffs went to the office of such attorney to repay the loan, the
attorney was not in, and, on being called by telephone, directed
plaintiffs to leave a check for the amount and said that he would
send them the papers to which they were entitled. and that
plaintiffs then left a check for the amount at the office of such
attorney, who cashed the same and disappeared, was sufficient

to justify a finding that such attorney was at no time acting as the agent of plaintiffs, but was the agent of the defendant. pp. 127, 135.

2. PRINCIPAL AND AGENT.—*Authority of Agent.—Evidence.—Letter Written by Agent.*—A letter written by an attorney, who had negotiated a loan for defendant, informing plaintiffs that he could not accept payment of the principal at a semi-annual interest date, that under the contract, from which he quoted, such payment could be made only at an anniversary date, and asking plaintiffs to remit the amount of the interest payment, though not constituting evidence establishing the agency of such attorney, is important as tending to show that he had possession of the papers connected with the loan and was assuming to act in the matter of the collection of the note in question previous to the time of its payment. p. 133.

3. PRINCIPAL AND AGENT.—*Authority of Agent.—Apparent Authority.*—Where the acts of a principal are such as to justify innocent third persons, who have relied thereon, in believing that the agent is authorized to do that which he does, although the agent in fact had no such authority, the principal is bound thereby, under the rule that where one of two innocent persons must suffer because of the betrayal of a trust reposed in a third, the person most at fault must bear the loss. p. 134.

From Vanderburgh Circuit Court; *C. A. DeBruler*, Judge.

Action by Henry F. McCool and another against Margaret Wagner. From a judgment for plaintiffs, the defendant appeals. *Affirmed.*

Henry Kister, W. D. Robinson and *W. E. Stilwell*, for appellant.

Albert W. Funkhouser and *Arthur F. Funkhouser*, for appellees.

HOTTEL, J.—The complaint in this case is in one paragraph and avers, in substance, that on the 6th day of January, 1908, appellees were the owners of certain described real estate, which they on said day, by a deed of general warranty, conveyed to appellant to secure the payment of a note, for the sum of $500, on said day executed by appellees as evidence of a loan then made by appellant to appellees: that at the same time and as a part of the same transaction the appellant by her agreement in writing, which is set out in said complaint, agreed to reconvey said real estate to appellees on full payment by them of the loan evidenced by said note according to the terms and conditions of said agreement; that said agreement provided that such note might be paid by appellees "on any annual anniversary of said contract;" that on the 5th day of January, 1909, appellees fully paid said note, and performed all the conditions of said contract on their part to be performed, and demanded a reconveyance of said real estate by quitclaim deed, which appellant refused.

Appellees ask that appellant be compelled to execute to appellees a deed to the real estate so conveyed by them, that they be declared to be the owners of the same, and that their title thereto be quieted. A demurrer to this complaint was overruled, and appellant filed her answer in denial and a cross-complaint. The cross-complaint alleges the execution· and delivery of the several instruments mentioned in the complaint, and sets out each, and avers, in substance, that the deed mentioned was executed to secure the payment of the note, and that it and the written agreement to reconvey were intended as a mortgage and should be so construed.

The averments of the complaint and cross-complaint are in substance and effect the same, except that the complaint avers the payment of the note and compliance with the terms of the agreement, and asks a reconveyance of the real estate according to the terms of the agreement, and that appellees' title be quieted therein, while the cross-complaint alleges that the note is unpaid and other violations of the terms of said agreement, and asks that the deed be declared a mortgage and for a foreclosure and sale of the mortgaged premises to satisfy the debt. A denial to the cross-complaint closed the issues. Pursuant to the request of appellant, the court made a special finding of facts and stated its conclusions of law thereon. On this finding there was judgment for appellees.

A motion for a new trial filed by appellant was overruled and exceptions properly saved.

The assigned error presenting the ruling on this motion is the only question discussed in appellant's brief. In fact, the only question presented by appellant's counsel in their brief under their points and authorities or discussed in their argument is the sufficiency of the evidence to sustain the decision.

There is little dispute between appellant and appellees as to any issue of law or of fact, except that relating to the question of the agency of the attorney to whom appellees executed the check given in payment of the debt represented by the note given by appellees to appellant. Inasmuch as the facts found by the court, except the ultimate fact of agency, hereinafter referred to, are, in effect, conceded by appellant to be supported by the evidence, instead of attempting to set out the evidence, we will set out the findings based thereon, which we think important in determining the question here involved. They are, in substance, as follows:

Appellees about the last of December, 1907, having theretofore been informed that Louis J. Herman, a practicing attorney of the city of Evansville, had a client or clients who had money to loan, applied to said Herman for a loan of $5C0, and on the 6th day of January, 1908, appellees borrowed of appellant said sum, for which they executed to appellant their note for that amount, payable three years after date at the Commercial Bank, Evansville, Indiana, with 7 per cent interest after date. Neither of appellees had any personal acquaintance with the appellant. They had never seen her, and had no conversation or dealings with her, except through said Herman. The execution and delivery of the other papers mentioned in the complaint are found and their contents set out, and the findings then proceed, in substance, as follows: (4) and (5) That before making said loan said Herman, on behalf of appellant, examined the abstract of title to the real estate described in said deed, and personally examined the property therein described, with a view of determining its value as security for said loan, prepared the note, the deed and the title bond hereinabove referred to, and took the acknowledgment on the deed as a notary public. (6) That on the delivery of the papers above set out said Herman gave to appellees his personal check for $490 retaining out of the loan $10 to cover his services in connection with making the loan. (7) That appellant made said loan to appellees through said Herman, either under instructions from herself directly or by one Bernard Ewers, in whose home appellant then lived as his housekeeper, and she continued to reside with said Ewers until his death on the 23rd day of December, 1908. (8) In making said loan appellant entrusted the preparation of the note and other papers securing the loan to said Herman, and relied solely on his judgment as to the title of the property described in the complaint and as to the value thereof, and as to its sufficiency as security for said loan. (9) and (10) On and continuously since the 6th day of January, 1908, appellees have resided in the city of Evansville, where the property described in the complaint is located. (11) Said Herman disappeared from Evansville on the 9th day of January, 1909, and has not since been seen or heard of by any of the parties to this suit. (12) On the 1st day of July, 1908, appellees by the check of Henry McCool payable to "Louis J. Herman, Atty.," paid to said Herman $17.50, the interest on said note, and appellant credited said payment by indorsement on the back of said note on the 6th day of July, 1908; said check was for $94.50, and included $77 interest on another loan which appellees then had from Bernard Ewers, as well as the $17.50 interest on the loan which they had received from appellant. (13) Shortly before the 30th day of June, 1908, appellees offered to pay said Herman said note, but he refused to accept the same, because said note was not then due, and under the terms of the contract and loan appellees had the privilege of paying said note only at an annual anniversary thereof, and January 6, 1909, was such anniversary. (14) At and since the time said loan of $500 was made to appellees, and from five to seven years prior thereto, said Herman had acted for appellant, as her agent and attorney for the negotiation and collection of other loans in Vanderburgh county. (15) Said note for $500 was never deposited at the Commercial Bank, Evansville, Indiana, for payment or collection. (17) On January 5, 1909, appellee Henry F. McCool called at the office of said Herman, in the city of Evansville, for the purpose of paying said note. Said Herman was not then at his office, but was at the courthouse, and by telephone directed said McCool to leave his check for $517.50, in full payment of said note and loan, at the office of said Herman, and promised said McCool to send to his (McCool's) office the papers in connection with said loan, and to which he was entitled on the payment of the same; that thereupon said McCool delivered to said Herman his check on the Mercantile National Bank of Evansville, Indiana, dated January 5, 1909, for $517.50, payable to "Louis J. Herman, Atty." A few days thereafter said papers, except a deed from appellant to appellees, were sent to appellees by the stenographer in charge of and employed in the office of said Herman. Said Herman had then left the city, and the stenographer was not authorized by appellant or by said Herman to send the papers to said McCool. (18) At the time of the execution and delivery of said check said Herman was in possession of said note for $500 and other papers connected with the loan, except a deed from said appellant to appellee. (19), (20) and (21) Said note, with other papers relating to the loan, had been delivered to said Herman by appellant on or about December 18, 1908, and remained continuously in his possession until delivered to appellees. At the time appellant delivered said note and other papers to said Herman he asked for them, and stated to appellant that he wanted to examine them and to "look something up," and she then knew that said Herman had prepared said deed and note, examined the abstract of title, and had collected from appellees the $17.50 interest on July 1, 1908, which he afterwards paid to appellant, and knew that appellees, under the terms of the contract and loan, had the privilege of repaying the same on January 6, 1909. (22) Appellees had no knowledge or notice and no means of knowing of any revocation or limitation of the authority of said Herman to act for appellant as her agent and attorney, until after their payment to him of said note. (23) Appellees, during the transaction of all the matters connected with said loan, and at the time of the delivery of said check of $517.50 in payment of said note, believed that said Herman was the duly-authorized agent and attorney for appellant to negotiate said loan and to collect the same. (24) Said note was payable on the day following the time said McCool delivered to said Herman the check for $517.50. (25) Said check was indorsed by said Herman and was duly paid by the Mercantile National Bank, Evansville, Indiana, on January 7, 1909. (26) Said Herman never paid or accounted to appellant for any part of said sum of $517.50. (27) Appellees had no agreement, contract or understanding with appellant or with said Herman that they should pay for any services rendered by said Herman in collecting said loan or in accounting therefor to appellant, and said Herman was not the agent or attorney of appellees or either of them in that behalf. (28) That in making said loan to appellees and in collecting the same on January 5, 1909, said Herman acted as the agent of appellant and not as the agent of appellees. (29) Appellant made no inquiry of said Herman as to said papers in connection with said loan, which she had delivered to him on December 18, 1908, until January 14, 1909, and after said Herman had disappeared from the city of Evansville, she made no inquiry or demand whatever from said McCool for the payment of said note until after she had learned of such disappearance of said Herman, and until after said McCool had written to her on or about January 23, 1909, demanding a reconveyance of said real estate, as in said contract provided. (30) Appellees in all things complied with the terms and conditions of the contract, and fully paid said note when due, and before the bringing of this suit. (31) That said written instrument, which on its face purports to be a deed, and said written instrument, which on its face is a bond and contract, were executed, delivered and accepted for the purpose of securing said loan. (32) That before the bringing of this suit, and after the repayment of said loan, appellant refused to execute and deliver to appellees a deed to the real estate described in their complaint, and no such deed was ever executed. As above stated, these facts are, in effect, conceded to be in accord with the evidence, except in so far as the court finds that in all the matters connected with said loan and its payment said Herman was not at any time acting as the agent of appellees, and finding 28 is especially relied on as having no evidence for its support.

It is insisted by appellant that if it can be said that the evidence tends to show that said Herman was acting for appellant at any time or in any capacity, that it at most only shows that he acted for her in the negotiation of the loan and the preparation of the papers evidencing and securing the same, and that appellees had no right to assume that he was acting for her in the collection of such loan.

In addition to the evidence which warranted the finding of said facts, in effect conceded by appellant to be correctly found, we have the following letter from Mr. Herman to Mr. McCool:

"Law office of
Louis J. Herman.
Rookery Bldg.
Telephone 324, 127 Fourth St.
Evansville, Indiana.

June 30, 1908.

Dr. Henry F. McCool,
    City.
Dear Sir:—

On my return to the office my stenographer informed me that you desired to pay off the entire loan held by Father Ewers and Mrs. Wagner. In looking over the papers I find the following clause in the Wagner loan:

'Said Henry F. McCool and Maggie N. McCool are hereby given the right to pay said Five Hundred ($500.00) Dollars on any annual anniversary of this contract.' I therefore see no way to accept this money until the end of the year, January 6th, 1909.

Upon examining the Ewers loan I find this clause:

'In the event that said Emery McCool and Anna McCool his wife, or their assigns or legal representatives desire to pay any portion of said Twenty-two Hundred ($2,200.00) Dollars prior to the end of said three (3) years, then they shall have the right to do so at any semi-annual interest bearing period upon the payment of all interest due at that time and the money so paid shall be credited on said principal of $2,200.00 represented by said notes.' The semi-annual interest bearing period referred to in this clause was June 16th, 1908, and as you made no tender on that date I cannot see my way clear to accept payment of this loan until the next interest bearing period, which will be December 16th, 1908.

I would therefore ask that you send me the six months interest due on the $500.00 and also the six months interest due on the $2,200.00.

Very truly yours,
[Signed]   Louis J. Herman."

Another letter, which tends strongly to show that appellant had depended wholly on either her attorney, Herman, or Father Ewers, who in turn evidently entrusted all of said matters to said attorney, is as follows:

"Princeton, Indiana, Jan. 23, 1909

Dr. H. McCool
  Evansville, Ind;
Dear Sir:—
  Miss Margaret Wagner of this city, has left with me for adjustment a claim against you for $500.00. It seems that Mr. Louis J. Herman had something to do with this claim.
  Will you please advise me the exact nature of the claim, as to whether same was secured and if so, how, and what has been done in the matter?
  An early reply will be appreciated.

Yours truly,

[Signed]   Henry Kister."

Mr. McCool testified that Mr. Herman did not prepare the papers connected with the loan at his request; that he (McCool) "wanted to give a mortgage and he (Herman) said his client would not accept a mortgage." Appellant testified, in effect, that she entrusted the entire matter of making and collecting this loan and four others to Father Ewers, in whose home she lived and for whom she kept house. In fact, she repeatedly stated and insisted with reference to all of said loans inquired about that she entrusted them all, both their making and collecting, to Father Ewers, and that she had nothing to do with Mr. Herman except through Father Ewers; yet on cross-examination she, in effect, admitted that she knew that said Ewers employed Herman to make the loans and prepare the papers, and that Herman collected the interest and principal of such loans and gave the same to Father Ewers, who would then turn such collections over to her; that she, before said loans were paid, gave the notes and securities to said Ewers to be surrendered, and that Herman made the collections.

While the letter of Mr. Herman to appellees could not be taken as evidence establishing his agency, it is an important item of evidence strongly tending to show that he 2. had possession of the papers and was assuming to act in the matter of the collection of the note in question previous to the time of its payment.

Appellee Henry F. McCool testified that in December before he paid the note, at a time when he was in Mr. Herman's office on another matter, Mr. Herman told him he had the Wagner papers, and that he (the witness) saw them and saw a deed from appellant to appellees, signed by her, and that he then told Mr. Herman he was not then ready to take up that note; that it was not due until January, but for him to keep the papers, that he would take care of the note later.

Another witness—Mr. Davenport—an abstractor, testified that on one occasion when he went to see Mr. Herman about an abstract of another tract of land on which Father Ewers had a loan, and in which appellees were interested, Mr. Herman in that connection said: " 'I have a deed to turn over to Dr. McCool.' And he said 'here is one Miss Wagner had a loan on.' That I said, 'I don't know anything about that, the doctor [McCool] didn't tell me a thing about that.' He said, 'well I have a deed to that too, that is due in a few days and I suppose he wanted to pay all.' "

It is apparent from the evidence that this was a case of "misplaced confidence" both on the part of appellant and appellees. It is one of the numerous cases "where
3. one of two innocent persons must suffer because of the betrayal of a trust reposed in a third, and where the person most at fault must bear the loss." Story, Agency (9th ed.) §127. See, also, *Bamberger* v. *Geiser*, (1893), 24 Or. 203, 33 Pac. 609; *Kasson* v. *Noltner* (1878), 43 Wis. 646; *McLeod* v. *Despain* (1907), 49 Or. 536, 90 Pac. 492, 92 Pac. 1088, 124 Am. St. 1066, 1079.

"The maxim of natural justice here applies with its full force, that he, who, without intentional fraud, has enabled any person to do an act, which must be injurious to himself, or to another innocent party, shall himself suffer the injury rather than the innocent party, who has placed confidence in him." Story, Agency (9th ed.) §127. The question in such cases seems to be, not "what was the authority actually given?" but, what was the party "in dealing with the agent justified in believing the authority to be?"

A rule which seems to be fundamental in the law of agency is stated in Mechem, Agency §§283, 284 as follows: It is well settled that "the authority of the agent must depend, so far as it involves the rights of innocent third persons, who have relied thereon, upon the *character* bestowed, and not upon the *instructions* given, or, in other words, the principal is bound to third persons who have relied thereon and in ignorance of any limitations or restrictions, by the *apparent* authority he has given to the agent, and not by the *actual* or *express* authority. * * * A principal is responsible, either when he has given to an agent sufficient authority, or, when he justifies a party dealing with his agent in believing that he has given to this agent this authority."

In view of the principles of law controlling in the case, we feel there can be no doubt but that there is at least some

1. evidence tending to support the decision of the court on the question in dispute. In fact, if we were required to weigh the evidence we are not prepared to say that we would not reach the same conclusion reached by the trial court. A hardship must necessarily result to one party or the other by any decision that may be made in the case, and we are inclined to the belief that the trial court let it fall where, under the evidence and the law applicable thereto, it should fall. As further supporting this conclusion see, *Over* v. *Schifling* (1885), 102 Ind. 191, 196, 26 N. E. 99; *Morehead* v. *Murray* (1869), 31 Ind. 418, 421; *Broadstreet* v. *McKamey* (1908), 41 Ind. App. 272, 273, 83 N. E. 773; *County of Macon* v. *Shores* (1877), 97 U. S. 272, 279, 24 L. Ed. 889; *Smith* v. *Kidd* (1877), 68 N. Y. 130, 141, 23 Am. Rep. 157; *Leo Austrian & Co.* v. *Springer*

(1892), 94 Mich. 343, 349, 350, 54 N. W. 50, 34 Am. St. 350.

Judgment affirmed.

NOTE.—Reported in 100 N. E. 895. See, also, under (1) 31 Cyc. 1667; (2) 31 Cyc. 1658; (3) 31 Cyc. 1331.

GENERAL CONVENTION OF THE NEW CHURCH IN
THE UNITED STATES ET AL. *v.* SMITH ET AL.

[No. 7,887. Filed January 9, 1913.]

1. TRUSTS.—*Establishment.*—*Complaint.*—*Sufficiency.*—A complaint to declare a trust in relation to real estate is insufficient under §4012 Burns 1908, §2969 R. S. 1881, where no writing, on which the action should be founded, is filed with or made a part thereof. p. 137.

2. TRUSTS.—*Creation.*—*Wills.*—*Construction.*—A bequest of a note for the express purpose of building a New Jerusalem Hall and Library on the lot devised by testator to his brother, with direction that the note be paid out of the first moneys derived from the estate does not create a trust in personalty. p. 137.

3. TRUSTS.—*Creation.*—*Wills.*—*Complaint.*—*Sufficiency.*—A complaint alleging that a bequest of a note for $2,000 had been made by a testator for the purpose of erecting a New Jerusalem Hall and Library for the benefit of plaintiffs on a lot devised by the testator to his brother, and that such brother used the proceeds of the note in erecting a hall and library on such lot, which was used by plaintiffs for about twenty years, but not averring that it was testator's intention that the title to the property should ever pass to plaintiffs, or that testator's brother ever promised him to convey such title to plaintiffs, and not showing that the alleged trust was to continue for any definite or indefinite period of time, is insufficient on demurrer, since, if any trust is shown to have been created, it is not shown that the same has not been fully terminated. p. 138.

4. TRUSTS.—*Establishment.*—*Parol Evidence.*—The rule that a trust in an absolute legacy may be shown by parol applies only in case of actual or constructive fraud. p. 138.

5. TRUSTS.—*Establishment.*—*Parol Evidence.*—Where money is intrusted in parol to one person to be invested in real estate for the benefit of another, a volunteer, such volunteer cannot, in the absence of fraud, enforce such trust. p. 139.

From Howard Circuit Court; *H. J. Paulus*, Special Judge.

Action by the General Convention of the New Church in the United States and others against Alzora Nativa Smith and others. From a judgment for defendants, the plaintiffs appeal. *Affirmed.*

Stanley W. Merrell and *Morrison & McIntosh,* for appellants.

M. Bell, John E. Moore and *Blacklidge, Wolf & Barnes,* for appellees.

IBACH, C. J.—This is a suit by appellants against appellees, the heirs of George W. Defenbaugh, on a complaint in six paragraphs. Each paragraph is long, and we deem it unnecessary to set them out in full. It is sufficient
1. to say that the first four paragraphs are clearly to declare a trust in a certain lot located in Kokomo, Indiana, which had been conveyed by Lewis Defenbaugh to his brother George W. Defenbaugh, and yet no writing of any kind, which is necessarily the foundation of such a suit, is filed with or made a part of any paragraph founded on this theory. To hold any of these paragraphs sufficient when assailed by demurrer would be in opposition to §4012 Burns 1908, §2969 R. S. 1881, and in direct conflict with the decisions of the Supreme Court. *Grimes' Execs.* v. *Harmon* (1871), 35 Ind. 198, 9 Am. Rep. 690; *Ransdel* v. *Moore* (1899), 153 Ind. 393, 399, 53 N. E. 767, 53 L. R. A. 753; *Ellison* v. *Ganiard* (1906), 167 Ind. 471, 486, 79 N. E. 450, and cases cited.

By the averments of the fifth and sixth paragraphs of the complaint, appellants seek to show facts establishing
2. lishing a trust in personalty, and rely principally on the third item of the will of Lewis Defenbaugh, which is as follows:

I give and devise to my beloved brother George W. Defenbaugh of Howard county, Indiana, a certain promissory note, given by myself to my brother for two thousand dollars, due one year from date hereof, and now in deposit with the banking house of Russell-Dol-

man and Company of Kokomo, Indiana. This bequeath-
ment is made for the express purpose of building a New
Jerusalem Hall and library on the lot I have bequeathed
to him, and direct that the note be paid out of the first
moneys derived from my estate, after,'' etc.

We fail to observe anything in this item of the will (and
this is the only part of the will referred to in the complaint)
which tends toward the establishment of a trust in favor of
plaintiffs or others.

The facts averred in the last two paragraphs of complaint,
and relied on as establishing a trust, when summed up briefly are that George W. Defenbaugh by the terms of
his brother's will obtained the sum of $2,000, which
he was to use, and promised to use, in building a
New Jerusalem hall and library for the benefit of appellants,
on the lot given to him by the same brother. It is nowhere
averred that it was Lewis Defenbaugh's intention that the
title to this property should ever pass to plaintiffs, nor
that George W. Defenbaugh ever promised him to convey
such title to plaintiffs. Nor does it appear that the trust
for the use and benefit of plaintiffs was to continue for any
definite or indefinite period of time. It is averred that
George W. Defenbaugh, with the proceeds of the note
bequeathed to him, in 1888 erected on the lot given
to him by his brother a hall and library which were used
by plaintiffs for about twenty years. So far as the averments of the complaint show, the purposes of the bequest
were fully carried out by the erection of this building, of
which plaintiffs had the use and benefit for nearly twenty
years, and it does not appear that they are still entitled to
its use and benefit. In other words, it does not appear that
the trust, if any was created, has not been fully terminated.

Appellant has cited several cases, among them *Ransdel* v.
Moore, supra, and *Winder* v. *Scholey* (1910), 83 Ohio St.
204, 93 N. E. 1098, 33 L. R. A. (N. S.) 995, to the
effect that a trust in an absolute legacy may be shown
by parol. This rule applies only in case of actual or

constructive fraud. But in the present case, appellants have not averred sufficient extrinsic facts to show that the legacy in the will was given on any further trust than was executed.

In the absence of fraud, it is held that where money is intrusted in parol to one person to be invested in real estate for the benefit of another, a volunteer, such volunteer

5. cannot enforce such trust. *Rooker* v. *Rooker* (1881), 75 Ind. 571; *Teele* v. *Bishop of Derry* (1897), 168 Mass. 341, 47 N. E. 422, 38 L. R. A. 629, 60 Am. St. 401; *Miller* v. *Coulter* (1901), 156 Ind. 290, 293, 59 N. E. 853; *Alexander* v. *Spaulding* (1903), 160 Ind. 176, 66 N. E. 694; *Orth* v. *Orth* (1896), 145 Ind. 184, 206, 42 N. E. 277, 44 N. E. 17, 32 L. R. A. 298, 57 Am. St. 185. The court did not err in holding that each paragraph of the complaint was insufficient.

Judgment affirmed.

NOTE.—Reported in 100 N. E. 384. See, also, under (1) 31 Cyc. 556; (2) 39 Cyc. 57; (3) 39 Cyc. 620; (4) 39 Cyc. 631; (5) 39 Cyc. 46. As to the creation of trusts in land, see 115 Am. St. 774. For a discussion of an implied trust arising from a testamentary gift secured by the promise of the donee to hold for the benefit of another, see 21 Ann. Cas. 1384.

ESPENLAUB ET AL. *v.* HEDDERICK

[No. 7,728. Filed January 10, 1913.]

1. **MASTER AND SERVANT.**—*Injury to Servant.*—*Unguarded Machinery.*—*Contributory Negligence.*—*Complaint.*—In a servant's action for personal injuries, the allegations of the complaint that the injury was caused by defendants' negligence in failing to guard the saw, that by reason of a defect in the saw-table a piece of wood became lodged near the saw, and that, while attempting to remove it, plaintiff's hand was caught in the saw and injured, but which neither show the distance of plaintiff's hand from the saw when he took hold of the wood, nor that he placed his hand in dangerous proximity to the saw, do not show affirmatively as a matter of law that plaintiff was guilty of contributory negligence. p. 141.

2. NEGLIGENCE.—*Contributory Negligence.—Complaint—Sufficiency.*
—A complaint in a negligence case need not negative contributory
negligence on the part of plaintiff, and will be held sufficient in
this respect, unless facts are specifically averred therein disclosing the defense of contributory negligence. p. 141.

3. NEGLIGENCE.—*Complaint.—Allegations.—Presumptions of Contributory Negligence.*—Contributory negligence of plaintiff will
not be presumed from allegations of the complaint tending to
disclose such defense. p. 141.

4. PLEADING. — *Presumptions Against Pleading.* — Presumptions
against a pleading relate only to the facts necessary to constitute a cause of action, and not to facts tending to disclose an
affirmative defense. p. 142.

5. MASTER AND SERVANT.—*Injury to Servant.—Unguarded Saw.—
Contributory Negligence.—Evidence.—Verdict.*—In a servant's
action for injury to his hand by coming in contact with an unguarded saw while he was attempting to remove a piece of wood
that had lodged in the saw-table, where there was evidence showing that plaintiff could have stopped the saw by going around
the table and using a lever provided for that purpose, while other
evidence showed that if he had attempted to do so he would
thereby have exposed himself to other serious dangers, and that
in attempting to remove the wood without stopping the saw
plaintiff was pursuing the usual course, the question of whether
he used due care was one of fact for the jury and its verdict
thereon will not be disturbed. p. 142.

6. APPEAL.—*Review.—Conflicting Evidence.—Verdict.—Conclusiveness.*—The verdict of a jury on a question of fact, where the evidence is conflicting or is of such character that reasonable minds
might draw opposite inferences therefrom, will not be disturbed
on appeal. p. 142.

7. APPEAL.—*Review.—Instructions.—Refusal.*—The refusal of requested instructions that are covered by instructions given, or
are inapplicable to the issues and the evidence, is not error. p. 142.

From Posey Circuit Court; *Herdis F. Clements*, Judge.

Action by Arthur Hedderick, by his next friend, John E.
Hedderick, against John W. Espenlaub and others. From
a judgment for plaintiff, the defendants appeal. *Affirmed.*

George A. Cunningham, for appellants.

John W. Spencer, John R. Brill and *Frank H. Hatfield*,
for appellee.

LAIRY, J.—Appellee by his next friend sued appellants
to recover damages for personal injuries alleged to have been

caused by appellants' negligence. Appellants' demurrer to the complaint was overruled, an answer in general denial filed, the cause tried by a jury, and a verdict returned in favor of appellee. Appellants' motion for a new trial was overruled, and judgment rendered in favor of appellee on the verdict. The rulings of the court on the demurrer to the complaint and the motion for a new trial are assigned as error here.

Appellants assert that the complaint is insufficient for the reason that its averments show affirmatively that the plaintiff was guilty of contributory negligence. It
1. appears from the allegations of the complaint that the plaintiff was injured while operating a buzz-saw in defendants' factory, by reason of the negligence of defendants in failing to guard the saw in obedience to §8029 Burns 1908, Acts 1899 p. 231, §9, commonly known as the factory act. It appears also that, by reason of a defect in the table or platform on which the saw was operated, a piece of wood became clogged or fastened near the teeth of the unguarded saw, and that while plaintiff was attempting with his left hand to remove this piece of wood, the revolving saw caught it and his hand was jerked against the teeth of the saw and thereby injured. From these averments the court cannot say as a matter of law that plaintiff was negligent. The complaint does not show that plaintiff in attempting to remove the piece of wood placed his hand in dangerous proximity to the saw, neither is the distance of his hand from the saw at the time he took hold of the piece of wood
2. shown. It was not necessary for plaintiff to allege that he was free from contributory negligence, and the complaint will be held good in this respect, unless facts are specifically averred therein disclosing the defense of contributory negligence. As to such facts, no pre-
3. sumptions are indulged against the pleader. Presumptions against a pleading relate only to the facts necessary to constitute a cause of action, and do not relate

to facts tending to disclose an affirmative defense.

4. *Cleveland, etc., R. Co.* v. *Clark* (1912), 51 Ind. App. 392, 97 N. E. 822; *Cole* v. *Searfoss* (1912), 49 Ind. App. 334, 97 N. E. 345. The court cannot say in this case that the facts stated in the complaint show affirmatively as a matter of law that plaintiff was guilty of contributory negligence. The demurrer to the complaint was properly overruled.

The evidence on the question of contributory negligence was conflicting. The testimony showed that plaintiff could have stopped the saw by going around the table and

5. using a lever provided for that purpose. Some of the witnesses said that this would have been the safer course to pursue, while others testified that an attempt to pursue this course would have exposed plaintiff to other dangers of a serious character, and that the way employed by plaintiff in his attempt to remove the piece of wood in question was the way in which it was usually done. Under the evidence, the question of whether the plaintiff used due care was one of fact for the jury. This court will

6. not disturb the verdict of a jury on a question of fact where the evidence is conflicting, or where it is of such a character that reasonable minds might draw opposite inferences therefrom in respect to such fact.

Appellants object to the fourteenth and seventeenth instructions, on the ground that they are not applicable to the evidence. An examination of the record shows that there was some evidence to justify these instructions. The fifteenth instruction, objected to by appellants, is not erroneous.

Error is predicated on the refusal of the court to give certain instructions tendered by appellant. An ex-

7. amination of these instructions shows that they were either covered by other instructions given or that they were inapplicable to the issues and the evidence.

Judgment affirmed.

Croan *v.* Myers—52 Ind. App. 143.

NOTE.—Reported in 100 N. E. 382. See, also, under (1) 26 Cyc. 1399; (2) 29 Cyc. 575; (3) 29 Cyc. 579; (5) 26 Cyc. 1482; (6) 3 Cyc. 348; (7) 38 Cyc. 1612, 1711. As to the contributory negligence of an employe as affecting his right to recover for personal injuries see 97 Am. St. 884; also, note to *Brazil Block Coal Co.* v. *Gibson* (Ind.) 98 Am. St. 289.

CROAN *v.* MYERS.

[No. 7,793. Filed January 10, 1913.]

1. BILLS AND NOTES.—*Action.—Answer.—Sufficiency.*—In an action on an ordinary promissory note, appearing on its face to be complete, an answer admitting its execution but alleging that an oral agreement was made at the time, whereby the note was not to be paid in the event an enterprise, in furtherance of which it was executed, should terminate unsuccessfully, and that such enterprise had failed, is insufficient in the absence of a showing that fraud or mistake entered into the transaction. p. 144.

2. EVIDENCE.—*Parol Evidence.—Variation of Terms of Written Instrument.*—In the absence of a showing of fraud or mistake, parol evidence is not admissible to annul or substantially vary the terms of a written instrument. p. 145.

3. BILLS AND NOTES.—*Action.—Defenses.*—Where a husband upon lending money took a note payable to his wife, the wife's delivery of the note to defendant after the death of the husband, pursuant to the husband's request, is no defense to an action thereon, in the absence of averments showing a gift, or that it was delivered pursuant to an agreement based on a sufficient consideration. p. 146.

4. BILLS AND NOTES.—*Note Payable to Wife for Money Loaned by Husband. — Consideration. — Presumptions.* — Where, a husband upon lending his money, took a note payable to his wife, it will be presumed, in the absence of any averment to the contrary, that the note was so made on a sufficient consideration. p. 147.

5. PLEADING.—*Presumptions.*—It is always presumed that a party's pleading is as strong in his favor as the facts will warrant. p. 147.

6. APPEAL.—*Review.—Harmless Error.—Amount of Recovery.*—While error in the amount of recovery, whether too large or too small, is a statutory cause for new trial, appellant cannot avail himself thereof, where the verdict against him was for $400 less than it should have been, as shown by the evidence, since it is manifest that he was not harmed thereby. p. 148.

7. APPEAL.—*Error Warranting Reversal.*—A judgment will be reversed for error only when it is shown to have been prejudicial to the complaining party. p. 148.

From Madison Circuit Court; *C. K. Bagot,* Judge.

Action by Florence S. Myers against William M. Croan. From a judgment for plaintiff, the defendant appeals. *Affirmed.*

Henry C. Ryan, for appellant.
Ellis & Ellison, for appellee.

ADAMS, J.—Appellee sued appellant on a lost or destroyed promissory note, shown to be in the words following:

"$500.   Anderson, Ind., June 15, 1897.
    Ten years after date I promise to pay to the order of Florence S. Myers, five hundred dollars ($500) value received, without any relief whatever from valuation or appraisement laws, with interest at 6% per annum from date, and attorneys' fees. The drawers and endorsers severally waive presentment for payment, protest, notice of protest and non-payment of this note.
                                        Wm. M. Croan."

Appellant answered the complaint in five paragraphs. Trial by jury; verdict and judgment for appellee in the sum of $575. Errors assigned and relied on for reversal are (1) sustaining a demurrer to the third paragraph of answer, and (2) overruling appellant's motion for a new trial.

The third paragraph of answer, in substance, alleges that the note sued on was executed in 1897 at a time when appellant and others had organized a corporation under
1. the name of "The Anderson Normal University", the object and purpose of which was the establishment of a normal school for general educational purposes in the city of Anderson, Indiana; that appellee's husband, William R. Myers, was a brother of appellant's wife, and was one of the incorporators of said institution; that for

the purpose of assisting appellant and his wife in promoting, conducting and carrying on said normal school, of which appellant was then president, said William R. Myers advanced the sum of $500; that the money so advanced was evidenced by a promissory note, and was the money of said William R. Myers, husband of appellee, and the note taken therefor was taken in the name of appellee; that it was agreed and understood when said money was advanced and said note given that if said school should be a success the money was to be repaid in accordance with the terms of the note, but if the same was not a success said money was to be a gift by said William R. Myers, and was never to be repaid; that the school was not a success; that William R. Myers died in April, 1907, having retained said note in his possession, and during said time never made demand for payment; that before his death he requested his wife, appellee herein, to carry out his promise, and to surrender said note to appellant; that within a few weeks after the death of said Myers, appellee did carry out the wish, request and agreement of her said husband, and surrendered said note to appellant, which he at the time destroyed; that by said surrender the note was canceled and satisfied, and said debt fully forgiven.

We think there was no error in sustaining the demurrer to this paragraph of answer. It will be observed that the note sued on was in form an ordinary promissory note. Appellant does not claim that the expressed consideration was not the true consideration, or that he did not receive the $500, which, by the note, he promised to repay. No element of fraud or mistake is shown to have entered into the transaction. The note appears on its face to be complete, and not dependent on or collateral to any other agree-

2. ment. Under such conditions, the elemental rule that parol evidence will not be received to annul or substantially vary the terms of a written instrument must be

held to apply. *Brunson* v. *Henry* (1894), 140 Ind. 455, 462, 39 N. E. 256.

In *Conant* v. *National St. Bank* (1889), 121 Ind. 323, 22 N. E. 250, the court said: "It is true that the actual consideration of a contract may be shown by parol evidence, but it is not true that where the acts that a party agrees to perform are expressly and specifically set forth, it may be shown by parol evidence that he agreed to do other things. Where the writing states specifically the acts which the parties are to perform, no other acts can be proved by parol except in cases of fraud or mistake. The writing takes up and retains the whole and every part of the contract, leaving nothing to be supplied by extrinsic evidence." Citing cases. Again, in the same case, the court said: "The provisions of the contract are specific, and these specific provisions cannot be supplanted by oral statements. To permit parties to substitute oral statements for written stipulations would render written instruments valueless, and leave to the uncertainty of human memory the terms of contracts. This would defeat the chief purpose of a written instrument, which is to furnish certain, reliable and permanent evidence of the contract. Where parties commit their contract to writing, by that writing they must stand, where there is neither fraud nor mistake. This must be true, or else the distinction between oral and written contracts will be utterly broken down." See, also, *Diven* v. *Johnson* (1889), 117 Ind. 512, 515, 20 N. E. 428, 3 L. R. A. 308; *Buckeye Mfg. Co.* v. *Woolley, etc., Works* (1900), 26 Ind. App. 7, 13, 58 N. E. 1069; *Pierse* v. *Bronnenberg* (1907), 40 Ind. App. 662, 668, 81 N. E. 739, 82 N. E. 126.

It is averred, however, in the third paragraph of answer "that within a few weeks after the death of said William R. Myers, the plaintiff, his widow, carried out the

3. wish, request and agreement of her said husband, and surrendered said note to the defendant." It is insisted that this averment makes the paragraph of answer

good. We cannot concur in this view. If the note was surrendered pursuant to any agreement, the answer is bad for
failing to show the consideration supporting such agreement.
If the note was surrendered as a gift to appellant, the answer is likewise bad, for want of proper averment showing
a gift. But assuming that the paragraph of answer is good,
as it stands, it must follow that proof of a surrender of the
note, even for the purpose of examination, would defeat a
recovery. Such a position is manifestly untenable. The
paragraph should have set out the consideration, if any,
supporting the surrender, and if the surrender was not made
pursuant to any agreement, then the purpose and intention
of appellee in surrendering the note should have been shown.
An issue of fact could then have been formed, on which the
rights of the parties could have been determined, but the
rights of the parties could not have been determined by
proof of a mere, naked surrender. It must be borne in mind
that this note was the property of appellee. Her title to
it was absolute. While the loan was made by her
4. husband out of his own funds, he had the note made
payable to his wife. In the absence of any averment
to the contrary, it must be presumed that the note
5. was so made on a sufficient consideration. 'It is always presumed that a party's pleading is as strong in
his favor as the facts will warrant.

In the case of *Sherman* v. *Sherman* (1852), 3 Ind. *337,
on which appellant relies, a different state of facts is shown.
That was a proceeding in equity to foreclose a mortgage
securing a note for $800, executed to a father by his two
sons. The defense was that the father had conveyed to said
sons a certain tract of land as a gift, but to secure to himself and his wife a maintenance during their lives, and for
no other purpose, the note and mortgage were executed;
that the father and his wife were supported by defendants
as long as the father lived, and his wife was still supported
by defendants; that a short time before his death, the father

surrendered the note and mortgage to one of the defendants to be canceled. This defense was held good, on the evident theory that the parties had a right to show the actual consideration moving in the transaction.

In support of his motion for a new trial, appellant
6. urges that there was error in assessing the damages, the same being too small. It is true that error in the amount of the recovery, whether too large or too
7. small, is a statutory ground for a new trial. In this case, it appears from all the evidence that the recovery should have been approximately $400 more than the amount found by the jury. Conceding, as we must, that there was error in the amount of recovery, it is well settled that a judgment will not be reversed for any error appearing in the record, but only for such error as may be shown to be prejudicial to the complaining party. It is obvious that appellant was not harmed by a verdict and judgment for less than the amount shown by the evidence to be due. *Redpath* v. *Nottingham* (1840), 5 Blackf. 267, 269; *Swain* v. *Hardin* (1878), 64 Ind. 85, 86; *Louisville, etc., R. Co.* v. *Argenbright* (1884), 98 Ind. 254, 255; *Hartwig* v. *Schiefer* (1897), 147 Ind. 64, 70, 46 N. E. 75; *Noftsger* v. *Smith* (1893), 6 Ind. App. 54, 55, 32 N. E. 1024; Elliott, App. Proc. §632.

The court did not err in overruling appellant's motion for a new trial.

The judgment is affirmed.

NOTE.—Reported in 100 N. E. 380. See, also, under (2) 17 Cyc. 567; (4) 8 Cyc. 222; (5) 31 Cyc. 79; (6) 3 Cyc. 384; (7) 3 Cyc. 383. As to parol evidence of conditions in promissory notes, see 128 Am. St. 609. As to subsequent parol agreements to vary a writing, see 56 Am. St. 659.

MODERN WOODMEN OF AMERICA v. JONES.

[No. 7,606. Filed June 27, 1912. Rehearing denied January 10, 1913.]

1. APPEAL.—*Ruling on Demurrer.— Waiver.— Briefs.*— Error alleged in the overruling of a demurrer is waived by appellant's failure to set out in its brief a copy of such demurrer, or to state its substance or the grounds thereof. p. 150.

2. TRIAL.—*Reception of Evidence.—Discretion of Court.*—Where, in an action on an insurance certificate, plaintiff rested her case without having shown that proofs of death had been made as provided for in the certificate, the action of the court in permitting plaintiff to reopen the case and introduce such proof and other evidence, after defendant had asked for a peremptory instruction, was a matter within the discretion of the trial court, and not erroneous. pp. 150, 151.

3. APPEAL.—*Review.—Discretion of Lower Court.—Order of Proof.*—The action of a trial court in permitting the introduction of evidence out of the usual order is a matter within its sound discretion, and will not be interfered with on appeal, unless it is made to appear affirmatively that there has been an abuse of such discretion which prevented the complaining party from having a fair trial. p. 151.

4. APPEAL. — *Review. — Evidence. — Refusal to Direct Verdict.* — Where there was some evidence to support each material averment of the complaint, it was proper to refuse to direct a verdict for defendant. p. 151.

5. TRIAL.—*Direction of Verdict for Plaintiff.—When Authorized.*—Where the evidence to support the material averments of the complaint is documentary and clearly makes out a case for plaintiff, and is susceptible of no other inference, and there is no evidence to contradict it or to establish a defense, an instruction to find for the plaintiff is proper. p. 151.

6. INSURANCE.—*Fraternal Insurance.—Defense.—Nonpayment of Dues.—Conditions Precedent.*—A fraternal insurance company may not defend an action on a certificate issued by it on the ground that a payment of dues was made too late, and at the same time retain the amount of such payment, but, to defend on such ground, it should show that it had refused to accept such payment, or had offered to return it and had kept the tender good by bringing the amount into court. p. 152.

7. INSURANCE.—*Fraternal Insurance.—Evidence.—Direction of Verdict.*—In an action on a fraternal benefit certificate, uncontradicted documentary evidence as to the issuance of the certificate,

the payment of dues and the death of the member, made a *prima facie* case for plaintiff, notwithstanding evidence showing an offer to return the last payment of dues, where defendant failed to keep the tender good, and, in the absence of any other evidence, an instruction to return a verdict for plaintiff was not erroneous. p. 152.

From Warrick Circuit Court; *Roscoe Kiper*, Judge.

Action by Mary Jones against the Modern Woodmen of America. From a judgment for plaintiff, the defendant appeals. *Affirmed.*

Benjamin D. Smith and *Edmund L. Craig*, for appellant.

R. E. Roberts, John W. Spencer, John R. Brill and *Frank H. Hatfield*, for appellee.

IBACH, J.—Action to recover on a benefit certificate issued to the husband of appellee by appellant.

Appellant argues error of the trial court in (1) overruling the demurrer to the second paragraph of reply to the fifth paragraph of answer, (2) refusing to direct a verdict for appellant at the close of appellee's evidence and in allowing appellee to reopen the case, and (3) directing the jury to return a verdict for appellee.

Appellant has failed to set forth in its brief a copy of the demurrer, its substance or the grounds thereof, and for this reason has waived consideration of the first error

1. argued. *Holliday* v. *Anheier* (1910), 174 Ind. 729, 93 N. E. 1; *Chicago, etc., R. Co.* v. *Walton* (1905), 165 Ind. 253, 74 N. E. 1090; *Knickerbocker Ice Co.* v. *Gray* (1905), 165 Ind. 140, 72 N. E. 869, 6 Ann. Cas. 607; *Wirrick* v. *Boyles* (1910), 45 Ind. App. 698, 91 N. E. 621; *Anderson* v. *Leonard* (1912), 51 Ind. App. 14, 98 N. E. 891.

Plaintiff rested her case, and thereupon defendant moved the court to instruct the jury to find for defendant, for the reason that the certificate introduced in evidence pro-

2. vides that before it becomes payable certain proofs of death must be made by the beneficiary, that no such proofs had been introduced and there was no evidence that

such were supplied, and until that is done there is no liability under the policy. Thereupon plaintiff asked leave to introduce such proofs, and over the objection and exception of defendant was permitted to introduce such proof and other evidence. When plaintiff again rested, defendant failed to offer any testimony, and the court on its own motion instructed a verdict for plaintiff.

It has been repeatedly held by this court and the Supreme Court that the reception of additional evidence out of the usual order is within the sound discretion of the trial court. Appellate courts therefore will not interfere with the action of trial courts in this respect, until it is made to appear affirmatively that there has been an abuse of such discretion, and thereby the complaining party has been prevented from having a fair trial. The courts have gone so far as to hold that after the trial has been concluded and after the argument of counsel it was not error for the trial court to admit additional testimony, opportunity being given the opposite party to offer rebutting evidence to oppose that received out of its regular or usual order. *Stewart* v. *Stewart* (1902), 28 Ind. App. 378, 383, 62 N. E. 1023. It has been held that there was no abuse of discretion in admitting further testimony several days after the evidence was closed *(Todd* v. *Crail* [1906], 167 Ind. 48, 57, 77 N. E. 402), or even two months after trial. *Beatson* v. *Bowers* (1910), 174 Ind. 601, 91 N. E. We find no abuse of discretion in the present case, nor that appellant was harmed. There was some evidence to support each and every material averment of the complaint, and the court did right to refuse the motion to instruct for defendant.

In regard to the giving of the peremptory instruction to find for plaintiff, the general rule is that where the evidence to support the material averments of the complaint is documentary and clearly makes out a case for the plaintiff, and no evidence has been introduced either to contradict it, or to establish a defense to plaintiff's action, so that there is absolutely no conflict in the evidence and all the evidence introduced is susceptible of no other inference, it is eminently proper for the court to instruct the jury to find for the plaintiff. *Porter* v. *Millard* (1862), 18 Ind. 502; *City of New Albany* v. *Ray* (1892), 3 Ind. App. 321, 29 N. E. 611; *Moss* v. *Witness Printing Co.* (1878), 64 Ind. 125, 131; *Haughton* v. *Aetna Life Ins. Co.* (1905), 165 Ind. 32, 73 N. E. 592, 74 N. E. 613. In this last cited case, and in the case of *Hynds* v. *Hays* (1865), 25 Ind. 31, in discussing a similar question, the Supreme Court said: "This was not usurping the province of the jury, but was simply a discharge of duty by the court."

In the present case, appellee had proved by documentary evidence the issuance of the benefit certificate, the payment of all dues, and the death of the member, and, as before stated, appellant introduced no evidence of any character to sustain the issue tendered by the answer, which was that the member had become suspended before the last payment was made, and that as he was in ill-health at the time he made such payment, appellant, under the by-laws of the order, had refused to reinstate him. Further, appel-

6. lant could not defend on the ground that a payment was made too late, and at the same time retain the amount of such payment, and in order to defend, it must show that it had refused to accept such payment, had offered to return it to the beneficiary, and had kept the tender good by bringing such amount into court. *American Cent. Life Ins. Co.* v. *Rosenstein* (1910), 46 Ind. App. 537, 92 N. E. 380.

The evidence showed that the amount of the last payment made by the member had been sent from appellant's head office to their local clerk with directions to tender it

7. to the heirs or legal representatives of decedent, that it had been offered to appellee, that she refused it, and thereupon it was returned to appellant's head banker.

There was no showing that the tender was kept good by bringing the amount into court for appellee. As the evidence was without contradiction as to the issuance of the certificate, the payment of dues, and the death of the member, a *prima facie* case was thus made out for appellee. Then, as appellant introduced no evidence, and could not maintain its defense in the absence of a showing that a tender had been made to the beneficiary, and had been kept good by bringing the amount thereof into court, the question of appellant's liability became one of law, and the court did not err in directing a verdict for the plaintiff.

Judgment affirmed.

NOTE.—Reported in 98 N. E. 1006. See, also, under (1) 2 Cyc. 1014; (2) 38 Cyc. 1360; (3) 3 Cyc. 336; (4) 38 Cyc. 1576; (5) 38 Cyc. 1574; (6) 29 Cyc. 194; (7) 38 Cyc. 1574. As to the waiver of the forfeiture of a beneficiary certificate for the non-payment of an assessment or dues by the acceptance of arrearages or a similar act, see 11 Ann. Cas. 539.

INDIANAPOLIS OUTFITTING COMPANY *v.* CHEYNE ELECTRIC COMPANY.

[No. 7,803.   Filed January 21, 1913.]

1. APPEAL.—*Review.*—*Harmless Error.*—*Ruling on Motion to Dismiss.*—Where an action was brought before a justice of the peace to recover $200 for material furnished and labor performed at the special instance and request of defendant, and, on appeal to the superior court, plaintiff filed an additional paragraph of complaint to recover the same amount on the theory of an express contract, error in overruling defendant's motion to dismiss the action, on the ground that the court had not jurisdiction of the subject-matter, was harmless, where, after such ruling the plaintiff dismissed such additional paragraph and proceeded to trial on the original complaint.   p. 154.

2. APPEAL.—*Review.*—*Harmless Error.*—*Affirmance.*—A judgment will not be reversed on account of an error which did not prejudice the substantial rights of the party complaining.   p. 155.

3. EVIDENCE.—*Account Books.*—*Ledger.*—In an action to recover for material furnished and labor performed, a ledger kept by

plaintiff's bookkeeper in the regular course of plaintiff's business, the entries in which were made from memoranda furnished by the employes who sent out the material and by the men who did the work, was admissible as affording some proof of the account, although such bookkeeper had no personal knowledge of the amount of material furnished or the amount of labor performed at the time such entries were made by him. ·p. 155.

4. APPEAL.—*Review.*—*Refusal to Direct Verdict.*—The refusal to direct a verdict for defendant was not error, where there was evidence tending to support a verdict for plaintiff. p. 156.

From Superior Court of Marion County (78,879); *Ulric Z. Wiley,* Special Judge.

Action by the Cheyne Electric Company against the Indianapolis Outfitting Company. From a judgment for plaintiff, the defendant appeals. *Affirmed.*

Wm. E. Reiley, for appellant.

Charles Alcon and *H. L. Wynegar,* for appellee.

LAIRY, J.—This case originated in the court of a justice of the peace of Marion county, and was appealed to the Superior Court of Marion county, where the judgment from which this appeal is taken was rendered in favor of appellee for the sum of $199.86. This action was brought to

1. recover for materials furnished and labor performed by appellee for appellant, and in the justice's court the complaint proceeded on the theory that the materials were furnished and the labor was performed at the special instance and request of defendant, and sought to recover the reasonable value of the materials and labor so furnished. After the case reached the superior court, plaintiff, by leave of court, filed a second paragraph of complaint, alleging an express contract and seeking to recover thereon. Each paragraph demanded $200. After the second paragraph was filed, defendant made a motion to dismiss the action, on the ground that the court had no jurisdiction of the subject-matter, which motion the court overruled; and, thereupon plaintiff dismissed the second paragraph of his complaint.

The case proceeded to trial, and judgment was rendered on the complaint originally filed before the justice of the peace.

If there was error in the ruling of the court on the motion to dismiss the action, such error was rendered harmless by the subsequent proceedings of the court. A judgment will not be reversed on account of an error which, as shown by the record, did not prejudice the substantial rights of the party complaining. *Vulcan Iron Works Co.* v. *Electric, etc., Min. Co.* (1913), 53 Ind. App. ——, 99 N. E. 429, 100 N. E. 307, and cases cited.

2.

On the trial of the case the court permitted the book-keeper of the plaintiff, over the objection of defendant, to refer to entries made by him in a ledger kept by him in the regular course of plaintiff's business. From the testimony of this witness it appears that he had no personal knowledge of the amount of material furnished or the amount of labor performed at the time the entries were made in this book, but that the entries were made from memoranda furnished by the employes who sent out the material and by the men who did the work.

3.

Shop books kept by a merchant or tradesman in the course of his regular business are admissible, under certain conditions, to prove the transactions between him and his customers. A discussion of the reasons on which such books are held to be admissible, or of the limitations affecting their admissibility, would not be profitable in this opinion. For a discussion of these questions we refer to the concurring opinion of Roby, J., in the case of *Johnson* v. *Zimmerman* (1908), 42 Ind. App. 165, 84 N. E. 541, and also to the case of *State, ex. rel.,* v. *Central States Bridge Co.* (1912), 49 Ind. App. 544, 97 N. E. 803. There has been much uncertainty as to the rule in this State, but recent decisions seem to justify us in holding that shop books, kept in the manner here shown, are admissible in evidence, and that they offered some proof of the account, the weight of which is for the consideration of the jury.

The trial court did not err in refusing to direct a
4. verdict for defendant, and there is evidence in the
record tending to support the verdict rendered.

Judgment affirmed.

NOTE.—Reported in 100 N. E. 468. See, also, under (1, 2) 3 Cyc.
383; (3) 17 Cyc. 393; (4) 38 Cyc. 1576. As to general requisites
to admissibility of account-books in evidence, see 138 Am. St. 445.
As to what is provable by books of account, generally, see 52
L. R. A. 680. On the question of party's books of account as evidence in own favor, see 52 L. R. A. 546.

THE CLEVELAND, CINCINNATI, CHICAGO AND ST. LOUIS RAILWAY COMPANY *v.* VAN LANINGHAM.

[No. 7,488. Filed February 14, 1912. Rehearing denied June 18,
1912. Transfer denied January 22, 1913.]

1. PLEADING.—*Demurrer.*—*Admissions.*—On demurrer to a complaint, all the material facts that are well pleaded must be taken
as true for the purposes of the demurrer. p. 163.
2. RAILROADS. — *Crossing Accident. — Contributory Negligence. —
Complaint.*—Where, in an action for the death of plaintiff's decedent, in a railroad crossing accident, the conclusions to be
drawn from the allegations of the complaint, with reference to
decedent's conduct in approaching the crossing, lead to no other
legitimate inference than that decedent was guilty of contributory
negligence, the existence of such contributory negligence will be
determined as a matter of law, but if the allegations are such
as might properly cause reasonable men to differ as to the existence of such negligence on the part of decedent, the question is
for the jury. p. 163.
3. NEGLIGENCE.—*Complaint.—Demurrer.—Contributory Negligence.
—Presumptions.*—On demurrer to a complaint in a negligence
case, it will be considered that plaintiff used due care, unless all
reasonable inferences drawn from the facts alleged show that
he was guilty of negligence as a matter of law. p. 163.
4. RAILROADS. — *Crossing Accident. — Contributory Negligence. —
Complaint.*—A complaint to recover for the death of plaintiff's
decedent in a railroad crossing accident, alleging that decedent
was sixty years old and had good hearing and eyesight, that
when about 100 feet from the crossing he stopped and looked
and listened for an approaching train, and, neither seeing nor
hearing any, he proceeded toward the crossing, that, from the
point where he stopped to a point five feet from the tracks, he

Cleveland, etc., R. Co. *v.* Van Laningham—52 Ind. App. 156.

could not see an approaching train because of obstructions which defendant negligently permitted to exist, that defendant negligently failed to give any signal or warning of the train's approach to the crossing by sounding the whistle or ringing the bell, and that the train was negligently run at a high rate of speed over said crossing, thereby causing the death, does not show contributory negligence as a matter of law and is sufficient to withstand a demurrer. pp. 164, 165.

5. RAILROADS. — *Crossing Accident. — Contributory Negligence. — Failure to Look and Listen.*—One, who, on approaching a railroad track fails to look and listen for an approaching train, is guilty of negligence as a matter of law. p. 164.

6. RAILROADS. — *Crossing Accident. — Contributory Negligence. — Jury Question.—Looking and Listening.*—Where a person, on approaching a railroad crossing, looked and listened in good faith, the question of whether he looked and listened enough is for the jury. p. 164.

7. RAILROADS.—*Crossing Accident.—Care by Persons Approaching Crossings.*—A person approaching a railroad crossing is required to use only ordinary care to avoid injury, and while he is required to use every reasonable precaution and to look and listen for an approaching train, he has a right to rely on the railroad company performing its duty and is not bound to anticipate that it will fail to give proper warning of the approach of its train. p. 164.

8. TRIAL.—*Verdict.—Answers to Interrogatories.*—A general verdict is overcome by answers to interrogatories only when they exclude every reasonable hypothesis consistent with the verdict which might have been proven under the issues. p. 166.

9. RAILROADS. — *Crossing Accident. — Contributory Negligence. — Verdict.—Answers to Interrogatories.*—In an action against a railroad company to recover for the death of plaintiff's decedent in a crossing accident, answers to interrogatories showing decedent was familiar with the crossing, that he stopped, looked and listened before approaching the same, that from where he stopped to a point within five feet of the track he could not have seen the approaching train, that when decedent arrived at the point in the highway where he could see the train he could not stop his horse in time to avoid injury, and had not space enough in which to turn the horse around, and that the whistle was not sounded until the engineer saw decedent crossing the track, do not show that decedent failed to use ordinary care and are not in conflict with the general verdict for plaintiff. p. 166.

10. RAILROADS. — *Crossing Accident. — Instructions. — Last Clear Chance.*—In an action against a railroad company for the death of plaintiff's decedent in a crossing accident, where there was

evidence that the engineer saw the decedent when he was some distance from the railroad, that decedent then disappeared behind an embankment which prevented decedent from seeing the train and hid him from the engineer's view, and that the engineer next saw the horse appear about fifteen feet from the track, an instruction that where a person traveling on a highway, and a train are each approaching a crossing under circumstances indicating if neither stops a collision is likely, the engineer, if he has signalled the approach of the train, has a right to presume that such person will stop and to proceed with the train until he sees that such person does not stop, and if, after making such discovery in time to stop the train and avoid a collision, his failure to do so will render the company liable for the resulting injury, was a proper instruction and applicable to the evidence, even under the view that the engineer was not bound to use the last clear chance to avoid accident until he saw the horse emerging from behind the embankment. pp. 167, 168.

11. RAILROADS.—*Crossing Accident.—Issues.—Last Clear Chance.— Complaint.*—A complaint, in an action for the death of plaintiff's decedent in a crossing accident, averring that the servants of defendant carelessly and negligently caused the train to strike decedent, while knowing that he did not and could not know of the approach of such train, is sufficient to bring into the case the doctrine of last clear chance. p. 167.

12. TRIAL.—*Instructions.—Negligence.*—Instructions on the question of negligence should apply only to the negligence charged in the complaint, where the acts charged are definite and specific. p. 169.

13. TRIAL.—*Instructions.—Refusal.*—The refusal of requested instructions on questions fully covered by the instructions given, is proper. p. 169.

14. RAILROADS.—*Crossing Accident.—Action.—Burden of Proof.*— In an action to recover for the death of plaintiff's decedent in a railroad crossing accident, plaintiff has the burden of showing negligence as charged, and the burden of showing contributory negligence by the decedent is on defendant. p. 169.

15. APPEAL.—*Review.—Evidence.—Verdict.*—The verdict for plaintiff in a negligence case will not be disturbed on the evidence, on appeal, where such evidence is conflicting on the question of defendant's negligence, and does not show contributory negligence as a matter of law. p. 169.

16. DEATH.—*Damages.—Excessive Damages.*—In an action for death against a railroad company, where decedent was sixty-two years old, able-bodied, living with and supporting his wife and daughter, and had a life expectancy of thirteen and one-half years, a verdict for $5,200 will not be held excessive, where there

is no showing that the jury adopted an improper method of calculating the damages, or was misled by sympathy, or influenced
by unfair means. p. 170.

From Johnson Circuit Court; *W. E. Deupree,* Judge.

Action by Carl Van Laningham, administrator of the estate of Cassius C. Van Laningham, deceased, against The
Cleveland, Cincinnati, Chicago & St. Louis Railway Company. From a judgment for plaintiff, the defendant appeals. *Affirmed.*

John W. Kern and *L. E. Slack,* for appellant.
Clarke & Clarke, for appellee.

IBACH, P. J.—This was a suit brought in the Superior
Court of Marion County by appellee as the administrator of
the estate of Cassius C. Van Laningham, on account of the
death of his decedent, which it is averred in the complaint
was caused by the negligence of appellant in running one
of its passenger-trains upon decedent at a highway crossing
in Marion county. The venue was subsequently changed to
Johnson county, where the cause was tried. The amended
complaint on which issues were joined was in two paragraphs. A demurrer to each paragraph for want of facts was
overruled, exceptions were taken and answer filed. Trial by
jury resulted in a verdict for appellee, assessing damages
at $5,200. With the general verdict were returned answers
to certain interrogatories. Appellant's motion for judgment on these answers was overruled, and judgment rendered on the verdict.

The errors assigned call in question the action of the trial
court in overruling appellant's separate demurrers to each
paragraph of the amended complaint, and in overruling appellant's motions for judgment on answers to interrogatories, and for a new trial.

The first paragraph of complaint sets out the following
alleged facts: Plaintiff is the administrator of the estate of
Cassius C. Van Laningham. Defendant is a railroad corpo-

ration, owning and operating a line of railroad passing
through the towns of Lawrence and Oaklandon, in Marion
county, Indiana. The course of said railroad from Lawrence to Oaklandon is straight. One mile west of Oaklandon
is a railroad crossing known as Springer's Crossing, where
said line of railroad tracks crosses a public highway at an
angle of about 45 degrees east, which highway had been
opened for many years prior to the construction of the railroad, and is used extensively by the traveling public.
Southwest of Oaklandon, for about three-quarters of a mile,
defendant's tracks go down grade until they cross a creek,
then ascend gradually, and where they intersect said public
highway they are about 10 or 15 feet below the original
grade of the highway. The grade of the highway has been
lowered to correspond to that of the railroad, and in lowering the highway grade north of the railroad defendant carelessly and negligently failed to remove the embankment
thus caused east of the highway and adjacent to the tracks
within its right of way. Defendant and others erected along
and near the railroad tracks a large number of telegraph
and telephone poles. A person approaching the track from
the north, walking, or driving in a buggy or wagon, cannot
see defendant's tracks or a train thereon to the east of said
highway at any time until he is within 5 feet of said railroad, owing to the presence of said embankment and poles.
A person in a buggy or wagon passing along said highway
in said cut going south cannot hear a train approaching at
any time until within 5 feet of said tracks, unless a good
and sufficient whistle is loudly sounded before said train
reaches said crossing and within 100 rods thereof, and
unless the bell on the locomotive drawing such train rings
continuously immediately before reaching said crossing, to
indicate the approach of the train, or other proper and necessary signals are made indicating the approach of a train
on said railroad. On December 18, 1907, plaintiff's decedent, a man of sixty years, of good health, good hearing

and eyesight, was passing south on said highway towards his home, which is situated about one-half mile south thereof. When he came to a place about 100 feet from the railroad tracks he stopped his horse, which he was driving to a buggy, and looked and listened. He did not see any train approaching, owing solely to the presence of said embankment and said poles, which obstructed his view. A line of interurban tracks parallels the railroad tracks at this place, and is separated therefrom by a high embankment. After decedent stopped, as related, an interurban car passed said crossing. Decedent drove on towards the south in said cut, and from where he could not see said railroad tracks and a train thereon to the east. Owing to said embankment, poles and wires, said decedent while so driving, could know of the approach of a train on said railroad only when a good and sufficient whistle on said locomotive was sounded and a bell rung continuously. When said decedent was within about five feet of said tracks he first saw and heard a train approaching from the east, but it was then too late to escape by any other means except by driving across said tracks. While decedent was attempting to escape, a train owned, operated and controlled by defendant ran into and against him, knocking and hurling him, his wagon and his horse for 100 feet, and so bruising and wounding decedent that he died a few minutes thereafter. The engine which struck and killed him was owned and operated by defendant, and in charge of one of its agents and employes, and such employe in charge of the engine carelessly, negligently and unlawfully failed and neglected to sound the engine whistle at a distance of not more than 100 and not less than 80 rods from such crossing, and negligently and carelessly failed to ring the bell on the locomotive continuously for at least 80 rods immediately before crossing said highway. Said acts of neglect and failure are the sole, immediate and direct cause of decedent's death. Then follow the averments as to those dependent on decedent, and judgment for $10,000 is asked.

The second paragraph is similar to the first, except that in this paragraph defendant is charged with negligence in allowing a pile of dirt, described as from 12 to 15 feet high, 30 feet wide, and 100 feet long, to remain adjacent to its right of way, so as to cause the obstruction of the view of the railroad tracks and trains thereon to persons using said highway. Defendant and its servants well knew the condition of said crossing, and knew that persons along the highway passing through said cut could not see or hear a train approaching on account of the embankment, poles and wires, unless such servants sounded loudly the whistle of the locomotive within a proper distance, and caused the bell on the locomotive to be rung continuously, and made such other noises, alarms or signals in such a manner that one within said cut would know or have the means of knowing of the approach of said train, and although defendant, its agents and servants knew these facts, they carelessly and negligently failed to erect alarm bells and signals at said crossing, and its agents and servants in charge of such locomotive negligently and carelessly failed to sound the whistle of said locomotive, to ring continuously the bell thereon, or give other signals or warnings of the approach of said train in such a manner and at such a time that plaintiff's decedent while using said crossing as aforesaid could be warned of the approach of such train in time to avoid injury therefrom, and such servants and agents of defendant carelessly and negligently caused said train to approach and dash over said highway at the rate of a mile a minute, without giving warning, as aforesaid, and to strike and hurl decedent and carry him along with said train for one-half mile or more, while knowing that he did not and could not know of the approach of such train. That such acts of negligence on the part of defendant's servants directly, proximately and solely caused decedent's death.

It is claimed by appellant that each paragraph of the complaint is bad because it affirmatively appears from the averments thereof that plaintiff's decedent was guilty of contributory negligence. By appellee it is insisted that whether decedent's conduct under the conditions averred as existing at the crossing at the time of the accident amounted to contributory negligence, was a question of fact for the jury, and not one of law for the court.

Since each paragraph of the complaint is tested by demurrer, all the material facts, which are well pleaded, regarding the conduct of decedent while approaching
1. the crossing in question, together with the conditions adjacent to the crossing and the character thereof at the time decedent was killed, must be taken as true for the purposes of the demurrer. If the conclusions which
2. we are forced to draw therefrom lead to but one legitimate inference, and that is that appellant by his own negligence materially contributed to bring about the accident complained of, it then becomes our duty to determine decedent's contributory negligence as a matter of law. *Greenawaldt* v. *Lake Shore, etc., R. Co.* (1905), 165 Ind. 219, 223, 74 N. E. 1081; *Indianapolis St. R. Co.* v. *Bolin* (1906), 39 Ind. App. 169, 78 N. E. 210. If, on the other hand, from the facts alleged it can be said that reasonable men might properly differ as to whether decedent was guilty of such conduct as to contribute to his own injury and death, then the question cannot be decided as a matter of law, but is a fact for the jury to determine under proper instructions from the court. The plaintiff will be considered to have used due care unless all reasonable
3. inferences drawn from the facts alleged show that he was guilty of negligence as a matter of law. *Cleveland, etc., R. Co.* v. *Harrington* (1892), 131 Ind. 426, 30 N. E. 37; *Cincinnati, etc., R. Co.* v. *Grames* (1893), 136 Ind. 39, 34 N. E. 714.

It will be observed that the complaint alleges that de-

cedent at the time of the accident was a man 60 years old,
having good hearing and eyesight; that while at-
4. tempting to cross appellant's railroad tracks in his
buggy he approached the highway crossing from the
north, and when about 100 feet from the crossing he stopped
his horse and looked and listened for an approaching train,
but was unable to see or hear one, he then proceeded to
drive toward the crossing, but could not see an approaching train while driving from the point where he stopped
until he arrived at a point five feet from appellant's tracks,
wholly on account of a high bank of earth and poles which
appellant had negligently allowed to be there. It is
averred, in addition to this act of negligence relative to the
obstruction of his view, that appellant negligently failed to
give any signal or warning of the approach of the train, by
sounding the whistle or ringing the bell in the manner, and
within the distance from such crossing required by statute,
when it knew that plaintiff, on account of said high embankment which obstructed his view, could not know of the approach of a train when the whistle was not blown or the
bell rung, and that the train was negligently run at the
high and dangerous rate of speed of a mile a minute over
said crossing and against decedent, and he was thereby
killed.

When a person before attempting to cross a rail-
5. road track does not heed the danger of his situation,
and fails to look and listen for an approaching train.
he is guilty of negligence as a matter of law, but when such
person looks and listens in good faith, the question
6. whether he looked and listened enough is for the
jury. The law requires such person to use ordinary
care to avoid injury. Nothing more is required of him.
While a traveler on a public highway on approach-
7. ing a railroad crossing is required to use every reasonable precaution and keep a lookout and to listen

attentively for an approaching train, still he is not bound
to anticipate that any railroad company will be so reckless
and so unmindful of its duty as to fail and neglect to give
the signals and alarms as required by law to warn all travelers approaching any of its crossings, and whose danger is
increased by reason of such neglect on its part, but rather
he may rely on the railroad company performing its duty.

    The averments in the complaint before us concerning
4. the negligence on the part of defendant company in
    approaching and passing over the crossing in ques-
tion, together with the other facts appearing in the complaint, are such that we cannot say that he did what no
ordinarily prudent person would do. The complaint is
sufficient.

    The author in Wharton, Negligence (2d ed.) §804, says:
"Even where a statute is in force requiring the use of a
bell or steam whistle or other signal at a crossing, while the
omission to comply may, under the statute, create a *prima
facie* case against the company, it is a good defense that
the plaintiff saw the train, and recklessly exposed himself
to the collision. When, however, the injury results from
the omission of the signals, then the railroad is liable."

    The Supreme Court of this State in considering a com-
plaint somewhat like the present said: "The signal required by law not being given, the view being obstructed,
and the plaintiff not being hard of hearing, he had no reason
to suppose that the train was within eighty rods of the
crossing; he was misled by the defendant's negligence in
omitting the proper signal, he was not guilty of negligence
in assuming, in the absence of any indication to the contrary, that the company was obeying the law, and that no
engine was advancing toward the crossing within a distance of eighty rods." *Pittsburgh, etc., R. Co.* v. *Martin*
(1882), 82 Ind. 476, 483. See, also, *Tabor* v. *Missouri Valley R. Co.*, (1870), 46 Mo. 353, 2 Am. Rep. 517; *Louisville,*

etc., R. Co. v. *Williams* (1898), 20 Ind. App. 583, 51 N. E. 128; *Chesapeake, etc., R. Co.* v. *Steele* (1898), 84 Fed. 93, 29 C. C. A. 81.

It is assigned as error that the court erred in overruling appellant's motion for judgment on the answers to interrogatories. A general verdict is overcome by an

8. swers to interrogatories only when such answers exclude every reasonable hypothesis consistent with the verdict which might have been proven under the issues. *Southern Ind. R. Co.* v. *Peyton* (1902), 157 Ind. 690, 61 N. E. 722; *Harmon* v. *Foran* (1911), 48 Ind. App. 262, 94 N. E. 1050, 95 N. E. 597.

By its answers to the interrogatories the jury found that decedent was of good hearing and good eyesight; that he was familiar with the crossing; that he stopped,

9. looked and listened before crossing the interurban track; that if he had stopped afterwards at any time before reaching a point where his horse's head was within five feet of the tracks he could not have seen the approach of the train which struck him; that the embankment immediately east of the highway entirely cut off the view of an approaching train; that the engineer failed to sound the whistle or ring the bell until with 150 feet or 200 feet of the crossing; that when decedent reached a point in the highway where he could see the train approaching on defendant's tracks he did not have time enough to stop his horse, nor was there space enough in the highway to turn his vehicle with safety, and thereby avoid a collision; that the first whistle which was sounded for the crossing where decedent was struck was the stock alarm or distress signal, sounded after the engineer had seen decedent crossing the tracks. These answers do not show that decedent failed to use ordinary care in approaching the crossing and in attempting to drive over the same. The general verdict finds that due care was used by him in that respect, and the answers specially made do not exclude the existence of suffi-

cient circumstances which justify the conclusion reached.
The court was right in overruling the motion for judgment
on the answers to interrogatories.

Error has been assigned in refusing to give to the jury
certain instructions requested by appellant and in giving
others on the court's own motion, and at the request
10. of the appellee. In view of the conclusion reached,
it will be unnecessary to discuss all the instructions
covered by these assignments. The one to which the strong-
est objection is made, is instruction No. 1 given at appellee's
request, which is as follows: "If a train of cars hauled by
a locomotive engine upon a railroad, and a citizen traveling
in a buggy upon a public highway are both approaching a
crossing of such highway with such railroad, under circumstances indicating that a collision between them is likely to
occur if they both proceed upon their way without stopping,
the engineer in charge of such train, if he has sounded the
required signals with the engine whistle, and in ringing the
bell of the engine, has a right to presume that the citizen
will stop before he drives upon the crossing, and has a right
to proceed on his way with his engine and train, until he
discovers that the citizen does not stop. And if the engineer makes the discovery that the citizen does not stop, in
time to stop his train and avoid the collision, and if after
making such discovery, the engineer could have stopped his
train, but did not do so, then in that view of the case the
railroad company would be liable for the injury inflicted
upon the citizen by such collision." This instruction was
based on the theory that appellant's engineer saw decedent
in a dangerous position, and was negligent in failing to
slow down or stop his train. The averments of the
11. complaint characterizing the manner in which it is
claimed the accident occurred are sufficient to bring
into the case the doctrine of last clear chance, for it is
averred "that the servants * * * of defendant carelessly and negligently caused said train to strike * * *

decedent while knowing that he did not and could not know of the approach of such train." *Indianapolis Traction, etc., Co.* v. *Croly* (1913), —— Ind. App. ——, 96 N. E. 973; *Evansville, etc., Traction Co.* v. *Johnson* (1913), —— Ind. App. ——, 97 N. E. 176; *Indiana Union Traction Co.* v. *Myers* (1911), 47 Ind. App. 646, 93 N. E. 888.

This instruction was based on the testimony of the engineer that he saw decedent before he crossed the interurban track, and that when he crossed such track he disap-

10. peared from sight behind the embankment; that he next saw the head of the horse emerge from behind the embankment, and then the buggy came into view, and he could see the lines going up and down as if the driver, whom he did not see, was urging the horse. He says that he saw the horse about fifteen feet from the track, when he first realized that decedent was attempting to cross, and was making no attempt to stop.

We cannot say from the engineer's evidence, that at this time, when he says he first realized that decedent was not going to stop, he could not have stopped his train in time to avoid the accident, or checked its speed to such an extent that decedent would have passed on over the track unhurt. Although the engineer states that he did what he could to stop the train, yet this was to be considered in the light of his testimony as to surrounding conditions, and it was for the jury to say whether the conditions were such that on seeing the horse emerge from behind the bluff the engineer still should have been able to avoid the accident, in view of his testimony as to the distance the horse was from the track and the train from the crossing, and the further fact that the horse passed over the track in safety, while the buggy was struck by the train. We consider the instruction applicable to the evidence offered by the engineer, even taking the view that the engineer was not bound to use the last clear chance to avoid accident until he saw the horse emerging from the cut.

It cannot be said as a matter of law that the engineer did not see decedent in a place of danger, or entering into a place of imminent danger, until after it was too late to check or stop the train. When he saw decedent pass from view behind the embankment, it then became the engineer's duty to exercise that ordinary care and prudence which the law imposed on him under the circumstances as they were shown by the evidence in the case to exist at the time of the accident. While we do not commend the language of the instruction generally, and can see where the same might be found to be even erroneous in certain cases when there were no obstructions to hide an approaching train, yet under the facts as disclosed by the record before us we must conclude that the instruction was as favorable as appellant could ask, and that no error was committed in submitting instructions embodying the doctrine of last clear chance.

In considering error assigned in giving certain other instructions, it is sufficient to say that the acts of negligence charged against the railroad company were definite
12. and specific, and the instructions given on the question of appellant's negligence should have applied only to the negligence charged in the complaint; but in view of all the instructions given, we cannot find reversible error in the giving of the instructions criticised.
13. Other instructions asked by appellant were rightly refused, because the same questions were covered by instructions given, and the jury was fully informed on the issue of contributory negligence.

It is assigned that the evidence is not sufficient to sustain the verdict. It is admitted that the train which ran upon and over decedent was a train of appellant, and was
14. being operated by its employes. There is a conflict as to whether the whistle was sounded or the bell rung before reaching the crossing, as provided by
15. statute. The burden of showing negligence on the part of appellant, as charged, was on appellee, and the bur-

den of showing contributory negligence on the part of decedent was on appellant. It seems, under the decisions, that the issue of contributory negligence in cases where the facts are similar to those in the present is left to the determination of the jury, and the questions both of the negligence of appellant and the lack of contributory negligence of decedent were determined by the jury in favor of appellee. The evidence is quite voluminous, and its sufficiency not free from doubt. Without setting it out, we feel justified in saying, after having carefully reviewed it, that it would be error to say as a matter of law that decedent was guilty of contributory negligence.

It is also claimed by appellant that the damages assessed are excessive. The evidence shows that decedent was sixty-two years old, able-bodied, living with and·support-
16. ing his wife and daughter. His expectancy of life was 13½ years. There is nothing to show that the jury adopted an improper method of calculating the damages, or was misled by sympathy, or influenced by unfair means, and the amount, though large, is not so large that we can say that it abused its discretion. Therefore, we would not be authorized to reverse the judgment on this ground.

Judgment affirmed.

NOTE.—Reported in 97 N. E. 578. See, also, under (1) 31 Cyc. 333; (2) 33 Cyc. 1111; (3) 29 Cyc. 596; (4) 33 Cyc. 1060; (5) 33 Cyc. 1000; (6) 33 Cyc. 1116; (7) 33 Cyc. 1027; (8) 38 Cyc. 1927; (9) 33 Cyc. 1142; (12) 38 Cyc. 1612; (13) 38 Cyc. 1711; (14) 33 Cyc. 1066, 1070; (15) 3 Cyc. 348; (16) 13 Cyc. 375. As to the duty of travelers on highways to use their senses to avoid accidents at railroad crossings, see 90 Am. Dec. 780. As to the presumption of the exercise of care, see 116 Am. St. 108. As to the presumption of negligence from the happening of an accident, see 113 Am. St. 986. As to what is an excessive verdict in an action for death by wrongful act, see 18 Ann. Cas. 1209. As to the failure to give customary signals as excusing nonperformance of duty to look and listen, see 3 L. R. A. (N. S.) 391. On the duty of traveler approaching railway crossing as to place and direction of observation, see 37 L. R. A. (N. S.) 186.

STUDABAKER v. FAYLOR ET AL.

[No. 7,592. Filed April 25, 1912. Rehearing denied June 27, 1912. Transfer denied January 22, 1913.]

1. WITNESSES.—*Communications to Physician.—Waiver of Privilege.*—The privilege conferred by §520 Burns 1908, §497 R. S. 1881, on communications by a patient to his physician, may be waived by the patient, or by those who stand in his place, or are authorized to represent him. p. 172.

2. WITNESSES.— *Competency.— Privileged Communications.— Communications to Physicians.—Waiver of Privilege.—Failure to Object.*—The privilege conferred by §520 Burns 1908, §497 R. S. 1881, on communications by a patient to his physician, is waived where the witness has been permitted without objection to testify at a former trial as to matters learned in such communications. p. 172.

3. APPEAL.—*Review.—Right to Search Record of Former Appeal.*—Appellate courts may search their own records on their own motion or the suggestion of counsel, and, while they may not go to the record of a former appeal in the same cause to compare the probative force of evidence given, they may look to such record in order to ascertain that a witness testified without objection to matters sought to be excluded in the pending appeal. p. 173.

4. WITNESSES.—*Privileged Communications.—Communications to Physician.—Waiver.—Persons Entitled to Waive Privilege.*—The right to waive the privilege of confidential communications after the death of the patient, in litigation affecting the estate, is lodged in those who represent and stand in the place of decedent, and the waiver may be express, or implied from the conduct of such persons in standing by and permitting the testimony to be given without objection. p. 174.

From Adams Circuit Court; *J. T. Merryman*, Judge.

Action by Thomas Faylor and others against David D. Studabaker. From a judgment for plaintiffs, the defendant appeals. *Affirmed.*

Eichhorn & Vaughn, Lesh & Lesh, D. E. Smith and *John Burns*, for appellant.

Mack & Sons, D. D. Heller & Son, C. J. Lutz, R. W. Stine and *Simmons & Dailey*, for appellees.

IBACH, P. J.—Appellees, all the heirs of Catherine Faylor, deceased, sued appellant to set aside a deed of conveyance of real estate made to appellant by Catherine Faylor, on the grounds that she was insane when the deed was made and that the conveyance was obtained through fraud of appellant. They also asked that their title be quieted to this real estate, and they be put in possession.

This appeal is taken on a reserved question of law as to the correctness of the court's action in allowing Dr. Cook, a witness at the trial, to testify, over the objection and exception of appellant, as to information gained as a physician while treating Mrs. Faylor.

Section 520 Burns 1908, §497 R. S. 1881, provides that physicians shall not be competent witnesses as to matters communicated to them as such by patients, in the

1. course of their professional business, or advice given in such cases. This privilege may be waived by the patient, or those who stand in his place or are authorized to represent him. *Towles* v. *McCurdy* (1904), 163 Ind. 12, 71 N. E. 129; *Heaston* v. *Krieg* (1906), 167 Ind. 101, 77 N. E. 805, 119 Am. St. 475; *Morris* v. *Morris* (1889), 119 Ind. 341, 21 N. E. 918. The reason for this statute is that communications may be made in the relation of physician

2. and patient which a due regard for the privacies and decencies of life should protect from being exposed to the public. This privilege may be waived, and when the matters have been once published to the world, no reason remains to hold the privilege in force. The statute was not enacted to enable persons to avoid liability or to win a suit by making it difficult to obtain evidence, but was made in order to allow them to prevent certain private affairs from becoming public property. So it has been held in this State and other states that when a witness has been permitted, without objection, in a former trial to testify to privileged communications, the bar of privilege is waived, and the testimony cannot be excluded on that ground at a

subsequent trial. *Pittsburgh, etc., R. Co.* v. *O'Connor* (1909), 171 Ind. 686, 693, 85 N. E. 969, and cases cited; *Elliott* v. *Kansas City* (1906), 198 Mo. 593, 96 S. W. 1023, 6 L. R. A. (N. S.) 1082, 8 Ann. Cas. 653 and note; *People* v. *Bloom* (1908, 193 N. Y. 1, 85 N. E. 824, 18 L. R. A. (N. S.) 898, 127 Am. St. 931, 15 Ann. Cas. 932.

This case was appealed to this court before and was transferred to the Supreme Court. See *Studabaker* v. *Faylor* (1908), 170 Ind. 498, 83 N. E. 747, 127 Am. St. 397. On referring to the record in that appeal, we find that Dr. Cook was permitted at that trial, without objection from any one, to testify to information gained while a professional relation existed between him and Mrs. Faylor. We do not need in this case to decide whether appellant had any right to object to his testimony on the ground of privilege, though many authorities uphold the doctrine that he had not, since he is not the personal representative of Mrs. Faylor *(Lockwood* v. *Lockwood* [1887], 56 Conn. 106, 110, 14 Atl. 293), and the privilege is personal. 3 Wigmore, Evidence §§2192, 2196; 4 Wigmore, Evidence §§2320, 2386. If appellant had the right to object to the admission of the evidence, such right has been waived by failure to object at the former trial, thus permitting the communications to become public.

Appellate courts may search their own records on their own motion or the suggestion of counsel. While we may not go to the record in a former appeal in order to 3. compare the probative force of the evidence there given with that given in the later trial *(Cleveland, etc., R. Co.* v. *Wynant* [1893], 134 Ind. 681, 34 N. E. 569), yet we may look to the record in a former trial and appeal of the same case in order to ascertain that a witness testified without objection to the same matters now sought to be excluded. *Hancook* v. *Diamond Plate Glass Co.* (1906), 37 Ind. App. 351, 75 N. E. 659; *Cluggish* v. *Koons* (1896), 15 Ind. App. 599, 43 N. E. 158; *Denney* v. *State, ex rel.*

(1896), 144 Ind. 503, 42 N. E. 929, 31 L. R. A. 726; *Mississinewa Min. Co.* v. *Andrews* (1902), 28 Ind. App. 496, 63 N. E. 231; *Westfall* v. *Wait* (1905), 165 Ind. 353, 73 N. E. 1089, 6 Ann. Cas. 788.

Furthermore, under authorities above cited, the right to waive the privilege of confidential communications, after the death of Mrs. Faylor, in litigation affecting her

4. estate, was lodged in those who represented her and stood in her place. Even if appellant could be considered her representative, he has, as we have seen, waived his right to object. It is generally conceded that heirs may waive this privilege. 4 Wigmore, Evidence §2391. However, the heirs or devisees seeking to overthrow a will may not waive it as against other heirs or devisees. *Towles* v. *McCurdy, supra.* In the case at bar all the heirs were plaintiffs, and they not only called Dr. Cook to testify, but the record in the present appeal shows that all of them expressly waived the privilege. It is unquestioned that the administrator has the power to waive the privilege in order to conserve the interests of the estate. *Scott* v. *Smith* (1908), 171 Ind. 453, 85 N. E. 774. The administrator of decedent's estate, though not a party to the suit, was present at the trial, testified, and likewise expressly waived the privilege. All the persons in whom there could be a right to insist on the privilege have either expressly waived the privilege, or have impliedly waived it by standing by and allowing the testimony to be given.

As before said, when once the matters ascertained in a privileged relation are published to the world without objection, no reason remains to uphold the bar of privilege. This suit was instituted nearly ten years ago, and the cause has been four times tried, and twice appealed. It seems to us that no good purpose would be served by a further trial, and that justice demands an end of litigation in this cause.

Judgment affirmed.

Note.—Reported in 98 N. E. 318. See, also, under (1, 4) 40 Cyc. 2397. As to when a physician may testify as to matters learned in the practice of his profession, see 17 Am. St. 565. As to the effect of the waiver of a privileged communication at one trial on the right to claim the privilege at a subsequent trial, see 8 Ann. Cas. 660; 15 Ann. Cas. 935.

OSBORN v. THE ADAMS BRICK COMPANY.

[No. 7,714   Filed October 29, 1912.   Rehearing denied January 22, 1913.]

1. TRIAL.—*Verdict.*—*Answers to Interrogatories.*—*Motion for Judgment.*—A motion for judgment on the answers to interrogatories can only be sustained where the facts thereby found are in irreconcilable conflict with the general verdict. p. 182.

2. TRIAL.—*Verdict.*—*Answers to Interrogatories.*—*Presumptions.*—Every reasonable presumption is indulged in favor of the general verdict, and nothing is presumed in favor of the answers to the interrogatories. p. 182.

3. TRIAL.—*Verdict.*—*Answers to Interrogatories.*—*Judgment.*—To authorize a judgment on the facts found by answers to interrogatories, such facts must be sufficient to overcome any evidence legitimately admissible under the issues. p. 182.

4. PLEADING.—*Complaint.*—*Determination of Theory.*—The theory of a complaint must be determined from its general scope and tenor, and not from fragmentary statements, detached parts or conclusions, and that theory which is most apparent and clearly outlined by the leading averments of the pleading will be adopted. p. 182.

5. MASTER AND SERVANT.—*Injury to Servant.*—*Complaint.*—*Construction.*—A complaint alleging that plaintiff was employed in defendant's shale bank or pit as a common laborer or shoveler, that defendant's shot-firer was discharged by defendant, and that defendant, knowing that the pit was unsafe, wrongfully and negligently ordered and directed plaintiff to go into such dangerous place and blast and loosen such shale and continue loading cars, does not show that plaintiff was employed as, or accepted the position of shot-firer, but that he was merely transferred temporarily from his employment as a shoveler to that of a shot-firer. p. 182.

6. MASTER AND SERVANT.—*Inexperienced Servant.*—*Duty to Warn and Instruct.*—Where the master requires a dangerous service at the hands of an inexperienced servant, it is the duty of the

master to warn him and to give him such instructions as will enable him to avoid injury, unless both the danger and the means of avoiding it are apparent. p. 183.

7. MASTER AND SERVANT.—*Assumption of Risk.—Work Outside Scope of Employment.*—The servant's implied assumption of risk, which is a part of the contract of hiring, is confined to the particular work or class of work for which he is employed, and if he is ordered temporarily to do other work, involving different or greater dangers than those incident to the work within the scope of his employment, he does not, by obeying such orders, necessarily assume the risk incident thereto. p. 183.

8. MASTER AND SERVANT.—*Hazardous Employment.—Assumption of Risk.*—One who enters upon an employment, which is from its nature necessarily hazardous, assumes the usual and ordinary risks and perils of such service. p. 184.

9. MASTER AND SERVANT.—*Employment to Make Dangerous Place Safe.—Assumption of Risk.*—One employed to do the work of making a dangerous place safe, assumes the risks ordinarily incident to such employment. p. 184.

10. MASTER AND SERVANT.—*Assumption of Risk.*—The risks assumed by an employe in any case are those ordinarily incident to the particular work covered by the contract of hiring. p. 184.

11. MASTER AND SERVANT.—*Assumption of Risk.—Right of Servant to Rely on Master Providing Safe Place to Work.—Employment to Make Dangerous Place Safe.*—A servant may ordinarily assume that the master has provided him a safe place in which to work, and rely on that assumption, except as to defects and dangers which he may ascertain by ordinary care for his own safety; and while one who undertakes to make a dangerous place safe may not presume that the master has already done the work he is employed to do, he does not assume all possible risks, but only those incident to such employment. p. 184.

12. MASTER AND SERVANT.—*Injury to Servant.—Work Outside Scope of Employment.—Assumption of Risk.*—Where a complaint against the master for personal injuries proceeds on the theory that plaintiff was employed as a common laborer and while working as such was called upon by defendant to perform temporarily the duties of shot-firer after the discharge of defendant's regular shot-firer, and alleges that plaintiff was assigned to such new duties after the regular shot-firer had reported to defendant that conditions in the place of work were unsafe and had refused to send the men back to work in such place unless he was first permitted to make the place safe, the rule as to assumption of risk, governing where one is employed to make a dangerous place safe, is not applicable. p. 185.

13. MASTER AND SERVANT.—*Injury to Servant.—Verdict.—Answers to Interrogatories.*—Where the allegations of the complaint in a servant's action for personal injuries showed that plaintiff was employed as a common laborer and while working as such was called upon by defendant to perform temporarily the duties of shot-firer in defendant's shale pit, that it was a dangerous place in which to work, but appeared to plaintiff to be safe, that the danger was such that without long experience it was impossible for a person of ordinary prudence and foresight to discern it, that plaintiff had no experience and did not know or appreciate the danger, all of which defendant knew, and that defendant wrongfully and negligently ordered plaintiff to proceed to blast and loosen shale and to load cars in said dangerous place, and that in performing such work plaintiff was injured, a verdict for plaintiff is a finding that such allegations are true, so that a recovery by plaintiff is authorized unless the answers to interrogatories are in irreconcilable conflict therewith. p. 185·

14. MASTER AND SERVANT.—*Injury to Servant.—Work Outside Scope of Employment.—Duty to Warn and Instruct.*—Where defendant, knowing of the dangerous condition of its shale pit, and knowing that plaintiff was a common laborer and did not understand and appreciate such danger, ordered him, in an emergency, to take the place of shot-firer in such pit, and plaintiff was injured within a few minutes after beginning such duties, the defendant's failure to warn and instruct plaintiff as to the dangers was inexcusable. p. 186.

15. MASTER AND SERVANT.—*Injury to Servant.—Verdict.—Answers to Interrogatories.*—Where the complaint in a servant's action for personal injuries is on the theory that plaintiff was employed by defendant as a common laborer, and that he was ordered by defendant to perform temporarily the duties of a shot-firer in defendant's shale pit, in the performance of which duties he was injured, a general verdict for plaintiff is not overcome by answers to interrogatories showing that plaintiff was given the position of, and proceeded to discharge the duties of, shot-firer in the place of a shot-firer who had been discharged, since such answers do not conclusively show that plaintiff was employed to take the position in any other sense or to any further extent than that charged in the complaint. p. 187.

16. APPEAL.—*Review.—Verdict.—Answers to Interrogatories.*—In considering a motion for judgment on answers to interrogatories nothwithstanding the general verdict, all evidence admissible under the issues will be treated as actually in the record, and the court will indulge every reasonable presumption in favor of the general verdict and reconcile such answers therewith, if possible on any reasonable theory within the issues. p. 188.

17. MASTER AND SERVANT.—*Injury to Servant.—Verdict.—Answers to Interrogatories.*—Where the complaint, in a servant's action for personal injuries, alleged that plaintiff was a common laborer employed in defendant's shale pit, that defendant discharged its shot-firer for refusing to obey defendant's order to have the men work in the pit while it was in a dangerous condition, and that defendant, knowing that the pit was unsafe, wrongfully and negligently directed plaintiff to perform the duties of shot-firer, with knowledge that plaintiff was inexperienced and did not know and appreciate the danger, answers to interrogatories showing that the shot-firer was discharged because of unsatisfactory work, though excluding the idea that he was discharged because he refused to obey orders as alleged in the complaint, do not negative the facts found by the general verdict, that defendant knew and plaintiff did not know the hidden dangers incident to the new duties to which plaintiff was assigned. p. 189.

18. APPEAL.—*Review.—Judgment on Answers to Interrogatories.—Disposition of Cause.*—Where, on appeal, the facts are complicated and close questions of law are involved, and reversible error is found in the action of the trial court in rendering judgment *non obstante veredicto*, a new trial will be ordered rather than judgment on the general verdict. pp. 189, 190.

19. COURTS.—*Appellate Court.—Powers.—New Trial.*—The Appellate Court has the power to order a new trial, and it is its duty to do so, where it appears that the ends of justice will be best subserved thereby. p. 190.

20. NEW TRIAL.—*Rights of Parties.*—The party against whom a general verdict has been rendered, on proper motion, has the right to have the trial court pass on the verdict before judgment thereon is rendered against him. p. 190.

From Fountain Circuit Court; *William B. Durborow,* Special Judge.

Action by William T. Osborn against The Adams Brick Company. From a judgment for defendant, the plaintiff appeals. *Reversed.*

O. B. Ratcliff, for appellant.

John B. Elam, James W. Fesler, Harvey J. Elam and *Lucas Nebeker,* for appellee.

FELT, J.—Appellant brought this action to recover damages for personal injuries received by him while in the employ of appellee. The case was tried by a jury, which returned a general verdict in favor of appellant together with answers to interrogatories. Appellee's motion for judgment in its favor on the answers to interrogatories was sustained, judgment rendered accordingly, and this appeal taken. The assignment of errors, in substance, raises but one question: Did the trial court err in sustaining appellee's motion for judgment on the answers to interrogatories, notwithstanding the general verdict?

The complaint is long and contains many repetitions. The substance of its material averments is as follows: On May 19, 1908, appellee owned and was operating a certain brick plant in the city of Veedersburg, Indiana; that in connection therewith it was operating a certain shale bank or pit, from which it was procuring "shale" for use in the manufacture of brick; that the top of said shale was irregularly intersected by horizontal and vertical seams and other defects hidden from view and unknown to appellant, and by reason of such defects it broke easily and unexpectedly when not supported; that said shale could be taken from said bank and pit with absolute safety to appellee's employes engaged in such work by first stripping said rock and yellow clay from the top of said shale and removing the shale from the top downward; that on May 19, 1908, appellant, as a common laborer and shoveler for appellee, was at work in said pit loading the shale into cars; that on the morning of said day said bank and pit, near the middle thereof, was in a dangerous condition, in that the yellow clay above the shale had not been stripped therefrom, but, together with the top of said shale stratum, projected about five feet over and beyond the lower part of said shale stratum, and was slowly working and breaking loose from the sandstone and clay above; that by reason of such condition the pit was a dangerous place in which to work, but the same appeared to appellant to be safe; that without long experience in working in and about such banks and pits it was impossible for a person of ordinary prudence and foresight to discern

the slow breaking of the top of such shale, or to appreciate
the dangers arising therefrom; that appellant had not had
any experience in the management of the work in such pits
or in guarding against the dangers thereof, and did not
know or appreciate said dangers until after his injury; that
on said date one Frank Dawson was in the employ of appellee as shot-firer and foreman in said pit, and as such was
doing the blasting and stripping in said pit; that prior
thereto said Dawson had several years' experience in operating and working said bank and pit, and similar banks and
pits, and by reason thereof knew the nature of said rock,
clay and shale, and said defects or seams in the top of said
shale, and at this particular time, by reason of his experience and knowledge, could see and did see the slow working
and breaking of the top of said shale, and knew and appreciated said dangers arising therefrom, and that such place was
unsafe and dangerous; that he immediately notified appellee
and its superintendent of said dangers, and although ordered and directed by appellee to put said shovelers to
work in such dangerous place, he refused so to do, unless
permitted first to make such place safe; that appellee.
through its said superintendent and vice principal, wrongfully and negligently ordered, directed and put said shovelers, including appellant, into said unsafe place to load the
cars with shale, and discharged Dawson at noon of said day.
by reason of his said refusal, and wrongfully and negligently
permitted and allowed such place to continue and remain
unsafe and dangerous while appellant and the other shovelers were so compelled to work as aforesaid; that appellee
knew that appellant did not understand or appreciate said
dangers, and wrongfully and negligently failed to notify
appellant thereof, and further wrongfully and negligently
ordered appellant to go into said dangerous place immediately to blast and loosen shale, and to continue loading cars:
that appellant in pursuance of said orders went into said
pit, and while working therein a large amount of said shale

and stratum fell upon and against him, and covered and crushed the lower part of his body.

The answers to the interrogatories, as far as material, in substance, show that the embankment around said shale pit was 30 or 40 feet high, and was made up of shale, sandstone, rock, gravel and earth; that at the time appellant was injured there was a projection of shale extending out from said embankment about 5 feet above the bottom of the pit, which had been there on said day from about 8 o'clock in the morning; that appellant was injured about 1:15 p. m. of said day, and had worked there from morning until that time; that there were three tracks running into said pit; that Frank Dawson "the shooter" fired a shot between 7 and 8 a. m. of said day, at the bottom of the pit near the end of the middle track and said projection; that about the middle of the forenoon of said day appellant, and his fellow workmen were ordered by said Dawson from the middle track to the east track, because of the danger from said projection; that Dawson was discharged at noon of said day by appellee, because his work was unsatisfactory, and for no other reason, and appellant was given his place as "shooter" on the same day and before the accident occurred, and accepted the place and proceeded to discharge his duties as such "shooter"; that appellant was an adult person, in the possession of all his senses; that he could not by looking have seen the "working" of shale and other substances; that it was the duty of the "shooter" to clear away the projection of shale, gravel and other substance above the place where the clay or shale was mined out; that appellant received no specific instructions from appellee as to the manner in which he should perform his duties as such shooter.

Appellant contends that the court erred in sustaining appellee's motion for judgment on the answers to the interrogatories, for the alleged reason that they do not show that he assumed the risk, or that he was guilty of negligence contributing to his injury.

The motion for judgment on the answers to interrog-
1. atories can only be sustained where the facts so
found are in irreconcilable conflict with the general
verdict. Every reasonable presumption is indulged in
2. favor of the general verdict, and nothing is presumed in favor of the answers to the interrogatories.
The facts found by such answers must be sufficient
3. to overcome any evidence legitimately admissible
under the issues before a judgment is authorized on
such finding of facts. *Indiana Union Traction Co.* v.
Scribner (1911), 47 Ind. App. 621, 628, 93 N. E. 1014;
Southern R. Co. v. *De Pauw* (1910), 174 Ind. 608, 614, 92
N. E. 225.

In determining whether the answers to interrogatories are
in irreconcilable conflict with the general verdict, we may
be assisted by first determining the theory of the
4. complaint. This must be determined from its general scope and tenor, and not from fragmentary statements, detached parts or conclusions. That theory will be
adopted which is most apparent and clearly outlined by the
leading averments of the pleading. *Oölitic Stone Co.* v.
Ridge (1908), 169 Ind. 639, 643, 83 N. E. 246; *State, ex
rel.,* v. *Scott* (1908), 171 Ind. 349, 354, 86 N. E. 409; *Flowers* v. *Poorman* (1909), 43 Ind. App. 528, 531, 87 N. E.
1107.

Tested by this rule, the complaint shows that appellant
was employed as a common laborer to shovel in appellee's
pit, and that on Dawson's discharge he was changed
5. from that position and ordered to discharge the duties
previously performed by Dawson. It is not averred
that he was employed as, or accepted the position of shot-
firer, or "shooter"; but after showing Dawson's discharge, it
is clearly averred that appellee "wrongfully and negligently
ordered and directed him to go into said dangerous place
immediately and blast and loosen such shale therein and
continue loading cars." In other words, he was employed

as a shoveler, and temporarily transferred from that employment to that of a "shooter", for the duties assigned him were those formerly discharged by Dawson.

This theory of the complaint makes it important to ascertain the duty of appellee when it placed appellant in the position of a shot-firer, which required knowledge, skill and experience not required of a common laborer. The 6. master may not expose an inexperienced servant, at whose hands he requires a dangerous service, to such dangers without giving him warning. He is also required to give him such instructions as will enable him to avoid injury, unless both the danger and the means of avoiding it are apparent. This duty does not extend to employes of mature age who are familiar with the work they are called on to do and the risks incident thereto, but it does extend to inexperienced employes of mature years as well as to those of tender age. *Atlas Engine Works* v. *Randall* (1885), 100 Ind. 293, 296, 50 Am. Rep. 798; *Republic Iron, etc., Co.* v. *Ohler* (1903), 161 Ind. 393, 402, 68 N. E. 901; 4 Thompson, Negligence §4065.

The servant's implied assumption of risks, which accompanies and is a part of the contract of hiring, is confined to the particular work or class of work for which he is 7. employed, and if the master orders him temporarily to do other work, involving different or greater dangers than those incident to the work within the scope of his employment, he will not by obeying such orders necessarily assume the risks incident to such other work. When 6. such change of employment takes place, the master owes the duty of warning the servant of the dangers incident to the work so required of him, and likewise the duty of giving him instructions, where he is not familiar with the new duties to which he is so assigned. Where the master knows the servant so intrusted with new duties involving other or greater hazards is inexperienced in such work, and ignorant of the dangers incident thereto, the duty to warn and instruct is imperative, and failure so to do makes him liable for an injury resulting from such failure, where the servant has not negligently contributed thereto. *Pittsburgh, etc., R. Co.* v. *Adams* (1886), 105 Ind. 151, 164, 5 N. E. 187; *Republic Iron, etc., Co.* v. *Ohler, supra,* 403; *Newcastle Bridge Co.* v. *Doty* (1907), 167 Ind. 259, 264, 79 N. E. 485; *Cincinnati, etc., R. Co.* v. *Madden* (1893), 134 Ind. 462, 471, 34 N. E. 227.

8.   It is true, as asserted by appellee, that where a person enters on an employment which is from its nature necessarily hazardous, he assumes the usual and ordinary risks and perils of such service. It is

9.   likewise the law that one employed to do the work of making a dangerous place safe, assumes the risks ordinarily incident to such employment. The very nature of such work enlarges or multiplies the risks assumed by such an employe, but the rule in such case is not essentially different in principle from that applicable to any em-

10.   ploye. In any case the risks assumed are those *ordinarily* incident to the particular work covered by the contract of hiring. The difference arises not from principle but from the character of the work the employe undertakes to do. The servant may ordinarily assume that the

11.   master has provided him a safe place in which to work, and rely on that assumption except as to defects and dangers which he may ascertain by ordinary care for his own safety. The one who undertakes to make a dangerous place safe may not presume that the master has already done the work he is employed to do. He represents the master in such work, but the relation of master and servant nevertheless exists between them, and he does not by virtue of his undertaking to make a dangerous place safe assume all possible risks, but only those ordinarily incident to such employment.

But in this case the theory of the complaint and the facts found do not justify the application of the rule invoked,

where an employe expressly or impliedly undertakes
12. to make a dangerous place safe. For, as already
shown, the complaint proceeds on the theory that appellant was employed and worked as a common laborer, and
while so doing was called on by appellee to discharge the
duties of shot-firer after Dawson's discharge. It is also
averred that he was assigned to these new duties after
Dawson had reported to the master that the conditions then
existing in the pit made it dangerous to continue working
therein, and that Dawson had refused to send the workmen
back · into the pit on account of such dangers, unless he
was first permitted to make the place safe. It is not directly
averred that appellant was employed as "shooter", and undertook generally or for any considerable length of time to
discharge the duties of that position, but it is charged that
he was ordered into the pit after Dawson's discharge at
noon, "immediately" to blast and loosen shale, which clearly shows the character of his work, the emergency and the
change in the kind of work appellant was called on to do.

It is further charged in the complaint that on the day
of the accident, the pit was a dangerous place in which to
work, but it appeared to appellant to be safe; that
13. the projecting part of said bank was slowly working
and breaking loose from the sandstone and clay
above; that without long experience in working in such a
pit it was impossible for a person of ordinary prudence and
foresight to discern the breaking and loosening of the shale,
or to know and appreciate the danger arising therefrom;
that appellant had no experience in such matters or in
guarding against the dangers thereof and did not know or
appreciate said danger; that appellee knew he did not have
such skill and experience or know of said dangers; that
Dawson, the "shooter", had such skill and knowledge, and
knew the peculiar properties of shale, and how to detect in
advance indications of an approaching cave or fall; that
he knew and appreciated the danger on the day of appel·

lant's injury, and notified appellee thereof; that appellee
discharged Dawson at noon of said day, and wrongfully and
negligently ordered appellant to proceed to blast and loosen
shale and to load cars in said dangerous place; that appellant
went to work in pursuance of said orders, and was injured
as alleged. The general verdict finds all of the foregoing
allegations to be true, and they are sufficient to warrant a
recovery, unless the answers to the interrogatories are in
irreconcilable conflict therewith. The answers to the interrogatories show that after Dawson's discharge at noon, appellant was given his place as "shooter"; that he accepted
the place, proceeded to his work, and was injured at 1:15
o'clock p. m.

Appellee knowing that appellant was a common laborer, in
the emergency put him in the place of the "shooter", whose
        duties required him to do the work of placing the pit
14. in shape for the removal of the shale; he accepted
        the place, went to work, and was injured about 15
minutes thereafter. He did not have the requisite skill and
experience to detect the latent dangers of the pit, and did
not know or appreciate the peculiar danger that resulted in
his injury. Appellee knew of said dangers, knew that the
pit was at that time an unsafe place in which to work, that
appellant did not know, understand or appreciate said dangers, and yet appellee wholly failed to warn him thereof.

On this state of facts, Did appellee owe appellant any
duty when it placed him in the position of "shooter"? This
question must be answered in the affirmative, and the fact
that he was called from one kind of work to another, requiring different knowledge and more skill and experience,
under all the authorities, instead of relieving appellee from
responsibility, only emphasizes its duty, enjoined by the
law, to warn appellant of known dangers and of those it
might ascertain by reasonable care and inspection. But
here appellee is shown to have received positive information
that the pit was dangerous, and also knew appellant was

a common laborer, that he did not know the peculiar dangers of the pit, and did not possess the skill and experience that would enable him to ascertain such dangers for himself. This makes appellee's failure to warn inexcusable.

But it is contended that notwithstanding appellee failed to warn appellant of the dangers known to it, judgment was rightfully rendered for appellee on the answers to the interrogatories. In support of this contention it is said that the answers show conclusively that appellant was employed as "shooter"; that he accepted the employment, and was injured while in the discharge of the duties of that position; that he assumed the risks of his new position, and cannot recover.

Conceding that appellant was regularly employed as "shooter", and that he accepted the place and undertook to discharge the duties of the position generally, there may be serious doubt, on the facts of this case, even on such theory, that appellant assumed the risks of which he was ignorant, which were known to appellee, who likewise knew that appellant did not know thereof and that he did not possess the requisite skill and experience to detect the dangers for himself, and yet failed to give him any warning or instruction. But in our view of this case we are not called on to decide that question, because of other reasons, some of which have already been pointed out, which show that it was error to sustain the motion for judgment on the answers to the interrogatories.

The answers do show that after Dawson's discharge, appellant was, in the afternoon, prior to the accident, given Dawson's place as "shooter", and that he proceeded to the discharge of the duties of the position, that he came into the pit at 1 o'clock and was injured at 1:15 o'clock p. m. But these facts are not necessarily in irreconcilable conflict with the general verdict. The verdict was a finding in appellant's favor as to all the material facts averred in the complaint, and the interrogatories do not conclusively show, as against such finding, that appellant was employed to take the position of shot-firer, in any other sense or to any further extent than that charged in the complaint, which, as already shown, was brought about by the emergency occasioned by Dawson's discharge, and falls within the rule of a change from one kind of employment to another kind involving greater and different hazards, and requiring more skill and experience than 'the employment from which the servant was called. Such change of employment does not evidence the contractual relation of one who undertakes the responsibility of making a dangerous place safe.

Standing alone and unexplained, the answers to the interrogatories are insufficient to overcome the general verdict, which amounts to a finding that appellant was, in the emergency, temporarily called on to discharge the duties of shot-firer. But under the issues, testimony was admissible to show that the arrangement by which appellant undertook to discharge the duties of "shooter" was only temporary, for the purpose of meeting the existing emergency and keeping the work going in the pit; that appellant was not to continue permanently in the position, but remained in appellee's employ under his original contract of hiring, and was by order of appellee temporarily transferred from the work he was employed to do and called on to discharge new and different duties.

Under the rule for considering a motion for judgment on the answers to interrogatories, we are to determine the question as though such testimony was actually in the
16. record, and, indulging every reasonable presumption in favor of the general verdict, reconcile the answers to the interrogatories therewith, if it can be done on any reasonable theory possible within the issues. When this is done, it is quite plain there is no such conflict between the special finding of facts and the general verdict as the law

declares sufficient to overcome the latter and warrant a judgment on the former.

The contention that Dawson's discharge was on account of his refusal to obey appellee's order to have the men under him work in the pit at the place where appellant was injured is not sustained, for the answers to the interrogatories show that he was discharged because of unsatisfactory work, and for no other reason. This excludes the idea that he was discharged because of his refusal to obey orders as alleged in the complaint, but does not negative the fact found by the general verdict, that appellee knew and appellant did not know the peculiar properties of shale and the hidden dangers incident to the new duties to which appellant was assigned. Nor does such finding negative the fact that appellee knew that appellant did not know or appreciate such peculiar and hidden dangers when he was sent back to work after Dawson's discharge.

17.

The so-called gravel pit cases to which reference has been made are not controlling in this case, because of the theory of the complaint.

For reasons already stated, the judgment is reversed, with instructions to the lower court to overrule the motion for judgment on the answers to the interrogatories, and to render judgment on the verdict of the jury.

Hottel, C. J., Adams, P. J., and Myers, Lairy and Ibach, JJ., concur.

ON PETITION FOR REHEARING.

FELT, P. J.—On reëxamination of the questions involved in this appeal we are satisfied with the conclusions announced in the original opinion, but we believe the mandate should be modified. Where a general verdict is returned in favor of one of the parties, and his adversary obtains judgment in his favor on the answers of the jury to interrogatories, notwithstanding the general

18.

verdict, this court cannot know, unless it be in exceptional cases, that a new trial would not have been granted the losing party on application, had the motion for judgment on the answers to the interrogatories been overruled.

In any event, this court has the power to order a 19. new trial, and it is its duty so to do, where it appears that the ends of justice will be best subserved by so doing.

The court, in sustaining the motion for judgment on the interrogatories, granted appellee relief of a different and higher character than that obtainable by a motion for a new trial, and which, but for the error of the court, left no occasion or necessity for a new trial. But appellee should not on account of such ruling have judgment rendered against it, without on opportunity to retry the case. The 20. party against whom a general verdict has been rendered, on proper motion has the right to have the trial court pass on the verdict before judgment thereon is rendered against him.

But for the action of the trial court in sustaining the motion for judgment on the answers of the jury to the interrogatories, appellee might have obtained a new trial on motion duly made for causes which may exist, and on which no court has passed judgment.

In a case where the facts are complicated and close questions of law are involved, and in which this court finds reversible error in the action of the trial court in 18. rendering judgment *non obstante veredicto,* the ends of justice will generally be best subserved by order- ing a new trial, unless it be in exceptional cases where the facts specially found of themselves clearly indicate that the party who obtained the general verdict is entitled to judg- ment. *Shoner* v. *Pennsylvania Co.* (1892), 130 Ind. 170, 179, 28 N. E. 616, 29 N. E. 775; *Brown* v. *Ohio, etc., R. Co.* (1894), 138 Ind. 648, 657, 37 N. E. 717, 38 N. E. 176; *Masterson* v. *Southern R. Co.* (1908), 170 Ind. 296, 298, 80 N. E.

505; *Citizens St. R. Co.* v. *Reed* (1902), 28 Ind. App. 629, 63 N. E. 770; *Columbia Creosoting Co.* v. *Beard* (1913), *post* 260, 99 N. E. 823.

Applying the foregoing propositions to the facts of this case, we believe the ends of justice will be best subserved by ordering a new trial.

The petition for rehearing is therefore overruled, and it is ordered that a new trial be granted, with leave to amend the pleadings if desired, and for further proceedings not inconsistent with this opinion, and that the mandate of the original opinion be, and the same is modified accordingly.

NOTE.—Reported in 99 N. E. 530, 100 N. E. 472. See, also, under (1, 2, 3) 38 Cyc. 1927; (4) 31 Cyc. 84; (5) 26 Cyc. 1384; (6) 26 Cyc. 1165; (7) 26 Cyc. 1221; (8) 26 Cyc. 1188; (9, 10) 26 Cyc. 1177; (11) 26 Cyc. 1182; (13, 15, 17) 26 Cyc. 1513; (14) 26 Cyc. 1165; (16) 38 Cyc. 1927; (18, 19) 3 Cyc. 454. As to assumption of risk as affecting an employe's right to recover for personal injuries, see 97 Am. St. 884. As to the duty to warn or instruct servant, see 44 L. R. A. 33. As to the duty of a master to adopt rules to protect servant, or to warn him against dangers not reasonably to be apprehended, see 21 L. R. A. (N. S.) 89. As to instructing minor servant who is of insufficient age or capacity to comprehend dangers of employment as affecting master's responsibility, see 8 L. R. A. (N. S.) 284. As to the assumption of obvious risks of hazardous employment, see 1 L. R. A. (N. S.) 272. Servant's assumption of risk of danger imperfectly appreciated, see 4 L. R. A. (N. S.) 990. As to the assumption of risk of dangers created by the master's negligence, which might have been discovered by the exercise of ordinary care on the part of the servant, see 28 L. R. A. (N. S.) 1250. On the question of a servant's right of action for injuries received in obeying a direct command, see 48 L. R. A. 753; 30 L. R. A. (N. S.) 436. As to servant's assumption of risk in obeying orders to perform obviously dangerous work, see 4 L. R. A. (N. S.) 830.

SOUTHERN RAILWAY COMPANY ET AL. *v.* FRIEDLEY.

[No. 7,794. Filed January 22, 1913.]

1. PLEADING.—*Complaint.—Theory.*—The theory of an action must be determined from the general character and tenor of the leading and controlling averments of the complaint. p. 195.

2. WATERS AND WATERCOURSES.—*Obstruction.—Injury to Property. — Complaint. — Sufficiency.* — A complaint in substance alleging that by the wrongful acts and negligence of defendants in obstructing a natural watercourse, excavations were washed in plaintiff's land, crops growing thereon were destroyed, the soil was washed away, the fertility of the land was destroyed, and that the stream was changed from its natural channel onto plaintiff's land, shows a complete loss or destruction of a part of plaintiff's land, and was sufficient on the theory of a permanent injury. p. 195.

3. WATERS AND WATERCOURSES.—*Obstruction.—Permanent Injury to Land.—Trial.—Exclusion of Evidence.*—In the trial of an action on the theory of permanent injury to land caused by the obstruction of a natural watercourse, testimony in support of any other theory was properly excluded. p. 196.

4. WATERS AND WATERCOURSES.—*Obstruction.—Permanent Injury to Land.—Damages.—Instructions.*—Where an action was based on the theory of a permanent injury to land by the obstruction of a natural watercourse, instructions, that the measure of damages was the depreciation in the rental value of the land, were properly refused. p. 196.

5. APPEAL.—*Review.—Instructions.—Defect Cured by Other Instructions.*—An instruction, that if plaintiff has proved both paragraphs of the complaint, the jury should find generally for plaintiff, is not objectionable for the omission of any reference to a preponderance of the evidence, where the jury was fully advised on that subject in other instructions given. p. 196.

6. APPEAL.—*Review.—Instructions.—Consideration as a Whole.*—On appeal instructions will be considered as a whole, and if, when so considered, they fairly state the law, an inaccuracy in a particular instruction will not cause a reversal. p. 196.

7. WATERS AND WATERCOURSES.—*Obstruction.—Permanent Injury to Land.—Verdict.—Answers to Interrogatories.*—In an action based on the theory of permanent injury to land caused by the obstruction of a natural watercourse, where there was evidence that defendants had placed piles so as to deflect the stream and cut plaintiff's bank, and had allowed the bed to become partially filled with stone and debris, thereby casting the water onto plain-

tiff's land and causing the same to cut, wash away, and cave in, answers to interrogatories showing that a large portion of the damage to plaintiff's property was caused by natural overflow, and that part of it was done by cutting, are not in irreconcilable conflict with a general verdict for plaintiff. p. 197.

From Floyd Circuit Court; *William C. Utz*, Judge.

Action by Laura B. Friedley against the Southern Railway Company and another. From a judgment for plaintiff, the defendants appeal. *Affirmed*.

Alex. P. Humphrey, Edward P. Humphrey, John D. Welman and *Walter V. Bulleit*, for appellants.

Evan B. Stotsenberg and *John H. Weathers*, for appellee.

IBACH, C. J.—Appellee recovered judgment below for $300 for injuries to her land caused by appellants.

Appellants assign error of the lower court in overruling their demurrers to each paragraph of the complaint, in overruling their separate motions for judgment in their favor on the answers to interrogatories returned with the general verdict by the jury, and in overruling their motions for a new trial.

It is insisted that the complaint is insufficient because it alleges no facts from which any permanent injury can be inferred, and does not allege in positive terms a permanent injury; further that it is not good for a continuing nuisance, because there is no allegation in either paragraph of the lessened rental value of the land in suit.

The first paragraph of the complaint charges, in substance, that defendants own and operate a steam railroad through certain real estate in Floyd county, Indiana, belonging to plaintiff, and described in the complaint; that there is a natural watercourse extending through plaintiff's real estate which drains and carries off the water from the premises of the plaintiff and others adjoining her; that the railroad of the defendants is constructed on an embankment on and across said watercourse and through the lands of plaintiff;

that the prior owners of said railroad built an opening in the embankment for said watercourse, and within the last six years defendants have rebuilt, changed and made smaller such culvert or opening so as to form a dam to such watercourse and to change the course thereof and allow no escape therefor except through such lessened culvert; that by reason of such acts of defendants the waters of such stream were diverted and changed from their natural course, and that said culvert was made smaller and insufficient to carry off the water of said stream and the course of the same was changed and part of the water was thrown over, upon and across the land of plaintiff, flooding said lands and washing excavations therein; that defendants have wrongfully and negligently permitted said watercourse to be filled with gravel, stone and other debris, and permitted the same so to remain, and that the waters of said stream have been diverted thereby, changed and thrown upon plaintiff's land, destroying the crops grown thereon, destroying the fertility of the land, preventing plaintiff from cultivating said land, washing away the soil and tearing holes in plaintiff's land, and causing the water to flow in a different channel on plaintiff's land from that formerly occupied by the creek, thereby washing holes and excavations therein and thereon, all without any fault or negligence on plaintiff's part.

The second paragraph charges, in substance, that plaintiff for two years past has been the owner of the real estate described therein, and that defendants maintained their railroad through said real estate; that running through said real estate of plaintiff there is a natural watercourse, draining plaintiff's land, and also a large area to the west; that said railroad of defendants is built and maintained on the north bank of said creek, for a distance of more than 500 feet through plaintiff's land, and part of said right of way is in the bed of said creek; that defendants have negligently and wrongfully permitted the bed of said creek on its right of way to become filled with brush, logs and debris, and have wrongfully permitted trees and bushes to grow on and in their right of way, which is occupied by said creek and watercourse, and have wrongfully used, appropriated and occupied the bed of said creek and watercourse, and by reason thereof the waters of said creek have been diverted and changed from the bed of said creek over and onto plaintiff's land, changing the course of said water from its natural course; that by reason thereof part of the waters of said creek have been thrown upon and across plaintiff's land, flooding the same and washing excavations therein, destroying the crops thereon, destroying the fertility of the soil, washing away the soil, causing the bank on the south side thereof to cave in and the soil to be washed away, preventing the cultivation of said land, and changing the natural course of the stream, all without any fault on plaintiff's part.

It is a well-established rule of law that the theory on which a cause of action is based must be determined by the court from the general character and tenor of the

1. averments of the complaint, that is, the theory to be adopted must be that which is most apparent from the leading and controlling averments, and not one which might be supported by isolated statements. *Oölitic Stone Co. v. Ridge* (1908), 169 Ind. 639, 83 N. E. 246.

The leading and controlling averments of the complaint before us are, in substance, that by the wrongful acts and negligence of appellants, excavations were washed in

2. appellee's land, crops growing thereon were destroyed, the soil was washed away, the fertility of the land was destroyed, and the creek was changed from its natural channel onto appellee's land. These charges, when associated with the other averments of the complaint, show that definite and specific physical injuries of a permanent character were done in the manner charged to the land itself, and they were to such an extent permanent that it may be said they show a complete loss or destruction of a

part of such land. The record shows that no evidence was introduced at the trial based on any other theory; also, in the light of the instructions given, there can be no doubt but that the trial court regarded each paragraph of the complaint as proceeding on the theory of permanent injury, and on such theory submitted the case to the jury. We hold that the complaint was sufficient on such theory, and that it stated a cause of action for specific physical injuries to appellee's land, of a permanent character, caused by appellants' negligent and wrongful acts, previous to the time of the filing of the suit, and subsequent to her purchase of the land. Since we have held that the theory of the

3. complaint is for permanent injury, rather than for a continuing trespass, the trial court very properly refused to receive any testimony on any other theory, and rightly refused to give to the jury the instructions

4. tendered by appellant based on the theory that the proper measure of damages was the depreciation in the rental value of the land.

Appellant also contends that the court erred in giving to the jury the following instruction, on its own motion: "If the plaintiff has proved both paragraphs of the com-

5. plaint, you should find generally for the plaintiff."

The objection urged is that by this instruction the jury is told to find for the plaintiff on both paragraphs of the complaint if proved, without reference to a preponderance of the evidence. This omission in this particular instruction could not have misled the jury, because it had been fully instructed on the matter omitted in the two instructions just preceding the one here objected to. In-

6. structions are to be considered together as a whole. The court is not bound to give all the law "in one breath," and if, when so considered, the instructions fairly state the law, an inaccuracy in one instruction is not cause for reversal, where the necessary addition or limitation to complete an instruction, which is correct as far as

it goes, may be found in other instructions given as a part of the same series. *Parry Mfg. Co.* v. *Eaton* (1908), 41 Ind. App. 81, 83 N. E. 510, and cases cited.

The court did not err in giving to the jury the instructions tendered by appellee, for each and all stated the proper rule to be applied in the ascertainment of liability and assessment of damages in cases of this character.

The jury found by answers to interrogatories that a large portion of the damage to appellee's property was caused by natural overflow, that part of it was done by cutting. 7. There was evidence to the effect that appellants had so placed piles and palisades in the bed of the stream at the culvert as to cause the water to be deflected and to cut appellee's bank, also, that they had allowed its bed to become partially filled with stones and debris, and had thus thrown the water over on appellee, and caused the land to cut, wash away and cave in. There is abundant evidence of damage to appellee's property, and some evidence that appellants were responsible for part of this damage. The answers to interrogatories are not irreconcilable with the general verdict, when considered with the evidence which was submitted at the trial. The evidence, which tends to prove that appellants' negligence caused damage to appellee, would, if it stood alone, be amply sufficient to support the verdict.

No error appearing, the judgment is affirmed.

NOTE.—Reported in 100 N. E. 481. See, also, under (1) 31 Cyc. 84; (2, 3) 40 Cyc. 579; (4) 40 Cyc. 580; (5) 38 Cyc. 1782; (6) 38 Cyc. 1778; (7) 38 Cyc. 1927. As to rights of owners of dams and their liability for resulting injury to others' property, see 57 Am. Dec. 684.

198   APPELLATE COURT OF INDIANA,

Great Council, etc., **Red Men** *v*. **Green**—52 Ind. App. 198.

GREAT COUNCIL OF INDIANA IMPROVED ORDER OF RED MEN *v*. GREEN ET AL.

[No. 7,692.   Filed January 22, 1913.]

1. APPEAL.—*Record.—Bill of Exceptions.—Evidence.*—The sufficiency of the evidence cannot be considered on appeal, unless it shall affirmatively appear, over the signature of the trial judge, that the bill of exceptions contains all the evidence. p. 198.
2. APPEAL.—*Record.—Bill of Exceptions Containing Evidence.— Form.*—A bill of exceptions containing the evidence, preceding the formal conclusion, should contain the words: "And this was all the evidence given in said cause." p. 198.

From Warrick Circuit Court; *Roscoe Kiper*, Judge.

Action by Cullen B. Green and others against the Great Council of Indiana Improved Order of Red Men. From a judgment for plaintiffs, the defendant appeals. *Affirmed.*

Richard M. Milburn and *Horace M. Kean*, for appellant. *E. A. Ely* and *E. F. Ely*, for appellees.

ADAMS, J.—The errors presented by the assignment in this appeal and relied on for reversal of the judgment require an examination of the evidence.   Appellees insist that the sufficiency of the evidence cannot be considered, for the reason that the bill of exceptions does not conclude with the statement "and this was all the evidence given in said cause," and the certificate of the trial judge does not state that the bill of exceptions contains all the evidence given in the cause.   Appellees' position is fully supported by authority.

It is well settled that this court cannot consider
1. the sufficiency of the evidence to sustain the decision, unless it shall affirmatively appear, over the signature of the trial judge, that the bill of exceptions contains all the evidence.   The bill of exceptions preceding
2. the formal conclusion should contain the words: "And this was all the evidence given in said cause."

Petree v. *Fielder* (1891), 3 Ind. App. 127, 131, 29 N. E. 271; *Ohio, etc., R. Co.* v. *Smith* (1892), 5 Ind. App. 36, 39, 31 N. E. 371; *Haynes, Spencer & Co.* v. *Erk* (1893), 6 Ind. App. 332, 335, 33 N. E. 637; *Miller* v. *Fuller* (1898), 21 Ind. App. 254, 256, 52 N. E. 101; *Brickley* v. *Weghorn* (1880), 71 Ind. 497, 499; *Seig* v. *Long* (1880), 72 Ind. 18; *Beatty* v. *O'Connor* (1886), 106 Ind. 81, 84, 5 N. E. 880; *Kleyla* v. *State, ex rel.* (1887), 112 Ind. 146, 13 N. E. 255; *Guenther* v. *State* (1895), 141 Ind. 593, 595, 41 N. E. 13.

The judgment is affirmed.

NOTE.—Reported in 100 N. E. 472. See, also, under (1) 3 Cyc. 167. As to the indication, by the filing of a bill of exceptions, that it has been allowed by the court, see 15 Am. St. 297.

KREITLEIN *v.* FERGER.

[No. 7,507. Filed March 8, 1912. Rehearing denied June 29, 1912. Transfer denied January 23, 1913.]

1. EVIDENCE.—*Discharge in Bankruptcy.*—A certificate of discharge in bankruptcy is evidence of the jurisdiction of the court, the regularity of the proceedings in the bankruptcy case, and the fact that such order of discharge was made therein. p. 203.

2. BANKRUPTCY.—*Discharge.*—*Debts Affected.*—Under the provisions of the bankruptcy act of 1898, as amended in 1903, a discharge in bankruptcy does not operate as a discharge of all the debts of the bankrupt, but releases him from all provable debts, except as therein otherwise specially provided. p. 204.

3. BANKRUPTCY.—*Provable Debts.*—*Judgment.*—A judgment is a provable debt under §63a(1) of the bankruptcy act of 1898 as amended in 1903. (1 Fed. Stat. Annot. 679.) p. 205.

4. BANKRUPTCY. — *Debts Discharged.* — *Notice.* — Under the bankruptcy act of 1898, as amended in 1903, providing that debts not duly scheduled in time for proof and allowance, with the name of the creditor, if known to the bankrupt, are not affected by a discharge in bankruptcy, unless the creditor had actual knowledge of the proceeding in bankruptcy, and providing that, in his list of creditors, the bankrupt shall show the residence of each creditor, if known, a debt was not discharged by a bankruptcy proceeding, where the schedule of the debt gave only the initial, instead of the full Christian name, of the creditor, and gave his

residence as Indianapolis, without any street or number, and such creditor received no actual notice of the proceedings. pp. 205, 206.

5. NAMES.—*Initials.*—The initial of a given name alone and unexplained is not recognized as a name. p. 206.

6. JUDGMENT. — *Action on Judgment. — Defense. — Discharge in Bankruptcy.—Proof.—Burden.*—In an action on a prior judgment, where defendant pleaded a discharge in bankruptcy, he had the burden of proving that the debt which he listed in his schedule of creditors in the bankruptcy proceeding was the debt of the plaintiff on which the action is brought, so that a judgment for plaintiff will not be disturbed on the ground that the decision is not sustained by sufficient evidence, or that it is contrary to law, where there was no proof in any way identifying the judgment sued on and the debt listed in the bankruptcy proceedings as being one and the same debt. p. 208.

7. JUDGMENT.—*Action on Judgment.—Review.—Form of Judgment. —Failure to Object.*—Although it was improper, in an action on a judgment with relief and without exemption, to render a judgment with benefit of exemption and without relief, the judgment will not be reversed, where appellant failed to make objections or take exception to the form of the judgment, and made no motion to modify same. p. 209.

8. APPEAL.—*Objection to Form of Judgment.—Presenting Question for Review.—Motion for New Trial.*—Questions arising on the form of a judgment are not presented by a motion for a new trial, on the ground that the decision is not sustained by sufficient evidence, except in cases where the facts are specially found and an error in the finding is carried into the judgment, but such questions are saved by objection and exception made at the time the judgment is rendered, or by a motion to modify or correct. pp. 209, 210.

9. APPEAL.—*Review.—Error in Form of Judgment.—Disposition of Cause.*—In an action on a judgment with relief and without exemption, error in rendering judgment with benefit of exemption and without relief, will not operate as a cause for reversal on appeal, but the judgment will be ordered cured by a modification. p. 211.

From Superior Court of Marion County (75,562) ; *Vincent G. Clifford,* Judge.

Action by Charles Ferger against George F. Kreitlein. From a judgment for plaintiff, the defendant appeals. *Affirmed.*

John B. Elam, James W. Fesler and *Harvey J. Elam,* for appellant.

Charles W. Appleman and *William E. Reiley*, for appellee.

HOTTEL, J.—Appellee brought this suit to recover on a prior judgment which he held against appellant. The complaint was in one paragraph, to which appellant filed a general denial, and also pleaded a discharge in bankruptcy as a defense. Appellee replied in denial, and the cause was tried by the court which rendered judgment for appellee in the sum of $508.50, without relief from valuation or appraisement laws.

The only error relied on for reversal is the overruling of appellant's motion for a new trial, the grounds of which motion are (1) that the decision of the court is not sustained by sufficient evidence, and (2) that the decision of the court is contrary to law.

The material facts in this case are as follows: On November 23, 1897, appellee recovered a judgment against appellant in the Superior Court of Marion county for the sum of $300 and costs, and said judgment is now the basis of this action. Thereafter, in 1905, appellant duly filed his petition in bankruptcy, and obtained a discharge therein, which discharge he pleaded in defense when this action was brought in 1908.

The only question presented by this appeal is whether the decision of the court is sustained by sufficient evidence. On this question the averments of the complaint are conceded to be proven. The question we have to determine is, therefore, whether appellant's answer of discharge in bankruptcy is supported by the evidence. Appellant's position is that "there is no dispute in the evidence," and that this court should therefore "determine that as a matter of law appellant is entitled to judgment" on the facts proven.

The only evidence introduced by plaintiff was the judgment, that part of which important to this decision is as follows: "Come again the parties, and the jury having returned their verdict herein, finding for the plaintiff and assessing his damages at the sum of $300.00, the court renders judgment thereon. It is therefore considered, adjudged and decreed by the court that the plaintiff recover of and from the defendant herein the sum of $300.00, collectible with relief from valuation and appraisement laws, but without exemption, and costs herein expended, taxed at $————.'' Charles Ferger testified on direct examination: "I own the above judgment and it has never been paid." On cross-examination he said: "I did not know that Mr. Kreitlein went through bankruptcy until lately, and did not get any notice of it."

Defendant introduced in evidence the record of the verdict, and the answers by the jury to interrogatories in the case, in which the judgment was rendered, on which this suit was brought. There were twenty-five of these interrogatories, the answers to which, important in determining the questions involved in this case, were, in effect, that defendant in that case—appellant here—was on November 4, 5, 6, 7, 1895, insolvent, and that on said dates he ordered the flour described in plaintiff's complaint; that said defendant, neither in person nor by or through any one representing him, either at the time of ordering said flour or prior thereto, made any representations to the plaintiff as to his (defendant's) financial condition; that neither defendant nor any one representing him had at either of said times made any representation to the public generally as to the solvency or insolvency of such defendant; that neither at the time defendant received said flour, nor prior thereto, had he, or any one representing him, made any false representations to the plaintiff or to the public generally as to the solvency or insolvency of defendant; that plaintiff in receiving the order for said flour and filling the same did not rely on any statements made to him or to the public generally by defendant, or by any one representing defendant; that plaintiff in that suit—appellee here—believed that the sale of said flour was a sale for cash, and sent his son to collect for the same, who received from defendant shoes, the value of which was to be credited on the account of plaintiff against defendant; that plaintiff, after the sale of said flour, sent an attorney to defendant, who demanded payment of the account, to whom defendant made a promise to pay the account within twenty-four hours, and said attorney, with knowledge of the facts under which the flour was purchased, agreed to wait, and did wait until the time promised by defendant. Appellant also introduced in evidence the original petition and schedule filed therewith in the bankruptcy proceedings, November 11, 1905. In the schedule, which was a statement of all creditors whose claims were unsecured, appears under the heading *"Names"*, "C. Ferger"; under the heading *"Residence"*, "Indianapolis"; under the heading *"Place and Date"*, "Indianapolis, 1895"; under the heading *"Nature"*, "Merchandise"; under the heading "Amount", "$271.85". The discharge in bankruptcy completed appellant's evidence, and it is as follows: "Whereas, George F. Kreitlein, in said district, has been duly adjudged a bankrupt, under the acts of Congress relating to bankruptcy, and appears to have conformed to all requirements of law in that behalf, it is therefore ordered by this court that said George F. Kreitlein be discharged from all debts and claims which are made provable by said acts against his estate, and which existed on the 11th day of November, A. D. 1905, on which day the petition for adjudication was filed by him; excepting such debts as are by law excepted from the operation of a discharge in bankruptcy." This discharge was evidence of the jurisdiction of the court and the regularity of the proceedings in the bankruptcy case, and the fact that such order of discharge was made therein. Bankruptcy Act, §21, subd. *c-f* (1 Fed. Stat. Annot. 589); *Hays* v. *Ford* (1876), 55 Ind. 52; *Begein* v. *Brehm* (1890), 123 Ind. 160, 23 N. E. 496; *Graber* v. *Gault* (1905), 103 App. Div. 511, 515, 93 N. Y. Supp. 76.

The provisions of the bankruptcy act of 1898, as amended
in 1903, applicable to the questions presented by this appeal,
are as follows: (1) Section 17 (1 Fed. Stat. Annot.
2. 578): "Debts not affected by a discharge.—A discharge in bankruptcy shall release a bankrupt from
all of his provable debts, except such as * * * ; (3)
have not been duly scheduled in time for proof and allowance, with the name of the creditor if known to the bankrupt, unless such creditor had notice or actual knowledge of
the proceedings in bankruptcy, * * * ." (2) Section
63 (1 Fed. Stat. Annot. 679): "Debts which may be proved.
—a1 Debts of the bankrupt may be proved and allowed
against his estate which are (1) [*fixed liability.*] A fixed
liability, as evidenced by a judgment or an instrument in
writing, absolutely owing at the time of the filing of
the petition against him, whether then payable or not,
with any interest thereon which would have been recoverable at that date or with a rebate of interest upon such as were not then payable and did not bear interest
* * * ." (3) That part of subd. 8, §7, which provides
that the bankrupt shall, "prepare, make oath to, and file in
court within ten days, * * * a list of his creditors,
showing their residences, if known; if unknown, that fact
to be stated, the amounts due each of them, the consideration thereof, the security held by them, if any, and a claim
for such exemptions as he may be entitled to (1 Fed. Stat.
Annot. 559)." Other sections provide for notices to be given
to the creditors of the bankrupt of certain steps to be taken
in such proceedings, the notices to be sent *by the referee in
bankruptcy by mail to the "respective addresses"* of such
creditors *"as they appear in the list of creditors of the bankrupt,* or as afterwards filed with the papers in the case by
the creditors unless they waive notice in writing." (Our
italics.) See §58, and also §33 subd. 4. In addition to the
above is a general order, §33, subd. 5, which provides "that
all of the schedules shall be printed or written out plainly

without abbreviation or interlineation, except when such abbreviation or interlineation may be for the purpose of reference.''

It will be seen from these provisions that a discharge in bankruptcy does not operate as a discharge of all the debts of such bankrupt, but that he shall be released from
3.   all of his *provable debts except those therein specially provided*. The debt herein sued on was a judgment, and under §63a(1), *supra*, was a provable debt.

It is insisted by appellant that the burden of proof is on appellee to prove that the debt sued on was included in any of the classes excepted from the discharge. On this question there is some conflict in the authorities both in our own State and in other jurisdictions. Under the bankruptcy law of 1841 our Supreme Court, in the case of *Sorden* v. *Gatewood* (1848), 1 Ind. *107, expressly held that the burden of proof in such a case is on the bankrupt, who pleads and relies on his discharge. This case has never been expressly overruled, and has been cited in the following cases. *Bivens* v. *Newcomb* (1850), 2 Ind. *98; *Slaughter* v. *Detiney* (1858), 10 Ind. 103; *Donald* v. *Kell* (1886), 111 Ind. 1, 4, 11 N. E. 782; *Madison Tp.* v. *Dunkle* (1888), 114 Ind. 262, 16 N. E. 593.

In this connection it is proper to say that while the case of *Sorden* v. *Gatewood, supra,* has never been expressly overruled by our Supreme Court, some doubt has been cast on it as an authority on this particular question by the later case of *Goddin* v. *Neal* (1885), 99 Ind. 334. In view, however, of our conclusion on the other questions presented by the appeal, we do not deem it important or necessary in this case to determine on whom rested the burden of proof as to said question.

Under the provision of §17, *supra*, the discharge in bankruptcy did not affect such debts of the bankrupt as
4.   had not been "*duly scheduled*" in time for proof and allowance, with the name of the creditor, if known to

the bankrupt, unless "such creditor had actual knowledge of the proceeding in bankruptcy," and subd. 8, §7, of said act, *supra,* provides that such bankrupt in his said list of creditors "shall show their residences if known, if unknown that fact to be stated." There can be no question under any of the authorities construing said provisions, but that it was at least necessary that such schedule should contain the name of such creditor or that such creditor should have actual knowledge of the proceedings, before it could be said that a discharge under such act would be a release as to such creditor. *Marshall* v. *English-American Loan, etc., Co.* (1906), 127 Ga. 376, 56 S. E. 449; *Custard* v. *Wigderson* (1907), 130 Wis. 412, 110 N. W. 263, 10 Ann. Cas. 740; *Columbia Bank* v. *Birkett* (1903), 174 N. Y. 112, 66 N. E. 652, 102 Am. St. 478.

In this State the initial of the given name alone and unexplained is not recognized as a name. *Bascom* v.
5. *Toner* (1892), 5 Ind. App. 229, 31 N. E. 856; *Shearer* v. *R. S. Peale & Co.* (1894), 9 Ind. App. 282, 286,
36 N. E. 455; *Louden* v. *Walpole* (1848), 1 Ind. *319.

The other section, providing that the schedule should
also contain the residences of such creditors, not being a
part of the section providing the debts to be affected
4. by the discharge and the exceptions therefrom, there
is ground for holding that such statement of the
residence is not a condition, the performance of which is
necessary to prevent the operation of the discharge, and
our attention is called to the case of *Steele* v. *Thalheimer*
(1905), 74 Ark. 516, 518, 86 S. W. 305, which so holds.
There are other cases, however, holding to the contrary.
Columbia Bank v. *Birkett, supra; Haack* v. *Theise* (1906),
99 N. Y. Supp. 905, 51 Misc. 3.

The purpose of this provision is manifest. The law of
1898 is different from the bankruptcy laws of 1841 and
1867, in the matter of the manner and kind of notice to be

given the creditors of such bankrupt. The law of 1898 provides for individual notices of the proceedings in bankruptcy to be given to each creditor by mail, and the purpose of requiring the bankrupt to furnish the names and residences of his creditors is that the referee may have the information necessary to give such notices. These notices are important, and it is necessary that the bankrupt be as accurate and certain as he can be in the furnishing of said information in order that the provisions for the personal notice to the individual creditors required by the act, be complied with. If he withholds, or for any reason fails accurately and correctly to perform this duty required by the statute, the provision for such notice may be thereby defeated. ''One of the fundamental principles in the jurisprudence of this country is that no man can be deprived of any legal right by a judicial proceeding to which he is not a party, and of which he has not received lawful notice or had actual knowledge.'' *In re Monroe* (1902), 114 Fed. 398. The court in the case just cited says further: ''Creditors who have not been notified of the proceedings in the manner prescribed by the bankruptcy law are not estopped from asserting their rights by reason of mere failure on their part to be diligent in discovering the insolvency of their debtors or their resort to a court of bankruptcy.''

In the case of *Columbia Bank* v. *Birkett, supra*, the court said on page 116: ''The schedule of debts, which the bankrupt is to file with his petition, furnishes the basis for the notices which the referee, or the court, is to give thereafter to the creditors, and, thus, the bankrupt appears to be made responsible for the correctness of the list of his creditors. That he is to suffer, in the case of his failure to state the name of the creditor, to whom his debt is due, if known to him, seems to me very clear from the reading of §17 of the act. * * * I think it was intended that the decree discharging the voluntary bankrupt should be confined in its operations to the creditors, who had been duly listed and who were enabled to receive the notices which the act provides for.''

On the question of the sufficiency of the statement in the schedule of the residence or address of the creditors, where they reside in large cities see *Haack* v. *Theise, supra;* *Cagliostro* v. *Indelli* (1907), 102 N. Y. Supp. 918, 53 Misc. 44.

As a matter of fact the proof shows that the information furnished by appellant in his schedule did not result in appellee's getting notice of said bankruptcy proceedings. We are of the opinion that, under the authorities cited and quoted from, appellee's debt was not duly scheduled according to the letter and spirit of said provisions of the bankruptcy act. But there is another reason why this judgment on its merits is correct. Under the answers of appellant, the burden was on him to prove that the debt which he listed in his said schedule of creditors was the debt of appellee herein sued on. The proof on this subject shows that the debt so listed by appellant in 1905 in said bankruptcy proceeding was the debt of C. Ferger, for $271.85 for merchandise. This suit was on a judgment rendered on November 23, 1897, for $300, amounting at the time of the judgment herein to $508.50. The record of said former judgment showed it to be a judgment in tort ''without exemption.'' There is no proof whatever showing that the C. Ferger whose name appears on said schedule of the bankrupt is the Charles Ferger herein sued, or that said debt for merchandise bought in 1895 was any part of or in anyway connected with said judgment for tort rendered some seven years before said debt on said schedule was so listed. There is no proof that in anyway connects the two debts as one and the same debt, unless it could be said that said answers to interrogatories furnish such proof, and we fail to see wherein they can be said to identify the two debts as one and the same debt. See *Louden* v. *Walpole, supra.*

Appellant next insists that the motion for a new trial should be granted because the court in rendering the judgment herein rendered. a judgment with benefit of

7. exemption and without relief, whereas the judgment on which the suit was predicated was with relief and without exemption. The judgment in this respect was wrong, but no objections were made or exceptions taken by appellant to the form of the judgment, and no motion was made to modify the same. Appellant insists that his

8. motion for a new trial presents the question, and re-lies on the cases of *Jarboe* v. *Brown* (1872), 39 Ind. 549, and *Polley* v. *Pogue* (1906), 38 Ind. App. 678, 78 N. E. 1051. We do not think either case cited supports appellant's contention. This court in *Polley* v. *Pogue, supra,* expressly bases its decision on the fact that the facts found by the court made it necessary that the judgment should be rendered in that case as it was, and says *"the finding in such respect is contrary to law as well as contrary to the evidence* and good cause arises therefrom for a new trial."

In *Jarboe* v. *Brown, supra,* there were reasons shown in the opinion for reversing the judgment in that case other than that a part of the same was rendered without relief. All of the more recent authorities hold that to save a question as to the form of the judgment some objection and exception must be made and saved at the time it is rendered, or a motion made to modify or correct. *Allen* v. *Studebaker Bros. Mfg. Co.* (1899), 152 Ind. 406, 53 N. E. 422; *Tucker* v. *Hyatt* (1898), 151 Ind. 332, 338, 51 N. E. 469, 44 L. R. A. 129; *Stalcup* v. *Dixon* (1893), 136 Ind. 9, 19, 35 N. E. 987; *Kelley* v. *Houts* (1903), 30 Ind. App. 474, 477, 66 N. E. 408; *Johnson* v. *Prine* (1876), 55 Ind. 351; *Lewis* v. *Edwards* (1873), 44 Ind. 333; Elliott, App. Proc. §§345, 346.

Judgment affirmed.

ON PETITION FOR REHEARING.

HOTTEL, C. J.—On a petition for rehearing it is very earnestly insisted that the original opinion herein discloses the necessity for a reversal of the case. This contention is predicated on the statement in the opinion that the judgment below was wrong, in that it was rendered with benefit of exemption and without relief, "whereas the judgment upon which the suit was predicated was with relief and without exemption." It is insisted that this court is in error in holding that such mistake in the judgment was not properly presented by the grounds of the motion for a new trial, that the decision was not sustained by sufficient evidence and is contrary to law, and in holding that the attention of the court below should have been directed to the mistake by a proper objection to the judgment and exception to the same, or by a motion to modify.

Counsel, in support of their position, insist that the finding in this case contained the same error as that carried into the judgment, and that therefore the error is properly raised by said ground of the motion for a new trial. The case of *Migatz* v. *Stieglitz* (1906), 166 Ind. 361, 77 N. E. 400, and others of similar import are relied on. It must be remembered that in the case at bar there is no special finding, but only a general finding for plaintiff that he shall recover $508.50 without relief. Appellant's contention that where the finding contains the error and the judgment correctly follows the finding, that such error is presented by said grounds of the motion for new trial, is correct, where there has been a finding of facts. It is so manifest that the error here relied on was the result of mistake and oversight, which would have been promptly corrected by the trial court if its attention had been directly called to the same, that the reason for the application of the general rule, which requires that the attention of the trial court should be called to the particular error relied on before it will be available on appeal, seems obvious.

9. But, in any event, the error is not one that should operate to reverse the case, but is one which this court can and should cure by a modification of the judgment below. *Merom Gravel Road Co.* v. *Pearson* (1904), 33 Ind. App. 174, 69 N. E. 694, 71 N. E. 54; *Harris* v. *Curtis* (1905), 34 Ind. App. 438, 72 N. E. 1102; *McAfee* v. *Reynolds* (1891), 130 Ind. 33, 28 N. E. 423, 18 L. R. A. 211, 30 Am. St. 194; *Daugherty* v. *Wheeler* (1890), 125 Ind. 421, 25 N. E. 542.

The court will allow its judgment of affirmance to stand, with directions to the court below so to amend its judgment as to make it with relief from valuation and appraisement laws.

Petition for rehearing overruled.

NOTE.—Reported in 97 N. E. 819, 98 N. E. 1005. See, also, under (1) 5 Cyc. 407; (2) 5 Cyc. 377; (3) 5 Cyc. 401; (4) 5 Cyc. 404; (5) 29 Cyc. 269; (9) 3 Cyc. 424. For a discussion of the sufficiency of the schedule of debts required by the bankruptcy law, see 10 Ann. Cas. 742.

GERMAN AMERICAN TRUST COMPANY, ADMINISTRATOR, *v.* LAFAYETTE BOX BOARD AND PAPER COMPANY.

[No. 7,712. Filed June 19, 1912. Rehearing denied December 13, 1912. Transfer denied January 23, 1913.]

1. DEATH. — *Action.* — *Limitation.*—*Statutes.*—Under §285 Burns 1908, Acts 1889 p. 405, providing that when the death of one is caused by the wrongful act or omission of another, the personal representatives of the former may maintain an action therefor against the latter, if the former might have maintained an action, had he or she lived, against the latter for an injury for the same act or omission, and providing that such action shall be commenced within two years, death is the foundation of the right given by the statute, and an action for death under such statute is not affected by the fact that the right of action for the injury in favor of decedent was barred before his death, but is governed by the rule of limitation therein contained. p. 213.

From Carroll Circuit Court; *James P. Wason,* Judge.

Action by the German American Trust Company, administrator of the estate of John Hall, deceased, against the Lafayette Box Board and Paper Company. From a judgment for defendant, the plaintiff appeals. *Reversed.*

Charles E. Thompson, Hanna & Hall and *Wilson & Quinn,* for appellant.

Kumler & Gaylor, William A. Ketcham and *Howe S. Landers,* for appellee.

ADAMS, P. J.—The determination of this appeal involves the construction of §285 Burns 1908, Acts 1889 p. 405, which reads as follows: ''When the death of one is caused by the wrongful act or omission of another, the personal representatives of the former may maintain an action therefor against the latter, if the former might have maintained an action, had he or she (as the case may be) lived, against the latter for an injury for the same act or omission. The action shall be commenced within two years. The damages cannot exceed ten thousand dollars; and must inure to the exclusive benefit of the widow, or widower (as the case may be), and children, if any, or next of kin, to be distributed in the same manner as personal property of the deceased.''

Appellant, as the personal representative of John Hall, decedent, brought this action on May 23, 1908, against appellee, to recover damages for the death of said Hall, which death, it is averred, was caused by the fault and negligence of appellee. The complaint discloses that appellant's decedent was injured on December 5, 1905, and died from his injuries on March 14, 1908. Appellee demurred to the complaint for want of sufficient facts, which demurrer the court sustained. Appellant refusing to plead over and electing to abide by its complaint and exception to the ruling of the court in sustaining the demurrer thereto, final judgment was rendered that appellant take nothing by its action and that appellee recover its costs.

The only error assigned is that the court erred in sustaining the demurrer of appellee to appellant's complaint. The evident theory on which the trial court held the complaint insufficient was that as the complaint affirmatively shows an interval of more than two years from the time decedent was injured until his death, he had no right to maintain an action immediately prior to his death for his own injuries, and, therefore, no right of action arose in favor of his personal representatives after his death.

It may be admitted that §285, *supra,* is the only authority in this State by which the personal representatives of a decedent may bring an action for death by the wrongful act or omission of another. It may also be admitted that in this case decedent's right to maintain an action for his injuries was barred by the statute of limitation after December 5, 1907, and that a right of action for personal injuries by the wrongful act or omission of another is one that does not survive, under the rule *actio personalis moritur cum persona.* But is this right to maintain an action, conferred by §285, *supra,* on personal representatives, the same right possessed by the decedent, or a new right conferred by statute for the benefit of the persons named and described therein? This is the single question presented by the record before us, and it is not now an open question in Indiana.

In *Wilson* v. *Jackson Hill Coal, etc., Co.* (1911), 48 Ind. App. 150, 95 N. E. 589, this court reviewed the history of
§285, *supra,* which is a substantial reënactment of
1. the Lord Campbell act of 1846, and the English and American decisions construing the same. Our holding then was and now is that death is the foundation of the right given by statute; that it is governed by the rule of limitation therein contained, and is exempt from the rule of limitation which barred the claim of the decedent. This action having been brought within two years from the death of John Hall, the complaint cannot be challenged success-

fully because the right of decedent to maintain an action for his injuries was barred at the time of his death.

For error in sustaining the demurrer to the complaint, the judgment is reversed, and the cause remanded, with instructions to the court below to overrule the demurrer to the complaint, and for further proceedings in consonance with this opinion.

NOTE.—Reported in 98 N. E. 874. See, also, 13 Cyc. 339. For a discussion of the commencement of the running of the statute of limitations against an action for death by wrongful act, see 17 Ann. Cas. 519.

BROTHERHOOD OF LOCOMOTIVE FIREMEN AND ENGINEMEN v. CORDER.

[No. 7,343. Filed January 12, 1912. Rehearing denied May 15, 1912. Transfer denied January 23, 1913.]

1. APPEAL.—*Assignment of Errors.—Waiver.—Briefs.*—Error assigned is waived by appellant's failure to present it either under points and authorities in the briefs, or by other discussaison. p. 216.

2. INSURANCE.—*Fraternal Insurance.—Parol Contract.—Complaint. —Sufficiency.*—A complaint against a fraternal order, stating that decedent applied to a local lodge for a beneficiary certificate, naming plaintiff, his sister, as beneficiary, that the application was accepted and approved, that he paid his fees, became a member and performed all the conditions required of him to entitle him to a certificate, that defendant agreed to insure his life for a specified sum to be paid to plaintiff on decedent's death, and that he was assessed as a member until his death, but that a certificate was never issued and that defendant refused to issue it, etc., sufficiently states a cause of action on the theory of a parol contract of insurance. pp. 216, 218, 219.

3. INSURANCE.—*Action on Parol Contract.—Complaint.—Testing Sufficiency.*—Although some writings are set out and made part of a complaint in an action against an insurance company, drawn on the theory of a parol contract, such fact does not require the sufficiency of the pleading to be tested by the rules applicable where the action is based on a certificate or policy actually issued. p. 218.

4. CONTRACTS.—*Contract Partly in Writing.—Parol Contract.*—A contract that is partly in writing and partly in parol will be treated as a parol contract. p. 218.

5. INSURANCE.—*Fraternal Insurance.—Parol Contract.—Complaint. —By-Laws.*—In an action against a fraternal insurance company, where the complaint was on the theory of a parol contract of insurance, it was not essential to the sufficiency of the complaint that copies of the constitution and by-laws be set out therein. p. 219.

6. INSURANCE.—*Parol Contracts.*—A parol contract of insurance is valid and enforceable. p. 219.

7. INSURANCE.—*Fraternal Insurance.—By-laws.—Conditions Precedent.—Waiver.*—Where the by-laws of a fraternal insurance society make an application for a beneficiary certificate a condition precedent to initiation in a local lodge, and provide that the same shall be in possession of the lodge at the time of the initiation, that before initiation a committee of the local lodge must pass on the qualification of the applicant and recommend him for membership, and that the local physician must make the required medical examination and report thereon before initiation, and that if the applicant has met the conditions and is initiated within the prescribed time, he is entitled to a beneficiary certificate, subject only to the approval of the grand medical examiner, the action of a local lodge in initiating a member after the expiration of the time prescribed in the by-laws, and the failure of the grand lodge to reject him as a member of the lodge, was a waiver of the objection that he was not initiated within the prescribed time following his medical examination. pp. 224, 225.

8. INSURANCE.— *Fraternal Insurance.— By-laws.— Construction.*— Where the object of a fraternal order is not the seeking of profit, but the protection of its members and their beneficiaries by means of indemnity, its constitution, by-laws and other writings are to be liberally construed to promote the benevolent objects of the organization. p. 224.

9. INSURANCE.—*Fraternal Insurance.—By-Laws.—Waiver.*—A fraternal insurance organization may waive compliance with a by-law or regulation made for its benefit, and it may ratify the action of a local lodge in waiving compliance with any such by-law or regulation. p. 225.

10. INSURANCE.—*Fraternal Insurance.—Medical Examiner.—Powers.*—Where the authority of the grand medical examiner of an insurance order, under its constitution and by-laws, extended to the determination of the physical qualifications of the applicant, and to the ascertainment that the application complies generally with the prescribed forms, rules and laws of the order, he had no authority to deny an applicant a beneficiary certificate because

he was not initiated within a certain time after medical examination, as prescribed by the laws of the order. p. 226.

11. APPEAL.—*Assignment of Errors.—Motion for New Trial.*—The
action of the trial court in denying a motion to require an answer returned by the jury to an interrogatory to be made more
specific, is not properly presented by assignment of error, but the
alleged error is ground for a motion for a new trial. p. 228.

From Gibson Circuit Court; *John W. Brady,* Special
Judge.

Action by Armedia Corder against the Brotherhood of
Locomotive Firemen and Enginemen. From a judgment for
plaintiff, the defendant appeals. *Affirmed.*

Thomas McDonald, Harvey Harmon and *H. L. Dickson,*
for appellant.

Henry Kister, W. D. Robinson and *W. E. Stilwell,* for
appellee.

FELT, C. J.—This is an action by appellee, Armedia
Corder, against appellant, Brotherhood of Locomotive Firemen and Enginemen, to recover on an alleged contract of
insurance.

The errors assigned are the following. (1) Overruling
the demurrer to the first paragraph of complaint; (2) the
same as to the second paragraph; (3) overruling appellant's demurrer to the second paragraph of reply to the
second paragraph of answer; (4) overruling the motion to
make the answer to interrogatory No. 32 more specific;
(5) overruling the motion for judgment on the answers to
the interrogatories; (6) overruling the motion for a new
trial. The first error is waived by appellant's fail-
1. ure to present it either under points and authorities
in the briefs or by other discussion.

The second paragraph of the complaint is alleged to be
insufficient because it avers conclusions and does not directly aver the material facts essential to a cause of
2. action; also for failure to plead certain sections of
the constitution and by-laws of appellant. This

paragraph is long, but, in substance, charges that appellant is a corporation, a fraternal order, and is authorized to take applications for and to deliver beneficiary certificates to its members; that on August 22, 1907, William R. Cox, applied to the local lodge for membership and for a beneficiary certificate in the sum of $1,500, and named in said application appellee, his sister, as beneficiary; that this written application is in the possession of appellant; that said application for membership and for a beneficiary certificate was duly accepted and approved by appellant; that Cox paid his fees, was duly initiated, and became a member of appellant; that he performed all the conditions to be by him performed under the constitution and laws of appellant to entitle him to a beneficiary certificate; that in consideration of the payment of the sum named and the further obligations assumed by Cox, appellant promised and agreed to insure his life in the sum of $1,500, and agreed to pay that sum to appellee, his beneficiary, in the event of his death, and agreed to issue to him a beneficiary certificate in said sum, entitling him to all the rights and benefits of such certificate; that he was admitted to membership and was recognized as a beneficiary member by the subordinate lodge, and was assessed as such member until the day of his death; that the beneficiary certificate was never issued to him, and appellant refused and still refuses to issue the same, though often requested so to do; that after the death of Cox, appellee demanded from appellant the sum of $1,500, and appellant refused to pay the same or any part thereof; that it refused on the ground that Cox, during his lifetime, was not a beneficiary member and was not entitled to the beneficiary certificate, and that appellant was not liable for the payment of said sum or any part thereof. It is further averred that said Cox during his lifetime did and performed all the conditions to be by him performed under said agreement aforesaid; that appellee has performed all conditions on her part to be performed by her as such beneficiary.

This paragraph proceeds on the theory of a parol contract for insurance; that decedent did everything required of him to entitle him to a beneficiary certificate, and that appellant wrongfully refused to issue the same to him.

The fact that some writings are set out and made a part of this paragraph of complaint is not sufficient to show
3. that it must be tested by the rules of pleading where the suit is on a beneficial certificate or policy actually issued and in the possession of the beneficiary.
4. If a contract is partly in writing and partly in parol, it will be treated as a parol contract. *Stauffer* v. *Linenthal* (1902), 29 Ind. App. 305, 64 N. E. 643.

The complaint shows the parties to the contract, its subject-matter, the insurable interest of appellee in the life of decedent, the amount of insurance, the premium
2. or fees paid, and compliance with the conditions requisite to obtaining a beneficial certificate. The certificate was not issued and is not the foundation of the action.

In *New England Fire, etc., Ins. Co.* v. *Robinson* (1865), 25 Ind. 536, 538, the court said: "The policy of insurance, which the company agreed to issue, was not the foundation of the action, and a copy thereof was not, under the code, required to be filed with the complaint. The company having refused to issue the policy, it was not necessary that the complaint should be special, and show the conditions complied with. *Tayloe* v. *Merchants' Fire Ins. Co.* [1850], 9 How. 390 [13 L. Ed. 187]. * * * The conditions precedent were waived by the refusal of the company to issue the policy. *Post* v. *Aetna Ins. Co.* [1864], 43 Barb. 351."

In *Eames* v. *Home Ins. Co.* (1876), 4 Otto 621, 629, 24 L. Ed. 298, it is said: "It is sufficient if one party proposes to be insured, and the other party agrees to insure, and the subject, the period, the amount, and the rate of insurance is ascertained or understood, and the premium paid if demanded. It will be presumed that they contemplate such form of policy, containing such conditions and limitations as are usual in such cases, or have been used before between parties.''

5. Appellee was not required to set out copies of the constitution and by-laws of appellant to state a cause of action on the theory of her complaint

The pleading shows that appellant's plan of insurance is carried on through and by means of local lodges subordinate to appellant, and that Air Line Lodge No. 2. 409, into which decedent was initiated, is one of such subordinate lodges; that said lodge has authority to receive and act on applications for membership, and beneficiary certificates, and that in so doing it represents and acts for appellant. It sufficiently appears that decedent's alleged contract for insurance was with appellant, and not with the local lodge, though the complaint in this respect is not a model pleading.

An oral contract for insurance is valid and enforceable. *Commercial Union Assur. Co.* v. *State, ex rel.* (1888), 113 Ind. 331, 15 N. E. 518; *New England Fire, etc., Ins.* 6. *Co.* v. *Robinson, supra; Posey County Fire Assn.* v. *Hogan* (1906), 37 Ind. App. 573, 77 N. E. 670; *Western Assur. Co.* v. *McAlpin* (1899), 23 Ind. App. 220, 55 N. E. 119, 77 Am. St. 423.

The second paragraph of complaint states a cause of action, and the court did not err in overruling the demurrer thereto.

The controlling questions in this case are: (1) Did the local lodge or the grand lodge waive the condition requiring candidates to be initiated within sixty days from the date of their medical examinations? (2) Did the local lodge have power to bind appellant by such waiver, independent of the grand lodge? (3) Did the grand medical examiner

have authority to reject a candidate solely on the ground
that he was not initiated within the prescribed time? (4)
Did appellant on the facts of this case have the right to
accept Cox's application for some purposes and reject it
for others? An intelligent consideration of these questions makes it necessary to state some additional and uncon-
troverted facts, and to give parts of the application made
by Cox and parts of the constitution and by-laws of appellant.

All persons seeking membership in appellant are required
to make the same application and pay the same fees; each
must take out a beneficial certificate if he becomes a member and has the physical qualifications; each applicant is
examined by a local physician selected by the lodge, and
this examination and the report on his application must be
on file in the lodge when the initiation takes place.

The second paragraph of answer admits that appellant
has local lodges, and that appellant issues beneficiary certificates. It seeks to avoid the complaint by showing that
the constitution of appellant requires an applicant to be
initiated within 60 days after his medical examination, and
that Cox was not initiated within that time, and that the
medical examination of the applicant must be approved by
the grand medical examiner before he can receive a beneficiary certificate; that said examiner disapproved Cox's
application, *for the reason* that he was not initiated within
60 days after the examination. This paragraph also sets
out certain sections of the constitution, and has, as exhibits,
copies of Cox's application for membership and his application for a beneficiary certificate.

The second paragraph of reply seeks to avoid this answer
by pleading facts tending to show a waiver of the requirement that the initiation must be within 60 days after the
medical examination, and also that the grand medical examiner has no authority to disapprove a medical examination solely on the ground that the applicant was not admitted

within 60 days after his examination. The reply pleads a number of sections of the constitution and by-laws in reply to certain sections of the constitution pleaded in the answer.

That part of the application material here is as follows: "I, William R. Cox, desiring to make application for membership in Air Line Lodge Number 409 of the Brotherhood of Locomotive Firemen and Enginemen, hereby agree to comply with all the laws, usages and regulations of said Brotherhood now in force. I understand and agree that neither I, nor any beneficiary * * * shall be entitled to participate in the beneficiary department of said Brotherhood, nor shall said Brotherhood incur any liability whatsoever to pay me or my beneficiary any sum of money whatever, by my becoming a member of said Brotherhood until the Grand Medical Examiner shall have first examined and approved this application for beneficiary certificate, and in the event that the Grand Medical Examiner, who shall be the sole judge thereof, does not approve but on the contrary disapproves this application for beneficiary certificate, then I agree to be classified as a non-beneficiary member entitled to all the rights, privileges and benefits of the Brotherhood of Locomotive Firemen and Enginemen except those of participating in the beneficiary department."

Section 61 of appellant's constitution provides, in part, as follows: "A candidate for admission shall at the time of applying for admission for membership, make application for a beneficiary certificate, in substance as follows."

Section 63 of the by-laws is, in part, as follows: "When an applicant has been duly elected to become a member of the lodge, he may be, as soon as practicable, initiated: Provided that the applicant shall have filed with the secretary of the lodge an application for beneficiary certificate of the form prescribed by the officers of the Grand Lodge, and such application for beneficiary certificate shall be in the lodge room in the possession of the secretary of the lodge, or in the hands of the acting secretary of the lodge at the time the applicant is initiated. Provided, also that an applicant upon initiation shall become a non-beneficiary member, and shall not become a beneficiary member until his application for beneficiary certificate is approved by the Grand Medical Examiner as provided herein. No applicant or beneficiary, or beneficiaries, shall be entitled to participate in the beneficiary department or in any other fund of the Brotherhood, neither shall the Brotherhood incur any liability to pay him or his beneficiary any sum of money whatever by reason of his becoming a member until the Grand Medical Examiner shall have examined and approved his application for beneficiary certificate; and in the event that the Grand Medical Examiner, who shall be the sole judge thereof, does not approve, but on the contrary, disapproves his application for beneficiary certificate, then such member shall be classed as a non-beneficiary member and entitled to the rights, privileges, and benefits of the brotherhood except those of participating in the Beneficiary Department.''

Section 64 is as follows: ''An applicant who has not been admitted by initiation or special dispensation within sixty days after the date of the medical examination required in his application for beneficiary certificate, shall forfeit his application fee and his right of admission into the lodge, and his application for beneficiary certificate shall become null and void; Provided that in case of sickness of the applicant or some unavoidable occurrence, the lodge may by the consent of the Grand Master, grant an extension of time, but when such an extension of time is granted, a new application for beneficiary certificate must be filed by the applicant under the same rules and requirements as before.''

Section 65 provides: ''Immediately upon the initiation of an applicant the secretary shall forward the application for beneficiary certificate to the Grand Secretary and Treasurer, who, after recording the membership shall refer it to the Grand Medical Examiner, who shall, as soon as practicable, examine it to ascertain the physical condition of the applicant and whether the application complies with the Constitution, Rules and Regulations of the Brotherhood.''

Section 39 provides: ''It shall be the duty of the Grand Medical Examiner to examine all applicants for beneficiary certificates and promptly pass upon the same. If the applicant possess the necessary qualifications prescribed by the Constitution, and can pass the required physical examination his application shall be approved by the Grand Medical Examiner, otherwise his application shall be disapproved.''

Section 163 provides: ''In case an applicant is unable to pass the required medical examination, or is over the age limit to participate in the Beneficiary Department, but is otherwise eligible to become a member he may be admitted as a non-beneficiary member.''

Decedent applied for membership in the local lodge and for a beneficiary certificate on August 22, 1907. He was examined by the local physician on August 22, 1907. The report of the committee approving his application was made on October 13, 1907. Notice of the approval of his application was mailed to Cox on October 14, 1907, stating that the initiations are held on Wednesday evenings and Sunday afternoons at the lodge room in Princeton, Indiana. Also calling attention to the fact that he should be initiated within 60 days from the date of his medical examination, and that he would be entitled to a beneficiary certificate after his initiation and the approval of his application by the grand medical examiner.

Cox was initiated on November 20, and on November 22, 1907, the grand medical examiner rejected his application for a beneficiary certificate, solely on the ground that he had not been initiated within 60 days from the date of his medical examination. Appellant on November 27, 1907, received and recorded the application, and on November

29, 1907, issued to Cox a non-beneficiary certificate, which he rejected and returned. He died on February 10, 1908. No question is raised as to the physical condition of Cox at the time of his application or initiation, nor as to the payment of fees and charges due up to the time of his rejection. No objection is made to his age, service or other requirements of the order entitling members to beneficiary certificates. If appellant wrongfully refused to issue to Cox a beneficiary certificate, to which he was entitled, it cannot take advantage of its own wrong, and thereby escape liability. The provisions of said section 63 make an application for a beneficiary certificate a condition precedent to initiation in a local lodge, and provide that the same shall be in the possession of the lodge at the time of the initiation. Before initiation a committee from the local lodge must pass on the qualifications of the applicant and recommend him for membership. The local physician must make the required medical examination and report thereon before initiation. When these conditions are met, the candidate may be initiated within the prescribed time, and if he has met the requirements of the laws and regulations of the order his right to a beneficiary certificate is then complete, subject only to the approval of the grand medical examiner on questions he is authorized to decide.

Appellant is a fraternal, mutual organization, not seeking profit, but the protection of its members and their beneficiaries by means of indemnity. Where this is the object, the constitution, by-laws and other writings affecting the rights of the parties are to be liberally construed to promote the benevolent objects of the organization. *Supreme Lodge, etc.,* v. *Schmidt* (1884), 98 Ind. 374, 381; *Supreme Lodge, etc.,* v. *Hutchinson* (1893), 6 Ind. App. 399, 406, 33 N. E. 816; *Schmidt* v. *German Mut. Ins. Co.* (1892), 4 Ind. App. 340, 344, 30 N. E. 939.

Section 64, *supra,* authorizes the local lodge, with the

consent of the grand master, to grant extensions of time for initiation beyond the sixty days from the date of the

7. medical examination, but in such case the applicant is required to file a new application. The local lodge had in its possession the application of Cox for a beneficiary certificate, when he was initiated, and he was necessarily present, giving opportunity for objections, and also subject to further examination. The sixty days having expired, the lodge could have refused to initiate him, and he would have been compelled to forfeit his right to a beneficiary certificate and the fees paid by him. To have proceeded further, he would then have been required to make a new application. But the lodge saw fit to initiate him, and thereby, to the extent of its authority, waived any right to a forfeiture or a new application. This action of the local lodge did not bind appellant to accept Cox as a member, for it could still reject him on account of the time of his initiation, as provided in said section sixty-four. But it could not accept him as a member of any class, without waiving this objection. Where a by-law or regulation is for the benefit of such an organization as appellant,

9. compliance therewith may be waived by it. Appellant could waive objection to the time of the initiation, or its right to insist on a forfeiture of the fees paid by Cox, and likewise its right to object to his initiation on the pending application. It could also ratify the action of the local lodge in waiving objection to initiating the candidate after the 60 days had expired. 3 Am. and Eng. Ency. Law, 1084 note 1; *Bruner* v. *Brotherhood, etc.* (1907), 136 Iowa 612, 619, 111 N. W. 977; *Supreme Lodge, etc.,* v. *Johnson* (1907), 81 Ark. 512, 514, 99 S. W. 834; *Manning* v. *Ancient Order, etc.* (1887), 86 Ky. 136, 5 S. W. 385, 9 Am. St. 270; *Splawn* v. *Chew* (1883), 60 Tex. 532; *Morrison* v. *Wisconsin, etc., Ins. Co.* (1884), 59 Wis. 162, 18 N. W. 13; *Bloomington Mut. Ben. Assn.* v. *Blue* (1887),

120 Ill. 121, 11 N. E. 331, 60 Am. Rep. 558; *Protection Life Ins. Co. v. Foote* (1875), 79 Ill. 361; *Metropolitan Life Ins. Co. v. Johnson* (1912), 49 Ind. App. 233, 94 N. E. 785.

Section 64, *supra,* provides that on failure to be initiated within the prescribed time the applicant "shall forfeit his application fee and his right of admission into the lodge, and his application for beneficiary certificate shall become null and void."

The report of the local lodge to the grand lodge and the action of the grand medical examiner gave to the grand lodge full knowledge of all the facts showing that the applicant was entitled to a beneficiary certificate, and the only objection that stood in his way was that of the grand medical examiner based on the time of his initiation. In this situation, the grand lodge was by the laws of the order required either to insist on its right to a forfeiture and reject him altogether, as provided in section 64, *supra,* or to accept him as a member and issue to him a beneficiary certificate to which he was entitled as shown by sections 39, 65 and 163, *supra.* He had met the requirements of the order as to service, age and health. The grand lodge could have elected to reject him on account of the time of his initiation, but having accepted him as a member, it waived its right so to do. Appellant is bound by its constitution and by-laws the same as its members. It could not arbitrarily place the applicant in a class different from that to which he belonged under the laws of the order. When it accepted him as a member, it did so with full knowledge of the facts, and must be held to have known that he was entitled to a beneficiary certificate.

But it is insisted that the grand medical examiner had the right and authority to deny the applicant a beneficiary

10. certificate because he was not initiated within 60 days from the date of his medical examination, and that his action justifies the refusal of appellant to issue him a beneficiary certificate.

As we have shown, the power to control the time of initiations is not vested in the grand medical examiner, but in the local lodge, with the consent of the grand master. It therefore appears that the grand medical examiner has no authority to reject an application on account of the time of his initiation, nor to work a forfeiture, nor to require a new application after the prescribed time has elapsed.

A careful consideration of the constitution, by-laws and form of application for members, leads us to the conclusion that the power and authority of the grand medical examiner extends (1) to the determination of the physical qualifications of the applicant, and (2) to the ascertainment that the application complies generally with the prescribed forms, rules and laws of the order.

As already shown, the authority to control the time of initiations is definitely fixed by the by-laws of the order and is vested in the local lodges by and with the consent of the grand master. There are no provisions conferring such authority on the grand medical examiner, and as the laws of the order clearly provide who shall exercise this power, it amounts to a denial of such authority to the grand medical examiner.

We therefore conclude (1) that the grand medical examiner exceeded his authority when he rejected the application of decedent because he was not initiated within the prescribed time; (2) that both the local and grand lodge waived objection on account of the time of the initiation; (3) that the applicant had met all the requirements and was entitled to a beneficiary certificate at the time a non-beneficiary certificate was issued to him, and the former was wrongfully withheld by appellant. These conclusions lead us to hold that the court did not err in overruling the demurrer to the second paragraph of reply to the second paragraph of answer, nor in overruling the motion for a new trial.

The fourth alleged error is not a proper assignment, but

is ground for a new trial, as the action complained of occurred at the trial below.   However, in view of our
11. conclusions as to the law of this case, it is apparent
that no harm came to appellant by reason of this
answer or the court's refusal to have it made more specific.

The answers to the interrogatories do not contradict, but
support the general verdict.   We find no available error
in the record.

Judgment affirmed.

NOTE.—Reported in 97 N. E. 125. See, also, under (1) 3 Cyc.
388; (2, 3, 5) 29 Cyc. 222; (4) 9 Cyc. 299; (6) 29 Cyc. 62; (8) 29
Cyc. 16. As to the validity of oral contracts of insurance, see 138
Am. St. 81. As to the waiver of stipulations that conditions and
forfeitures in insurance policies shall not be waived, or shall be
waived in writing only, see 107 Am. St. 99. On the question of the
waiver by a subordinate lodge of right of benefit association to insist upon forfeiture of benefit because of violation of laws of association, see 10 L. R. A. (N. S.) 136.

CAMPBELL, RECEIVER, v. MARYLAND CASUALTY
COMPANY OF BALTIMORE, MARYLAND.

[No. 7,874. Filed March 29, 1912. Rehearing denied June 20, 1912
Transfer denied January 23, 1913.]

1. INSURANCE. — *Action on Policy.* — *Proof.* — *General Denial.* —
Where, in an action on an employer's liability policy, it is essential to a recovery by plaintiff that he allege and prove payment of a judgment against him in favor of the employe, it may
be shown under the general denial that such payment was not in
good faith and that the money claimed to have been paid was
advanced by the agents and attorneys of the employe and had
since been returned to them. p. 231.

2. APPEAL.—*Review.*—*Harmless Error.*—*Ruling on Demurrer.*—
Overruling a demurrer to an answer is harmless where the facts
alleged are provable under the general denial. p. 231.

3. INSURANCE.—*Employer's Liability Insurance.*—*Indemnity Contract.*—*Proof.*—In an action on an employer's liability policy, if
the contract is one to indemnify against loss, plaintiff must show
a damage before he can recover. p. 231.

4. INSURANCE. — *Employer's Liability Insurance.* — *Insurance
Against Liability.*—*Right of Action.*—Where an employer's lia-

bility policy is a contract to protect the assured against liability merely, an action may be brought and recovery had thereon as soon as the liability is legally imposed, regardless of whether any actual loss or damage has been suffered. p. 231.

5. INSURANCE.—*Employer's Liability Insurance.*—*Construction of Policy.*—*Insurance Against Liability.*—Where an employer's liability policy stated that the company agreed to indemnify the assured against loss from liability for damages on account of bodily injuries to an employe caused by the negligence of the assured, and provided that no action should lie against the company unless brought by the assured himself to reimburse him for loss actually sustained and paid by him in satisfaction of a judgment after trial of the issue, the language indicates an intention to indemnify against loss only; but, when construed in connection with a rider providing that the policy should "only cover losses sustained by and liabilities for any claims against the assured as a result of the risk specified in the contract," the policy insured against liability as well as against loss and the employer could recover thereon without showing an actual loss. p. 232.

From Morgan Circuit Court; *Joseph W. Williams*, Judge.

Action by Joseph H. Campbell, receiver of the Clear Creek Stone Company, against the Maryland Casualty Company of Baltimore, Maryland. From a judgment for defendant, the plaintiff appeals. *Reversed.*

J. E. Henley and *R. H. East*, for appellant.

Duncan & Batman and *Miller, Shirley & Miller*, for appellee.

LAIRY, J.—Appellant brought this action to recover on an employer's liability policy of insurance issued by appellee to the Consolidated Stone Company and assigned to the Clear Creek Stone Company, of which appellant is receiver. There was a trial resulting in a judgment for appellee, from which this appeal is taken.

The Clear Creek Stone Company at the time of the assignment of said policy was a corporation engaged in operating a stone-quarry, and, during the time such policy was in force, employed a number of men, among whom was Frank Carmichael. While so employed and during the life of such policy Frank Carmichael received an injury to his person, for which he brought suit aganst the Clear Creek Stone Company, and recovered a judgment in the sum of $2,500, which was appealed, and finally affirmed by the court of last resort. Before said judgment was affirmed the Clear Creek Stone Company became insolvent and passed into the hands of a receiver. All the assets of said company were taken under a foreclosure of mortgage, and no property or other assets of said company ever came into the hands of the receiver. The receiver brought this action to recover on the policy issued by appellee for the amount of the Carmichael judgment and interest. The complaint avers that the receiver under the order of the court borrowed money and paid the Carmichael judgment before the commencement of the action.

The third paragraph of answer admits the execution of the policy sued on and its assignment to the Clear Creek Stone Company with the consent of appellee, but it avers that, long before the Carmichael judgment was affirmed the Clear Creek Stone Company became insolvent, and that it possessed no assets from which its receiver could pay such judgment; that such judgment was not paid in good faith by the receiver or by the Clear Creek Stone Company, but that the money with which the pretended payment was made was furnished and procured by and through the agents and attorneys of Carmichael for the purpose of being paid to the clerk of the Brown Circuit Court, and that said clerk was thereby induced to enter a formal satisfaction of said judgment, after which the money was turned over to Carmichael's attorneys, who receipted to the clerk therefor, and returned said money to the person who had advanced it to the receiver. A demurrer for want of sufficient facts was filed to this paragraph of answer, which demurrer was overruled, and this ruling is assigned as error.

The facts stated in this paragraph of answer show that the Carmichael judgment was not paid in good faith before

the commencement of this action. If it is necessary
1. to a recovery by plaintiff that he should allege and
   prove that the judgment on which he bases his claim
or some part of it has been paid, then the facts alleged in
   this paragraph of answer could have been properly
2. proved under the general denial, and a ruling on
   demurrer, if wrong, would be harmless. *Good* v.
Elwood Lodge, etc. (1903), 160 Ind. 251, 66 N. E. 742;
State v. *Hindman* (1903), 159 Ind. 586, 65 N. E. 911.

If the policy sued on is a contract to indemnify against
loss, it is necessary to show a damage before there can be
   a recovery. *Carter* v. *Aetna Life Ins. Co.* (1907),
3. 76 Kan. 275, 91 Pac. 178, 11 L. R. A. (N. S.) 1151;
Allen v. *Aetna Life Ins. Co.* (1906), 145 Fed. 881,
76 C. C. A. 265, 7 L. R. A. (N. S.) 958; *Connolly* v. *Bolster*
   (1905), 187 Mass. 266, 72 N. E. 981. On the other
4. hand, if the policy sued on is a contract to protect
   the assured against liability merely, an action may
be brought and a recovery had as soon as the liability is
legally imposed, regardless of the question as to whether
any actual loss or damage has been suffered. *Fenton* v.
Fidelity, etc., Co. (1899), 36 Or. 283, 56 Pac. 1096, 48 L.
R. A. 770; *Anoka Lumber Co.* v. *Fidelity, etc., Co.* (1895),
63 Minn. 286, 65 N. W. 353, 30 L. R. A. 689.

The distinction observed between contracts to indemnify
against loss and contracts to protect against liability is
recognized by practically all the cases cited. The decision
of this case must depend on the meaning of the policy sued
on. If this policy is to be construed as a contract to indemnify the assured against loss, then the judgment of the
trial court is correct; but if it is to be construed as a contract to protect against liability, then the judgment is erroneous and must be reversed. The contract must speak for
itself. In the body of the policy appellee agreed to indemnify the assured for the period of twelve months against
loss from common-law or statutory liability for damages

on account of bodily injuries, fatal or non-fatal, accidentally suffered by an employe or employes of the assured while on duty, caused by the negligence of the assured. On the reverse side of the policy is printed a number of conditions, one of which is as follows: No. 8. "No action shall lie against the company as respects any loss under this policy unless it shall be brought by the assured himself to reimburse him for loss actually sustained and paid by him in satisfaction of a judgment after trial of the issue. * * *."

The language quoted from the body of the policy, as well as the language of provision No. 8, heretofore set out, would seem to indicate that the purpose of the contract was to indemnify the assured against loss and not to protect it against liability. A number of cases has been called to the attention of the court in which policies containing similar provisions to those quoted have been construed and held to be contracts for indemnity against loss. *O'Connell* v. *New York, etc., R. Co.* (1905), 187 Mass. 272, 72 N. E. 979; *Allen* v. *Aetna Life Ins. Co., supra; Carter* v. *Aetna Life Ins. Co., supra; Stenbom* v. *Brown-Corliss Engine Co.* (1909), 137 Wis. 564, 119 N. W. 308; 20 L. R. A. (N. S.) 956.

The case of *Sanders* v. *Frankfort Marine, etc., Co.* (1904), 72 N. H. 485, was one in which a policy containing similar provisions was construed, and held to constitute a contract for protection against liability, but this case seems to be out of line with the current of authority, and we are not inclined to follow it.

If the contract in question were to be construed solely from a consideration of the provisions heretofore referred to, and in the light of the authorities cited, we should have no doubt as to its meaning; but the policy in this case carries a slip or rider, which, to the mind of the court, materially affects its meaning. The slip referred to is as follows: "This policy shall only cover losses sustained by and liabilities for any claims against the assured as a result of the risk specified in the contract or contracts hereto attached, and is issued and accepted upon the condition that all the provisions printed on the slip, or slips attached to this policy are accepted and shall be fulfilled by the assured as part of this contract as fully as if they were recited at length over the signatures hereto affixed.''

In attaching this slip to the policy, the parties no doubt intended to modify in some manner the force and effect of the language of the policy. This slip seems to have the effect so to modify the body of the policy and condition No. 8 as to make the policy cover not only *losses sustained by the assured,* but also *liabilities for any claims against the assured.* If the language of the slip is to be given any meaning at all, it must have the effect stated; and it certainly will not be presumed that the parties took the trouble to attach a slip to the policy without intending thereby to change its effect. By virtue of the slip, the policy sued on was made to cover liabilities against the assured as well as losses. The plaintiff may recover on this policy under the authority of the cases cited without showing an actual loss. It is sufficient if he show that a liability has become legally fixed.

Judgment reversed, with directions to grant a new trial and to sustain a demurrer to the third paragraph of answer.

Felt, C. J., Myers, Hottell and Ibach, JJ., concur, Adams, J., dissents.

DISSENTING OPINION.

ADAMS, J.—I am unable to join my associates in holding the contract sued on to be one of insurance against liability as well as against loss. I am thus impelled, not from any erroneous statement of the law contained in the majority opinion, but from a fair construction of the provisions of the policy itself, and the slip attached thereto. The policy is clearly one of insurance against loss, and does not raise a liability against appellee until there has been a loss to the assured.

By condition No. 8 it is expressly provided that no action shall lie unless brought by the assured himself to reimburse him for loss actually sustained and paid.   This slip is shown to have been attached to the policy four days after its execution, and must be considered in connection with the policy.   Manifestly it is not a separate contract of insurance in itself, although the majority opinion gives it that effect.

To hold that the slip by its terms enlarges the engagements of appellee would be doing violence to the plain meaning of its words, which imply a limitation, rather than an enlargement of appellee's liability on its contract of insurance.   The slip provides that "this policy shall *only* cover losses sustained by and liabilities for any claims against the assured as' a result of the risk specified in the contract or contracts hereto attached."   What is the risk specified in the contract attached?   Undeniably it is the risk arising from a loss, which is the only risk assumed.

As I read the policy, with the conditions attached, it is not one for liability insurance, and the reference to liability set out on the slip can have no meaning or application, unless it is held to raise a new and different contract between the parties, and one wholly at variance with the terms of the policy.

In my opinion, the judgment shou'd be affirmed.

NOTE.—Reported in 97 N. E. 1026, 1028.   See, also, under (2) 31 Cyc. 358; (3, 4) 25 Cyc. 224 f. Anno.; (5) 25 Cyc. 224 d. Anno.

I. F. Force Handle Company *v.* Hisey.

[No. 7,152. Filed November 23, 1911. Rehearing denied January 25, 1912. Transfer denied January 23, 1913.]

1. Master and Servant.—*Injury to Servant.—Complaint.—Sufficiency.*—In a servant's action for personal injuries, a complaint alleging that plaintiff was employed as a common laborer in and about defendant's factory, and that while so employed, and while he was engaged in his duties as such common laborer, and while he was so standing in the yards of said defendant, he was injured through the negligence of defendant, is not insufficient on the ground that it does not show that plaintiff at the time of his injury was acting in the line of his duty as an employe of defendant, or that defendant owed him any duty, since the word "duties" refers to any work which his employment required him to perform as common labor, and the word "so," in the allegation that the injury occurred while he was "so" standing in the yards, refers back to the statement that he was engaged in his duties. p. 239.

2. Master and Servant.—*Injury to Servant.—Place of Work.—Duty of Master.—Complaint.—Necessary Allegations.*—Where the relation of master and servant exists, the law imposes on the master the general duty to furnish the servant a reasonably safe place in which to perform his work, so that a complaint in a servant's action for personal injuries, showing that the relation of master and servant existed at the time of the injury and that the servant was performing the work which he was employed to do, need not specifically aver that the masterial duty was owing to him; but the allegation of facts showing the existence of such duty is necessary where the complaint discloses that the servant's employment required him to do a particular work in a particular place, and that at the time of the injury he was not in such place, but in a different one where the performance of the particular work could not have called him. p. 240.

3. Master and Servant.—*Injury to Servant.—Existence of Relation.—Complaint.*—The statement in a complaint for injuries to a servant, that plaintiff was in the employ of defendant as a common laborer, fixes the relation of master and servant, and sufficiently shows the existence of the legal duty owing to plaintiff by defendant to use ordinary care to furnish him a reasonably safe place in which to work, and reasonably safe appliances with which to work. *South Bend, etc., Plow Co. v. Cissne* (1905), 35 Ind. App. 373, is overruled. p. 242.

4. TRIAL.—*Verdict.—Answers to Interrogatories.*—On a motion for judgment on answers to interrogatories notwithstanding the general verdict, all reasonable intendments are taken in favor of the general verdict, and no intendments are made in favor of the moving party, and, in order to grant such motion, the special findings must be in such conflict with the general verdict that the two cannot be reconciled. p. 242.

5. MASTER AND SERVANT.—*Injury to Servant.—Verdict.—Answers to Interrogatories.*—In an action by a servant for injuries sustained by the breaking of a defective link in a chain used by defendant in moving a car, the general verdict for plaintiff amounted to a finding that the defect would have been apparent to one making a reasonably careful inspection of the chain, and one with knowledge of which defendant was chargeable, and answers to interrogatories showing that the link was defective because of imperfect weld, that a slight darkness in it at one point of the weld was the only thing to indicate any imperfections in the link or to distinguish its appearance from any other link in the chain, are not inconsistent with such general verdict, since it cannot be said therefrom that an inspection would have been useless, nor that the defect was a hidden one which defendant could not have discovered by the exercise of proper care, nor that the accident was inevitable and one which defendant could not anticipate. p. 243.

6. MASTER AND SERVANT.—*Injury to Servant.—Assumption of Risk. —Instructions.*—Where the complaint, in a servant's action for personal injuries, alleged facts sufficient to constitute a cause of action and showing nonassumption of risk, an instruction that if plaintiff has proved the material allegations thereof by a preponderance of the evidence, he is entitled to a verdict, provided the evidence does not show that he was guilty of contributory negligence, was not erroneous on the ground that it omitted the question of assumption of risk by plaintiff, and especially where the jury was fully informed on that subject by other instructions. p. 246.

7. MASTER AND SERVANT.—*Injury to Servant.—Assumption of Risk. —Negligence of Master.—Instructions.*—An instruction, that while a servant assumes the ordinary risks incident to his master's business, in which he is engaged, he does not assume those risks occasioned by the master's negligence, unless such risks were occasioned by defects of which the servant had knowledge, or of which he is chargeable with knowledge, is correct. p. 246.

8. MASTER AND SERVANT.—*Injury to Servant.—Knowledge of Defect.—Instructions.*—Where the complaint in a servant's action for personal injuries, caused by the breaking of a chain, charged that the chain was defective and also that it was not sufficient

to stand the strain to which it was put and for which it was used, and the law governing the necessity of showing knowledge of the danger on the master's part was sufficiently stated to the jury, an instruction that if plaintiff has proved by a preponderance of the evidence either of such allegations, and if under the evidence he is otherwise entitled to recover, and was not guilty of contributory negligence and had not assumed the risk, he has made a case, is not open to the objection that the element of knowledge or means of knowledge on defendant's part is ignored. p. 247.

9. TRIAL.—*Instructions.—Construction.*—Instructions should all be construed together and not separately. p. 247.

10. TRIAL.—*Instructions.—Assumption of Facts.*—An instruction in a personal injury action, that if the jury finds for plaintiff, it becomes its duty to assess his damages at such sum as the evidence relating thereto shows him to be entitled, not exceeding the sum of $15,000, and that the elements of damage which the jury may consider consist of all the effects of the injury complained of, if any, as shown by the evidence relating thereto, is not objectionable as assuming the truth of facts in issue, or that certain facts have been proved. p. 248.

From Clark Circuit Court; *Harry C. Montgomery,* Judge.

Action by Edward F. Hisey against the I. F. Force Handle Company. From a judgment for plaintiff, the defendant appeals. *Affirmed.*

Elmer E. Stevenson, Stannard & Howard and *Jewett & Jewett,* for appellant.

Stotsenburg & Weathers and *George H. Voigt,* for appellee.

IBACH, J.—This is a suit commenced in the Floyd Circuit Court by appellee against appellant, a corporation operating a factory at New Albany, Indiana, to recover damages for personal injuries alleged to have been sustained while in its employ, and caused by its negligence. On request of appellee, the venue was changed to Clark county.

The amended complaint is in a single paragraph, and, omitting the formal parts, states "that on the 23d day of June, 1905, the plaintiff was in the employ of said defendant as a common laborer, in and about its factory; that on said day, while this plaintiff was so employed, and while he

was engaged in his duties, as such common laborer, and
while he was in the yards of said defendant, this plaintiff
was injured by the negligence of the defendant as hereinafter set out; that on said date, and prior to the time of this
plaintiff's injury, said defendant rigged up a rope, which
was fastened at one end to a freight car standing on a switch
controlled by the defendant, and the other end was attached to the drum of the engine; that said rope about the
middle of its length ran through a pulley or tackle block
fastened by a chain to a post, in such a way as to make said
rope in the shape of a right angle, and in such way as to
put the strain of said engine and of the load attached to the
other end of the rope, when said engine was started, on the
chain; that said rope was so rigged for the purpose of moving said car on said switch; that said chain, with which said
pulley was fastened to said rope, was old, rusted, defective
and insufficient to stand said strain, all of which was then
and there well known to the said defendant in ample time to
either repair said chain, or furnish another and sufficient
one in its place, or to warn this plaintiff of the danger, but
notwithstanding the same was well known to the defendant,
said defendant then and there negligently used the said
chain for said purpose; that the defective and insufficient
condition of said chain was unknown to this plaintiff; that
while said plaintiff was so standing in the yards of said
defendant's factory, said defendant started said engine,
thereby tightening the said rope, and thereupon said chain,
by reason of and as a result of said defective condition suddenly and without any warning, broke and said chain, rope
and block, on account of being released, were thrown with
great force and violence against and around the body of
the plaintiff, causing the plaintiff thereby to be thrown with
great force and violence to the ground." It is further
averred that on account of his said injuries, caused wholly
by defendant's negligence, plaintiff is permanently crippled.

A demurrer to the complaint for want of facts was overruled, to which ruling appellant excepted. The cause was put at issue by an answer in denial, and a further answer in which was pleaded the statute of limitations. Trial by jury resulted in a general verdict for appellee in the sum of $5,000. The jury also returned special findings of facts in the form of answers to interrogatories submitted to it. Appellant moved for judgment on the answers to interrogatories, which motion was overruled, likewise its motion for a new trial, and judgment was rendered for appellee on the general verdict.

Errors relied on for reversal are that the complaint does not state facts sufficient to constitute a cause of action, overruling the demurrer to the amended complaint, overruling the motion for judgment on the answers to interrogatories and special findings of facts notwithstanding the general verdict, and overruling the motion for a new trial.

Appellant's counsel claim that the amended complaint does not state a cause of action, as no facts are alleged showing that appellee at the time he was injured was act-

1. ing in the line of his duty as an employe of appellant, or that appellant owed him any duty. They argue that the allegation of the complaint on this point, in the following words, is only the conclusion of the pleader: "That on said day, while this plaintiff was so employed, and while he was engaged in his duties as such common laborer, and while he was in the yards of said defendant, this plaintiff was injured by the negligence of the defendant as hereinafter set out." They insist that it is nowhere shown what appellee was doing, all that is alleged as to his employment being that he "was in the employ of said defendant as a common laborer in and about said factory," and that in spite of the later allegation that the accident occurred "while plaintiff was so standing in the yards of said defendant's factory," still the complaint is absolutely silent as to facts showing why he was there. They urge that it is not sufficient to allege in general terms that it was the duty

of a plaintiff or a defendant to do or not to do a certain thing, but that the facts must be alleged from which a duty may be inferred, for, charging that it was the duty of plaintiff or defendant to do a certain thing is the averment of a mere conclusion of law.

But it seems to us that, on a reasonable construction, the complaint in the present case is sufficient. From the allegations objected to by appellant as being general, it appears that appellee was employed as a common laborer in and about appellant's factory, and that at the time he was injured he was engaged in his duties as such in the yards of the factory. Here the word "duties" refers to any work which his employment required him to perform as a common laborer. A later allegation is that the injury occurred while he was "so" standing in the yards, the word "so" seemingly being used by the pleader to refer back to the statement that he was engaged in his duties. It is true that it nowhere appears from a specific allegation what was the particular task embraced under the head of common labor, which appellee was performing.

A complaint by a servant seeking to hold his master liable for an injury received by him on account of the failure on the part of the master to furnish him a safe place in 2. which to work must aver facts which show that at the time he was injured the relation of master and servant existed between them. When such facts appear, the law at once imposes the general duty on the master to furnish to the servant a reasonably safe place in which to perform his work. In addition to this, however, it must be made to appear, from the facts averred, that at the time of his injury he was in a place where the master owed such duty to him. This may be made to appear by an allegation that at the time he received the injury complained of he was actually engaged in the duties to which he had been assigned by his master. So when the allegations of the complaint show that the servant when he received the injury complained of was performing the work which he was employed to do, this will be held to be a sufficient averment that he was rightfully at the place where he was injured. Where it appears from a complaint that the employment of the servant required him to perform a particular work, and that the performance of such work required him to be in a particular place, if it further appears from such complaint that when he received the injury complained of he was not in that particular place, but in a different one, where the performance of the particular work could not have called him, then such a complaint would not be good unless it contained additional facts showing that the master owed him a duty while at the place where the injury actually occurred. Such is, in effect, the holding in the case of *Pittsburgh, etc., R. Co.* v. *Lightheiser* (1904), 163 Ind. 247, 71 N. E. 218, 71 N. E. 660. In the case now under consideration it does not appear that the work which appellee was directed to do compelled him to be in any particular place, and it does not appear affirmatively from the complaint that he was at any place where the work which he was employed to do did not require him to be. It was therefore only necessary in order to show a duty owing by his master to appellee to allege such facts as show that at the time he was injured he was engaged in the work assigned to him by the master. The allegations that appellee was employed as a common laborer in and about appellant's factory, and was engaged in his duties as such in the yards of such appellant, fully show that he was where he had a right to be, for, the place and the character of his work and the reason why he was in the place where he was injured are alleged with sufficient particularity. This holding is supported by the holdings in *Pittsburgh, etc., R. Co.* v. *Rogers* (1910), 45 Ind. App. 230, 87 N. E. 28; *Cleveland, etc., R. Co.* v. *Morrey* (1909), 172 Ind. 513, 88 N. E. 932; and *Cleveland, etc., R. Co.* v. *Heineman* (1910), 46 Ind. App. 388, 90 N. E. 899.

VOL. 52—16

The statement in the complaint, that appellee was in the employ of appellant as a common laborer, fixes the relation
of master and servant, and thus sufficiently shows the
3. existence of a legal duty owed to appellee by appellant, namely, to use ordinary care to furnish him a
reasonably safe place in which to work, and reasonably safe appliances with which to work. As the place of his employment is alleged to be in and about his master's factory, his master must use reasonable care to make this place reasonably safe for him. The law imposes this duty on the master, and it is unnecessary specifically to allege its existence in the complaint. We therefore hold the complaint sufficient to withstand demurrer for want of facts.

Appellant's counsel base their argument for the insufficiency of the complaint mainly on the decision in the case of *South Bend, etc., Plow Co.* v. *Cissne* (1905), 35 Ind. App. 373, 74 N. E. 282. On the authority of that case the complaint in the present case would clearly be insufficient to withstand demurrer for want of facts, and in so far as the opinion in the present case is in conflict with the decision in the case of *South Bend, etc., Plow Co.* v. *Cissne, supra,* that case is expressly overruled.

In the case of *McCoy* v. *Kokomo R., etc., Co.* (1902), 158 Ind. 662, 64 N. E. 92, the court discussed very fully the
general principles governing a judgment on answers
4. to interrogatories notwithstanding a general verdict, and a portion of the opinion in that case was quoted
with approval in the case of *Harmon* v. *Foran* (1911), 48 Ind. App. 262, 94 N. E. 1050, 95 N. E. 597. Suffice it to say, that in order to grant a motion for judgment on answers to interrogatories notwithstanding the general verdict, the special findings must be in such conflict with the general verdict that the two cannot be reconciled, that all reasonable intendments are taken in favor of the general verdict, and no intendments are made in favor of the moving party.

The interrogatories and answers thereto show the follow-

ing facts, in substance: There was a post planted in the
ground west of the engine, and a chain was main-
5. tained around this post, in order that the hook of
sheave or pulley could be attached thereto when a car
was to be pulled on the railroad track by the engine. The
links of the chain were made of $\frac{3}{8}$-inch metal. There was
one link defective because of an imperfect weld. A rope
passed from the engine to the drawbar of the car and
through the pulley, and defendant, by using its engine, attempted by pulling on the rope to pull cars on the track.
When the power was applied to the rope the chain broke,
because of the defective link, the rope struck plaintiff on the
legs and caused him to trip and fall. There was no evidence
as to whether there was anything in the appearance of the
chain before it broke to indicate that the link which gave
·way was defective. The link was defective because of an
imperfect weld, a portion of the inner part of it having
failed to unite where the parts of the metal of which it was
made lapped one on the other, a portion of the two surfaces
having united and a portion having failed to unite. The
link which broke was similar in size and form to the other
links in the chain, and a slight darkness in color at one
point on the weld was all there was in the appearance of the
link to indicate that there was any imperfection in it, or
to distinguish its appearance from any other link in the
chain. The chain had been maintained around the post, for
the purpose mentioned, for from eight to nine months prior
to June 23, 1905, and had been used during that time at
intervals of about twice each month to pull cars on the
track. In so doing the defective link had stood the strain.
After the chain broke on June 23, its severed parts were reunited by passing a link of one part through the opening in
a link of the other part, and inserting an iron pin in the
opening of the first mentioned link, and thus reunited, the
chain was used to pull cars until the spring of 1907, during
which time the chain stood without breaking, even when the

same car was pulled which defendant was attempting to pull when the chain broke on June 23. Plaintiff continued to work for defendant as a laborer from June 23, 1905, until October, 1905, and did not inform defendant at any time that he had sustained any injury by the fall, mentioned in the complaint, until he filed his suit. After quitting defendant's service plaintiff drove a coal cart for several weeks, worked at the veneer mill for several weeks, at the rolling-mills, drove a grocery wagon, handled iron for the Hedgewald Iron Works, worked on a farm for several months, all before the time of filing this suit. The place where plaintiff fell was covered five or six inches deep with sawdust. There was no visible mark on his person to indicate that he had been injured, until an abcess appeared. Plaintiff had a physician, and was at the time of the trial suffering with "Potts disease." Seventy per cent of the · cases of Potts disease are caused by tuberculosis; but the medical profession is in doubt as to what is the true cause of the remaining cases of Potts disease. The case from which plaintiff suffered was caused by the injury occasioned by said fall. The chain was strong enough for the purpose for which it was used, with the exception of the one defective link, having no other apparent defect. Plaintiff had suffered with his back for some time prior to June 23, 1905, and supposed his affliction to be rheumatism, his suffering being evidenced by a pain in the left side of his back, and for several weeks in April, 1904, he was confined to his home on account thereof. Defendant did not inspect the chain when it was placed around the post.

We cannot say that these answers are in irreconcilable conflict with the verdict. Some of them are in conflict with each other. Appellee's case hinges on a determination of whether the defect in the link would have been apparent to one making a reasonably careful inspection of the chain, and was a defect with knowledge of which appellant was chargeable. The jury by its general verdict found such fact for appellee. The interrogatories and answers bearing on this point are set out below: ''(13) If you answer the foregoing interrogatories in the affirmative, state whether there was anything in the appearance of the chain, before it broke, to indicate that the link which gave way was defective? A. No evidence. (14) If you answer interrogatory No. 13 in the affirmative, then state what there was in the appearance of the chain, before it broke, to indicate that the link which gave way was defective? A. No evidence. * * * (19) If you answer that the link which broke was defective on account of an imperfect weld, state whether a slight darkness in color, at one point on the weld, was all there was in the appearance of the link to indicate that there was any imperfection in the link? A. Yes. (20) If you answer interrogatory No. 19 in the negative, then state what, besides the slight darkness in color, there was in the appearance of the link to indicate that there was any imperfection in the link, or to distinguish its appearance from any other link in the chain? A. No other appearance. * * * (53) Did the defendant inspect the chain when it was placed around the post? A. No. (54) If you answer interrogatory No. 53 in the affirmative, state whether when defendant so inspected the chain there was anything in the appearance of the link open to ordinary observation to indicate that the link which afterwards gave way on June 23d, had the defect in it which caused it to break? A. No.''

The answer to No. 19 tends to support the general verdict. Its effect is to nullify the findings of (13), (14) and (54), which are favorable to appellant. It is clearly set out in finding No. 53 that defendant failed to inspect the chain. In this it was negligent. Bearing in mind the answer to 19, as to the existence of a small discolored spot on the defective link, we can neither say that such inspection would have been useless, nor that the defect in the chain was a hidden one which defendant could not have known by the exercise of proper care, nor that the accident was inevitable and one which defendant could not anticipate. Such being the case, the general verdict must stand, and the trial court committed no error in overruling the motion for judgment on answers to interrogatories.

Appellant assigns among the reasons for a new trial, the giving of instructions Nos. 1, 9, 13 and 16 at appellee's request. Instruction No. 1 is as follows: "If the plaintiff has proved the material allegations of his amended complaint by a preponderance of the evidence, then he is entitled to a verdict against the defendant for not exceeding $15,000, provided of course, the evidence does not show the plaintiff to have been guilty of contributory negligence." Appellant claims this instruction to be defective because omitting the question of assumption of risk by appellee. We have said the amended complaint contains facts sufficient to constitute a good cause of action, the facts alleged show a nonassumption of risk, and the expression "the material allegations of the amended complaint" included the nonassumption of risk, which must have been proved before the jury could find for appellee under this instruction. The instruction was not erroneous, and the jury was fully informed as to assumption of risk by other instructions given.

Instruction No. 9 is as follows: "While a servant assumes the ordinary risks incident to his master's business, in which he is engaged, he does not assume those risks occasioned by the master's negligence, and in this case, I instruct you that while the plaintiff assumed the ordinary risks incident to the work he was called upon to perform, he did not assume the risks, if any such, arising from the negligence of the defendant, unless such risks were occasioned by defects of which the plaintiff had knowledge, or of which he is chargeable with knowledge."

Appellant's counsel state in their brief that their conception of the law is that an employe assumes not only the risks ordinarily incident to the business, but the risk of all open and obvious dangers and those of which he has knowledge or of which he could have knowledge by the exercise of reasonable care. This is substantially a restatement in different language of the very things which the jury was told by instruction No. 9. And in instructions Nos. 13 and 19, given at appellant's request, the court fully covered all the points regarding the servant's assumption of risk. There was no error in giving instruction 9.

Instruction No. 13 is as follows: "The amended complaint in this case charges that the chain in question was defective and also that it was not sufficient to stand the

8. strain to which it was put and for which purpose it was used. In order to entitle the plaintiff to recover, it is not necessary that the plaintiff should prove both of these allegations. If the plaintiff has proved to your satisfaction by a preponderance of the evidence either of these allegations of his complaint, and if under the evidence he is otherwise entitled to recover, and the plaintiff is not guilty of contributory negligence and has not assumed the risk, and then I instruct you the plaintiff has made his case." This instruction is not open to the objection made against it, that the element of knowledge or means of knowledge on appellant's part is ignored, because it expressly states that before the jury can find for the plaintiff he must be otherwise entitled to recover under the evidence. Instructions Nos. 6, 9 and 17, given at appellant's request, sufficiently state the law governing the necessity of showing knowledge of the danger on the master's part.

9. Instructions should all be construed together, and not separately. Under the allegations of the complaint appellee could recover whether the chain was defective or whether it was insufficient, and the use of the word "sufficient" in the instruction does not raise a question outside of the issues.

The portion of instruction No. 16 objected to is as follows: "You are instructed if you find for the plaintiff it becomes

your duty to assess his damages at such sum as the
10. evidence relating thereto shows him to be entitled,
      not exceeding the sum of $15,000. The elements of
damages you are entitled to take into consideration consist
of all the effects of the injury complained of, if any, as
shown by the evidence relating thereto.'' This instruction
does not, as appellant alleges, assume the truth of facts in
issue, or that certain facts have been proven, for it begins
with the condition, ''If you find for the plaintiff,'' and the
jury could not find for him without finding that he was
injured.

There is evidence fairly tending to support the verdict,
and, as no reversible error appears, the case is affirmed.

Lairy, C. J., Hottel and Felt, JJ., concur.

Adams and Myers, JJ., concur in conclusion reached.

CONCURRING OPINION.

MYERS, J.—I concur in the conclusion reached by the
majority opinion in this case, but I cannot agree to follow
an unnecessary and erroneous path in order to reach that
conclusion.

The complaint was challenged by a demurrer for want
of facts. The statement in the complaint, ''that while said
plaintiff was so standing in the yards of said defendant's
factory,'' lends no aid, nor does it weaken the facts, theretofore alleged, tending to show the relation of the parties,
occupation and situation of the plaintiff at the time he was
injured.

The facts directly stated show plaintiff's employment by
defendant, the character of the employment, the place he
was employed to work (in and about defendant's factory),
and that while so employed as a common laborer in defendant's yards he was injured. These facts cast on defendant
the duty to protect plaintiff from the claimed injuries, alleged to have been caused by defendant's negligence. The
complaint was sufficient.

It is argued that the complaint does not show that at the time of the injury plaintiff was at a place where he was employed to work, and in support of this insistence the case of *South Bend, etc., Plow Co.* v. *Cissne* (1905), 35 Ind. App. 373, 74 N. E. 282, is cited. In that case the plaintiff was employed to propel a truck from place to place *in the factory,* and to see that the screws and bolts, which were a part of the truck, were kept "tight in place". This was the extent of his employment. There is not one word or combination of words in the complaint that can be twisted into a statement that the injury occurred while plaintiff was propelling the truck, or while he was engaged in tightening the bolt. It does appear that the injury happened while plaintiff was preparing to tighten the bolt.

If it be conceded that preparation to tighten the bolt was necessary as an incident of his employment to keep the bolts tight, it should further appear that he was in a place at the time of such preparation where he might reasonably be expected to be in the the performance of the work he was thus employed to do. The pleading is silent on that subject. What was he to do in the way of preparation? The complaint does not answer, but it is plain that when the bolt became loose plaintiff was *then* using the truck, and *there,* in the factory, "engaged in his work as aforesaid." The work aforesaid was propelling the truck from place to place in the factory. The bolt was loose, and he was preparing to fasten it, not that he was "then and there" preparing to fasten it, for it would hardly be said that he was at the same time both propelling the truck and doing some physical act in the way of preparing to fasten a bolt on it. Plaintiff at said time (January 21) of said preparation was where? In the factory? No, he "was at and near a certain pile of manufactured ware," which is not shown to be in or out of the factory, nor in a place where plaintiff was employed to work.

The majority opinion in the case at bar, holding the complaint in the case of *South Bend, etc., Plow Co.* v. *Cissne, supra,* good as to the point herein referred to, is in conflict with the rule of pleading as old as the common law, and incorporated in the civil code of this State, requiring a statement of the facts constituting the cause of action in plain and concise language. Certainty in pleading was the rule at common law. It is the rule now, and should not be unsettled. *City of Logansport* v. *Kihm* (1902), 159 Ind. 68, 64 N. E. 595; *Speeder Cycle Co.* v. *Teeter* (1897), 18 Ind. App. 474, 48 N. E. 595; *Indiana Rolling-Mill Co.* v. *Livezey* (1911), 47 Ind. App. 396, 94 N. E. 732.

NOTE.—Reported in 96 N. E. 643, 649. See, also, under (1) 26 Cyc. 1384; (2) 26 Cyc. 1389; (3) 26 Cyc. 1384, 1389; (4) 38 Cyc. 1927; (5) 26 Cyc. 1513; (6, 7) 26 Cyc. 1503; (8) 26 Cyc. 1497; (9) 38 Cyc. 1778; (10) 38 Cyc. 1657. As to the doctrine of assumption of risk and contributory negligence as affecting the right of an employe to recover for personal injuries, see note to *Brazil Block Coal Co.* v. *Gibson* (Ind.) 98 Am. St. 289; 97 Am. St. 884. On the question whether a servant may assume the risk of dangers created by the master's negligence, see 4 L. R. A. (N. S.) 848; 28 L. R. A. (N. S.) 1215. As to assumption of risk of dangers created by the master's negligence, which might have been discovered by the exercise of ordinary care on the part of the servant, see 28 L. R. A. (N. S.) 1250.

CAMP, ADMINISTRATOR, *v.* CAMP, EXECUTOR.

[No. 8,311.   Filed January 23, 1913.]

1. APPEAL.—*Assignment of Errors.—Waiver.*—Errors assigned, but not discussed, are waived. p. 251.

2. APPEAL.—*Record.—Briefs.—Sufficiency.*—Where the transcript and briefs substantially comply with the rules of court, they are sufficient to prevent a dismissal of the appeal. p. 252.

3. JURY.—*Right to Trial by Jury.—Refusal.*—Where a cause is triable by jury, the court's refusal to permit it to be so tried is error. p. 252.

4. JURY.—*Right to Trial by Jury.—Equity.—Trusts.*—Under §418 Burns 1908, §409 R. S. 1881, providing how causes shall be tried, where the complaint in an administrator's action disclosed that plaintiff's decedent was the mother of defendant's decedent, and

that the mother and son lived for many years in relations of the greatest trust and confidence, during which time the son marketed the products of the mother's land for her benefit, and deposited and loaned out the proceeds in his own name in trust for her, by reason of which the son's estate was indebted to the mother's estate in a certain sum, the refusal of the trial court to submit the entire cause to a jury was not erroneous. pp. 252, 254.

5. TRUSTS.—*Creation.*—*Creation by Parol.*—A trust in personal property may be created by parol. p. 253.

From DeKalb Circuit Court; *D. R. Best,* Special Judge.

Action by Luther Camp, administrator of the estate of Susan Camp, deceased, against Jesse W. Camp, executor of the last will of Oliver Camp, deceased. From a judgment for defendant, the plaintiff appeals. *Affirmed.*

Charles H. Bruce and *Mountz & Brinkerhoff,* for appellant.

P. V. Hoffman and *Link & Atkinson,* for appellee.

SHEA, J.—Appellant in this case was the plaintiff below. As the administrator of the estate of Susan Camp he filed a claim in the form of a complaint against the estate of appellee's decedent for rents and profits received and held in trust by Oliver Camp for his mother Susan Camp. To this complaint no answer was filed. Appellant (claimant and plaintiff below) demanded a jury trial, which was refused on the objection of appellee (defendant below). On the court's own motion a jury was called to hear the evidence and answer certain questions submitted to it, on the theory, as stated, that a parol trust was disclosed by the allegations of the complaint, tendering an equitable issue rather than one at law. Appellant duly excepted. The cause was tried, and the court rendered judgment for appellee. Appellant filed a motion for a new trial, assigning as reason therefor the overruling of his motion for a trial of the issues

1. by a jury. It is also assigned that the decision of the court is contrary to law, and is not supported by sufficient evidence, but said errors are not discussed, and are therefore waived.

Appellee makes vigorous attack on appellant's brief, as
well as the transcript filed, as not conforming to the rules
of this court. The transcript and briefs are by no
2. means models of neatness, but there is a substantial
compliance with the rules, and the court does not
feel justified in dismissing the appeal for that reason.

The refusal of the trial court to submit the cause to a
jury for trial presents a serious question. If the plaintiff
was entitled to a trial by jury on the issue as pre-
3. sented, it was error to refuse it. In the case of *Morgan* v. *Squier* (1856), 8 Ind. 511, the court uses this
language: "We think the mode prescribed for filing claims,
entering them upon the appearance, and afterwards, if
necessary, upon the issue docket, etc., is a mode of getting
them into court to receive final adjudication, as in a suit
at law."

The complaint discloses that appellant's decedent, Susan
Camp, was the mother of appellee's decedent, Oliver Camp;
that for a great number of years they resided to-
4. gether, and that there existed between Oliver Camp
and his mother, Susan Camp, during her lifetime,
relations of the greatest trust and confidence; that Susan
Camp was the owner of a large amount of real estate, the
products of which Oliver Camp took possession during
all of said years, and marketed for her, for her use and
benefit and in trust for her, and received and collected all
the moneys arising from the sale of his mother's share of
the products of said land; that the moneys so received by
Oliver Camp were by him deposited in various banks, in
his own name, and loaned by him to persons on notes and
other evidences of indebtedness which were taken in his own
name, and all of which he at all times held for the use and
benefit of his mother, and in trust for her; that the proceeds of all of said lands were at all times taken by Oliver
Camp in trust for the use and benefit of his mother; that

during 1892 he farmed 160 acres of land in DeKalb county, belonging to Susan Camp, with the agreement that she should have one-half of the proceeds thereof, which he was to hold in trust for her use; that large quantities of hay, corn and other farm products were produced and marketed; that Oliver Camp, acting as trustee and agent for his mother, performed the business of selling said farm products and live stock, and collected all the moneys received from the sale thereof, which moneys he kept and held in trust for his mother, and in his own name deposited the same from time to time in banks, and loaned the same to various persons, but in all his dealings therein he took, held, kept and handled the money for the benefit and use of his mother, in trust and not otherwise; that he received in trust for his mother during said years a total sum from proceeds of said farms of about $10,000, for which he never accounted to his mother during her lifetime, or to her heirs or representatives after her death. The complaint alleges that on account of the moneys so received and held by Oliver Camp in trust for his mother, he was at the time of his death, and his estate is now indebted to the estate of his mother in the amount of $10,600. Judgment for $15,000 is prayed.

In this case the subject-matter of the action was personal property. It has often been held that a trust in personal property may be created by parol. *Taber* v. *Zehner*

5.   (1911), 47 Ind. App. 165, 93 N. E. 1035; *Cowan* v. *Henika* (1897), 19 Ind. App. 40, 48 N. E. 809; *Woods* v. *Matlock* (1898), 19 Ind. App. 364, 48 N. E. 384; *Stanley's Estate* v. *Pence* (1903), 160 Ind. 636, 66 N. E. 51, 67 N. E. 441.

The court in *Taber* v. *Zehner, supra*, says: "It is elementary that no particular form of words is necessary in order to create a trust, so that each case usually depends upon its own facts and circumstances from which the intention of the parties to create a trust is to be determined."

It was held on facts pleaded very similar to those in the case now being considered, that a trust was created, and that the case was one of equitable cognizance.

In *Stanley's Estate* v. *Pence, supra*, the facts alleged, briefly stated, were that Stanley received certain sums of money during the lifetime of his wife, in trust for her children by a former marriage. Stanley kept the money and managed it during his lifetime, and at his death a claim was filed against his estate for the amount of money. The court held under the facts that "the trust so created was a direct and continuing one, not cognizable at law, but exclusively within the jurisdiction of equity."

We think the action of the court in calling a jury to answer the interrogatories submitted was all appellant was entitled to under the facts as pleaded. No error

4. was committed by the court in refusing to call a jury in such a case, in view of the authorities cited. §418 Burns 1908, §409 R. S. 1881.

Judgment affirmed.

NOTE.—Reported in 100 N. E. 478. See, also, under (1) 3 Cyc. 388; (5) 39 Cyc. 51. As to waiver of appeal or right of review, see 13 Am. Dec. 546.

STATE OF INDIANA, EX REL. BOARD OF COMMISSIONERS OF THE COUNTY OF MONROE, v. JACKSON ET AL.

[No. 7,758. Filed January 23, 1913.]

1. APPEAL.—*Assignment of Errors.*—*Waiver.*—Errors assigned, but not discussed, and in support of which no authorities are cited, are waived. p. 256.

2. LIMITATION OF ACTIONS.—*Concealment of Cause of Action.*—To constitute concealment of a cause of action so as to prevent the running of the statute, of limitations, some trick or artifice must be employed to prevent inquiry or elude investigation, or which is calculated to mislead and hinder the party who has the cause of action from obtaining information, by the use of ordinary diligence, that a right of action exists, and the acts relied on must be of an affirmative character and fraudulent. p. 258.

3. LIMITATION OF ACTIONS.—*Concealment of Cause of Action.— Entries on Public Records.—Special Findings.—Sufficiency.*—In an action by the state on relation of the board of county commissioners against a former official and the sureties on his bond to recover money wrongfully appropriated, special findings, showing that an entry had been made by the board of commissioners authorizing the dismissal of a former action for the recovery of such money, stating that it had been compromised and settled, and showing its dismissal, and findings showing that nothing had ever been paid pursuant to such compromise, and that the persons constituting the board of commissioners at the time of the latter action had no knowledge of the indebtedness until shortly before bringing the action, were insufficient to show a concealment of the cause of action so as to avoid the statute of limitations pleaded by such sureties. pp. 259, 260.

4. LIMITATION OF ACTIONS.—*Concealment of Cause of Action.— Knowledge of Existence of Cause of Action.—Board of County Commissioners.*—Where a board of county commissioners had knowledge of the existence of an indebtedness to the county, the subsequent change in the personnel of the board could not affect the question of knowledge thereof by the board, since such board is a perpetual body not affected by changes in its membership. p. 259.

5. LIMITATION OF ACTIONS.—*Concealment of Cause of Action.— Entries on Public Records.*—Entries on public records, that may tend to mislead, cannot of themselves constitute a concealment of a cause of action, where, on investigation, such records reveal facts showing that such cause of action does exist. p. 259.

6. LIMITATION OF ACTIONS.—*Concealment of Cause of Action.— Burden of Proof.*—One who alleges and relies on concealment to avoid the statute of limitations has the burden of proving same. p. 259.

7. LIMITATION OF ACTIONS.—*Concealment of Cause of Action.— Special Findings.*—Special findings, to be sufficient to avoid the statute of limitations on the ground of concealment, should show such concealment as an ultimate fact, or it must appear therefrom as a necessary inference from the facts found. p. 259.

8. TRIAL.—*Special Findings.—Failure to Find Material Fact.— Effect.*—Where a special finding of facts is made, the failure to find a material fact is the equivalent of finding such fact against the party having the burden of proving the same. p. 260.

9. APPEAL.—*Review.—Exceptions to Conclusions of Law.—Admissions.*—An exception to the conclusions of law concedes, for the purpose of the exception, that the facts are fully and correctly found. p. 260.

From Monroe Circuit Court; *Rufus H. East*, Special Judge.

Action by the State of Indiana, on the relation of the Board of Commissioners of the County of Monroe, against James W. Jackson and others. From a judgment in favor of certain defendants, the relator appeals. *Affirmed.*

R. L. Morgan, for appellant.

Miers & Corr, Ira C. Batman, Robert G. Miller and *James W. Blair*, for appellees.

FELT, P. J.—Appellant brought this suit against James W. Jackson and his sureties on an official bond to recover fees alleged to have been collected and unlawfully converted to the use of said Jackson while serving as recorder of Monroe county, Indiana. Jackson, the principal, was defaulted, and from a judgment in favor of appellees, Duncan and Farr, this appeal is prosecuted. Appellees answered the complaint by a general denial, the five years' statute of limitations and a plea of *res judicata*. Appellant replied to the special answers by general denial and by a special paragraph which sought to avoid the statute of limitations by averring that appellees had concealed the cause of action against them.

On request the court made a special finding of facts and stated its conclusions of law thereon, to which appellant duly excepted.

Appellant has assigned several errors, but those properly assigned raise the same question as that presented by the assignment that the court erred in its second conclusion of law, and appellant in its brief states that "the question involved in this appeal is whether or not the operation of the statute of limitations has defeated the appellant's right to recover against the appellees, Duncan and Farr, the sureties on appellee Jackson's official bond." Furthermore,

1. appellant has only discussed the questions raised by the exception to the conclusions of law and only cited

authorities in support of the questions so presented. Other questions, if any, are therefore waived. *Indianapolis, etc., Traction Co.* v. *Arlington Tel. Co.* (1911), 47 Ind. App. 657, 659, 95 N. E. 280; *Hoover* v. *Weesner* (1897), 147 Ind. 510, 45 N. E. 650, 46 N. E. 905; *Franklin* v. *Lee* (1902), 30 Ind. App. 31, 34, 62 N. E. 78.

The facts found show, in substance, that James W. Jackson was elected and served a term as recorder of Monroe county, Indiana, ending November 18, 1898; that during said term he taxed and collected fees and costs of said office in the sum of $1,992.10, which he wrongfully failed to pay the treasurer of said county, and converted to his own use; that in June, 1901, the board of commissioners of said county caused a suit to be commenced against said Jackson and appellees to recover the amount due as aforesaid; that appellees on June 16, 1902, filed answers to the complaint in said cause, to which appellant filed demurrers; that said cause was continued in said court; said demurrers were not ruled on, and on April 20, 1903, the case was dismissed at the cost of defendants, and judgment rendered therefor in appellant's favor; that prior to the dismissal of said cause the board of commissioners of said county, by agreement of the members thereof and the defendants in said suit, made and entered of record an order, showing that "the above cause of action having been compromised and settled, the Board of Commissioners find that the same ought to be dismissed", and thereupon ordered the county attorney to have the proper entry of dismissal entered in the Monroe Circuit Court; that no part of the indebtedness for which said suit was brought was at any time paid the treasurer of said county by any person; that in August, 1908, the board of commissioners of said county ordered an investigation of the records of the recorder's office of said county, and employed expert accountants who made an investigation thereof, and on December 12, 1908, reported to said board that said Jackson owed the county, for fees collected and retained by him, the sum of $1,992.10; that said board on December 17, 1908, made demand therefor, payment was refused, and this suit was begun on December 23, following said demand; that the individual members of the board of commissioners, as constituted on December 12, 1908, first learned of said indebtedness on the filing of said report, as aforesaid.

The court stated as its conclusions of law (1) that appellant is entitled to recover against Jackson, the principal on the bond, the sum of $1,992.10, with six per cent interest from November 18, 1908, and costs of suit; (2) that appellant's cause of action is barred by the five years' statute of limitations as to appellees, Duncan and Farr, and they are entitled to recover costs. Appellant does not deny that the statute of limitations has barred a recovery from appellees, unless the cause of action was concealed by them so as to prevent the running of the statute of limitations until the filing of the report of the expert accountants in December, 1908.

To constitute concealment of a cause of action within the meaning of the statute, it must be alleged and proved that some trick or artifice has been employed to prevent inquiry or elude investigation, or calculated to mislead and hinder the party who has the cause of action from obtaining information, by the use of ordinary diligence, that a right of action exists.

2.

The acts relied on must be of an affirmative character, calculated to prevent a discovery of the cause of action by the person in whose favor it exists. Mere silence on the part of the person against whom such cause of action exists is insufficient to show concealment. The concealment recognized by the statute arises out of fraud, and there can be no sufficient showing of concealment to avoid the statute of limitations in the absence of fraud. *Stone* v. *Brown* (1888), 116 Ind. 78, 81, 18 N. E. 392; *Miller* v. *Powers* (1889), 119

Ind. 79, 89, 21 N. E. 455, 4 L. R. A. 483; *Bower* v. *Thomas* (1899), 22 Ind. App. 505, 508, 54 N. E. 142; *Jackson* v. *Jackson* (1898), 149 Ind. 239, 242, 47 N. E. 963.

The findings relied on to show concealment are those showing the entry by the Board of Commissioners of the County of Monroe, authorizing the dismissal of the former 3. suit and its dismissal in the circuit court; also the fact that the persons serving as county commissioners in 1908 had no knowledge of the indebtedness until they were informed thereof by the report of the experts.

The change in the personnel of the members of the 4. board could not affect the question of the knowledge by the board of the cause of action, for the board is a perpetual body not affected by changes in its membership.

It has been held that entries in public records that may tend to mislead, cannot of themselves constitute the concealment of a cause of action, where, on investigation, 5. such public records reveal the facts which show that the particular cause of action in question does exist. *Board, etc.,* v. *Lods* (1894), 9 Ind. App. 369, 374, 36 N. E. 772.

If it can be said that the facts relied on tend to show concealment at all, it is equally apparent that the slightest investigation of the records in the public offices of 3. Monroe county would have proven conclusively that nothing had been paid to the county, and that the cause of action, if any existed, was not terminated by 6. the dismissal aforesaid. Furthermore, as appellant alleged and relied on concealment, it had the burden of proving it.

Under the issues, concealment was an ultimate or inferential fact that must be found by the court, or it must appear as a necessary inference from the facts found. 7. to enable appellant thereby to avoid the statute of limitations. *Perkins* v. *Hayward* (1890), 124 Ind. 445. 450, 24 N. E. 1033; *American Bonding Co.* v. *State, ex rel.*

(1907), 40 Ind. App. 559, 562, 82 N. E. 548; *Taylor* v. *Cana-day* (1901), 155 Ind. 671, 675, 57 N. E. 524, 59 N. E. 20.

Where a special finding of facts is made, the failure to find a material fact is the equivalent of finding such fact against the party having the burden of proving the 8. same. *Temster* v. *Warner* (1894), 137 Ind. 79, 36 N. E. 900; *State Bank* v. *Backus* (1903), 160 Ind. 682, 693, 67 N. E. 512.

An exception to the conclusions of law concedes, 9. for the purposes of the exception, that the facts are fully and correctly found.

The special finding does not contain a finding of the ultimate fact of concealment of the cause of action nor do 3. the facts found compel such inference. Appellant had the burden of showing this fact, and its absence from the finding of facts is conclusive against appellant.

No available error appearing in the record, the judgment is affirmed.

Note.—Reported in 100 N. E. 479. See, also, under (1) 3 Cyc. 388; (2, 3) 25 Cyc 1218; (4) 25 Cyc. 1217; (6) 25 Cyc. 1427; (8) 38 Cyc. 1924. As to estoppel of right to plead the statute of limitations, see 104 Am. St. 746. For a discussion of assumption of risk on the failure of the employer to perform a statutory duty, see 4 Ann. Cas. 599; 13 Ann. Cas. 36; Ann. Cas. 1913 C 210. As to burden of proof on plea of statute of limitations, see 81 Am. Dec. 725.

COLUMBIA CREOSOTING COMPANY ET AL. *v.* BEARD ADMINISTRATOR.

[No. 7,748. Filed November 22, 1912. Rehearing denied January 24, 1913.]

1. APPEAL.—*Review.*—*Verdict.*—*Answers to Interrogatories.*—*Motion for Judgment on Answers.*—In determining whether the trial court in overruling a motion for judgment on the answers to interrogatories notwithstanding the general verdict, the investigation is confined to the complaint, the interrogatories and the answers thereto, and the general verdict. p. 262.

2. TRIAL.—*Verdict.—Answers to Interrogatories.—Presumptions.*—
To support a general verdict for plaintiff, as against the facts
found by the answers to interrogatories, every intendment and
presumption that plaintiff has proved the allegations of his complaint constituting a cause of action will be indulged. p. 262.

3. TRIAL.—*Verdict.—Answers to Interrogatories.—Control of General Verdict.*—Where the jury's answers to interrogatories are in
irreconcilable conflict with any fact or facts of the complaint,
essential to recovery, the general verdict must yield to the facts
found by such answers. p. 263.

4. MASTER AND SERVANT.—*Injury to Servant.—Complaint.—Verdict.
—Answers to Interrogatories.*—In an action for the death of a
servant by being crushed by an electric motor, allegations of the
complaint to the effect that the device for controlling the motor
was defective and that defendant placed an incompetent person
in charge of the motor, cannot be reconciled with facts specially
found showing that the accident was not caused by defects in
the motor, that a competent motorman was employed by defendant to operate such motor, but that defendant's switchman, without the direction or knowledge of defendant, or of any person
representing it, undertook to and was operating such motor at
the time of the accident. p. 265.

5. MASTER AND SERVANT.—*Injury to Servant.—Work Outside Regular Employment.—Liability.*—Where a servant employed to do
certain work, was injured while performing work which he voluntarily undertook to perform without direction, request or acquiescence of the employer, and which was not included in the
service which he was employed to perform, recovery for such
injury is precluded. p. 265.

6. MASTER AND SERVANT.—*Injury to Servant.—Incompetent Fellow
Servants.—Verdict.—Answers to Interrogatories.*—No recovery
can be had against the master for injury to a servant, on the
theory of the master's negligence in employing an incompetent
fellow servant, where the injury resulted from the act of an
intoxicated, inexperienced and incompetent servant in starting an
electric motor backward instead of forward, and the special findings show that such incompetent servant was not employed to
operate the motor and was not placed in charge thereof by defendant, or anyone representing defendant, but that he took
charge of same at the request of defendant's regular and competent motorman, without the knowledge or consent of defendant
or any person representing it. p. 266.

7. MASTER AND SERVANT.—*Injury to Servant.—Proximate Cause.—
Furnishing Employes Beer.*—The act of defendant's superintendent in furnishing beer on his own account to defendant's employes
as a reward for accomplishing an unusual amount of work, was

not the proximate cause of injury to an employe who was crushed by an electric motor operated by an incompetent and intoxicated person, who was not the regular motorman, but was in control thereof at the request of the regular motorman, without the knowledge or acquiescence of defendant, or of any of its officers or agents, and such regular motorman was not intoxicated and had not partaken of the beer.   p. 266.

8. NEGLIGENCE.—*Proximate Cause.—Efficient Cause.*—The proximate cause of an injury is not necessarily the immediate cause, but must be the efficient cause, which is the cause that sets in motion the chain of circumstances leading up to the injury. p. 267.

From Hancock Circuit Court; *Robert L. Mason,* Judge.

Action by Clarence M. Beard, administrator of the estate of John B. Gordon, deceased, against the Columbia Creosoting Company and another.   From a judgment for plaintiff, the defendants appeal.   *Reversed.*

John B. Elam, James W. Fesler and *Harvey J. Elam,* for appellants.

Eli F. Ritter, for appellee.

MYERS, J.—Appellee brought this action against appellants to recover damages for negligently causing the death of John B. Gordon.   The issues, joined by a general denial to the complaint, were submitted to a jury for trial, and a general verdict, with answers to 145 interrogatories, was returned in favor of appellee.   These answers formed the basis for a separate motion by each appellant for judgment notwithstanding the general verdict.   The overruling of each motion is separately assigned as error.

In the decision of the questions here presented our investigation is confined to the complaint, the interroga-

1. tories and the answers thereto, and the general verdict. *Consolidated Stone Co.* v. *Summit* (1899), 152 Ind. 297, 53 N. E. 235; *Chicago, etc., R. Co.* v. *Fretz* (1910), 173 Ind. 519, 90 N. E. 76.   The burden was

2. on appellee to prove allegations of his complaint constituting a cause of action, and in this respect he is entitled to every intendment and presumption as against

the facts found by the answers to interrogatories. But if
from the answers of the jury facts are shown in irrec-
3. oncilable conflict with any essential fact or facts of
the complaint, and without which there could be no
recovery, then the general verdict must yield to the facts
found by such answers, for the general verdict amounts to
no more than a finding that all the material allegations of
the complaint are true.

Looking to the complaint, it appears, in substance, that
on July 14, 1906, appellant company was operating a creosoting factory in the town of Shirley, Indiana, and appellant James Craven was its superintendent and manager, and
in charge of the work and workmen, in number thirty-six,
including decedent, John B. Gordon. The company's plant
included a building in which were located two large retorts
made of steel, through each of which was constructed a
track for railroad cars. These retorts had a capacity of
fifteen cars loaded with railroad ties, lumber or material
to be creosoted. The retorts were provided with heavy iron
doors, from which a movable track twelve feet long extended
to other tracks leading in various directions into the yard,
and over which materials to be creosoted were brought to
the retorts by means of a motor-car, supplied with power
by an underground cable. The movable track permitted
said doors to be opened and closed. The motor was equipped
with a device whereby the motorman in charge was enabled
to turn on and off the power, and to regulate the speed and
direction of its movements. On said day, and for two months
prior thereto, said device was defective, making it difficult
to stop and start the motor, of which defects appellants for
all that time had knowledge, and decedent had no knowledge thereof. The work of decedent was to move the track,
open and close the doors, and assist in moving the cars in
and out of the retorts, and to hook and unhook the cable
connecting the motor to the train of cars. On the day of
the accident, as an inducement for the workmen there em-

ployed to do an unusual amount of work, appellant Craven brought to the factory a sixteen-gallon keg of beer, and invited and permitted said employes to drink said beer at their will; that immediately prior to the accident the employe regularly engaged in running said motor and moving the cars was replaced by another employe, who was without experience and incompetent for that work, and was highly intoxicated from the excessive use of said beer; that while said inexperienced, incompetent and intoxicated motorman was engaged in running the motor and moving the cars, Gordon, in the performance of his work, unhooked the cable connecting the motor with the cars, and signaled the motorman to move it away, so that the track could be removed and the doors to the retorts opened, but instead of moving it away from the doors of the retorts, by reason of his inexperience, incompetency and intoxicated condition, and without any warning whatever, he applied the power to the motor and started it with a jerk and great force toward and against decedent, crushing him between the motor and the door, thereby injuring him, and from which injuries he died within fifteen minutes; that at the time of the accident Gordon did not know the regular motorman was not in charge of the motor, nor that the man in charge was inexperienced, incompetent and in an intoxicated condition; that the sole cause of Gordon's death was the furnishing of intoxicating liquors to said employes while they were engaged in the dangerous business of handling the motor and cars; that appellants failed in the performance of a duty they owed to Gordon by permitting the defective motor to be used; by knowingly placing it in charge of an inexperienced, incompetent and drunken motorman, and by permitting the regular motorman to leave the motor in charge of said intoxicated person.

It will be noticed that the complaint does not characterize any of the acts of appellant as having been negligently done, or that any act was negligently omitted, but assuming that the complaint states facts sufficient to constitute a cause of action, our attention will be directed to the findings of the jury in connection with the allegations of the complaint.

From a careful reading of the complaint it would seem that the pleader proceeded on the theory that the beer furnished by Craven to the employes in and about the plant was the proximate cause of Gordon's death. Other 4. allegations, to the effect that the device for controlling the motor was defective, that the company placed an inexperienced, incompetent and intoxicated person in charge of the motor, that the regular and competent motorman was displaced by the company and an incompetent person given charge of it, cannot be reconciled with the facts specially found by the jury. By reference to the answers it will be seen that the accident was not caused by any defect in the motor, for it was expressly found that the motorman then in charge of it, by mistake in handling the device controlling its running direction, ran it backward instead of forward, thereby crushing decedent between the dummy-car and the ties on the truck next to it. As to the other allegations, the findings show that Ramer, a competent motorman, was employed by the company to operate the motor, and that the company had not, nor had its superintendent or other person representing it, displaced Ramer or put in charge of the motor any other person, nor was any change made at its direction or to its knowledge. Asbury was employed as switchman, and it was his duty to unhook the cable, but it appears that Ramer, a few minutes before the accident, without the knowledge or consent of any officer, agent or other person representing the company, turned the motor over to Asbury, who, without appellants' knowledge, was engaged in operating it at the time of the accident. Decedent was employed as a doorman, and had 5. never been assigned the work of hooking or unhooking the cable connecting the trucks with the dummy-car. His employment did not include the service at which

he was engaged when injured, and which he voluntarily undertook to perform, without direction, request or acquies-
cense of the company.   Under these circumstances a recovery is precluded. *Robertson* v. *Ford* (1905), 164 Ind. 538,
74 N. E. 1; *Pittsburgh, etc., R. Co.* v. *Adams* (1886), 105
Ind. 151, 5 N. E. 187.

These answers also preclude any question relative to the
master's employment or retention of incompetent fellow
servants, or as to liability for the death of Gordon,
6. on the theory of negligence in knowingly running
the motor by the agency of a careless or incompetent
person.

As to the beer, it is found that it was furnished at the
suggestion of some of the employes in the yard engaged in
loading ties, and on the afternoon of the day of the
7. accident, which occurred about 6 o'clock, in consideration of their doing a certain amount of work on
that day.   The beer was not for the tie loaders alone, it
was free for all.   While it was bought to be drunk after
the day's work was done, it was delivered before, was opened
by said loaders and drunk before the day's work was completed.   It was not the duty of Craven, nor did the company authorize him to buy beer for any one, and no officer
of the company knew he had bought it for any of the employes, before Gordon was killed.   The beer was furnished
by Craven at his own expense, and as his own personal treat.
While the beer was being drunk by the men about the plant,
decedent was 100 feet or more away, and did not drink any
of it himself, yet he knew that beer was being drunk by
some of the men about the plant.

The general verdict finds that by reason of Asbury's inexperience, incompetency and intoxicated condition he applied
the power to the motor, and started it backward instead of
forward.   But the findings show that he was not at that
time acting in the line of his employment.   He was the
switchman, and the running of the motor was the work of

Ramer. No facts are stated in the complaint from which it can be said that Ramer drank any of the beer, nor does the complaint proceed on the theory that the furnishing of beer by Craven to the workmen, and the drinking thereof by Asbury, influenced Ramer to surrender the motor, or induced Asbury to abandon his employment, take charge of the motor and attempt to run it. The motorman, switchman and the decedent, at the time of the accident, were coemployes, and according to the findings they were not engaged in the work they were employed to do, but the furnishing of beer is not claimed to be the cause of the unauthorized engagements. Nor can it be said that the complaint proceeded on the theory that the accident happened because appellants negligently permitted conditions to exist or continue from which some injury to another might reasonably be anticipated to result, and the resulting injury was the natural and reasonable consequence of such negligence.

In actions of this character this court has held that "the proximate cause of an injury is not necessarily the immediate cause, but must be the efficient cause, and the 8. efficient cause is that which sets in motion the chain of circumstances leading up to the injury." *Cleveland, etc., R. Co.* v. *Carey* (1904), 33 Ind. App. 275, 278, 71 N. E. 244. See, also, *Pittsburgh, etc., R. Co.* v. *Cozatt* (1907), 39 Ind. App. 682, 79 N. E. 534; *Chicago, etc., R. Co.* v. *Dinius* (1908), 170 Ind. 222, 84 N. E. 9; *Indianapolis St. R. Co.* v. *Schmidt* (1904), 163 Ind. 360, 71 N. E. 201.

From the record before us it must be said that the death for which damages in this case are claimed was caused by the negligence of coemployes, and not the furnishing of the beer.

The judgment is reversed. Believing that justice will best be subserved by a new trial, it is therefore ordered that a new trial be granted, with leave to amend the complaint, if appellee so desires, and for such other proceedings not inconsistent with this opinion.

NOTE.—Reported in 99 N. E. 823. See, also, under (2, 3) 38 Cyc. 1927; (4, 6) 26 Cyc. 1513; (5) 26 Cyc. 1224; (7) 26 Cyc. 1092; (8) 29 Cyc. 488. As to the liability of an employer to an employe who volunteers upon a duty with which he is not charged, see 85 Am. St. 622. As to the doctrine of proximate and remote cause, see 36 Am. St. 807. Injury to servant in performance of duties outside scope of original employment, see 48 L. R. A. 796. Liability of master for injury to volunteer, see 13 L. R. A. (N. S.) 561; 16 L. R. A. (N. S.) 963.

GRIFFITH v. FELTS ET AL.

[No. 7,717. Filed October 8, 1912. Rehearing denied January 24, 1913.]

1. APPEAL.—*Briefs.—Omission of Error Relied on for Reversal.—Affirmance.*—Where appellant's brief does not contain a statement of the errors relied on for reversal, and does not inform the court, except by inference, that any assignment of errors is in the record, the judgment must be affirmed. p. 269.

2. APPEAL.—*Briefs.—Rules of Court.—Force and Effect.*—The rule of the Supreme and Appellate Courts requiring appellant's brief to contain a statement of the errors relied on for reversal, has the force and effect of law, binding alike on litigant and the Court. p. 269.

3. APPEAL.—*Review.—Harmless Error.—Exclusion of Evidence.—Affirmance.*—Where it appears that the trial court reached a correct result which would not have been affected by the admission of evidence which was excluded, the error, if any, is not cause for reversal. p. 270.

From Whitley Circuit Court; *Joseph W. Adair*, Special Judge.

Action by Louise Felts Griffith against Frank E. Felts and others. From a judgment for defendants, the plaintiff appeals. *Affirmed.*

Lesh & Lesh and *C. F. McNagny*, for appellant.

Eichhorn & Vaughn and *Bowers & Feightner*, for appellees.

FELT, J.—This is an action to quiet title to and obtain possession of real estate.

At the conclusion of the evidence the trial court, on motion of appellees, defendants below, instructed the jury to find for defendants. The jury returned its verdict in accordance with the instruction, and judgment was rendered on the verdict, from which this appeal is taken.

Under the established rules of this court and our Supreme Court the judgment must be affirmed for the failure of appellant to set out in her brief the errors relied on 1. for reversal. The brief wholly fails in this respect, and does not inform the court, except by inference, that any assignment of errors is in the record. The rule is definite and clear, and has the force and effect of 2. law, binding alike on litigant and on the court. *Schrader* v. *Meyer* (1911), 48 Ind. App. 36, 95 N. E. 335; *King* v. *State, ex rel.* (1911), 47 Ind. App. 595, 93 N. E. 1082; *Albaugh Bros., etc., Co.* v. *Lynas* (1911), 47 Ind. App. 30, 33, 93 N. E. 678; *Ferdinand R. Co.* v. *Bretz* (1911), 47 Ind. App. 642, 94 N. E. 1046; *Magnuson* v. *Billings* (1899), 152 Ind. 177, 180, 52 N. E. 803; *American Fidelity Co.* v. *Indianapolis, etc., Fuel Co.* (1912), 178 Ind. 133, 98 N. E. 709; *Chicago, etc., R. Co.* v. *Newkirk* (1911), 48 Ind. App. 349, 93 N. E. 860.

It does appear, however, from appellant's brief, that the relief prayed for depends on proof that a deed executed by the father of appellant's husband and placed in escrow to be delivered to appellant's husband, now deceased, on the death of the grantor, was, after being placed in escrow and before delivery to the grantee, altered by the insertion therein of a clause which changed the title conveyed from a fee simple to a life estate.

Neither the evidence set out in appellant's brief as admitted nor that alleged to have been erroneously excluded by the court tends to prove that the deed when placed of record was not in the identical form and condition that it was in when signed and acknowledged by the grantor nor that it was altered in any respect by any person.

On the issues as disclosed by appellant's brief it appears that the trial court reached a correct result, which would not

3. have been affected by the admission of the evidence excluded. Where the result reached is clearly right on the merits, the judgment will not be reversed for intervening errors not substantially affecting the merits of the case.

From appellant's brief it appears that this case falls within the above rule, and that no assignment of error, on the facts of the case disclosed by the brief, should work a reversal of the judgment. *City of Logansport* v. *Jordan* (1908), 171 Ind. 121, 133, 85 N. E. 959, 37 L. R. A. (N. S.) 1036, 17 Ann. Cas. 415; *Germania Fire Ins. Co.* v. *Pitcher* (1903), 160 Ind. 392, 405, 64 N. E. 921, 66 N. E. 1003; *Hedrick* v. *Robbins* (1903), 30 Ind. App. 595, 600, 66 N. E. 704.

The judgment of the lower court is therefore affirmed.

Hottel, C. J., Lairy, Myers and Ibach, JJ., concur. Adams, P. J., not participating.

NOTE.—Reported in 99 N. E. 432. See, also, under (1, 2) 2 Cyc. 1014; (3) 38 Cyc. 1450.

SOUTHERN RAILWAY COMPANY *v.* UTZ.

[No. 7,586. Filed May 8, 1912. Rehearing denied January 24, 1913.]

1. APPEAL.—*Review.*—*Ruling on Motion for Judgment on Answers to Interrogatories.*—In determining questions presented by an assignment of errors in overruling a motion for judgment on the answers to interrogatories notwithstanding the general verdict, only the general verdict, the complaint and answer, and the interrogatories and the answers thereto, will be considered. p. 272.

2. TRIAL.—*Verdict.*—*Effect.*—A general verdict for plaintiff is a finding that every material averment of the complaint was proved. p. 272.

3. APPEAL.— *Assignment of Errors.— Briefs.— Questions Determined.—Evidence.—Instructions.*—Although appellant's brief is an effort to disclose by the instructions that the court below tried the case on the wrong theory, the court is not required to determine such question where there is no assignment presenting error in the instructions or questioning the sufficiency of the evidence to support the verdict. p. 274.

4. APPEAL.—*Review.—Ruling on Motion for Judgment on Answers to Interrogatories.—Evidence.—Instructions.—Consideration.*—In considering the question presented on appeal by the ruling of the trial court on a motion for judgment on the answers to interrogatories notwithstanding the general verdict, the court will look neither to the evidence nor to the instructions given. p. 275.

5. CARRIERS.—*Injury to Passengers.—Verdict.—Answers to Interrogatories.—Construction.*—In an action by a railway mail clerk for personal injuries sustained while transferring mail from one of defendant's trains to another, affirmative answers to interrogatories propounded to the jury asking whether the fact that plaintiff was a railway mail clerk was sole reason for plaintiff being on the train and on the platform, and answers to other questions showing that he had paid nothing to ride, are not equivalent to a finding that plaintiff was not a passenger. p. 275.

6. TRIAL.—*Interrogatories to Jury.—Interrogatories Calling for Conclusions.*—Interrogatories to the jury calling for legal conclusions are objectionable. p. 277.

7. CARRIERS.—*Injury to Passengers.—Railway Mail Clerk.—Complaint.—Verdict.—Answers to Interrogatories.*—In an action by a railway mail clerk for injuries sustained while transferring mail from one of defendant's trains to another, the averments in the complaint that plaintiff was being carried on defendant's train in the character of a postal clerk in the service of the United States, in charge of United States mail, under a contract between defendant and the United States, were sufficient, under §4000 R. S. U. S. making it the duty of railroad companies carrying mail to carry without extra charge the person in charge thereof, to show the relation of passenger and carrier, so that a general verdict for plaintiff was equivalent to a finding that he was a passenger at the time of his injury and answers to interrogatories, showing that plaintiff was on the train solely because of his position as a railway mail clerk, are consistent, rather than inconsistent, with such verdict. p. 277.

8. TRIAL.—*Verdict.—Answers to Interrogatories.—Inconsistent Answers.*—A general verdict is not overcome by answers to interrogatories which are in themselves inconsistent and contradictory. p. 279.

9. TRIAL.—*Verdict.—Answers to Interrogatories.*—A general verdict will not be set aside on the answers to interrogatories, unless there is an apparent conflict between it and such answers that cannot be reconciled on any theory, or on any supposable state of facts provable under the issues, whether actually proved or not. p. 279.

From Floyd Circuit Court; *Joseph H. Shea,* Special Judge.

Action by Archie Utz against the Southern Railway Company. From a judgment for plaintiff, the defendant appeals. *Affirmed.*

Alex. P. Humphrey, Edward P. Humphrey, John D. Welman and *Walter V. Bulleit,* for appellant.

Stotsenberg & Weathers, for appellee.

HOTTEL, J.—This is an appeal from a judgment against appellant for $1,500 damages, rendered in favor of appellee on account of alleged personal injuries. The issues were tendered by a complaint in one paragraph and a general denial thereto. There was a trial by a jury and a general verdict for appellee, accompanied by answers to interrogatories. Appellant filed a motion for judgment on such answers, which was by the court overruled, and this ruling presents the only error relied on.

1. The determination of the questions presented by the ruling on this motion requires this court to consider only the general verdict, the complaint, the answer; and said interrogatories and the answers thereto.

2. The only answer being a general denial, it need not be considered, and the general verdict is a finding that every material averment of the complaint was proven.

The complaint is lengthy, and inasmuch as its sufficiency is not questioned, we will set out only the substance of such averments as we deem necessary to an understanding of the case and a consideration of the question presented by the motion.

After the averments showing that defendant is a corporation, the complaint alleges that as such it controlled and operated a main line of railroad from the city of Louisville to the city of St. Louis, and also another line known as the "Evansville Branch," running between the city of Huntingburg, Indiana, on the main line, and the city of Evansville; that on December 12, 1906, it ran and operated over both its main line and said branch passenger and freight trains between said cities, as a common carrier of passengers, freight, baggage and United States mail. Then follow averments alleging in detail the operation by appellant of train No. 3 over its branch, and train No. 23 over its main line; the existence of an arrangement or agreement between appellant and the United States Government by which appellant was carrying the United States mail over its said lines; the carrying of such mail on said trains No. 3 and No. 23 from the city of Evansville to said city of Louisville on the day of appellee's injury; the necessity for transferring such mail at the city of Huntingburg from train No. 3, on the branch line, to train No. 23, on the main line, and the provision by appellant of a platform between said lines at the city of Huntingburg for the transfer of passengers, mail and express matter from one train to the other; the employment by the government of appellee as a postal clerk in charge of such mail, together with his duties and work in connection therewith; the fact that appellee was on said day in charge of the mail carried on train No. 3 to Huntingburg, to be there transferred to train No. 23 on the main line and then carried on said train to Louisville; the arrival of train No. 3 at Huntingburg, where it stopped to transfer its passengers, mail, baggage, etc., to train No. 23; that appellee there proceeded to transfer all the mail pouches and mail matter under his charge from the mail car on train No. 3 to the mail car on train No. 23, and that while performing said duty he was injured as set out. In connection with the

manner in which appellee received his injury, details of the
employment by appellant of its baggage man on train No.
3 and his duties and work as such baggage man are averred,
viz., that he was in charge of the baggage and express matter
carried on said train No. 3, and that it was his duty to assist
in loading and unloading said express car so situate in said
train; that while appellee was performing his said duty of
transferring said mail from train No. 3 to train No. 23, and
while passing along said platform, as he was compelled to
do, and while passing the express and baggage car, in
charge of E. F. Shawler, baggage man, and servant of appellant, and while using due care and caution, and while
appellee was in the proper discharge of his duties, and without any fault or negligence on his part, said E. F. Shawler
in unloading the baggage and express matter from the
express car of the appellant, and while in the discharge of
his duties, carelessly and negligently threw a heavy piece
of iron from the baggage and express car, striking appellee
on the head, thereby injuring him, etc.

Appellant insists that this case was tried by the lower
court on the theory "that when a person is commissioned as
a postal clerk or mail agent to handle United States mail on
railroad trains, such person becomes a passenger *ipso facto*
on such railroad, and the railroad has nothing to say either
to create or prevent such relation."

Numerous instructions given and refused by the court
are copied into appellant's brief and commented on to support this contention. In fact, the brief in the main
3. is an effort to disclose by the instructions that the
court below tried the case on such alleged wrong
theory. It is not necessary that we should express any
opinion as to the theory on which the case was tried as disclosed by said instructions or the evidence. It is sufficient
to say, in this connection, that if the instructions were erroneous, or the evidence insufficient to support the verdict,

the law makes plain the manner and method of obtaining a consideration of said questions by this court.

In considering the question presented by the ruling on the motion for judgment on the answers to the interrogatories, this court will look neither to the instructions
4. nor to the evidence. But, appellant insists that this same alleged error was carried into the ruling of the court on the motion for judgment on the answers to the interrogatories, in that said answers show (we quote
5. from appellant's brief) "only that a mail clerk was injured, which means no more than that a traveling man or drummer was injured * * *, that plaintiff at the time of his injury was not a passenger, and that the relation of passenger and carrier did not exist, and therefore no recovery could be had under the complaint." Appellant bases this contention practically on the answers of the jury to interrogatories 7, 8, 9, 10 and 21 which are as follows: "(7) Did the plaintiff ride on train number three at the time in question for the *sole* reason that he was a railway postal clerk in the service of the United States? A. Yes. (8) Did the plaintiff ride on train number twenty-three at the time in question for the *sole* reason that he was a railway postal clerk in the service of the United States? A. Yes. (9) Was the plaintiff on the station platform at Huntingburg at the time he was injured for the *sole* reason that he was at that time a railway postal clerk in the service of the United States? A. Yes. (10) Did the plaintiff pay anything to ride upon said train number three and twenty-three, and if so, what? A. No. * * *
(21) At the time he was injured was plaintiff using a platform in transferring himself *as* a postal clerk from train No. 3 to train No. 23? A. Yes." Other questions asked the jury and the answers given are as follows: "(11) Was there any contract between the defendant and the United States or its postal authorities under which the mail was

being carried on train No. 3 and No. 23 at the time and place in question? A. Yes. * * * (22) At the time he was injured was the plaintiff using a platform furnished by the defendant for the purpose of transferring passengers from train No. 3 to train No. 23? A. Yes. (23) At the time he was injured was it necessary for the plaintiff to transfer from train No. 3 to train No. 23? A. Yes. (24) Did the defendant furnish the platform plaintiff was using at the time he was injured for the purpose of transferring passengers and United States mails, agents or clerks between train No. 3 and train No. 23? A. Yes."

We are unable to reach the conclusion which appellant insists must follow from these answers. Great emphasis is placed on the word "sole" in interrogatories Nos. 7, 8 and 9 and it is insisted that this word, and the word "as" in interrogatory No. 23 negative the idea that appellee was on either train or the platform for any reason other than that he was a postal clerk, and that therefore he was not a passenger.

We do not think the word "reason" as used in these interrogatories imports the meaning that appellant seeks to give it, or that it was, by the jury, understood to have such meaning. Reason is frequently used in the sense of "efficient cause" or motive. These answers simply import that the only reason appellee had for being on the train at all was that he was postal clerk, that he was on no other errand, and had no other business on the train, and that the "sole" and efficient reason for his being on the train and on the platform was because he was postal clerk.

Grant that by these answers the jury intended to say that appellee was not on the train for the same "reason" that the ordinary passenger was on the train, but was there solely because his vocation or employment required him to be there—and this is an interpretation as favorable to appellant as the answers will permit—still the answers do not import that appellee was not on the train or platform as a passen-

ger, or that as such postal clerk he did not sustain the relation of a passenger to appellant. If it could be
6. said that the interrogatories in fact required the
jury to determine and answer whether, in its judgment, appellee was or was not, by virtue of his being postal
clerk, also a passenger, then they would be susceptible to
the objection made by appellee, namely, that they called for
a legal conclusion rather than a fact.

The complaint in this case contains the general averment that appellee was a passenger on appellant's said train.
The theory of the pleading, however, in this respect
7. is manifest, and it is apparent that this general averment rests on the special averments with reference to
his being a postal clerk in the service of the United States,
and in that character being carried on appellant's train, in
charge of United States mail, under the contract between
appellant and the United States Government, by the terms
of which appellant was carrying said United States mail, with
appellee in charge thereof. These averments were sufficient
to show that appellant owed to appellee at the time of his
injury "the same duty it owed a passenger riding on the
train, that the relation of passenger and carrier existed between them" by reason of the special facts so pleaded.
Malott v. *Central Trust Co.* (1907), 168 Ind. 428, 435, 79
N. E. 369, 11 Ann. Cas. 879; *Cleveland, etc., R. Co.* v. *Ketcham* (1893), 133 Ind. 346, 354, 33 N. E. 116, 19 L. R. A. 339,
36 Am. St. 550.

Section 4000 R. S. U. S. makes it the duty of railroad
companies carrying mail to "carry on any train which may
run over its road and without extra charge therefor all
mail matter directed to be carried thereon *with the person
in charge of the same.*" It certainly cannot be seriously
contended that a railroad company contracting with the
government for the carrying of United States mail does not
do so with reference to the provision of the law that requires
that, in carrying the same, it shall also carry a person in

charge of such mail, and that by such contract it agrees and undertakes to carry such person.   While it is doubtless true that the commission, by the government, of such person as a postal clerk or mail agent does not, *ipso facto,* create the relation of passenger and carrier between such person and the railroad carrying such mail at all times and under all circumstances yet, it must follow that such railroad company by undertaking, under its contract with the government, to carry the person in charge of such mail thereby creates the relation of passenger and carrier between itself and the person in charge of mail, which it in fact carries with such person in charge.   We do not understand that the appellant contradicts that under such circumstances the relation of passenger and carrier exists between the mail agent and the carrying company.   In fact, it is, in effect, conceded by appellant that where the carrying company *accepts such postal clerk in charge of mail carried by it under its contract with the government to carry such mail,* it thereby creates the relation of carrier and passenger between such postal clerk and such company, while such mail is being so carried with such person in charge thereof.   This admission, we think, is sufficient, in view of the presumptions which this court must indulge in favor of the general verdict, to prevent a reversal of the case.   Under the averments of the complaint the jury may have found, and for the purpose of the motion being considered it, by its general verdict, did find, that appellant railroad, at the time of appellee's injury, was under contract with the United States Government to carry United States mail on its two trains, No. 3 and No. 23; that appellee at the time of his injury was in the employ of the United States Government, as one of its mail agents or postal clerks in charge of the mail to be carried from Evansville to Louisville on defendant's said trains No. 3 and No. 23; that on said day defendant accepted, at the city of Evansville. United States mail destined for the city of Louisville, with appellee in charge thereof, and received and took said mail, with appellee in charge, on said train No. 3, and undertook to and did safely transport said mail and appellee to the city of Huntingburg, Indiana, there to be transferred from said train No. 3 on its branch line, to train No. 23 on its main line; that appellee, while so in charge of said mail, transferring the same from defendant's said train No. 3 to train No. 23, and while using appellant's platform between said trains, provided for that purpose, among others, was injured, as set out in his complaint. Such facts being treated as found, the most that could be said, giving to appellant the advantage of a construction of said answers to interrogatories most favorable to its

8. contention, would. be that the answers to the interrogatories were inconsistent and contradictory, but this will not permit them to override the general verdict. *Fitzmaurice* v. *Puterbaugh* (1897), 17 Ind. App. 318, 323, 45 N. E. 524; *Davis* v. *Reamer* (1886), 105 Ind. 318, 323, 4 N. E. 857; *Shuck* v. *State, ex rel.* (1893), 136 Ind. 63, 76, 35 N. E. 993. These answers when considered in connection with the theory of the complaint and its special averments mentioned herein, to us seem consistent with the general verdict, but in any event they are not so inconsistent as to entitle appellant to a judgment thereon, in view of the many and different announcements of the Supreme Court and this court, indicating the presumptions indulged by said courts in favor of the general verdict, as against the answers to interrogatories.

Where a general verdict is returned with answers to special interrogatories, the general verdict controls, unless there is a conflict between such verdict and answers,

9. apparent on the face of the record, which is irreconcilable on any theory or on any supposable state of facts provable under the issues, whether such facts were actually proved or not. *Ohio, etc., R. Co.* v. *Trowbridge* (1890), 126 Ind. 391, 398, 26 N. E. 64; *Evansville, etc., R. Co.* v. *Marohn* (1893), 6 Ind. App. 646, 653, 34 N. E. 27;

Indianapolis Union R. Co. v. *Neubacher* (1896), 16 Ind. App. 21, 64, 43 N. E. 576, 44 N. E. 669; *Shoner* v. *Pennsylvania Co.* (1892), 130 Ind. 170, 181, 28 N. E. 616, 29 N. E. 775; *Consolidated Stone Co.* v. *Summit* (1899), 152 Ind. 297, 304, 53 N. E. 235.

Many other announcements, equally favorable to the general verdict as against the answers to interrogatories, might be quoted, but enough has been indicated to require an affirmance of this judgment.

Judgment affirmed.

Shea, J., did not participate in any ruling herein.

NOTE.—Reported in 98 N. E. 375. See, also, under (3) 3 Cyc. 980; (5) 38 Cyc. 1030; (6) 38 Cyc. 1900; (7, 8, 9) 38 Cyc. 1927. On the question of the liability of a carrier for injury to mail clerk, see 26 L. R. A. (N. S.) 1058; 6 Ann. Cas. 683; 11 Ann. Cas. 882.

AILES v. MILLER.

[No. 7,935. Filed January 24, 1913.]

1. PRINCIPAL AND SURETY.—*Creation of Contract.*—*Consideration.*— Where a note is signed by a surety at the time of its execution by the principal, the surety's undertaking will be deemed to be a part of the original transaction supported by the consideration moving to the principal but if his undertaking is entered into at a time subsequent to the execution by the principal, it is a new contract, and not binding on the surety, unless supported by a new consideration. p. 282.

2. PRINCIPAL AND SURETY.—*Creation of Contract.*—*Ratification.*— Where, on borrowing money, the maker of the note told the payee that his father would become surety thereon, and subsequently to the death of the maker, the payee presented the note to maker's father, who signed same, saying that if the son had signed it for him it would have been all right, and that he would sign it then just the same as if the son were living, the acts of the father constituted a ratification of the agreement made by his son as of the date when the agreement was made, and rendered him liable as surety. p. 282.

From Boone Circuit Court; *James V. Kent*, Special Judge.

Action by Samuel Ailes against Matthew G. Miller. From a judgment for defendant, the plaintiff appeals. *Reversed.*

Charles M. Zion, for appellant.

B. S. Higgins, for appellee.

ADAMS, J.—Appellant relies for reversal of the judgment rendered in this cause on an exception to the overruling of his motion for a new trial.

The evidence shows that on February 2, 1909, Joseph S. Miller applied to appellant for a loan of $420, representing that he had immediate use for that amount of money. He said he was about to sell a carload of cattle, and would repay the loan at any time. He further said that he would secure the note, and would give his father, appellee, as surety thereon. Appellant agreed to make the loan, and at once gave Miller a check for $420. A note was then prepared by appellant at the direction of Miller, payable one day after date, and immediately signed by Miller. Appellant then asked Miller whether he (appellant) should retain the note and have appellee sign it, or should he (Miller) take the note and secure his father's signature as surety thereon, to which Miller replied: "You take it, possibly you will see dad before I will, and the first time you see him, tell him to sign the note." Appellant agreed to do this. About six weeks later Joseph S. Miller died, up to which time appellant had not been able to see appellee. A few days after the death of Joseph S. Miller, appellant called on appellee in reference to becoming surety on said note, pursuant to the agreement between appellant and Joseph S. Miller. Appellant informed appellee that a loan of $420 had been made to his son, and also informed appellee of the agreement between appellant and appellee's said son in reference to appellee becoming surety on his son's note. Appellant said he had come over to see appellee and ask him if he was then willing to carry out the agreement made by his son, and become surety on said note, to which appellant replied: "Yes, I will. If Joe had signed it for me it would have been all right. I will sign it now just the same as if Joe was living." Appellee then signed the note.

The only question presented and argued by the parties in their briefs is whether a note made under the circumstances shown by the evidence in this case is binding on a surety who was not present at the time of making the note, who knew nothing about it until long after the consideration passed to the principal and after the maturity of the note, and who received no new consideration at the time the note was executed by the surety.

It is earnestly insisted by appellee that where a note is signed by a surety at the time of its execution, the undertaking by the surety will be deemed to be a part of

1. the original transaction, and supported by the consideration moving to the principal, but if the undertaking of the surety is entered into at a time subsequent to the execution by the principal, it is a new contract, and is not binding on the surety, unless supported by a new consideration. In support of this principle appellee cites the following cases: *Bingham* v. *Kimball* (1861), 17 Ind. 396; *Crossan* v. *May* (1879), 68 Ind. 242; *Clodfelter* v. *Hulett* (1880), 72 Ind. 137; *Favorite* v. *Stidham* (1882), 84 Ind. 423; *Owens* v. *Tague* (1892), 3 Ind. App. 245, 29 N. E. 784; *Brant* v. *Barnett* (1894), 10 Ind. App. 653, 38 N. E. 421; *Wipperman* v. *Hardy* (1897), 17 Ind. App. 142, 46 N. E. 537. No one will question the foregoing as being a correct statement of the law, and fully supported by the cases cited; but we do not think the rule announced can be held to apply to the facts before us.

It is true that the principal had received the full consideration, had signed the note, and put the same in-

2. to the possession of appellant for the purpose of securing the signature of appellee long before the note

was presented to appellee. But the agreement of the principal to give his father as security on the note was not consummated until the note was actually signed by appellee. While appellee was not a party to the agreement, and knew nothing of it until the note was presented to him, such facts do not relieve him from the burden assumed. He was not compelled to ratify and carry out his son's agreement. He could have repudiated the agreement, but he did not do so. On the contrary, with full knowledge of the same, he said to appellant that if his son had signed his name to the note it would have been all right, and that he would sign it, the same as if his son were living. We think but one construction can be placed on this statement—that of affirmance and ratification of his son's agreement, as of the date when made.

We have been unable to find any case in this State where the facts are identical with the facts before us, but we think the law is well settled by the text-books and adjudicated cases in other jurisdictions. In 1 Brant, Suretyship and Guaranty (3d ed.) §24, it is said: "A principal signed an undertaking, and at the time it was agreed between the principal and creditor that certain other parties should sign it as sureties. The writing was delivered by the principal to the creditor when it was signed, and the creditor afterwards and at another time presented it to the sureties who signed it, and it was held that they were bound." This refers to the case of *Williams* v. *Perkins* (1860), 21 Ark. 18, wherein that court said: "Although the signatures of the principal obligors were procured at one time, and those of the sureties afterwards, nevertheless, in contemplation of law, their promises were contemporaneous, and formed a part of one and the same general transaction; and the same consideration which supports the promise of the one also supports that of the other."

In *Winders* v. *Sperry* (1892), 96 Cal. 194, 31 Pac. 6, the court said: "It is true, in general, that one who adds his signature to a promissory note after its execution and delivery is not bound unless there is a new consideration. But this is not that case. The execution and delivery were not complete until it was signed by appellant. But if we are bound to conclude that it had been executed and delivered as to one of the makers, there was a consideration for the subsequent signature of the appellant. As the contract was that he should sign the note, and the note was accepted only upon that understanding, the payee could have cancelled it or tendered it back if appellant had refused to sign, and maintained a suit at once for his money."

In *Deposit Bank, etc.,* v. *Peak* (1901), 110 Ky. 579, 62 S. W. 268, 96 Am. St. 466, it was held that a surety cannot escape liability on the ground that his undertaking was without consideration, because he signed the note after its delivery to the payee, where the note had been accepted on condition that he should sign it.

In *Bowen* v. *Thwing* (1894), 56 Minn. 177, 57 N. W. 468, the court said: "It is true that the agreement that the surety should sign in this case was not made with her, and until she signed she was in no way bound by it; but, as any one who executes a contract binding on its face must be presumed to do so in order to bind himself, her signing must, if necessary to bind her, be referred to what took place when the note had its inception—to the agreement then made by the principal that she should sign. In signing, she in fact carried out that agreement, and she must be conclusively presumed to have so intended when she signed —to have intended to carry out any agreement with respect to her signing which the principal, who requested her to sign, had made."

In *Smith* v. *Molleson* (1896), 148 N. Y. 241, 42 N. E. 669, the court held that where a building contract is entered into on the contractor's promise to furnish a bond as a guaranty of faithful performance, it becomes complete and binding on the other party thereto only on delivery of the bond, and the mutual obligations imposed on the parties furnish a consideration for the bond, even if it is not given until after the execution and delivery of the contract, and after the contractor has entered on its performance.

In *Hawkes* v. *Phillips* (1856), 7 Gray (Mass.) 284, it was held that one not a party to a promissory note, who, after its delivery to the payee, indorses the same, pursuant to an agreement made with the payee before the making of the note, and without the maker's knowledge, is liable on the note as a joint promisor.

Steers v. *Holmes* (1890), 79 Mich. 430, 44 N. W. 922, was in some respects similar to the case at bar. In that case, a sale of personal property was made by the vendor on an expectancy that a brother of the vendee would sign his note given for the same, of which fact the brother had notice, having been asked by the vendee if he would sign the note, and although he did not promise to sign it, told his brother he "would see about it." After the note was signed by the principal, the payee took it to the brother of the principal, and asked him to sign it, saying, "I expect your brother spoke to you about this." Without making any reply, the brother took the note and signed it. The court said on page 439: "Knowing, as he did, that plaintiff expected him to sign the note as security for the payment of the sum mentioned therein, and signing it as he did, his act furnished a sufficient consideration; and it would make no difference in his liability upon it whether he signed before or after the property passed. He would be considered in law, as well as in justice, as having placed his name on the note at the time it bears date, if that should be necessary to give effect to his engagement." See, also, *Moies* v. *Bird* (1814), 11 Mass. *436, 6 Am. Dec. 179; *Childs* v. *Wyman* (1857), 44 Me. 433, 69 Am. Dec. 111; *McNaught* v. *McClaughry* (1870), 42 N. Y. 22, 1 Am. Rep. 487; *Standley* v. *Miles & Adams* (1858), 36 Miss. 434. We think the foregoing authorities conclusively show that appellee was liable on the note in suit as a surety. The decision of the court was therefore not sustained by the evidence, and was contrary to law.

The judgment is reversed and the cause remanded to the Boone Circuit Court, with instructions to sustain appellant's motion for a new trial, and for further proceedings in accordance with this opinion.

NOTE.—Reported in 100 N. E. 475. As to when an apparent principal may show himself to be a surety, see 17 Am. Dec. 416.

CLINE *v.* STRONG ET AL.

[No. 7,789.   Filed January 28, 1913.]

1. SPECIFIC PERFORMANCE. — *Contracts Enforceable.* — Courts of equity will decree the specific performance of a contract only when it is for an adequate consideration, and is in writing, certain and definite in all its provisions, fair and mutual in its terms, and is capable of being performed. p. 287.

2. SPECIFIC PERFORMANCE.—*Contract for Sale of Real Estate.—Sufficiency.—Right to Enforce.*—A letter from a real estate agency stating that it has, from the owner of certain real estate, an agreement to accept a certain sum for same, if taken on or before a certain date, that it was obtained after an offer made by the addressee, and that the agency would be glad to hold the offer open for the addressee's account until the date specified, together with the addressee's written acceptance, and the agency's receipt for one dollar as earnest money, does not constitute a contract capable of being specifically enforced in a court of equity, since it is uncertain as to terms and time of payment and assumption of liens, and is susceptible of being construed as merely an option. p. 288.

3. SPECIFIC PERFORMANCE.—*Contracts Enforceable.*—In suits for specific performance, the equitable doctrine is that the enforcement must be mutual, and before a vendee is entitled to specific performance, the vendor must likewise be able to compel the acceptance of a deed and the payment of the stipulated consideration. p. 290.

From Superior Court of Marion County (76,511); *Vinson Carter,* Judge.

Action by Benjamin F. Cline against Wendell M. Strong and others. From a judgment for defendants, the plaintiff appeals. *Affirmed.*

John O. Spahr, James A. Ross and *Harding & Hovey,* for appellant.

Whitcomb, Douden & Stout, for appellees.

IBACH, C. J.—Appellant sued appellees to enforce the specific performance of a written contract for the sale of certain real estate located in the city of Indianapolis, and to compel the execution of a deed therefor. The amended complaint of one paragraph was tested by a demurrer, and held to be insufficient by the trial court. The ruling on this demurrer presents the only ground for contention here.

This is an equitable action, and in cases like this it has been uniformly held, and it is well understood, that courts of equity will decree a specific performance only

1. when the contract is in writing, is certain and definite in all its provisions, is fair and mutual in its terms, is for an adequate consideration, and is capable of being performed. In the case of *Colson* v. *Thompson* (1817), 2 Wheat. *336, 340, 4 L. Ed. 253, quoted by our Supreme Court in *Burke* v. *Mead* (1902), 159 Ind. 252, 257, 64 N. E. 880, the court announces the rule in this language: "The contract which is sought to be specifically executed, ought not only to be proved, but the terms of it should be so precise as that neither party could reasonably misunderstand them. If the contract be vague or uncertain, or the evidence to establish it be insufficent, a court of equity will not exercise its extraordinary jurisdiction to enforce it, but will leave the party to his legal remedy."

If we find that there is such certainty in the language of the writing relied on here as to leave the intention of the parties clear and definite respecting the substantial terms of the contract, and also the other necessary qualities are found therein, then the case becomes one for specific performance, but if such contract is in any essential particular incomplete, uncertain or ambiguous, then it will not be specifically enforced in equity, and the party will be left to his legal remedy. If this were not the rule, courts might enforce precisely what the parties never intended or contemplated. See 6 Pomeroy, Eq. Jurisp. §764; *Van Dyke* v. *Norfolk, etc., R. Co.* (1911), 112 Va. 835, 72 S. E. 659; *Krum* v. *Chamberlain* (1898), 57 Neb. 220, 77 N. W. 665; *Taylor* v. *Williams* (1869), 45 Mo. 80; *Mossie* v. *Cyrus* (1912), 61 Or. 17, 119 Pac. 485 and 624; *Wilks* v. *Burns* (1882), 60 Md. 64.

We quote from the complaint so much of it as appellant insists sets out a contract entitling him to the relief prayed
2. for: "That prior to said date, said defendant, Wendell M. Strong, engaged and employed C. F. Sayles & Company, a real estate brokerage firm of the City of Indianapolis, Indiana, as his agents, to sell said above described real estate and to procure for him a purchaser therefor for the sum of six thousand dollars, and that said agents and brokers were authorized and directed by said defendant to make a sale of said real estate and to procure a binding contract with some person for the purchase of the same, or to accept an offer of six thousand dollars for said real estate. That thereafter, to wit, on the 26th day of May, 1908, said defendant, Wendell M. Strong, by and through his said duly authorized agents and brokers, made, executed and delivered to this plaintiff the following written proposition, an instrument for the sale of said real estate, which said proposition was afterwards, to wit, on the 13th day of June, 1908, duly accepted in writing by plaintiff, and the sum of one dollar was paid by plaintiff to said defendant as a part of the purchase price for said real estate, which said proposition so made by said defendant and the acceptance thereof, as aforesaid, is in the words and figures as follows:

'Indianapolis, Indiana, May 26, 1908;
B. F. Cline, Esq.,
    City.
Dear Sir:—
    We have from the owner of lots 1, 2, 3, 4, 5, 6, in
block 1; lots 3, 4, 5, 6, 7, 8, 16, 17, 18, 19, 20, 21, and 22
in block 3; lots 4, 5, 12, 13, 14, 17, 18, 19, 20, 21, and
22 in block 8; lots 1, 2, 3, 4, 5, 6, 23, 24, 25, 26, 27 and
28 in block 7, all in Cleveland's addition City of Indianapolis, Indiana, an agreement to accept the sum of
six thousand ($6000) dollars for said lots if taken on
or before June 22nd, 1908. As this offer was obtained
after an offer made by you for said lots, we will be
pleased to hold this open for your account until this
date.   [Signed] C. F. Sayles & Co.

I hereby accept the above proposition June 12th, 08.
                    [Signed] Benj. F. Cline.

Received of Benjamin F. Cline ($1.00) as earnest
money on the above proposition, June 12, 1908.
                    [Signed] C. F. Sayles & Co.' ''

The terms of this writing, when considered as a contract,
are so indefinite and the form of the acceptance so doubtful
that it ought not to be specifically enforced in a court of
equity. We are unable to say whether the language of the
letter is sufficiently definite and certain to constitute a proposition for an actual sale of the lots mentioned therein, or
whether thereby merely an option to purchase was extended
to appellant; nor are we able to say that by the terms of
the so-called acceptance appellant bound himself, by such a
memorandum as is required by the statute of frauds, to
purchase appellee's real estate, in such certain terms that
appellee could have obtained a decree of specific performance against appellant if he failed to pay the consideration
and accept a deed. We are also unable to determine what
force or effect is to be given the receipt for $1, executed by
the real estate agents, when considered in connection with
the other writings heretofore set out. Whether such payment shows that appellant intended thereby to enter into

a binding contract for the purchase of the lots, or whether
it was paid merely in consideration of the agreement on
the part of such agents to hold the proposition contained
in the letter open for him for some days, remains a question of much doubt and uncertainty.   There are too many
details, such as time of payment, amount of payment, terms
of payment, assumption of liens, if any, and many others,
which are not within the authority of a real estate agent to
arrange for, but which are essential to show certainty in the
contract, and mutuality of the parties, which are entirely
left to conjecture, and are wholly unprovided for by the
parties themselves, so that it is not possible to determine
what was their real intent and purpose.

Appellant might contend, and such contention might well
be supported, if he himself were sued, that he never agreed
in writing to purchase the property in suit, but that his
sole intention was, when he paid $1 and accepted the prop-
osition, to obtain from the agents a number of days within
which he himself might obtain purchasers for the property
at a profit to him, as soon as he would obtain a deed to
himself therefor, or to acquire sufficient time to determine
for himself the advisability of making the purchase for any
purpose.   In short, appellant, if sued for an enforcement
of the agreement, might quite properly insist, in view of
the uncertainty of the language of the writings, that he
sought and obtained for $1 an option to purchase the lots
before June 22, 1908, and that he declined to avail himself
of the opportunity to consummate such purchase.

The equitable doctrine in such cases is that the enforcement of contracts must be mutual, and before the vendee
        is entitled to a specific performance, his vendor must
3.   likewise be able in equity to compel the acceptance
        of a deed and the payment of the stipulated con-
sideration.   *Migatz* v. *Stieglitz* (1906), 166 Ind. 361; 26 Am.
and Eng. Ency. Law (2d ed.) 106, and cases cited.

The conclusion which we have reached on this proposition makes it unnecessary for us to consider the remaining questions presented by appellant, in which he insists that the agreement should be specifically enforced, and that the demurrer should have been overruled.

While we give to appellant the benefit of all the facts well pleaded in his amended complaint, to which he is entitled on a demurrer, yet he has not set out a completed contract with that degree of certainty and definiteness which the general principles of specific performance require, for it does not appear that the minds of the parties met on the essential particulars of any contract with that degree of certainty which is necessary to enable the court to determine with any sort of accuracy what the parties intended.

The demurrer was properly sustained, and the judgment is affirmed.

NOTE.—Reported in 100 N. E. 569. See, also, under (1) 36 Cyc. 587, 609, 612; (2) 36 Cyc. 587, 597; (3) 36 Cyc. 622. As to the certainty necessary in a contract to warrant a decree for its specific performance, see 26 Am. Dec. 601; 140 Am. St. 58. For a discussion of the specific performance of optional contracts, see 1 Ann. Cas. 990; 12 Ann. Cas. 90; Ann. Cas. 1913 A 362.

PAUL, EXECUTOR, *v.* SNYDER.
[No. 7,806. Filed January 28, 1913.]

1. WILLS.—*Contract to Bequeath or Devise.*—*Evidence.*—*Sufficiency.*—Evidence showing that shortly after plaintiff moved onto the farm of decedent, he and the decedent went together to a justice of the peace, where a will was prepared by decedent by which he devised and bequeathed to plaintiff and his heirs all his real and personal property, and that at that time decedent said he wanted plaintiff and his heirs to have his property, that he loved plaintiff and his children and wanted them to have his farm, and that he wanted plaintiff to come and run it until he died and take care of him in his old age, was sufficient to warrant the jury in drawing an inference that the will was made in consideration

of an agreement on the part of plaintiff to move on decedent's farm and run it so long as decedent lived, and to take care of him in his old age. p. 293.

2. APPEAL. — *Review.* — *Evidence.* — *Verdict.* — *Conclusiveness.* —Where the evidence is of such a character that opposite inferences may reasonably be drawn therefrom, a finding by the jury of a fact, sustained by either of such inferences, is supported by evidence and will not be disturbed on appeal. p. 294.

3. WILLS.—*Contracts to Bequeath or Devise.—Breach.—Remedy.*— Where a person has fully performed his contract to perform services and board and care for another during his lifetime, in consideration of the other's promise to will all his property to him, he may, upon the failure of the other party to leave such a will in force at his death, recover as damages for such breach the reasonable value of the services rendered under such contract. p. 295.

4. LIMITATION OF ACTIONS.—*Accrual of Cause of Action.—Breach of Contract to Bequeath or Devise.*—Where a person fully performs his contract to perform services and to board and care for another during his lifetime, in consideration of the other's promise to will all his property to him, and the other party fails to leave such a will in force at his death, the breach occurs immediately prior to his death, at which time the cause of action accrues and the statute of limitations begins to run. p. 295.

5. LIMITATION OF ACTIONS.—*Accrual of Cause of Action.—Breach of Contract to Bequeath or Devise.*—Where a party who has agreed to will all his property to another, in consideration of the other's services in running his farm and providing him board and care during life, prevents performance on such person's part by so mistreating him that he is compelled to abandon his efforts to perform, the contract is terminated at the time of such abandonment and thereupon the statute of limitations begins to run against the right of action for the value of services rendered under the contract. p. 296.

From Carroll Circuit Court; *James P. Wason,* Judge.

Action by Cary Snyder against Earl P. Paul, executor of the will of Jeremiah Snyder, deceased. From a judgment for plaintiff, the defendant appeals. *Reversed.*

Boyd & Julien, for appellant.

Charles R. Pollard and *James O. Obear,* for appellee.

LAIRY, J.—Appellee filed a claim against the estate of Jeremiah Snyder, deceased, in which he alleged that he lived on the farm of decedent from February, 1897, to November, 1898, during which time he furnished board and performed services for decedent, and provided materials for the construction of improvements to the farm. An itemized statement of the materials provided, the services rendered, and the board and care furnished is set out in the claim, and it is alleged that all of the items set out were provided and furnished at the special instance and request of decedent, under a contract whereby decedent agreed to pay therefor by the execution of a will, by the terms of which he would devise and bequeath to the claimant all the real estate and personal property of which he was the owner. It is further alleged that on February 5, 1897, a will was executed in accordance with the terms of such contract, but that it was afterward revoked by said decedent, without the knowledge or consent of claimant, and that decedent died on March 4, 1909, without having paid claimant and without having made any provision by will for the payment of the indebtedness due him.

A trial resulted in a verdict for appellee. Appellant's motion for a new trial was overruled, and judgment rendered on the verdict. Several errors are assigned on appeal, but the only one presented by appellant's brief is the action of the court in overruling the motion for a new trial.

The first contention of appellant is that the evidence wholly fails to establish the contract set out in the complaint. It is true that there is no direct evidence of any ne-

1. gotiations between appellee and Jeremiah Snyder resulting in the contract alleged, but the evidence shows that appellee and his wife moved on the farm of decedent in February, 1897, and that shortly after, appellee and decedent went together to a justice of the peace, where a will was prepared by Jeremiah Snyder, by which he devised and bequeathed to Cary Snyder and his heirs all of his real and personal property. The evidence further

shows that decedent said at the time of making the will that he wanted Cary Snyder and his heirs to have his property, that he loved Cary and loved his children, and wanted them to have his farm, and that he wanted Cary to come and run it until he (decedent) died, and take care of him in his old age.

The fact that the will was executed about the time appellee moved to the farm of decedent, when considered in connection with the statements made by decedent at the time, and the services performed by appellee, as shown by the evidence, was sufficient to justify the jury in drawing an inference that the will was made in consideration of an agreement on the part of appellee to move on the farm, and run it so long as decedent lived, and to take care of him in his old age. The jury evidently did infer such a contract from the evidence, and while it is possible that an opposite inference might have been drawn from the evidence, the one drawn by the jury is certainly legitimate and reasonable. Where the evidence is of such a

2. character that opposite inferences may reasonably be drawn therefrom, a finding by the jury of a fact sustained by either of such inferences is supported by evidence and will not be disturbed on appeal. *Siebe* v. *Heilman* (1906), 38 Ind. App. 37, 77 N. E. 300; *Knoefel* v. *Atkins* (1907), 40 Ind. App. 428, 81 N. E. 600.

The statute of limitations was relied on as a defense at the trial of this case, and it is asserted on appeal that the evidence shows without dispute that the right of action in favor of appellee accrued more than six years before this action was commenced. Both parties to this appeal agree that the evidence shows, without conflict, that appellee moved away from the farm of Jeremiah Snyder in November, 1898, and that the items sued for were all furnished and provided prior to that date. Appellant contends that the right of action in favor of appellee accrued at the time he left the farm and ceased to render services or to provide board under the contract, while appellee claims that the contract to pay him by executing a will in his favor was a contract to pay at the date of the death of decedent, and that his right of action for services rendered under such agreement did not accrue until that date.

The contract, which the evidence in this case tends
3. to establish, was to the effect that Cary Snyder should live on the farm and run it so long as Jeremiah Snyder lived, and that during that time he would
4. board the latter, and care for him in his old age. In consideration of these services to be so rendered by appellee, Jeremiah Snyder was to will all his property to appellee and his heirs. If this contract had subsisted unbroken by either party until the death of Jeremiah Snyder, and if he had complied with its terms by executing his will in accordance therewith, appellee would have received the compensation for his services at that time. Jeremiah Snyder had his entire lifetime in which to perform his part of the contract, and this he might have done by executing his will in accordance with his promise, and leaving it unrevoked until his death. If appellee had fully performed the contract on his part, and decedent had broken it by failing to leave such a will in force at his death, appellee would have been entitled to recover, as damages for such breach, the reasonable value of the services rendered under such contract. In such a case the breach of contract which gives rise to a cause of action occurs immediately prior to the death of the party who has agreed to leave the property by will, and the cause of action accrues at that time, and the statute of limitations runs from the date of death. *Purviance* v. *Purviance* (1896), 14 Ind. App. 269, 42 N. E. 364; *Riddle* v. *Backus* (1874), 38 Iowa 81; *Hull* v. *Thoms* (1909), 82 Conn. 647, 74 Atl. 925.

In this case, however, the evidence most favorable to ap-

pellee shows that Jeremiah Snyder committed a breach of
the contract on his part more than ten years before

5.   his death, by so mistreating appellee and his wife as
to make it impossible for appellee to perform the contract on his part, and that, by reason of the misconduct of
decedent, appellee was compelled to abandon his efforts to
perform the contract on his part and to move away from
the farm, which he did in November, 1898.   In view of
these facts, we think that the contract was terminated by
breach in November, 1898, and that appellee's right of action
to recover for the value of the services rendered up to the
time of such breach accrued at that time.   In such a case,
the statute of limitations runs from the date of the termination of the contract by breach.   *Bonesteel* v. *Van Etten*
(1880), 20 Hun (N. Y.) 468; *Henry* v. *Rowell* (1900), 64
N. Y. Supp. 488, 31 Misc. 384; *Taggart* v. *Tevanny* (1891),
1 Ind. App. 339, 27 N. E. 511; Wood, Limitations (2d ed.)
§120.   We quote the following language of the court in the
case first cited: "The contract between these parties, if
any existed, was at an end in 1859.   The defendant's testator had terminated it with offensive language and driven the
plaintiff from his house.   There was a breach of the contract by the father.   He would not allow plaintiff to earn
the wages agreed upon.   By such breach of the contract, by
such refusal to perform, the father became liable to plaintiff for the value of the services already rendered.   The
plaintiff could have brought his action for his damages immediately."   In the case of *Henry* v. *Rowell, supra,* the
court used the following language: "It needs to be kept in
mind that this case is not like cases where the agreement
was only a general one to make fair compensation by will
for such services as might be or were to be rendered, the
amount of the compensation, and sometimes the length or
extent of the services, not being fixed by the agreement; as
in *Patterson* v. *Patterson* [1816], 13 Johns *379, *Martin* v.

Wright's Admrs. [1835], 13 Wend. *460, 28 Am. Dec. 468; *Reynolds* v. *Robinson* [1876], 64 N. Y. 589; and *Collier* v. *Rutledge* [1892], 136 N. Y. 621, 32 N. E. 626. In such cases the only breach that can occur is the failure of the decedent to leave a will providing for an adequate compensation; unless, indeed, he gives notice in his lifetime of a repudiation of the contract, and of his refusal to make compensation by will, in which case a cause of action for the value of the services rendered accrues immediately.''

No contract to compensate appellee by will for such services as he might render at any time during the lifetime of Jeremiah Snyder can reasonably be inferred from the evidence. When appellee was denied the right to perform his part by the conduct of the other party thereto, it would be absurd to hold that he would have to wait until the death of appellee to get, not what was provided for by the contract, but only the reasonable value of the services rendered.

The verdict is not sustained by the evidence and is contrary to law, and the judgment must be reversed.

Judgment reversed, with directions to grant a new trial.

NOTE.—Reported in 100 N. E. 571. See, also, under (1) 40 Cyc. 1072; (2) 3 Cyc. 348; (3) 40 Cyc. 1070; (4) 25 Cyc. 1065; (5) 25 Cyc. 1068. As to a contract to make a will, see note to *McCoy* v. *McCoy* (Ind.), 102 Am. St. 240. As to the bar of the statute of limitations in will contests, see 49 Am. St. 710. As to the running of the statute of limitations against an action for services performed in consideration of an oral agreement to compensate by will, see 8 Ann. Cas. 118.

TOWN OF CICERO ET AL. *v.* LAKE ERIE AND WESTERN
RAILROAD COMPANY.

[No. 7,494. Filed January 3, 1912. Rehearing denied May 15, 1912.
Transfer denied January 28, 1913.]

1. PLEADING.—*Complaint.—Demurrer.—Inferences.*—Where a complaint is tested by demurrer, no inferences or intendments are indulged in favor of its sufficiency. p. 307.
2. PLEADING.—*Complaint.—Sufficiency.—Initial Attack After Judgment.*—Where a complaint is tested for the first time after judgment, all inferences and intendments are indulged in favor of the pleading, and if there is not a total failure to aver some essential fact, and it is sufficient to bar another action for the same cause, it will be held sufficient to support the judgment. p. 307.
3. PLEADING.—*Complaint.—Sufficiency.—Motion in Arrest of Judgment.—Appeal.*—Where an omission or defect in a complaint is one that may be supplied by proof, and the facts alleged will bar another action for the same cause, the complaint will be held sufficient on motion in arrest of judgment, or when first tested by assignment of error on appeal. p. 308.
4. APPEAL.—*Questions Presented for Review.—Exceptions to Conclusions of Law.*—Where there is a special finding in which the facts have been fully and correctly found within the issues, and on which the trial court has stated its conclusions of law, to which the appellant has duly excepted, such exceptions will present the same question as the overruling of a demurrer to the complaint. p. 308.
5. PLEADING.—*Complaint.—Sufficiency.—Initial Attack on Appeal. —Exceptions to Conclusions of Law.*—Where the sufficiency of a complaint is attacked for the first time on appeal, and appellant's exceptions to the conclusions of law raise the same questions as are raised by the assignment challenging the complaint, the sufficiency will be tested by the rule applicable after verdict. p. 308.
6. INJUNCTION.—*Action to Enjoin.—Municipal Corporations.—Appropriation of Railroad Property for Street.—Complaint.—Sufficiency.—Initial Attack on Appeal.*—In an action by a railroad company to enjoin a town and its officers from laying out a street over railroad property, a complaint alleging the acquisition of the property for railroad purposes, and the use thereof for over twenty years, that the town acquired a strip along the railroad property and began the construction of a street thereon

and that it intended to and would construct such street over a portion of the railroad right of way, etc., is sufficient when attacked for the first time on appeal. p. 308.

7. APPEAL.—*Review.*—*Special Findings.*—*Conclusions of Law.*—Although a complaint, attacked for the first time on appeal, is found sufficient, the question of whether the facts provable thereunder have been so fully and correctly found as to sustain the conclusions and support the judgment of the trial court must be determined on the exceptions to the conclusions of law. p. 308.

8. TRIAL.—*Special Findings.*—*Failure to Find Material Fact.*—*Effect.*—The failure to find a material fact, of which the burden of proof is on the plaintiff, is equivalent to a finding against plaintiff as to such fact. p. 309.

9. INJUNCTION.—*Actions to Enjoin Municipal Corporations.*—*Appropriation of Railroad Property for Street.*—*Complaint.*—*Proof.*—In an action by a railroad company to enjoin a town from appropriating a portion of the right of way for a street, plaintiff must allege and prove facts showing that the town and its officers were acting without warrant of law. p. 309.

10. EVIDENCE.—*Presumptions.*—*Performance of Official Duty.*—The law presumes the acts of public officers to be legal and regular, and until the contrary is made to appear, they are presumed to have done their duty according to law. p. 309.

11. INJUNCTION.—*Actions Against Municipal Corporations.*—*Appropriation of Railroad Property for Street.*—*Special Findings.*—*Sufficiency.*—In an action by a railroad company to enjoin a town from appropriating a portion of its right of way for a street, a special finding of facts which fails to show that the town or its officers acted wrongfully or unlawfully, or that the proceeding was not pursuant to some legal procedure authorizing such action, even if sufficient to exclude the theory of a street by dedication or prescription, is not sufficient to sustain a judgment for permanent injunction, but such omission amounts to an affirmance that the acts of defendant were lawful. p. 309.

12. EMINENT DOMAIN.—*Railroads.*—*Right of Way.*—*Dedication to Public Use.*—Land held by a railroad corporation for a right of way, when in actual use as such, is dedicated to a public use. p. 310.

13. EMINENT DOMAIN.—*Land Appropriated to Public Use.*—*Subsequent Appropriation.*—Where land is once appropriated to an important public use, it cannot again be devoted to another public use wholly inconsistent with the former, and which must necessarily supersede or destroy such former use, unless it is shown that the right to the second appropriation is authorized by an act

of the legislature, either expressly or by necessary implication; but, where the two uses may coexist, and the second does not destroy or seriously impair the use for which the first appropriation was made, the second appropriation may be had under a general statute authorizing the condemnation of ground for public purposes. p. 310.

14. EMINENT DOMAIN.—*Railroads.*—*Right of Way.*—*Subsequent Appropriation for Street.*—Under general statutory authority to lay out and establish streets, a street may be laid out through railroad grounds, unless the use for railroad purposes would thereby be destroyed or materially impaired. p. 313.

15. EMINENT DOMAIN.—*Railroads.*—*Right of Way.*—*Subsequent Appropriation for Street.*—Although §§8700, 8759 Burns 1908, Acts 1905 p. 219, §§97, 265, providing that towns may appropriate or condemn, for the public use, any property, real or personal, and may open, change, lay out or vacate any street, etc., including proposed street or alley crossings of railways or other rights of way, are general in their terms, and do not specifically authorize the taking of a longitudinal strip of a railroad's right of way for other public purposes, it cannot be held as a matter of law that a town cannot by proper proceedings acquire such a strip for highway purposes, and its right to do so will be upheld in the absence of proof that it had not acquired the right in any of the ways recognized by the law. p. 313.

16. APPEAL.—*Review.*—*Evidence.*—*Exceptions to Conclusions of Law.*—Technical objections as to the sufficiency of appellants' exceptions to conclusions of law will not be considered, where the evidence fails to prove the same essential facts omitted from the findings, thereby showing that the motion for a new trial should have been sustained. p. 314.

From Tipton Circuit Court; *Lex J. Kirkpatrick,* Judge.

Action by the Lake Erie and Western Railroad Company against the Town of Cicero and others. From a judgment for plaintiff, the defendants appeal. *Reversed.*

John F. Neal and *Phil J. Fariss,* for appellants.
John B. Cockrum and *Shirts & Fertig,* for appellee.

FELT, C. J.—Appellee brought this suit to enjoin appellants from constructing a street or highway over a strip of ground in the town of Cicero, which appellee claims as a part of its right of way.

NOVEMBER TERM, 1912. 301

Town of Cicero *v.* Lake Erie, etc., R. Co.—52 Ind. App. 298.

Issues were joined, and the court, on request, made a special finding of facts, stated its conclusions of law thereon in favor of appellee, and granted appellee a permanent injunction.

Appellants appealed to this court, and rely on the following errors for reversal: (1) The complaint does not state facts sufficient to constitute a cause of action; (2) the court erred in its conclusion of law on the special finding of facts; (3) the court erred in overruling appellants' motion for a new trial.

The special finding of facts is, in substance, as follows: That appellee is a railroad corporation and owns and operates a line of road from Indianapolis to Michigan City, Indiana, through the town of Cicero; that appellee's predecessor, the Peru and Indianapolis Railroad Company, prior to 1851, began the construction of said line of road; that in 1851, Elias Van Buskirk contracted with William A. Spurgin for the sale to the latter of certain real estate, including that in controversy, and in 1847 said Spurgin executed to said Peru and Indianapolis Railroad Company a relinquishment for a right of way across land which includes that in controversy, but the same did not designate the width thereof, and the instrument was not placed of record; that on November 8, 1851, said Spurgin executed to said Van Buskirk a deed of general warranty for the east half of said quarter section of land across which said release granted a right of way; that said deed made no reference to said road or said right of way, and was duly recorded; that after said railroad had been surveyed and located across said tract of real estate, said Van Buskirk, in 1851, platted said ground, as an addition to the town of Cicero, immediately north of Jackson street which runs east and west across the south end of said 80 acres, which street, and Cass street north thereof, are crossed by said railroad; that said railroad runs through blocks one and two in said addition,

bearing slightly from a north and south direction, as shown
by the following diagram:

that said plat was duly signed and acknowledged, and on
November 11, 1857, was duly recorded in the office of the

recorder; that said Van Buskirk marked on said plat said railroad as a strip 80 feet wide, and thereby intended to and did designate and set aside said strip of 80 feet as the right of way of said railroad, and the same was accepted as such by said road; that said railroad company took possession of said right of way, and about 1852 or 1853 constructed its road along the center line of said strip of 80 feet, and it and its successors have continuously maintained and operated said road thereon to the present time; that in the space between Jackson and Cass streets, next to and on the west side of the main track, there is a public street of said town, which the general public has used since said addition to said town was laid out, and since the location and construction of said railroad; that said railroad has maintained a cattle-guard since 1870 at a point on its road about 275 feet north of the north line of said lot two, block one; that when said road was constructed, the land along said right of way north of Cass street was in a forest, and the trees were cut and removed from a strip about 30 feet wide along said right of way, and shortly thereafter there was a fence erected along the west side of the railroad, and fifteen or twenty feet from the track extending north from Cass street the entire length of the strip of ground in controversy; that said Van Buskirk while owning the property erected said fence, and it was removed prior to 1868; that neither appellee nor any one of its predecessors ever erected or maintained a fence along the west side of the main track through the land in controversy; that immediately north of the ground in dispute the railroad company maintains, and has for a long time maintained, a fence connected with the wing fence at the cattle-guard, and located 26.7 feet west of the center of the track; that prior to 1870 lots two and three, west of the railroad and north of Cass street, were enclosed and improved, and buildings erected on the east ends of the lots, but none nearer than 40 feet from the center of the railroad track; that prior to 1870, the owner of the land west of the railroad, and immediately north of block one, fenced the same, leaving an alley between his ground and said lot two, block one, and erected a dwelling on his ground immediately north of said alley, more than 40 feet from the center of the railroad track, and a small barn 38.9 feet from said center; that said alley has been closed for more than 20 years; that prior to 1870 some use was made of the ground east of said buildings by the persons living therein, and the railroad used the space west of its tracks and north of Cass street for storing wood and ties, and for other purposes, and the same was open on the south; that since the closing of said alley a fence has been maintained by adjoining landowners, connecting with the fence on the east line of lots two and three, block one, and extending north to the wing fence at the cattle-guards, and there has never been any road or any wagon crossing over the railroad between Cass street and the first cattle-guard north thereof; that after the closing of said alley, the space north of that point between the railroad and the fence west thereof was occasionally used by the owners of the real estate in reaching their property, but no general use thereof was made by the public; that for more than twenty years before this suit was begun, successive owners of land west of the railroad and north of said block one conveyed the same by deeds, describing the ground as beginning at the northwest corner of said lot two, block one; thence north ten rods; thence east to the railroad (distance not given) ; thence south along the railroad to the northeast corner of said lot two; thence west to the place of beginning; that fences on the east line of the ground so conveyed were recognized and used as the boundary line fence continuously for more than thirty years prior to the removal of the fence by appellants, which fence extends from the wing fence at the cattle-guard at a point 26.7 feet west of the center of the railroad track in a straight line bearing west to the northeast corner of a barn, where the same is 38.9 feet distant from said center; thence extending south to the north line of Cass street 37.6 feet west of said center line; that at various times covering a period of twenty-five years the officers of the town of Cicero exercised some limited authority over the ground in controversy, but by what right or to what extent does not appear; that for more than thirty years appellee and its predecessors have maintained and operated a siding on the east side of its main track across Cass street, extending north to a point near the cattle-guards, which siding, with an elevator and coal-shed, has for more than thirty years occupied and used a strip of ground forty feet wide on the east of said railroad and north of Cass street; that appellee, as successor of the former owners of said railroad property, by divers mortgages, foreclosures, sales and transfers, has acquired all the property, rights and franchises of said former owners, but in none of said foreclosures or transfers was any particular description of the right of way in controversy given, nor was the width thereof stated; that shortly before this suit was begun, the town of Cicero acquired from adjacent landowners a strip of ground 18 feet wide along the west side of said right of way, north of said cattle-guards, and began the construction of a roadway thereon, intending and undertaking to extend the same south to Cass street; that in so doing appellants tore down the line fence on the west side of said right of way south of said cattle-guards, and moved the same east to a point within 15 feet of the railroad tracks; that appellants are preparing to construct a public road or street along the west side of the fence so located, and are claiming the right to appropriate for that purpose the ground up to a line within 15 feet of said tracks from said cattle-guards south to Cass street; that the removal of said fence, and the appropriation of said ground, as aforesaid, were without the consent or authority of appellee; that unless restrained, appellants will establish said fence within 15 feet of appellee's track, and construct said highway as aforesaid. On the foregoing finding of facts, the court stated its conclusions of law, in substance, as follows: That appellee is entitled to a permanent injunction against appellants, enjoining them and each of them from establishing and maintaining a street or public highway on the west line of appellee's right of way, describing the same, by the fence line south from said cattle-guard to Cass street, as it was before being disturbed by appellants.

The principal objections urged against the complaint are as follows: (1) The averments showing that appellee was the owner and had been in possession of the ground in question for more than twenty years is insufficient, for the reason that the right to establish a highway is not inconsistent with appellee's title to the land in controversy; (2) that the acts of public officers are presumed to be legal and regular, and to make the complaint good, it was necessary to aver facts showing that their acts complained of by appellee were without authority of law and not in pursuance of some legal procedure for the establishment of the proposed street or the condemnation of the ground in controversy for highway purposes; that it was not a part of a highway already existing by virtue of some grant, dedication or prescription, recognized by the law; (3) that the statement that appellants' acts, of which complaint is made, were wrongful and unlawful is a mere conclusion and not the averment of a fact.

The averments of the complaint are in general indicated by the finding of facts, but the parts especially challenged aver ''that plaintiff is and for more than twenty years last past has been the owner of said portion of right of way included within the boundaries of said west line and the center of said track, as above described, and it and its predecessors have been in the exclusive and continuous possession and use thereof, as such owners, and maintained a fence on the above-described west line of said described right of way, until September —, 1907, when the defendant wrongfully, unlawfully and without the consent of plaintiff, removed said fence from said west line, * * * and it is the intention of the defendants and they are about to construct said alleged highway or street over and through a portion of plaintiff's said described right of way and defendants are wrongfully claiming the right to construct, grade and maintain said alleged highway or street on such portion of such right of way.''

The rule is firmly established, that where a complaint is tested by demurrer, no inferences or intendments are indulged in favor of the pleading, but where it is tested

1. for the first time after judgment, all inferences and intendments are indulged in favor of the pleadings.

If there is not a total failure to aver some essential fact necessary to the existence of the cause of action at-

2. tempted to be stated, though some of such facts may be defectively stated, and the complaint is sufficient

to bar another suit for the same cause of action, the verdict, or finding and judgment of the trial court cures all other defects, and the complaint will be held sufficient to support the judgment. *Peoria, etc., R. Co.* v. *Attica, etc., R. Co.* (1900), 154 Ind. 218, 220, 56 N. E. 210; *Du Souchet* v. *Dutcher* (1888), 113 Ind. 249, 251, 15 N. E. 459; *Noblesville Foundry, etc., Co.* v. *Yeaman* (1892), 3 Ind. App. 521, 524, 30 N. E. 10; *Heyde* v. *Sult* (1899), 22 Ind. App. 83, 85, 52 N. E. 456; *Stevens* v. *Howerton* (1911), 49 Ind. App. 151, 96 N. E. 968.

The averments of the complaint, showing that appellants in opening the street were acting without legal authority, are defective in stating conclusions instead of pleading facts showing that appellants did not have the legal right to do the things complained of, but there was some averment of such facts, and though defective, in the absence of a demurrer, or a motion to make the complaint more specific, the defective averments were sufficient to admit evidence showing that appellants acted without legal warrant. Where the omission or defect is one that may be supplied

3. by proof, and the facts alleged will bar another suit

for the same cause of action, the complaint will be held sufficient on motion in arrest of judgment, or when first tested by assignment of error on appeal, as in this case. *Loeb* v. *Tinkler* (1890), 124 Ind. 331, 334, 24 N. E. 235; *Reed* v. *Browning* (1892), 130 Ind. 575, 578, 30 N. E. 704; *Chapell* v. *Shuee* (1889), 117 Ind. 481, 486, 20 N. E. 417; *Spitzmesser* v. *Spitzmesser* (1901), 26 Ind. App. 532, 534, 60 N. E. 315; *Palmer* v. *Logansport, etc., Gravel Road Co.* (1886), 108 Ind. 137, 142, 8 N. E. 905; 12 Ency. Pl. and Pr. 1033; 17 Ency. Pl. and Pr. 189.

It has frequently been held that where there is a special finding of facts on which the trial court has stated its con- clusions of law, to which appellant has duly excepted,

4. if the facts are fully and correctly found within the issues, the exceptions to the conclusions of law will

present the same question as the overruling of a demurrer to the complaint. *Runner* v. *Scott* (1898), 150 Ind. 441, 50 N. E. 479; *Philip Zorn Brewing Co.* v. *Malott* (1898), 151 Ind. 371, 51 N. E. 471; *Ross* v. *Van Natta* (1905), 164 Ind. 557, 74 N. E. 10; *Fry* v. *Hare* (1906), 166 Ind. 415, 77 N. E. 803; *Timmonds* v. *Taylor* (1911), 48 Ind. App. 531, 96 N. E. 331; *Sell* v. *Keiser* (1911), 49 Ind. App. 101, 96 N. E. 812.

In the case at bar there was no demurrer, but the com- plaint is questioned for the first time by independent as- signment of error. Where this is done, the excep-

5. tions to the conclusions of law present the same ques- tion as the assignment of error challenging the suffi-

ciency of the complaint, but the complaint in such case will be tested by the rule applicable after verdict.

Tested by this rule, the complaint is sufficient, but

6. whether the facts provable under the complaint so construed have been so fully and correctly found

7. as to sustain the conclusions and support the judg-

ment of the trial court, must be determined on the exceptions to the conclusions of law.

8. The failure to find a material fact, the burden of proving which is on plaintiff, is equivalent to a finding against him as to such fact. *Mug* v. *Ostendorf* (1911), 49 Ind. App. 71, 96 N. E. 780.

To entitle appellee to injunctive relief against the town of Cicero and its officers, it was necessary to allege and prove

9. that in removing the fence and taking a portion of appellee's right of way for a street they were doing so without warrant of law. It has been held that to enjoin a city from using a strip of ground as a street, the complaint must show, not only that there has been no grant, or condemnation of the land for a street, but also that there has been no implied dedication of, or prescriptive right acquired to, the ground for highway purposes. *Faust* v. *City of Huntington* (1883), 91 Ind. 493; *Jackson* v. *Smith* (1889), 120 Ind. 520, 527, 22 N. E. 431; *City of Lafayette* v. *Wabash R. Co.* (1902), 28 Ind. App. 497, 501, 63 N. E. 237; *Carr* v. *Kolb* (1884), 99 Ind. 53, 55.

The law presumes the acts of public officers to be legal and regular, and until the contrary is made to appear, they

10. are presumed to have done their duty according to law. *Faust* v. *City of Huntington, supra,* 495; *Town of Woodruff Place* v. *Raschig* (1897), 147 Ind. 517, 521, 46 N. E. 990; *Cummins* v. *City of Seymour* (1881), 79 Ind. 491, 496, 41 Am. Rep. 618.

The finding of facts does not show that the town or its officers acted wrongfully or unlawfully; nor does it show

11. that the town was not proceeding to remove the fence and open the highway in pursuance of some legal procedure which authorized such action, though it is probably sufficient to exclude the idea of a street by dedication or prescription.

The law places the burden on appellee to aver and prove facts showing that appellants were proceeding without lawful authority to do the things complained of by appellee, in order to meet and overcome the legal presumption in favor of the legality and regularity of the acts of appellants.

The complaint could not be upheld without some averment of such essential facts, and the failure to find facts showing the acts complained of to be wrongful or unlawful shows that the facts found are insufficient to sustain the judgment against appellants for a permanent injunction.

For the purposes of this appeal, the case comes to this court on a finding of facts which does not remove or disturb the presumption of the law as to the legality of the acts of the officials of the town of Cicero, but, in legal effect, affirms that their acts were lawful.

Appellee insists, however, that as the complaint and findings show appellants are seeking to take a longitudinal strip of its right of way for highway purposes, it was unnecessary to aver or prove that there had been no condemnation or other proceedings by the town to obtain the ground in controversy for such purposes; that the law absolutely forbids

12. such second appropriation for a public use. Our courts have decided that land held by a railroad corporation for a right of way, when in actual use as such, is dedicated to a public use. *City of Valparaiso* v. *Chicago, etc., R. Co.* (1890), 123 Ind. 467, 24 N. E. 249.

The general doctrine is recognized in this State, that where land is once appropriated to an important public use, it cannot again be devoted to another public

13. use wholly inconsistent with the former, and which, under the circumstances of the particular case, must necessarily supersede or destroy such former use, unless it is shown, either expressly or by necessary implication, that the right to subject the land to the second appropriation or use is authorized by an act of the legislature. *Cincinnati, etc., R. Co.* v. *City of Anderson* (1894), 139 Ind. 490, 38 N. E. 167, 47 Am. St. 285; *Steele* v. *Empson* (1895), 142 Ind. 397, 406, 41 N. E. 822; *City of Terre Haute* v. *Evans-*

ville, etc., R. Co. (1897), 149 Ind. 174, 176, 46 N. E. 77, 37
L. R. A. 189; *Gold* v. *Pittsburgh, etc., R. Co.* (1899), 153
Ind. 232, 242, 54 N. E. 802.

But on the question of the necessity of a special legislative enactment specifically authorizing such second appropriation for a public use, the rule is somewhat relaxed from the earlier decisions.

In *Baltimore, etc., R. Co.* v. *North* (1885), 103 Ind. 486, 3 N. E. 144, it was held that the circuit court, under the general drainage law, had no power to establish a public ditch along and on the right of way of a railroad, for the reason that lands once taken for an important public use cannot, under general laws, be appropriated to another public use, and that such second appropriation cannot be made except by express legislative authority, clearly and definitely granted, or arising by necessary implication.

In the case of *Baltimore, etc., R. Co.* v. *Board, etc.* (1901), 156 Ind. 260, 58 N. E. 937, 59 N. E. 856, it was stated that the doctrine of the case of *Baltimore, etc., R. Co.* v. *North, supra,* is incompatible with the later decision in *Gold* v. *Pittsburgh, etc., R. Co., supra,* and that *Baltimore, etc., R. Co.* v. *North, supra,* was overruled in so far as it is in conflict with *Baltimore, etc., R. Co.* v. *Board, etc., supra.* In that case a large public ditch was located along and over the right of way of the railroad for a distance of 8,400 feet, to a width of from 4 to 7 feet, and about 35 feet from the center of the railroad tracks, and the Supreme Court sustained the action of the lower court in so locating it, though the drainage statute under which the ditch was established did not expressly provide that a ditch could be constructed along and over such right of way.

Since the decision of the case of *Baltimore, etc., R. Co.* v. *Board, etc., supra,* the case of *City of Valparaiso* v. *Chicago, etc., R. Co.* (1890), 123 Ind. 467, 24 N. E. 249; *City of Seymour* v. *Jeffersonville, etc., R. Co.* (1891), 126 Ind. 466, 26 N. E. 188; *City of Fort Wayne* v. *Lake Shore, etc., R. Co.*

(1892), 132 Ind. 558, 32 N. E. 215, 18 L. R. A. 367, 32 Am.
St. 277; and other cases, following the doctrine of *Baltimore,
etc., R. Co.* v. *North, supra,* must be regarded as modified,
on the proposition of the right under a general statute to
appropriate ground to another and different public use
which is already devoted to an important public use. The
rule, as now established, is that if the two uses may coexist,
and the second does not destroy or seriously impair the use
first granted, the second may be secured in a proper proceeding under a general statute, authorizing the condemnation
of ground for public purposes.

In *Postal Tel., etc., Co.* v. *Chicago, etc., R. Co.* (1903), 30
Ind. App. 654, 66 N. E. 919, this court held that a telegraph company could by condemnation proceedings acquire
the right to erect and maintain its poles and lines along
and over the right of way of a railroad company, and, among
other things, said on page 660: "If the court, upon all
the facts, finds that the two uses can coexist, it is the duty
of the court to hold that the condemnation may be had
under the general grant for the purpose."

In *Steele* v. *Empson* (1895), 142 Ind. 397, 405, 41 N. E.
822, the court said: "It is claimed by appellant that the
ditch is partly located on the right of way of the O. & M.
R. W. Co., and that such location is not authorized, for the
reason, that property once taken and appropriated to one
public use cannot again be appropriated to another public
use. * * * The rule urged by appellant only applies
when the second public use would naturally injure or destroy the uses for which such right of way was employed,
and when the same could not exist without impairing the
first uses." See, also, *Indianapolis, etc., R. Co.* v. *Indianapolis, etc., Transit Co.* (1904), 33 Ind. App. 337, 341, 67
N. E. 1013.

The rule as it now exists in Indiana with reference to railroads and highways is well stated by an eminent law writer

as follows: "The general rule to be deduced from
14. the cases is that under a general authority to lay out
and establish highways and streets, a road may be
laid out across or through railroad grounds, unless the use
for railroad purposes would thereby be destroyed or materially impaired. The question is whether the establishment
of the highway will be so inconsistent with the use of the
property for railroad purposes, that the two uses cannot
reasonably and practically coexist." 2 Lewis, Eminent Domain (3d ed.) §417.

The act of 1905 (Acts 1905 p. 219, §§97, 265, §§8700, 8959
Burns 1908), relating to cities and towns, provides, in substance, that a town or city may appropriate or con-
15. demn for the use of the city or town "any property,
real or personal", and may "open, change, lay out
or vacate any street, alley or public place within such city,
including proposed street or alley crossings of railways or
other rights of way." This statute is general in its terms,
and does not specifically authorize the taking of a longitudinal strip of a railroad's right of way for other public
purposes.

Appellants propose to take a strip off appellee's right of
way, varying in width from about 12 to 23 feet, and up to
a line uniformly fifteen feet from the center of its tracks,
between Cass street and the cattle-guard north thereof, a
distance of about 400 feet. This requires us to determine
the right and power of the town of Cicero, under the general
statute for opening, vacating and changing highways, to take
a longitudinal strip off appellee's right of way for a public
street.

Following the foregoing authorities, we hold (1) that it
cannot be said as a matter of law that the town cannot by
proper proceedings acquire the strip in question for highway
purposes, but that in a proper proceeding and upon sufficient proof the law will enable it so to do; (2) that to en-

join the town and its officers from proceeding to open the highway as alleged in the complaint the burden rests on the appellee to prove that the town of Cicero had not acquired the right to open said highway in any of the ways recognized by the law; (3) that the finding of facts fails to show that appellants were not proceeding according to law, and the presumption in favor of the regularity and legality of their acts, in opening the highway in question, is therefore not overcome by the finding; (4) that the conclusions of law are erroneous.

Appellees have questioned the sufficiency of the exceptions to the conclusions of law, on the ground that the court made such amendments to the finding, after the exceptions were taken, as to render them unavailing.

16.

But the motion for a new trial challenges the sufficiency of the evidence to support the findings; also alleges that the decision of the court is not supported by sufficient evidence, and that the decision is contrary to law. *Scott* v. *Collier* (1906), 166 Ind. 644, 648, 78 N. E. 184; *Weaver* v. *Apple* (1897), 147 Ind. 304, 306, 46 N. E. 642.

As we have shown, the finding omits certain facts material to appellee's right to the relief prayed, and on examination of the evidence we find a total failure of evidence to prove the same essential facts. Therefore the motion for a new trial should have been sustained, and this makes it unnecessary to consider the technical objections to the conclusions of law, as any view taken of such questions could not avert the necessity of a reversal.

The judgment is therefore reversed, with instructions to the lower court to sustain the motion for a new trial, to permit the parties to amend their pleadings if desired, and for further proceedings in accordance with this opinion.

NOTE.—Reported in 97 N. E. 389. See, also, under (2, 3, 5) 31 Cyc. 82; (4) 2 Cyc. 730; (6) 22 Cyc. 924; (8, 11) 38 Cyc. 1924; (9) 22 Cyc. 936; (10) 16 Cyc. 1076; (13) 15 Cyc. 612; (14, 15) 15 Cyc. 622. As to the sort of defects in pleading that a verdict cures, see 1 Am. Dec. 210. As to right of eminent domain in respect of a town's taking or crossing the track of a railroad company, see 9 Am. St. 142. As to a railroad as a public use for which the power of eminent domain may be invoked, see 102 Am. St. 822. On the question of taking railroad lands for municipal purposes, see 2 L. R. A. (N. S.) 227; 41 L. R. A. (N. S.) 828.

KOEHLER v. HARMON, RECEIVER.

[No. 7,675. Filed June 26, 1912. Rehearing denied December 20, 1912. Transfer denied January 28, 1913.]

1. MASTER AND SERVANT.—*Injury to Servant.—Unguarded Machinery.—Complaint.—Sufficiency.*—A complaint, in a servant's action for personal injuries, alleging that a lathe used in defendant's shops, and which plaintiff was employed to operate, was of dangerous character, that the same could have been guarded, without impairing its usefulness, so as to protect the eyes and face of the operator from injury, that on the day of the injury the dog-plate on said lathe had been removed and plaintiff was directed to use a face-plate thereon instead, that said lathe was thereby rendered unsafe and dangerous, that defendant furnished a defective file to be used in connection with the work on said lathe, and negligently failed to guard said lathe, and that while operating said lathe the file was, by reason of its defective condition and the absence of a guard on said lathe, hurled against plaintiff's face, causing the injury complained of, sufficiently states a cause of action within the provisions of §8029 Burns 1908, Acts 1899 p. 231, requiring certain machinery to be guarded. p. 316.

2. MASTER AND SERVANT.—*Injury to Servant.—Complaint.—Violation of Statutory Duty.—Assumption of Risk.*—The doctrine of assumption of risk does not apply in a servant's action for personal injuries, where the complaint alleges facts showing the master's violation of a statutory duty, and in such case it is unnecessary to allege facts showing that the risk was not assumed. p. 318.

3. APPEAL.—*Review.—Harmless Error.—Exclusion of Evidence.*—Error, if any, in the exclusion of evidence, is harmless, where the record discloses that substantially the same facts were proved in another way. p. 318.

From Superior Court of Marion County (75,703); *Pliny W. Bartholomew*, Judge.

Action by Paul Koehler against Judson Harmon, receiver
of the Cincinnati, Hamilton & Dayton Railway Company.
From a judgment for defendant, the plaintiff appeals. *Reversed.*

George W. Galvin, for appellant.
John B. Elam, James W. Fesler and *Harvey J. Elam,* for
appellee.

FELT, J.—Appellant brought this action to recover damages for personal injuries sustained by him while in the employ of appellee.   The complaint was in two paragraphs, to
the second of which a demurrer was sustained and the case
was tried on the first.   At the close of appellant's evidence
the trial court, on motion by appellee, instructed the jury
to find for appellee, and also overruled appellant's motion
for a new trial.

The first error assigned and relied on by appellant is that
the court erred in sustaining appellee's demurrer to the second paragraph of the complaint.

Omitting the formal allegations this paragraph, in substance, charges that appellee operated large and extensive
shops in the city of Indianapolis for the manufac-

1. ture and repair of appliances used in the operation
of a railway; that in said shops appellee operates
much machinery; that one of said machines was a lathe, composed of many parts, and having planers, cogs, gearing, belting and set screws; that said lathe was operated by applied
power and run at high speed; that the material which was
worked on said lathe was caused to revolve with great veloc-
ity, and the work required close attention; that said machine was of a dangerous character, by reason of the great
speed at which it was operated; that the danger to the workmen using such machine could have been greatly lessened
by the use of a shield or guard over the same; that such
guard would have wholly protected the eyes and face of the
operator from coming in contact with the instrument or

tools used in the work on said machine if thrown therefrom by its rapid motion; that such machine could have been so guarded without in any way interfering with or impairing its usefulness; that on August 8, 1907, appellant was in the employ of appellee, and his work was to operate said lathe; that on coming to work on said date he found that the dog-plate on said lathe, which he had been operating, had been removed; that one Roesner was foreman in said shop, and directed appellant to use a face-plate on said lathe in doing his work, which rendered said machine unsafe for the performance of such labor thereon; that the file furnished to appellant was without a handle, and was difficult to hold and dangerous to work with on the rapidly-revolving material in the machine, all of which was known to appellee; that said machine could have been so guarded as to have been safe in its defective condition caused by the use of said face-plate, but appellee negligently and carelessly failed to supply such guard; that appellant "began work upon such machine and attempted to perform his labor as directed by said foreman, but the defects in said machine and the absence of a handle to his file caused said file to be thrown from his hand and the absence of a guard suffered and permitted such file to come in contact with his left eye," whereby the sight of the same was destroyed and he was otherwise severely injured.

Appellant asserts, and appellee denies, that the lathe or machine on which appellant was working when injured comes within the provisions of the statute (§8029 Burns 1908, Acts 1899 p. 231) requiring certain machinery to be guarded.

In the light of recent decisions of this court and the Supreme Court, we hold that the averments make a case within the purview of the statute. *United States Cement Co.* v. *Cooper* (1909), 172 Ind. 599, 612, 88 N. E. 69; *Green* v. *American Car, etc., Co.* (1904), 163 Ind. 135, 139, 71 N. E. 268; *Baltimore, etc., R. Co.* v. *Cavanaugh* (1905), 35 Ind.

App. 32, 36, 71 N. E. 239; *Hoffmeyer* v. *State* (1906), 37 Ind. App. 526, 77 N. E. 372.

Appellee in his brief states: "The second paragraph of complaint was insufficient because the burden was on the plaintiff to allege facts sufficient to show that the plaintiff did not have knowledge and hence assume the risks from which the injury resulted." Since the averments are sufficient to charge a violation of a statutory duty, the doctrine of assumption of risk has no application to this paragraph of the complaint. *Jenney Electric Mfg. Co.* v. *Flannery* (1913), 53 Ind. App. ——, 98 N. E. 424; *American Car, etc., Co* v. *Clark* (1904), 32 Ind. App. 644, 648, 70 N. E. 828.

The following language in *United States Cement Co.* v. *Cooper, supra*, 613, is applicable here: "It is alleged * * * that the offending machine was dangerous from being uncovered and exposed; that the same might have been covered at a reasonable cost and without affecting its efficiency. We think these averments are sufficient to send these questions to the jury." The second paragraph states a cause of action under the statute, and the court erred in sustaining the demurrer thereto.

The case was tried on the first paragraph of the complaint, and at the close of appellant's evidence the court directed a verdict for appellee. This action of the court is made a cause for a new trial and the overruling of the motion for a new trial is assigned as error.

The sufficiency of the first paragraph of the complaint is not questioned by this appeal. Our decision on the sufficiency of the second paragraph of the complaint compels a reversal of the judgment.

3. The alleged error in refusing to admit certain evidence of a conversation between appellant and appellee's storekeeper, if error at all, is rendered harmless for the record shows that substantially the same facts were proved in another way.

Further consideration of the other questions raised by the motion for a new trial can serve no good purpose, for in the event the case is retried the evidence may not be the same and the questions here presented may not again arise.

The judgment is therefore reversed, with instructions to sustain the motion for a new trial, overrule the demurrer to the second paragraph of the complaint, and for further proceedings in accordance with this opinion.

NOTE.—Reported in 98 N. E. 1009. See, also, under (1) 26 Cyc. 1384; (2) 26 Cyc. 1397; (3) 38 Cyc. 1457. As to risks assumed by servants, see 52 Am. Rep. 737; 24 Am. St. 320. As to the master's duty to guard or enclose dangerous machinery. See note to *Brazil Block Coal Co.* v. *Gibson* (Ind.), 98 Am. St. 299. As to servant's assumption of risk of master's breach of statutory duty, see 6 L. R. A. (N. S.) 981; 19 L. R. A. (N. S.) 646; 22 L. R. A. (N. S.) 634; 33 L. R. A. (N. S.) 646; 42 L. R. A. (N. S.) 1229.

BARTON ET AL. *v.* BARTON.

[No. 7,840.   Filed January 30, 1913.]

1. PLEADING.—*Complaint.—Sufficiency.—Defects Curable by Motion to Make Specific.—Demurrer.*—A complaint is not demurrable for defects that may be reached by a motion to make more specific, and will be held good if it states facts entitling plaintiff to any relief. p. 321.

2. PLEADING.—*Complaint.—Sufficiency.*—A complaint alleging facts from which it may readily be determined that defendant was the agent of plaintiff in buying and selling real estate, that on account of moneys advanced by plaintiff, interest collected, and profits derived from the sale of real estate, defendant became indebted to plaintiff, that defendant, as attorney in fact for plaintiff, wrongfully and without any consideration, conveyed certain real estate to his wife for the purpose and with the intent to cheat and defraud plaintiff, and which demands an accounting and the setting aside of such conveyance, is sufficient to withstand a demurrer. p. 321.

From Clinton Circuit Court; *Lee Nash*, Special Judge.

Action by Daniel J. Barton against John D. Barton and another. From a judgment for plaintiff, the defendants appeal. *Affirmed.*

Joseph Claybaugh, for appellants.

Thomas M. Ryan and *James V. Kent,* for appellee.

SHEA, J.—This was an action brought by appellee against appellants for an accounting and to set aside a deed.

The complaint was in one paragraph, to which a demurrer for want of facts was overruled. Appellants answered by a general denial. The cause was submitted to the court for trial. The court found the facts specially, and stated conclusions of law thereon, which are a part of the record. Judgment for appellee.

The ruling of the court in passing on the sufficiency of the complaint is the only error assigned. The complaint charges, in substance, that for a period of fifteen years appellant, John D. Barton, was the agent of appellee, Daniel J. Barton, and during said time he bought and sold real estate and personal property for the latter; that appellee furnished money for that purpose, and said appellant received said sums, and as agent for appellee, used them for the purchase of real estate and other purposes, for appellee's benefit; that during said time appellee advanced to said appellant the sum of $2,000, which sum, with interest thereon, and profits derived from the sale of real estate purchased with the same, is now due and owing to appellee from said appellant; that on April 18, 1908, appellee revoked the agency, and thereafter demanded an accounting, and the amount so due him as interest and profits, which demand was refused by appellant, John D. Barton; that said John D. Barton, as the attorney in fact of appellee, transferred and warranted to his wife, Anna B. Barton, appellant herein, certain real estate described in the complaint, belonging to appellee; that said conveyance was voluntary and without any consideration whatever, and appellee has received no proceeds from the sale thereof. It is prayed that an accounting be had; that the conveyance to Anna Barton be declared fraudulent and void; that a trustee be appointed to reconvey to appellee and that he have judgment for $3,500, and that said sum be declared a special lien on said real estate.

The complaint is subject to much criticism on account of lack of clear statement, which might readily have been cured in the court below by a motion to make more specific.

1. Appellants failed to resort to that method to cure the evils from which they now seek relief in this court.

It is a well-settled principle of law that if the complaint states a cause of action entitling plaintiff to any relief, it will not be obnoxious to a demurrer. *Gowdy Gas Well, etc., Co.* v. *Patterson* (1902), 29 Ind. App. 261, 64 N. E. 485; *Levi* v. *Hare* (1894), 8 Ind. App. 571, 36 N. E. 369; *Jessup* v. *Jessup* (1893), 7 Ind. App. 573, 34 N. E. 1017; *Scott* v. *Cleveland, etc., R. Co.* (1896), 144 Ind. 125, 43 N. E. 133, 32 L. R. A. 154; *United States Sav., etc., Co.* v. *Harris* (1895), 142 Ind. 226, 40 N. E. 1072, 41 N. E. 451; *Shepardson* v. *Gillette* (1892), 133 Ind. 125, 31 N. E. 788; *Coleman* v. *Floyd* (1892), 131 Ind. 330, 31 N. E. 75; *Bennett* v. *Preston* (1861), 17 Ind. 291; *Domestic Block Coal Co.* v. *DeArmey* (1913), 179 Ind. —, 100 N. E. 675, 102 N. E. 99.

It may readily be determined from the allegations of the complaint that appellant, John D. Barton, was for the period of fifteen years agent for appellee, Daniel J. Barton,

2. and during that time, on account of moneys advanced, interest collected, and profits derived from the sale of real estate, became indebted to appellee in a large sum of money; that during the period of the agency appellant John D. Barton wrongfully, as attorney in fact, conveyed a parcel of real estate, described in the complaint, to his wife, Anna B. Barton, appellant, without any consideration, "for the purpose of cheating plaintiff and with intent to cheat and defraud plaintiff." There is a demand for an accounting, and that the conveyance to Anna B. Barton be set aside and declared fraudulent and void. These allegations were sufficient to withstand a demurrer.

The facts specially found by the trial court show that a correct result was reached on the theory as stated.

Judgment affirmed.

Note.—Reported in 100 N. E. 688. See, also, under (1) 31 Cyc. 281; (2) 31 Cyc. 288. As to the doctrine that an agent to sell can not sell to himself, and its application to a sale by him to his wife, see 80 Am. St. 559.

SOUTHERN RAILWAY COMPANY ET AL. *v.* ADAMS.

[No. 7,767.   Filed February 11, 1913.]

1. CARRIERS.—*Injury to Passengers.—Negligence.—Derailment of Train.—Res Ipsa Loquitur.—Complaint.*—Where the complaint, in an action against a railroad company for personal injuries, clearly shows that the relation of carrier and passenger existed, and that the plaintiff was injured by the derailment of the train, the rule of *res ipsa loquitur* applies, notwithstanding several causes are alleged to have produced the derailment. p. 326.

2. CARRIERS.—*Injury to Passengers.—Derailment of Train.—Complaint.—Allegation of Particular Defects.—Proof.*—Where the complaint, in a passenger's action for injuries caused by the derailment of a train, alleges the particular defects that caused the derailment, the carrier is relieved from the burden of disproving or meeting any other negligence in regard to the derailment than that alleged, nor can the plaintiff prove any other causes than those alleged. p. 327.

3. CARRIERS.—*Injury to Passengers.—Complaint.—Sufficiency.*—Where the complaint, in an action for injury to a passenger by the derailment of a train, charged negligence in three respects, namely, defective track, defective axles and excessive speed, and further alleged that thereby and on account of the negligent and careless manner in which the train was run and managed, it was derailed and plaintiff was thereby injured, sufficiently charged that the derailment was caused by the negligence of defendant and that such negligence was the proximate cause of the injury. p. 328.

4. CARRIERS.—*Injury to Passengers.—Derailment of Train.—Particular Defects.—Proof.*—Where a passenger, in an action for injuries caused by the derailment of a train, alleged a number of defects as cause for the derailment, proof that the derailment was occasioned by any one or more of the causes alleged would warrant a finding for plaintiff. p. 328.

5. TRIAL.—*Argument.—Statement of Counsel.—Objection.—Motion.*—Where a party objects to a statement made by counsel in argument, a part of which is proper and warranted by evidence, he should direct his motion to the objectionable part and not to the whole statement. p. 329.

6. APPEAL.—*Review.—Harmless Error.—Misconduct of Counsel.— Refusal to Set Aside Submission of Cause.*—Where counsel indulged in improper remarks in argument, and the court instructed the jury to disregard them, the refusal of the court to set aside the submission of the cause will not work a reversal, where there is nothing in the record to overcome the presumption that the instructions were heeded, or indicating that appellants were thereby prevented from having a fair trial. p. 329.

7. CARRIERS.—*Injury to Passengers.—Derailment of Train.—Negligence.—Presumptions.*—In a passenger's action for injuries caused by the derailment of a train, proof of the relation of carrier and passenger, and a derailment resulting in injury to the passenger, creates a presumption of negligence on the part of the carrier, entitling plaintiff to recover, unless it is removed by evidence, and plaintiff is not deprived of such presumption by the fact that he has alleged specific acts of negligence as causing the derailment. p. 330.

8. CARRIERS.—*Injury to Passengers.—Derailment of Train.—Instructions.—Refusal.*—Where, in a passenger's action for injuries caused by the derailment of a train, plaintiff alleged that the derailment was caused by defective axles, defective tracks and excessive speed, a requested instruction that to be entitled to recover the plaintiff must prove that the derailment was the result of the three causes combined, was properly refused. p. 330.

9. TRIAL.—*Instructions.—Refusal of Instructions.*—The refusal of requested instructions that are covered by other instructions given is not error. p. 330.

10. APPEAL.—*Review.—Harmless Error.—Instructions.* — An instruction that although a common carrier of passengers does not insure the safety of its passengers the law will not tolerate any negligence on the part of the carrier, though inaccurate in failing to limit the negligence to that charged in the complaint, is harmless where the omission was covered by other instructions given. p. 331.

From Harrison Circuit Court; *William Ridley*, Judge.

Action by Leander C. Adams against the Southern Railway Company and another. From a judgment for plaintiff, the defendants appeal. *Affirmed.*

Alex. P. Humphrey, Edward P. Humphrey, John D. Welman, Thomas J. Wilson, Frank Self, Walter V. Bulleit and *Major W. Funk,* for appellants.

Stotsenberg & Weathers, Paris & Trusty, W. T. Zenor and *Ewing & Roose,* for appellee.

FELT, P. J.—This is a suit by appellee against appellants for damages alleged to have been sustained by reason of appellants' negligence.

The facts not in dispute show that appellants are common carriers of passengers; that appellee was a passenger on one of their trains, and while riding as such passenger, the train was derailed and appellee was injured. The jury returned a general verdict in favor of appellee, and with it, answers to 67 interrogatories.

Appellants have assigned as error the overruling of the demurrer to the complaint, the overruling of the separate motions of each appellant for judgment on the answers of the jury to the interrogatories, notwithstanding the general verdict, and the overruling of the motion of each appellant for a new trial.

The complaint charges, in substance, that appellee was a passenger on one of appellants' trains on January 28, 1909; that at that time appellants' track was defective at a point about three miles west of the city of New Albany, in this. that the rails were insufficient, were not properly spiked to the cross-ties, and that the ties were decayed and rotten: that the locomotive and cars comprising the train on which appellee was a passenger were old and out of repair and the axles of the same were imperfect and weak; that while appellee was such passenger and riding from the town of Corydon Junction to the city of New Albany, appellants ran said train carelessly and negligently at a high and unusual rate of speed to wit, 50 miles an hour; that said train was so carelessly, negligently and dangerously run over said defective and insufficient track, cross-ties and rails aforesaid.

and on a down grade without applying the brakes as should have been done; that appellants carelessly and negligently so ran said train at said high and dangerous rate of speed with said defective and insufficient locomotive and cars, "that thereby and by reason of all of which acts of carelessness and negligence on the part of said defendants as aforesaid, * * * said train and the car in which this plaintiff was riding while same was so negligently run as aforesaid and while so negligently run and being run at a down grade at and in the county of Floyd and State of Indiana, were so negligently and carelessly run and managed, that the car in which plaintiff was so riding together with other cars comprising the said train, were thrown from the said track and from said road down an embankment and * * * by reason of its sudden and immediate derailment * * * and without any fault or negligence on the part of this plaintiff, he was * * * greatly and severely injured."

It is asserted by appellants that the complaint does not charge either a negligent derailment or a negligent injury; that three interdependent causes of the derailment are alleged, viz.: defective track, defective axles and excessive speed. and that not one is shown to be the proximate cause of the injury; that under such a charge, though made in a passenger case, the rule of *res ipsa loquitur* has no application, and the complaint is bad because it fails to show a negligent derailment of the train, but does show that the derailment was the proximate cause of the injury; that the complaint is also insufficient to show a cause of action on any one of the alleged causes of the derailment, because it fails to show that any one of them was the proximate cause of the injury, but charges that all taken in combination, caused the derailment.

The complaint in this case proceeds on the theory of an injury by a common carrier to a passenger, caused by the

derailment of the train on which the passenger was
1. riding. While several causes of the derailment are
    alleged, we do not think the complaint falls within the
rule applicable, where several distinct acts of negligence are
charged as separately causing the injury, or within the rule
applicable where several negligent acts are alleged to have
operated jointly, or in combination, to produce the injury
complained of.

The complaint clearly shows that the relation of carrier
and passenger existed between appellants and appellee, and
where this is shown, and it also appears from the pleading
that the complaining passenger was injured by the derailment of the train, the rule of *res ipsa loquitur* applies, notwithstanding several causes are alleged to have produced the
derailment.

In the case of *Terre Haute, etc., R. Co. v. Sheeks* (1900),
155 Ind. 74, 56 N. E. 434, the court had under consideration
a case of a passenger alleged to have been injured by the
derailment of a train. The complaint charged several specific
defects with reference to a switch as the cause of the derailment, and it was contended that without proof of all of the
specific defects alleged there could be no recovery, and the
court, in discussing the question, said on page 91: "It
cannot be successfully asserted that because she by her complaint has been more particular and specific in describing
the deficiences of the switch in controversy than was necessarily required therefore she cannot recover unless she proves
all the particular defects as charged in the complaint." Also
on page 93 it is said: "Upon no view of the case can it be
said, we think, that appellee, in order to succeed, must prove
all of the particular infirmities or deficiences alleged in regard to the switch. As heretofore stated, proof of the
essence or gravamen of her cause of action would be sufficient. The facts alleged in the complaint, disclosing as they
do the relation of passenger and carrier, also the occurrence
of the accident and the injuries sustained by appellee there-

by, enable her to avail herself of the benefit of the rule which authorizes, upon the consideration of such facts, the presumption of negligence upon the part of the carrier. The charge as to appellant's negligence in the construction and maintenance of the switch was notice to it to bring forward facts to show that there was no negligence in this respect, but it certainly cannot be affirmed that, by the particular averments in her complaint, she thereby relieved appellant of the burden of showing, under the circumstances, what the law exacted of it. The duty of a railroad company engaged in carrying passengers is one well defined. While the company, as a carrier of passengers, is not an insurer of their safety, still, in consideration of the great danger to human life consequent upon the neglect of duty upon the part of the company, the law exacts of it the exercise of the highest practicable care for the safety of its passengers in the operation of its trains, and in keeping its road, machinery and appliances in a safe condition; and for any failure to exercise such care, and for slight neglect of its duty in this respect, it is liable to a passenger, who is himself without fault, for an injury sustained as the result of such negligence."

In the case from which the foregoing is quoted it is also stated, in substance, that the effect of alleging in a pleading the particular defects that caused a derailment
2. resulting in an injury to a passenger, is to relieve the carrier from the burden of disproving or meeting "any other negligence in regard to the derailment of the train" than that alleged, for the reason that having specified the particular defects or acts of negligence, the plaintiff will be confined to them, and not allowed to prove other causes of the derailment than those alleged.

Appellants concede that the complaint shows that the derailment was the proximate cause of the alleged injury, and that it would be sufficient if it charged in general terms a negligent derailment or a negligent injury.

The complaint charges negligence in three respects, viz.: defective track, defective axles and excessive speed, and further alleges that thereby and on account of the negligent and careless manner in which said train was run and managed it was thrown from the track, down an embankment, and by reason thereof appellee was injured without any fault or negligence on his part. These averments, when fairly construed, charge that the derailment was caused by the negligence of appellants, and show that such negligence was the proximate cause of appellee's alleged injury. *Domestic Block Coal Co.* v. *De Armey* (1913), 179 Ind. ——, 100 N. E. 675, 102 N. E. 99. The complaint states a cause of action, and the trial court did not err in overruling the demurrer thereto.

Appellants insist that their motion for judgment on the answers of the jury to the interrogatories, notwithstanding the general verdict, should have been sustained, and in support of this contention refer to the answers which, in substance, show that the derailment of the train on which appellee was a passenger was not caused by any axle or axles of said train; that the derailment was "not caused by something else than said track, speed and axles;" that the derailment was caused by the condition of the track and the speed of the train. Conceding, but not deciding, that appellants are right in their contention that the answers to the interrogatories show that the derailment was caused by the speed of the train and the condition of the track, and not by those two causes acting jointly in combination with the defective axle, under our construction of the complaint the motion was rightly overruled, for the negligent derailment of the train by one or more of the alleged causes was sufficient on this· point to warrant a finding for appellee.

One of the grounds for a new trial is the alleged misconduct of one of appellee's counsel in his closing argument to the jury, in referring to the extent of the road and the

property of appellants. Objection is also made to the
5. following remarks: "I take the side of the people
against the corporations, and no truer thing was ever
said by Billy Bryan and reiterated by Teddy Roosevelt, than,
if the railroads and corporations of this country cannot be
curbed and controlled that this Republic must fail." On
the trial, appellants moved the court to withdraw each of
said remarks from the jury, with instructions not to consider them, and also moved the court to set aside the submission of the case and to discharge the jury. As to the
statement in regard to the extent of the property, there was
evidence tending to show appellants' road master had under
his supervision over 500 miles of road. This evidence warranted at least a part of the statement complained of on
the subject of the extent of property, and the motion was
directed to the whole statement. Where it is possible to
separate the objectionable from the unobjectionable part of
a statement, the motion should be directed to the objectionable part only.

The court sustained the motion to withdraw each of said
remarks from the jury and instructed it to disregard the
same. While such remarks are not commendable,
6. and should not be indulged in by counsel, in view of
the action of the trial court in withdrawing the remarks and instructing the jury to disregard them, we are
not convinced that appellants were harmed by the refusal
of the court to set aside the submission of the cause. On
the showing made in this case it will be presumed that the
instructions of the court were heeded, and that the improper remarks did not prevent appellants from having a
fair trial. *Southern R. Co.* v. *Bulleit* (1907), 40 Ind. App.
457, 459, 82 N. E. 474; *Pigg* v. *State* (1896), 145 Ind. 560,
564, 43 N. E. 309; *Board, etc.,* v. *Redifer* (1903), 32 Ind.
App. 93, 98, 69 N. E. 305; *Southern Ind. R. Co.* v. *Davis*
(1904), 32 Ind. App. 569, 581, 69 N. E. 550.

Appellants also complain of the refusal of the court to

give several instructions tendered, and of the giving of a
number of instructions. Instruction No. 4, tendered
7. by appellants, in so far as it was applicable to the
issues, was covered by other instructions given. We
cannot approve the instruction as tendered, for the reason
that it, in effect told the jury that because appellee had
alleged specific acts of negligence as causing the derailment
he was not entitled to the benefit of the presumption of
negligence of appellants on proof of the relation of carrier
and passenger, and a derailment resulting in an injury to
the passenger. Proof of such facts makes a *prima facie* case
of negligence on the part of the carrier, and entitles the
injured passenger to a recovery, unless such presumption
is removed by the evidence.

Instruction No. 5, tendered and refused, in effect stated
that to be entitled to recover, the plaintiff must prove
by a preponderance of the evidence that the derail-
8. ment was the result of the imperfect track, imperfect
and defective axles and of the speed of the train,
combined. This instruction is erroneous, and was rightly refused for reasons already stated in this opinion.

Instructions Nos. 7 and 17 refused, as far as ap-
9. plicable to the issues, were covered by others given,
and no error was committed in refusing them.

Most of the objections to the instructions given by the
court are based on appellants' construction of the complaint,
and under our view are not tenable, for reasons apparent
from our discussion of the complaint.

The jury was clearly instructed on the burden of proof,
and the burden of maintaining the affirmative of the issue
of negligence charged in the complaint was not shifted to
appellants, as asserted by them. The jury was also told that
if it found that the car in which appellee was riding was
derailed bv something not alleged in the complaint as causing its derailment, or by some unforeseen or unexplainable

accident, and appellants were exercising the highest practical care and skill for the safety of their passengers, there could be no recovery. This gave appellants the full benefit of the limitations of proof set by the specific allegations of the causes of the derailment.

Complaint is also made that the court by its fourth instruction told the jury that although a common carrier of passengers does not insure the safety of its passengers, the law will not "tolerate any negligence on the part of said carrier." The instruction is not technically accurate, as it fails to limit the negligence to that charged in the complaint. In view of the other instructions given on the subject of the proof required to authorize a finding against appellants, they could not have been harmed by this omission. Furthermore, the error is rendered harmless in this case by reason of the fact that the jury expressly finds in its special verdict that appellants were guilty of negligence in causing the derailment in the manner and by the means charged in the complaint. *Baum* v. *Palmer* (1905), 165 Ind. 513, 518, 76 N. E. 108; *Pittsburgh, etc., R. Co.* v. *Higgs* (1906), 165 Ind. 694, 76 N. E. 299, 4 L. R. A. (N. S.) 1081. The instructions considered as a whole fairly and accurately state the law applicable to the issues and the evidence, both on the subject of liability and the measure of damages.

We find no available error in the record, and the judgment is therefore affirmed.

NOTE.—Reported in 100 N. E. 773. See, also, under (1, 3) 6 Cyc. 626; (2, 4, 8) 6 Cyc. 628—New Anno.; (5) 38 Cyc. 1508; (6) 3 Cyc. 386; (7) 6 Cyc. 628; (9) 38 Cyc. 1711; (10) 38 Cyc. 1782. As to derailed car or broken rail as *res ipsa loquitur*, see 20 Am. St. 491. As to legal theory of causal connection in respect of proximate cause, see 36 Am. St. 807. As to counsel's misconduct in course of argument as ground for reversal, see 9 Am. St. 564. On the question of pleading particular cause of injury as waiver of right to rely on *res ipsa loquitur*, see 24 L. R. A. (N. S.) 788. As to the relation of doctrine *res ipsa loquitur* to burden of proof, see 16

L. R. A. (N. S.) 527. Upon the presumption of negligence from injury to passenger, see 13 L. R. A. (N. S.) 601; 29 L. R. A. (N. S.) 808. For a discussion of the derailment of a train or car as evidence of negligence on the part of a carrier of passengers, see 12 Ann. Cas. 1045.

LAKE ERIE AND WESTERN RAILROAD COMPANY ET AL. *v*. MAROTT.

[No. 7,800.   Filed February 11, 1913.]

1. INJUNCTION.—*Act Involving Violation of Contract.—Complaint. —Sufficiency.—Exhibit.*—In an action by the assignee of a contract, granting the right to lay and maintain a gas main along the right of way of a railroad company, to enjoin the company from removing the main, the complaint was not demurrable on the ground that it contained an insufficient statement of the contract and that the defect was not cured by making the contract an exhibit thereto, since the contract was the foundation of plaintiff's right and was properly incorporated into the complaint by attaching thereto and filing therewith a copy as an exhibit, as provided by §308 Burns 1908, §362 R. S. 1881, requiring, where a pleading is founded on a written instrument, that the original, or a copy thereof, must be filed with such pleading. p. 337.

2. INJUNCTION.—*Nature of Remedy.*—Injunction is a form of proceeding in which the relief sought is negative in character, that is, it is to prevent the commission of some threatened act involving the violation of a contract or duty. p. 337.

3. CONTRACTS.—*Written Agreements.—Nature.—Determination.*—In determining the nature of a written agreement, the courts will look to the engagements of the parties as therein set out, rather than to the designation of the instrument. p. 338.

4. CONTRACTS.—*Grant of Right to Lay Gas Main.—Assignability.*—An agreement by a railroad company specifically providing that for a definite consideration, the company grants to a named company the right to lay and maintain a gas main along and across its right of way for a certain number of years, subject to certain supervisory control by the chief engineer of the railroad company, though designated both as an agreement and a license, constitutes an assignable agreement in the absence of an express covenant against assignment. p. 338.

5. CONTRACTS.—*Grant of Right to Lay Gas Main.—Covenant Against Assignment.—Construction.*—Where a contract granting

the right to lay a gas main along the right of way of a railroad company, provided that it should not be assigned without the written consent of the railroad company, an assignment by a receiver of the grantee passed to the assignee all rights of the grantee under such contract, since such covenants are not favored, and do not operate against an assignment by operation of law, but will be held to be directed only against a voluntary assignment by the grantee. p. 339.

6. APPEAL.—*Review.*—*Theory of Action.*—Where the assignee of a contract, granting the right to maintain a gas main on the right of way of a railroad company, sued to enjoin the company from removing such main, and the company defended on the theory that the contract was not assignable and that plaintiff obtained no rights by virtue of such assignment, it will be held to such theory on appeal, and cannot adopt the theory that plaintiff has no rights because the evidence fails to show that the stipulated rental was paid. p. 341.

From Marion Circuit Court (18,475); *Charles Remster,* Judge.

Action by George J. Marott against the Lake Erie & Western Railroad Company and another. From a judgment for plaintiff, the defendants appeal. *Affirmed.*

John B. Cockrum and *Shirts & Fertig,* for appellants.
Ralph Bamberger and *Isadore Feibleman,* for appellee.

ADAMS, J.—This action was brought by appellee against appellants, to enjoin and restrain the latter from taking up, removing, or in any manner interfering with, a certain pipeline constructed along and across the right of way of said appellants, near the town of Eaton, Delaware county, Indiana.

On a verified showing made to the court, a temporary restraining order was issued. Appellants filed a motion to dissolve the restraining order, which motion was overruled. Issue of law was formed by appellants' demurrer to the complaint. which demurrer was overruled. Issue of fact was formed by answer of general denial. Trial by the court, and on request the court made a special finding of facts and stated conclusions of law thereon. To the conclu-

sions of law and to each conclusion appellants separately
and severally excepted. Motion for a new trial was overruled, and judgment rendered on the conclusions of law,
enjoining appellants from taking up, removing or in any
way interfering with the pipe-line in question until February 11, 1917.

Errors relied on for reversal are (1) overruling motion
to dissolve temporary restaining order; (2) overruling demurrer to the complaint; (3) error in the conclusions of
law; (4) error in each conclusion of law; (5) error in overruling motion for a new trial. As the motion to dissolve the
temporary restraining order was based on the alleged insufficiency of the complaint, the first two errors assigned
may be considered together.

After averring that appellant, Lake Erie and Western
Railroad Company, was operating the Fort Wayne, Cincinnati and Louisville Railroad, and owned the entire capital
stock of the latter company, the complaint proceeds substantially as follows: That on February 11, 1907, the Fort
Wayne, Cincinnati and Louisville Railroad Company entered into a certain agreement with the United Box Board
and Paper Company, a corporation having a factory located
at Eaton, Indiana, wherein and whereby the Fort Wayne,
Cincinnati and Louisville Railroad Company granted to
said United Box Board and Paper Company the right to
lay, maintain and use one six-inch pipe for gas along and
across the right of way and under the tracks of said Fort
Wayne, Cincinnati and Louisville Railroad Company, near
the town of Eaton, Delaware county, Indiana; "that a full,
true and correct copy of said agreement is hereto attached,
herewith filed, and made a part of this complaint, marked
'Exhibit A' ''; that in accordance with said agreement, the
United Box Board and Paper Company, of Eaton, Indiana,
laid and caused to be laid a line of six-inch pipe along and
across the right of way and under the track of said Fort
Wayne, Cincinnati and Louisville Railroad Company, for a

distance of about 24,100 feet, near said town of Eaton; that said pipe was, ever since has been, and now is a part of a pipe-line running from said gas wells, then owned by the United Box Board and Paper Company, and located in Blackford county, Indiana, through said town of Eaton, and thence to the city of Muncie Indiana; that at said time the United Box Board and Paper Company used natural gas for fuel in the operation of its factories at Eaton, Indiana, and also sold the output of its wells, conveyed as aforesaid through said pipe-line, to various factories in and about said city of Muncie; that in a certain action then pending in the chancery court of the State of New Jersey, wherein the Lockport Felt Company was complainant, and the United Box Board and Paper Company was defendant, Thomas L. Raymond and Sidney Mitchell were appointed receivers of all the assets of said United Box Board and Paper Company, and said receivers were authorized to sell to appellee leases covering the gas field in Blackford county, and the right of way, pipe-line, gas and gas wells, including the right of way mentioned in the agreement heretofore referred to, executed between the Fort Wayne, Cincinnati and Louisville Railroad Company and the United Box Board and Paper Company. It is also averred in the complaint that in a certain action then pending in the circuit court of the United States for the district of Indiana, between the same parties, said court on July 6, 1908, appointed Sidney Mitchell as ancillary receiver of the United Box Board and Paper Company, and thereafter, an order was entered permitting and authorizing said ancillary receiver to sell to appellee the leases covering the gas field, situate in Blackford county, and the right of way, pipe-lines, gas, gas wells, pipe and fittings therein and thereto; that in conformity with said order the receiver did, on or about December 31, 1908, sell and convey to appellee all the property above mentioned, including the right of way granted by the agreement executed between the Fort Wayne, Cin-

cinnati and Louisville Railroad Company and the United
Box Board and Paper Company; that ever since said time
appellee has been and now is the owner of all of said property; that said pipe-line has for a long time been used to
convey gas to factories in Delaware county, and particularly in the city of Muncie; that appellee owns and operates
the property and property rights herein set out, and that
the same are of great value, not only to appellee but to the
industries using gas conducted through appellee's pipe-
lines, acquired as aforesaid; that such industries are constructed for the use of gas and for no other fuel, and are
entirely dependent on said pipe-line for the conveyance of
said fuel, and without which said industries would be compelled to close, throwing out of employment a large number
of employes, and causing great and irreparable injury and
loss to appellee, by reason of damages to which said industries would be entitled by appellee's failure to deliver such
fuel gas.

It is further averred that appellee has paid the full consideration and performed all the conditions of the agreement between the Fort Wayne, Cincinnati and Louisville
Railroad Company and the United Box Board and Paper
Company; that appellants knowing that said agreement
does not, by its terms, expire until February 10, 1917, and
with full knowledge of the facts herein set out, threaten
to, and, unless restrained by the court, will remove said
pipe-line, thereby causing appellee great and irreparable
damage, and making the balance of said pipe-line and all
of said gas wells, leases and contracts for the sale of gas,
now belonging to appellee, of no value whatever; that such
threatened action in the removal of said pipe-line would be
in violation of the agreement between the Fort Wayne, Cincinnati and Louisville Railroad Company and the United
Box Board and Paper Company. The complaint further
shows an emergency for the immediate issuance of a restrain-

ing order, and prays for a perpetual writ of injunction on the final hearing.

The contract, set out as an exhibit to the complaint, is shown to have been executed on February 11, 1907, for a term of ten years. No question arises on any part of this contract, except the sixth section, which provides that "the said pipe shall be used for the sole purpose of conveying gas, and this license shall not be assigned without the written consent of said first party being first obtained."

Appellants insist that the court erred in overruling the several demurrers to the complaint on the ground that the contract between the Fort Wayne, Cincinnati and

1. Louisville Railroad Company and the United Box Board and Paper Company not being the foundation of the action, could not be brought into the complaint by filing it as an exhibit thereto, and that no sufficient statement of the contract is contained in the complaint without the exhibit.

It is true that under §368 Burns 1908, §362 R. S. 1881, "when any pleading is founded on a written instrument * * * the original, or a copy thereof, must be filed with the pleading." This statutory requirement has been held to be imperative. In some cases, however, it is not always clear that the right declared on is directly founded on a written instrument. Injunction is a form of pro-

2. ceeding in which the relief sought is negative in character; that is to say, it is to prevent the commission of some threatened act involving the violation of a

1. contract or duty. When the threat is carried out, and becomes an accomplished fact, the remedy of the aggrieved party is an action for damages for violation of the contract. In such a case, the written contract is clearly the foundation of the action, and must be copied into the complaint or set out as an exhibit to the complaint. We fail to see wherein a proceeding to enjoin a threatened act,

whereby the complainant's rights under a contract are about
to be violated, is in any essential particular different from
a direct action for damages for the breach of such contract, in so far as the contract in each case constitutes the
foundation of the action.

In this case the complaint shows that a contract was entered into between the Fort Wayne, Cincinnati and Louisville Railroad Company and the United Box Board and
Paper Company, by the terms of which appellee acquired
certain property rights, for the preservation of which and
to avoid irreparable injury, this action was brought. Without the written contract, appellee would have no right of
action, either for injunction or for damages. We think the
contract was essentially the foundation of appellee's right,
and was a proper exhibit to be filed with the complaint as
a part thereof. *Old* v. *Mohler* (1890), 122 Ind. 594, 596,
23 N. E. 967; *Clupper* v. *Clupper* (1904), 163 Ind. 418, 421,
72 N. E. 125; *Williams* v. *Frybarger* (1894), 9 Ind. App.
558, 560, 37 N. E. 202; *State, ex rel.,* v. *Adams* (1896), 15
Ind. App. 310, 312, 44 N. E. 47.

Appellants make the further point that even if the contract is to be deemed a part of the complaint, still no right
of action is shown, for the reason that the same provides
that "this license shall not be assigned without the written
consent of said first party being first obtained," and hence
the instrument by its nature, as well as by its terms, is
simply a license and therefore not assignable.

It is elemental that courts in determining the
3. nature of a written agreement will look to the engagements of the parties as therein set out, rather than to
the designation of the instrument. The agreement
4. before us, while characterized both as an agreement
and a license, specifically provides that for a definite
consideration the Fort Wayne, Cincinnati and Louisville
Railroad Company grants to the United Box Board and
Paper Company the right to lay, maintain and use a six-

inch pipe for gas along and across its right of way for a
period of ten years from February 11, 1907, subject to certain supervisory control by the chief engineer of the railroad company. This would clearly constitute an
5. assignable agreement, but by its terms there is an
express covenant against assignment without the
written consent of the railroad company, and as there is
no averment that such consent was first obtained, it is
urged that the complaint states no cause of action in favor
of appellee. This would doubtless be true, if appellee were
claiming a right by virtue of an assignment, from the United
Box Board and Paper Company. The complaint, however,
shows that he obtained title to the property and leases
through a judicial sale, and the rule generally applicable
does not obtain in cases where title is taken by operation
of law.

Covenants in leases against assignment or subletting, having the force of conditions, are not favored by the courts.
It is said in Jones, Landlord and Tenant §464: "Covenants against assignments, or underletting, are not favorably regarded by the courts, and are liberally construed in
favor of lessees, so as to prevent the restriction of extending any further than necessary." This proposition is stated
even more strongly in *Riggs* v. *Purcell* (1876), 66 N. Y.
193, 198, wherein it is said: "Such covenants are re-
straints which courts do not favor. They are construed with
the utmost jealousy, and very easy modes have always been
countenanced for defeating them." Again, in Jones, Landlord and Tenant §466, it is said: "An ordinary covenant
against sub-letting and assignment is not broken by a transfer of the leased premises by operation of law, but the covenant may be so drawn as to expressly prohibit such transfer, and in that case the lease would be forfeited by an
assignment by operation of law. Where a lessee cove-
nanted 'not to let, set, assign, transfer, make over, barter,
exchange or otherwise part with the premises,' and after-

wards gave a warrant of attorney to confess judgment, on which the lease was taken and sold; this was held to be no forfeiture, for all the words used in the lease point to some act to be done by the tenant himself, and there is a distinction between acts that a party does voluntarily and those that pass *in invitum;* and judgments in contemplation of law always pass *in invitum.''*

In McAdam, Landlord and Tenant (4th ed.) §141, the rule is thus stated: ''A covenant not to assign is broken by a voluntary assignment for the benefit of creditors, but is not infringed by an assignment by operation of law, as, for instance, under the bankrupt laws in case of the tenant's bankruptcy, or under the insolvent laws in case of his insolvency, or by means of an execution sale, for in such cases the assignment is not the act of the tenant, but of the law.''

This is not a new legal principle, but has been a recognized rule for more than a century. In *Doe* v. *Bevan* (1815), 3 M. & S. 353, Bayley, J., said: ''In *Doe* v. *Carter* [(1798), 8 T. R. 57], it was decided that a proviso, that if the lessee, his executors, administrators, or assigns should assign, the landlord might re-enter, contemplated only a voluntary assignment, and not one which passed *in invitum* of the lessee, and where the party making the assignment acted in discharge of a duty cast upon him by the law. It has never been considered that the lessee's becoming bankrupt was an avoiding of the lease within this proviso; and if it be not, what act has the lessee done to avoid it? All that has followed upon his bankruptcy is not by his act but by the operation of law, transferring his property to his assignees. Then shall the assignee have capacity to take it, and yet not to dispose of it? Shall they take it only for their own benefit, or be obliged to retain it in their hands to the prejudice of the creditors for whose benefit the law originally cast it upon them? Undoubtedly that can never be.'' Many other authorities support the propositions above stated, among which are the following:

Doe v. *Carter, supra; Jackson* v. *Corliss* (1811), 7 Johns.
*531; *Jackson* v. *Silvernail* (1818), 15 Johns. *278; *Smith*
v. *Putnam* (1825), 3 Pick. (Mass.) 221; *Bemis* v. *Wilder*
(1868), 100 Mass. 446; *Farnum* v. *Hefner* (1889), 79 Cal.
575, 21 Pac. 955, 12 Am. St. 174; *Gazlay* v. *Williams* (1906),
147 Fed. 678, 77 C. C. A. 662, 14 L. R. A. (N. S.) 1199;
Wood, Landlord and Tenant (2d ed.) 714; 1 Taylor, Landlord and Tenant §408.

It is averred in the complaint before us that appellee
purchased the right granted by the lease at a receiver's sale,
made pursuant to an order of the chancery court of New
Jersey, and the circuit court of the United States for the
district of Indiana. Under the authorities herein quoted
and cited, the covenant which would have been broken by
an assignment of the lease by the United Box Board and
Paper Company would not be broken where the lease was
sold on decree in a proceeding against the original lessee.
We must, therefore, hold that the rights under the lease
originally granted to the United Box Board and Paper Company passed to appellee, and that the complaint is not bad
on account of the covenant in the lease against assignment.

Appellants also rely for reversal on error of the court in
stating its conclusions of law. We deem it sufficient to say
that an examination of the findings discloses that the substance of the contract was set out therein, as was also a description of the leased premises, from which a surveyor
might locate the same. The law requires no greater exact-
ness.

It is finally urged that the trial court erred in overruling
appellants' motion for a new trial, in that there was no evidence that the stipulated rental was paid. This
6. seems to be true. There was no proof of the payment
of $1 per annum in advance, as provided in the agree-
ment. Appellee, however, did prove by letters received from
officers and agents of appellants that in 1909, a demand was
made that appellee execute a new contract providing for

the payment of an annual rental of $535, and appellee was notified that failure to execute such contract would result in the removal of the pipe-line from the railroad property.

It was fairly shown by the evidence that appellants did not recognize that appellee had any right in the leased premises. On July 28, 1909, the chief engineer of appellants wrote appellee, in part, as follows: ''We have a pipe-line located on our right of way extending for a distance of 24,100 feet north of Eaton, Indiana, which formerly belonged to the United Box Board and Paper Company. This pipe-line is not covered by an agreement, and it will be necessary to either have an agreement executed covering this pipe-line, or have the pipe-line removed.'' In a subsequent letter appellants fixed the rental at $535 per annum, and still later appellee was notified that if he could not see his way clear to pay the rental named, steps would be taken to have the pipe-line removed from the railroad company's right of way.

The evidence shows that appellants were acting throughout on the assumption that appellee had no right of any kind under the grant to the United Box Board and Paper Company. The threat of appellants to remove the pipe-line from their right of way was not made on account of appellee's failure to pay an annual rental of $1, but clearly on account of his refusal to execute a new lease at an annual rental of $535. This was the theory on which the action was brought and defended. Another theory cannot be adopted on appeal.

Finding no reversible error in the record, the judgment is affirmed.

NOTE.—Reported in 100 N. E. 865. See, also, under (1) 22 Cyc. 932; (2) 22 Cyc. 741; (4, 5) 4 Cyc. 20; (6) 2 Cyc. 670. As to the construction of a restrictive covenant in a lease against an assignment or subletting, see Ann. Cas. 1913 B 889.

DAVIS v. BRYANT.

[No. 7,824. Filed February 11, 1913.]

1. APPEAL.—*Presentation of Questions for Review.—Errors Occurring During Trial.*—No question is presented on appeal by assignment that the trial court erred in overruling a motion to dismiss the action for want of certain proof, and that it erred in sustaining certain objections to questions asked a witness, since errors occurring during the trial, to be available, must be saved by assigning them as causes for a new trial. p. 344.

2. REPLEVIN.—*Action.—Necessity for Demand.*—Where the possession of goods sought to be replevied was wrongfully obtained, no demand is necessary before bringing the action. p. 344.

3. APPEAL.—*Review.—Insufficient Briefs.*—On appeal from a judgment for plaintiff in replevin, the court cannot determine if proof of a demand was necessary where appellant's brief does not contain any of the evidence in the case. p. 344.

4. APPEAL.—*Ruling on Motion for New Trial.—Waiver of Error.—Briefs.*—An assignment of error in overruling a motion for a new trial, based on the insufficiency of the evidence, will not be considered, where neither the motion nor any of its grounds are set out in appellant's brief, and no statement of the evidence is contained therein. p. 344.

From Superior Court of Marion County (78,160); *Charles J. Orbison,* Judge.

Action by Sanford Bryant against Sherman Davis. From a judgment for plaintiff, the defendant appeals. *Affirmed.*

George M. Russell and *R. Breckenridge Smith,* for appellant.

James T. V. Hill, for appellee.

HOTTEL, J.—This is an action in replevin begun before a justice of the peace.

From a judgment in appellee's favor, appellant appeals and assigns as errors:

(1) The court erred in overruling appellant's motion to dismiss for want of proof of demand; (2) the court erred in sustaining appellee's objection to questions propounded to Sherman Davis, as to whether or not he was a common

carrier; (3) the court erred in overruling appellant's motion for a new trial.

If either of the rulings of the trial court indicated by the first two of the assigned errors could be said to furnish a ground for reversible error in the form in
1. which the questions ruled on were presented to the trial court, the manner of their presentation to this court prevents their consideration.

Errors occurring during trial must be saved by assigning them as cause for a new trial. *Rhodius* v. *Johnson* (1900), 24 Ind. App. 401, 56 N. E. 942; *Stephens* v. *Smith* (1901), 27 Ind. App. 507, 61 N. E. 745; *Martin* v. *Motsinger* (1892), 130 Ind. 555, 30 N. E. 523; *Herrick* v. *Flinn* (1896), 146 Ind. 258, 45 N. E. 187.

If the matters assigned as error are only causes for a new trial, no questions are raised. *Singer* v. *Tormoehlen* (1898), 150 Ind. 287, 289, 49 N. E. 1055; *Migatz* v. *Stieglitz* (1906), 166 Ind. 361, 365, 77 N. E. 400; *George* v. *Robinson* (1905), 36 Ind. App. 310, 312, 75 N. E. 607.

We might add, with reference to the first alleged error assigned, that the complaint in this case avers both a pos-
2. session without right and an unlawful detention of the property sought to be replevied. Where the possession of the goods sought to be replevied was wrongfully obtained, no demand is necessary before the action for possession is commenced. *Ahlendorf* v. *Barkous* (1898). 20 Ind. App. 657, 659, 50 N. E. 887; *Bates* v. *State, ex. rel.* (1881), 75 Ind. 463; *Robinson* v. *Skipworth* (1864), 23 Ind. 311.

Appellant has failed to set out in his brief any part
3. of the evidence in the case, and in its absence this court cannot determine whether proof of a demand was necessary. The only questions discussed in ap-
4. pellant's brief under the third error assigned relate to the admission or sufficiency of the evidence, and neither the motion for a new trial nor any of its grounds

are set out in appellant's brief, nor is any of the evidence set out in such brief. These omissions, under the rules of the Supreme Court and this court, deprive appellant of a consideration of this assigned error. Clause 5, Rule 22, Supreme and Appellate Courts. See *Bartholomew* v. *Grimes* (1912), 51 Ind. App. 614, 100 N. E. 12, and authorities cited.

Judgment affirmed.

NOTE.—Reported in 100 N. E. 1062. See, also, under (1) 29 Cyc. 736; (2) 34 Cyc. 1406; (3) 2 Cyc. 1013. As to the demand and refusal preliminary to proceedings in replevin, see 80 Am. St. 753.

MASCARI *v.* HERT.

[No. 7,836. Filed February 11, 1913.]

1. APPEAL.—*Vacation Appeal.*—Where judgment was rendered on the eighteenth judicial day of the October term, 1909, and a motion to modify was filed on the twenty-second judicial day of such term, and overruled on the nineteenth judicial day of the January term, 1910, and the precipe bears date of January 31, the certificate to the transcript is dated February 14, and the record on appeal was filed October 20, 1910, the appeal must be regarded as a vacation appeal. p. 347.

2. APPEAL.—*Parties.*—*Dismissal.*—Where a party to the judgment below, in so far as the record discloses, is not a party to the appeal, and has not been served with notice as required by §674 Burns 1908, Acts 1899 p. 5, providing that, in case of appeal by a part of several coparties, notice of the appeal must be served on all the copa ties not appealing, the appeal cannot be entertained for want of jurisdiction. pp. 347, 348.

3. APPEAL.—*Vacation Appeal.*—*Parties.*—In a vacation appeal, all those against whom a judgment has been rendered, either *in rem* or *personam*, or who, in any manner are bound or affected thereby, must be made coappellants. p. 347.

4. APPEAL.—*Judgment.*—*Parties.*—Although the only question involved in an appeal is one of costs adjudged against appellant, and by the judgment appellant's codefendant recovered her costs, such codefendant is a necessary party to the appeal, since any order changing the judgment of the lower court must affect her interest. p. 348.

From Superior Court of Marion County (75,812); *Lawson M. Harvey*, Judge.

Proceedings supplementary to execution brought by Jacob Hert against Antonio Mascari and another. From a judgment against him for costs, the defendant, Antonio Mascari, appeals. *Appeal dismissed.*

Charles E. Averill, for appellant.
C. E. Fenstermacher, for appellee.

SHEA, J.—This was a proceeding supplementary to execution brought by appellee against appellant, Antonio Mascari, and Anna Mascari, his wife.

Appellee filed his affidavit or complaint in two paragraphs, alleging in each facts sufficient to authorize the issuance of an order requiring the defendants therein to appear. The proceeding was summary, and no pleadings affecting the allegations of the affidavit were filed.

The court made the following finding: "Come the parties and the court having heretofore taken this cause under advisement and being duly advised finds for the defendants and that plaintiff take nothing by this action except his costs expended herein. It is therefore considered, and adjudged by the court that defendant Antony Mascari pay the costs of this action taxed at $——." Appellant Antonio Mascari filed his separate motion, praying for a modification of the judgment by retaxing the costs. This motion was by the court overruled, which ruling is assigned as error in this court.

Appellee presents a motion to dismiss the appeal on the following grounds: (1) The motion to modify the judgment was a part of the main action from which no appeal lies. (2) In vacation appeals all parties to the judgment must be parties to the appeal, or the appeal will be dismissed for want of jurisdiction. Both Antonio Mascari and Anna Mascari, his wife, were parties to the record in the court below. Appellee's attorney, in his motion to dismiss, and in his argument, asserts that this is a vacation appeal.

This statement is not disputed by appellant's attorney, either in his brief or otherwise.

The judgment was rendered on October 23, 1909, being the eighteenth judicial day of the October term of the court.

1. The motion to modify the judgment was filed on October 28, 1909, the twenty-second judicial day of the October term of the court. On January 24, 1910, the nineteenth judicial day of the January term of the court, motion to modify the judgment was overruled. The precipe bears date of January 31, 1910. The certificate to the transcript bears date of February 14, 1910. The record was filed in this court on October 20, 1910, so that this must be regarded as a vacation appeal.

Section 674 Burns 1908, Acts 1899 p. 5, contains the following language: "A part of several co-parties may appeal to the supreme or appellate court, but in such case

2. they must serve written notice of the appeal upon all of the other co-parties or their attorneys of record, and file proof thereof with the clerk of such court * * *."

Anna Mascari, who was a party to the judgment in the court below, in so far as the record in this case discloses, is not a party to the appeal, and in so far as the record discloses was not served with the notice required.

In the case of *Haymaker* v. *Schneck* (1903), 160 Ind. 443, 67 N. E. 181, the court uses this language: "Under the circumstances, any one of the defendants in this

3. action had the right to appeal in term time from this judgment, without joining as a coappellant any of his codefendants, but the rule is otherwise, when an appeal is taken, as is this, in vacation, for in such cases all of the defendants against whom a judgment has been rendered, either *in rem* or *personam*, or who, in any manner, are bound or affected thereby must be made coappellants. Merely making them appellees in the appeal does not comply with the rule. All must be made appellants, otherwise the appeal

cannot be entertained for want of jurisdiction. It
2. is evident, under the circumstances, that appellant in
    this case has omitted to comply with this well-settled
rule of appellate procedure, and therefore this court is without power to hear and determine the appeal upon its merits.
Consequently all we can do is to sustain the motion to dismiss, as we are absolutely without authority to waive the
rule and assume jurisdiction in the case.   The following
decisions, among many others, fully affirm and support the
rule which appellee herein demands shall be enforced: *Mc
Kee* v. *Root* [1899], 153 Ind. 314 [54 N. E. 802], and cases
there cited; *Gregory* v. *Smith* [1894], 139 Ind. 48 [38 N. E.
395]; *Abshire* v. *Williamson* [1898], 149 Ind. 248 [48 N. E.
1027]; *Crist* v. *Wayne, etc., Loan Assn.* [1898], 151 Ind.
245 [51 N. E. 368]; *Michigan Mut. Life Ins. Co.* v. *Frankel*
[1898], 151 Ind. 534 [50 N. E. 304]; *Owen* v. *Dresback*
[1900], 154 Ind. 392 [56 N. E. 22, 56 N. E. 848]."

The only question involved in this appeal is one of
costs？ By the judgment in the lower court, Anna Mascari
        recovered her costs in the action against Antonio
4. Mascari.   Any order of this court changing the judg-
    ment of the lower court must affect her interests.   She
was therefore a necessary party to this appeal.

The appeal is dismissed for want of jurisdiction.

NOTE.—Reported in 100 N. E. 781. See, also, under (2) 2 Cyc.
804; 3 Cyc. 185; (3) 2 Cyc. 758; (4) 2 Cyc. 756. As to who may
appeal as an interested or injured party, see 119 Am. St. 740. For
a discussion of the parties entitled to a notice of appeal, see 13
Ann. Cas. 181; 21 Ann. Cas. 1277.

THE CLEVELAND, CINCINNATI, CHICAGO AND ST. LOUIS RAILWAY COMPANY *v.* NICHOLS, ADMINISTRATOR.

[No. 7,726. Filed October 16, 1912. Rehearing denied February 11, 1913.]

1. RAILROADS.—*Crossing Accidents.—Complaint.—Sufficiency.* — A complaint to recover for the death of plaintiff's decedent in a crossing accident, alleging that as decedent approached the crossing he had an unobstructed view for half a mile to the east, and that, when fifty feet from the crossing, he looked to the east and saw no train approaching, that the view to the west was obstructed by freight cars on defendant's tracks, and that decedent was thereby required to keep a close watch to the west until he was upon defendant's right of way to ascertain if a train were approaching from that direction, and that on ascertaining that no train was approaching from the west, he attempted to cross, that the crossing was defective and was dangerous to cross without going slowly, that while he was on the crossing a train approached from the east at the rate of sixty miles per hour and without ringing a bell, in violation of city ordinances regulating the operation of trains through the city, and, though he made every effort to get out of its way, he was struck by such train and killed, sufficiently states a cause of action. p. 351.

2. RAILROADS. — *Crossing Accidents. — Complaint. — Contributory Negligence.*—Where the complaint, in an action against a railroad company, alleged that decedent, as he approached a crossing, was obliged to keep a close watch to the west, on account of obstructions, and that, relying on a previous look to the east which gave him a clear view for a distance of one-half mile and disclosed no approaching train, he traveled the last fifty feet of the approach without looking to the east, that the crossing was defective, making progress over the track slow, and that while he was on the crossing a train from the east approached the crossing without warning, and at an unlawful rate of speed, and killed decedent. It cannot be said, as a matter of law, that decedent was guilty of contributory negligence. p. 352.

3. EVIDENCE.—*Judicial Notice.—Noise of Approaching Train.*—The court may take judicial notice of the fact that an approaching train will make some noise. p. 353.

4. RAILROADS.—*Crossing Accidents.—Care in Approaching Crossings.*—A person approaching a railroad crossing must use ordinary care to avoid injury, and whether ordinary care was used in a given case must be determined from a consideration of the

situation of the party at the time, his surroundings, and the
apparent danger. p. 354.

5. *Negligence.—Contributory Negligence.—Jury Question.*—Where
the facts are of a character to be reasonably subjected to more
than one inference or conclusion, the ultimate fact of contributory negligence, or due care, should be determined by the jury.
p. 354.

6. *Railroads.— Crossing Accidents.— Contributory Negligence.—
Jury Question.*—Where decedent failed to stop his horse after
he had reached a point within five feet of defendant's tracks, and
from there look in both directions before attempting to cross, it
is for the jury to determine from the evidence, under proper instructions, whether he was guilty of contributory negligence.
p. 354.

7. *Appeal.—Review.—Harmless Error.—Instructions.—Refusal.—*
The refusal of requested instructions is not reversible error,
where the instructions given were applicable to the issues and
fully and fairly stated the law. p. 355.

8. *Railroads.—Crossing Accidents.—Evidence.—Verdict.—Conclusiveness.*—Where, in an action against a railroad company to
recover for the death of plaintiff's decedent in a crossing accident, defended on the ground of contributory negligence, appellant's negligence and decedent's care were, under the evidence,
controverted questions of fact, a verdict for plaintiff cannot be
disturbed on the ground of insufficient evidence. p. 356.

From Marion Circuit Court (17,318); *Charles Remster,*
Judge.

Action by Baxter G. Nichols, administrator of the estate
of John A. Shewmon, deceased, against The Cleveland, Cincinnati, Chicago and St. Louis Railway Company. From a
judgment for plaintiff, the defendant appeals. *Affirmed.*

*John W. Kern, John J. Kelly, Leonard J. Hackney, Frank
L. Littleton* and *W. F. Elliott,* for appellant.

M. M. Bachelder, for appellee.

Felt, J.—Suit by appellee to recover damages for the
death of his decedent, John A. Shewmon, alleged to have
been caused by appellant's negligence. Trial by a jury resulted in a verdict for appellee in the sum of $2,500. Ap-
pellant's motions for judgment on the special findings and

for a new trial were overruled, and this appeal taken from the judgment on the general verdict.

The first error assigned and relied on by appellant is that the trial court erred in overruling the demurrer to appellee's complaint. The complaint sets forth much detail and is lengthy, but, in substance, charges that about 3 o'clock on the afternoon of September 28, 1908, appellee's decedent, while driving a one-horse wagon along Keystone avenue in the city of Indianapolis, was struck and killed by one of appellant's trains at a point where appellant's railroad crosses said Keystone avenue; that as said decedent approached said crossing he had an unobstructed view of appellant's tracks for half a mile to the east of Keystone avenue; that he looked to the east when fifty feet from appellant's right of way, and saw no train approaching him from that direction; that when fifty feet south of said crossing he looked to the west to ascertain whether any cars or locomotives were approaching from that direction; that his view of appellant's tracks to the west from that point and until he got within five feet of said crossing was obstructed by freight cars standing on one of appellant's tracks; that decedent was obliged to and did keep close watch to the west, to determine whether any cars were approaching him from behind said obstructions, until he was upon appellant's right of way, when he ascertained that none was coming from that direction; that he relied on his previous view to the east and the fact that appellant would not violate the laws of the State or the ordinances of said city in the operation of its trains within the city limits; that appellant maintained its Keystone avenue crossing in an unlawful and negligent manner, in this: that it was not planked, that the space between the rails was not filled, and the rails protruded some six or eight inches above the level of the ground at said point of intersection, making it very dangerous and hard for one to cross

1.

over said tracks without going very slowly; that at the time decedent attempted to cross said Keystone avenue crossing, appellant negligently, carelessly, unlawfully and wrongfully operated a passenger train on its said right of way from the east in the corporate limits of said city at a high rate of speed, to wit, sixty miles an hour; that decedent did not observe said train and did not know it was approaching until he was on said crossing; that he used all diligence and care within his power immediately to get out of the way of said train and across said tracks; that on account of the unlawful speed at which said train was running and the rough and unlawful condition of said crossing it was impossible for him to do so; that appellant did not ring any bell, blow any whistle, or attempt to stop or check the speed of said train, but negligently ran the same at the unlawful rate of speed, to wit, sixty miles an hour; that said train collided with decedent and killed him. The complaint then avers that certain ordinances of the city of Indianapolis were in force on the date of said accident, governing the establishment and maintenance of grade crossings, requiring a bell to be rung when a locomotive is moving in said city, and limiting the speed of trains within the city limits to four miles per hour, and alleges appellant's violation of the same. While some averments in appellee's complaint are by way of recital, and there is much detail and some repetition, a fair interpretation of the facts well pleaded shows that a cause of action is stated, and the complaint is sufficient to withstand the demurrer.

But appellant asserts that the facts alleged show that as a matter of law decedent was guilty of contributory negligence; that he was negligent in not keeping a proper

2. lookout for trains from the east while he traveled the last fifty feet of the approach to the Keystone avenue crossing, and that after he reached a point five feet from said crossing he had an unobstructed view of appellant's tracks, both to the east and to the west, but did not at that

time look to the east. Appellant further contends that this court will take judicial notice of the noise which is made by a train running at a speed of sixty miles an hour; that such noise must have been heard by decedent, and no reason is shown for his apparent failure to heed its warning; that the complaint also alleges a physically impossible state of facts, in that a train, running at a speed of sixty miles an hour, would not travel half a mile in the time taken by a horse, driven in a walk, to traverse fifty feet.

We cannot concur in appellant's view. The averments show that decedent looked to the east when about fifty feet from the right of way, and saw down the track for about half a mile and no train was in sight; that his view to the west was obstructed, making it necessary for him to keep a close watch in that direction for approaching trains; that the crossing was defective and impeded his progress in attempting to cross appellant's tracks; that no warnings were given of the approach of the train, and that it was running at a high and unlawful speed. On this state of facts we cannot hold that the complaint affirmatively shows decedent guilty of negligence contributing to his injury and death. Considering only the distance alleged and the absence of special warnings, it may be that the collision is thus shown to be improbable, if not impossible; but these averments must be considered in the light of the other allegations showing the obstructions to the west and the defective condition of the crossing, and when so considered, a cause of action is stated and the question of decedent's contributory negligence remains one of fact to be submitted to the jury.

This court may take judicial notice of the fact that an approaching train will make some noise, but on the facts alleged we cannot go to the extent of holding as a 3. matter of law that the warning given by such noise was sufficient to show decedent guilty of contributory negligence. A person approaching a railroad crossing must

use ordinary care to avoid injury, but what is such
4. care in any given case, or the precise distance from
the crossing at which the traveler must look and listen,
cannot ordinarily be stated as a matter of law. The test being, Did he, in view of his situation, surroundings and apparent danger, use ordinary care?

The principle involved is always the same, but each case
must be determined by its own peculiar facts and circumstances. If the facts are of a character to be reason-
5. ably subject to more than one inference or conclusion, the ultimate fact of contributory negligence, or
of due care, should be determined by the jury. *Baltimore,
etc., R. Co.* v. *Rosborough* (1907), 40 Ind. App. 14, 18, 80
N. E. 869; *Pittsburgh, etc., R. Co.* v. *Lynch* (1909), 43 Ind.
App. 177, 186, 87 N. E. 40; *Chicago, etc., R. Co.* v. *Turner*
(1904), 33 Ind. App. 264, 268, 69 N. E. 484; *Greenawaldt* v.
Lake Shore, etc., R. Co. (1905), 165 Ind. 219, 223, 74 N. E.
1081; *Stoy* v. *Louisville etc., R. Co.* (1903), 160 Ind. 144, 152,
66 N. E. 615; *Pittsburgh, etc., R. Co.* v. *Wright* (1881), 80
Ind. 236.

The alleged contributory negligence of decedent in failing
to stop his horse after he had reached a point within five
feet of appellant's tracks, and there looking in both
6. directions before attempting to cross, cannot be declared as a matter of law, but it is a question for the
jury to determine from the evidence, under proper instructions from the court as to the law. *Cincinnati, etc., R. Co.*
v. *Grames* (1893), 136 Ind. 39, 49, 34 N. E. 714. On the
facts averred, in the light of the foregoing decisions, it cannot be declared as a matter of law that decedent did not use
ordinary care to avoid injury as he approached the crossing
where he was injured.

The answers to the interrogatories are not in irreconcilable
conflict with the general verdict, and we cannot say from our
examination of the evidence that the jury in its answers

shows wilful disregard of the evidence, or that it was influenced by passion or prejudice.

After a careful examination of the instructions given by the court and those tendered by appellant, we are of the opinion that no error prejudicial to appellant was 7. committed by the trial court either in giving or in refusing instructions. The instructions given were applicable to the issues, and so fully and fairly state the law as to render harmless the refusal of the instructions tendered by appellant.

No good purpose can be subserved by setting out the instructions given or refused on which error has been assigned, or by a detailed discussion of the questions raised, which in this case could only mean the restatement of propositions many times declared by this court and our Supreme Court.

We find no reversible error in the admission or exclusion of evidence. Some questions are suggested where no exceptions are shown, and the other questions show no errors or relate to matters that could not possibly have harmed appellant.

Appellant earnestly insists that the verdict is not supported by sufficient evidence; that the undisputed physical facts show that decedent's own negligence contributed to his injury; that his view to the west was not obstructed, and that he could by looking have seen the approaching train from the east, and that he could have heard its approach, by reason of the necessary noise of the moving train, independently of any warning bell or whistle, had he exercised the care the law imposes on a person approaching a railroad crossing; that the alleged obstructions were so far from the crossing as not to obscure decedent's view or require his exclusive attention after he turned north on Keystone avenue.

The theory of appellant is correct, but the evidence was not so conclusive on the facts asserted as to preclude the

finding by the jury to the contrary. There was evi-
8.   dence warranting the inference or finding that decedent, before or at the time he turned north on
Keystone avenue, about 75 feet from appellant's tracks,
looked and could see no train approaching from the east
for such a distance as to give him reasonable assurance that
there was no danger of injury from a train from that direction before he could cross the tracks; that after he turned
north his view to the west was obstructed by box-cars until
he was within a few feet of the tracks; that his attention
was attracted by the noise and the ringing of the bell of a
switch engine operating a short distance west of the Keystone avenue crossing, all of which caused him to look west
for approaching trains; that from the time he was forty or
fifty feet from the tracks his view was obstructed by piles
of cross-ties, until he was within five feet of the tracks;
that he saw no train approaching from the east when 75
feet from the tracks, and relied on the fact that appellant
would not violate the city ordinance, or approach without
proper warning; that he drove upon the tracks and found
the crossing defective, which retarded his progress, and he
was on account thereof and by reason of the speed of the
approaching train, which came upon him without warning,
struck and injured as alleged. In this view of the evidence,
appellant's negligence and decedent's care were controverted questions of fact, which were properly submitted to
the jury, and under the established rules of our appellate
procedure we cannot disturb the verdict of the jury in such
a case.

Appellant insists that there is such inconsistency in the
fact of an unobstructed view to the east for more than
2,000 feet down the track when decedent was some 75 feet
from the crossing, and the finding of a collision as alleged.
as to compel the conclusion that decedent either did not
look or if he looked he did not heed the warning he must
have received. But there was evidence that in approaching

the track decedent passed over an ascending grade; that his horse halted when on the tracks, which may have been due to the alleged defects, all of which, when considered with the uncertainty of accurately measuring distance with the eye, presents a situation where the law requires the ultimate facts to be determined by the jury from the evidence. Considering the inferences that may possibly and lawfully be drawn from the facts of this case, we find no warrant for disturbing the finding of the jury or reversing the judgment of the lower court.

Judgment affirmed.

Note.—Reported in 99 N. E. 497. See, also, under (1) 33 Cyc. 1053; (2) 33 Cyc. 1111; (3) 16 Cyc. 852; (4) 33 Cyc. 981; (5) 29 Cyc. 631; (6) 33 Cyc. 1116; (7) 38 Cyc. 1816; (8) 33 Cyc. 1143. As to the duty of company's servants, in charge of train, to persons on or near the track, see 20 Am. St. 114. As to contributory negligence in failing to be on lookout for approaching cars, see 51 Am. Rep. 360. As to matters within the course and laws of nature of which a court takes judicial notice, see 124 Am. St. 27. As to the question of contributory negligence being one for the jury, see 8 Am. St. 849. For the duty of a traveller approaching railway crossing as to place and direction of observation, see 37 L. R. A. (N. S.) 136.

OHLWINE ET AL. *v.* PFAFFMAN.

[No. 7,819. Filed February 13, 1913.]

1. **Fraud.**—*Action for Damages.*—*Waiver of Fraud.*—*Ratification of Contract.*—*Effect.*—The retention of property by a party who has suffered loss through another's fraud does not preclude him from maintaining an action for damages, nor does an express waiver of the fraud and explicit ratification of the contract, unless of such a character as to imply a release from the consequences of such fraud. p. 361.

2. **Fraud.**—*Remedies.*—A person who has been induced by fraud to enter into a contract, may either repudiate the contract *in toto*, return or offer to return whatever of value he has received under it, and recover the property he has parted with, or its value; or he may affirm the contract, keep what property or advantage he has obtained under it, and recover the damages he has sustained by reason of such fraud. p. 362.

3. APPEAL.—*Review.*—*Harmless Error.*—*Refusal of Instructions.*—
Reversible error cannot be predicated on the refusal of a requested instruction that was fully and properly covered by instructions given. p. 362.

4. FRAUD.—*Waiver.*—*Acts Constituting.*—The fact that plaintiff,
in an action for damages resulting through fraud, had instituted
a former suit to rescind the contract and to obtain a reconveyance of the land, which was thereafter dismissed by him at his
own costs, and that he thereafter retained the stock he had received for the land, and continued to act as a director of the
corporation, was not inconsistent with his right to affirm the
contract and rely on his action for damages. p. 362.

5. FRAUD.—*Action.*—*Issues.*—*Instructions.*—In an action to recover damages for fraud perpetrated on plaintiff in the exchange of
corporate stock for plaintiff's land, where the complaint alleged
that T. and the other defendant conspired to induce plaintiff to
believe that T. owned the stock exchanged, that the other would
retain his stock and control the business with plaintiff, and that
T. in fact owned no stock, but that the stock exchanged was a
part of the stock owned by the other defendant, the question of
the ownership of the stock was material, so that an instruction
stating that it was wholly immaterial who was the owner of
such stock, provided plaintiff acquired a good title to same, was
properly refused. p. 362.

6. FRAUD.—*Statements of Value.*—*Opinion.*—Statements by defendants that they had paid par for their stock in a corporation,
made to induce plaintiff to exchange land therefor, were representations as to material, existing facts, and not the mere expression of opinions as to value, and constitute actionable fraud,
if they were false and were relied upon by plaintiff to his
damage. p. 364.

7. FRAUD.—*Statements of Value.*—*Representations by Vendor.*—
Reliance.—Representations of value by a vendor, who has, or
assumes to have, special knowledge of the value of property sold,
made as a basis of a contract between the parties, and with
knowledge that the vendee is ignorant of the value and is relying
on such representations, are binding on the vendor. p. 364.

8. EVIDENCE.—*Value.*—*Assessed Value of Corporation.*—*Record of
County Board of Review.*—Under §§10233, 10234 Burns 1908, Acts
1903 p. 49, requiring corporations to make out and deliver to the
assessor a sworn statement showing the value of all tangible property, and the market value, or if no market value, the actual
value of the shares of stock, and providing that such statement
shall be laid before the county board of review, it will be presumed, in the absence of a showing to the contrary, that the
board of review in fixing the assessment has regarded such state-

ment as true and correct and has fixed the true cash value of the property in accordance with the facts thereby shown, so that the record of such board showing the assessed value of corporate stock, unless made too remotely, is admissible as affording some evidence of its value. p. 365.

9. EVIDENCE.—*Presumptions.—Regularity of Corporate Acts.*—It will be presumed that the officers of a corporation, in preparing a statement of the value of all its tangible property, and of the shares of stock, as required by §10233 Burns 1908, Acts 1903 p. 49, made a true statement. p. 368.

10. NEW TRIAL.—*Misconduct of Juror.*—The fact that a juror, who had instituted an action which was compromised and dismissed before issues were formed, on being asked on his *voir dire* if he had ever had any litigation, answered "no," was not ground for a new trial, since the question was not calculated to call to his mind a case which was only filed and dismissed. p. 369.

From Noble Circuit Court; *Andrew A. Adams,* Special Judge.

Action by Philip Pfaffman against David F. Ohlwine and another. From a judgment for plaintiff, the defendants appeal. *Affirmed.*

Leonard, Rose & Zollars, T. A. Redmond and *McNagny & McNagny,* for appellants.

Deahl & Deahl and *Prickett & Carver,* for appellee.

FELT, P. J.—This is a suit by appellee to recover damages from appellant for alleged fraud in the exchange of a farm for certain stock in the Specialty Case Company, a corporation.

The complaint is in two paragraphs, but the allegations of each are similar, and, in substance, charge that in November, 1907, appellee was the owner of a farm in DeKalb county, of the value of $8,000; that in November, 1907, appellants falsely and fraudulently represented to appellee that appellant Ohlwine was the owner of 178 shares of the capital stock of the Specialty Case Company, of Kendallville, Indiana, of the par value of $8,900, for which he had paid one hundred cents on the dollar, and had purchased said stock from the Specialty Case Company; that appellant, Thomas, was the owner of 128 shares of the capital stock of said company, for which he had paid one hundred cents on the dollar; that said stock was then worth par; that appellants, in order to persuade and induce appellee to purchase said 128 shares of capital stock in said company, further falsely and fraudulently represented to him that the Specialty Case Company was then making money over and above the operating expenses; that if appellee would purchase said 128 shares of stock from appellant, Thomas, appellant, Ohlwine, would retain his 178 shares of stock, and appellee and said Ohlwine would then control the business and make from $10,000 to $15,000 annually; that appellants colluded and conspired together for the purpose of defrauding and cheating appellee out of his said farm; that the statements made to him by appellants as to the ownership of the capital stock alleged to belong to Thomas, as to the actual price paid for the stock and as to the value thereof at said time, were wholly false and untrue, and were made to appellee by appellants for the purpose of deceiving and defrauding him; that appellee had no knowledge of their falsity, and believed all said statements to be true as made by appellants, and he relied on them and purchased, as he then thought, 128 shares of capital stock from appellant, Thomas, and paid therefor the sum of $6,400, being the full par value of said stock; that Thomas did not in fact own any stock in said company, and the stock so purchased was a part of the stock of appellant, Ohlwine; that the stock at the time, viz., November 14, 1907, was worth only thirty-five or forty per cent of its face value, and appellee was thereby defrauded out of $4,000.

Appellants answered the complaint by general denial, and by a paragraph of special answer which set up the facts relating to the trade, and also alleged that appellee had prosecuted a former suit to rescind the contract under which the exchange was made, and to obtain a reconveyance of the land to him; that appellee knew all the facts connected with

said transaction when he instituted the same; that said
suit was prosecuted to final judgment against appellee; that
he continued to act as a director of the corporation, par-
ticipated in its business, and had, with full knowledge of
all the facts, ratified and confirmed the original transaction; that the facts alleged in the former suit to rescind
are substantially the same as those alleged in this suit. To
this special answer a reply was filed in general denial. On
the issues so formed the cause was submitted to a jury
for trial, and thereupon a verdict was returned for appellee
in the sum of $2,617. Appellants' motion for a new trial
was overruled, and this action of the court is the only error
relied on or discussed on appeal.

Appellants complain of the refusal of the court to give
instruction No. 22 tendered by them, which, in substance,

> informed the jury that if with full knowledge of all
1. the facts of the transaction appellee retained all the
> proceeds thereof and ratified the same, the "verdict
must be for the defendants."

In *Johnson* v. *Culver* (1888), 116 Ind. 278, 285, 19 N. E.
129, the Supreme Court declared the law applicable to the
question presented by the refusal of an instruction, as follows: "The retention of property by a party who has
suffered loss from the fraud of another does not preclude
the loser from maintaining an action for damages, nor does
even an express waiver of the fraud and explicit ratification
of the contract have the effect to deprive the party of his
action, unless, indeed, the ratification is of such a character
as to imply a release from the consequences of the fraud.
In the case of *St. John* v. *Hendrickson* [1882], 81 Ind. 350,
it was said: 'It is undoubtedly the law, that there may be
a waiver of a right to recover damages for loss resulting
from false and fraudulent representations by an express
affirmance. It is essential to such a waiver that the party
should possess full knowledge of the fraud practiced upon
him; that he should intend *to* confirm the contract and

abandon all right to recover for the loss resulting from the fraud.' "

Where a person has been induced by fraud to enter into a contract, he has his choice of remedies. He may repudi-
2. ate the contract *in toto*, return or offer to return whatever of value he has received under it, and re-cover the property he has parted with or its value; . or he may affirm the contract, keep whatever of property or advantage he has obtained under it, and recover the damages he has sustained by reason of the fraud perpetrated on him in the transaction. *Nysewander* v. *Lowman* (1890), 124 Ind. 584, 588, 24 N. E. 355; *Johnson* v. *Culver, supra,* 283; 20 Cyc. 87.

To affirm the contract, retain the actual consideration received under it and ratify the transaction falls short of a ratification with full knowledge of the fraud intending thereby to abandon all right to recover damages sustained on account of such fraud. Furthermore, in instruc-
3. tions Nos. 8 and 12, tendered by appellee and given by the court, the jury was properly instructed on the question of ratification involved in this case under the issues and the evidence.

It appeared from the evidence without dispute that the former suit was dismissed by appellee, at his own costs be-fore the issues were formed and without any trial.
4. The other things alleged to have been done by ap-pellee in relation to the business and property of the corporation were not at all inconsistent with his right to affirm the contract and rely on his action for damages.

Appellants allege error in the refusal of the court to give instruction No. 18 tendered by them, which, in sub-stance, told the jury that it was wholly immaterial
5. who was the owner of the stock transferred to ap-pellee, provided he acquired a good title to the same. It may be conceded that as a general rule the contention of appellants would be correct, but in this case the com-

plaint contained a charge that appellants conspired together to cheat and defraud appellee out of his farm; that they represented that appellant, Thomas, owned the 128 shares of stock he proposed to transfer to appellee for his farm; that, appellant, Ohlwine would not sell his 178 shares of stock if appellee would purchase said 128 shares of Thomas, but would continue to hold his stock and be active in the management of the business of the company, and he and appellee would thereby have control of a majority of the stock of the company, manage its business, and make from $10,000 to $15,000 per year; that appellant, Ohlwine, would not sell any of his stock at any price; that in fact appellant, Thomas, did not own any stock, and the stock transferred to appellee was a part of the 178 shares owned by Ohlwine; that appellee had no knowledge of the business of said company; that he had been acquainted with appellant, Ohlwine, for many years, had confidence in his honesty and in his ability to manage the business of said company; that he relied on said statements, believed them to be true, had no knowledge to the contrary, and but for such representations and his reliance thereon, he would not have executed said contract. The evidence shows that Thomas had no interest in the business of the company, owned no stock, and after obtaining from the appellee a deed for the farm, conveyed the same to appellant, Ohlwine, without any consideration. This and other evidence warranted the inference that Thomas was only a tool of Ohlwine, and that they fraudulently conspired to deceive appellee, and obtain from him his farm for a grossly inadequate consideration. On this state of facts it cannot be said that the ownership of the stock was immaterial, for it was essential to the perpetration of the fraud that appellee be deceived on this point, and be made to believe that Thomas owned the stock he was purchasing, and that Ohlwine would not sell his stock and would continue in the business.

Appellants complain of the giving of instructions Nos.

3, 4 and 5, at the request of appellee, on the ground that the instructions, in effect, told the jury that mere representations as to the price paid for stock amounted to fraud. Appellants assert that representations of the seller that he paid a certain price for an article are only trade talk, on which the purchaser has no right to rely.

The statements that appellants paid par for their stock were representations as to material, existing facts, and not the mere expression of opinions as to value. If the

6.   statements were false and appellee did not know them to be false, but relied on them to his damage, actionable fraud is shown. *Grover* v. *Cavanagh.* (1907), 40 Ind. App. 340, 346, 82 N. E. 104; *New* v. *Jackson* (1912), 50 Ind. App. 120, 95 N. E. 328, 331.

If the statements be viewed as representations of value, on the facts of this case, appellants are in no position to complain, for the reason that it is the law that if a vendor

7.   has, or assumes to have, special knowledge of the value of the property sold, and the vendee is ignorant of the value, which fact is known to the vendor, who also knows the vendee is relying on his representations as to value, representations of value made under such conditions, as a basis for a contract between the parties, are binding on the vendor. *Judy* v. *Jester* (1913), 53 Ind. App.——, 100 N. E. 15, and cases cited; *Kramer* v. *Williamson* (1893), 135 Ind. 655, 660, 35 N. E. 388.

Furthermore, the instructions complained of are not based entirely on the statement of the price paid for the stock, but connect that representation with the statement that the stock was then worth par, that said statements were false, and appellee was ignorant of their falsity, relied thereon, believed them to be true, and was thereby induced to purchase said stock at par value, to his damage as alleged.

The objection urged to instructions Nos. 6 and 9 given by the court are similar to those already considered, and are not tenable, for the reasons already apparent from this opinion. Complaint is also made of instructions Nos. 1 and 13 given by the court, but these instructions fairly construed are not open to the objections urged. The instructions taken as a whole are clear and correct statements of the law applicable to the issues and evidence of the case.

Over appellants' objection, the trial court admitted in evidence the record of the county board of review of Noble county, showing the assessed valuation of the property and capital stock of the Specialty Case Company made in 1907. Appellant, Ohlwine, purchased his stock in the company on June 27, 1907, the record of the board of review bore date of July 10, 1907, and the trade with appellee was made on November 18, 1907. The gist of the objection is that the assessment was made by persons not parties to this suit, that it is hearsay evidence, that it does not tend to show the value of the stock at the time of trade, and that the entry does not show on what property of the company the assessment is based. The question presented by this objection is one of importance, and we find no decisions that are conclusive on the proposition involved.

Under the earlier decisions of this court and our Supreme Court it was held that assessment lists of personal property were admissible as evidence to prove ownership, and the amount and kind of property owned by the person assessed at the time of the assessment, but were not competent as original evidence to prove the value of such property for any purpose other than taxation. The assessments were regarded as made for a special purpose, and could not be used to prove value except for such special purpose.

In the case of *Indiana Union Traction Co.* v. *Benadum* (1908), 42 Ind. App. 121, 83 N. E. 261, this court held that under the provisions of the taxation law of 1891, and subsequent acts, the party assessed is required to make oath that his assessment sheet contains a correct list of his personal property and shows the true cash value of the same; that under this statute assessment sheets become sworn statements of the persons assessed, showing not only ownership, but the cash value of the property listed, and are admissible as tending to show the value of the property.

In the case of *Brotherhood, etc.,* v. *Barton* (1910), 46 Ind. App. 160, 92 N. E. 64, in an action on a benefit certificate providing for a forfeiture if the assured should come to his death by his own improper conduct, it was held that a record kept by the board of health, and required by the state law or by municipal ordinance, showing that the decedent died from a particular disease, is not admissible as tending to show the cause of death. Roby, J., wrote a dissenting opinion in the case, which was concurred in by Hadley, J.

In the case of *Calahan* v. *Dunker* (1912), 51 Ind. App. 436, 99 N. E. 1021, this court recently held that it was error to receive in evidence the record of the assessed value of real estate. In that case reference was made to the decision in the case of *Indiana Union Traction Co.* v. *Benadum, supra,* and to the statutes providing for the assessment of both personal and real property. It was there observed that while the statute had been so changed as to warrant the decision relating to the admissibility of the assessment sheets of personal property, in so far as the assessment of real estate is concerned, the statute had remained practically unchanged, and for that reason this court was bound by the earlier decisions of the Supreme Court, which are cited at length in that opinion. In the assessment of personal property the owner himself determines its value and verifies it by his oath. It is on this ground that the assessment list is held to be evidence of value. In the assessment of real estate the value is fixed primarily by the assessor and ultimately by the board of review.

Under the present, as well as under former statutes the assessor is required to give a memorandum of the assess-

ment to the owner of the real estate, showing the time of
meeting of the board of review, but the owner has nothing
to do with fixing the value, though he may appear before
the board of review and become a witness in his own behalf.
In that event his evidence before the board might be competent as an admission, but that fact would not make the
record of the assessment evidence of value.

Section 10233 Burns 1908, Acts 1903 p. 49, requires corporations, such as the one involved in this controversy, between March 1 and May 15 of each year, in addition to the
ordinary listing of property for taxation, to make out and
deliver to the assessor a sworn statement showing the amount
of their capital stock and certain other facts.

The fourth subdivision of this section requires the statement to show "the market value, or if no market value,
then the actual value of the shares of stock," and the sixth
subdivision requires the statement to show "the value of
all tangible property." This statement is to be made out
by the president or other accounting officer of the corporation, and the assessor is required to return the same to the
office of the county auditor, who, at the meeting of the
board of review, is required to lay such statement and schedule before that board, and thereupon the board of review,
acting on such statement and schedule, and other information, if deemed essential, proceeds to fix the value of the
property of the corporation, and the value of the stock, in
case the value of the stock exceeds the value of the tangible
property. The value so fixed becomes the assessment for
taxation, and stands unless changed on appeal. §10300
Burns 1908, Acts 1895 p. 74.

A corporation can act only by and through its officers
and agents. Such officers and agents necessarily represent
the stockholders. In the assessment of the property and
stock of a corporation a statement is required as above indicated. The owner of real estate is not required to make
any statement or to determine the value of his land. In the

assessment of personal property the owner verifies the list and value of property returned by him. In the assessment of the property or stock of a corporation, such as the one now under consideration, the list and value is determined primarily by the officer of the corporation designated by the statute. In making this statement he acts for the corporation. The analogy between the assessment of the personal property of an individual or partnership and the assessment of the property or stock of such corporation is so strong as to warrant the conclusion that if one is to be received as some evidence of value, the other is admissible for the same purpose. The board of review acts under oath, and has authority under the statute to fix and determine values for the purpose of taxation. The present law requires the assessment to be made according to the true cash value of the property assessed. Notice of the meeting of the board of review is required to be given, and opportunity is afforded aggrieved property holders to be heard. We cannot presume that the law requiring the verified statement from the officers of a corporation, preliminary to the assessment of its property, intends such statement to be a mere formality or to be disregarded in making the assessment. On the other hand, in the absence of any showing to the contrary, we must presume not only that the statement

was honestly made as required by the statute, but

9.   that the board in fixing the assessment regarded the

statement as true and correct, and fixed the true cash value of the property in accordance with the facts shown by such statement.

In view of the foregoing facts, the record of the assessment of the property of the Specialty Case Company cannot be considered hearsay evidence, nor devoid of probative value. The objection that the record does not show on what property of the company the assessment was based is not tenable. We must presume that the officers of the company made a true statement, as required by the statute, and that the board acted with due regard to the facts shown in such statement. There is no showing of any kind that rebuts this presumption. The assessment was made near the time of the transactions in question, and is not so remote as to be without probative value. The absence of the particular facts on which the board based its valuation may affect the weight, but not the admissibility of the evidence.

The board of review acts under oath in an official capacity. Its records and procedure are open to the public. The values fixed by it are not conclusive, except for the purposes of taxation when there is no appeal, but in any case where the value of stock in a corporation like the one under consideration is in issue, the record of the assessment regularly made in pursuance of the statute, unless too remote in point of time, is some evidence of value, and proper to be considered, like other competent evidence tending to show value, in determining the ultimate fact of value.

One of the grounds for a new trial is the alleged misconduct of one of the jurors who tried the case. It is charged that the juror on his *voir dire* testified that he had never had any litigation; that after the trial appellants learned that in May, 1909, the juror had brought a suit in the Noble Circuit Court to recover damages for false representations made to him in the sale of a horse.

10.

In a counter affidavit filed by the juror it appears that he in fact had not been a party to any litigated lawsuit, but that in May, 1909, he instituted a suit to recover the purchase price of a horse that had been sold to him, alleging misrepresentation made to him in the sale; that before any issues were formed or any steps taken except the beginning of the suit the case was compromised, settled and dismissed. The examination of the juror, his affidavit and the other facts relating to the trial of the case show that the juror was fair and honest in his statements, had no intention of misleading appellants, and that he in fact gave true answers to the questions asked him. The examination was formal and not calculated to bring out any fact except an answer that he either had or had not been party to a lawsuit actually tried and determined in court. The question asked and the answer complained of are as follows: "Ever had any litigation? A. No, sir."

If counsel desired to develop facts from which to determine the advisability of exercising a peremptory challenge. the inquiry should have proceeded further and the questions should have been of a character that would indicate to the mind of a fair and reasonable man the information sought to be obtained. The one question asked was not calculated to bring to the mind of the juror a case that was only filed, never litigated, and settled by the parties out of court. The conduct of the juror as shown by the record affords no cause for a new trial. *Pearcy* v. *Michigan Mut. Life Ins. Co.* (1887), 111 Ind. 59, 12 N. E. 98, 60 Am. Rep. 673; *Johnson* v. *Tyler* (1891), 1 Ind. App. 387, 27 N. E. 643.

Some objections are urged to the admissibility of certain exhibits tending to show the value of the stock in the Specialty Case Company, but the objections urged properly relate to the weight of the testimony and not to its admissibility, and therefore do not merit extended consideration. The damages assessed are not excessive, and evince moderation and conservatism on the part of the jury, rather than a disposition to go to extremes. Other minor questions are discussed, but no reversible error is pointed out. It appears from the record that the case was fairly tried and a correct result reached.

Judgment affirmed.

Adams, J., not participating.

NOTE.—Reported in 100 N. E. 777. See, also, under (1, 4) 20 Cyc. 92; (2) 20 Cyc. 87; (3) 38 Cyc. 1711; (5) 20 Cyc. 127; (6) 20 Cyc. 17; (7) 20 Cyc. 51; (8) 17 Cyc. 308; (10) 29 Cyc. 767. As to action for fraud not being barred by plaintiff's retaining proceeds, see 18 Am. St. 562. As to the proof necessary in actions for fraud, see 65 Am. Dec. 157. As to extent and scope of examination of jurors in civil actions in contemplation of exercise of the right of challenge, see 109 Am. St. 567. For a discussion of the misrepresentation by the vendor of the price paid for property as actionable deceit, see 8 Ann. Cas. 1062.

THE CLEVELAND, CINCINNATI, CHICAGO AND ST. LOUIS RAILWAY COMPANY *v.* RUMSEY.

[No. 7,804.   Filed February 13, 1913.]

1. PLEADING.—*Complaint.—Sufficiency.—Initial Attack on Appeal.* —A complaint is good as against attack made for the first time on appeal, if it is sufficient to bar another action on the same state of facts. p. 372.

2. RAILROADS. — *Crossing Accident. — Contributory Negligence. — Complaint.*—A complaint for personal injuries in a crossing accident, alleging that plaintiff approached the crossing with care and caution, and that before driving onto the tracks he stopped his horse and looked in both directions and listened for approaching trains, that he continued to look and listen as he drove onto the tracks, but neither saw nor heard a train approaching, that when plaintiff's vehicle was upon defendant's track, plaintiff was struck by defendant's train which was negligently run at a high and dangerous rate of speed and without giving any signal of its approach to the crossing, is not open to the objection that it affirmatively shows that plaintiff was guilty of contributory negligence. p. 373.

3. RAILROADS.—*Crossing Accident.—Verdict.—Answers to Interrogatories.*—Where the complaint, for injuries received at a railroad crossing, alleged that before driving onto the tracks plaintiff stopped his horse and looked and listened and that he continued to look and listen as he drove onto the tracks, but neither saw nor heard a train approaching, and that when plaintiff's vehicle was upon defendant's tracks, plaintiff was struck by defendant's train, which was being negligently operated at a dangerous rate of speed, and which approached without the sounding of whistle or ringing of bell, answers to interrogatories showing that plaintiff knew the crossing was dangerous, that plaintiff's hearing and sight were good, that he drove his horse under full control upon the north track, and before his horse had entered on the track farthest south, he saw the train approaching on such south track at a rapid rate of speed, and that he did not see

the train in time to have stopped the horse and avoid the collision, are not in irreconcilable conflict with a verdict for plaintiff,
as showing contributory negligence, since, under the issues, evidence was admissible showing a state of facts on which it could
not be said that plaintiff was guilty of contributory negligence in
crossing in front of the train he saw approaching. pp. 374, 376.

4. TRIAL.—*Verdict.—Answers to Interrogatories.*—A general verdict must stand, unless the answers to interrogatories are in such
irreconcilable conflict with it, as to be beyond the possibility of
removal by any evidence legitimately admissible under the issues.
p. 375.

5. NEGLIGENCE.—*Questions of Law or Fact.—Different Inferences.*
—Negligence is not a matter of law, where different inferences
may be drawn from the facts. p. 376.

6. RAILROADS.—*Crossing Accident.—Contributory Negligence.—Reliance on Railroad's Performance of Duty.*—A person approaching a crossing is not bound to anticipate and act on the theory
that the railroad company will be negligent, but he may assume
that it will obey the law. p. 376.

7. RAILROADS.—*Crossing Accident.—Contributory Negligence.*—It
is not necessarily contributory negligence in every case to cross a
track in front of a locomotive which one sees approaching rapidly. p. 376.

From Boone Circuit Court; *Willett H. Parr,* Judge.

Action by George Z. Rumsey against The Cleveland, Cincinnati, Chicago and St. Louis Railway Company. From a
judgment for plaintiff, the defendant appeals. *Affirmed.*

*Leonard J. Hackney, Frank L. Littleton, Samuel M. Ral-
ston* and *John W. Kern,* for appellant.

Wymond J. Beckett and *A. J. Shelby,* for appellee.

IBACH, C. J.—Appellee brought action against appellant
for damages for personal injuries, and recovered judgment
Appellant assigns as error that the complaint does not state
facts sufficient to constitute a cause of action, and that the
court erred in overruling appellant's motion for judgment
on answers to interrogatories.

A complaint, attacked for the first time on appeal.
1. is held good if sufficient to bar another action on the
same state of facts. *Cleveland, etc., R. Co.* v. *Beard*
(1913), *ante,* 105, 100 N. E. 392, and cases cited.

The present complaint, in substance, alleges that appellant was on September 26, 1908, operating a railway across
Liberty street, a public highway in the city of Indian-

2. apolis; that plaintiff on said day was riding in an
open spring wagon, drawn by a gentle horse, and
was driving south in said Liberty street, and that the buildings on either side of said street extended to within two or four feet of said railway; that at the point where said street crosses said tracks, the line of railway on which said defendant operates its said trains curves to the northwest around said buildings on the east side of said Liberty street; that plaintiff approached said railway crossing with care and caution, and before driving onto said tracks stopped his horse and looked and listened in both directions for approaching trains, and that he continued to look and listen for approaching trains as he drove onto said tracks, and that he did not hear or see defendant's train approaching said crossing from the east; that he drove onto said tracks with due care and caution, and with the exercise of reasonable care, looking and listening for trains at all times, but that when his said horse had passed onto said track on which defendant ran its said trains, and when his said vehicle in which he was riding was on said track, defendant negligently ran one of its locomotive engines attached to a passenger train against plaintiff's said horse and vehicle, and negligently overturned said vehicle, and threw plaintiff out of said vehicle onto the track and ground, and thereby negligently injured plaintiff without his fault. It is further averred that defendant negligently approached and ran onto said crossing with its passenger train from the east at a high and dangerous rate of speed, to wit, at the rate of from twenty to thirty miles per hour, and that it ran its locomotive at said high and dangerous rate of speed toward and onto said crossing and against plaintiff, as aforesaid, without giving any signal of its approach by whistle or bell, all in violation of an ordinance of the city of Indianapolis, which ordinance.

making it unlawful to run an engine at a speed greater than
four miles an hour, or without ringing the bell, is set out in
full in the complaint.

The only objection urged to the sufficiency of this complaint is that it affirmatively shows that appellee was guilty
of contributory negligence. We do not think this objection
has any merit. It is averred that plaintiff used due care
and caution, that he stopped and looked and listened before
he drove onto the track, and continued to look and listen as
he drove onto the track, and that he did not hear or see
the train approaching.

The jury found the following facts in answer to interrogatories. The plaintiff received physical injuries on September 26, 1908, by reason of one of defendant's
3. engines attached to a passenger train running into a
one-horse wagon which plaintiff was driving across
railroad tracks in front of said engine at a point where said
tracks cross Liberty street in the city of Indianapolis. This
street ran north and south, and was crossed by four railroad
tracks at or near the place where plaintiff was injured. The
engine and passenger train which collided with plaintiff's
wagon was running on the track farthest to the south,
which was known as the west bound main track. The distance
from the north rail of the track, on which plaintiff was injured, to the south rail of the track farthest north and nearest Washington street was about 30 feet. Plaintiff's place
of business at the time of the injury was within a few hundred feet of the place where he was injured. He had frequently theretofore driven over the tracks at that point, and
on said date was familiar with said crossing and with the
buildings and structures adjacent to the same, and knew
that engines, trains and cuts of cars frequently passed backward and forward over said crossing, knew that the crossing was a dangerous one, and that the crossing of said tracks
with a vehicle was attended by danger. He was possessed

of good hearing and eyesight. On the date named he drove south from Washington street on Liberty street to the tracks before mentioned. He was driving a gentle horse attached to an open spring wagon about ten feet in length, and when he drove on the track where the collision occurred, his horse was under full control. After he had driven across the track farthest to the north, so that the rear of his wagon had cleared that track, the head of his horse was less than four or five feet from the track on which he was injured. After crossing the track farthest to the north, and before his horse had entered on the track farthest south, he saw the engine which collided with him approaching from the northeast, and observed that it was approaching at a rapid rate of speed. The engine had a lighted headlight on the front end, and the bell on the engine was ringing as it approached and collided with plaintiff. After seeing said engine and train approaching rapidly on the west bound main track, the plaintiff drove onto said track in front of said engine. If he had stopped his horse before entering on said west bound main track he would not have been injured by said engine. After he had cleared the north track with his horse and wagon, he did not see the train that collided with him in time to stop his horse and avoid the injuries complained of.

By the general verdict the jury found that appellant was guilty of negligence, and that appellee was not guilty of contributory negligence. By this verdict it found

4. that appellee was injured without his fault by reason of appellant running its trains through the city at the rate of twenty or thirty miles per hour, in violation of the ordinance of the city of Indianapolis which limits the rate of speed to four miles an hour. This general verdict must stand, unless the answers to interrogatories are in such irreconcilable conflict with it that it cannot be removed by any evidence legitimately admissible under the issues. *Har-*

mon v. *Foran* (1911), 48 Ind. App. 262, 94 N. E. 1050, 95 N. E. 597; *McCoy* v. *Kokomo R., etc., Co.* (1902), 158 Ind. 662, 64 N. E. 92.

Appellant claims that the answers which show that appellee saw the engine approaching at a rapid rate, and after seeing it, drove onto the track in front of it, show that he was guilty of contributory negligence. However, any apparent conflict between these answers and the general verdict is practically removed by the answer to the last interrogatory, in which the jury finds that he did not see the train in time to stop his horse before going on the track, and thus avoid the injuries complained of.

Negligence is not a matter of law where different inferences may be drawn from the fact. *City of Franklin* v. *Harter* (1891), 127 Ind. 446, 448, 26 N. E. 882;

5.   *Cleveland, etc., R. Co.* v. *Harrington* (1892), 131 Ind. 426, 431, 30 N. E. 37; *Lowden* v. *Pennsylvania Co.* (1908), 41 Ind. App. 614, 619, 82 N. E. 941; *Greenawaldt* v. *Lake Shore, etc., R. Co.* (1905), 165 Ind. 219, 74 N. E. 1081.

Nor was appellee bound to anticipate appellant's negligence and act accordingly, and he was entitled to assume that appellant would obey the law, and these princi-

6.   ples must be kept in mind in considering whether appellee was guilty of contributory negligence. *Cleveland, etc., R. Co.* v. *Lynn* (1909), 171 Ind. 589, 594, 85 N. E. 999, 86 N. E. 1017, and cases cited; *Chicago, etc., R. Co.* v. *Stephenson* (1904), 33 Ind. App. 95, 104, 69 N. E. 270; *Indianapolis St. R. Co.* v. *Hoffman* (1907), 40 Ind. App. 508, 510, 82 N. E. 543.

It is not necessarily in every case contributory neg-

7.   gence to cross a track in front of a locomotive which one sees approaching rapidly. Evidence was admissible under the issues, and we have the right to pre-

3.   sume that such evidence was introduced, to show that when appellee drove up to the north track and stopped and looked and listened for trains, a cut of cars

on the second track from the north was moving to the east, and he waited until that cut of cars had passed the crossing, and then looked and listened again for cars that might be on the other tracks west as well as east, and then attempted to pass over the crossing, and when he reached a point where he could see to the east, his horse was then very close to the track on which he was injured, and he then saw the train from 300 to 500 feet away, but at that time could not stop his horse before entering upon the track, or if he had stopped he would have been struck by the train which had just passed east and was backing to the west, so that he was caught between a train on the second track, backing to the west, and a train on the south track approaching the west, but at some distance, and it was a question what to do—stop his horse, if he could, and be run over by the backing train, or attempt to cross over in front of the train approaching at some distance, which he had a right to believe was not approaching so rapidly but that he could cross the track and be out of danger. The very fact that he was familiar with the crossing might have led him to believe that as trains were not in the habit of passing it at a rate prohibited by law, this particular train or any other train would not do so. The evidence may have shown that because of other noises at the crossing he could not hear the bell. It was not necessarily contributory negligence for him to attempt to get out of the way by passing over the track in front of the train on the south track, when he did not know how far away it was, nor how fast it was running. And if it were in fact a choice between two dangers, as the evidence may have shown—between absolutely certain injury by the backing freight train and a reasonable chance to escape by passing over in front of the passenger train—it was for the jury to say whether, under the circumstances, he did what a man of ordinary prudence would have done. The jury found that in attempting to pass over he did what a man of ordinary prudence would have done, and we cannot say as a matter of law that it was wrong.   See *Lake Shore, etc., R. Co.* v. *Myers* (1912), *ante*, 59, 98 N. E. 654, 100 N. E. 213.

It is not found that plaintiff was in a place of safety when he first discovered the train which collided with him approaching from the northeast, and there is no finding that he could have remained in a place of safety at any time after he saw the engine approaching on the west bound track, but, on the contrary, the jury finds expressly that after appellee cleared the north track with his horse and wagon, he did not see the train which collided with him in time to stop his horse and avoid the injuries complained of. If he could not have stopped, he was not guilty of negligence for not stopping, and there is nothing in the answers to interrogatories to show that he was negligent prior to crossing the north track.   Having found no error, the judgment is affirmed.   Appellee having died since this appeal was taken, the cause is affirmed as of date of submission.

NOTE.—Reported in 100 N. E. 782. See, also, under (1) 31 Cyc. 82; (2) 33 Cyc. 865; (3) 33 Cyc. 1142; (4) 38 Cyc. 1927; (5) 29 Cyc. 630; (6) 33 Cyc. 1027; (7) 33 Cyc. 1038. As to contributory negligence in failing to be on lookout for approaching cars, see 51 Am. Rep. 360. As to the question of contributory negligence being for the jury, see 8 Am. St. 849. As to the duty of traveler on highways to use his eyes and ears to avoid danger on railroad crossings, see 90 Am. Dec. 780. On the question of contributory negligence of trespassers or persons on railroad track generally, see 36 L. Ed. U. S. 1064. As to care and precaution necessary in crossing a railroad track, see 24 L. Ed. U. S. 403. For the duty of a traveler approaching railway crossing as to place and direction of observation, see 37 L. R. A. (N. S.) 136. For a discussion of the right of a traveller to recover for injuries received in crossing a railroad track ahead of a train known to be approaching, see 21 Ann. Cas. 1171.

SANITARY CAN COMPANY *v.* McKINNEY.

[No. 7,808. Filed February 13, 1913.]

1. MASTER AND SERVANT.—*Injury to Servant.—Complaint.—Theory.*—Where the complaint, in a servant's action for personal injuries, although alleging in general terms that defendant directed plaintiff to go to work on a certain machine, without giving proper instructions as to the use and operation thereof, averred that the gearing and cogs were not guarded, and that the injury was caused solely by the failure and neglect of defendant to guard same, the failure to guard such gearing and cogs must be deemed to be the theory on which the right to recover is predicated. p. 382.

2. MASTER AND SERVANT.—*Injury to Servant.—Complaint.—Sufficiency.—Initial Attack on Appeal.*—A complaint for injuries to an employe, which was sufficient to bar another action for the same injury, was good as against an objection, first made on appeal, that it did not state facts sufficient to constitute a cause of action, although its averments do not clearly show how the machine was constructed or operated, nor the manner in which plaintiff received his injury. p. 383.

3. APPEAL.—*Review.—Presumptions.—Verdict.—Answers to Interrogatories.*—On appeal all reasonable presumptions are indulged in support of the general verdict and against the answers to interrogatories, and if the general verdict, thus aided, is not in irreconcilable conflict with such answers, it must stand. p. 383.

4. APPEAL.—*Review.—Verdict.—Answers to Interrogatories.*—The antagonism between the general verdict and the answers to interrogatories must be apparent on the face of the record and beyond the possibility of being removed by any evidence within the issues, before the court is authorized to direct a judgment on such answers. p. 383.

5. MASTER AND SERVANT.—*Injury to Servant.—Verdict.—Answers to Interrogatories.*—In a servant's action for injuries to his hand by being caught in the unguarded cogs of a machine, a verdict for plaintiff is not overcome by answers to interrogatories showing that such cogs were covered by a box, which plaintiff had removed, that such removal was necessary in doing the work that he was doing at the time of the injury, and that if he had not removed it, he could not have received the injury, since the general verdict amounted to a finding that such box was not a proper guard. pp. 384, 385.

6. MASTER AND SERVANT.—*Injury to Servant.—Guarding Machinery.—Sufficiency of Guards.—Question for Jury.*—Since §8029

Burns 1908, Acts 1899 p. 231, providing for the guarding of dangerous machinery, does not describe the manner in which dangerous machinery shall be guarded or what shall be deemed a proper guard, the question of whether the statutory requirement has been complied with is, in each case, one of fact to be determined by the jury from the character of the machine and the nature of the peril. p. 385.

7. MASTER AND SERVANT.—*Injury to Servant.—Contributory Negligence.—Verdict.—Conclusiveness.—Motion for Judgment on Answers to Interrogatories.*—Where an employe was injured by his hand being caught in the cogs of a machine, the question of whether he was guilty of contributory negligence in attempting to remove certain receptacles while the machine was running, was determined in his favor by the general verdict, and cannot be considered under a motion for judgment on answers to interrogatories which presents the question as to whether such answers, which showed that the cogs were guarded by a box and that the injury could not have happened if plaintiff had not removed the box, were in conflict with the general verdict. p. 385.

8. MASTER AND SERVANT.—*Injury to Servant.—Instructions.—Evidence.—Damages.*—In an action by an employe for personal injuries, where there was evidence that plaintiff was living at home with a widowed mother, who had six children, that plaintiff began working at the age of fourteen, and that two of his sisters were working in defendant's factory, an instruction that the amount of damages should be determined "from all the facts and circumstances in the case as shown by the evidence," was erroneous, since such evidence was not competent on the question of damages. p. 386.

9. MASTER AND SERVANT.—*Injury to Servant.—Instructions.—Damages.*—Where, in an employe's action for damages, there was evidence that was not competent on the question of the amount of damages, an instruction, that in determining the amount of damages, "every particular and phase of the injury may enter into consideration in estimating such damages," was erroneous. p. 387.

10. INFANTS.—*Personal Injuries.—Recovery by Child.—Damages.*—A minor, having a widowed mother, cannot, in an action against his employer for injuries, recover for loss of time, loss of wages, or decreased earning power during minority, since his wages during such time belong to his mother. p. 388.

From Superior Court of Marion County (79,152); *Clarence E. Weir*, Judge.

Action by Thomas McKinney, by his next friend, Mauda

McKinney, against the Sanitary Can Company. From a judgment for plaintiff, the defendant appeals. *Reversed.*

John B. Elam, James W. Fesler and *Harvey J. Elam,* for appellant.

Vincent G. Clifford and *Adolph G. Emhardt,* for appellee.

ADAMS, J.—Suit by appellee against appellant for damages on account of personal injuries alleged to have been caused by the negligence of appellant in failing to guard certain cogwheels, and failing properly to instruct appellee as to the use and operation of the machine at which he was put to work.

The averments of the complaint are substantially, that appellee, on August 12, 1908, the date of his injury, was an infant fourteen years of age, without mechanical training, and without experience in the use and operation of machinery; that he was employed by appellant about June 20, 1908, for the purpose of picking up cans, carrying water and watching can chutes; that he performed such duties until about the ——— day of ———————, 1908, at which time the foreman, under whose orders he worked, directed and ordered him to operate a machine commonly known as a "lock seamer", without properly instructing him as to the use and operation of said machine; that the machine was operated by power conveyed through a system of shafting and belts; that it consisted of a large, iron frame, in front of which, at the heighth of about four feet from the floor, was a wooden apron or table about eighteen inches wide projecting out in front of said machine, on which the persons operating said machine placed pieces of tin, which were by said machine automatically trimmed, moulded and soldered into bodies of cans; that the tin chips or trimmings from the pieces of tin fed into the machine fell into cans or receptacles underneath the machine, below and beyond the table or apron, which cans or receptacles rested on a framework of the machine about two feet from the floor; that directly

in front of and slightly below the place where the receptacles were located were the gearing and cogwheels by which
the power was transmitted; that these cogwheels were not
guarded, but were carelessly and negligently left uncovered
and exposed by appellant, and were very dangerous to persons operating the machine, as was well known to appellant
for a long time prior to the injury to appellee; that the
same might have been guarded and made safe at a reasonable cost, so as to protect employes from injury in the operation of the machine, without impairing its usefulness or
efficiency; that it was a part of the duty of persons operating said machine to remove and empty the cans or receptacles whenever they became filled; that on August 12, 1908,
while appellee was feeding and operating the machine, the
receptacles became filled and were running over with tin
chips or trimmings, and in order to empty the same it was
necessary for appellee to, and he did, remove an old box
which stood below the table attached to said machine, and
reached underneath the body or frame of the machine, and
while so reaching his clothing was caught in the unguarded
cogwheels, and he was injured in the manner specifically set
out; that the injury suffered by appellee was caused solely
by the failure and neglect of appellant carefully to guard
the gearing and cogs, as required by law.

While it is averred in general terms that appellant directed appellee to go to work on a certain machine, "without
properly instructing him as to the use and operation
1. of said machine," it will be noted from the concluding averment that the injury was caused solely by
the failure and neglect of appellant carefully to guard the
gearing and cogs. If the failure to guard was the sole
cause of the injury, then such failure must be deemed to
be the theory on which the right to recover is predicated.

Appellant did not file a demurrer to the complaint, but
challenges its sufficiency to state a cause of action by assignment of errors in this court. While it does not clearly

appear from the averments of the complaint how the
2. machine was constructed or operated, or the manner
in which appellee was caught in the gearing, the
complaint is sufficient to bar another action for the same
injury. This is the test applied to complaints when questioned for the first time in this court. *Indianapolis Traction, etc., Co.* v. *Miller* (1907), 40 Ind. App. 403, 404, 82
N. E. 113; *Elwood State Bank* v. *Mock* (1907), 40 Ind. App.
685, 686, 82 N. E. 1003.

The jury returned a general verdict for appellee, and
with the general verdict returned answers to numerous interrogatories. Appellant moved the court for judgment on
the answers to interrogatories notwithstanding the general
verdict. The motion was overruled, and this ruling is the
second error assigned and relied on for reversal.

It is well settled that all reasonable presumptions will be
indulged in support of the general verdict and against the
special answers, and if the general verdict thus aided,
3. is not in irreconcilable conflict with the answers, it
must stand. This rule is general, and the reason
therefor is that the jury is required to find on all issuable
facts proved in the case, while the court, in determining the
force of isolated facts disclosed by the answers to interrogatories, cannot know what other facts relating to the same
matters were properly before the jury to warrant its general verdict. *City of South Bend* v. *Turner* (1901), 156
Ind. 418, 423, 60 N. E. 271, 54 L. R. A. 396, 83 Am. St. 200.

The antagonism between the general verdict and the
special answers must be apparent on the face of the record
and beyond the possibility of being removed by any
4. evidence admissible under the issues, before the court
is authorized to direct a judgment in favor of the
party against whom a general verdict has been returned.
Harmon v. *Foran* (1911), 48 Ind. App. 262, 266, 94 N. E.
1050, 95 N. E. 597; *Ittenbach* v. *Thomas* (1911), 48 Ind.
App. 420, 427, 434, 96 N. E. 21; *Indianapolis Union R. Co.*

v. Ott (1895), 11 Ind. App. 564, 568, 38 N. E. 842, 39 N. E. 529; *McCoy* v. *Kokomo R., etc., Co.* (1902), 158 Ind. 662, 663, 64 N. E. 92, and cases cited.

In *McCoy* v. *Kokomo R., etc., Co., supra,* the court said: "In passing upon a motion for judgment notwithstanding the verdict, it should be borne in mind that the verdict necessarily covers the whole issue, and that it solves every material fact against the party against whom it is rendered. To enable the latter successfully to interpose the special findings of the jury upon particular questions of fact, as a reason for judgment in his favor, he must, at least, have special findings that stand in such clear antagonism to the general verdict that the two cannot coexist."

In the case at bar, the jury by its general verdict found that the cogwheels were not guarded; that it was the duty of appellee to empty the receptacles whenever they became filled with tin clippings; that to perform this duty it was necessary for appellee to remove an old box which stood below the table of the machine, and while in the performance of this duty he was injured, on account of the neglect of appellant properly to guard the cogwheels. By its special answers, the jury found that during the time of appellee's employment in operating the machine, the cogs had been covered by a box; that when the box was placed over the cogwheels it completely covered them; that immediately prior to his accident, appellee removed the box, and that he could not have been caught in the cogwheels, as he was, had he not removed the box; that appellee attempted to remove the receptacles while the machine was running, and that the machine was one that could readily be stopped.

It is manifest that the question presented by the motion for judgment turns on whether the general finding that the cogs were not properly guarded is in irreconcilable conflict with the special finding that the same were covered, by a box, and that appellee could not have been caught, as he was, had he not removed the box. The statute §8029

Burns 1908, Acts 1899 p. 231, does not describe the
6.   manner in which dangerous machinery shall be
guarded or what shall be deemed a proper guard.   It
follows, therefore, that in every case the question of compliance with the statutory requirement is a question of fact
to be determined by the jury from the character of the
machine and the nature of the peril.   Localized to
5.   this case, the jury by its general verdict found that
the box was not a proper guard, and this finding is
conclusive, unless in irreconcilable conflict with the special
verdict. *Green* v. *American Car, etc., Co.* (1904), 163 Ind.
135, 140, 71 N. E. 268.

While the jury by its special answers found that the
wooden box covered the cogs, and that appellee would not
have been injured had he not removed the box, it was also
found by the special answers that it was appellee's duty to
empty the receptacles, and that in the discharge of that duty
it was necessary to remove the box.   There was no finding
that a proper guard might not have been installed and maintained that would have rendered appellee's duty in empty-
ing the receptacles wholly free from danger.   Whether appellee was guilty of contributory negligence in at-
7.   tempting to remove the receptacles while the machine
was running was a question of fact for the jury, to
be determined from all the evidence, and having determined
the same by its general verdict in favor of appellee that
feature of the case cannot be considered under this motion.
We think there was no error in overruling the motion for
judgment.

Appellant further assigns as error and relies for reversal
on the overruling of its motion for a new trial.   Under this
specification, many questions are presented, but in view of
the conclusion we have reached, it will be necessary to consider only the seventeenth instruction given by the court,
which it as follows: ''If, under the evidence and under the

instructions of the court, you find that the plaintiff is entitled to recover, it will then be your duty to assess the amount of damages to which, in that case, he will be entitled. In determining this amount, every particular and phase of the injury may enter into consideration in estimating such damages; you may consider whether or not the injury complained of is permanent or temporary only, to what extent, if any, plaintiff has suffered permanent impairment of his physical power, by reason of such injuries, his pain and suffering, both physical and mental, already endured, and that to be endured as a result of the injuries complained of, and from all the facts and circumstances in the case, as shown by the evidence, determine upon such sum as will fully compensate plaintiff for the injuries received, not, however, exceeding the amount named in the complaint."

It will be noted that a part of this instruction re-
8.   quires the jury to determine the amount of recovery "from all the facts and circumstances in the case as shown by the evidence." The giving of such an instruction has been often condemned, and held to be reversible error. *City of Delphi* v. *Lowery* (1881), 74 Ind. 520, 527, 39 Am. Rep. 98; *Monongahela River, etc., Co.* v. *Hardsaw* (1907), 169 Ind. 147, 151, 81 N. E. 492; *Broadstreet* v. *Hall* (1904), 32 Ind. App. 122, 128, 69 N. E. 415; *Knoefel* v. *Atkins* (1907), 40 Ind. App. 428, 441, 81 N. E. 600; *Mesker* v. *Leonard* (1911), 48 Ind. App. 642, 644, 96 N. E. 485.   In *Pittsburgh, etc., R. Co.* v. *Reed* (1909), 44 Ind. App. 635, 88 N. E 1080, an instruction similar to the one before us was given, and the words "all other facts and circumstances" held to be harmless, for the reason that appellant failed to point out in its brief any fact or circumstance shown by the evidence that might be considered as improperly influencing the jury. This case did not change the general rule that where an erroneous instruction is given, in order to prevent a reversal it must appear from the record on appeal that the error did not prejudice the complaining

party. It simply held that the general rule does not relieve
the appellant from the primary duty of pointing out error.
Mesker v. *Leonard, supra.*

In the case at bar, evidence was offered and received, over
the objection of appellant, that appellee was living at home,
with a widowed mother, who had six children; that appellee
went to work when he was fourteen years of age, and that
two of his sisters were working in appellant's factory. Assuming that this evidence was competent for some purpose,
such evidence was not competent in determining the amount
of appellee's damages. The jury cannot determine the
amount of the recovery ''from all the facts and circumstances in the case, as shown by the evidence,'' but only from
such facts as form proper elements in fixing the amount of
damages.

Vandalia Coal Co. v. *Yemm* (1911), 175 Ind. 524, 539, 92
N. E. 49, 94 N. E. 881.

Again, in the same instruction, the court told the jury
that in determining the amount of damages, ''every particular and phase of the injury may enter into consideration in estimating such damages.'' The court could
hardly have used more comprehensive language than
''every phase and particular of the injury.'' By this part
of the instruction the jurors were told that they might take
into consideration not only every particular of the injury,
but might consider the injury in its every aspect. The verdict was for $5,000. The court, over appellant's objection,
permitted proof to be made that appellee at the time of his
injury was earning $4 per week; that at the time of the
trial he was unable to do heavy work, and had, in fact, been
compelled to give up a position on account of his injury.
The loss of wages and diminished capacity to earn wages
would naturally and properly be considered by the jury as
phases of the injury. The vice of such an instruction is
peculiarly apparent in this case, where it appears that appellee at the time of his injury was a boy of the age of four-

teen years. While there was no demand for special
10. damages on account of loss of time, loss of wages and
    decreased earning power, in no event could appellee
have recovered for loss of wages during minority. His
wages during such time belonged to his mother, and she
alone had the right to recover for such loss. *Cole* v. *Searfoss* (1912), 49 Ind. App. 334, 97 N. E. 345.

Other questions presented by the record are not considered, as they may not arise again. The judgment is reversed, with instructions to the court below to sustain appellant's motion for a new trial, with leave to appellee to file an amended complaint, if desired.

NOTE.—Reported in 100 N. E. 785. See, also, under (1) 26 Cyc.
1384; (2) 26 Cyc. 1384; 31 Cyc. 82; (3, 4) 38 Cyc. 1927; (5) 26
Cyc. 1513; (6) 26 Cyc. 1463; (8) 13 Cyc. 234; (9) 13 Cyc. 238.
As to master's duty to guard or enclose dangerous machinery, see
note to *Brazil Block Coal Co.* v. *Gibson* (Ind.), 98 Am. St. 299. As
to plaintiff's family ties and obligations as a measure of damage,
see 85 Am. St. 835. As to the right of an infant to recover damages for loss of services or diminished earning capacity, during
minority, from personal injuries, see 6 L. R. A. (N. S.) 552.

CITY OF INDIANAPOLIS v. RAY.

[No. 7,517. Filed March 7, 1912. Rehearing denied December 31,
1912. Transfer denied February 13, 1913.]

1. MUNICIPAL CORPORATIONS.—*Defective Sidewalks.*—*Injury to
   Pedestrian.*—*Complaint.*—In an action against a municipal corporation for personal injuries caused by a defective sidewalk, a
   paragraph of complaint alleging facts showing that the sidewalk
   had been unsafe for a number of years, that defendant, by the
   exercise of proper care and diligence, could have known of such
   unsafe condition and could have made the same safe before the
   injury, that, for a period of two years before the injury, employes of defendant inspected the basement of a building adjacent to such sidewalk, and, if such inspections had been made
   with proper care, the defect could have been discovered, and
   that plaintiff had no knowledge of such defective condition, and
   could not have discovered it in the exercise of ordinary care,
   shows a violation of a duty owing to plaintiff and is sufficient to
   withstand a demurrer. p. 390.

2. MUNICIPAL CORPORATIONS.—*Care of Sidewalks.—Notice of Defects.—Liability.*—It is the duty of a municipal corporation to keep its sidewalks in a reasonably safe condition for the use of the public, and it is liable for all defects therein of which it had actual knowledge, or which were so obvious, or had existed for such a length of time, that its officers would be apprised of them, if they were diligent in the performance of their duty. p. 391.

3. MUNICIPAL CORPORATIONS.—*Defective Sidewalks.—Injury to Pedestrian.—Notice of Defect.—Evidence.*—In an action for injuries in falling through a defective sidewalk, evidence that the defect could not be discovered from any outward appearance of the walk, that the walk broke and allowed plaintiff to fall at the given point, because the foundation thereunder had been washed out, that the sand and gravel composing the foundation had gradually washed into the basement of an adjacent building, through an opening where a waterpipe penetrated the basement wall, that some years prior to the injury a similar defect in the walk had been caused by the giving way of the basement wall, and that for two years prior to plaintiff's injury a member of the city fire department entered such basement at various times to direct the removal of paper and rubbish, was insufficient to show that the city had either actual or constructive notice of the defect which caused the injury. p. 392.

4. MUNICIPAL CORPORATIONS.—*Defective Sidewalks.—Liability.*—In the absence of actual notice, municipal corporations are only liable for such defects in sidewalks as are apparent, or are suggested by appearances, or are disclosed by a test in the nature of the ordinary use of such walks. p. 395.

5. MUNICIPAL CORPORATIONS.—*Defective Sidewalk.—Notice of Defect by City Fireman.—Liability.*—Knowledge of the defective condition of a sidewalk by a member of the city fire department, will not of itself constitute notice to the city of such defect. p. 396.

From Superior Court of Marion County (73,810); *Clarence E. Weir,* Judge.

Action by Sarah Ray against the city of Indianapolis. From a judgment for plaintiff, the defendant appeals. *Reversed.*

Frederick E. Matson, Crate D. Bowen, James D. Peirce, Joseph B. Kealing, Merle N. A. Walker and *Newton J. McGuire,* for appellant.

Gay R. Estabrook, for appellee.

IBACH, P. J.—This was a suit brought by Sarah Ray, appellee, against the city of Indianapolis, appellant, to recover damages for injuries received by falling through a defective sidewalk, which, it is alleged, appellant had allowed to remain for a number of years on Georgia street, one of the principal streets of said city. The complaint as originally filed was in three paragraphs. A demurrer was sustained as to the first and overruled as to the second and third. The cause was put at issue by answer in general denial. There was a trial by jury and a verdict for plaintiff. The court overruled a motion for a new trial, and rendered judgment on the verdict. The errors assigned and argued are the overruling of the demurrer to the third paragraph of complaint, and the overruling of the motion for new trial.

The third paragraph, instead of charging that the city had actual knowledge of the defect in the walk complained of, as was charged in the second paragraph, avers that

1. the foundation on which such walk had been originally constructed was washed out at that place about one year before plaintiff was injured; that nearby said place and about two years previous to the time of her injury, a part of the walk had given way on account of the support thereof being washed out, and the same was not repaired for some months thereafter; that such defects could readily be seen during all that time; that the sidewalk where plaintiff fell had been unsafe and insecure for a number of years, and dangerous by reason of the foundation or support under the same having been washed out, and that defendant, by the exercise of proper care and diligence, could have known of such unsafe condition, and could have made the same safe long before. It is also charged that for a period of two years before plaintiff's injury, employes of the city inspected the basement of the building adjacent to such sidewalk, and if the inspection had been made with proper care, the hole under the sidewalk at the point where the section of the cement walk broke under plaintiff's weight, causing her to

fall and injuring her, could have been discovered and the defect remedied.   It is further charged that a certain drain had been constructed some years before leading from the building on the Georgia street side, and before the same was completed a large amount of the foundation of the sidewalk had been washed out by a heavy rain, and had not been properly replaced, and that by the exercise of proper care and diligence, after the drain was completed, the city could have discovered the unsafe condition of the walk; that plaintiff had no knowledge of its defective condition, and by the exercise of ordinary and reasonable care she could not have discovered it.   The defective condition of the sidewalk is made clear and specific, the absence of knowledge on plaintiff's part of any defect in the walk is also made to appear. Facts are also clearly pleaded tending to show constructive knowledge of the defect which caused plaintiff's injury for a sufficient length of time before the accident to have repaired it and to have made it safe, and nothing is specially pleaded tending to show that any act on plaintiff's part in passing over the walk contributed to her injury.   On the contrary, all the facts averred tend to show a violation of a duty toward plaintiff imposed by law on defendant, and for the violation of which an injury resulted to plaintiff.   We therefore think the third paragraph is sufficient to withstand the demurrer.

Appellant insists that the verdict is not sustained by sufficient evidence.   It is first contended that it is not shown that the city had any notice, either actual or constructive, of the defective condition of the sidewalk in question.

It is the duty of a municipality to keep its sidewalks in a reasonably safe condition for the use of the public, and it is liable for all defects therein of which it had

2.   actual knowledge or which were so obvious or had existed for such a length of time prior to the accident as to apprise the officers of such municipality, if they were diligent in the performance of their duty.   This rule has

been approved by our courts in the following or similar language: " 'Where the duty to keep its streets in safe condition rests upon the corporation, it is liable for injuries caused by its neglect or omission to keep the streets in repair, as well as for those caused by defects occasioned by the wrongful acts of others, but as, in such case, the basis of the action is negligence, notice to the corporation of the defect which caused the injury, or facts from which notice thereof may reasonably be inferred, or proof of circumstances from which it appears that the defect ought to have been known and remedied by it, is essential to liability.' For, in such cases, 'the corporation, in the absence of a controlling enactment, is responsible only for a reasonable diligence to repair the defect or prevent accidents after the unsafe condition of the street is known or ought to have been known to it or to its officers having authority to act respecting it.' " *Turner* v. *City of Indianapolis* (1884), 96 Ind. 51. See, also, *Town of Rosedale* v. *Ferguson* (1892), 3 Ind. App. 596, 30 N. E. 156; 2 Dillon, Mun. Corp. (5th ed.) §§789-790.

It must be conceded that it definitely appears from all the evidence in the case that the defect which caused appellee's injury was a latent one, under the walk, a defect

3.   which could not be discovered from any outward appearance of the portion of the walk which gave way. Indeed, there seems to be no contention that the city had actual knowledge of the existence of any washout prior to the accident. Plaintiff testified that the accident happened about 10 o'clock in the forenoon; the day was bright; she did not discover any depression or cracks or that the sidewalk was sunken; if it had been she would have noticed it, for she was "looking where she was going"; "the slab which broke was as smooth as a floor;" no defect in the walk could be seen. These statements are supported by all the witnesses who testified in the case.

It is not contended that the walk was not properly built

when first constructed, and it is definitely shown by all the
evidence that the walk broke and allowed plaintiff to fall
at the given point, because the foundation thereunder had
in some manner been washed out and left this particular
part of the walk unsupported, and when appellee and her
companion stepped upon it, it broke, and appellee fell with
it to the bottom of the hole thus made, a distance of about
four feet.

It is also made to appear that the walk was built at least
seven years before the date of the injury; that in 1904, owing to a large amount of rain causing high water, the cel-
lars of many buildings were filled with water, and at that
time some water flowed under and over the walk in question. The point where plaintiff fell is at the northeast corner of Georgia and Illinois streets, one of the public corners
of the city, where the walks are used extensively by the
traveling public, and there was nothing about the sidewalk
in the locality where the accident occurred to indicate that
it was in a dangerous condition until three years thereafter,
and then only at the time when plaintiff was injured. Prior
to that time there was nothing in the appearance of the
particular slab which broke and caused her fall that would
indicate danger to any one passing over it.

Considering the evidence alone most favorable to appellee,
including all reasonable inferences arising therefrom, can
we say then that there is any evidence of notice to the city
at any time before the accident of the dangerous condition
of the walk?

It is quite clear that the foundation gave way by reason
of the removal of the sand and gravel underneath, and on
no other account, and it was removed either at the time of
the high water of 1904, or it was carried away in the manner described by appellee's witness, Thomas Mobley, who
testified that he went into the basement of the Stubbins Hotel
on April 19, 1907, the day of the accident, and found, as he
had before, sand which had been washed out from under the

sidewalk; that the water-pipe which supplied the elevator with water from the main pipe had been brought through the brick wall; and an opening of about one-half inch had been left around the entire six-inch pipe. Witness had been called to "pack the elevator," and said: "I found the sand had worked out around the pipe that supplies the elevator, and I shoveled it back, you can see it there, as much as two wagon loads. The sand found there came from under the sidewalk. It came through the foundation of the building near the floor of the basement. Whenever there was a little bit of rain it would seep right in there, and the time most of it came in was when we had the flood in 1904." The facts proven show that the foundation of the building formed a retaining wall on the north and east to hold in place the sand and gravel forming the support for the cement walk, and the curb made the retaining wall on the Illinois street and Georgia street sides. This witness was the first to arrive at the point where appellee was hurt, and assisted her out of the hole, and he says that the amount of sand necessary to fill the hole would be two or three wagon loads, and that this excavation was near to the part of the walk where the water-pipe was located, being the same pipe referred to by the witness around which pipe an opening had been left in the basement wall.

Witness, Ohms, also testified to the effect that a washout had occurred five years before plaintiff's injury, and at that time sand and gravel had been removed from under the walk. We have carefully reviewed all the testimony given by this witness, and find it wholly wanting in the elements necessary to sustain the verdict, since it does not show actual notice to the city of such defect, and no conditions of any kind surrounding the place that would indicate that the walk was defective beneath its surface, or anywhere else.

There was some evidence tending to show that some distance from the slab which broke, and immediately adjacent to the building, and at a point where an outside stairway leads to the basement, the walk had previously given way. This is shown to have been occasioned by reason of the basement wall at this place giving way, for some reason unexplained, thereby allowing some of the foundation under the walk next to the building to be sunken and depressed. It nowhere appears, however, that there was anything in this circumstance that would indicate that there was any defect in the walk at any other point, or that there was anything in its appearance that would require the city to make an inspection, or that the hole under the walk could have been discovered even if an ordinary inspection had at any time been made by the proper city authorities. Such defect could only have been discovered by an extraordinary inspection, which is not required.

In the case of *Hembling* v. *City of Grand Rapids* (1894), 99 Mich. 292, 58 N. W. 310, the supreme court of Michigan said: "Respecting the ordinary sidewalks, there is

4.   no such duty of substructure inspection as is imposed in case of bridges or other elevated ways. In the absence of actual notice, municipalities are only liable for such defects in sidewalks as are apparent, or are suggested by appearances, or which are disclosed by a test in the nature of the ordinary use of such walks." This general doctrine is so well supported by the decisions of our own courts that it is unnecessary to cite authority.

It seems to us that the probable and active cause of the accident was the "seeping away of the sand and gravel from under the walk into the cellar around the water-pipe after each rain." The evidence discloses no other way in which such a portion of the foundation could have been removed. No other opening of any kind is shown to have been in either of the retaining walls, but, on the other hand, it is made to appear that the amount of such materials as did work out from under the walk into the adjacent building was the amount necessary to fill the hole under the walk where appellee fell.

Apparently, for the purpose of showing an opportunity to obtain knowledge of the defect if ordinary care had been used to discover it, appellee averred in her complaint "that for a period of more than two years prior to said injury servants and employes of the city inspected the basement of the building adjacent to such sidewalk, and if such inspection had been made with proper care the said hole could have been discovered." The only evidence on this branch of the case is that at various times for years a member of the city fire department went into the basement of such adjacent building, and directed persons in charge there to remove all paper and rubbish and all other combustible material. This evidence is wholly insufficient, con-

5. ceding that for some purposes it may have been competent, for if any inspection made by such fireman with a view to having rubbish removed from such basement revealed any defect in the walk, and he, by the exercise of ordinary care, observed or might have observed a washout under such walk, such knowledge on the part of the fireman would not of itself constitute notice to the city of such defective condition of the walk and foundation thereof. In cases of this character, the notice, either actual or constructive, must come to some officer or agent of the city other than a fireman. As a matter of law, appellant was not required to make search for such a defect as is conceded by the evidence existed in the foundation of the sidewalk in question. It is conceded that the city had no actual notice of such defective condition, neither was such condition apparent, and from a just examination of the whole record we come to the conclusion that the facts and circumstances are not sufficient to show that the defect complained of was suggested to appellant by the general appearance of the walk, or that it was discoverable by any one using the walk in the usual and ordinary way, or that appellant had any con-

structive notice that the walk was faulty. A new trial should have been granted.

Judgment reversed, and cause remanded for new trial.

NOTE.—Reported in 97 N. E. 795. See, also, under (1) 28 Cyc. 1465; (2) 28 Cyc. 1388; (3) 28 Cyc. 1498; (4) 28 Cyc. 1384; (5) 28 Cyc. 1397. As to a municipality's liability for injuries due to street defects, see note to *Mordhurst* v. *Ft. Wayne, etc., Co.* (Ind.), 106 Am. St. 264; 103 Am. St. 258. As to the notice to be given the municipality of the defect, see 103 Am. St. 258. On the question of notice of claim and cause of injury as condition of municipal liability for defect in highway, generally, see 20 L. R. A. (N. S.) 757.

VANDALIA COAL COMPANY v. HAVERKAMP.

[No. 7,520. Filed May 31, 1912. Rehearing denied November 20, 1912. Transfer denied February 13, 1913.]

1. MASTER AND SERVANT.—*Injury to Servant.—Complaint.—Proximate Cause.*—A complaint, in an action by a coal miner for personal injuries, alleging that defendant failed to furnish him a reasonably safe place in which to work, and failed to perform its statutory duty of sprinkling the roadways and entries of its mine, so that the air therein became charged with dust, that the same could have been sprinkled and the dust allayed without interfering in the operation of the mine, that the concussion and fire, resulting from illegal shots fired by other miners, acted on the air in the roadways and entries so as to produce a dust explosion in which plaintiff was injured, and that such explosion could not have occurred if defendant had sprinkled the dust and if such illegal shots had not been·fired, shows that the combined negligence of the defendant and the miners was the proximate cause of the injury, and was sufficient to withstand a demurrer. p. 399.

2. MASTER AND SERVANT.—*Injury to Servant.—Complaint.—Negligence of Fellow Servant.*—A complaint, from which it affirmatively appears that the injury was the proximate result of the negligence of a fellow servant, is bad and there can be no recovery thereon, but the rule does not apply where the negligence of the master, combined with the negligence of the fellow servant, was the proximate cause of the injury. p. 400.

3. NEGLIGENCE.—*Proximate Cause.*—There may be several elements combining to make up the proximate cause of an injury. p. 401.

4. APPEAL. — *Review.* — *Verdict.—Evidence.*—In determining the sufficiency of the evidence to support a verdict, the court will not weigh the evidence, but will consider only that most favorable to appellee. p. 402.

5. APPEAL.—*Review.—Verdict.—Evidence.*—The fact that the evidence may be weak, or unsatisfactory, will not authorize a reversal, if there is some evidence to support the verdict in every material respect. p. 402.

6. APPEAL.—*Review.—Instructions.—Refusal.*—The refusal of requested instructions, that were covered by others given, was not error. p. 403.

From Putnam Circuit Court; *John M. Rawley,* Judge.

Action by Edward Haverkamp, by his next friend, Karl Haverkamp, against the Vandalia Coal Company. From a judgment for plaintiff, the defendant appeals. *Affirmed.*

U. Z. Wiley, A. H. Jones, James P. Hughes and *John P. Allee,* for appellant.

Knight & Knight, S. A. Hays and *B. F. Watson,* for appellee.

ADAMS, P. J.—Appellee was injured by an explosion while employed in appellant's coal mine. By the same explosion one Yemm was injured, and prosecuted an action for damages against appellant, and recovered judgment, from which judgment appellant appealed to the Supreme Court, where the judgment was affirmed. See *Vandalia Coal Co.* v. *Yemm* (1911), 175 Ind. 524, 92 N. E. 49, 94 N. E. 881. It is admitted that the complaint in the Yemm case is identical with the complaint in this case, and that many of the errors originally relied on in this appeal for reversal have been definitely determined against the contention of appellant by the decision in the Yemm case. The court in that case, however, did not pass on the sufficiency of the second paragraph of complaint, as it affirmatively appeared from the record that the judgment was based on the first paragraph, which was held sufficient. It will, therefore, be unnecessary to consider the points raised in this appeal which have been directly decided in the above case.

Counsel for appellant insist that the verdict in this case rests on the second paragraph of complaint, and that as said paragraph is insufficient, the court should have sustained a demurrer thereto. The second paragraph of amended complaint, after showing appellee's employ-

1.   ment, avers that appellant violated its duty to furnish to appellee a reasonably safe place in which to perform his work; that appellant failed to use reasonable care and diligence in seeing that the roadways and entries through which appellee was required to pass in going to and from his work were kept in a reasonably safe condition; that under the laws of Indiana it was the duty of appellant to see that the roadways and entries of said mine were regularly and thoroughly sprinkled, whenever they became so dry that the air became charged with dust; that appellant did not, by itself or its agents, regularly and thoroughly sprinkle the roadways and entries, but negligently and in violation of a statutory duty imposed on it failed to sprinkle said roadways and entries; that it was practicable for appellant so to sprinkle said entries as to allay the dust, without interfering with the operation of said mine; that by reason of such failure and negligence the roadways and entries at the time of the accident, and for a period of six months prior thereto, had been permitted to become so dry that the air therein was charged with dust to such an extent as to render the same dangerous, and likely to create a dust explosion at any time; that appellant carelessly and negligently permitted such dust to accumulate on the floors of said roadways to a depth of from two to six inches, and made no effort to allay the same by sprinkling; that while appellee was going from his working place in said mine on the date of the injury, through said roadways and entries, for the purpose of leaving said mine, an explosion of dust occurred in the roadways and entries, enveloping him in a sheet of fire and flame, burning and injuring him, as specifically set out. Appellee also averred that a short time before

the explosion, some miner or miners, working as employes of appellant, whose identity is unknown to appellee, had negligently, carelessly and in violation of the mining laws of the State, fired certain illegal shots, particularly describing the same; that as a result of said shots a great concussion resulted, and much fire and flame were emitted; that such concussion and fire, acting on the air in the roadways and entries charged and filled with dust, produced and effected such explosion; all without any fault or negligence on the part of appellee. It is also averred that if appellant had performed its duty in regularly and thoroughly sprinkling said dust on or before the date of the explosion, and if said miner or miners had not fired such illegal shots in the manner described, the accident and resulting injuries to appellee would not and could not have occurred; that the accident did occur and appellee was injured thereby solely through the combined negligence of appellant and said miner or miners.

Appellee does not admit that the verdict rests on the second paragraph of complaint, and calls our attention to the answer to the sixtieth interrogatory, submitted by the court, wherein the jury answered that the explosion would have occurred if the unlawful shots had not been fired. This would indicate that the jury based its verdict on the first paragraph of complaint. But assuming that the verdict was returned on the second paragraph of complaint, or that it does not clearly appear on which paragraph the verdict rests, we think there was no error in overruling the demurrer to the second paragraph.

It is true, as contended by the learned counsel for appellant, that where it affirmatively appears from the complaint that the injury was the proximate result of 2. the negligence of a fellow servant the complaint is bad, and there can be no recovery. But we think this principle is not applicable to the paragraph of complaint before us. Facts are averred which show that the immediate and proximate cause of the injury was the negligent omission of appellant to perform a statutory duty, combined with the negligence of appellee's fellow servants in firing the illegal shots.

3.   It may be strictly accurate to say, as contended by appellant, that there can be but one proximate cause of an injury, but it is clear that there may be several elements combining to make up the proximate cause.

In *Beaning* v. *South Bend Electric Co.* (1910), 45 Ind. App. 261, 279, 90 N. E. 786, this court said: "There may be several proximate causes of a particular injury, some of them innocent, and for which no liability exists on the part of any one; others may be the result of tortious acts of one or more. When this is true, each of the tortfeasors is jointly and severally liable for the injury resulting, and the fact that accidental or innocent causes or conditions and concurring wrongful acts of other parties join to produce the given injury does not affect the liability of any one of the wrongdoers."

In *Vandalia Coal Co.* v. *Yemm, supra,* the court on page 532 said: "It is expressly averred in the first paragraph 'that if said defendant company had performed its duty, by regularly and thoroughly sprinkling said dust on or before the date of the explosion, the accident, and injuries herein complained of would not and could not have occurred, and that they did occur solely and proximately by reason of its neglect in that behalf.' The fact could hardly be more directly stated."

It will be observed that substantially the same averment appears in the second paragraph of the complaint, with the addition that the negligence of appellant combined with the negligence of the miners in firing the illegal shots producing the injury to appellee, and that appellee was injured solely through the combined negligence of appellant and said miners.

In *Princeton Coal, etc., Co.* v. *Lawrence* (1911), 176 Ind. 469, 483, 95 N. E. 423, the court said: "The fact that the negligence of another miner, or other miners, concurred with the negligence of appellant in producing the injury, will not exonerate appellant, if its negligence in failing to sprinkle was the proximate cause of the injury, and the jury so found." See also, *Fort Wayne, etc., Traction Co.* v. *Roudebush* (1909), 173 Ind. 57, 62, 66, 88 N. E. 676, 89 N. E. 369; *Romona Oölitic Stone Co.* v. *Shields* (1909), 173 Ind. 68, 74, 88 N. E. 595; *Lake Erie, etc., R. Co.* v. *Charman* (1903), 161 Ind. 95, 98, 99, 67 N. E. 923; *Hymera Coal Mining Co.* v. *Mahan* (1909), 44 Ind. App. 583, 587, 588, 88 N. E. 108.

No question is raised as to the extent of appellee's injury or the amount of the recovery, but it is earnestly insisted that there was no evidence to support the verdict. While the complaint proceeds on the theory of a coal-dust explosion, and the jury expressly found by its answers to interrogatories that there was a coal-dust explosion, appellant says that the evidence, without contradiction, shows a gas explosion. If this is true, the verdict is unwarranted, as there would be no causal connection shown between the negligence charged—that of failing to sprinkle the entries and roadways—and the injury resulting. If the explosion was from gas alone, then the negligent failure to sprinkle and allay the dust had nothing to do with the accident.

We have carefully examined the record, and find evidence from which the jury might fairly have concluded that
the explosion was due to coal dust. This was a
4. question of fact to be determined by the jury, and
the court on appeal will not weigh the evidence, but will consider only that most favorable to appellee. *Diamond Block Coal Co.* v. *Cuthbertson* (1906), 166 Ind. 290, 300,
76 N. E. 1060. The fact that the evidence may be
5. weak or unsatisfactory will not authorize a reversal,
where there is some evidence supporting the judg-

ment in every material respect. *Republic Iron, etc., Co.* v. *Berkes* (1904), 162 Ind. 517, 526, 70 N. E. 815.

It is also urged that the trial court erred in giving certain instructions and in refusing to give certain other instructions tendered by appellant. Without setting

6. out the instructions given and refused, it is sufficient to say that those refused were covered by others given by the court, and the instructions given, of which complaint is made, have been approved by the Supreme Court in the case of *Vandalia Coal Co.* v. *Yemm, supra.*

Finding no reversible error in the record, the judgment is affirmed.

Note.—Reported in 99 N. E. 648. See, also, under (1) 26 Cyc. 1384; (2) 26 Cyc. 1302; (3) 29 Cyc. 496; (4, 5) 3 Cyc. 348; (6) 38 Cyc. 1711. As to the effect of an irregular, improvident or fraudulent sale by trustee, see 19 Am. St. 293. As to laches, and equity's intolerance of stale claims, see 2 Am. St. 795.

INDIANAPOLIS SOUTHERN RAILROAD COMPANY *v.* EMMERSON.

[No. 7,581. Filed June 19, 1912. Rehearing denied December 31, 1912. Transfer denied February 13, 1913.]

1. CARRIERS.—*Passengers.*—*Contract Relation.*—The law implies a contract between passenger and carrier, that the latter shall carry the passenger safely, so far as human foresight, reasonably exercised, can guard against disaster. p. 409.

2. CARRIERS.—*Duty.*—*Injury to Passengers.*—*Liability.*—A carrier is required to exercise the highest degree of care to secure the safety of passengers, and is responsible for the slightest neglect which is the proximate cause of injury to a passenger who is himself without fault. p. 409.

3. NEGLIGENCE. — *Acts Constituting Negligence.* — *Operation of Train.*—The sudden or violent motion or jerking of a train may be negligence. p. 410.

4. CARRIERS.—*Injury to Passengers.*—*Complaint.*—In a passenger's action for injuries caused by being thrown from a train while standing near the door of the car preparatory to alighting, a complaint alleging that after defendant's agents had called the

station, and at a time when, according to usage and custom, passengers were making preparation to leave the train at said station, defendant's agents, well knowing such custom and that passengers were preparing to leave the train, and that they were likely to be standing in the aisles, "negligently, unnecessarily and suddenly increased the speed of said train and unnecessarily and negligently jerked said coach," etc., whereby plaintiff was thrown and injured, sufficiently charges negligence so as to withstand a demurrer, in the absence of specific averments that overcome the effect of those constituting such charge. p. 410.

5. CARRIERS.—*Injury to Passengers.—Presumption of Negligence.—Instructions.—Reference to Complaint.*—An instruction, in a passenger's action for personal injuries from being thrown from a train, that if plaintiff has proved by a fair preponderance of the evidence that she was a passenger on defendant's train, "and that she was jerked or thrown therefrom and injured as charged in her complaint, without any fault on her part," such facts would raise a presumption of negligence on the part of defendant, and that defendant would have the burden of proving that the injury could not have been avoided by the highest practical care and diligence, in order to rebut such presumption, did not tell the jury that proof of the injury alone would create a presumption of negligence, but stated as an express condition that the injury must be shown to have occurred in the manner charged in the complaint, and without fault on plaintiff's part, and therefore was not erroneous. p. 411.

6. CARRIERS.—*Injury to Passengers.—Presumption of Negligence.—Instructions.*—In a passenger's action for injuries, an instruction that if a carrier provides perfect machinery, cars and roadbed, and the servants in charge of same are negligent, there is a breach of duty, and a presumption of negligence arises in favor of the passenger injured without fault by the negligent operation of the train, the same as it would in case the injury flowed from defective track, cars, or machinery, is not open to the objection that it tells the jury that defendant's negligence will be presumed from the injury regardless of the circumstances under which it was received. p. 413.

7. CARRIERS.—*Injury to Passengers.—Contributory Negligence.—Children.—Instructions.*—Where, in a passenger's action defended on the ground that plaintiff contributed to her injury by leaving her seat before the train had stopped, there was evidence that plaintiff was sixteen years of age and had comparatively no experience in riding on trains, that the brakeman had twice announced the station, that the train had slowed down, and that plaintiff, believing that it was nearing the station, and with information that it stopped but a few seconds, left her seat and

Indianapolis Southern R. Co. *v.* Emmerson—52 Ind. App. 403.

walked to the door through which the brakeman had passed, when, by a sudden jerk of the train, she was thrown and injured, an instruction that recovery could not be defeated on the ground of contributory negligence, if considering her age and experience and all the surrounding circumstances, plaintiff acted as a reasonably prudent person, similarly situated, would have acted, was proper and applicable to the evidence. p. 413.

8. CARRIERS.—*Injury to Passengers.—Negligence.—Instructions.*— An instruction, in a passenger's action for injuries, that if defendant was guilty of other negligence than that charged, there can be no recovery, was properly refused, since its effect was that, even though defendant was guilty of the negligence charged, and it was the proximate cause of the injury, plaintiff could not recover if the jury found that defendant was also guilty of other negligence. p. 415.

9. TRIAL.—*Instructions.—Refusal.*—An instruction open to criticism on account of being inaccurate, ambiguous, uncertain or misleading, may be properly refused,' even when its giving might not constitute reversible error. p. 415.

10. TRIAL.—*Conflicting Evidence.—Assumption of Facts.—Instructions.—Refusal.*—A requested instruction stating that the evidence shows certain facts, where the evidence as to such facts is conflicting, invades the province of the jury and is properly refused. p. 415.

11. APPEAL.—*Review.—Refusal of Instructions.*—The refusal of instructions, that are covered in their essential features by the instructions given, is not error. p. 416.

12. TRIAL.—*Answers to Interrogatories.—Motion for Judgment.— Grounds.*—The fact that the jury's answers to interrogatories are not consistent with the evidence, or with each other, furnishes no ground for sustaining a motion for judgment thereon. p. 416.

13. APPEAL.—*Review.—Verdict.—Answers to Interrogatories.*—In determining the correctness of the trial court's ruling on a motion for judgment on answers to interrogatories, only the pleadings, the general verdict, and the interrogatories and answers, will be considered. p. 417.

14. APPEAL.—*Review.—Presumptions.—Verdict.—Answers to Interrogatories.*—Every presumption is indulged in favor of the general verdict as against the answers to interrogatories, and it is only when the conflict between them and the general verdict is irreconcilable on any theory, or on any supposable state of facts provable under the issues, that such answers will control. p. 417.

15. APPEAL.—*Review.—Verdict.—Evidence.—Sufficiency.* — Where there is some evidence on each fact essential to its support, a verdict will not be set aside on the ground of insufficient evidence. p. 418.

16. APPEAL.—*Questions Presented for Review.—Motion for New Trial.—Grounds.—Special Verdict.*—No question is raised on appeal by the grounds of a motion for a new trial, that the special verdict is not sustained by sufficient evidence, and is contrary to law. p. 419.

17. CARRIERS.—*Injury to Passengers.—Evidence.—Admissibility.— Contributory Negligence.*—In a passenger's action for injuries in being thrown from a train by the sudden jerking of the train while plaintiff was standing near the door preparatory to alighting at a station, evidence in relation to plaintiff's experience in riding on trains, and her information as to the length of time the train stopped at the station, was admissible as affecting the question of whether she was guilty of negligence contributing to her injury. p. 419.

From Monroe Circuit Court; *James B. Wilson,* Judge.

Action by Maude E. Emmerson, by her next friend, Sarah E. Yockey, against the Indianapolis Southern Railroad Company. From a judgment for plaintiff, the defendant appeals. *Affirmed.*

Duncan & Batman, James E. Kepperley, Robert G. Miller and *James W. Blair,* for appellant.

Joseph E. Henley, Rufus H. East and *Anderson Percifield,* for appellee.

HOTTEL, C. J.—Appellee recovered a judgment in the court below for $5,000 for injuries which she alleged she received by being thrown from one of appellant's trains when a passenger thereon. The cause was tried by a jury which returned a general verdict for appellee in the above amount, with answers to interrogatories.

Appellant's demurrer to the complaint, its motion for judgment on the answers to interrogatories and for a new trial were each overruled, and these rulings present the alleged errors assigned and relied on.

That part of the complaint necessary to present the objection made thereto and other questions presented by the appeal is, in substance, as follows: That when said train was about half a mile east of Trevlac, said defendant, by its agents in charge of said train, sounded the whistle for

NOVEMBER TERM, 1912. 407

Indianapolis Southern R. Co. *v.* Emmerson—52 Ind. App. 403.

said station, and materially checked the speed of said train
as it approached a sharp curve then and there in defendant's railroad track at said point; that thereupon said agents
aforesaid passed through the train and through the coach
in which this plaintiff was riding, and twice announced in
a loud tone of voice "Trevlac"; that at said time said train
was passing over said sharp curve, and the speed was greatly reduced as though said train was about to come to a
stop; that it was then dark, and the plaintiff, observing
lights in houses near the track, believed she was very near
said station; that so believing, she arose from her seat, took
up her baggage, consisting of a suit case and a hat, walked
down the aisle between the seats in said coach to the rear
end thereof, in the same direction the servant of said defendant had gone as he announced said station; that plaintiff stopped when near the last seat in said coach, and while
so standing in said coach at said point near the rear door
of said coach, waiting for said train to come to a full stop
at said station, and while in the exercise of due care for
her own safety, and without any fault on her own part and
without any notice or warning whatever, said defendants,
by its agents in charge of said train, carelessly and negligently and with great force and violence so negligently
managed and operated said train as to cause the coach in
which said plaintiff was riding to be suddenly and violently
jerked forward, the speed thereof suddenly and violently
increased, causing said coach and train to be instantly
drawn forward with a lurch, and thereby this plaintiff, by
reason of such negligence, was instantly jerked and thrown
from her position out of the rear door of said car, and was
suddenly and violently jerked and thrown from said car and
off said train while it was thus running at such greatly-in-
creased and high and dangerous rate of speed, causing her
to fall and be thrown into a cattle-pit and against some
fencing on defendant's right of way, with great force and
violence, from which she sustained permanent and lasting

injuries; that plaintiff at the time of her injuries was almost wholly without experience in riding on trains, having been a passenger on trains only two or three times in her life, and did not know anything about the management and operation of passenger trains; that as she approached the station of Trevlac on said train, and at the time she left her seat to go to the rear of said car, she was led to believe and did believe the train was very near said station; that she was unacquainted with defendant's track at said point, and said defendant's servant having passed through said coach and having twice called ''Trevlac'', and having opened the doors of said coach, thereby inviting passengers to leave the train, and knowing that said train stopped at the small stations only a few seconds, she believed that it was necessary for her to get her baggage and go to the rear of the coach to alight from said train; that by custom and usage on defendant's line, passengers desiring to alight at the small stations. such as Trevlac, took up their baggage and made preparations to leave the train as soon as such stations were called, and so believing, plaintiff walked to the rear of said coach, as aforesaid. Plaintiff further avers that said defendant, its agents and servants in charge of said train, well knowing such custom, and that passengers were preparing to leave said train at said station on said date, and knowing that passengers were likely to be standing in the aisles, *negligently, unnecessarily* and *suddenly increased the speed of said train* and *unnecessarily* and *negligently jerked said coach* as aforesaid and thus threw her from said car and said train, injuring her as aforesaid.

The objection urged to the complaint is that (we quote from appellant's brief) ''there is no charge of bad track, defective equipment, incompetent servants, or of any mishap to the train, the car, the crew, or the passengers. There is no allegation of a collision, derailment, break, or any accident to the train or to any part thereof, or to a single passenger of the train, or to any one operating it, or to any one connected with it except appellee. * * * Saying a thing is negligent does not make it so. It requires the statement of some act which is averred to have been improperly done. * * * The fact of the plaintiff's injuries would not raise a presumption of the defendant's negligence.''

Appellant either misconstrues the cases cited and relied on in support of its contention, or fails to give proper force and effect to the averments of the complaint.

"By the sale of a ticket, or the receipt of the price for transportation, from one point to another, a railway company expressly contracts to carry such person to the point covered by the contract, and in addition to that,

1. a contract arises by implication, between the company and the passenger, that the latter shall be carried safely, so far as human foresight, reasonably exercised, can guard against disaster.'' *Kentucky, etc., Bridge Co.* v. *Quinkert* (1891), 2 Ind. App. 244, 247, 28 N. E. 338; 2 Wood, Railway Law 1178. See, also, *Grand Rapids, etc., R. Co.* v. *Ellison* (1889), 117 Ind. 234, 237, 20 N. E. 135; *Prothero* v. *Citizens St. R. Co.* (1893), 134 Ind. 431, 439, 33 N. E. 765; *Knauss* v. *Lake Erie, etc., R. Co.* (1902), 29 Ind. App. 216, 219, 64 N. E. 95. In such cases the carrier is required to exercise the highest degree of care

2. to secure the safety of passengers and is responsible for the slightest neglect which is the proximate cause of injury to a passenger who is himself without fault. *Kentucky, etc., Bridge Co.* v. *Quinkert, supra; Sherlock* v. *Alling* (1873), 44 Ind. 184; *Louisville, etc., R. Co.* v. *Kelly* (1884), 92 Ind. 371, 47 Am. Rep. 149; *Bedford, etc., R. Co.* v. *Rainbolt* (1885), 99 Ind. 551; *Louisville, etc., R. Co.* v. *Thompson* (1886), 107 Ind. 442, 8 N. E. 18, 9 N. E. 357, 57 Am. Rep. 120; *Grand Rapids, etc., R. Co.* v. *Ellison, supra; Louisville, etc., R. Co.* v. *Snyder* (1889), 117 Ind. 435, 20 N. E. 284, 3 L. R. A. 434, 10 Am. St. 60; *Louisville, etc., R. Co.* v. *Lucas* (1889), 119 Ind. 583, 21 N. E. 968, 6

L. R. A. 193; Thompson, Carriers 200-204; *Cincinnati, etc.,
R. Co. v. Worthington* (1903), 30 Ind. App. 663, 666, 65
N. E. 557, 66 N. E. 478, 96 Am. St. 355; *Terre Haute, etc.,
R. Co. v. Buck* (1884), 96 Ind. 346, 49 Am. Rep. 168; *Jef-
fersonville R. Co. v. Hendricks* (1866), 26 Ind. 228; *Cleve-
land, etc., R. Co. v. Hadley* (1908), 170 Ind. 204, 207, 82
N. E. 1025, 84 N. E. 14, 16 L. R. A. (N. S.) 527, 16 Ann.
Cas. 1; *Perc Marquette R. Co. v. Strange* (1908), 171 Ind.
160, 165, 84 N. E. 819, 85 N. E. 1026, 20 L. R. A. (N. S.)
1041.

The *sudden* or *violent* motion or *jerking* of a train *may
be* negligence. *Kentucky, etc., Bridge Co. v. Quinkert,
supra,* 244, 249; *Louisville, etc., R. Co. v. Crunk
3.* (1889), 119 Ind. 542, 21 N. E. 31, 12 Am. St. 443; 2
Wood, Railway Law 1125; *Dougherty v. Missouri R.
Co.* (1884), 81 Mo. 325, 51 Am. Rep. 239; *Wood v. Lake
Shore, etc., R. Co.* (1882), 49 Mich. 370; *Cincinnati, etc., R.
Co. v. Revalee* (1897), 17 Ind. App. 657, 671, 672, 46 N. E.
352; *Consolidated Traction Co. v. Thalheimer* (1896), 59 N.
J. L. 474, 37 Atl. 132.

The complaint shows that the sudden jerking of the train,
alleged to be negligent, was after appellant's agents had
called the station for which appellee had purchased
4. her ticket, and at a time when, according to usage
and custom, passengers were making preparations to
leave the train at said station, and that the agents of appellant, ''well knowing such custom and that passengers were
preparing to leave said train at said station on said date,
and knowing that passengers were likely to be standing in
the aisles, *negligently, unnecessarily* and *suddenly* increased
the speed of said train and unnecessarily and negligently
jerked said coach,'' etc.

The negligent operation of the train by appellant's servants, the manner of such negligent operation, and appellee's injury, resulting as a consequence, are averred. These
general averments of negligence and their causal connection

with the injury are sufficient as against a demurrer, unless the specific averments overcome their effect. *Pittsburgh, etc., R. Co. v. Richardson* (1907), 40 Ind. App. 503, 82 N. E. 536; *Standard Forgings Co. v. Saffel* (1911), 176 Ind. 417, 96 N. E. 321; *Cincinnati, etc., R. Co. v. Worthington, supra.*

The specific acts pleaded, above indicated, tend to support rather than overthrow the general averment that the train was negligently jerked, and therefore furnish no ground or reason for the court to say as a matter of law that such jerking was not negligent. The complaint is not open to the objections made against it.

Appellant objects to instructions Nos. 6 and 7, given at the request of appellee. It is insisted, in effect, that by
5.   these instructions the jury was told that the presumption of the defendant's negligence arises in all cases of injured passengers, and that the burden was cast on defendant to prove that the proper degree of care was exercised by it, regardless of the circumstances under which the injury was received; in other words, that the trial court "applied the rule of *res ipsa loquitur* in this case; while that rule does not apply where the action of the passenger might contribute to the injury."

Instruction No. 6 is as follows: "While the plaintiff here has the burden of proving the negligence charged, and all other material facts which constitute the cause of action alleged in her complaint, yet, if she has proven by a fair preponderance of the evidence that she was a passenger, that she had paid her fare and was admitted as a passenger on defendant's train, and that *she was jerked or thrown therefrom and injured as charged in her complaint, without any fault on her part,* then I instruct you that *such facts would raise a presumption of negligence* on the part of the defendant railroad company, and would place upon said defendant the burden of proving, in order to rebut the presumption of negligence, that the injury could not have

been avoided by the exercise of the highest practical care
and diligence, and in the absence of such proof on the part
of said defendant, such presumption of negligence would
prevail.'' (Our italics.)

We do not think the instruction open to the objection
urged against it. It will be observed that instruction No. 6
contains, as an express condition necessary to raise the presumption of negligence against appellant, the following provision: ''And that she was jerked or thrown therefrom
and injured as charged in her complaint without any fault
on her part.'' Under this instruction the jury was not
told that proof of the injury alone created a presumption
of negligence, but that such injury, in connection with proof
that it resulted in the manner charged in the complaint and
without appellee's fault, would give rise to such presumption. We think that, under the authorities, the instruction might have told, and was probably intended by its
author to tell, the jury, in effect, that proof of the relation
of carrier and passenger between appellant and appellee,
together with proof of appellant's negligence as charged,
and appellee's injury, would create a presumption that the
injury resulted from such negligence, and, subject to the
condition that appellee was herself without fault, would
impose on appellant, in order to avoid liability, the necessity
of proving that the injury could not have been avoided by
the exercise of the highest practical care and diligence, but
the instruction as worded falls far short of being thus favorable to appellee. This instruction, considered in connection with the averments of the complaint, was certainly as
favorable to appellant in this regard as the authorities warrant. *Kentucky, etc., Bridge Co.* v. *Quinkert, supra,* 252;
Memphis, etc., Packet Co. v. *McCool* (1882), 83 Ind. 392,
397, 398, 43 Am. Rep. 71; *Terre Haute, etc., R. Co.* v. *Buck,
supra; Louisville, etc., R. Co.* v. *Snyder, supra; Louisville,
etc., R. Co.* v. *Thompson, supra; Consolidated Traction Co.*
v. *Thalheimer, supra; Cleveland, etc., R. Co.* v. *Hadley,*

supra, and authorities cited; *Pere Marquette R. Co.* v. *Strange, supra,* and authorities cited.

So with instruction No. 7, the provision is simply that "if the carrier provides perfect machinery, cars and road

6. bed *and the servants in charge of the same are negligent,* there is a breach of duty, and a presumption of negligence arises in favor of the passenger *injured without his fault by the negligent operation of the train,* the same as it would in case the injury flowed from defective track, cars, or machinery." (Our italics.) This instruction probably does not express what it was intended to express, but it does not tell the jury that appellant's negligence will be presumed from the injury, and, therefore, is not open to the objection urged against it, and certainly could not have harmed appellant.

Instruction No. 8, given at appellee's request, is objected to on the ground that it "undertakes to make experience and age an element in determining the question of

7. contributory negligence." That part of the instruction objected to is as follows: "If you find from a fair preponderance of all the evidence given in the cause that the plaintiff acted as a reasonably prudent person, similarly situated, would have acted *considering her age and experience* and all the surrounding circumstances, then her case cannot be defeated on the ground of contributory negligence alone." It was a part of appellant's defense that appellee by getting up out of her seat and going to or near the door of the car contributed to her injury, and on this account was not entitled to recover. There was evidence showing that appellee at the time she was injured was only sixteen years of age, and had comparatively no experience in riding on trains; that before she left her seat the brakeman passed through the car, twice announcing the station to which she had bought her ticket; that the train had slowed down; that appellee, believing that it was nearing the station, and with information that it stopped but a few

seconds, got up preparatory to getting off, and walked to the seat nearest the door through which the brakeman had passed, leaving the same open, when by a sudden increase of speed of the train, she was jerked off her feet, thrown out of the door, and injured as alleged. We think under the evidence the instruction was applicable and supported by authority. *Cleveland, etc., R. Co.* v. *Miles* (1904), 162 Ind. 646, 658, 70 N. E. 985; *Baltimore, etc., R. Co.* v. *Hickman* (1907), 40 Ind. App. 315, 318, 81 N. E. 1086; *Consolidated Traction Co.* v. *Scott* (1896), 58 N. J. L. 682, 689, 34 Atl. 1094, 33 L. R. A. 122, 55 Am. St. 620; 4 Am. and Eng. Ency. Law 46; *Van Natta* v. *People's St. Railway, etc.* (1896), 133 Mo. 13, 22, 23, 34 S. W. 505; *Pittsburgh, etc., R. Co.* v. *Moore* (1903), 110 Ill. App. 304, 306, 307.

In the case last cited the court said: "It is further claimed that instruction eleven, quoted in the statement, is erroneous because it uses the word 'child' instead of 'person' but we are of opinion that the jury could not have been misled by the instruction for that reason. We think, however, that the instruction is subject to criticism in that it omits the element of the intelligence of the child. The instruction instead of the phrase 'for one of his age and experience' should have been 'for one of his age, capacity and experience.' *R. R. Co.* [Illinois Cent. R. Co.] v. *Slater* [1889], 129 Ill. 91-99 [21 N. E. 575, 6 L. R. A. 418, 16 Am. St. 242]; *City of Chicago* v. *Keefe* [1885], 114 Ill. 222, 229 [2 N. E. 267, 55 Am. Rep. 860]."

In the case of *Consolidated Traction Co.* v. *Scott, supra*, the court said: "And when a child has reached the age of discretion, and is considered *sui juris* as a matter of law, the degree of care and caution required of him will be no higher than such as is usually exercised by persons of similar age, judgment and experience. And whether that degree of care and caution has been exercised by the child in a given case, is usually, if not always, a question of fact for the jury. 4 Am. and Eng. Ency. Law 46, and cases cited.''

The refusal of appellant's instruction No. 2 is urged as error. This instruction contains a positive statement and direction to the jury that ''if the defendant was

8. guilty of other negligence than that charged, there can be no recovery.'' The effect of this statement was to tell the jury that even though appellant was guilty of the negligence charged, and that the same was the proximate cause of appellee's injury, yet she would not be entitled to recover if it found that appellant was also guilty of other negligence. Taking the instruction as a whole, this court understands that it was doubtless the intent of appellant to have the instruction tell the jury that on the question of appellant's negligence it should not consider any negligence other than that charged in the complaint, and that if appellee's injuries in fact resulted from, and were caused solely by some negligence of appellant other than that charged and relied on in the complaint, there could be no recovery.

But, to say the least, the instruction as tendered was not an accurate statement of the law, and the statement above quoted made it so misleading that it might have been harmful, and therefore furnished sufficient ground for the court's refusal to give it. An instruction open to

9. criticism on account of being inaccurate, ambiguous, uncertain or misleading, may be properly refused when the giving of the same might not constitute such harmful error as to necessitate reversal.

Instruction No. 3, tendered by appellant and refused, is completely covered in all its parts by other instructions.

The refusal to give appellant's instruction No. 6 is urged. This instruction, as preliminary to rules of law an-

10. nounced therein governing appellee's conduct, contained the following: ''The evidence shows the plain-

tiff *voluntarily* left the seat in which she was sitting and, with her baggage, went toward or onto one of the platforms on the defendant's train while it was still in *rapid motion,* and while a *very considerable distance from the station* to which she was going; that there were unoccupied seats in said car, specially provided for passengers; that there was *no necessity* for her leaving her seat at that time and going toward or onto said platform; there is no evidence that others who remained in their seats until said train arrived at Trevlac were injured or hurt, or that other passengers left their seats.''

This instruction clearly invaded the province of the jury. Whether or not appellee *voluntarily* left her seat; whether the train was at such time in "rapid" or "slow motion"; whether it was a *"considerable"* or a short "distance" from the station when she left her seat, and whether there was or was not *"necessity"* for her leaving when she did, were, under the conflicting evidence in this case, all questions of fact to be determined by the jury.

The refusal to give other instructions is urged, but we deem it unnecessary to set them out, or refer to them further than to say of them generally that such as cor-

11. rectly stated the law were in their essential features covered by other instructions given at appellee's request stated in language more appropriate to the facts of the case, and less likely to mislead the jury than those refused.

It is next insisted that the court erred in overruling appellant's motion for judgment on the answers to interrogatories. It is insisted that to support its general ver-

12. dict, "the jury went to the limit in answering the interrogatories," and that the answers are a marvel of inconsistencies and contradictions of each other and of the evidence. These answers, as we view them, while apparently inconsistent in some respects, may be, in the main, when considered together, reconciled with each other and

with the evidence, and are not open to the severe criticism made upon them. But in any event, the fact that all or either of the same are not consistent with the evidence, or with each other, furnished no ground for sustaining a motion for judgment thereon. *McCoy* v. *Kokomo, R. etc., Co.* (1902), 158 Ind. 662, 64 N. E. 92; *Flutter* v. *New York, etc., R. Co.* (1901), 27 Ind. App. 511, 57 N. E. 337; *Pittsburgh, etc., R. Co.* v. *Lightheiser* (1907), 168 Ind. 438, 78 N. E. 1033.

In determining the correctness of the ruling of 13. the court below on this motion, this court does not look to the evidence, but considers only the pleadings, the general verdict, and the interrogatories and 14. answers thereto. Every presumption is indulged in favor of the general verdict, and it is only when the conflict between such answers and the general verdict is irreconcilable on any theory, or on any supposable state of facts, provable under the issues, that such answers will control. *Consolidated Stone Co.* v. *Summit* (1899), 152 Ind. 297, 53 N. E. 235; *Shoner* v. *Pennsylvania Co.* (1892), 130 Ind. 170, 28 N. E. 616, 29 N. E. 775; *Peru Heating Co.* v. *Lenhart* (1911), 48 Ind. App. 319, 95 N. E. 680; *Southern R. Co.* v. *Utz* (1913), *ante*, 270, 98 N. E. 375.

It is urged that the verdict is contrary to law. In support of this ground of the motion for a new trial it is insisted in effect that the trial court instructed the jury that if the plaintiff was lawfully on the train, there would arise in her favor a presumption that her injury was caused by defendant's negligence and that such presumption could only be removed by defendant's proving by a preponderance of the evidence that "it could not have been avoided by the exercise of the highest possible degree of care."

We have already indicated in the discussion of the instructions that neither of them is open to the criticism so assumed against them, but on the contrary they separately and in their entirety clearly told the jury that the appellee was required to prove as one of the elements necessary to a recovery, appellant's negligence as charged in her complaint, and expressly recognized the principle that appellee, by getting out of her seat and moving to the rear of the car, and there standing while the same was in motion, thereby assumed all the risks of injury incident to the usual and ordinary operation of the train, and that if by her own act she in any way contributed to the proximate cause of her injury she could not recover.

The insufficiency of the evidence to sustain the verdict is urged, but we think we have already, in this opinion, indicated enough of the evidence to show that there was some evidence on each fact essential to its support.

The evidence in this case is meagre and unsatisfactory as to the actual manner in which appellee's injury occurred, and the real or proximate cause thereof. It was of
15. a character that should, and doubtless did raise in the mind of the trial court, with opportunity to weigh the evidence, serious doubt as to whether appellee's injury occurred, in fact, from any negligent omission or commission of appellant's servants in the operation of said train, rather than from the additional risk which she herself assumed by getting up and walking, with both hands full of packages, to or near the rear door of the coach in which she was riding while said train was in motion, unaffected by any act of appellant other than that of the usual and ordinary operation of its train. This court has no such question to determine.

The only question we are called on to determine is whether there was any evidence on said question, and we cannot say that there was no evidence on this or any other fact necessary to be proven under the issues.

The grounds of the motion for a new trial, that the special verdict is not sustained by sufficient evidence and is contrary to law, raise no question in this court. *Con-*

solidated Stone Co. v. *Williams* (1901), 26
16. Ind. App. 131, 135, 57 N. E. 558, 84 Am.
St. 278.

Lastly, it is urged that evidence by appellee in relation
to her experience in riding on railroad trains and her information as to the length of time the train stopped at
17. the station of Trevlac was improperly admitted.

While it is true that appellee's experience or lack of
experience could have nothing to do with appellant's negligence in the absence of averments showing some special duty
arising on account thereof, yet we think under the authorities cited, *supra*, in discussing the instruction tendering the
same question, that this evidence was proper as affecting the
question of appellee being guilty of negligence contributing
to her injury. So we think as affecting the same question,
especially in view of the averments of the complaint, that
appellee's information as to the length of time the train
stopped at the station for which she had purchased her ticket
was competent.

We find no error in the record, and the judgment below
is therefore affirmed.

NOTE.—Reported in 98 N. E. 895. See, also, under (2) 6 Cyc.
591; (3) 6 Cyc. 624; (4) 6 Cyc. 626; (5, 6) 6 Cyc. 628; (7) 6 Cyc.
637; (9) 38 Cyc. 1598, 1599, 1602; (10) 38 Cyc. 1657; (11) 38 Cyc.
1711; (14) 38 Cyc. 1927; (15) 3 Cyc. 648; (17) 6 Cyc. 628—New
Anno. On the question of the liability of a carrier for injuries to
passenger inside car from sudden starting or stopping of car or
train, see 34 L. R. A. (N. S.) 225. On the presumption of negligence from sudden start, stop, jolt, or jerk of car, see 13 L. R. A.
(N. S.) 611.

ANGOLA RAILWAY AND POWER COMPANY *v.* BUTZ, ADMINISTRATRIX.

[No. 7,618. Filed June 6, 1912. Rehearing denied December 18, 1912. Transfer denied February 13, 1913.]

1. MASTER AND SERVANT.—*Injury to Servant.—Failure to Comply with Factory Act.—Complaint.—Sufficiency.*—A complaint, in an action for the death of a servant who was caught in an unguarded belt, alleging that defendant furnished electricity to various customers, and that, as a part of the machinery in its plant, it had boilers, dynamos and engines, sufficiently shows that defendant was engaged in the generation of electricity, so as to be within the provisions of §8029 Burns 1908, Acts 1899 p. 231, for the guarding of certain dangerous machinery. p. 423.

2. WORDS AND PHRASES.—*"Dynamo."*—A dynamo is a machine for generating or converting mechanical energy into electricity. p. 424.

3. EVIDENCE.—*Judicial Notice.—Matters of Common Knowledge.—Matters of Science.*—Courts take judicial notice of such matters of common knowledge and science as are known to all men of ordinary understanding and intelligence, and they judicially know that a dynamo is used for generating electricity and not merely for the purpose of transmitting or storing the same. p. 424.

4. ELECTRICITY.—*Generation of Electricity.—"Manufacturing Establishment".—Factory Act.*—A plant for the generation of electricity is a manufacturing establishment, as contemplated by the provisions of the factory act, §§8021, 8029 Burns 1908, Acts 1899 p. 231, §§1, 9. p. 424.

5. MASTER AND SERVANT.—*Injury to Servant.—Violation of Statutory Duty.—Negligence.—Complaint.—Sufficiency.*—A complaint for the death of an employe, alleging that the death was caused by the employer's omission, in violation of statute, to guard a dangerous belt, sufficiently charges negligence without averring such failure to be a negligent failure, since the failure to discharge a duty imposed by statute is negligence *per se.* p. 425.

6. MASTER AND SERVANT.—*Injury to Servant.—Violation of Statutory Duty.—Assumption of Risks.*—The doctrine of assumed risk has no application when the death or injury of an employe is caused by the employer's failure to safeguard machinery as required by statute. p. 425.

7. MASTER AND SERVANT.—*Injury to Servant.—Complaint.—Allegations.—"Duty".*—In an action for the death of a stationary engineer, whose arm was caught by an unguarded belt, the allega-

Angola R., etc., Co. v. Butz—52 Ind. App. 420.

tion of the complaint, that it was a part of decedent's duty to adjust such belt, is not the statement of a conclusion, but is the allegation of an ultimate fact. p. 426.

8. APPEAL.—*Review.—Verdict.—Answers to Interrogatories.—Conclusions.—Ruling on Motion for Judgment.*—The objection that some of the findings included in the answers to interrogatories are statements of conclusions, and not facts, does not affect the question presented by the motion for judgment on such answers, where the general verdict includes a finding of facts covering practically the same proposition. p. 428.

9. MASTER AND SERVANT.—*Injury to Servant.—Contributory Negligence.*—Contributory negligence is not necessarily established against an employe by showing that he continued to use defective machinery after he knew it was out of repair. p. 429.

10. MASTER AND SERVANT.—*Injury to Servant.—Contributory Negligence.—Jury Question.*—In an action for the death of a stationary engineer, whose arm was caught by an unguarded belt while he was attempting to adjust the idler, where it was shown that he was attempting to do the work by the means provided and in the usual way, but that the place where he was attempting to adjust the idler was more dangerous than other places where he could have done the same work, the question of his contributory negligence was for the jury. p. 429.

11. MASTER AND SERVANT.—*Injury to Servant.—Verdict.—Answers to Interrogatories.*—In an action for the death of a servant, whose arm was caught by an unguarded belt while he was attempting to adjust the idler, the general verdict for plaintiff is not overcome by answers to interrogatories showing that he was attempting to do the work with the means provided, and in the usual way, but that the place where he was attempting to adjust such idler was more dangerous than other places where he could have done the same work. p. 430.

12. TRIAL.—*Instructions.—Incorporating Complaint.*—The incorporation of the whole complaint in an instruction to the jury, while not to be commended, is not ground for reversal. p. 430.

13. TRIAL. — *Instructions. — Incomplete General Instruction.*—A general instruction when incomplete, but correct as far as it goes, may be completed by other instructions. p. 430.

14. APPEAL. — *Review. — Harmless Error.—Instructions.*—A judgment will not be reversed for error in an instruction, where, by answers to interrogatories, it is shown that appellant was not harmed. p. 431.

15. APPEAL. — *Review. — Instructions. — Refusal.*—The refusal of tendered instructions is not error, where the law applicable to the issues was correctly and fully stated in the instructions given. p. 431.

10. APPEAL.—*Review.*—*Harmless Error.*—*Admission of Evidence.*—Error, if any, in the admission of evidence which was not of a character to harm appellant, will not work a reversal. p. 431.

From Steuben Circuit Court; *E. A. Bratton,* Judge.

Action by Della Butz, administratrix of the estate of William H. Butz, deceased, against the Angola Railway and Power Company. From a judgment for plaintiff, the defendant appeals. *Affirmed.*

Elmer E. Stevenson and *Leonard, Rose & Zollars,* for appellant.

Brown & Carlin and *Powers & Yeagley* for appellee.

FELT, J.—This was an action by appellee, as administratrix of the estate of William H. Butz, deceased, against appellant, to recover damages for personal injuries resulting in the death of said Butz. The cause was tried by a jury which returned a verdict in favor of appellee in the sum of $4,000, together with answers to interrogatories. Appellant's motions for judgment on the answers to the interrogatories and for a new trial were overruled and this appeal taken.

The first error relied on for reversal is that the trial court erred in overruling appellant's demurrers to the complaint. The complaint is in one paragraph, and, after showing appellee's right to maintain the action, charges that appellant "is a corporation duly organized under the laws of the State of Indiana, and is the owner and operator of a plant for the furnishing of electric light and water to the city of Angola; * * * that the machinery in said plant consists of boilers for the generation of steam, two engines, dynamos, pumps, shafts, belting, etc.; that a shaft runs through the building in which said plant is located, which shaft is used in transmitting power and motion to the machinery in said plant." The complaint then shows the construction of a certain pulley in said plant and the usual method of adjusting the same by means of certain screws, and then alleges ''that on the 9th of January, 1909, the deceased, William H. Butz, was and for fourteen years prior thereto had been engineer in said plant and it was a part of his duty as such engineer to adjust said belt by raising or lowering said pulley according as it was desired to loosen or tighten the same; that on said day while attempting to adjust said belt by turning down said screws and thereby tightening said belt and while standing on the west side of said belt and in close proximity thereto, as he was compelled to do in order to reach said screws, and while engaged in the discharge of his duties as such engineer and without any fault or negligence on his part and in consequence of the negligence of said defendant in not guarding said belt and machinery, the arm of said William H. Butz was caught by said belt and carried under said pulley and his body was thereby drawn between said post and said pulley or wheel and so jammed, bruised and crushed that he was instantly killed; that at the time the deceased was killed as aforesaid he was in the employment of the defendant as engineer in said plant and had been continuously in such employment for five years or more; that said belt at the time said deceased was killed, as aforesaid, was and for a long time immediately prior thereto had been wholly unguarded; that said belt, at the time of said killing, and during all of the time it remained unguarded as aforesaid was very dangerous; that said belt could have been guarded without rendering the same useless for the purpose for which it was used and intended, to wit: the transmission of power and motion from said engine to said shaft, and without in any way interfering with the efficiency of said belt or of said machinery.''

Counsel for appellant first contend that the complaint is insufficient for the reason that it does not show that at the time of the injury to appellee's decedent, appellant was engaged in the generation or manufacture of anything, and for the further reason that appel-

1.

lant's plant is not of such a character as to come within
the statute requiring machinery to be guarded.

The complaint does not directly state that appellant was
engaged in the generation of electricity, but that it "furnished" electricity to various customers, and that as a part
of the machinery in said plant it had boilers, dynamos and
two engines. A dynamo has been defined to be a
2. machine for generating or converting mechanical
energy into electricity. *Thomson-Houston Electric
Co.* v. *Western Electric Co.* (1895), 65 Fed. 615; Standard
Dict. (20th Century ed.) 567; Webster's New International
Dict. 689; 3 Century Dict. and Cyc. 1867; 8 Ency. Britan-
nica (11th ed.) 764. Courts will take judicial notice
3. of such matters of common knowledge and science
as are known to all men of ordinary understanding
and intelligence. *Eureka Vinegar Co.* v. *Gazette Printing
Co.* (1888), 35 Fed. 570; *Brown* v. *Piper* (1875), 91 U. S.
37, 42, 23 L. Ed. 200.

In the case of *City of Crawfordsville* v. *Braden* (1892),
130 Ind. 149, 158, 28 N. E. 849, 14 L. R. A. 268, 30 Am.
St. 214, it is stated that courts will not take judicial notice
of the various methods of generating and transmitting electricity, but this statement is not inconsistent with the proposition that courts may know judicially that a dynamo is
used for generating electricity and not merely for transmitting or storing the same. From the averments of the complaint, the reasonable and necessary inference to be drawn
is that at the time of the alleged injury appellant owned
and operated the plant, where decedent was employed, for
the purpose of generating electricity as well as furnishing
the same to its patrons. *Indianapolis St. R. Co.* v. *Ray*
(1906), 167 Ind. 236, 241, 78 N. E. 978.

The authorities are not in harmony as to whether a plant
for the generation of electricity is a manufacturing
4. establishment, but the better reason and the spirit of
our statute require that it be so classified. §§8021,

8029 Burns 1908, Acts 1899 p. 231, §§1, 9; *Hoffmeyer* v. *State* (1906), 37 Ind. App. 526, 531, 77 N. E. 372; *Burke* v. *Mead* (1902), 159 Ind. 252, 260, 64 N. E. 880; *Wells* v. *Christian* (1906), 165 Ind. 662, 76 N. E. 518; *People, ex rel.,* v. *Wemple* (1892), 129 N. Y. 543, 29 N. E. 808, 14 L. R. A. 708; *People, ex rel.,* v. *Campbell* (1895), 88 Hun 527, 34 N. Y. Supp. 711; *Bates Mach. Co.* v. *Trenton, etc., R. Co.* (1904), 70 N. J. L. 684, 58 Atl. 935, 103 Am. St. 811; *Beggs* v. *Edison Electric, etc., Co.* (1891), 96 Ala. 295, 11 South. 381, 38 Am. St. 94; *Lamborn* v. *Bell* (1893), 18 Colo. 346, 32 Pac. 989, 20 L. R. A. 241.

Appellant next urges that the complaint is insufficient for the reason that it does not charge that appellant negligently failed to guard the belt. The complaint alleges

5. appellant's omission, in violation of statute, to guard a dangerous belt. This was a sufficient charge of negligence, since a failure by the owner of a manufacturing establishment to discharge a duty specifically imposed on him by statute is negligence *per se*. *Davis* v. *Mercer Lumber Co.* (1905), 164 Ind. 413, 420, 73 N. E. 899; *Monteith* v. *Kokomo, etc., Co.* (1902), 159 Ind. 149, 152, 64 N. E. 610, 58 L. R. A. 944; *Indiana Mfg. Co.* v. *Wells* (1903), 31 Ind. App. 460, 462, 68 N. E. 319; *Buehner Chair Co.* v. *Feulner* (1902), 28 Ind. App. 479, 483, 63 N. E. 239.

The doctrine of assumed risk, contended for by appellant, has no application when the death, or injury, of an employe is caused by a failure on the part of his

6. employer to safeguard machinery, as required by statute. *Jenney Electric Mfg. Co.* v. *Flannery* (1913), 53 Ind. App. ——, 98 N. E. 424; *American Car, etc., Co.* v. *Clark* (1904), 32 Ind. App. 644, 648, 70 N. E. 828; *Chamberlain* v. *Waymire* (1904), 32 Ind. App. 442, 447, 68 N. E. 306, 70 N. E. 81.

Appellant also contends that the allegation that "it was a part of his [decedent's] duty as such engineer to adjust said belt" is a conclusion, and that the complaint is there-

fore insufficient for failure to show that decedent's
7. employment required him to come in close contact
with the unguarded belt.

"There are instances where the word 'duty' may be used
in a pleading to designate the character of work to be done,
or act to be performed, in pursuance of an employment,
and when so used the allegation is one of ultimate fact,
and not subject to the criticism that it states only a conclusion of the pleader. There is, however, a clear distinction between such use of the word 'duty' and its use in a
general statement charging that it is the duty of a person
to do, or to refrain from doing, a certain act or thing, intending thereby to charge that by reason of contractual
relations, or by implication of law, such person is obligated
to do or not to do the particular thing averred. In the
latter case the weight of authority is decidedly to the effect
that such averments state conclusions of law and not facts.
But the use of the word 'duty' in the case at bar clearly
comes within the former class, and is employed in the sense
of work or labor." *Chicago, etc., R. Co.* v. *Hamerick*
(1912), 50 Ind. App. 425, 434, 96 N. E. 649, and cases
cited. The trial court did not err in overruling the demurrer to the complaint.

With the general verdict the jury returned answers to
265 interrogatories, which describe in detail the construction and operation of appellant's plant and machinery, and
find the facts leading up to and attending the accident to
appellee's decedent. The answers show, in substance, that
at the time of his death, said William H. Butz was the
chief engineer and machinist in appellant's plant, and had
occupied that position in the same plant for many years;
that he was in charge of the engines, boilers and other machinery in the plant and was authorized to make needed
repairs to the same and to purchase materials therefor; that
he had charge of the men in the plant and was authorized
to use them in making repairs; that Carver Woods was gen-

eral manager of appellant's business and of said plant;
that he was not a machinist or engineer; that the line shaft
in said plant, to which the belt ran from the drivewheel
on the engine, was out of line, which fact was known to
both decedent and said Woods for about two months prior
to the death of said Butz; that the belt had a tendency to
run off the drivewheel on account of said shaft being out
of line, and decedent overcame said tendency by adjusting
the "idler"; that he had been ordered by said manager
sometime before his injury to adjust the line shaft, but did
not do so; that in adjusting the idler decedent usually, and
upon the occasion of his injury, stepped upon the top of
a brick wall located just south of the idler pulley and between said pulley and the flywheel of the engine, and
reached down ten inches or more to turn the adjusting
screws by using the handles attached thereto; that at the
time of the accident the belt leading from the flywheel of
the engine to the drivewheel of the line shaft was running;
that decedent could have adjusted the idler before starting
the engine, and while the belt and idler pulley were stationary; that it was necessary to adjust the idler while the machinery was in motion to obtain the best results; that decedent could not have gone down on the floor of the pit and
adjusted the idler by using the handle on the screw while
standing in the pit on the west side of the brick wall without coming in contact with the pulley on the belt; that he
could have gone into the pit, stood on the brick wall immediately west of the post and collar, and adjusted the idler
without coming in contact with the pulley; that it was
not practicable and feasible to go down into the pit to a
point immediately west of the post and idler and there make
the necessary adjustment; that it was more dangerous to
step upon the brick wall from the doorway or step and
adjust the idler from that position than to go down on the
floor of the pit and get upon the wall immediately west of
the post and idler; that decedent could have gone down

on the floor of the pit and from there have adjusted the idler in safety, by turning the set screws in the west collar of said idler but the boxing could not readily be moved in that manner; that it was more dangerous to attempt to adjust the idler by the use of the screw above the idler while standing on the brick wall than to attempt to adjust it by means of two set screws in the collar while standing on the floor of the pit west of the wall; that the floor of the dock above the pit was easily accessible from the floor of the engine room by means of a stairway; that the screws of the idler protruded above the floor of the dock about nine inches, were easily accessible, and could be adjusted by using a wrench; that said idler was ordinarily adjusted by using the handles on said screws, and decedent when injured was attempting to adjust the screw on said idler in the usual and ordinary way; that the belt and idler were without guard at the place where decedent was required to go to adjust the idler; that it was practicable to guard said belt and idler, and decedent's injury was caused by failure of appellant properly to guard the belt and idler at the point where he was caught and killed; that the failure to guard said belt and idler was the proximate cause of his death, and he was at the time acting without any fault on his part.

Appellant insists that some of the findings were conclusions and not facts, but as the general verdict includes a finding of facts covering practically the same propositions, the objection does not affect the question presented by the motion for judgment on the answers to the interrogatories. Appellant insists that the interrogatories show (1) that the conditions making necessary the work decedent was doing when killed were caused wholly by his own failure to adjust the line shaft; (2) that decedent was doing the work in a negligent manner, in that he voluntarily chose a dangerous method when safer methods had been provided.

The first objection is answered by the proposition that the question of assumption of risk has no application to a case arising under the statute requiring belts and 9. other machinery to be guarded, and the further proposition that contributory negligence is not necessarily established against an employe by showing that he continued to use defective machinery after he knew it was out of repair. *American Car. etc., Co.* v. *Clark, supra; Davis* v. *Mercer Lumber Co., supra.* In the recent well-considered case of the *Jenney Electric Mfg. Co.* v. *Flannery, supra,* it is said: "Contributory negligence cannot in all cases, be imputed to a servant from the mere fact that he chooses the more dangerous way or method of performing a duty when a safe method, or one less dangerous, was open to his choice. * * * In many cases, however, the question must be one of fact for the jury." The propositions, reasoning and authorities in the case just cited are applicable to the case at bar to such an extent as to render unnecessary an extended discussion or consideration in this opinion of many of the propositions there considered.

The decedent is shown to have undertaken to adjust the idler by using the handles on the screws specially provided by his employer for that purpose. The answers also 10. show that he could have taken other positions safer than the one he was in when killed, and could have adjusted the idler by set screws not so provided with handles; but that he was attempting to do the work by the means provided and in the usual way. Several possible ways of doing the work are indicated, but some of these are shown to be impractical. He was not required by any order or rule to do the work in any particular manner. The contention that he was guilty of contributory negligence is not based on the proposition that he was attempting to do the work by improper means or in a forbidden or unusual way, but that the place where he was attempting to adjust the idler was more dangerous than other places where he could have done the same work. Some of the answers are contradictory and nullify each other. The jury, both by the general verdict and by answers to interrogatories, found that decedent acted with due care and was not guilty of any negligence contributing to his death. On the facts of this case the question of decedent's contributory negligence was for the jury and cannot be declared as a matter of law. The answers are not in irreconcilable conflict with the general verdict, and the motion for judgment thereon was properly overruled.

11.

Appellant complains of the giving of certain instructions and of the refusal of the court to give instructions tendered by appellant. The first objection is to the giving of instruction No. 1 on the ground that the court incorporated into the instruction the entire complaint. While the practice of reading the whole complaint to the jury as a part of the instructions is not generally to be commended, it does not afford ground for reversing a judgment. *Blair-Baker Horse Co.* v. *First Nat. Bank* (1905), 164 Ind. 77, 84, 72 N. E. 1027; *Collins* v. *Williams* (1898), 21 Ind. App. 227, 232, 52 N. E. 92. It is also stated that the instruction is erroneous because it did not include a statement of the doctrine of assumption of risk. We have already shown that the doctrine of assumption of risk has no application to this case, because the action is based on the statute requiring certain machinery and belting to be guarded. A general instruction when incomplete, but correct as far as it goes, may be completed by other instructions. *Harness* v. *Steel* (1902), 159 Ind. 286, 293, 64 N. E. 875; *Aspy* v. *Botkins* (1903), 160 Ind. 170, 175, 66 N. E. 462.

12.

13.

By instruction No. 25 tendered by appellant and given by the court, the jury was told that if it found defendant had violated the statute in failing to guard the belting, as alleged, and decedent was injured on account thereof, this alone would not justify a recovery if decedent by his own negligence proximately contributed to his injury. This and other instructions clearly cured any alleged omission in instruction No. 1.

Where the answers of the jury to interrogatories show that an alleged erroneous instruction was harmless,
14. the judgment will not be reversed on account of such error. *Clear Creek Stone Co.* v. *Dearmin* (1903), 160 Ind. 162, 169, 66 N. E. 609.

Many of the instructions tendered by appellant and refused by the court, in practical effect asked the court to instruct the jury, as a matter of law, that decedent was guilty of negligence contributing to his death, and that the plaintiff could not recover. These instructions were refused, and the court gave others which submitted the question of the care or want of care of the decedent to the jury to be determined from the evidence. The instruc-
15. tions given, when considered as a whole, state the law fully and correctly under the issues, and those tendered which were correct statements of the law applicable to the facts and issues of the case were fully covered by those given.

Appellant also complains of the admission and exclusion of certain testimony. We have examined these questions and do not consider them of sufficient importance to
16. set them out in this opinion, for the alleged error, if any, in this respect was not of a character to in any sense harm appellant. The final contention that the judgment is not sustained by sufficient evidence is fully answered by the discussion of other questions already considered.

Finding no error prejudicial to appellant, the judgment is in all things affirmed.

NOTE.—Reported in 98 N. E. 818. See, also, under (1, 5) 26 Cyc. 1392; (2) 14 Cyc. 1129; (3) 16 Cyc. 852, 856; (4) 26 Cyc. 529; (6) 26 Cyc. 1180; (7) 31 Cyc. 49; (9) 26 Cyc. 1239; (10) 26 Cyc. 1482; (11) 26 Cyc. 1513; 88 Cyc. 1927; (13) 38 Cyc. 1782; (14) 38 Cyc. 1809; (15) 38 Cyc. 1711; (16) 38 Cyc. 1411. As to scientific facts and principles of which courts take judicial notice, see 124 Am. St.

31. As to duties and liabilities of electric companies under the law of master and servant, see 100 Am. St. 537. As to the rule of assumption of risk, as applied to dangerous machinery, see 119 Am. St. 434. As to the distinction to be marked between assumption of risk and contributory negligence, see note to *Brazil Block Coal Co. v. Gibson* (Ind.), 98 Am. St. 314. As to when contributory negligence is a question for the jury, see 8 Am. St. 849. On the question of servant's assumption of risk of master's breach of statutory duty, see 6 L. R. A. (N. S.) 981; 19 L. R. A. (N. S.) 646; 22 L. R. A. (N. S.) 634; 33 L. R. A. (N. S.) 646; 42 L. R. A. (N. S.) 1229. As to whether a servant may assume the risk of dangers created by the master's negligence, see 4 L. R. A. (N. S.) 848; 28 L. R. A. (N. S.) 1215.

NORTHERN ASSURANCE COMPANY OF LONDON *v.*
CARPENTER, TRUSTEE.

[No. 7,029. Filed April 18, 1911. Rehearing denied December 14, 1911. Transfer denied February 14, 1913.]

1. APPEAL.— *Review.* —*Harmless Error.— Instructions.— Damages.* —In an action on a fire policy, which stipulated that the company would not be liable in the event of loss for an amount greater than three-fourths of the actual cash value of the property covered by the items of the policy at the time of the loss, error in an instruction which did not accurately state the rule for the measurement of damages, was harmless, where the damages assessed were in a sum less than the amount of the aggregate three-fourths of the value of the items, as shown by the evidence, together with interest on the sum that would be properly chargeable against defendant. p. 434.

2. INSURANCE.— *Fire Insurance.— Actions.— Presumptions.— Presumption Against Forfeiture.*—Every presumption is indulged in favor of the good faith of the parties to fire policy, and inconsistencies on its face will be resolved in favor of the actual contract, and against forfeiture. p. 436.

3. INSURANCE.—*Fire Insurance.—Provisions of Policy.—Waiver.*— Where the insuring clause of a fire policy stated that for the consideration named the company insures the owner of the property described against loss by fire for a definite term, and the policy contained defeasance clauses inconsistent therewith and providing that before the policy shall take effect the insured shall make an inventory, and requiring him to keep books of account, etc., the provisions of such clauses were waived and the risk attached at once, where the company delivered the policy and

accepted and retained the full premium, without calling the attention of the insured to such clauses or making any inquiry as to an inventory, or as to his method of doing business. pp. 436, 439.

4. INSURANCE.—*Fire Insurance.—Construction of Contract.*—A fire insurance policy will not be interpreted with the strictness which ordinarily obtains in written instruments, since the insured has no part in drawing the contract. p. 437.

5. INSURANCE.—*Fire Insurance.—Inconsistent Provisions.—Waiver.—Fraud.*—Where the insurer receives pay for a valid and binding policy, and the insurer believes that he has such a policy, the law will not impute to the insurer a fraudulent intent not to deliver that kind of a policy, but will hold that conditions therein inconsistent with the risk were either waived or overlooked, and that the insurer is estopped from setting up a breach thereof. p. 440.

From Greene Circuit Court; *Charles E. Henderson,* Judge.

Action by Enos W. Carpenter, trustee of the estate of Sherman Hash, bankrupt, against the Northern Assurance Company of London. From a judgment for plaintiff, the defendant appeals. *Affirmed.*

A. C. Ayres, A. Q. Jones, J. E. Hollett and *Frank C. Ayres,* for appellant.

W. L. Slinkard and *H. W. Letsinger,* for appellee.

ADAMS, J.—This was an action by appellee, as the trustee of the estate of Sherman Hash, bankrupt, to recover on a fire insurance policy issued by appellant to said Hash, insuring a store building, fixtures and a stock of merchandise against loss by fire.

The policy separately insured the store building for $300, the fixtures for $50, and the stock of goods for $1,200, and provided that the company should not be liable, in the event of loss, for more than three-fourths of the value of the goods destroyed.

The insuring clause in said policy reads as follows:

"In consideration of the stipulation herein named and of Twenty Five and 58/100 Dollars premium, does

VOL. 52—28

insure Sherman Hash for the term of one year from
the 12th day of December, 1905, at noon, to the 12th
day of December, 1906, at noon, against all direct loss
or damage by fire, except as hereinafter provided. To
an amount not exceeding Fifteen Hundred Fifty Dollars; to the following described property, while located
and contained as described herein, and not elsewhere.''

Then follows a description of the property insured and the
location of the same, together with the separate amount of
insurance on the building, fixtures and stock.

The policy further provides:

''It is expressly stipulated that the assured shall, before this policy shall take effect (provided no inventory has been taken within twelve months), make an
inventory of the stock to be covered hereby, and shall
keep books of account, correctly detailing purchases
and sales of said stock, from and after the date of said
inventory, both for cash and credit, and shall keep said
inventory and books securely locked in an iron safe, or
away from the building containing the property hereby insured, during the hours that such store is closed
for business. Failure to observe these conditions, shall
work a forfeiture of all claims under this policy.''

Appellant insists that instruction No. 11 given to the
jury was erroneous. By this instruction the court told the
jury that if the plaintiff was entitled to recover, it
should allow him, as damages, three-fourths of the
aggregate value of the insured property destroyed by
fire, within the aggregate sum of the insurance on the building, stock and fixtures. It was stipulated in the policy that
in the event of loss the company would not be liable for
an amount greater than three-fourths of the actual cash
value of the property covered by each item of the policy at
the time of such loss. In view of this stipulation, the instruction does not give the jury a strictly accurate rule for
the measurement of damages; still the error was harmless,
for the reason that the damages assessed by the jury are in
a sum less than the amount of the aggregate three-fourths
of the value of the building, of the stock of goods, and of

the fixtures, as shown by the evidence, together with interest on the sum that would be properly chargeable against appellant.

The insufficiency of the evidence to sustain the verdict is also insisted on as ground for reversal. The evidence in the record shows, without dispute, that the insured was the owner of a country store, carrying a stock of general merchandise; that on December 12, 1905, appellant, by its agent J. O. Walker solicited said Sherman Hash for fire insurance on his property; that said agent called on Hash at his store, and, after making inquiry as to the company represented by said agent and the rates, Hash agreed to take insurance; that the agent thereupon looked over the building, stock and fixtures, and agreed to insure the same for the several amounts and for the term herein set out, in consideration of the payment of a premium of $25.58; that no written application was made by Hash, and no questions were asked with reference to any inventory or the methods employed by Hash in the conduct of his business, nor did said agent state to the insured that before said insurance would become effective it would be necessary for him to make out an inventory and keep books of account; that the agent while on the premises, wrote out and delivered the policy, and took the notes of the insured for the premium; that said notes were paid before the fire, and that the company received and still retains said premium. It further appears from the evidence that the policy was not read to said Hash, nor did he read it, although he was an experienced business man, and was able to read; that the stock of goods on which the policy was written had recently been opened for sale; that Hash had not made an inventory, and did not thereafter make an inventory, or keep books of account detailing purchases and sales of stock, and did not have an iron safe in his store; that said agent at the time of delivering said policy knew that there was no iron safe in the store of the insured. It is also shown by the evidence that from the time the policy was written and delivered until February 13, 1906, when the property was destroyed by fire, said agent was at the store of the insured once or twice a week, and was in said store on the day before the night in which it was burned.

Every presumption will be indulged in favor of good faith in construing the contract on which this action is founded, and any inconsistencies appearing on the

2. face of the policy will be resolved in favor of the actual contract of the parties, and against a forfeiture. *McMaster* v. *New York Life Ins. Co.* (1901), 183 U. S. 25, 22 Sup. Ct. 10, 46 L. Ed. 64; *Glens Falls Ins. Co.* v. *Michael* (1907), 167 Ind. 659, 666, 74 N. E. 964, 79 N. E. 905, 8 L. R. A. (N. S.) 708.

It will be noted that the insuring clause is inconsistent with the defeasance clause, and the defeasance clause is inconsistent in itself. The insuring clause states that

3. for the consideration named, appellant insures Sherman Hash against loss or damage by fire for the term of one year from December 12, 1905, at noon, to December 12, 1906, at noon, in the total sum of $1,550. This clause is complete and easily understood. It needs no explanation or construction. But the defeasance clause in effect says that Sherman Hash is not insured until he shall make an inventory of his stock, and shall thereafter keep books of account, correctly detailing purchases and sales. Hash could not be protected and unprotected at the same time. He was either insured, as provided in the insuring clause, or he was not. That he believed he was insured is evident from the fact that he paid his money. That the insurance company shared this belief is evident from the fact that it accepted the premium for one year's insurance, and delivered the policy. That the risk attached, and was intended to attach at the time the policy was delivered, is evident, from the further condition in the defeasance clause that ''failure to observe these conditions shall work a for-

feiture of all claims under this policy." If making the inventory and keeping books as provided constituted a condition precedent to the attaching of the risk, then the risk never attached, and there was no insurance. If there was no insurance, there could be no forfeiture. There was nothing to forfeit.

Again, the defeasance clause is inconsistent in another particular. While providing that before the policy shall take effect an inventory shall be made, it also provides that the inventory shall be kept in an iron safe, or "away from the building containing the property *hereby insured*" during the hours such store is closed. If the insurer did not consider itself bound from the time of receiving the premium and delivering the policy, and the property "hereby insured" was not, in fact, insured, nor intended to be insured, then the transaction cannot be characterized as anything other than fraudulent. No such construction can be placed on the policy in suit as long as it is possible to construe the same as an honest and fair contract, by taking and considering all of its parts together.

The conclusion following such construction is that the risk attached at noon on December 12, 1905, the day on which the policy was written, delivered and the premium paid. It would be unconscionable to collect and retain the full consideration of the contract, and then permit the insurance company to say that no liability accrued, and no protection was given the insured until he should, at some future time, comply with the stipulation relating to the inventory. The insured had no part in drawing the

4. contract, and such contract will not be interpreted with the strictness which generally obtains in written instruments.

It is said in the well-considered case of *Glens Falls Ins. Co.* v. *Michael, supra,* on page 677: "Insurance policies are prepared in advance by insurance and legal experts, having in view primarily the safeguarding of the interests

of the insurer against every possible contingency. The insurer not only fully knows the contents of the writing, but
also adequately comprehends its legal effect. The insured
has no voice in fixing or framing the terms of his policy, but
must accept it as prepared and tendered, usually without
any knowledge of its contents, and often without ability to
comprehend the legal significance of its provisions. The
meeting of the minds ordinarily deemed essential to a valid
contract, as to many of its terms and conditions, is wanting
in fact, and a mere fiction of law.'' In the same case at
page 702, on petition for rehearing, the court, quoting from
1 Wood, Fire Ins. (2d ed.) §176, says: ''When a policy is
issued upon a verbal application, without any representations in reference thereto, all information relative to the
risks, except such as is unusual and extraordinary, is waived,
and the policy is valid.''

In the case of *Ohio Farmers Ins. Co.* v. *Vogel* (1906), 166
Ind. 239, 245, 76 N. E. 977, 3 L. R. A. (N. S.) 966, 117 Am.
St. 382, the court said: ''There is nothing mysterious or
peculiarly venerable about the ordinary insurance policy,
with its long list of provisions and conditions of defeasance.
All these, and singular, must be construed like similar provisions in other written instruments, upon sound and well-
established principles—principles that support the integrity
of the contract, and that forbid an insurer from taking the
money of another for a policy which he knows at the time
of delivery contains a provision which, under the facts, will
enable him to avoid it, if a loss occurs. Such provisions in
insurance policies have been before the courts a great many
times, and, so far as we have observed, courts have everywhere in the absence of fraud, refused to enforce a condition of forfeiture in favor of an insurer who has knowledge
of the condition broken when he delivered the policy. One
reason is this: having accepted a premium to take the risk
of indemnifying the insured against loss, it is incompatible
for the insurer to attach to the policy a condition that will

from the beginning relieve him of that risk. Another reason is that, although so expressed in the instrument, a violation of such condition does not in fact make the policy void,
but voidable only, at the election of the insurance company.
* * * And when an election has been once exercised the
company will be confined to its choice. * * * In short
it had the right to elect between two inconsistent courses,
and, having chosen one, it will be excluded from all rights
and benefits of the other. In such case, in the absence of
fraud, it will be conclusively presumed that the insurer,
while he keeps the premium, waives the inconsistent provision.''

Appellant, through its agent, having knowledge of the
provisions of the policy contract, was bound to make inquiry
as to the inventory, and to explain to the insured the
3. terms of the policy, particularly if it was the purpose of the insurer to defer the attaching of the risk
until the insured should comply with certain of its terms.
Failing to make such inquiry, the company must be deemed
to have waived the condition relating to the time when the
insurance should be effective; and by retaining the premium
the company must be deemed to have waived other inconsistent provisions set out in the policy. *Glens Falls Ins.
Co.* v. *Michael, supra; Ohio Farmers Ins. Co.* v. *Vogel,
supra; Farmers Ins. Assn.* v. *Reavis* (1904), 163 Ind. 321,
70 N. E. 518, 71 N. E. 905; *German Mut. Ins. Co.* v.
Niewedde (1895), 11 Ind. App. 624, 39 N. E. 534; *Hanover
Fire Ins. Co.* v. *Dole* (1898), 20 Ind. App. 333, 50 N. E. 772;
Modern Woodmen, etc., v. *Vincent* (1907), 40 Ind. App.
711, 80 N. E. 427, 82 N. E. 475; *Aetna Life Ins. Co.* v *Bock-
ting* (1907), 39 Ind. App. 586, 79 N. E. 524.

In the case of *Short* v. *Home Ins. Co.* (1882), 90 N. Y. 16,
19, 43 Am. Rep. 138, it is held that failure on the part of
the insured to make known the fact that a building is unoccupied is not a breach of a condition in the policy avoiding
it, for failure to make known every fact material to the

risk; that the applicant has a right to assume that the insurer will make proper inquiries, and that in making inquiries as to material facts he considers all others as immaterial, or assumes to know or waive information in regard to them.   The law will not impute to the in-
5.   surer a fraudulent intent not to give a valid and binding policy, although receiving pay for such a policy, and the insured believing that he had such a policy. Such imputation can be avoided only on the theory that the condition was overlooked or was waived, and the insurer held himself estopped from setting it up.   See, also, *Van Shoick* v. *Niagara Fire Ins. Co.* (1877), 68 N. Y. 434; *Woodruff* v. *Imperial Ins. Co.* (1880), 83 N. Y. 133, 140.

"When the insurer issues a policy to the assured without any written application, containing conditions inconsistent with the risk; * * * it is estopped from setting up a breach of such conditions in defense to an action upon the policy, and the insured may maintain an action for loss under the policy, without seeking its reformation, as the doctrine of estoppel and waiver comes in aid of the assured." 2 Wood, Fire Ins. 1163.   See, also, *Mershon* v. *National Ins. Co.* (1871), 34 Iowa 87; *Viall* v. *Genesee Mut. Ins. Co.* (1854), 19 Barb. (N. Y.) 440.

In *Mershon* v. *National Ins. Co., supra,* the court said: "Receiving the premium on the policy, with full knowledge, and after the occurrence of the facts upon which defendant might declare it forfeited, would amount to a waiver of defendant's right to treat it as forfeited."

In *Viall* v. *Genesee Mut. Ins. Co., supra,* it is said: "After they had, with knowledge of the facts, received the assessment, and thus again declared themselves entitled to enforce performance of the contract, on the part of the plaintiff, they were not at liberty, when called upon by the plaintiff to perform on their part, to insist that the contract had become void immediately after it was made.   They had long afterwards recognized its existence.   They had shown themselves willing to receive the advantages which it tendered to them. They had taken its fruits, and must not now be relieved from its obligations.''

In the case of *Caldwell* v. *Fire Assn., etc.* (1896), 177 Pa. St. 492, 502, 35 Atl. 612, the court said: ''Where, at the time of issuing an insurance policy, the company knows that one of the conditions thereof is inconsistent with the facts, and the insured has been guilty of no fraud, the company is estopped from setting up the breach of said condition. The same rule prevails when the insurance company ought to have known the facts constituting the alleged breach.''

While no Indiana case has been based on facts identical with the case at bar, our decisions have been so numerous, and the principles declared in construing policies of insurance have been laid on such broad and equitable lines, as to cover and include the facts before us.

We find no reversible error in the record. The judgment is affirmed.

Myers, C. J., Lairy, P. J., Hottell, Ibach and Felt, JJ. concur.

NOTE.—Reported in 94 N. E. 779. See, also, under (1) 38 Cyc. 1809; (2) 19 Cyc. 936; (3) 19 Cyc. 796; (4) 19 Cyc. 656. As to how generally fire insurance policies are to be construed, see 10 Am. St. 390.

TISHBEIN *v.* PAINE.

[No. 7,847. Filed February 14, 1913.]

1. PLEADING. — *Complaint.* — *Duplicity.* — *Remedy.* — Where each paragraph of complaint contains two separate and distinct causes of action, that may be properly joined, the defect cannot be reached by a demurrer for want of facts, but the remedy is by a motion to require that the causes be separated and stated in separate paragraphs. p. 442.

2. CONTRACTS.—*Contracts Partly in Writing.—Action.—Complaint.* —*Sufficiency.*—A contract, partly in writing and partly in parol,

rests entirely in parol, and a complaint thereon is not rendered insufficient by failure to set out therein the portion of the contract that is written, or to make the same an exhibit thereto. p. 443.

3. CONTRACTS.—*Action.—Complaint.—Sufficiency.—Bill of Particulars.*—Where, in an action on a building contract, each paragraph of complaint stated facts sufficient to constitute a cause of action on the contract, plaintiff's failure to file a bill of particulars of items claimed as extras in each paragraph, does not render the complaint demurrable. p. 443.

4. PLEADING.—*Complaint.—Demurrer.*—A complaint is sufficient to withstand a demurrer, if it states facts sufficient to entitle plaintiff to some relief. p. 443.

5. APPEAL.—*Record.—Bill of Exceptions Not Signed.—Questions Not Considered.*—Questions presented by a motion for new trial, and depending on the evidence, cannot be considered where the bill of exceptions containing the evidence, as shown by the record, is not signed by the trial judge. p. 443.

From Lake Circuit Court; *Willis C. McMahan,* Judge.

Action by Henry A. Paine against John Tishbein. From a judgment for plaintiff, the defendant appeals. *Affirmed.*

Sheehan & Lyddick, for appellant.
Franklin T. Fetterer, for appellee.

LAIRY, J.—Appellee filed an amended complaint in the trial court, by which he sought to recover from appellant a balance claimed to be due him on a contract, by the terms of which he was to furnish material and erect a building for appellant for the agreed price of $4,000. The amended complaint was in two paragraphs, to each of which a demurrer for want of sufficient facts was addressed and overruled. This ruling is assigned as error, and presents the first question for our consideration.

Both paragraphs seek to recover a balance of $225 due on the contract, and also an amount claimed to be due for extra labor performed and extra material furnished.

1. The first objection pointed out is that each paragraph contains two separate and distinct causes of action.

If it be conceded that appellant is correct in this contention, the defect could not be reached by a demurrer for want of facts. It could be reached only by a motion for an order requiring plaintiff to separate his causes of action and to state them in separate paragraphs of complaint. *Lane* v. *State, ex rel.* (1866), 27 Ind. 108; *Carger* v. *Fee* (1895), 140 Ind. 572, 39 N. E. 93; *Baddeley* v. *Patterson* (1881), 78 Ind. 157; *Leak* v. *Thorn* (1895), 13 Ind. App. 335, 41 N. E. 602; *Shroyer* v. *Pittenger* (1903), 31 Ind. App. 158, 67 N. E. 475.

Appellant makes a further objection to the sufficiency of the complaint on the ground that the part of the contract which is alleged to be in writing is not set out therein or made an exhibit thereto. This is not required.

2. Neither paragraph of the amended complaint is based on a written contract. The contract alleged in each paragraph of the complaint, being partly written and partly oral, rests entirely in parol. *Board, etc.,* v. *Shipley* (1881), 77 Ind. 553; *Stauffer* v. *Linenthal* (1902), 29 Ind. App. 305, 64 N. E. 643.

Each paragraph of the complaint states facts sufficient to constitute a cause of action in plaintiff on the contract for the erection of the building, and to entitle him to recover the balance due thereon. The failure of plain-

3. tiff to file a bill of particulars of the items claimed as extras in each paragraph would not render the complaint or either paragraph thereof demurrable. A

4. complaint which is sufficient to entitle the plaintiff to some relief is good as against a demurrer. *Gilman* v. *Fultz* (1906), 37 Ind. App. 609, 77 N. E. 746; *Owen School Tp.* v. *Hay* (1886), 107 Ind. 351, 8 N. E. 220.

The bill of exceptions containing the evidence, as shown by the record, is not signed by the trial judge. We can-

5. not, therefore, consider any question presented by the motion for a new trial, as all the questions so pre-

sented depend on the evidence. We find no reversible error. Judgment affirmed.

Note.—Reported in 100 N. E. 766. See, also, under (1) 31 Cyc. 124; (2) 31 Cyc. 556; (3) 31 Cyc. 302; (4) 31 Cyc. 288; (5) 3 Cyc. 43. As to the necessity of filing bill of exceptions, see 15 Am. St. 297.

THOMPSON *v.* NEWSOM ET AL.

[No. 8,488. Filed February 14, 1913.]

1. APPEAL.—*Jurisdiction.*—*Parties.*—*Notice.*—Notice to all necessary parties is essential to jurisdiction of an appeal, and unless such notice is given, or there is an appearance, a submission may be set aside and the appeal dismissed. p. 445.

2. APPEAL.—*Notice.*—*Service on Attorneys.*—Although under §681 Burns 1908, §640 R. S. 1881, notice of an appeal may be served on the attorneys of record of the parties sought to be made appellees, such notice is not perfected by an attempt to serve same on attorneys, who, to the knowledge of appellants at the time of the attempted service, no longer represent such parties. p. 446.

3. APPEAL.—*Jurisdiction.*—*Parties.*—*Death.*—The court cannot acquire jurisdiction of an appeal prosecuted against parties who have died after the rendition of the judgment appealed from, and before the filing of the appeal, but under §677 Burns 1908, §636 R. S. 1881, in such case the proper method of appealing is to serve notice of the appeal on the persons against whom the action might have been revived, if death had occurred before judgment. p. 446.

4. APPEAL.—*Void Appeal.*—*Substitution of Parties.*—Where an appeal was void for want of jurisdiction, because of the death of a party to the judgment before the appeal was filed, an order substituting his administrator as an appellee is also void. p. 447.

5. APPEAL.—*Substitution of Parties.*—*Assignment of Errors.*—*Failure to Amend.*—If, after a valid order substituting as a party to the appeal the administrator of a deceased appellee, the appellant permits the time for appeal to expire without amending the assignment of errors by substituting the name of the administrator for that of the decedent, the court will not permit such amendment to be thereafter made. p. 447.

From Owen Circuit Court; *Joseph W. Williams*, Judge.

Action by Stephen B. Thompson against John W. Newsom and others. From a judgment for defendants, the plaintiff appeals. *Appeal dismissed.*

S. J. Gee and *Spangler & Rundell,* for appellant.
Charles E. Henderson, for appellees.

IBACH, C. J.—Certain appellees have made a special appearance and asked that this appeal be dismissed, (1) because notice of appeal was not properly served on the persons named as appellees; (2) because there is a defect of parties appellees in the assignment of errors, in that John W. Newsom, named as an appellee, died after judgment was rendered below and before the appeal was taken.

The judgment of the lower court was rendered on October 7, 1911, and the transcript on appeal was filed in this court on October 5, 1912. It appears, from affidavits accompanying the motion to dismiss, that appellant's attorneys came to two attorneys who had represented the defendants in the trial of the cause before the lower court, and asked them to acknowledge service of notice on October 5, 1912, and these attorneys informed appellant's attorneys that they had long since been discharged by defendants, and had no further connection with the cause, and that defendant, Newsom, was dead. It is shown by the record that the attorneys for appellant delivered a copy of notice of appeal to each of these attorneys, but they did not acknowledge service, and have never entered an appearance in this court. It also appears by affidavit that defendant, Newsom, died on May 12, 1912, and that Fred E. Dyer was appointed his administrator on May 18, 1912. On December 31, 1912, this court granted appellant's motion to substitute Fred E. Dyer, administrator, for John W. Newsom, deceased.

In order to give this court jurisdiction of an appeal, notice must be given to all necessary parties, and if no notice
1.   is given and there is no appearance, a submission may be set aside and the appeal dismissed. *Tate* v. *Hamlin* (1895), 149 Ind. 94, 41 N. E. 356, 41 N. E. 1035; *Abshire* v. *Williamson* (1898), 149 Ind. 248, 48 N. E.

1027; *Bozeman* v. *Cole* (1894), 139 Ind. 187, 35 N. E. 828; *Kreuter* v. *English Lake Land Co.* (1902), 159 Ind. 372, 65 N. E. 4; *Slusser* v. *Palin* (1905), 35 Ind. App. 335, 74 N. E. 17.

2. The notice attempted to be given in this case was the notice of the first character provided for by §681 Burns 1908, §640 R. S. 1881, or what is known as the unofficial notice. This notice may be served on the attorneys of record of the parties sought to be made appellees, but notice cannot be perfected by an attempt to serve notice on attorneys who, to the knowledge of appellants at the time of the attempted service, no longer represent such parties. *Richardson* v. *Pate* (1884), 93 Ind. 423, 47 Am. Rep. 374; *Rose* v. *Owen* (1906), 37 Ind. App. 125, 76 N. E. 412.

3. But even if notice had been served on attorneys who at the time of service represented defendants, this court has failed to acquire jurisdiction of this attempted appeal, for another reason. An appellate court has no jurisdiction of an appeal prosecuted against a party who has died after the rendition of the judgment from which the appeal was taken and before the filing of the appeal in the appellate court. Such an attempted appeal is a nullity. Section 677 Burns 1908, §636 R. S. 1881, provides that "in case of the death of any or all the parties to a judgment before an appeal is taken, an appeal may be taken by, and notice of an appeal served upon, the persons in whose favor and against whom the action might have been revived, if death had occurred before judgment." Under this statute, and the decisions construing it, hereinafter referred to, the only proper method in which appellant could bring an appeal was to serve notice on the administrator of defendant Newsom. *Doble* v. *Brown* (1898), 20 Ind. App. 12, 50 N. E. 38; *Moore* v. *Slack* (1894), 140 Ind. 38, 39, N. E. 237.

Since such administrator was not served with notice before the expiration of the year for perfecting appeal, this

court acquired no jurisdiction, and the order of the
4. court made on December 31, 1912, substituting Fred
E. Dyer, administrator, as appellee, in the place of
John W. Newsom, was void, because the appeal was void,
and conferred on this court no jurisdiction over the cause.

And even if that order had been valid, still appellant
5. would be in no better situation, because he had made
no effort to amend his assignment of errors by substituting the name of the administrator for his decedent, and
since the year for appeal has expired, this court will not
permit the amendment of the assignment of errors as to a
material matter. In respect to the second question presented by the motion to dismiss, this case is ''on all fours''
with *Doble* v. *Brown, supra,* and on the authority of that
case the submission is set aside, and the cause is ordered
stricken from the docket.

Appeal dismissed.

NOTE.—Reported in the 100 N. E. 772. See, also, under (1) 2
Cyc. 863, 873; (2) 2 Cyc. 868; (3) 2 Cyc. 769; (5) 2 Cyc. 788. As to
administrators as appellants, see 119 Am. St. 754.

SOUTHERN RAILWAY COMPANY *v.* TOWN OF FRENCH LICK ET AL.

[No. 7,826. Filed February 14, 1913.]

1. MUNICIPAL CORPORATIONS.—*Streets.—Vacation.—Procedure.*—To
be entitled to the rights and privileges given by §§8910, 8910
Burns 1908, Acts 1907 p. 617, §§3, 9, providing for the vacation of
streets, and the method of proceeding, the parties must bring
themselves within the provisions of the statute. p. 452.

2. MUNICIPAL CORPORATIONS.—*Streets.—Vacation.—Remonstrance.
—Time for Filing.*—Under §8910 Burns 1908, Acts 1907 p. 617, §3,
providing that notice of the filing and pendency of a petition
for the vacation of a street "shall be given as in this act provided," and if no objection within such time be made in writing,
the court shall grant the prayer of such petition, construed with
§8916 Burns 1908, Acts 1907 p. 617, §9, providing for the giving
of such notice by publication for ten days by two successive
weekly publications which shall state the time and place when

and where the petition shall be heard, where the notice was first published on November 29, and stated that the hearing would be had on December 10, a remonstrance filed on December 10 was filed in time. p. 452.

3. PLEADING.—*Special Statutory Procedure.*—While, in all special statutory enactments, the procedure prescribed by the statute must be followed, the practice authorized by the civil code may be followed, where it is not inconsistent with the procedure so prescribed. p. 452.

4. MUNICIPAL CORPORATIONS.— *Streets.— Vacation.— Procedure.— Demurrer to Petition.*—Filing a demurrer to a petition for the vacation of a street is a permissible means of objecting to its sufficiency, and is not inconsistent with the provisions of §§8910, 8916 Burns 1908, Acts 1907 p. 617, §§3, 9, providing for the vacation of streets and the method of procedure, since, if the petition is insufficient under the statute, no remonstrance is necessary, and, if it is sufficient, the right to file a remonstrance within the specified time is not thereby lost. p. 453.

5. PLEADING.—*Demurrer.—Questions Raised.—Defect of Parties.—* Under the code, a demurrer for want of facts presents no question concerning a defect of parties plaintiff or defendant. p. 453.

6. MUNICIPAL CORPORATIONS.—*Streets.—Vacation.—Petition.—Sufficiency.*—A petition for the vacation of a street, alleging that the petitioner is the owner of all the ground on both sides of that part of the street to be vacated, and that other streets particularly described "afford proper ingress and egress to the citizens of said town and the residents of said street," sufficiently complies with the requirement of §8910 Burns 1908, Acts 1907 p. 617, §3, requiring such petition to state the names of the persons "particularly interested" in the vacation of the street "who shall be affected thereby". pp. 453, 454.

7. WORDS AND PHRASES.—*"Proper."*—The word "proper" is a usual word in pleadings to show ordinary and sufficient means of ingress to and egress from property. p. 454.

8. PLEADING.—*Statement of Cause of Action.—Requisites.—Construction.*—A pleading is required to state facts constituting the cause of action in plain and concise language, in such manner as to enable a person of common understanding to know what is intended, and, in construing the same, the words used will be taken in their plain, ordinary and usual meaning, unless they have some peculiar and technical significance. p. 454.

9. PLEADING.—*Demurrer.—Admissions.*—For the purposes of a demurrer to a pleading, the facts alleged are to be taken as true. p. 454.

10. MUNICIPAL CORPORATIONS.—*Streets.—Vacation.—Persons Entitled to Object.—Statutes.*—While §§8910, 8916 Burns 1908, Acts

1907 p. 617, §§3, 9, providing for the vacation of streets and the method of procedure, do not limit the right to object to the vacation of a street to those persons who own property abutting on that part of the street to be vacated, persons, who have sufficient or "specially suited" means of ingress or egress, have no more than a general interest common to all the citizens, and are not required to be named in the petition. p. 455.

11. MUNICIPAL CORPORATIONS. — *Streets.* — *Vacation.* — *Damages.* — A person claiming damages by reason of the vacation or obstruction of a street must show that he has suffered, or will suffer, an injury different in kind, and not simply in degree, from that suffered by the community in general. p. 456.

12. COURTS.—*Appellate Court.*—*Jurisdiction.*—*Constitutional Questions.*—Where appellant's petition for the vacation of a street proceeds on the theory that appellant is the only one having any special interest in that part of the street to be vacated, the Appellate Court has jurisdiction, since a decision does not involve the question of the taking of property without compensation, in which any one is specially interested, and no constitutional question is presented. p. 456.

13. APPEAL.—*Review.*—*Scope.*—On reversing a judgment and ordering further proceedings, the court will not anticipate and decide questions not presented by the record, and which may never arise. p. 456.

From Orange Circuit Court; *Thomas B. Buskirk,* Judge.

Petition by the Southern Railway Company to vacate a street in the town of French Lick, and contested by the town and certain citizens. From an adverse judgment, the petitioner appeals. *Reversed.*

John D. Welman and *Perry McCart,* for appellant.

B. Harvey, H. A. Carnes and *Talbott & Roland,* for appellees.

FELT, P. J.—This proceeding was instituted by appellant by the filing of an *ex parte* petition in the Orange Circuit Court to vacate a portion of a street in the town of French Lick.

Appellant has separately assigned error in the overruling of each separate and several objection made by it to the filing of a number of several and separate demurrers to its petition, and the same as to the filing of each of several separate remonstrances. Also that the court erred in sustaining the separate demurrer of appellee, Flick, and others to its petition, and the same as to the separate demurrer of the town of French Lick.

The petition filed by appellant, after formal averments, alleges, in substance, that it is the owner of a railroad track and right of way in the town of French Lick, Orange county, Indiana, which right of way intersects a street or alley in Belview addition to said town, which street appellant asks to be vacated for a distance of 200 feet; that the petitioner owns all the lots on both sides of that portion of said street sought to be vacated; that at the intersection of said street or alley and said right of way there are five railroad tracks which form the terminus and southern end of petitioner's yards; that said tracks will be in almost constant use for the switching and running of engines and cars; that said tracks are 6 or 8 feet below the level of said street; that if said street is not vacated its use by the public will be very dangerous. It is then averred "that the main street of said Belview addition is one block south and parallel to said street or alley about two hundred feet therefrom. That said main street is about sixty feet in width and extends parallel to said street or alley its entire length, and that the cross streets running north from said main street to said street or alley afford proper ingress or egress to the citizens of said town and the residents of said street or alley."

Appellant indorsed on the petition that the same was set for hearing on December 10, 1910, and gave notice by publication of the pendency of said petition, and stated therein that "this petition is filed for hearing on the 10th day of December, 1907."

Section 8910 Burns 1908, Acts 1907 p. 617, §3, provides: "Whenever any person or persons interested therein, or the owner or owners of any lot or lots * * * in any incorporated city or town * * * shall desire to vacate any

Southern R. Co. v. Town of French Lick—52 Ind. App. 447.

street, alley or public ground therein or any part thereof adjoining such lot or lots or part or parts thereof, such person or persons shall file with the circuit court in the county in which such lands, or some part thereof, are situate, his, their or its petition setting forth the particular circumstances of the case, giving a distinct description of the property sought to be vacated and the names of the persons particularly interested therein and who shall be affected thereby, and notice of the filing and pendency of said petition shall be given as in this act provided. If no objection within such time be made in writing by any party interested the court shall grant the prayer of said petition. If objection thereto be made the court shall set the same down for trial and hearing by the court, and if, in its opinion, justice shall require it the court shall grant the prayer of said petition in whole or in part. No vacation of any street, alley or other public ground or part thereof shall take place over the objection of any person or persons owning the property immediately adjoining the part of such street or alley sought to be vacated until the damages, if any, of ·such objecting parties, by such vacation, be first assessed by the court and paid to the clerk thereof for their use and benefit by the petitioner or petitioners for such vacation.''

Section 8916 Burns 1908, Acts 1907 p. 617, §9, provides: ''Whenever notice is required to be given for any purpose by any of the provisions of this act, notice [shall be given] by publication for ten days by two successive weekly publications in some newspaper * * * of general circulation, published in the city or town affected by any such proceeding, * * *. Said petition shall set forth the substance of the matter and things in issue, and shall designate the property affected by the proceedings without setting forth the names of the persons affected, but shall be addressed to the city or town and the citizens thereof and shall state the time and place when and where and by whom the things in issue shall be heard and determined.''

The first publication was made on November 29, 1907, and the second on December 6, 1907. Appellees filed remonstrances, in accordance with the statute (§8911 Burns 1908, Acts 1907 p. 617, §4), on December 10, 1907. Appellant contends that the ten days' notice expired on December 9, and that the remonstrances filed on December 10 cannot be considered, because filed too late, notwithstanding the indorsement on the petition and the notice designated December 10 as the date for appearance and the hearing on the petition.

1. This is a special statutory proceeding, and parties must bring themselves within the provisions of the statute to be entitled to the rights and privileges given thereby. *City of Peru* v. *Cox* (1909), 173 Ind. 241, 243, 90 N. E. 7.

2. To determine whether the remonstrances filed on December 10 were filed after the time allowed by the statute, we must construe §§8910, 8916, *supra,* together. The former section provides that "notice of the filing and pendency of said petition shall be given as in this act provided." The latter section provides for the giving of a notice "by publication for ten days by two successive weekly publications," which "shall state the time and place when and where" the petition shall be heard. Construing these two provisions together, a remonstrance filed on December 10, the date stated in the notice, was within the time specified by §8910, *supra.* The case of *City of Peru* v. *Cox, supra,* decides nothing contrary to this conclusion, but incidentally recognizes the proposition that a remonstrance filed on the day named in the notice is in compliance with the statute.

3. Appellant insists that as this is a special statutory proceeding, the filing of a demurrer was not permissible practice. In all special statutory enactments the procedure prescribed by the statute must be followed,

but when not inconsistent with the procedure so prescribed, the practice authorized by our civil code may be followed. *Evans* v. *Evans* (1886), 105 Ind. 204, 5 N. E. 24, 5 N. E. 768; *Weakley* v. *Wolf* (1897), 148 Ind. 208, 220, 47 N. E. 466; *In re Griffin* (1904), 33 Ind. App. 153, 69 N. E. 192.

The testing of the sufficiency of the petition by demurrer is not inconsistent with or contrary to the statute providing that "if no objection within such time be made 4. in writing by any party interested therein, the court shall grant the prayer of said petition," nor with the provisions authorizing the filing of a remonstrance for certain specified reasons. The statute contemplates objections, and provides for remonstrances. The filing of a demurrer is a permissible means of objecting to the sufficiency of the petition. If insufficient, there is no necessity for remonstrating. If the petition be sufficient under the statute, a party interested may still file a remonstrance within the specified time. We therefore conclude that the court did not err in overruling the objections to the filing of the demurrers and remonstrances, nor in overruling the motions to strike out the several demurrers and remonstrances. The demurrers in this case were for insufficiency of the facts alleged to state a cause of action.

Under the code a demurrer for want of facts presents 5. no question concerning a defect of parties plaintiff or defendant. *Boseker* v. *Chamberlain* (1903), 160 Ind. 114, 117, 66 N. E. 448.

But this is a special statutory proceeding, and the petitioner must aver facts sufficient to bring himself 6. within the provisions of the statute. To comply with this rule the names of the parties "particularly interested" must be stated in the petition, the same as any other facts required by the statute.

The principal objection urged against appellant's petition

is that it fails to state the names of persons "particularly interested" in the vacation of the street "who shall be affected thereby." The petition shows that appellant owns all the ground on both sides of that portion of the street sought to be vacated, and that the other streets particularly described "afford proper ingress and egress to the citizens of said town and the residents of said street or alley."

The word "proper" is a usual word to use in a pleading to show ordinary and sufficient means of ingress to and egress from property. Webster defines the word as
7. meaning "suitable in all respects—appropriate— right." March's Thesaurus Dictionary of the English language (1910 ed.) gives as its meaning or synonym, "specially suited."

A pleading is required to state facts constituting the cause of action, in plain and concise language, in such manner as to enable a person of common understand-
8. ing to know what is intended. Words are to be taken in their plain, ordinary and usual meaning, unless they have some peculiar and technical significance.

Viewed in this light, appellant's petition gives the name of the owner of all the property abutting on that part of the street proposed to be vacated, and shows that the
6. citizens of the town and all the residents of said street have ingress and egress suitable in all respects, appropriate and right, or "specially suited" to their needs, without that portion of the street asked to be vacated. For the purposes of the demurrer, these facts are taken as true, and when so considered the petition names those particularly interested and affected by the proposed va-
9. cation as required by the statute. This view of the pleading is more liberal to appellee than the construction placed on a somewhat similar, though more definite statute as to those who may object (§§3647-3650 Burns 1901. §§3184-3187 R. S. 1881), under which it was held that a

person competent to object to the vacation of the street, as a property owner, must be the owner of property abutting immediately on that part of the street to be vacated. *House* v. *City of Greensburg* (1884), 93 Ind. 533, 536; *Hall* v. *City of Lebanon* (1903), 31 Ind. App. 265, 268, 67 N. E. 703.

The statute under which this proceeding is maintained does not expressly limit property owners who may object to the vacation of a street to those owning property 10. abutting on that part of the street to be vacated, and it is apparent that no such limitation can reasonably be made. Persons owning property abutting on the street may be, and in many instances are, particularly interested and affected by the vacation of a portion of the street other than that part on which their property abuts. *O'Brien* v. *Central Iron, etc., Co.* (1902), 158 Ind. 218, 221, 63 N. E. 302, 57 L. R. A. 508, 92 Am. St. 305. But persons who have sufficient or "specially suited" means of ingress and egress, as alleged in appellant's petition, do not have more than a general interest common to the citizens of the particular vicinity, city or town. For these reasons we conclude that the court erred in sustaining the several demurrers to appellant's petition. With this error corrected there will be before the trial court a sufficient petition, and remonstrances filed within the time specified by the statute.

Appellees have suggested that the questions presented by this appeal involve a constitutional question, on the ground that the statute authorizes the taking of property in which persons, other than the abutting property owners of the part of the street to be vacated, have a special interest, which is to be taken without compensation.

The decisions in this State establish the proposition that the owner of property claiming damage by reason of the vacation or obstruction of a street must show that he has

suffered, or will suffer, an injury different in kind
11. and not simply in degree, from that suffered by the
community in general. *Dantzer* v. *Indianapolis Union
R. Co.* (1895), 141 Ind. 604, 610, 39 N. E. 223, 34 L. R. A.
769, 50 Am. St. 343; *O'Brien* v. *Central Iron, etc., Co.
supra; Pittsburgh, etc., R. Co.* v. *Noftsger* (1897), 148 Ind.
101, 104, 47 N. E. 332; *Strunk* v. *Pritchett* (1901), 27 Ind.
App. 582, 586, 61 N. E. 973.

The petition proceeds on the theory that no person other
than appellant has any special interest in that part
12.   of the street to be vacated, and that all other property owners have only such interest as belongs to the
general public of that vicinity.

Our decision does not therefore involve the question of
the taking of property without compensation, in which any
one is specially interested. No constitutional question is
therefore duly raised and presented by this appeal. We are
not called on to decide any question relating to the remonstrance, except the time for filing and presenting the same.
However, the second ground of remonstrance is that the
proposed vacation will leave the real estate of the remon-
strants without means of ingress to or egress from a public
way or street, and the third is that it will cut off the public's
access to some church, school or other public buildings or
grounds.

As the case must be reversed for the reasons already
shown, the questions raised by the remonstrance can be
tried and determined on the evidence. If the re-
13. monstrance is sustained, the street cannot be vacated.
If the proof sustains the petition and fails to sustain
the remonstrance, the court will proceed in accordance with
the statute, but we cannot now anticipate and decide questions not presented by the record and which may never arise.

For reasons already stated, the judgment is reversed, with
instructions to the lower court to overrule the demurrers to

appellant's petition and for further proceedings not inconsistent with this opinion.

NOTE.—Reported in 100 N. E. 762. See. also, under (1, 6, 10) 28 Cyc. 840; (3) 31 Cyc. 92; (7) 32 Cyc. 637; (8) 31 Cyc. 86; (9) 31 Cyc. 333; (12) 11 Cyc. 818; (13) 3 Cyc. 223. As to the exercise. by a city of the power to vacate streets, see 46 Am. St. 494. As to the persons entitled to compensation for the vacation of a street, see 15 Ann. Cas. 687.

THE PITTSBURGH, CINCINNATI, CHICAGO AND ST. LOUIS RAILWAY COMPANY *v.* JOHNSON ET AL.

[No. 7,671. Filed October 18, 1912. Rehearing denied February 14, 1913.]

1. EXECUTION.—*Action to Enjoin Enforcement.—Irregularity in Rendition of Judgment.—Cross-Complaint.*—In an action to enjoin the enforcement of an execution on the ground that no judgment had been rendered, or, that if rendered, the record entry thereof had not been signed, a cross-complaint seeking to cure irregularity in the rendition of such judgment by having the same read in open court and signed by the court *nunc pro tunc,* is a proper pleading and germane to the subject-matter of the complaint. p. 465.

2. APPEAL.—*Review.—Harmless Error.—Overruling Demurrer to Answer.*—Overruling a demurrer to a paragraph of answer, even if erroneous, is harmless, where the finding is for plaintiff on the complaint. p. 466.

3. TRIAL.—*Conclusions of Law.—Conformity to Issues.*—The conclusions of law announced by the trial court are not improper, where they are within the issues tendered by a cross-complaint and the answer thereto, although they may be outside the issues tendered by the complaint. p. 467.

4. JUDGMENT.—*Validity.—Failure to Read and Sign.*—While the rendition of a judgment by the trial court, its entry on the order book by the clerk, and its final approval and authentication by the judge's signature, after it has been read in open court, are separate, independent acts essential to support an execution issued on such judgment, the failure of the court to cause the order book entry to be read in open court, and to sign same, as required by §1450 Burns 1908, Acts 1885 p. 124, will not render the judgment void. p. 467.

5. TRIAL.—*Special Findings.—Conclusions of Law.*—In an action to enjoin the enforcement of an execution, where the special findings show that a judgment had been rendered, but that the order book entry had not been read in open court and signed, a conclusion of law that such judgment is valid, but that no execution may issue thereon until the record is read and signed in open court, is not inconsistent with a conclusion that the enforcement of the existing execution should be enjoined. p. 468.

6. JUDGMENT.—*Rendition During Pendency of Motion for New Trial.—Validity.*—A judgment is not void because it is rendered while a motion for a new trial is pending, but such pending motion merely operates to suspend the effect and enforcement of the judgment. p. 469.

7. JUDGMENT.—*Failure to Read and Sign.—Findings.—Conclusions of Law.—Nunc Pro Tunc Proceedings.*—Where, in an action to enjoin the enforcement of an execution, the special findings show that the judgment on which the execution issued had been rendered, and that it had been properly entered by the clerk, but had not been read and signed, a conclusion of law stated thereon that such judgment and record entry "should be and the same now is read and signed in open court *nunc pro tunc,* and said judgment may now be enforced by proper writ", is not open to the objection that it is a *nunc pro tunc* rendition of the judgment. p. 469.

8. JUDGMENT.—*Failure to Read and Sign.—Reading and Signing Nunc Pro Tunc.—Effect.*—Where the only irregularity in the rendition of a judgment consisted of the failure to read and sign the order book entry of same, as required by §1450 Burns 1908, Acts 1885 p. 124, the *nunc pro tunc* reading and signing thereof, as authorized by §1451 Burns 1908, §1331 R. S. 1881, gave to it regularity authorizing its enforcement by execution as of the date of its rendition. p. 470.

9. JUDGMENT.—*Rendition.—Evidence—Sufficiency.*—In an action to enjoin the enforcement of an execution, wherein defendant secured a *nunc pro tunc* reading and signing of the judgment, special findings that a judgment was rendered and entered, and that the only irregularity consisted of a failure to read and sign the entry in open court, are sufficiently supported by the evidence, where, besides the testimony of witnesses to the effect that the judgment had been rendered and entered in the order book, there was some record and documentary evidence to support every material part of each and all the findings made by the court. p. 471.

10. JUDGMENT.—*Nunc Pro Tunc Entries.—Evidence.*—As a general rule a *nunc pro tunc* entry cannot be made on oral testimony alone. p. 476.

11. APPEAL.—*Invited Error.*—Invited error cannot be taken advantage of on appeal. p. 477.

12. APPEAL.—*Review.*—*Harmless Error.*—*Admission of Testimony.*—Error, if any, in the admission of testimony, is not cause for a reversal, where the findings and judgment of the trial court show that such testimony was disregarded. p. 477.

From Pulaski Circuit Court; *Francis J. Vurpillat,* Judge.

Action by The Pittsburgh, Cincinnati, Chicago and St. Louis Railway Company against Carl Johnson and another to enjoin the enforcement of an execution. From a judgment against it on a cross-complaint seeking to cure the defect of the judgment on which the execution was issued, by reading and signing the record thereof *nunc pro tunc,* the plaintiff appeals. *Affirmed.*

G. E. Ross, for appellant.

M. M. Hathaway and *M. Winfield,* for appellees.

HOTTEL, C. J.—This is a suit begun by appellant to enjoin the enforcement of an execution in favor of appellee, Johnson, in the hands of appellee, Sanders, sheriff. Appellee, Johnson, will be referred to as appellee.

The issues of fact in the case were presented by a complaint in two paragraphs, the first of which was dismissed after trial; neither paragraph was denied, but each was specially answered. A demurrer to each answer was overruled. A reply in denial and special replies were filed. After the case had proceeded to trial appellee, over appellant's objection, filed a cross-complaint in two paragraphs. After a motion to strike out each of these paragraphs had been overruled, a general denial was filed, and the trial of the cause concluded. To set out the substance of these various pleadings would extend this opinion to an unreasonable length. We think it sufficient to say that the issue tendered by the complaint was, as expressed by appellant in its brief, "whether any judgment had ever been rendered" in the original action in which the execution was issued.

The issue on the first paragraph of the cross-complaint was whether the trial court in said original action had, in fact, announced and rendered the judgment in said action appearing in the record entry of October 8, 1908, prepared by the clerk of said court, and whether the same should be read in open court and signed by the court *nunc pro tunc*. The second paragraph of the complaint differed from the first, in that it proceeded on the theory that the judgment on which the execution had issued was announced and rendered in open court on October 8, 1908, and had been entered by the clerk under the order of court, and that the court in term, to wit, on October 9, 1908, intending to sign the record of the entire proceedings had on October 8, by inadvertence and mistake, signed the same before the close of the day's proceedings and immediately before the entry containing said judgment here involved. At the request of the parties the court made a special finding of facts with conclusions of law thereon, and entered judgment enjoining appellees "from levying said execution on the property of the plaintiff", and ordered that the judgment rendered on October 8, 1908 (being the judgment in said original action upon which the execution was issued), "be and the same is a valid and subsisting judgment and that the same be read in open court and signed by the judge which is now done and said proceedings on the 8th day of October, 1908, are now read in open court by the judge *nunc pro tunc* which reading and signing are now done in open court."

This appeal is prosecuted from that part of said judgment rendered on the cross-complaint. The errors relied on are: (1) In overruling appellant's motion to strike out the cross-complaint of appellee; (2) in permitting the paper called a cross-complaint to be filed by appellee; (3) in overruling appellant's demurrer to the second paragraph of the answer of appellee to the second paragraph of appellant's complaint; (4) in its second conclusion of law on the facts specially found; (5) in its third conclusion of law on the facts specially found; (6) in overruling appellant's motion for a new trial; (7), (8), (9), (10) in the rulings of the court on the several specifications of appellant's motion to modify the judgment; (11) in that the cross-complaint does not state facts sufficient to constitute a cause of action.

The facts controlling on the questions involved in the appeal are presented by the court's finding of facts, and are, in substance, as follows: (2) On October 8, 1908, appellant filed in the original action its bills of exceptions Nos. 1 and 2, and its written motion and causes for a new trial, and "on the same day, while this motion was pending and undisposed of, the appellee, by his attorney, moved the court for judgment upon the verdict of the jury", which motion the court at the time sustained, and announced from the bench and rendered judgment on such verdict in favor of appellee for $6,000 and costs; that on October 10, the court overruled the motion for a new trial, and granted appellant ninety days in which to file a bill of exceptions, and appellant then prayed an appeal to the Appellate Court, which was granted on the filing within 90 days of an appeal bond in the sum of $8,000, with the American Surety Company of New York as surety. (3) At the time of the filing of said amended complaint, and subsequent thereto, the court used a bench docket, on which he personally noted in writing minutes or memoranda of the court's proceedings in said cause: that the minutes or memoranda made by the trial court itself upon said bench docket, relative to the proceedings had in said case, and set out in the last preceding finding are in the words and figures following: "Oct. 4. Jury return answer to interrogatories and general verdict in the sum of $6,000. Oct. 8. Dft. files bills of except. No. 1 and No. 2. Deft. also files written causes and motion for new trial. Oct. 10. Motion for new trial overruled and exception and 90 days to file bills of exceptions. Dft. prays an appeal to Appellate Court which is granted upon filing bond in sum of $8,000 with the American Surety Company as surety within 90 days.'' (4) The trial court failed to make minutes on its bench docket of the motion for judgment on the verdict, the sustaining of such motion, and the rendition of such judgment, all of which were done by the trial court on October 8, 1908, as shown in finding No. 3; that on that day, after such proceedings were had and judgment rendered, M. M. Hathaway, as one of the attorneys for Johnson, prepared a formal record entry of all the proceedings had in said cause on October 8, ''including in such entry the proceedings of which the trial court made minutes on its bench docket as well as those proceedings of which the trial court failed to make such minutes * * * and presented to the judge such formal record entry which was thereupon examined and * * * approved by Judge Nye, the trial court; that such entry so prepared, was placed with the other papers filed in the case, but was not itself marked filed;'' that this entry so prepared was afterwards duly entered of record by the deputy clerk of said court, and now appears of record in order-book No. 34, page 402, of the records of Pulaski Circuit Court, and filed at the clerk's office at Pulaski County, Indiana; the record of such proceedings, as so prepared and recorded, is as follows: ''Carl Johnson vs. P., C., C. & St. L. Railway Company, No. 7180. Comes now the defendant by counsel and files Bills of Exceptions No. 1 and No. 2 in words following, to-wit; (Insert). Defendant also files written cause and motion for new trial in words and figures following, to-wit: (Insert). Plaintiff now moves the court for judgment on the verdict which motion is by the court sustained. It is therefore ordered, adjudged and decreed by the court that plaintiff recover of and from the defendant the sum of Six Thousand Dollars as and for his damages, together with his costs made and taxed in this cause at $———.'' (5) The record of the day's proceedings had by the Pulaski Circuit Court on October 8, 1908, appears of record in order-book No. 34, pages

399-403; that such record was never read or signed in open court; that the trial judge, Judge Nye, signed said record in the clerk's office during vacation; that said judge did not sign the record of said day's proceedings at the close thereof, but signed the same on the bottom of page 401, the record of the case of appellee v. appellant, set out in the last preceding finding, and record entries of other cases, appearing after said trial judge's signature. (6) That the clerk of the Pulaski Circuit Court entered said judgment of appellee Johnson v. appellant, set out and referred to in the preceding finding, in judgment docket H, page 235 of the records of the Pulaski Circuit Court, such judgment docket being as follows, to wit: then follows said entry. (7) On December 31, 1908, appellant filed with the clerk of the Pulaski Circuit Court an appeal bond according to the directions of the court made on October 10, 1908, which appeal bond recites, in substance, among other things, the following: ''That whereas said Carl Johnson, who is defendant in this cause, on the 9th day of October, 1908, recovered judgment in the Pulaski Circuit Court against the appellant in the sum of $6,000 and costs and the said defendant Railway Company appeal from said judgment, now if the defendant, the Pittsburgh, Cincinnati, Chicago and St. Louis Railway Company shall duly prosecute said appeal and pay the judgment that may be rendered against it in the Appellate Court of Indiana, then the bond shall be void, otherwise to remain in full force and effect; that said bond was endorsed as follows: No. 7180 Carl Johnson vs. P., C., C. and St. L. Ry. Co. Appeal Bond, Amount $8,000, filed Dec. 31, 1908. Frank Wittmer, Clerk Pulaski Circuit Court, George E. Ross, Attorney for defendants.'' (8) On October 18, 1909, appellant commenced this action against appellees by a complaint duly sworn to by George E. Ross, attorney for appellant, and in said complaint alleged ''that on the 8th day of October, 1908, the plaintiff in this case, filed its motion and causes for a new trial; and after the filing of said moti: n and causes for a new trial and pending said motion and before said motion had been ruled upon, and without ruling on said motion of the defendant for a new trial, the said Pulaski Circuit Court, on said 8th day of October, 1908, entered a judgment in favor of said Carl Johnson and against this plaintiff, on said verdict of the jury, for the sum of $6,000 and that no other judgment or different judgment has ever been rendered in said cause; that afterwards, to wit, on the 15th day of November, 1909, the plaintiff filed a second paragraph of complaint not verified, wherein it alleges that said judgment was void; that no judgment had ever been rendered by the court and that the entry was simply the entry of the clerk, and, on the trial of said cause, to wit, on the 2d day of December, 1909, the plaintiff dismissed his cause of action as to said first paragraph of complaint.''

On the foregoing facts the court announced the following conclusions of law: (1) That plaintiff, The Pittsburgh, Cincinnati, Chicago and St. Louis Railway Company, is entitled to the relief prayed for in the second paragraph of complaint, that is, that defendants and each of them be forever enjoined from executing the execution now in the hands of defendant, William Sanders, sheriff of Pulaski county, Indiana, and that the plaintiff is entitled to recover its costs in this action. (2) That the judgment appearing of record in order-book No. 34, page 402, of the records of the Pulaski Circuit Court, and set out in finding No. 4, is a valid, subsisting judgment in favor of defendant and cross-complainant, Carl Johnson, and against plaintiff, The Pittsburgh, Cincinnati, Chicago and St. Louis Railway Company, and that said judgment was duly and legally rendered by the Pulaski Circuit Court and entered of record by the clerk thereof; but that no execution may issue thereon until said judgment record is read and signed in open court. (3) That the judgment and record entry in the case of Carl Johnson v. The Pittsburgh, Cincinnati, Chicago and St. Louis

Railway Company appearing in order-book No. 34, at page 402, of the records of the Pulaski Circuit Court, and set out in finding No. 4, should be and the same now is read and signed in open court *nunc pro tunc,* and said judgment may now be enforced by proper writ.

The first, second and eleventh of the above errors present in different form practically the same question, and may be disposed of together. It is insisted by appellant (1) that the cross-complaint does not grow out of and is not germane to the subject-matter of the complaint; (2) that the relief sought therein is such as could be obtained only in the original action, and hence not proper by way of cross-complaint in this action; (3) that a cross-complaint must not only arise out of the same subject-matter as the original action, but that it must also be between the same parties.

Without discussing the reasons urged by appellant in support of its contention, it is sufficient to say that practically the exact procedure here followed was approved by

1. the Supreme Court in the case of *Kent* v. *Fullenlove* (1872), 38 Ind. 522, which was a suit to enjoin the enforcement of an execution on a judgment signed by the judge in vacation, and before it had been read in open court. This case, so far as we have been able to find, has never been overruled, modified or criticised. Since the decision of the case just cited, the legislature passed an act (§1451 Burns 1908, §1331 R. S. 1881), which provides as follows: "In all cases where business of any kind has been or shall be transacted by any circuit or superior judge and put of record, and the judge, from death, resignation, or any other cause, has left or may leave the record of such proceeding or proceedings unsigned, the successor of such judge shall have the same power and authority to sign such record, at any subsequent term of the court, as if such record has been made by such judge." The evident purpose of this act was to meet a condition like, or similar to, that presented by the cross-complaint in this case, and furnishes additional authority

for the action of the trial court in permitting the filing of said cross-complaint. *Beitman* v. *Hopkins* (1887), 109 Ind. 177, 9 N. E. 720; *Mayer* v.: *Haggerty* (1894), 138 Ind. 628, 38 N. E. 42.

The third error relied on, which calls in question the sufficiency of the second paragraph of answer to the second paragraph of complaint, may be disposed of by saying that this answer also substantially follows the answer in the case of *Kent* v. *Fullenlove, supra*. The court said with reference to the answers filed in that case that they "did not set up any matter which was a bar to the action. They admitted the facts to be substantially as alleged in the complaint. *Regarded, however, in the nature of motions or cross-complaints to have the record amended, by having it read and signed in open court, we are inclined to hold them sufficient."* (Our italics.)

But, even if it could be said that the overruling of the demurrer to the answer in this case was error, it was rendered harmless by the court's finding for appellant on its complaint, and the rendition of the judgment thereon enjoining the levying of the execution on appellant's property. Such a ruling will furnish no ground for reversal. *Gilliland* v. *Jones* (1896), 144 Ind. 662, 43 N. E. 939, 55 Am. St. 210; *Walling* v. *Burgess* (1890), 122 Ind. 299, 22 N. E. 419, 23 N. E. 1076, 7 L. R. A. 481; *Vulcan Iron Works Co.* v. *Electric, etc., Min. Co.* (1913), 54 Ind. App. —, 99 N. E. 429, 100 N. E. 307; *Beasley* v. *Phillips* (1898), 20 Ind. App. 182, 50 N. E. 388.

Alleged errors four and five will be considered together. In support of the contention that the court erred in its second and third conclusions of law, it is insisted, in effect, (1) that no issue presented by the complaint and answer warrants either of said conclusions, and that each conclusion is inconsistent with the first conclusion, because if the judgment was valid appellant was not entitled to an injunction; (2) that it appears from the findings that the judgment attempted to be rendered was rendered after the filing of the motion for a new trial, and while the same was pending and undisposed of, and that a judgment so rendered "was ineffective for any purpose, * * * and absolutely void;" (3) that as to the third conclusion of law, the court had no jurisdiction of the subject-matter, and therefore "no power in this action to adjudge and decree or to make said entry in order-book 34, page 402, an entry of proceedings had in that cause, or to cause the same to be read in open court, and then sign it *and make it an entry nunc pro tunc in said cause;*" that such conclusion is "inconsistent with and in irreconcilable conflict" with conclusion one.

In answer to that part of the first ground of appellant's objection that the conclusions in question are outside the issues tendered by the complaint and answer, it is sufficient to say that they are not outside the issues tendered by the cross-complaint and answers thereto,. and if we were right in holding that the court below properly permitted the filing of such cross-complaint, it follows that this ground of appellant's objection is not tenable.

3.

As to the remaining ground of this first contention, we think it fails to distinguish between an invalid or void judgment and a judgment merely irregular, because it lacks the authentication, necessary under the statute, to support an execution issued thereon. For the purposes of an execution a judgment must be read and signed by the judge of the court rendering the same. This is so by reason of §1450 Burns 1908, Acts 1885 p. 124, which provides, in substance, that the clerk shall draw up each day's proceedings at full length on the proper order-book; that the court shall cause the same to be read in open court, after which the same shall be signed by the judge, and that "no process shall issue on any judgment or decree of court until it shall have been so read and signed." .The rendition of the judgment by the court, its entry on the order-book by the clerk, and its final approval and authentication by the

4.

judge's signature, after it has been read in open court, are separate, independent acts, all of which may be necessary under the above statute to support an execution issued on such judgment. It does not follow, however, that all of the above steps are necessary to the validity of a judgment. *Anderson* v. *Mitchell* (1877), 58 Ind. 592; *Pittsburgh, etc., R. Co.* v. *Johnson* (1911), 49 Ind. App. 126, 93 N. E. 683, 95 N. E. 610.

The purpose of the reading and signing is to verify and approve the record entry, and see that it correctly sets out the judgment before announced and rendered by the court, and the judge's signature thereto is required as certification and authentication that the judgment as entered was in fact rendered by the court.

A judgment entered of record and not signed is not necessarily invalid or void, depending on whether the judgment was in fact rendered by a court with jurisdiction and authority to render the same. *Catterlin* v. *City of Frankfort* (1882), 87 Ind. 45, 56; *Griffith* v. *State* (1871), 36 Ind. 406, 408; *Jaqua* v. *Harkins* (1907), 40 Ind. App. 639, 82 N. E. 920; *Pittsburgh, etc., R. Co.* v. *Johnson, supra.* But, under the law, the signature thereto of the judge of the court which rendered the judgment furnishes the evidence of its rendition and the authentication thereof necessary to support an execution issued thereon. §1450 Burns 1908, Acts 1885 p. 124; *Griffith* v. *State, supra;* 23 Cyc. 850; *Pittsburgh, etc., R. Co.* v. *Johnson, supra.*

The legislature by passing §1451 Burns 1908, §1331 R. S. 1881, providing that a judgment may be signed at any subsequent term of court, after its rendition, recognized that an unsigned judgment was not void, because if void there was no necessity for such an act.

The facts found show that a valid judgment had in fact been rendered by the court on October 8, 1908, but that

5.   the same had not been read in open court and signed by the judge thereof in term, and for this reason,

under the above authorities, conclusion of law No. 2 was proper and consistent with conclusion No. 1.

As to the second ground of contention above, appellant is in error in assuming that a judgment rendered after a motion for new trial is filed, and while such motion is 6. pending undisposed of, is absolutely void.   The authorities cited by appellant on this subject are to the effect that so long as a motion for a new trial remains undisposed of, there can be no final judgment within the meaning of the statute regulating appeals. *Colchen* v. *Ninde* (1889), 120 Ind. 88, 22 N. E. 94; *New York, etc., R. Co.* v. *Doane* (1886), 105 Ind. 92, 4 N. E. 419. These authorities lend no support to appellant's position, but simply hold, in effect, that the undisposed-of motion for a new trial operates to suspend the effect and enforcement of the judgment only during the pendency of such motion, implying that the judgment is valid and will become effective and enforceable after such motion has been overruled.   In this connection see *Davison* v. *Brown* (1896), 93 Wis. 85, 87, 67 N. W. 42; *Pittsburgh, etc., R. Co.* v. *Johnson, supra.*

The third ground of appellant's contention also proceeds on an erroneous assumption, viz., that the court adjudged and decreed *"and made said entry in order-* 7. *book No. 34, page 402, an entry of proceedings had in that cause,* or after having caused the same to be read and signed in open court, *made it an entry nunc pro tunc."* The theory of the finding of facts and the conclusions of law, as we understand them, is that the judgment had already been rendered, and that it had been properly entered by the clerk, but had not been read and signed, that there was no necessity for a *nunc pro tunc* rendition of the judgment, or for a *nunc pro tunc* entry of the same, but that the reading and signing alone should be *nunc pro tunc*. With this view, the court's conclusions of law are consistent throughout and supported by the finding of facts.   The judgment being unsigned, it would not, by reason of an express statute, support the execution, and therefore the first conclusion of law was correct. It being found that the judgment had in fact been rendered and entered but not signed, the second and third conclusions of law were warranted, and were entirely consistent with No. 1 and with each other. This second conclusion may be open to the criticism that it is in part in the nature of a finding of fact rather than a conclusion of law, but that part which is a conclusion of law is justified by the facts found and entirely consistent with conclusion No. 1.

It may be open to doubt whether it is strictly and technically accurate to say that the manual signing of a judgment after term by the trial judge, under the authority of §1451, *supra,* is a signing *nunc pro tunc,* but for the purposes of the questions here presented, this language in the conclusion of law and in the pleading was not of controlling importance. The questions involved are whether the facts of this case warranted the trial court in having such record read and signed, and whether when so read and signed it was effective from its rendition.

When considered in connection with the statute and decisions, there was no inconsistency between the conclusion that the enforcement of the present execution should be enjoined, and the conclusion that the judgment was valid and "should be and is now read and signed in open court *nunc pro tunc* and said judgment may now be enforced by proper writ."

The execution, the enforcement of which was enjoined, was issued before signing the judgment, and, therefore, under the statute could not be enforced. Said §1451, 8. *supra,* authorized the court to cause the judgment to be read and signed, which the court did, and then authorized its enforcement by proper writ. The reading and signing of the judgment gave it the regularity that authorized its enforcement by execution as of the date of its rendition. *Mayer* v. *Haggerty* (1894), 138 Ind. 628, 631, 38 N.

E. 42; *Kraus* v. *Lehman* (1908), 170 Ind. 408, 426, 83 N. E. 714, 84 N. E. 769, 15 Ann. Cas. 849; *Pittsburgh, etc., R. Co.* v. *Johnson, supra.*

In support of its contention that the court erred in overruling the motion for new trial, it is first insisted that "oral testimony alone will not be sufficient on which to make an entry *nunc pro tunc* after the case has ceased to be *in fieri*," and in this connection counsel assert that "there is no evidence except the oral testimony of M. M. Hathaway that any judgment was ever rendered, hence nothing to sustain that part of the findings that a judgment was rendered."

Numerous authorities are cited to support the legal proposition relied on, but the trouble with appellant's position is not in its proposition of law, but in its assumption
9. that there was "no evidence except the oral testimony of M. M. Hathaway" that any judgment was ever rendered. In this connection appellant insists that parts of several of the findings are not sustained by sufficient evidence. Without setting out the several parts of the findings questioned, we will indicate enough of the evidence to show that there was some evidence to support every material part of each and all the findings made by the court. Page 402 of order-book 34 of the Pulaski Circuit Court was read in evidence. The caption of this order is as follows:

"September Term, 1908. October 8, 28th day. Carl Johnson vs. P. C. C. & St. L. Railway Company. No. 7180."

The body of the order is just as set out in finding No. 4 above. This, we think, was some record evidence of the rendition and entry of the judgment.

There was read in evidence the order-book entry of October 10, 1908, which is as follows: "Carl Johnson vs. P. C. C. & St. L. Railway Company. No. 7180.

Come now again the parties, by counsel, and motion by defendant for new trial is overruled, to which ruling of the court defendant excepts and 90 days given in which to

file bill of exceptions. The defendant now prays an appeal
to the Appellate Court which is granted upon filing bond in
the sum of $8,000 with the American Surety Company as
surety within 90 days.''

This order shows a prayer for appeal granted, and the
fixing of the amount and sureties of the appeal bond. This
entry contained no judgment. The trial court had a right
to infer from this item of evidence that appellant would
not do a foolish or useless thing, and appeal merely from
the ruling on a motion for a new trial, but that it was appealing from a final judgment before rendered.

The appeal bond given by appellant was also offered and
read in evidence, which was the usual appeal bond given in
such cases and contained among its other provisions the following: ''The condition of the above obligation is such,
that whereas, heretofore, to wit: On the 9th day of October, 1908, the said Carl Johnson in the Pulaski Circuit
Court, recovered a judgment against the said The Pittsburgh, Cincinnati, Chicago & St. Louis Railway Company
for the sum of six thousand dollars, in damages and costs
of suit, etc., from which said judgment of said Pulaski Circuit Court, the said The Pittsburgh, Cincinnati, Chicago &
St. Louis Railway Company appeal to the Supreme Court
of Indiana. Now the said The Pittsburgh, Cincinnati, Chicago & St. Louis Railway Company shall and will duly prosecute said appeal, and abide by and pay the judgment and
costs, which may be rendered or affirmed against it then the
above obligation to be null and void, otherwise to be and remain in full force and virtue in law. The Pittsburgh, Cincinnati, Chicago and St. Louis Railway (seal) Company by
G. E. Ross, Solicitor The American Surety Company (seal)
of New York by John F. Brookinger, (seal), Its Attorney in
fact.'' This bond is indorsed as follows: ''No. 7180. Carl
Johnson vs. The P. C. C. & St. L. Ry. Co. Appeal Bond.

Amount $8,000. Filed in open court, Dec. 31, 1908. Frank Wittmer, Clerk Pulaski Circuit Court. (Recorded.) G. E. Ross, Attorney for Deft.''

It was admitted by appellant and appellee that this bond is the appeal bond which was filed on December 31, 1908, in cause No. 7180 in the Pulaski Circuit Court. This bond expressly recognizes that a judgment had been before rendered in the case.. True, it refers to a judgment rendered on October 9 instead of October 8, and indicates that the appeal was to the Supreme Court instead of the Appellate Court, as provided by order granting the appeal. At all events this bond was some evidence from which the trial court might infer that a judgment had been in fact rendered in the case sometime before October 10, 1908, and after the rendition of the verdict on October 4, 1908.

The above indorsement on the appeal bond and other various entries showed that George E. Ross was one of appellant's attorneys, representing it at various steps and stages of the original action. The original complaint on which the restraining order was granted herein was introduced and read in evidence. It was a verified complaint sworn to by George E. Ross and contained the averments as found by the court in its finding of facts, No. 8 above. The theory of this complaint at the time it was filed and sworn to was that the court in said original action did render judgment on October 8, 1908, but that the same was rendered after a motion for a new trial had been filed, and while such motion was pending undisposed of, and for this reason the judgment was invalid and void.

The oral testimony of Mr. Ross shows that this original complaint sometime later, and when the second paragraph was filed, was amended, with the consent of the court, by inserting the words ''clerk of the'' before the words ''Pulaski Circuit Court,'' but that the same was never resworn to. The complaint as amended showed that the clerk of the court entered the judgment, and that no other or different judgment was ever rendered in said cause. There was also offered and read in evidence the record of said judgment contained in the judgment docket of said court, which entry is that usually contained in a judgment docket, showing, under the usual headings, the number of the cause —7180; attorneys—Hathaway and Winfield; O. B. 402 F. B. U. page 96. Parties—Carl Johnson v. P. C. C. & St. L. Ry. Co.; against whom judgment is rendered—defendants; amount of judgment and costs—$6,000 and costs; date of rendition—October 8, 1908.

In addition to the record and documentary evidence above indicated, there was oral evidence as follows: M. M. Hathaway testified that he was one of the attorneys for appellee Johnson in the original case against appellant, viz., No. 7180 in the Pulaski Circuit Court; and among other answers he made the following: "The rulings of the court were as they appear in that order-book; that is the order-book entry Judge Ross, that you and I compared. * * * The court announced his rulings from the bench, just as they appear in that order-book, and I prepared the order-book entry. * * * As attorney for the plaintiff I orally made a motion that the court * * * render judgment on the verdict by the jury and the court announced from the bench that the motion was sustained and judgment on the verdict, is the substance of what he said. * * * I prepared the order-book entry in the matter. I have it with me. It was that among the files and papers here. I prepared the order-book entry and handed it to Judge Nye, and he, after reading it, to the clerk of this court * * *. Judge Burson, [one of the appellant's attorneys in the trial of the case] was present at the time the judgment was rendered. This order-book entry was among the papers in the case."

Appellant's witness, M. J. O'Connell, the deputy clerk who made the entry in the order-book, testified, among other things, that the entry was prepared for her by the attorney for appellee; that she thought Mr. Hathaway gave her the entry; she also identified exhibit No. 4 as the paper furnished her by Mr. Hathaway, and testified further, in substance: That is where the court signed on the morning of October 8. There are two paragraphs of the record that have not been signed, and was the entry of the proceedings of October 8. She prepared the entry from an entry furnished by Mr. Hathaway.

This prepared entry was introduced in evidence, and is the same as of the record entry above of date October 8, 1908. The clerk testified: "I was in court * * * I remember about the judgment being entered. I remember there was a judgment but I paid no particular attention to it."

John C. Nye, the trial judge, testified. He identified his signature to the record at bottom of page 401 of order-book 34, and said with reference to the same: "I signed it in the belief I was signing the day's proceedings. * * * I can say clearly this: that when I put my signature there it was my intention to sign the proceedings of the day and I thought I was doing so."

We think we have indicated enough of the evidence to show that every finding had at least some evidence to support it. It is admitted by both parties, and in fact appellant bases its contention on the fact, that this entry of October 8, 1908, purporting to be a judgment, is the only judgment ever entered in the case. From some judgment appellant prayed an appeal to the Supreme Court. The appeal was granted conditioned on the filing of a bond in the sum of $8,000 as directed by the court. On December 31, 1908, appellant filed its appeal bond as directed by the court, reciting therein that judgment had been rendered in said cause on October 9, 1908. By this bond, recognizing said judgment and the appeal therefrom, appellant obtained a stay of execution, and allowed the year to go by without appeal, and then when appellee caused an execution to be issued on said judgment, appellant filed its complaint under oath, alleging therein that judgment was rendered in said cause on October 8, 1908, but that such judgment was rendered pending a motion for a new trial, and before the same had been ruled on, and for this reason such judgment was void. We have this and other items of record evidence supporting the court's finding. In addition, we have the entry prepared by appellee's attorney Hathaway, given to the court and found with the files, though not itself filed, and the testimony of Hathaway and the other witnesses.

But it is insisted that the court erred in admitting the evidence of M. M. Hathaway, that a record entry may not be proven by oral testimony. It is true that as a general rule a *nunc pro tunc* entry cannot be made on oral testimony alone. Counsel cite no authorities, and we have been unable to find any, that go to the extent of holding that the correctness of a record entry entered in the proper record kept for the purpose by the clerk of the court, whose duty it was to make the same, when itself offered in evidence in connection with other entries and files tending to prove its correctness, may not also be supported by oral testimony. But if it be conceded that appellant is right in its contention that such entry should be based solely on record and documentary evidence on file in the case, there would certainly be as good or better reason for applying the same rule to evidence tending to dispute the entry or its correctness. Appellant in this case, to make his case in chief, introduced both the clerk of the court and his deputy, and tried to show by them that the entry was made by the deputy clerk in vacation without the sanction or authority of the court, and that the judgment contained in the entry was never in fact announced or rendered by the court in open court

He who invites error may not take advantage of it on

appeal. *Nitche* v. *Earle* (1889), 117 Ind. 270, 275, 19 N.
    E. 749; *Perkins* v. *Hayward* (1890), 124 Ind. 445,
11. 449, 24 N. E. 1033; *Louisville, etc., R. Co.* v. *Miller*
    (1895), 141 Ind. 533, 563, 37 N. E. 343; Elliott, App.
Proc. §628.

      The evidence of John C. Nye, above quoted, was
12. objected to and a motion made to strike out the
    same. These rulings are relied on as error.

The finding and judgment herein in favor of appellant
on his complaint show that the trial court wholly disregarded the intent and belief of the witness, and in fact
found that the judge's signature appearing on page 401 of
the entry was placed there in vacation, before the judgment
and not after it, and that the judgment would not support
an execution until read and signed, so that any error in the
admission of that part of the evidence which might be said
to be objectionable was rendered harmless by the finding
and judgment. Such an error will not work a reversal of
a case. *Vulcan Iron Works Co.* v. *Electric, etc., Min. Co.,
supra,* and cases cited.

Finally, appellant insists that the court erred in overruling
the several specifications of its motion to modify the judgment. These several assigned errors present in a different
form questions already considered, and for the reasons
herein indicated in discussing the other errors relied on we
think no reversible error is presented by any of the several
specifications. We find no reversible error in the case and
are of the opinion that the judgment of the lower court
was authorized both by the evidence and the law.

    Judgment affirmed.

NOTE.—Reported in 99 N. E. 508. See, also, under (2) 31 Cyc.
358; (5) 38 Cyc. 1986; (6) 23 Cyc. 784; (10) 23 Cyc. 845; (11) 3
Cyc. 242; (12) 38 Cyc. 1411. As to *nunc pro tunc* entries of judgment, see 4 Am. St. 828. As to the facts or conditions that render
a judgment void, see 20 Am. St. 78. As to injunction against execution sale generally, see 111 Am. St. 97. As to stay, otherwise than
statutory, of execution and what court may direct, see 127 Am.
St. 712.

PARK v. MORGAN.

[No. 7,823.   Filed February 18, 1913.]

1. INJUNCTION.— *Closing Passway.— Complaint.— Sufficiency.*— A complaint to enjoin defendant from closing a passway, from which it is apparent that no prescriptive right exists in the easement claimed, and which alleges that defendant, with the consent of his son, who was then the owner of the land now owned by plaintiff, opened the passway in lieu of another which had been purchased by a remote grantor, and had since kept the same open as a passway from the land now owned by plaintiff to the public highway, but that defendant is now threatening to and will close same unless restrained from doing so, does not show a right of action in favor of plaintiff. p. 478.

2. INJUNCTION.—*Closing Passway.—Right to Relief.*—An action to enjoin the closing of a passway cannot be maintained where it does not appear from the complaint that plaintiff has any right therein that is about to be invaded. p. 479.

From Morgan Circuit Court; *Henry C. Barnett,* Special Judge.

Action by Sarah B. Morgan against William P. Park. From a judgment for plaintiff, the defendant appeals. *Reversed.*

McNutt & Bain and *E. K. Thomas,* for appellant.
James M. Bishop and *D. E. Watson,* for appellee.

ADAMS, J.—Judgment was rendered for appellee in this action, restraining and enjoining appellant from closing or in any manner interfering with appellee's use of a certain passway over the lands of appellant, and declaring said passway to be a permanent easement.

The first error assigned calls in question the sufficiency of the complaint to state a cause of action. The complaint

1. alleges that appellee is the owner of a certain forty-acre tract of land, which lies about one-fourth of a mile north of the Mooresville and Waverley gravel road; that appellee cannot reach said highway without

going over the lands of appellant or the lands of one Carpenter. It is further averred "that more than 25 years
ago the plaintiff's grantor purchased a passway over the
lands of said Carpenter, and a few feet west of where it is
now located, to said highway, and the said grantor continued to use the same as a means of ingress and egress until
the real estate now owned by plaintiff, as aforesaid, was purchased by a son of the defendant, which occurred in the
year 1892, when the defendant changed said passway from
the lands of Carpenter across the fence onto his own land,
by and with the consent of said son, who is a grantor of this
plaintiff, and said passway has ever since been maintained
and used as a passway by the owners of said real estate up
to the —— day of 1908 without objection, and as a passway from the land now owned by plaintiff to said public
highway."

The passway claimed is particularly described in the complaint, and it is averred that appellant is threatening to
close the same, and will do so unless restrained by the court.

It is apparent that no prescriptive right is shown in the
easement claimed. The possession and use of the way does
not appear to have been adverse, under claim of right, or
for a sufficient length of time to ripen into absolute right.
Nor does the averment that appellant in 1892 changed the
way from the Carpenter lands to his own, with the consent
of his son, make the complaint good. Had appellant sold a
right of way on his own lands, and subsequently changed
the same to another part, with the consent of the owner of
the easement, a different case would be presented. But it
is not shown by what authority appellant presumed to close
up the way on the Carpenter lands, or that there was any
agreement that the new way was to pass by virtue of the
consideration moving for the old way. In short, it does not
appear from the averments of the complaint that
2.   appellee had any right that was about to be invaded,
and was, therefore, not entitled to the relief de-

manded. The court erred in overruling appellant's demurrer to the complaint. *Smith* v. *Miller* (1909), 44 Ind. App. 168, 170, 88 N. E. 859.

The judgment is reversed, and the cause remanded to the Morgan Circuit Court, with instructions to sustain appellant's demurrer to the complaint.

NOTE.—Reported in 100 N. E. 861. See, also, under (1, 2) 22 Cyc. 926. As to easements, and whether they may be acquired by operation of the statute of limitations, see 11 Am. Dec. 663. As to the necessity of something more than mere nonuser to extinguish easement, see 14 Am. St. 282.

MARION IRON AND BRASS BED COMPANY *v.* THE EMPIRE STATE SURETY COMPANY.

[No. 7,898. Filed February 18, 1913.]

1. BONDS.—*Fidelity Bonds.—Conditions in Application.—Breach.— Effect.*—Where a bond to secure an employer against embezzlement by a sales manager, was issued by a surety company on such employer's representation in the application that daily reports and monthly statements would be required of such manager, and that a representative would check up his accounts, such representations were conditions precedent, a breach of which would prevent a recovery on the bond, in the absence of a waiver thereof by the surety. p. 484.

2. BONDS.—*Fidelity Bonds.—Liability.—Estoppel.—Failure to Return Premium.*—A surety company is not estopped, by failure to return premium, from setting up the defense of forfeiture of a bond securing an employer against embezzlement by his sales manager, occasioned by the employer's breach of conditions binding him to require such manager to furnish daily reports, monthly statements, etc., where the bond was valid and in force when issued. p. 484.

3. BONDS.—*Fidelity Bonds.—Breach of Conditions.—Forfeiture.— Waiver.*—The right of a surety company to declare the forfeiture of a bond, executed to secure an employer against embezzlement by his employe, because of the employer's breach of conditions binding him to require the employe to furnish daily reports, monthly statements, etc., is not waived by the company's request for the prosecution of the defaulting employe, in the ab-

sence of a showing that it knew of such breaches by the employer prior to the time of requesting the prosecution of such employe. p. 487.

From Grant Circuit Court; *H. J. Paulus,* Judge.

Action by the Marion Iron and Brass Bed Company against The Empire State Surety Company. From a judgment for defendant, the plaintiff appeals. *Affirmed.*

J. F. Charles, for appellant.

Bamberger & Feibleman and *Stein, Mayer & Stein,* for appellee.

SHEA, J.—Action by appellant against appellee on a surety bond executed by the latter, for damages sustained by appellant through dishonesty and infidelity of its employe indemnified thereby. The complaint was in one paragraph. Appellee answered in two paragraphs; the first a general denial, and the second setting up an affirmative defense. A demurrer to the second paragraph of appellee's answer was overruled, and appellant then filed a reply thereto in general denial. The cause was submitted to the court for trial, and a special finding of facts was made and conclusions of law stated thereon. Appellant excepted to the conclusions of law, and filed a motion requesting the court to restate same, which motion was overruled, and judgment rendered in favor of appellee.

The errors assigned are : (1) the overruling of the demurrer to the second paragraph of appellee's answer; (2) the court erred in its conclusions of law on the facts specially found; (3) the overruling of appellant's motion requesting the court to restate its conclusions of law; (4) the court erred in rendering judgment for appellee.

In substance, the complaint alleges that appellant had in its employ George H. Besancon, an agent located in Los Angeles, California, who represented it as its sales manager in California, and who was charged with the duty of selling

appellant's goods and remitting to it money received on
account thereof. Appellant on November 15, 1906, purchased and paid for a certain indemnifying bond, securing
it from loss on account of any embezzlement or misappro-
priation of its funds by said California agent. Certain
breaches of said bond, aggregating the sum of $933.30, are
set out in the complaint. There is no dispute as to the execution of the bond, the defalcation of the agent, nor that
the bond was in force at the time of the defalcation.

Appellant insists that error was committed by the court
in overruling the demurrer to the second paragraph of appellee's answer, and on the determination of this question
this action must be decided.

The averments of this paragraph are, in substance, as follows: Appellee admits the execution of the contract on
November 15, 1906, and its extension until November 15,
1908, as shown by the complaint; that on October 24, 1906,
at the time the execution of the bond was under consideration, it submitted to appellant certain questions in writing,
the answers to which were to be taken as conditions precedent, and as a basis of the bond applied for or any continuation thereof; that the answers returned by appellant were
for the purpose of inducing appellee to execute the obligation in suit, and relying on the same and believing them to
be true, appellee did execute the bond. These questions
and answers were by the agreement of both parties made
conditions precedent; that they are warranties, and entered
into and became a part of the contract sued on. It is averred
that appellant's business is carried on in the city of Marion,
Indiana, and that it had a salesman in Los Angeles, California, one George H. Besancon, who had charge of its
property and effects in that city; that among certain condition specified in the bond was the following: "No. 5. The
business of the Employer shall continue to be conducted,
and the duties of the Employe shall remain, in accordance

NOVEMBER TERM, 1912.   483

Marion, etc., Bed Co. r. Empire State Surety Co.—52 Ind. App. 480.

with the written statements made by the Employer to the
Surety relative thereto, and the Surety may at any time
either before or after loss inspect the. Employe's books,
papers and accounts.'' Among the questions which formed
a basis for the execution of the contract are the following:
''(11) To whom and how frequently will he account for the
handlings of funds and securities? A. Send in cash each day
and makes monthly reports of stock. (12) What means
will you use to ascertain whether his accounts are correct?
A. Send our own representative from Marion to check up
each day and do all our shipping. How frequently will
they be examined? A. He will remain in Oakland. His
name is Frank Bethel, of this city.'' It is averred that
these questions and answers were conditions precedent to
said obligation, and a warranty that appellant would require its agent and accountant, Frank Bethel, to remain in
Oakland and daily check up the accounts of said Besancon,
and do all of its shipping; that appellant wholly failed
and neglected to have said Bethel do this, and for six months
after the extension of the obligation he made no examination of said agent's cash account, did no shipping for appellant, and the agreement that he should do so was by
appellant wholly abandoned and neglected; that no daily
account of the cash of said agent was ever taken by appellant; that it permitted him to do all of his own shipping, and
took no steps to examine his accounts or ascertain the
amount of cash or stock on hand; that immediately on the
execution of the obligation sued on, appellant wholly abandoned the proposed and agreed method of conducting its
business, and left the agent to his own procedure; that
during the time of the failure of appellant to carry out
and perform its part of the agreement, the agent's defalcation occurred; that appellee had no knowledge thereof, but
relied wholly on appellant's written condition and warranty, and that the failure to carry on its business in accordance therewith contributed to and caused the defalca-

tion; that by reason of such failure, appellant violated the obligation sued on, and ought not to recover; that appellant represented by said answers that Besancon would receive a salary or commission of $750 per month during the term of his employment, which would be paid the first day of each month, and these conditions were made warranties under and by virtue of the application and bond; that appellant failed to pay Besancon said sum, under said warranty, and by reason thereof cannot recover.

A consideration of the general legal propositions presented, and an application of the principles to the questions in this case, will very much shorten this opinion.

It is insisted by appellee that the questions and answers set out in the second paragraph of answer present a condition precedent, and an obligation and warranty that

1. the matters and things therein set out would be fulfilled, and that the failure so to do avoided the legal liability of appellee on said bond. There is no serious contention that there was a compliance with said conditions. Daily reports were not furnished, monthly statements were not furnished, and an agent of appellant was not on the ground supervising the business. Unless there has been a waiver of said breach, or some failure on the part of appellee changing the legal status, these must be held to be conditions precedent, to the fulfillment of which appellant was bound before it could recover.

Appellant argues (1) that the bond was valid and in force when issued; (2) that appellee is estopped from setting up the defense of forfeiture on account of such breaches, since it has not returned the premium received since the delivery of the bond.

As to the first proposition, there is no division of opinion. To the consideration of the second, therefore, we will give attention. When and under what circumstances is

2. it necessary for the insurer to tender back the premium before it can maintain the defense herein set out?

NOVEMBER TERM, 1912.   485

Marion, etc., Bed Co. r. Empire State Surety Co.—52 Ind. App. 480.

The application of the doctrine of estoppel to this case, especially, would seem to impose an undue burden on appellee. The precaution was resorted to to impose on appellant certain careful business obligations in connection with its agent indemnified. Those promises made by appellant were in no sense unreasonable, and imposed no undue hardship or duty on it, simply wise, sensible business precautions. It and it alone had knowledge as to whether those obligations were fulfilled. Appellee in this case had no knowledge, in so far as the record discloses, of any misconduct on the part of Besancon, until a demand was made on it to respond in damages for the alleged loss sustained by appellant. Under such conditions, it is the judgment of this court that the policy having taken effect, the insured is not entitled to a return of the premium, as in such cases it is only when the policy is void *ab initio* that the premium must be tendered or returned to the insured. On this proposition the authorities in this State seem to be in harmony. In the case of *Continental Life Ins. Co.* v. *Houser* (1883), 89 Ind. 258, the court said: "The policy was valid in its inception, and there was for a time a risk, and the general rule is that where the risk attaches premiums cannot be recovered from the company." The same case, on a second trial, was affirmed. *Continental Life Ins. Co.* v. *Houser* (1887), 111 Ind. 266, 12 N. E. 479. In the case of *Standley* v. *Northwestern, etc., Ins. Co.* (1884), 95 Ind. 254, 258, it is said: "Premiums paid to secure insurance cannot be recovered if the risk has once attached. If a policy is valid in its inception, then the company cannot be required to refund the premiums received." The case of *Metropolitan Life Ins. Co.* v. *McCormick* (1898), 19 Ind. App. 49, 49 N. E. 44, 65 Am. St. 392, is to the same effect, also *Northwestern, etc., Assn.* v. *Bodurtha* (1899), 23 Ind. App. 121, 53 N. E. 787, 77 Am. St. 414. In the latter case the application recited that the insured would not use intoxicating liquors thereafter. There was a breach of this condition, and because of the failure of the insurer to return the premium, it was contended that it could not maintain a defense of forfeiture. The court in answering this contention held that the company was not estopped from maintaining that the bond was forfeited, and said on page 130: ''We are not unmindful of the rule that forfeitures are not favored in law, and that the insurance company is asking the enforcement of a rule which is, ordinarily, a harsh one, while it retains the premiums for which the insurance was carried. But the courts do declare forfeitures when the insurer is clearly entitled thereto.''

In the case of *Medley* v. *German Alliance Ins. Co.* (1904), 55 W. Va. 342, 367, 47 S. E. 101, 2 Ann. Cas. 99, the court said: ''Nor is there any evidence of waiver on the part of the company, unless its failure, or offer, to return the premi-- um could so operate, but it cannot. As to this condition, violated after the policy became effective and operative, the return of the premium is not a prerequisite to an assertion of forfeiture. It does not render the policy void *ab initio*. It is not cause for rescission, in the execution of which the parties must be put in *statu quo*, nor is it a case of the ratification of an unauthorized contract, made by an agent, by retention of benefits thereunder. If it were not a breach of a promissory warranty, but a violation of a stipulation as to a fact relating to title or condition of the property, or to some other matter affecting the inception of the contract, retention of the premium might, on sound principle, amount to a waiver of the breach, for the ground of defense there would be the want of a valid contract to start with, and not the cessation of a contract, in the manner therein appointed by the parties for putting an end to it, after it has gone into effect.''

In *Georgia Home Ins. Co.* v. *Rosenfield* (1899), 95 Fed. 358, 37 C. C. A. 96, the court held that if the risk attached and the policy became void, subsequently, through the conduct of the insured, no part of the premium can be re-

NOVEMBER TERM, 1912. 487

Marion, etc., Bed Co. r. Empire State Surety Co.—52 Ind. App. 480.

covered. See, also, *National Surety Co.* v. *Schneiderman* (1911), 49 Ind. App. 139, 96 N. E. 955; *Robinson* v. *Aetna Fire Ins. Co.* (1902), 135 Ala. 650, 34 South. 18; *United States Fidelity, etc., Co.* v. *Ridgley* (1903), 70 Neb. 622, 97 N. W. 836; *Capital Fire Ins. Co.* v. *Shearwood* (1908), 87 Ark. 326, 112 S. W. 878; *Hendricks* v. *Commercial Ins. Co.* (1811), 8 Johns. (N. Y.) *1; *Everett-Ridley-Ragan Co.* v. *Traders Ins. Co.* (1904), 121 Ga. 228, 48 S. E. 918, 104 Am. St. 99; Joyce, Insurance (1897 ed.), §§1397, 1407; *Bartlett* v. *British America Assur. Co.* (1904), 35 Wash. 525, 77 Pac. 812.

We have carefully examined the cases cited by appellant on this point, and find they are easily distinguishable in their facts from the case at bar, hence the principle contended for has no application in this case.

Appellee requested that appellant proceed to prosecute its defaulting employe. It is now urged that this amounted to a waiver of the forfeiture. This involves an examination of the record to determine the facts in connection herewith. The application was signed and delivered October 23, 1906. The first bond was executed November 15, 1906, and remained in force one year. A renewal certificate was issued November 4, 1907, under which the bond continued in force until November 15, 1908. The loss occurred after November 15, 1907, and before June 26, 1908. Appellant notified appellee of the defalcation July 15, 1908. On December 7, 1908, appellee wrote appellant stating that it desired the arrest and prosecution of Besancon for the larceny and embezzlement charged.

There is no evidence to show that appellee, prior to the date requesting the prosecution of Besancon, had any knowledge that appellant had been guilty of the breaches herein charged, and the special findings of the court do not show that appellee had any knowledge on this question. It is therefore the opinion of this court that there was no waiver of appellee's rights shown by the evidence in this case, and it cannot be said to have been estopped, because no misleading act on its part is charged or proved. *Traders Ins. Co.* v. *Cassell* (1900), 24 Ind. App. 238, 56 N. E. 259; *Northern Assur. Co.* v. *Grand View Bldg. Assn.* (1902), 183 U. S. 308, 22 Sup. Ct. 133, 46 L. Ed. 213; *Sun Life Ins. Co.* v. *United States Fidelity, etc., Co.* (1902), 130 N. C. 129, 40 S. E. 975; *United States Fidelity, etc., Co.* v. *Ridgley, supra;* *Everett-Ridley-Ragan Co.* v. *Traders Ins. Co., supra; Georgia Home Ins. Co.* v. *Rosenfield, supra; Gibson Electric Co.* v. *Liverpool, etc., Ins. Co.* (1899), 159 N. Y. 418, 54 N. E. 23; Cooley, Briefs on Ins. 2467; Elliott, Insurance (1907 ed.) §177; *Bartlett* v. *British America Assur. Co., supra.*

The demurrer to the second paragraph of appellee's answer was properly overruled. The court did not err in its conclusions of law.

Judgment affirmed.

NOTE.—Reported in 100 N. E. 882. See, also, under (1) 19 Cyc. 521, 523. As to whether employer's lack of diligence operates to release a fidelity-bond surety, see 100 Am. St. 787.

FULLER *v.* FULLER.

[No. 7,832. Filed February 19, 1913.]

1. APPEAL.—*Weight of Evidence.—Statutes.*—Where the evidence on which the finding of the trial court rests consists in whole or in part of oral testimony, §698 Burns 1908, Acts 1903 p. 338, providing that in causes not triable by jury, the court on appeal shall weigh the evidence, etc., does not apply, even though the cause was not triable by jury. p. 488.

2. APPEAL.—*Review.—Evidence.—Findings.*—On appeal the court will not weigh conflicting evidence consisting of oral testimony, but will consider only that which is favorable to the finding in determining the sufficiency of the evidence to support same. p. 490.

3. APPEAL.—*Review.—Evidence.—Findings.*—Where there is some evidence to justify a finding of the trial court, such finding is sustained by sufficient evidence. p. 490.

4. PLEADING.—*Complaint.—General Denial.*—The general denial puts in issue every material allegation of the complaint. p. 490.

5. VENDOR AND PURCHASER.—*Vendor's Lien.—Issues.—Evidence.*— In an action to enforce a vendor's lien, the plaintiff, under the

issues formed by the general denial, must prove that the vendee
is still indebted for some part of the purchase price. p. 490.

6. EVIDENCE.—*Admissions.*—*Testimony in Another Action.*—Testimony of a party, given in another action, is admissible as an
admission. p. 491.

7. APPEAL.—*Review.*—*Objections to Evidence.*—*Availability.*—Objections to evidence, which do not state the grounds on which
they are based, are unavailing on appeal. p. 491.

From Fulton Circuit Court; *Enoch Myers*, Special
Judge.

Action by Major Fuller against Mary Fuller. From a
judgment for defendant, the plaintiff appeals. *Affirmed.*

Rowley & Mattice and *I. Conner*, for appellant.
Montgomery & Emmons and *Holman, Stephenson &
Bryant*, for appellee.

LAIRY, J.—As disclosed by the record in this case, appellee is the daughter-in-law of appellant, being the widow of
his deceased son, Arthur C. Fuller. In the lifetime of
Arthur C. Fuller, appellant conveyed to him a farm of
eighty acres in Fulton county, Indiana, which was devised
by Arthur C. Fuller to appellee. The action was brought
by appellant to enforce a vendor's lien against this real
estate in the hands of appellee, for $1,400 and interest as the
unpaid purchase price of the land.

Appellee filed three paragraphs of answer. The first was a
general denial, the second set up the statute of limitations,
and the third was an answer of former adjudication. There
was a general finding and judgment for appellee. The only
error assigned in this court is the action of the trial court
in overruling appellant's motion for a new trial.

The first question presented under this assignment relates
to the sufficiency of the evidence to sustain the finding.
As this is a case not triable by a jury, we are asked

1. by appellant to consider and weigh the evidence given
in the cause and to give judgment according to the
clear weight of such evidence, as provided by §8 of an act

concerning proceedings in civil cases, approved March 9, 1903 (Acts 1903 p. 338, §698 Burns 1908). It has frequently been decided by this court and the Supreme Court that this statute does not apply to cases where the evidence on which the finding of the trial court rests consists in whole or in part of oral testimony of witnesses delivered at the trial. *Karges Furniture Co.* v. *Amalgamated, etc., Union* (1905), 165 Ind. 421, 75 N. E. 877, 2 L. R. A. (N. S.) 788, 6 Ann. Cas. 829; *Hudelson* v. *Hudelson* (1905), 164 Ind. 694, 74 N. E. 504; *Maitland* v. *Reed* (1906), 37 Ind. App. 469, 77 N. E. 290.

As the evidence in this case consists largely of oral testimony, we are governed by the well-settled rule which forbids a court on appeal to weigh conflicting evidence.
2.   We can consider only the evidence favorable to the finding, and if there is some evidence tending to support it in every essential, it must be permitted to stand, regardless of evidence to the contrary. *Klein* v. *Ninde* (1910), 45 Ind. App. 672, 91 N. E. 611; *Schmidt* v. *Zahrndt* (1897), 148 Ind. 447, 47 N. E. 335.

There were three issues of fact formed by the pleadings and submitted to the court for trial. If there is
3.   some evidence to justify a finding in favor of defendant on any one of these issues, such finding is sustained by sufficient evidence. It seems to be conceded by both parties to this appeal that no evidence was introduced to sustain the second paragraph of answer setting up the statute of limitations. The finding cannot, therefore, rest on this issue. But it is contended by appellee that there is evidence to sustain the finding on both of the other issues tendered by the pleadings.

The general denial put in issue every material allegation of the complaint. Under the averments of
4.   the complaint, as one of the facts authorizing a recovery, it was necessary for plaintiff to prove by a
5.   preponderance of the evidence that Arthur C. Fuller

at the time of his death was indebted to plaintiff in some amount, as the purchase price of the lands conveyed to Arthur C. Fuller by plaintiff. On this issue the evidence is conflicting, and justifies a finding in favor of defendant.

In view of the conclusions we have reached, we need not consider or decide whether the evidence in the record is sufficient to sustain the answer of former adjudication.

Appellant also complains of the ruling of the trial court in permitting the witness C. K. Bitters, the official court reporter, to testify as to statements made by appellant 6. while testifying in another action to which he was a party. We think that the evidence was admissible as an admission of the plaintiff; but in any event, no available objection to its decision was interposed in the trial court.

An objection to evidence which does not state the 7. grounds on which such objection is based is unavailing. *Russell* v. *Branham* (1846), 8 Blackf. 277; *City of Delphi* v. *Lowery* (1881), 74 Ind. 520, 39 Am. Rep. 98. Objections were made to several questions, but in only one instance was the ground of objection stated, and in that instance the answer was not prejudicial to appellant.

Appellant has presented no error for which the judgment should be reversed.

Judgment affirmed.

NOTE.—Reported in 100 N. E. 869. See, also, under (1, 2, 3) 3 Cyc. 360; (4) 31 Cyc. 687; (5) 30 Cyc. 1868; (6) 16 Cyc. 970; (7) 38 Cyc. 1378. As to extent to which the vendor's lien is recognized in America, see 127 Am. St. 873. As to admissibility of testimony given by party in another action, see 91 Am. St. 198.

PENN AMERICAN PLATE GLASS COMPANY v. POLING,
ADMINISTRATRIX.

[No. 7,681.   Filed December 10, 1912.   Transfer denied February
19, 1913.]

1. APPEAL.—*Term-time Appeal.—Bond.—Approval of Surety.*—The
failure to name and approve sureties on an appeal bond during
the term at which the final judgment was rendered, is an omission of a necessary step to be taken in order to perfect a term-
time appeal, under §679 Burns 1908, §638 R. S. 1881, providing
that when an appeal is taken during the term at which the judgment is rendered, it shall operate as a stay of all further proceedings on the judgment, upon an appeal bond being filed by
appellant, with such penalty and surety as the court shall approve, and within such time as it shall direct, and requires a dismissal of the appeal unless it has been perfected as a vacation
appeal. p. 493.

2. APPEAL. — *Term-time Appeal. — Bond. — Approval of Surety. —
Waiver.*—The requirement that, to perfect a term-time appeal
under §679 Burns 1908, §638 R. S. 1881, the sureties on the bond
must be named and approved by the court during the term at
which the final judgment is rendered, is not waived by appellee's
failure to object to the order fixing the penalty without naming
the sureties. *Price v. Huddleston* (1905), 36 Ind. App. 450, and
Yanthis v. Kemp (1907), 40 Ind. App. 649, overruled. p. 494.

From Tipton Circuit Court; *Leroy B. Nash,* Judge.

Action by Anna B. Poling, administratrix of the estate of
Henry E. Poling, deceased, against the Penn American Plate
Glass Company.   From a judgment for plaintiff, the defendant appealed and on June 30, 1911, the appeal was dismissed
per curiam, and thereafter a petition for a rehearing was
granted.   *Appeal dismissed.*

John W. Lovett and *G. B. Slaymaker,* for appellant.
Kittinger & Diven, for appellee.

ADAMS, J.—Motion by appellee to dismiss this appeal, on
the ground that appellant has not complied with the statute authorizing a term-time appeal and has failed to perfect
a vacation appeal.

The record discloses that on January 15, 1910, and at the November, 1909, term of the Tipton Circuit Court, a judgment was rendered against appellant and in favor of appellee. Appellant prayed an appeal to this court, which was granted, and the penalty of the appeal bond was fixed at $3,000, with sureties to be approved by the court, and ninety days given within which to file said bond. On April 13, 1910, and at the February, 1910, term of said court, appellant filed its appeal bond in the sum of $3,000, with the National Surety Company as surety thereon, which bond on said last date was approved by the court.

There is no claim that this is a vacation appeal, but, on the contrary, it is insisted that the proceedings had in the court below were in substantial compliance with §679

1   Burns 1908, §638 R. S. 1881, the statute governing term-time appeals. This section is in part as follows: "When an appeal is taken during the term at which the judgment was rendered, it shall operate as a stay of all further proceedings on the judgment, upon an appeal-bond being filed by the appellant, with such penalty and surety as the court shall approve, and within such time as it shall direct." It clearly appears that all the provisions of this statute were complied with except one—the sureties were not named and approved during the term at which the judgment was rendered. Failure to name and approve sureties on a bond of this character during such term has been held to be an omission of one of the necessary steps to be taken in order to effect a term-time appeal.

In *Michigan Mut. Life Ins. Co.* v. *Frankel* (1898), 151 Ind. 534, 537, 50 N. E. 304, the court said: "The statute provides the steps which must be taken in order to effect a term-time appeal, and thereby relieve the appellant from giving the notice required by law in vacation appeals. The penalty of the appeal bond must be fixed and the surety named and approved by the court during the term at which the final judgment is rendered, and the bond, conditioned according to law, must be filed within the time directed by the court.''

In *Ashley* v. *Henderson* (1904), 32 Ind. App. 242, 69 N. E. 469, this court, quoting from Elliott, App. Proc. §246, said: ''To perfect a term-time appeal the following steps must be taken: '(1) An appeal must be prayed during the term at which the judgment was rendered, and it must be granted during that term. (2) The penalty of the bond must be fixed and the surety named during the term at which the judgment was rendered. (3) The bond must be filed during that term and approved by the court, or the court must during that term fix a time within which the bond shall be filed, and it must be filed and approved by the court within the time designated. (4) The transcript must be filed in the office of the Clerk of the Supreme Court within sixty days after the filing of the bond.' '' See, also, Buskirk's Practice 61; 2 Works' Practice §1088; Thornton & Ballard's Practice §639, note 1; Ewbank's Manual §175. Among other cases requiring the sureties to be named at the term in which the judgment is rendered are the following: *McKinney* v. *Hartman* (1896), 143 Ind. 224, 227, 42 N. E. 681; *Thompson* v. *Connecticut Mut. Life Ins. Co.* (1894), 139 Ind. 325, 328, 38 N. E. 796; *Holloran* v. *Midland R. Co.* (1891), 129 Ind. 274, 275, 28 N. E. 549; *Hartlep* v. *Cole* (1889), 120 Ind. 247, 251, 22 N. E. 130.

In *Price* v. *Huddleston* (1905), 36 Ind. App. 450, 75 N. E. 972, the penalty of the bond was fixed by the court, but the approval of the sureties left to the clerk. Appel-

2. lees were in court when the order was made, and having offered no objection to the same as made were held to have waived the statutory requirement.

This court in *Yanthis* v. *Kemp* (1907), 40 Ind. App. 649, 82 N. E. 926, held that to perfect a term-time appeal the same must be prayed and granted, the penalty of the bond must be fixed, and the sureties named by the court during the term at which the judgment was rendered. But the court also held that as appellees were present in court when the judgment was rendered and the appeal granted, and interposed no objection to the order fixing the penalty, but naming no sureties, and where the bond was approved by the court at a subsequent term within the time allowed, they waive the naming of the sureties within the term at which the judgment was rendered; following *Price* v. *Huddleston, supra.*

In *Daugherty* v. *Payne* (1911), 173 Ind. 603, 95 N. E. 233, the doctrine of waiver by failure to object, as announced in *Price* v. *Huddleston, supra,* was held to be erroneous. Continuing, the court said: "A party is not required to assist his adversary in perfecting his appeal, and waives nothing on that question by mere silence, unless he is required to speak." It is said in *Yanthis* v. *Kemp, supra,* and in several other cases, that an appeal bond is for the benefit of the appellee. This is true to the extent that the bond insures to appellee the collection of his judgment; but, manifestly, the bond is also for the benefit of the appellant, in that it enables him to appeal without notice, and protects his property from seizure and sale, upon execution pending a final determination on appeal.

The cases of *Price* v. *Huddleston, supra,* and *Yanthis* v. *Kemp, supra,* are not in harmony with the other cases herein cited, and especially with *Daugherty* v. *Payne, supra,* which is the latest expression of the Supreme Court on this subject.

It would be possible to distinguish the case at bar, since the record does not show that appellee was present in court at the time the appeal was prayed and granted, but this would only be postponing the day when the rule must be declared and the conflict in the cases cleared up. Where a question of practice only is involved, it is not so important how the question is decided, as that it should be decided.

It is due to *nisi prius* courts and to the profession generally that the rules of appellate procedure should not be left in doubt or confusion, and to that end, we find it necessary to overrule *Price* v. *Huddleston, supra*, and *Yanthis* v. *Kemp, supra*, in so far as these cases hold that an appellee, by offering no objection to the failure of the court to name the sureties on the appeal bond during the term at which the judgment was rendered, shall be deemed to have waived the naming of such sureties.

In this case there was a failure to perfect a term-time appeal, and the motion must be sustained.

Appeal dismissed.

NOTE.—Reported in 100 N. E. 83. See, also, under (1) 2 Cyc. 842.

NAVE *v*. POWELL.

[No. 7,175. Filed November 15, 1911. Rehearing denied March 15. 1912. Transfer denied February 19, 1913.]

1. APPEAL.—*Briefs.—Sufficiency—Statement of Substance of Pleadings.*—Where appellant makes a good faith effort to set out the substance of each of the pleadings and gives a reference to the page and lines of the record where the entire pleading is found. so that the court can know by reference to the brief alone the real question attempted to be raised as to the sufficiency of such pleadings, the brief is sufficient to require a consideration of such question. p. 498.

2. SALES.—*Rescission.—Common Law Rule.*—The right to return a warranted article and rescind the contract does not exist at common law, except in cases of fraud or where there is a special contract to that effect, and the purchaser is limited in his remedy to a recovery of damages for the breach of warranty. p. 504.

3. SALES.—*Warranty.—Return of Property and Rescission of Contract.—Exclusiveness of Remedy.*—Contracts of sale containing provisions for the return of the property and a rescission of the contract, or for the substitution of other property for that which fails to comply with the warranty, are not treated as exclusive in the remedy provided, unless such intention is clearly expressed by the language and terms of the warranty. p. 505.

4. SALES.—*Warranty.—Breach.—Limitation of Remedy.*—In a contract of sale, the parties may provide all and entire the remedies contemplated and agreed upon to be applied in the event of a breach of the warranty, in which case they are bound thereby and limited to the remedy, or remedies, so provided. p. 505.

5. SALES. -- *Warranty. — Construction Against Warrantor. —* The rule, that an express warranty should be construed most strongly against the party in whose interest the contract was prepared, applies only where there is ambiguity or uncertainty in ascertaining the intent of the parties. p. 506.

6. SALES.— *Warranty.— Construction.— Intention of Parties.—* In construing an express warranty, the object to be attained is the intention of the parties, and such intention must be ascertained, if possible, by the language used, and not by reading into it words that import an understanding wholly unintended and unexpressed when the contract was written, but suggested by some apparent hardship in the enforcement thereof. p. 506.

7. SALES.—*Warranty.—Construction.—Exclusiveness of Remedy.—* A contract of sale, in which the seller of a horse contracted that "in the event the above named stallion, in perfect health with proper usage * * * does not get with foal 50 per cent. * * * then on return * * * in good health and condition I agree to furnish another," etc., and which stated that should the stallion thereafter become injured or disabled through accident or disease, the warranty should be null and void and of no effect and all obligations of the seller considered fulfilled and ended, and that the contract contained all the agreements of warranty connected with such sale, construed in its entirety, limits the buyer's remedy for a breach of the warranty, and an action for damages for such breach will not lie. pp. 506, 508.

8. CONTRACTS.—*Construction.*—The true meaning of any contract is to be ascertained from a consideration of all its provisions in their entirety, and not from a literal or technical construction of any isolated or special clause. p. 508.

From Miami Circuit Court; *Joseph N. Tillett*, Judge.

Action by Alton P. Nave against Oliver M. Powell. From a judgment for defendant, the plaintiff appeals. *Reversed.*

Charles R. Milford, for appellant.
Cox & Andrews, for appellee.

HOTTEL, J.—Action on two promissory notes for $500 each, given by appellee to appellant in payment for a stallion.

Numerous pleadings, by way of special answers and special replies thereto and cross-complaints and special answers thereto, were filed in the case, the sufficiency of each of which was tested by demurrer by each party respectively, and exception to each ruling properly saved. The cause was tried by a jury and resulted in a verdict for appellee in the sum of $98. A motion for a new trial was filed by appellant and overruled by the court with exception to appellant. From a judgment on the verdict this appeal is prosecuted.

The rulings on the pleadings adverse to appellant and the ruling of the court on the motion for new trial are assigned as errors. These rulings on the pleadings are numerous, but inasmuch as it is conceded by appellant that each ruling presents practically the same question, viz., the effect to be given to a written warranty given to appellee at the time of said sale of said horse, and for the further reason hereinafter indicated, we deem it unnecessary to set out each particular pleading and ruling on the demurrer thereto.

Appellant in his original brief concedes that there are but two questions presented by this appeal. "(1) Whether or not the expense put on the horse for his care, etc., is a legitimate item of damage. (2) The construction to be put on said written warranty of the stallion." Appellee, however, insists that appellant, on account of failure to comply with the rules of this court in the preparation of his brief, is not entitled to have either question considered. Appellant in his reply brief in effect concedes that he has not in his original brief incorporated therein the motion for new trial, or any of its grounds, and that he has by such omission deprived himself of the consideration of any of the questions presented by such motion, but, on the other hand, earnestly insists that as to the question presented by the pleading he has not only made a good faith effort to, but has, in fact, set out enough of the substance of each respective pleading to present the real question involved in the ruling of the court on the demurrer thereto, and has thereby fully brought himself within the spirit of the rules of the court as interpreted by its decisions; that this is especially true with respect to the first paragraph of his reply to appellee's first paragraph of answer, and also with respect to the sixth paragraph of appellee's answer, and the third paragraph of his cross-complaint, the last two being practically the same.

Appellant sets out in his original brief a copy of the written warranty and a copy of a contract of insurance contained in each of said pleadings, and while the respective pleadings are not set out in detail, yet there is such a good-faith effort on the part of appellant to set out the substance of each, with a reference to the page and lines of the record where the entire pleading will be found, that we think that to deprive him of a consideration of the question of the construction to be placed on such warranty and insurance contract, in so far as said pleadings are controlled by the same, would be to require a strictness of compliance with said rules never contemplated or intended by their makers, and wholly unwarranted by the previous decisions of this court.

We think it clear that each member of this court can know by a reference to appellant's brief alone, and without reference to the record, the real question therein attempted to be raised as to the sufficiency of said respective pleadings, in so far as they are affected by said written instruments, which, we think, under the holdings, is sufficient to require a consideration of said question. *Houpt* v. *Dutton* (1908), 170 Ind. 69, 71, 83 N. E. 634; *Hay* v. *Bash* (1906), 37 Ind. App. 167, 169, 76 N. E. 744; *Roberts* v. *Fort Wayne Gas Co.* (1907), 40 Ind. App. 528, 532, 82 N. E. 1135.

A summary of the material allegations of the first paragraph of appellee's answer, to which appellant's said special reply is addressed, is as follows: That plaintiff had been and was on April 21, 1904, engaged in breeding horses, and in importing and selling horses for breeding purposes; that defendant through plaintiff's agent made application to buy such stallion of plaintiff, and that plaintiff through his agent

sold to defendant the horse Major McKinley; that plaintiff
was informed and knew the purpose for which said stallion
was wanted by defendant, and so knowing sold said stallion for breeding purposes, and said horse so sold constituted the only consideration given for each of said notes;
"that plaintiff thereby impliedly warranted said horse to be
fit and suitable for breeding purposes and a reasonably sure
foal getter." Said paragraph then alleges that defendant
"stood said horse for the breeding season of 1904," and advertised him by posting and newspaper notices; that the
horse was well patronized by the public; that sixty fruitful
mares were bred to him during said breeding season, none
of which were gotten in foal; "that said horse was utterly
barren and unprolific * * * and * * * incapable of
getting any mares with foal" at the time of said sale or
thereafter; "that relying on said statements, representations
and warranty so made by plaintiff, and believing the same to
be true," defendant "purchased said horse for breeding purposes;" that the fact that said horse was "barren and unprolific" could not be detected by a "person of ordinary
prudence and skill exercising ordinary care," and was for
this reason unknown to defendant, but such facts were well
known to plaintiff when he sold defendant the horse; that
said horse was wholly worthless, and that therefore the consideration for said horse had wholly failed. The theory of
this paragraph of answer is an implied warranty of the
breeding qualities of said stallion by plaintiff at the time of
the sale, and a breach thereof.

By way of avoidance of the matters alleged in said answer.
said first paragraph of reply avers the sale of said stallion
for $1,000, for which the notes in suit are alleged to have
been given, and avers further the execution and delivery to
defendant, as part of said contract of sale of said stallion,
"a certain writing" which is set out in said reply and is
as follows:

"Walnut Grove Stock Farm, A. P. Nave, Proprietor, Breeder of High Class Percheron Horses.

Attica, Indiana, April 21, 1904.

Know all men by these Presents, That I A. P. Nave, of Attica, Fountain County, Indiana, have this day sold to O. M. Powell of Wagoner of County, State of Indiana the Percheron Stallion Major McKinley No. 19858. For extended pedigree See Certificate of Registry. For the consideration of one thousand dollars ($1000.00) the receipt whereof is hereby acknowledged. In the event that the above named stallion, in perfect health, with proper usage, and the mares to him regularly returned and tried or bred on one full service season's trial does not get with foal 50 per cent, of the producing mares regularly tried and bred to him, then on return of the said staliion to me at Attica, Fountain County, Indiana, during the first week in the month of April next following the full service season first concluded after the date thereof, in good health and condition I agree to furnish the above named purchaser without further charge, another imported or pure bred stallion of equal quality in exchange; but it is expressly provided as a condition of this warranty, that the tally sheet accompanying and delivered with this bill of sale shall be accurately filled out, with date of each service and trial to enable identification of all mares bred, and after being so filled out shall be returned to me at Attica, Fountain County Indiana by registered letter, not later than July 15th, 1905. It is hereby stipulated that a stallion's full service season shall be considered as the period commencing the first day of May and ending the first day of July.

In the event the conditions of the above agreement are not faithfully performed, or should the above named stallion hereafter become injured or disabled through accident or disease, or should any change or alteration be made in this Bill of Sale, not shown by the press copy of same preserved by me, this warranty shall be null and void and of no effect and all obligations incurred by me herein shall be considered fulfilled and ended.

This bill of sale contains all the agreements of warranty or guaranty made by me in the sale of the above mentioned stallion, and it is expressly provided that I shall not be liable for any claim that may hereafter be

made alleging any verbal agreement of myself or agent
in the sale of said horse.

In witness whereof I have hereto set my hand and
seal this the twenty-first day of April in the year of
our Lord Nineteen Hundred Four.

A. P. Nave [Seal]."

The reply then alleges that as a part of the same transaction "plaintiff executed and delivered to defendant a
certain written instrument in the following words."

"Walnut Grove Stock Farm, A. P. Nave, Proprietor,
Breeder and Importer of Percheron Horses of high class
and purest lineage.

Attica, Indiana, April 21, 1904.

This indenture witnesseth:

That whereas O. M. Powell has purchased of the un-
dersigned Alton P. Nave, of Attica, Indiana, the Percheron Stallion, named Major McKinley, numbered
19858, the said Nave hereby agrees with said Powell
that if the stallion should die on or before April 21,
1905, from natural causes, said death not to be due from
lack of proper care, feed or attention, nor negligence of
any kind on the part of said Powell, then on proper
proof of the death of said animal, said Powell will be
given a credit of ($500.00) on his promissory note
drawn in favor of said Nave.

A. P. Nave."

This paragraph of reply then alleges that "said warranty
and bill of sale and said bond" as herein set out "were accepted by the defendant as controlling in said transaction
at the time of said sale," and were retained by him and
"accepted * * * as the only warranty of any kind or
character under which said animal was bought and sold,
either express or implied, and that there was no verbal
agreement subsequent thereto that in anyway affected said
warranty" or its terms as set out in said instrument; that defendant at no time demanded another stallion; that plaintiff was at all times ready and in a situation to comply with
said warranty by furnishing another stallion on compliance
by defendant with the terms of said warranty; that said
stallion was delivered to defendant in April, 1904, and at

all times thereafter until his death on November 26, 1904, remained in the care, custody and control of defendant.

The sixth paragraph of defendant's answer alleges "that on the 21st day of April, 1904, and as part of the sale and delivery by plaintiff to this defendant of a percheron stallion, Major McKinley, * * * said plaintiff executed to said defendant his written warranty and obligation or bond in these words and figures to wit." Then follows said contracts of warranty and insurance above set out. This answer then alleges further, that by said writing plaintiff warranted to defendant "all and singular the qualities and usefulness of said stallion as in said warranty and bond set out;" that he (defendant) received and took said horse into his possession, and took him to his home in Fulton county, and "performed all and singularly the obligations of said warranty which devolved * * * upon him" between said date of purchase and November 26, 1904, at which last date said horse died; that defendant immediately notified plaintiff by telegram of the death of said horse, and inquired what to do, and received no answer; that said horse was not injured or disabled by accident or disease, and no change or alteration was made in said bill of sale; that defendant gave said horse proper and sufficient food three times a day (describing the food), and gave him daily exercise (describing it); that defendant relied on said warranty, believed it to be true, advertised said horse for breeding purposes, and had bills and circulars printed, posted and distributed, and publications in newspapers, all at a cost of $300; that defendant engaged help, who together with himself took care of and fed said horse, and "exhibited him and stood him throughout the period of time aforesaid, to defendant's costs in the sum of $500; * * * that said horse was wholly barren and unprolific, and of no value for breeding purposes;" that he was bred to sixty-nine "fruitful mares," none of which "became with foal;" that by reason of the breach of said warranty defendant was damaged in the sum of $800. "Wherefore defendant files his counterclaim, and prays damages in the sum of $800, with costs."

It will be observed that this paragraph, while denominated an answer, is in fact a counterclaim, and seeks affirmative relief, but the designation or name of the pleading is unimportant for the purposes of the question here involved.

The third paragraph of cross-complaint alleges substantially the same facts above set out as contained in said sixth paragraph of answer, and alleges that if the horse "had been as warranted he would have been of the value of $1,000; but in the condition in which he actually was he was of no value; that by the breach of the warranty" defendant has been damaged in the sum of $1,000, and demands judgment in said sum.

It will be seen from the above summary of said pleadings, that the question presented by the rulings on the demurrers thereto turns on the construction to be placed on said contract of warranty. Appellant insists that the warranty is express, and provides all its terms and conditions, and fixes and limits the remedy of appellee for its violation; that under such warranty appellee's only remedy was the return of the horse in good health and condition, with the privilege of getting another. Appellee, on the other hand, insists that the remedy provided in said warranty is not exclusive, but that he has in addition to that provided in the contract his remedy at law for damages for the breach of the warranty.

At common law the remedy allowing the return of the warranted article and rescission of the contract does not exist except in cases of fraud or by special contract 2. to that effect, and the purchaser is limited in his remedy to a recovery of damages for the breach of the warranty. Mechem, Sales §1805; *Lynch* v. *Curfman* (1896), 65 Minn. 170, 68 N. W. 5; *Close* v. *Crossland* (1891), 47 Minn. 500, 50 N. W. 694; *Hoadley* v. *House* (1859), 32

Vt. 179, 76 Am. Dec. 167; *Hoover* v. *Sidener* (1884), 98 Ind. 290; *Marsh* v. *Low* (1876), 55 Ind. 271.

Contracts, therefore, which contain a provision for the return of the property and a rescission of the contract, or

3. for the substitution of other property for that which fails to comply with the warranty, are not treated as exclusive in the remedy provided, unless such intention is clearly expressed by the language and terms of the warranty. 30 Am. and Eng. Ency. Law (2d ed.) 197; Mechem, Sales §1807; *Elwood* v. *McDill* (1898), 105 Iowa 437, 442, 75 N. W. 340; *Jas. H. Love & Co.* v. *Ross, Crawford & Graham* (1893), 89 Iowa 400, 402, 56 N. W. 528; *Fitzpatrick* v. *D. M. Osborne & Co.* (1892), 50 Minn. 261, 52 N. W. 861; *Douglass Axe Mfg. Co.* v. *Gardner* (1852), 10 Cush. (Mass.) 88.

Giving this rule its broadest application, we are unable to place on this contract the construction and meaning contended for by appellee, and evidently placed on it by the

4. lower court. It must not be forgotten that in contracts of warranty, the same as in all other contracts, the contracting parties have a perfect right to put into such contract all its terms and conditions, and provide all and entire the remedies contemplated and agreed on by the parties. On this subject the Supreme Court of this State said in the case of *Brown* v. *Russell & Co.* (1886), 105 Ind. 46, 52, 4 N. E. 428: "Of course, it was competent for the parties to contract with each other in relation to the extent, terms and conditions of the warranty, and to impose such limitations and restrictions thereon as they might mutually agree upon." The same rule is expressed in the case of *Bomberger, Wright & Co.* v. *Griener* (1865), 18 Iowa 477, 480. When the parties do agree on such remedies, and their contract by its terms expresses a clear intent and purpose in that respect, they are bound thereby and limited to the remedies or remedy so provided. *F. C. Austin Mfg. Co.*

v. *Clendenning* (1899), 21 Ind. App. 459, 465, 52 N. E. 708;
Nichols-Shepard Co. v. *Rhoadman* (1905), 112 Mo. App.
299, 87 S. W. 62; *Main* v. *Griffin* (1906), 141 N. C. 43, 53
S. E. 727; *Avery Planter Co.* v. *Peck* (1902), 86 Minn. 40,
89 N. W. 1123.

But it is insisted by appellee that there is another rule
which should be observed in construing this contract, viz.,
 That it should be construed most strongly against the
5. party by whom or in whose interest it was prepared.
 It is only where there is ambiguity or uncertainty
that this rule of construction is called into operation. The
rules for the interpretation of express warranties do not essentially differ from those applied to other contracts.
6. In construing such contracts the object to be attained
 is the intent of the parties, but this intent must be ascertained if possible by the language which the parties have
themselves adopted and used in such contract, and not by
reading into it words that import an intent and understanding wholly unintended and unexpressed when the contract
was written, but suggested by some apparent hardship in
the enforcement thereof. *Brown* v. *Russell & Co., supra;
Conant* v. *National State Bank* (1889), 121 Ind. 323, 324-
327, 22 N. E. 250; *Shirk* v. *Mitchell* (1894), 137 Ind. 185,
190, 36 N. E. 850; *Reeves & Co.* v. *Byers* (1900), 155 Ind.
535, 58 N. E. 713; *Sullivan Mach. Co.* v. *Breeden* (1907), 40
Ind. App. 631, 82 N. E. 107.

It will be observed that there is in fact no absolute unconditional warranty provided by the terms of this contract.
 In other words, appellant did not expressly warrant
7. the stallion Major McKinley *to be a good breeder or
 foal getter, etc.,* but the warranty is a conditional or
qualified and a limited warranty only, viz., ''In the event
that the above named stallion, in perfect health, with proper
usage * * * does not get with foal 50 per cent, * * *
then on return * * * in good health and condition I
agree to furnish * * * another,'' etc.

On the interpretation of this language the case of *Davis
v. Iverson* (1894), 5 S. Dak. 295, 58 N. W. 796, is in point.
The warranty in that case was in the words following:
" 'Colman, D. T., June 25, 1887. Know all men by these
presents, that we have this day sold to the Colman Horse
Company one gray Norman stallion, "Count Rotrow, 487,"
and he is free from all incumbrance, and their title to said
horse is good, and the above named horse warranted by his
importer, George E. Case of St. Peter, Minn., to be, with
proper care and handling, an average foal getter; and should
the above-named horse prove to be barren, a horse of equal
size and value to be put in his place. Whippel, Farley &
Co.' " The court in construing the language of this warranty, at page 297 of their opinion, said: "Reading this
paper with the purpose of getting its meaning from its
language, we should say without hesitation that the sellers
for themselves warranted that the horse was free from incumbrance, and their title was good, and that the horse
'was warranted by his importer, George E. Case, of St.
Peter, Minnesota, to be, with proper care and handling, an
average foal getter.' To make the warranty mean anything
different from this would require us to essentially change its
terms, which, of course, we can not do. * * * By the
terms of the papers the sellers did not warrant the horse to
be an average foal getter. They only said that the horse
was so warranted by its importer. But they did undertake
for themselves that if the horse should prove barren, then
that another of equal size and value should be put in its
place." Counsel for appellee say that in this case the holding turns on the fact that the representation in the warranty was that the importer and not the seller warranted the
horse to be an average foal getter. But the contract in that
case contains all that the contract in the case at bar contains.
It has a very similar provision for the return of the horse
in case of his failure to prove a good foal getter. The fact
that the contract contains a provision that the importers war-

ranted his foal getting qualities certainly would not make the contract any weaker in this respect than the one at bar, which wholly omits an absolute warranty by either seller or importer.

While we recognize the force of the reasons given for the holding in the case of *Davis* v. *Iverson, supra,* we might hesitate to follow it to the extent of holding that damages for a breach of the warranty could be defeated in this case because of the omission of such words of general warranty alone, unsupported by any other language of the contract evidencing such intention of the parties thereto, but taken in connection with the other provisions of this contract, hereinafter referred to, we think such omission significant.

The true meaning of any contract is to be ascertained from a consideration of all its provisions in their entirety, and not from a literal or technical construction of any isolated or special clause of the same. *Wilson* v. *Cooper* (1899), 95 Fed. 625, 628; *Indiana, etc., Oil Co.* v. *Grainger* (1904), 33 Ind. App. 559, 562, 70 N. E. 395; *Beard* v. *Lofton* (1885), 102 Ind. 408, 411, 2 N. E. 129.

There is another clause of this contract which we think must have a material influence in arriving at a correct interpretation of the same. Its provisions are as follows: "should the above named stallion hereafter become injured or disabled through accident or disease, * * * *this warranty shall be null and void and of no effect and all obligations incurred by me herein shall be considered fulfilled and ended.*" (Our italics.)

Another provision is as follows: "This bill of sale contains all the agreements of warranty or guaranty made by me in the sale of the above mentioned stallion."

This stallion was not merely "injured or disabled by disease," but was killed thereby. It will be observed that in case such injury or disability results in death, that it is provided by the above clause not merely that the provision as to the

return of the stallion and his replacement by another shall
be avoided, but the provision is that *"this warranty* shall be
null and void and of no effect, and all *obligations incurred
by me herein shall be considered fulfilled and ended."* (Our
italics.)   This language to us seems as definite and certain
as it could well have been made.   Indeed, we are forced to
the conclusion that appellee was not altogether ignorant of
or in doubt as to its meaning when he accepted the warranty, and for this reason he obtained a contract whereby
he forced on appellant the assumption of one-half the risk
in case such injury or disability should in fact result in the
death of such stallion.   Considering the several provisions
of this contract of warranty together, and construing the
contract in its entirety, and in connection with the contract
of insurance executed at the same time, we are forced to
the conclusion that in the matter of the provision for the
remedy for the breach of the warranty the contract is exclusive, and that appellee is restricted to the remedies
therein contained, and that the court below therefore erred
in overruling appellant's demurrers to the sixth paragraph
of answer and the third paragraph of cross-complaint, respectively, and also in sustaining appellee's demurrer to appellant's special reply to the first paragraph of answer.

Inasmuch as this case must be reversed for these errors,
we have not examined the other paragraphs of the pleadings
with a view of determining their sufficiency, and express no
opinion thereon, further than to say that the construction
placed on the written warranty and contract of insurance
is the law of the case applicable to all the pleadings the
same as to those expressly considered and ruled on.

The judgment is therefore reversed, with instructions to
the court below to sustain the demurrer to appellee's sixth
paragraph of answer and third paragraph of cross-
complaint, and to overrule the demurrer to appellant's

special reply to appellee's first paragraph of answer, and for further proceedings not inconsistent with this opinion.

NOTE.—Reported in 98 N. E. 395. See, also, under (2) 35 Cyc. 434; (3, 4) 35 Cyc. 437; (5) 35 Cyc. 412; (8) 9 Cyc. 579. As to rescission of sale for fraud in obtaining credit, see 18 Am. St. 302. As to what defects constitute breaches of warranty of soundness, see 53 Am. Dec. 173.

CITY OF BLOOMINGTON *v.* CHICAGO, INDIANAPOLIS AND LOUISVILLE RAILWAY COMPANY.

[No. 7,580.   Filed April 19, 1912.   Rehearing denied June 25, 1912. Transfer denied February 19, 1913.]

1. MUNICIPAL CORPORATIONS.—*Streets and Public Ways.—Defects.* —*Liability.*—Cities have complete jurisdiction over all streets and public ways within their respective limits, under §§8655. 8960-8966 Burns 1908, Acts 1905 p. 219, §§53, 266-271, and consequently are liable for failure to keep such public highways in reasonably safe condition for travel. p. 515.

2. MUNICIPAL CORPORATIONS. — *Defective Streets. — Liability of Abutting Owners.*—A property owner, who, by some affirmative wrongful act, causes the defective condition of a street, is liable to the city or town for any amount which it may be required to pay as damages on account of such defect. p. 515.

3. MUNICIPAL CORPORATIONS.—*Defective Streets.—Railroad Crossings.—Liability of Railroad Company.—Statutes.*—Under §5250 *et. seq.* Burns 1908, Acts 1895 p. 233, requiring railroad companies to properly grade and plank their roads at all street crossings, so as to afford security for life and property at such crossings, providing for the collection of penalties for failure so to do, and also providing that the municipality may, on their failure so to do, have the work done at the expense of such railroads, it is the primary duty of a railroad company so to construct and maintain all street crossings as to make them reasonably safe for travel, and a railroad company is primarily liable for injuries resulting from its failure to perform such duty. p. 515.

4. MUNICIPAL CORPORATIONS.—*Defective Streets.—Railroad Crossings.—Liability.*—One, who is injured by a defective street caused by the failure of a railroad company to properly repair such street at the intersection of its tracks therewith, may bring an action against the railroad company, or he may bring it against the city, since, as between the city and the public, the city stands as a guarantor that the company will not be negligent, and, it is

NOVEMBER TERM, 1912. 511

City of Bloomington r. Chicago, etc., R. Co.—52 Ind. App. 510.

therefore primarily liable for such negligence; and where the city has been obliged to pay, the company is primarily liable to it for such damages, together with the costs and expenses fairly incurred. pp. 517, 518.

5. RAILROADS.—*Street Crossings.—Approaches.—Duty to Maintain.* —The approaches of a street to a railroad crossing constitute a part of such crossing, and the company is bound to maintain such portion of the street as well as that which crosses the tracks. p. 518.

6. MUNICIPAL CORPORATIONS.—*Action for Personal Injuries.—Defective Railroad Crossing.—Judgment.—Res Judicata.—Matters Directly in Issue.*—In an action by a pedestrian against a city for injuries caused by the defective condition of a railroad street crossing, where the railroad company, after notice, failed to appear and defend, the only matters adjudicated, so far as the right of the railroad company is concerned, were such as were essential to support the verdict, namely, the existence of the defect, the liability of the city to plaintiff, and the amount of damages which the city was required to pay; so that in an action by the city against the railroad company to recover the amount of the judgment rendered against it, the company was not prevented from showing that it was under no duty to repair the defect, and that the injury was not caused by any negligence on its part. p. 519.

7. MUNICIPAL CORPORATIONS.—*Streets.—Duty to Light.—Liability for Failure.*—The lighting of streets by a muncipality is merely the exercise of a governmental function, and negligence cannot be imputed for a failure to exercise such power. p. 520.

From Lawrence Circuit Court; *James B. Wilson,* Judge.

Action by the City of Bloomington against the Chicago, Indianapolis and Louisville Railway Company. From a judgment for defendant, the plaintiff appeals. *Reversed.*

Duncan & Batman, Michael T. Poling and *Miers & Corr,* for appellant.

E. C. Field, Brooks & Brooks and *H. R. Kurrie,* for appellee.

IBACH, P. J.—Appellant brought this action to recover from appellee the amount of a judgment which it had been required to pay to Minnie Woodworth, a pedestrian, who had been injured by falling through a defective sidewalk which appellant, with knowledge, had allowed to remain in one of its streets, and in whose case appellee had been notified to appear and assume the defense. The complaint consists of one paragraph, and avers substantially the same facts as are contained in the special finding made by the trial court. It was answered by a general denial. The cause was submitted to the court, who at the request of both parties, made a special finding of facts and stated his conclusion of law thereon against appellant. The only error assigned is in the court's conclusion of law.

The special finding of facts, so far as essential to the determination of the question before us, is as follows: Appellant was a city duly organized under the laws of Indiana. Appellee was a railroad corporation also duly organized under the laws of Indiana, and for a number of years operated a line of railroad which passed through Monroe county and the city of Bloomington, and transported passengers and freight over its line of road for hire. Said road in passing through the city of Bloomington runs practically north and south, crossing certain streets of said city at right angles, until it arrives at Sixth street, a street running east and west, where it turns toward the northwest, crossing Seventh street, which runs parallel with and lies immediately north of Sixth street. Said streets are crossed at grade. Before the construction of the grade of the railroad in 1853 there was a stream of water running practically south across Seventh street, and which street crossed through the bed of the stream without any superstructure. In constructing the grade for said railroad the course of said stream was deflected from the west side of said grade, beginning at the outer edge of the walk in the north line, and a culvert was constructed in a southeasterly direction to the south line of said Seventh street, said culvert being about six feet deep. In making the grade, the railroad company graded the whole width of the street on both the east and west sides thereof back from 150 to 250 feet over said culvert, and to the depth of 1 or 2 feet, over which and by means of said grade the public passed over said stream, railroad track and culvert in using the street. The south end of said culvert was flush with the south line of the pavement at the south side of Seventh street, and was 20 feet east of the east rail of the track. Said culvert entered an open drain walled on the west side by a stone wall, built by appellee, and extended south and 10 or 15 feet east of said east rail of said railroad about 132 feet. Prior to February 9, 1905, appellant had built a brick sidewalk on the east side of Seventh street and adjacent to the south line thereof to within about 50 feet of the east side of the railroad track, and appellee had built a board walk from the end of said brick walk over and across said culvert and grade to the east rail of the track. It put a wooden banister, about 35 feet long, on the south side of such walk, which banister extended to within 10 feet of said east rail. This walk, so constructed, had been used for a number of years by the traveling public. On the evening of February 9, 1905, Minnie Woodworth, while passing over such wooden portion of the walk, and between appellee's east rail and the culvert, got her foot in a hole in such board sidewalk, was thrown, and permanently injured. On March 23, 1905, she brought suit against appellant. Then follows a copy of her said complaint, as well as copies of the other pleadings filed in such court. The result of the trial was the awarding to said plaintiff of damages in the sum of $5,000. Appellee failed to appear, and appellant was required to pay and did pay on December 3, 1907, on account of such judgment, interest and expense of the court, the sum of $5,966.70. The conclusion of law is: ''The law is with the defendant and the plaintiff is not entitled to recover in any sum.''

It is contended by appellant that both by the principles of the common law and by statute a duty is imposed on appellee, both to construct and to maintain all highway crossings and the approaches thereto in a reasonably safe condition for the traveling public, and that it is liable to respond in damages to one who has sustained injuries on account of neglect to perform any of such duties; and since the railroad company is primarily liable for such damages, any judgment which the city has been required to pay on account of said injury, together with costs, and all reasonable expenses of making the defense, can be recovered back from such railroad company, and since notice was served on it to appear and defend the original action, it is bound by the matters litigated in that cause.

In the original complaint defendant city was charged with negligence in failing sufficiently to light the defective portion of the walk in suit. As to this charge appellant contends that lighting a street of a city is a governmental function, and that since a city cannot be held liable for a failure to perform a governmental function, the conclusion announced by the court could not have been based on that fact as constituting an act of negligence.

In answer to these contentions appellee says that a property owner is not liable to return to the city the amount of the judgment which it was required to pay out on account of the defective walk, where it appears that the property owner has done nothing more than fail to make improvements or repairs. Also, that it was not the effect of legislative enactment on this subject to place on railroad companies the primary duty of maintaining the streets and alleys over which it crosses. Furthermore, because in the original suit brought by Minnie Woodworth the city was charged with an independent act of negligence in failing to maintain a sufficient light near the dangerous walk, so that its dangerous condition might be discovered, and as it was no part of the duty of the railroad company to maintain lights, it must be concluded that the judgment of the court was based on the whole complaint which included the absence of the light. Cities of this State have, under existing statutes, complete jurisdiction over all streets and public

ways within their respective limits (§§8655, 8960-
8966 Burns 1908, Acts 1905 p. 219, §§53, 266-271);

1. consequently they are held liable on the failure of
their officers to perform the duty of keeping such public
highways in a reasonably safe condition for travel. *Wickwire* v. *Town of Angola* (1892), 4 Ind. App. 253-56, 30 N.
E. 917; *McNaughton* v. *City of Elkhart* (1882), 85 Ind. 384,
388.

The property owner, however, who is guilty of some
affirmative wrongful act in causing the defective condition
of the street, is liable to the city or town for any

2. amount which it may have been required to pay to
any one as damages on account of the defective condition which he produced. This doctrine is so well established that we consider citation of authorities unnecessary.

As to crossings over railroads, the statute provides: "That
it shall be the duty of each railroad company whose road or
tracks cross, or shall hereafter cross, any street

3. * * * in any incorporated town or city * * *,
which said street * * * has been or shall hereafter be, by addition, plat or otherwise, dedicated to the
public use, to properly grade and plank its said road or
tracks at its intersection with and crossing of said street
* * * in accordance with the grade of said street, in
such manner as to afford security for life and property at
said intersection and crossing." §5250 Burns 1908, Acts
1895 p. 233.

The following sections of the statute provide for the collection of a penalty for failure to comply with the provisions of this section, and also provide that the municipality
may, on failure of the railroad so to do, have the work done
at the expense of such railroad company.

By the enactment of §§5250-5254 Burns 1908, Acts 1895 p.
233, §§1-5, it was the evident intention of the legislature to
place the primary duty on all railroad companies so to construct and maintain all street crossings as to make them rea-

sonably safe for travel. For this reason the numerous authorities cited by appellee, holding that abutting lot owners are liable for damages where injury occurs to a person on account of the owner not making repairs in the street, are not in point, for in those cases there is no duty resting on such abutting lot owners to maintain the street on which the property abuts in a reasonably safe condition for travel, while in the case at bar appellee is charged with the violation of an express legal duty, a fundamental obligation imposed by law to maintain the crossings over its right of way in a safe condition for travel.

In the case of *Wabash R. Co.* v. *De Hart* (1903), 32 Ind. App. 62, 67, 65 N. E. 192, the court said: "If it [railroad company] does not restore the highway which it crosses in such a manner as to comply substantially with the statutory requirement, the dangerous condition thus resulting will constitute a public nuisance, or there is negligence *per se.*" After further discussing the duties of the railroad to repair its crossings, the court continues: "The duty devolved upon it, the nonperformance of which constitutes actionable negligence, is an obligation to exercise carefulness, measured not only by the danger, but also by the privilege it enjoys of encumbering a public highway for its private benefit; and the manner in which the duty is to be performed is expressly enjoined and described by statute."

In the case of *Evansville, etc., R. Co.* v. *State* (1898), 149 Ind. 276, 278, which was a suit by appellee to compel appellant by writ of mandamus to construct a suitable and safe crossing over its tracks at a street crossing, the court said: "This duty is imposed by statute in this State and also exists independent of any statute."

In the case of *City of Elkhart* v. *Wickwire* (1882), 87 Ind. 77, in which the city had sued Wickwire to recover over what it had been required to pay, the law is thus declared: "It results from these general principles that if the facts stated in the special verdict can be regarded as showing that the appellee made the sidewalk unsafe, or was charged with a duty respecting it and negligently omitted to perform that duty, the judgment should have been for the appellant."

In the later case of *City of Anderson* v. *Fleming* (1903), 160 Ind. 597, 602, 66 L. R. A. 119, Judge Monks, speaking for the Supreme Court, said: "The established rule in this State is that when a street of a municipal corporation is rendered unsafe by the wrongful act or negligence of a third person, and the corporation is compelled to pay for injuries caused by such unsafe streets, it has a right of action over against the person who rendered the same unsafe, for the amount so paid. * * * In such cases, as between the municipal corporation and the one who created the dangerous condition which occasioned the injury, the latter is primarily liable, and said corporation, having been compelled to pay such damages to the one injured, becomes subrogated to the remedy of the injured party."

In the case at bar the injured party might have brought her suit against the railroad company, whose neglect to repair the street caused the injury, or against the city.

4.   Both were liable. As between the city and the public, the city occupies the position of a guarantor for the company that it will not be negligent, and the city is primarily liable to a traveler on its streets who becomes injured on account of a defect therein, but as between the city and the one whose neglect to repair the street caused the injury, the latter is primarily liable to indemnify the city for the damages it has been compelled to pay, together with the costs and expenses fairly incurred. These propositions are well supported by the following authorities: Tiedeman, Mun. Corp. §306; 2 Dillon, Mun. Corp. (2d ed.) §§795, 796; *City of Portland* v. *Atlantic, etc., R. Co.,* (1877), 66 Me. 485; *Catterlin* v. *City of Frankfort* (1881), 79 Ind. 547, 41 Am. Rep. 627; *Inhabitants of Lowell* v. *Boston, etc., R. Corp.* (1839), 23 Pick. (Mass.) 24; *Cleveland, etc., R. Co.* v. *Miller*

518   APPELLATE COURT OF INDIANA,

City of Bloomington v. Chicago, etc., R. Co.—52 Ind. App. 510.

(1905), 165 Ind. 381, 74 N. E. 509; *Cincinnati, etc., R. Co.* v. *City of Connersville* (1908), 170 Ind. 316, 83 N. E. 503; *Pennsylvania Co.* v. *Frund* (1892), 4 Ind. App. 469, 30 N. E. 1116; *Western, etc., Railroad* v. *City of Atlanta* (1885), 74 Ga. 774.

In the last case the court said: "If railroad companies are required by law, as well as by public policy, to keep in good order, at their own expense, public roads and private ways, where the same cross the right-of-way of the various railroads of this State, much stronger should be the reason for keeping in proper order and repair street crossings in cities and towns, which are likely to be thronged with persons."

In 3 Elliott, Railroads §1092, the author, in discussing the duties devolving on railroads to construct and maintain highway crossings, says: "This is not performed by merely restoring the street to the condition in which it was at the time the track was laid, for it is a continuing duty to keep such portion of the street in repair. The city may also be liable in such a case if it negligently suffers the defect or obstruction to remain in the street. But it may have its remedy over against the company." The approaches to a railroad crossing constitute a part of such crossing,

5. and the duty rests on the railroad company to maintain this portion as well as that part which crosses the railroad tracks. *Cincinnati, etc., R. Co.* v. *Claire* (1893), 6 Ind. App. 390, 33 N. E. 918.

The trial court finds that the walk in question was constructed by appellee on the approach or fill made at the time the road was built across the street, and it

4. further finds that the plaintiff in the original suit was injured on such walk by having her foot caught "in a hole and defect in said board walk so erected, and maintained on said culvert and grade, by said defendant [railroad company] by which she was violently thrown down and permanently injured, which was caused by the danger-

NOVEMBER TERM, 1912. 519

City of Bloomington r. Chicago, etc., R. Co.—52 Ind. App. 510.

ous and defective condition of said board walk, so erected and maintained as aforesaid."

Under the law it was the duty of appellee to keep the sidewalk at the point where Minnie Woodworth was injured in a reasonably safe condition for travel, and for a failure to perform this duty it became negligent, and became liable to respond to her in damages for the injury she sustained. Appellant having been required to pay such damages is entitled to recover from appellee the amount so paid, and the trial court should have stated its conclusion of law in favor of appellant on the facts found.

The matters adjudicated in the case of Minnie Woodworth against appellant, so far as the rights of the parties to the present suit are concerned, are such as were essential 6. and necessary to support the verdict returned, and these were (1) the existence of the defect in the street, (2) the liability of the city to the plaintiff, and (3) the amount of the damages which the city was compelled to pay. *Catterlin* v. *City of Frankfort, supra; Chicago City* v. *Robbins* (1862), 2 Black (U. S.) 418, 17 L. Ed. 298. Those matters which were not necessary to the disposal of the real question in issue in that suit were not involved in it, and were therefore not adjudicated thereby. 2 Black, Judgments §615. Consequently the facts on which the suit at bar is predicated were not adjudicated between the parties hereto by the original suit against the city, and the city is not prevented from bringing this suit against the railroad company to recover the money it was compelled to pay on account of such suit, and neither was the railroad company when sued by the city prevented from showing that no duty devolved on it to keep the walk in repair, and that the accident did not happen by reason of any act of negligence on its part. All these matters were left open for determination in the suit at bar.

In the original suit one of the averments of the complaint was that the city failed to maintain sufficient lights near the

defective sidewalk, so that its dangerous condition
7. could have been discovered. This was an allegation
of failure to light its streets sufficiently, rather than
a charge of negligently failing to guard the particular defective portion of the walk, by placing a danger light at
that point.   The lighting of streets by a municipality is
merely the exercise of a governmental function and for a
failure to exercise such a power, negligence cannot be imputed against any city or town.

In the case of *City of Vincennes* v. *Thuis* (1902), 28 Ind.
App. 523, 528, 63 N. E. 315, the court said, ''It is not negligence *per se* for a city to fail to exercise its authority, conferred upon it by law, to light its streets. * * * So
that a failure to light the street is not a sufficient charge of
negligence to render the city liable.'' See, also, *City of Vincennes* v. *Spees* (1905), 35 Ind. App. 389, 74 N. E. 277.
The greater weight of authority in our own State as well as
in other states, is against the contention of appellee.

The judgment of the trial court is therefore reversed, with
instructions to restate its conclusion of law in favor of appellant, and to render judgment for appellant in the sum of
$5,966.70, with interest thereon from December 3, 1907.

Note.—Reported in 98 N. E. 188. See, also, under (1) 28 Cyc.
1342; (3) 28 Cyc. 1434; (5) 33 Cyc. 273; (6) 23 Cyc. 1309; (7)
28 Cyc. 1403. As to a city's liability for injuries resulting from defects in streets, see 103 Am. St. 260. As to the right of a municipality which has been held liable for injuries from unsafe condition
of street to recover over against the owner or occupant of abutting
property, see 12 L. R. A. (N. S.) 949. On the right of a municipality to recover indemnity or contribution from one for whose
tort it has been held liable, see 40 L. R. A. (N. S.) 1165. On the
question of the duty of a municipality to light streets, see 13 L. R.
A. (N. S.) 1166. For a discussion of the exoneration between a
municipality and abutting owners as to damages paid on account
of an unsafe highway, see 1 Ann. Cas. 945; 14 Ann. Cas. 1047.

MITTEN ET AL. *v.* CASWELL-RUNYAN COMPANY.

[No. 7,615. Filed June 28, 1912. Rehearing denied November 27, 1912. Transfer denied February 19, 1913.]

1. JUDGMENT.—*Record.*—*Pleadings.*—The pleadings filed in a cause are a part of the record, though not required to be copied at length into the order-book entries. p. 525.
2. JUDGMENT.—*Res Judicata.*—A judgment determines all material issues involved between the parties to the action and all matters which might have been properly litigated and settled within the issues tendered or made by the pleadings, and is *res judicata* in a subsequent action, though the form of the two actions is not the same. p. 525.
3. JUDGMENT.—*Res Judicata.*—*Issues.*—*Pleading.*—What was in issue in a former action must generally be determined by the pleadings therein, and everything which might have been adjudged under such issues will be presumed to have been adjudicated. p. 527.
4. JUDGMENT.—*Res Judicata.*—*Parol Evidence.*—Parol evidence is not admissible to determine what was in fact adjudicated in a former action, where the pleadings in such action are definite and unambiguous. pp. 528, 530.
5. PRINCIPAL AND SURETY.—*Judgment.*—*Res Judicata.*—Where, in an action by a building contractor to recover on the contract, defendant filed a cross-complaint to recover on the contractor's bond and recovered judgment thereon, such judgment was the measure of the contractor's liability, and is conclusive in a subsequent action on such bond as to the liability of the sureties. p. 530.

From Huntington Circuit Court; *Charles E. Sturgis,* Judge.

Action by the Caswell-Runyan Company against Lewis C. Mitten and others. From a judgment for plaintiff, the defendants appeal. *Reversed.*

Watkins & Butler and *Lesh & Lesh,* for appellants.

John M. Sayler and *Wm. F. McNagny,* for appellee.

FELT, J.—This was an action brought by the Caswell-Runyan Company against Lewis C. Mitten and his sureties upon a certain contractor's bond, given for the construction of certain buildings. ·

From a judgment for $2,000 this appeal was taken. The errors assigned are: (1) The overruling of appellants' demurrer to the amended complaint; (2) the overruling of appellants' demurrer to the second paragraph of appellee's reply to the second and third paragraphs of appellants' answer; (3) error in the conclusion of law; (4) error in overruling appellants' motion for a *venire de novo;* (5) overruling the motion for a new trial.

Appellants, other than Mitten, also made the same assignments of error, and each appellant separately excepted to each conclusion of law and separately assigned error thereon.

The complaint sought a recovery on a contractor's bond, and alleged a breach thereof in suffering and permitting certain mechanics' liens to be filed against the buildings erected for appellee by appellant Mitten. The complaint states a cause of action against all the appellants. To this complaint all the appellants answered by general denial. They also filed second and third paragraphs of answer as pleas of former adjudication. The second was a partial answer, in which the execution of the building contract and the bond sued on was admitted, but it was further averred, in substance, that on or about January 23, 1908, appellant Mitten sued appellee on said contract, and alleged full performance therof on his part and the furnishing to appellee of a large amount of extra labor and material not covered by the original contract; that in said action appellee filed an answer in seven paragraphs, the last of which was by way of counterclaim and set-off; that in said answer it made said contract and the bond here sued on exhibits, and alleged that said Mitten had violated said contract and bond in this, that he had failed to pay for the labor and material used in the construction of the buildings covered by the contract; that he had not kept the same free from mechanics' liens, but had suffered bills to be and remain unpaid, and liens therefor in the sum of $1,500 to be filed against said property. It is also averred that the contract and bond mentioned in this suit are the identical contract and bond set out in and made a part of said counterclaim in said other suit, and the liens mentioned and described in said counterclaim are the identical liens and claims mentioned and described in the complaint in this suit; that appellant Mitten demurred to said counterclaim filed in said former suit; that his demurrer was overruled, and he thereupon filed a reply in general denial; that said cause was thereafter duly tried in the Huntington Circuit Court, and on June 17, 1908, the court made a general finding against said Mitten on his complaint and for said Caswell-Runyan Company on its special answer in the sum of $184.57, and accordingly rendered judgment in its favor against said Mitten for that amount; that said judgment was never appealed from and is in full force and effect, and is *res judicata* of the claim sued on in this action.

The third paragraph of answer set up the plea of former adjudication in general terms, and averred the identity of the parties and the subject-matter of the two suits.

The sureties on said bond—appellants other than said Mitten—set up a special paragraph of answer, in which they admitted the execution of said bond to secure the performance of said builder's contract by said Mitten, but alleged that thereafter and without their consent the buildings were materially changed by alterations and additions, and the cost thereof materially increased, so that the same were wholly different from the buildings for which said contract was executed and for which they became bondsmen; that by reason thereof they are released from liability on said bond.

Appellee's second paragraph of reply to the second and third paragraphs of answer admits that in the suit by said Mitten against appellee mentioned in said paragraphs of answer, it did file the answer as alleged, and that in said suit there was a finding and judgment for said Caswell-

Runyan Company, but it further avers that there was a
large number of other issues in said cause, including answers by general denial and payment, paragraphs of set-off
and counterclaim, besides the paragraph of set-off and
counterclaim described in the answer as aforesaid; that said
finding and judgment in favor of said company were on
said other issues and not on the answer referred to as aforesaid; that the court which tried said former cause expressly
refused to receive any evidence on any of the matters set
forth in said counterclaim and in the complaint herein, and
refused to pass on, consider or decide any of said matters,
but on the contrary said cause was decided "by said court
wholly upon the evidence adduced by plaintiff under its
other answers in said cause, as to the value of the labor and
material furnished by said Lewis C. Mitten to the plaintiffs and the payments made to him thereon by the plaintiffs. And the plaintiff further avers that the judgment in
said former cause does not show, on its face, upon what
issues in the cause it was rendered and what issues the court
considered and adjudicated. And so the plaintiff says that
none of the matters set forth in the complaint in this cause
were heard, tried, determined or adjudicated in said former cause."

A demurrer for want of sufficient facts was overruled to
said paragraph of reply. The court heard evidence in support thereof and made a special finding of facts, in which
it found the facts to be substantially as therein alleged.
The finding states in detail facts showing a breach of the
bond, failure to pay bills and certain mechanics' liens on
the buildings for which said contract was executed and said
bond given; that liens for labor and material amounting to
$1,579.89 have been foreclosed, and said Mitten has paid no
part thereof; but has himself filed a lien on said buildings
for $3,200. The court also found that changes were made
in said building, but were immaterial matters of detail; that
in said former suit said Mitten sought to recover the con-

tract price aforesaid and additional compensation for labor and material made necessary by said changes and alterations; that the issues in said former suit were tried by the Hon. Samuel E. Cook, judge of the Huntington Circuit Court; that both parties adduced evidence on the subject of the alterations and changes aforesaid; that as a result of such trial judgment was rendered for Caswell-Runyan Company against said Mitten for $184.57, which is unreversed and unappealed from. On .the facts so found the court stated its conclusions of law in favor of said appellee, and gave judgment in this suit in its favor for $1,579.89.

The controlling question, raised in different ways by the several assignments of error, is that of former adjudication. Put in another form the question is, May a trial court, where matter is plainly in issue by unambiguous pleadings, make a general finding on all the issues, so far as shown by the record, and render judgment accordingly, and in a subsequent suit the same matter be put in issue by pleadings, and parol testimony be admitted to show that the matter though in issue in the first suit was not in fact adjudicated, and that the judgment so rendered was on other issues, and the matter so in issue was not in fact considered and adjudicated?

1. In this State the pleadings filed in a cause are a part of the record, though not required to be copied at length into the order-book entries.

In *Ryan* v. *Rhodes* (1906), 167 Ind. 121, 126, 76 N. E. 249, 78 N. E. 330, it is said: "The rule is well settled since the decision of this court in *Fischli* v. *Fischli* (1825), 1

2. Blackf. *360, 12 Am. Dec. 251, that a judgment in an action or proceeding determines or settles all material issues involved between the parties to the action and all matters which might have been properly litigated and settled within the issues tendered or made by the pleading." To the same effect are numerous decisions, among them the following: *Finley* v. *Cathcart* (1898), 149 Ind. 470, 477, 48

N. E. 586, 49 N. E. 381, 63 Am. St. 292; *Wright* v. *Anderson* (1889), 117 Ind. 349, 354, 20 N. E. 247; *Kurtz* v. *Carr* (1886), 105 Ind. 574, 583, 5 N. E. 692; *Faught* v. *Faught* (1884), 98 Ind. 470.

In *Van Camp* v. *City of Huntington* (1906), 39 Ind. App. 28, 37, 78 N. E. 1057, it is said: "To constitute a former adjudication, it is not necessary that the form of action be the same in both cases. It is sufficient if the question in controversy has been once litigated between the same parties. *Pittsburgh, etc., R. Co.* v. *Noftsger* (1897), 21 Ind. App. 599 [46 N. E. 360]. * * * In the suit for an injunction to restrain the appellant herein from interfering with the property of the city, the defendant therein pleaded the contract for the service which constituted the alleged interference. There was an answer in denial, and the execution of this contract was not effectually denied, and therefore, for the purposes of the cause, it was admitted. The judgment was on the merits and was a general judgment for the appellant herein. The execution of the contract was adjudicated in that suit, voluntarily prosecuted by the city to such result. Such matter could not properly be brought into controversy in the subsequent action on the contract."

In *Griffin* v. *Wallace* (1879), 66 Ind. 410, 416, it is said: "But, in any given case, where the plaintiff has sued in assumpsit, or in any action, for a number of separate causes of action which might be joined, making the aggregate of such causes the amount for which he demands judgment, if neglecting to withdraw any of those causes from the jury or court on the trial, he fails to establish any of them by proof, he cannot afterward bring another suit for those items." In the same case on page 419, it was also said that if a party "fail in the proof of all that is within the issues in the cause, but such failure is not shown by the record," the rule of former adjudication is applicable.

In *Howe* v. *Lewis* (1889), 121 Ind. 110, 113, 22 N. E. 978, the court said: "That a matter once adjudicated and

finally determined by a court of competent jurisdic-
3. tion is considered at rest, is a rule which prevails in
all civilized nations, with very few exceptions, is not
denied. Without such rule the repose of society would be
materially disturbed, and communities and courts would be
constantly disturbed and harassed by repeated contests, in
court, over the same subject of litigation. The difficulty
always arises in determining just what has been litigated
and settled and in the application of the rule, and never
exists in ascertaining what the rule is. The difficulties in
applying the rule are largely increased in this State by
reason of the fact that the defendant, under our system of
practice, is permitted to plead, in separate paragraphs, all
the defenses he may have whether legal or equitable. Under
this rule defenses are often pleaded which seem to be an-
tagonistic to each other. In such cases where there is a
general verdict, or a general finding for the defendant followed by a judgment, the effect of such finding, verdict and
judgment is left in some doubt. What was in issue must
always be determined by the pleadings. *Sharkey* v. *Evans*
[1874], 46 Ind. 472. Everything which might have been
adjudged under the issues in a cause will be presumed to
have been adjudicated. *Griffin* v. *Wallace* [1879], 66 Ind.
410; *Bottorff* v. *Wise* [1876], 53 Ind. 32; *Goble* v. *Dillon*
[1882], 86 Ind. 327 [44 Am. Rep. 308]. If a cause of action
was involved in a former action either as a set-off, counterclaim or defense, it is barred by the judgment. *Goble* v.
Dillon, supra; Green v. *Glynn* [1880], 71 Ind. 336. A
party is not bound, when sued, to plead a set-off or counterclaim, but if the issues are so formed as that a counterclaim
is, in fact, litigated, the defendant will not be permitted
afterward to sue and recover on the same."

The general rule is that what was in fact in issue in the
former action is to be determined from the pleading. *Howe*
v. *Lewis, supra,* 114; *Goble* v. *Dillon, supra; People's Sav.,*
etc., Assn. v. *Spears* (1888), 115 Ind. 297, 300, 17 N. E. 570,

Green v. *Glynn, supra; Sharkey* v. *Evans, supra; Fromlet* v. *Poor* (1892), 3 Ind. App. 425, 428, 29 N. E. 1081; *Beaver* v. *Irwin* (1893), 6 Ind. App. 285, 287, 33 N. E. 462. In the last case cited it is said: "Where the pleadings are unambiguous parol evidence is not admissible to show what was actually litigated, or what cause of action or defense the judgment is based upon." See, also, *Gentry* v. *Purcell* (1882), 84 Ind. 83; *Pickrell* v. *Jerauld* (1891), 1 Ind. App. 10, 27 N. E. 433, 50 Am. St. 192; *Furry* v. *O'Connor* (1891), 1 Ind. App. 573, 28 N. E. 103.

There are exceptions to the general rule where parol testimony may be received to determine what was in fact adjudicated, but the case before us does not fall

4. within any of such exceptions. The pleadings are definite and unambiguous, and the case falls within the general rule of former adjudication. Appellee does not claim that there is any ambiguity in the pleadings, but asserts that the rule is in all cases that the judgment is only *prima facie* proof of what was adjudicated, and that parol proof may be heard to show that matter clearly embraced within the issues was not in fact adjudicated. It may be conceded that there is language in some Indiana cases and some decisions tending to support this view. But the rule as declared by numerous decisions of the courts of last resort of this State and by the prevailing weight of authority elsewhere, is as above indicated, and the exceptions by no means warrant the sweeping rule contended for by said appellee. To open the door to parol proof in every case would be to destroy the binding force and stability of the judgments of our courts and to change the effect of the record by parol proof. The cases where parol proof is admissible are generally cases where such proof is necessary on the question of the identity of parties or the subject-matter, where the pleadings are indefinite or ambiguous, or for some reason it cannot be ascertained from the record and pleadings what was in fact adjudicated. Where the record, including the

pleadings, is clear and unambiguous, it is the best evidence, and controls. 2 Van Fleet, Former Adjud. §§422-435.

The case most confidently relied· on by appellee company is *Bottorff* v. *Wise, supra.* The court in that case passed on the sufficiency of a reply of former adjudication and held it good, and stated that a possessory action to recover lands and *mesne profits,* followed by a judgment thereon, was not a bar to an action for waste and `injury to land. This was all that the case actually decided, but the rule is broadly stated that the presumption that all matters within the issues were determined is not conclusive. This language as applied to the facts of that case may have been correct, and under the well-recognized rule we are not warranted in making a broader application of the rule than the facts of that case warrant. The case is cited in *Goble* v. *Dillon, supra,* where the rule is more fully and accurately stated on page 332. Appellee company also relies on the case of *Russell* v. *Place* (1876), 94 U. S. 606, 24 L. Ed. 214, and it may be admitted that its contention is, to some extent, sustained by some of the language there employed. But the rule as generally declared in this State and other states is recognized, and on page 608 it is said: "To apply the judgment, and give effect to the adjudication actually made, when the record leaves the matter in doubt, such evidence is admissible. * * * The record wants, therefore, that certainty which is essential to its operation as an estoppel, and does not conclude the defendants from contesting the infringement or the validity of the patent in this suit."

In 2 Van Fleet, Former Adjud. §422, it is stated that there is some confusion in the decisions over the question of admissibility in evidence of the secret deliberations of the judge or jury to determine that an issue was or was not decided, but the cases cited by the author show the weight of authority to be against their admissibility except in unusual cases unlike the one at bar. In 2 Van Fleet, Former Adjud.

§428, the author quotes with approval from *Chapman* v. *Smith* (1853), 16 How. 114, 133, 14 L. Ed. 868, as follows: "If the facts in issue appear upon the record, either expressly or by necessary intendment, it is not competent to contradict them, as this would be contradicting the record itself. The judgment is conclusive upon these facts, between the same parties or privies, whenever properly pleaded."

It is also asserted that the plea of former adjudication must fail because appellants, other than Mitten, who were the sureties on the bond, were not parties to the first 5. suit. But for the fact of suretyship, this claim would present a serious question. The bond was given to secure the performance of the building contract and save appellee company harmless from the liens that might be placed against its property. The identical contract, bond and liens were set up in the former suit against Mitten, the principal on the bond, and appellee company secured judgment against him. This judgment was the measure of the principal's liability, and when his liability is extinguished the sureties are released.

The answer of former adjudication was partial, and covered all amounts in excess of the former judgment. 2 Van Fleet, Former Adjud. §572 *et seq.; City of Anderson* v. *Fleming* (1903), 160 Ind. 597, 603, 67 N. E. 443, 66 L. R. A. 119.

The contention that the evidence is not in the record cannot be sustained. The foregoing discussion and authorities show that it was error to admit the testimony of 4. the judge who tried the former suit, to contradict the record or change the effect of the judgment rendered in that case.

Judgment reversed, with instructions to the lower court to sustain the motion for a new trial, to sustain the demurrer to the second paragraph of the reply to the second and third paragraphs of the answer, and for further proceedings in accordance with this opinion.

Hottel, C. J., Myers and Lairy, JJ., concur. Adams, P. J., and Ibach, J., absent.

NOTE.—Reported in 99 N. E. 47. See, also, under (2) 23 Cyc. 1221; (3) 23 Cyc. 1295; (4) 23 Cyc. 1538, As to the conclusiveness of a judgment, see 15 Am. St. 142. As to judgment as subject of counterclaim, see 47 Am. St. 591. For a discussion of the application of the doctrine of *res judicata* to issues in an action as to which the judgment is silent, see 6 Ann. Cas. 104.

GRUBB *v.* BRENDEL ET AL.

[No. 8,351. Filed February 20, 1913.]

1. NEW TRIAL.—*New Trial as of Right.*—*Action for Money Judgment.*—A complaint alleging that a deed executed by plaintiff was in fact a mortgage, and seeking the recovery of a money judgment for the difference between the actual value of the land and the debt secured by the alleged mortgage, states a cause of action that is not within the provisions of the statute (§1110 Burns 1908, §1054 R. S. 1881) authorizing a new trial as of right. p. 534.

2. NEW TRIAL.—*New Trial as of Right.*—Where two or more substantive causes of action proceed to judgment in the same case, and a new trial as of right is authorized by §1110 Burns 1908, §1054 R. S. 1881, as to one or more of such causes, but not as to others, a new trial as of right must be denied. p. 534.

3. DEEDS.—*Action to Declare Deed a Mortgage.*—*Evidence.*—*Burden of Proof.*—In an action to have a deed declared to be a mortgage, the burden of proving that the deed, and a contract executed at the same time, evidenced a loan with security, rather than a purchase of the land by defendant and an option to sell to plaintiff, rests on plaintiff. p. 536.

4. DEEDS. — *Operation.* — *Presumptions.* — *Evidence.* — *Mortgage.*—The presumption is that a deed, absolute on its face, is what it purports to be, and, unless the evidence proves it to be a mortgage, it will operate as a conveyance of the fee. p. 536.

5. DEEDS.—*Action to Declare Deed a Mortgage.*—*Evidence.*—*Debt.* —In an action to have a deed declared a mortgage, the absence of any written evidence of a debt due defendant from plaintiff, is a circumstance tending to support the theory of a sale. p. 536.

6. DEEDS.—*Action to Declare Deed a Mortgage.*—*Evidence.*—*Consideration.*—In determining whether a deed, absolute on its face,

is in fact a mortgage, the adequacy of consideration supports the theory of a sale, and inadequacy supports that of a loan with security. p. 536.

7. APPEAL.— *Review.*— *Evidence.*— *Weight and Sufficiency.*— Although the evidence is conflicting on some of the material issues, the decision of the trial court will not be disturbed, if there is evidence tending to support every fact essential thereto, since the court on appeal will not weigh conflicting evidence. p. 536.

From Boone Circuit Court; *Willett H. Parr,* Judge.

Action by Nola S. Grubb against James W. Brendel and others. From a judgment for defendants, the plaintiff appeals. *Affirmed.*

David A. Leach, for appellant.

R. P. Bundy, J. W. Hornaday and *S. M. Ralston,* for appellees.

FELT, P. J.—Appellant filed suit in two paragraphs against appellees to declare a deed a mortgage and for other relief.

The undisputed facts show that on March 16, 1909, appellant and his wife by a warranty deed conveyed to James W. Brendel, 36½ acres of real estate in Boone county, Indiana, for the consideration of $3,000; that on the same day said Brendel and appellant entered into a written agreement, wherein it was stipulated that said Brendel had sold to appellant said real estate for the sum of $2,951.75, to be paid on or before September 16, 1909, and further provided that "the conditions of this sale are such that if the said second party shall not at the time herein set forth be able to pay first party the full amount of the herein named purchase price then the said sale shall be null and void and of no effect and first party shall not be bound by any of the terms of this said sale." By the terms of said instrument appellant was given the right to sell the real estate to a third person if sold within six months, and appellee Brendel agreed to execute to such purchaser a quitclaim deed for the land, provided the price paid was not less than $2,951.75.

On September 29, 1909, appellees, Brendel and Brendel, as husband and wife, conveyed said real estate to appellees, John S. and Milton Hussey, for a consideration of $3,000. Appellant failed to pay any part of the purchase money designated in said contract of sale, but continued in possession of the land.

The gist of the first paragraph of complaint is that the deed executed by appellant to appellee Brendel is in fact a mortgage, given to secure a debt for money loaned, and the court is asked so to declare, and to fix the amount due said appellee from appellant. It is further alleged that appellees Hussey and Hussey purchased said real estate knowing said deed was a mortgage, and with full knowledge of appellant's rights in the land. This paragraph also prays that appellant be given a reasonable time within which to pay the amount found to be due appellee Brendel, or, in lieu thereof, that he be required to foreclose his mortgage evidenced by said deed.

The allegations of the second paragraph of complaint are substantially like those of the first paragraph, and in addition thereto it is alleged that appellees Hussey and Hussey are innocent purchasers for value; that the purchase money due from them had not been paid to said Brendel; that appellant is entitled to recover the difference in amount between said mortgage, and $4,500, the alleged value of the land. Prayer that appellant be subrogated to the rights of said Brendel, in the recovery of the purchase money due from said Hussey and Hussey, and that he be given judgment for $1,500.

The complaint was answered by general denial of all the appellees. Appellees Hussey and Hussey filed a special answer, in which they allege that they purchased the land from said Brendel for $3,000, for which amount they executed their note, without any knowledge of appellant's claim. Appellees, Hussey and Hussey, also filed a cross-complaint against appellant, in which they allege ownership in fee simple of said real estate, and ask to have their title quieted. Appellant replied to said special answer by general denial, and issues were joined on the cross-complaint by denial of its averments. The court found for appellees on appellant's complaint and also found for said Hussey and Hussey on their cross-complaint, and gave judgment quieting their title as against appellant. Appellant moved for a new trial as of right, which was overruled, and also moved for a new trial for cause, which was likewise overruled. The ruling on each of said motions is assigned as error. The case proceeded to trial and judgment on the issues joined on both paragraphs of the complaint and the cross-complaint.

The second paragraph of complaint seeks to obtain a money judgment for the difference between the actual value of the land and the debt secured by the alleged mortgage. Such a cause of action is clearly not within the provisions of the statute authorizing a new trial as of right.

1.

Where two or more substantive causes of action proceed to judgment in the same case, and a new trial as of right may be had as to one or more of such causes, but the statute (§1110 Burns 1908, §1054 R. S. 1881) does not authorize such new trial as to one or more of the causes so associated, a new trial as of right must be denied. *Henry* v. *Frazier* (1913), 53 Ind. App. —, 100 N. E. 770, and cases cited; *Roeder* v. *Keller* (1893), 135 Ind. 692, 697, 35 N. E. 1014; *Seisler* v. *Smith* (1898), 150 Ind. 88, 92, 46 N. E. 993; *Nutter* v. *Hendricks* (1898), 150 Ind. 605, 607, 50 N. E. 748; *Butler University* v. *Conard* (1884), 94 Ind. 353; *Studabaker* v. *Alexander* (1913), 179 Ind. —, 100 N. E. 10; *Larrance* v. *Lewis* (1912), 51 Ind. App. 1, 98 N. E. 892.

2.

No error was committed in overruling appellant's motion for a new trial as of right. The motion for a new trial for cause alleges that the decision of the court is not sustained by sufficient evidence; also that it is contrary to law. Appellant contends that the transaction of March 16 shows a loan to appellant, with the deed to Brendel as security, while appellees assert that it was an absolute sale of the land to Brendel, with an option to appellant to buy the land within six months at a stipulated price. In addition to the writings offered in evidence, the court heard oral testimony to assist in the determination of the controversy.

The evidence shows without dispute that appellant's land was mortgaged for about $1,800, and that this, and other past-due indebtedness of appellant aggregated $2,865.66 on the day the deed to Brendel was executed; that on the same day he gave his check to appellant for that amount, and the money so obtained was used in the payment of said indebtedness; that prior to the transaction of March 16 appellant tried to borrow money with which to meet his obligations, but was unable so to do; that no note or other evidence of a debt due appellee Brendel from appellant was given, but the amount received by appellant, plus six per cent interest thereon for six months, equals the price stated in the option agreement. The execution of the written instruments in the form shown is not disputed. The oral testimony is more or less conflicting. Some of it tends to show that the transaction was a loan, with the deed as security for its payment, while, on the other hand, there is ample evidence tending to prove that appellee Brendel refused to make a loan, and purchased the land, taking an absolute title, but at the same time gave to appellant an option to buy or sell the land within six months. On the question of the value of the land, some of the evidence tends to show that the price paid by Brendel was less than its fair value, while much of it tends to prove the price paid was the full value of the land.

Many admissions of appellant were proven to show that he understood the transaction to be a sale, and made no claim to the contrary until after Brendel sold the land. A number of these statements were made to or in the presence of disinterested witnesses before this suit was begun, and were strongly corroborative of appellee Brendel's testimony and of his interpretation of the transaction. This theory of the case was not in contradiction of, but in harmony with, the written instruments. The burden of prov-

3. ing that the deed and contract evidenced a loan with security, rather than a purchase of the land by Brendel, with an option to sell to appellant, or a purchaser secured by him, rested on appellant. *Deadman* v. *Yanthis* (1907), 230 Ill. 243, 82 N. E. 592, 597, 120 Am. St. 291; *Stevens* v. *Hays* (1856), 8 Ind. 277.

A deed absolute on its face, will operate as a conveyance of the fee, unless the evidence proves it to be a mort-

4. gage. The presumption is that it is what it purports to be—a general warranty deed. *Rogers* v. *Beach* (1888), 115 Ind. 413, 415. The absence of any written evidence of a debt due Brendel from appellant is a cir-

5. cumstance tending to support the theory of a sale, though not conclusive. *Hays* v. *Carr* (1882). 83 Ind. 275, 283; *White* v. *Redenbaugh* (1907), 41 Ind. App. 580, 583, 82 N. E. 10. Adequacy of consideration tends

6. to support the theory of a sale and inadequacy that of a loan with security. *Calahan* v. *Dunker* (1912), 51 Ind. App. 436, 99 N. E. 1021.

The contention and argument of appellant on the motion for a new trial for cause serve only to establish the proposition that there is a conflict in the evidence on some

7. of the material questions in the case. There is ample evidence tending to support every material fact es- sential to the decision of the trial court. It is fundamental that it is not the province of this court to weigh conflicting evidence in any case of the class to which the one at bar belongs. We find no error in the record.

Judgment affirmed.

NOTE.—Reported in 10 N. E. 872. See, also, under (1) 29 Cyc. 1034; (7) 3 Cyc. 360. As to equitable mortgages generally, and forms of them in particular, see 4 Am. St. 696; 131 Am. St. 914.

As to when a deed, with a contract to reconvey, is a mortgage, see 3 L. Ed. U. S. 321. On the question of parol evidence admissible to show deed a mortgage, see 3 L. Ed. U. S. 321; 6 L. Ed. U. S. 142. The question whether a deed absolute on its face, but intended as a mortgage, conveys the legal title is treated in 11 L. R. A. (N. S.) 209. For a discussion of price as a consideration in determining whether a deed was intended as a mortgage, see 20 Ann. Cas. 1199.

BARTON *v.* BARTON.

[No. 7,820. Filed February 20, 1913.]

1. PRINCIPAL AND AGENT.—*Husband and Wife.—Power of Attorney. —Construction.—Death of Wife.—Revocation.*—A power of attorney executed by a husband and wife directly authorizing the attorney in fact to convey the property of "any one of us," etc., and not containing any power to convey joint property, is several and is not revoked by the death of the wife. p. 539.

2. PRINCIPAL AND AGENT.—*Power of Attorney.—Payment of Money to Authorized Agent.—Recovery.*—One who pays money to an agent authorized to receive it is entitled to his credit without tracing the fund through the hands of the agent and into those of his principal, so that where an agent, authorized by a power of attorney to borrow money on "the note, notes, mortgage or mortgages" of the principal, borrowed money on his promise to give the note of the principal therefor, a recovery may be had by the lender against the principal, although no note was ever executed. p. 540.

3. PRINCIPAL AND AGENT.—*Existence of Relation.—Evidence.—Instructions.*—In an action for money loaned, where it was alleged that defendant borrowed the money through an agent, evidence that the alleged agent received a check from plaintiff and deposited same to defendant's credit, and was constantly loaning money for defendant, and performed other and similar acts for defendant, an instruction by which the question of whether he was the defendant's agent in the making of such loan was left wholly to the jury, after a consideration of all the facts shown, was proper. p. 541.

4. PRINCIPAL AND AGENT.—*Power of Attorney.—Recovery of Money Paid to Agent.—Instructions.*—In an action to recover money alleged to have been loaned to defendant through his agent, an instruction that if the jury determined from all the evidence that a power of attorney from defendant to such agent was in force during the time of the business dealings between plaintiff and such agent, and that such agent borrowed the money under the

authority therein granted, defendant would be liable, was not erroneous. p. 541.

5 APPEAL.—*Review.*—*Instructions.*—*Refusal.*—The refusal of requested instructions is not error, where they are fully covered by others given, or where they are not applicable to the evidence. p. 541.

6. APPEAL.—*Review.*—*Affirmance.*—Where there is ample evidence to support the verdict, and no prejudicial error is shown by the record, the judgment must be affirmed. p. 542.

From Hamilton Circuit Court; *Meade Vestal*, Judge.

Action by Dennis Barton against Patrick Barton, Sr. From a judgment for plaintiff, the defendant appeals. *Affirmed.*

J. F. Neal and *N. C. Neal*, for appellant.

James V. Kent, Thomas M. Ryan and *Shirts & Fertig*, for appellee.

IBACH, C. J.—This action was brought by a complaint in two paragraphs. The first is for money had and received and the second for money loaned to appellant at his instance and request. Each paragraph is based on alleged transactions between appellee and appellant by and through John D. Barton, who, it is claimed by appellee, was the attorney in fact of appellant. The issues were finally joined by an answer in general denial. There was a trial by jury, resulting in a verdict and judgment for appellee in the sum of $1,785.58 and costs. The only error assigned and relied on for reversal is the action of the trial court in overruling appellant's motion for a new trial. At the trial appellee introduced and had read in evidence a certain power of attorney executed by appellant and his wife, which is in the following words:

"Know all men by these presents, that we, Patrick Barton and his wife Bridget Barton, all of Coles county in the State of Illinois, have made constituted and appointed, and by these presents do make constitute and appoint John D. Barton of Clinton county in the State of Indiana, our true and lawful attorney for us and in our name and stead to make, sign each of our names thereto, execute and deliver general warranty deeds for any and all real estate of whatsoever kind or description owned by any one of us, and situated in Clinton county, in the State of Indiana, to any and all person or persons or corporations to whom the said John D. Barton may desire to sell or trade any and all of said real estate, and the said John D. Barton shall have power and he is hereby expressly authorized to sell and convey any and all of said real estate owned by any one of us in said county, and to collect and receipt to said parties in full for all purchase money or other consideration received for the same. And the said parties above named do hereby expressly authorize and empower the said John D. Barton and for that purpose he is constituted their true and lawful attorney, to make sign each and all of our names thereto to execute and deliver to any person or persons from whom the said John D. Barton may desire, to obtain the loan of any money, any note, notes, mortgage or mortgages, whatsoever, to obtain any said loan and to secure the payment thereof giving and granting unto said attorney full power and authority, to do and perform all and every act and thing whatsoever requisite and necessary to be done in and about the premises as fully to all, intents and purposes as we might or could do if personally present, with full power of substitution and revocation hereby ratifying and confirming all that our said attorney or his substitute shall lawfully do or cause to be done by virtue hereof. In Witness Whereof, We have hereunto set out hands and seals this 10 day of December, 1903.

P. Barton (Seal)
'Budget B.' (Seal)
Bridget Barton (Seal)."

It is first contended by appellant that the court erred in permitting the introduction of the instrument in evidence, because it does not tend to support any issue presented by the pleadings, that the instrument shows on its face that it is a power of attorney given by Patrick Barton and wife Bridget, and only empowers and authorizes said John D. Barton to act as attorney in fact for the two persons who executed it, jointly, and not for either of them separately, and that it was revoked by the death of the wife and therefore has no bearing on the case.

If it could be said that this power of attorney was the joint act of appellant and his wife, and was not severable in its character, the position of appellant would be upheld. *Hawley* v. *Smith* (1873), 45 Ind. 183; *Rowe* v. *Rand* (1887), 111 Ind. 206, 12 N. E. 377.

But we can scarcely conceive of an instrument more severable in its character. The parties could not have selected words more appropriate nor of greater force to constitute a several instrument than those used in the writing under construction. By its terms the agent is directly authorized to convey the property of "any one of us", and is given no power to convey property held by them jointly; he is by its terms directed to "sign each and all of our names to any note, notes, mortgage or mortgages whatsoever," to obtain any said loan and to secure the payment thereof. We therefore hold that the instrument under consideration was several and not joint, and therefore it was not revoked by the death of appellant's wife, Bridget Barton.

It is also argued that by this power of attorney the agent was only authorized to borrow money on the "note, notes, mortgage or mortgages" of the parties, and

2. therefore he had no power to borrow money to be charged to the account of the principal, as in the present case. But even if the construction contended for by appellant could be placed on the power of attorney, there was evidence to show that the money sued for had been borrowed on the promise of the agent to give the note of the principal therefor, and that he had failed to make the note. After receiving the money for the use of the principal, and after placing the same in the bank to his principal's credit, he refused to execute a note therefor. The agent was by the power of attorney authorized to receive the money. "One who pays money to an agent authorized to receive it is entitled to his credit without tracing the fund through the hands of the agent and into those of his principal. Of course, without regard to authority of agent,

money had and received may be recovered, but payment having been once made to an authorized agent, the principal cannot avoid its effect because of the delinquency of the agent." *Indiana Trust Co.* v. *International, etc., Assn.* (1905), 36 Ind. App. 685, 690, 74 N. E. 633.

Complaint is also made of certain instructions given by the court at the request of appellee. By the first instruction objected to, the jury was, in substance, told
3. that if it found from the evidence that John D. Barton was the agent of appellant, and had power to make loans in his behalf, and that he did borrow money from appellee for the express use and benefit of appellant, the verdict should be for appellee for the amount so borrowed, with interest. Many facts outside of the power of attorney itself, tending to prove agency, were shown at the trial. Among the most important are the facts that John D. Barton received a check from appellee and deposited it in the bank to appellant's credit; that said agent was constantly loaning money for appellant, and that at the time the money in question was borrowed, other and similar acts were performed by him for appellant. By the instruction the determination of the question of agency is left wholly to the jury after a consideration of all the facts shown, and it was not erroneous.

The second instruction was likewise applicable to the evidence, and a correct statement of the law, for by it the jury was told that if it determined from all the evi-
4. dence that the power of attorney was in force during the time of the business dealings between appellee and the agent of appellant, and such agent borrowed the money in suit under the authority granted him therein, then appellant would be liable. The remaining instruction, given at appellee's request, is not objectionable, and was quite proper for a correct determination of the merits
5. of the case, in view of the undisputed evidence. We find no error in the refusal of the court to give

certain instructions tendered by appellant, for those which were applicable to the evidence were fully covered by other instructions given by the court of its own motion and other instructions requested by appellant, and instructions Nos. 5, 9 and 10 were properly refused, for the reason that they were not applicable to the evidence and placed an entirely erroneous construction on the instrument, which gave to appellant's agent the power of borrowing money for the use and benefit of appellant.

6. There is ample evidence in the record to support the verdict, and since the record fails to show any error prejudicial to appellant the judgment must be affirmed. Appellant having died since this appeal was taken, the judgment is affirmed as of date of submission.

NOTE.—Reported in 100 N. E. 870. See, also, under (1) 31 Cyc. 1407; (3) 31 Cyc. 1672, 1678; (5) 38 Cyc. 1711; (6) 3 Cyc. 418. As to how joint powers of attorney are to be construed, see 22 Am. St. 726. As to power of attorney, given by a married woman, see 84 Am. St. 765. As to what power an agent has to borrow money, also as to ratification, see 29 Am. St. 93, 96. As to imputation to principal of notice given agent, see 24 Am. St. 228. On the question of the effect of a provision in a power of attorney declaring that it shall not be revoked by death, see 6 L. R. A. (N. S.) 855.

JORDAN *v.* INDIANAPOLIS COAL COMPANY.

[No. 7,859.   Filed February 21, 1913.]

1. PLEADING.—*Complaint.—Sufficiency.—Initial Attack on Appeal.* —A complaint is good as against an attack made for the first time by assignment of errors on appeal, if it contains facts sufficient to bar another action for the same cause. p. 543.

2. PLEADING.—*Complaint.—Bill of Particulars.—Objections on Appeal.*—The objection that a bill of particulars filed with a complaint is not properly referred to or identified by the complaint cannot be successfully presented for the first time on appeal. p. 544.

3. JUDGES.—*Judge Pro Tem.—Appointment.—Validity.—Judge De Facto.*—Where the regular judge appointed a judge *pro* tem. to preside over the court during his illness, and the court has jurisdiction of the subject-matter of the action and of the person of

the defendant, and the judge so appointed took the oath and assumed the duties of a judge *pro tem.*, he was a judge *de facto*, if not *de jure*, notwithstanding the failure of the regular judge to sign the order of appointment. pp. 544, 545.

4. APPEAL.—*Assignment of Errors.—Questions Presented.—Validity of Appointment of Judge Pro Tem.*—An assignment of error grounded on the proposition that the trial court had no jurisdiction to render the judgment from which the appeal is taken presents no question as to the right and authority of the presiding judge of such court to act as such. p. 544.

5. JUDGES.—*Judge Pro Tem.—Appointment.—Objections.—Waiver. —Appeal.*—Where a judge has been called, or an attorney appointed as judge, to try a cause, and no objection is made at the time, or to his sitting in the cause when he assumes to act, all objections thereto will be deemed waived on appeal, and the same rule applies as to the appointment of a judge *pro tem.* p. 545.

6. PRINCIPAL AND AGENT.—*Authority of Agent.—Evidence.—Verdict.*—A verdict for plaintiff, in an action for the price of a car of crushed stone, is sustained by sufficient evidence, where the evidence shows that a landscape gardener employed by defendant, after a conversation with defendant on the subject, ordered the stone from plaintiff, and that the car was billed to defendant and used in the improvement of a driveway on his premises. p. 545.

From Superior Court of Marion County (80,383); *Charles J. Orbison,* Judge *Pro Tem.*

Action by the Indianapolis Coal Company against Arthur Jordan. From a judgment for plaintiff, the defendant appeals. *Affirmed.*

T. J. Moll and *Edmund B. Walker,* for appellant.
Jesse W. Potter, for appellee.

LAIRY, J.—Appellee filed its complaint in the trial court and recovered a judgment against appellant for the value of a carload of crushed stone, alleged to have been delivered by it to appellant at his special instance and request. Appellant did not challenge the sufficiency of the complaint in the trial court by demurrer or otherwise; but its sufficiency is questioned for the first time by an assignment of errors. When so presented the objections urged against this complaint are unavailable. The complaint is sufficient to bar another action for the same cause.

Town of Knightstown v. *Homer* (1905), 36 Ind. App. 139, 75 N. E. 13; *Lewis Tp. Improv. Co.* v. *Royer* (1906), 38 Ind. App. 151, 76 N. E. 1068.

The objection that the bill of particulars filed with the complaint is not properly referred to in or identified by the complaint cannot be successfully presented for the first time on appeal. *Chamness* v. *Chamness* (1876), 53 Ind. 301; *Douglass* v. *Keehn* (1880), 71 Ind. 97.

2.

It appears from the record that on May 31, 1910, the regular judge of the court in which this action was pending, on account of sickness, appointed the Hon. Charles J. Orbison to preside as judge of such court until such time as the regular judge should be able to resume his duties. The order of appointment was entered on the order-book of the court, but it was not signed by the regular judge. Charles J. Orbison took the oath and assumed the duties of judge *pro tem.* As such he assumed jurisdiction of this case, and proceeded to final judgment. At no time during the course of the proceedings in the trial court did appellant make any objection to the appointment of the judge *pro tem.*, and no question was raised as to his right or authority to act as such. The question is presented for the first time on appeal by an assignment of errors.

3.

The assignment of errors presenting this question is grounded on the proposition that the trial court had no jurisdiction to render the judgment from which this appeal is taken. The position of appellant on this proposition cannot be maintained. It is not contended that the Superior Court of Marion County did not have jurisdiction of the class of cases to which this one belongs; and its jurisdiction of the person of appellant is not questioned. It is therefore apparent that the court had jurisdiction of the subject-matter of the action and of the person of appellant, and had power to proceed to judgment. The defect pointed out was not affecting the juris-

4.

diction of the court, but the right and authority of its presiding judge to act as such. The judge who pre-

3. sided at the trial of this case was acting under color of authority, and he was a judge *de facto* if not a judge *de jure.*

It has been held repeatedly by this court and the Supreme Court that when a judge has been called or an attorney appointed to try a cause, and no objection is made

5. at the time, or to his sitting in the cause when he assumes to act, all objections thereto will be deemed waived on appeal. *Perry* v. *Pernet* (1905), 165 Ind. 67, 74 N. E. 609, 6 Ann. Cas. 533; *Crawford* v. *Lawrence* (1900), 154 Ind. 288, 56 N. E. 673; *Lillie* v. *Trentman* (1891), 130 Ind. 16, 29 N. E. 405; *Lewis* v. *Albertson* (1899), 23 Ind. App. 147, 53 N. E. 1071. We see no reason why the rule announced and applied to special judges should not apply with equal force to a judge *pro tempore.*

The evidence in this case shows that one McDougal was employed by appellant as landscape gardener to make certain improvements on lands owned by appellant, and

6. that during the progress of the work McDougal, after a conversation with appellant on the subject, ordered from appellee the carload of crushed stone in question, and that the car was billed to appellant and the stone used for the improvement of a driveway on his premises. Appellant asserts that the verdict is not sustained by the evidence, for the reason that there is no evidence showing that McDougal in ordering the carload of stone was acting as the agent of appellant. In this we think appellant is mistaken. It is not necessary to extend this opinion by a statement of the evidence bearing on this question. It is sufficient to say that we have examined the record and find abundant evidence to sustain the verdict of the jury in this respect.

Judgment affirmed.

NOTE.—Reported in 100 N. E. 880. See, also, under (1) 31 Cyc. 82; (2) 2 Cyc. 689; (3) 23 Cyc. 618; (5) 23 Cyc. 616; (6) 31 Cyc.

1667. As to the validity of acts of *de facto* judicial officers, see 140 Am. St. 169. As to the general rules for defining the limits of an agent's authority, see 16 Am. St. 493. As to the waiver of objections to the jurisdiction of a special or substituted judge, see 19 Ann. Cas. 94.

ANTIOCH BAPTIST CHURCH ET AL. *v.* MORTON ET AL.

[No. 8,499. Filed Feburary 21, 1913.]

1. APPEAL.—*Notice of Appeal.—Sufficiency.*—By §681 Burns 1908, §640 R. S. 1881, two methods of giving notice of an appeal are provided for, one official and the other unofficial, either of which, if followed, constitutes sufficient notice. p. 547.

2. APPEAL.—*Notice of Appeal.—Service.—Sufficiency.*—Under §681 Burns 1908, §640, R. S. 1881, providing the method of giving notice of an appeal, unofficial notice may be served on appellees personally, or their attorney of record and the clerk of the court below, but if service is sought through an official notice, resident appellees must be served in person, and non-residents by publication notice, and service on appellees' attorney of record is insufficient. p. 547.

3. APPEAL.—*Notice of Appeal.—Dismissal.*—The court has no jurisdiction and an appeal must be dismissed, where notice of the appeal has not been served in one of the methods provided by §681 Burns 1908, §640 R. S. 1881. p. 548.

From Marion Circuit Court (18,500); *Charles Remster,* Judge.

Action by Emma G. Morton and others against the Antioch Baptist Church and others. From a judgment for plaintiffs, the defendants appeal. *Appeal dismissed.*

Wm. E. Henderson and *Asa H. Boulden,* for appellants. *Robert W. McBride* and *Caleb S. Denny,* for appellees.

IBACH, C. J.—Appellees, Emma G. Morton, Kate Morton Carroll, Chester Morton and David Morton, appear specially and move to dismiss this appeal, and assign as reasons therefor that, in addition to the four appellees who join in the motion, James Morton and Minnie Morton Anderson are named as appellees in the assignment of errors, and as they had jointly with these four appellees obtained a judgment in the Marion Circuit Court against appellants, that both of said parties were necessary parties to this appeal, but had not been brought before this court by proper notice.

It appears from the record before us that the transcript and assignment of errors were filed in the office of the clerk of this court on October 19, 1912. Pursuant to the written precipe filed by appellants with the transcript and assignment of errors, the clerk of this court issued to the sheriff of this court the notice of appeal, and the names contained therein were Emma G. Morton, Kate Morton Carroll, Minnie Morton Anderson and son Chester Morton, David Morton, and Caleb S. Denny, attorney of record for appellees. The precipe and the notice did not contain the name of James Morton, and it is admitted by appellants that at the time of the filing of the transcript and assignment of errors, Minnie Morton Anderson was and is now a nonresident of the State of Indiana.

Appellants contend, however, that the statute has been complied with, and that both of the last-named parties have been properly brought into court by reason of the fact that their attorney of record had been properly served by the sheriff of this court. The record bears out the contention of appellants, but the notice thus served on their attorney of record is not service on appellees under the facts of this 1. case. By §681 Burns 1908, §640 R. S. 1881, two methods of giving notice of an appeal are provided for, either one of which methods may be adopted by appellant, and will constitute sufficient notice. The first is an unofficial notice, because there is no necessity for any official acts, while the second form of notice must be issued by the clerk of this court and must be served by the sheriff 2. of this court or his deputy. The notice relied on by appellants in this case was an official notice, and was issued to and served only on the attorney who had represented the two omitted parties, and who were necessary parties to this appeal. Such service of the official notice was without authority of law, and is not legal notice to appellee of the appeal. This holding is fully supported by the case of *Tate* v. *Hamlin* (1895), 149 Ind. 94, 41 N. E. 356, 41 N. E. 1035. If the party adopts the first method of serving an unofficial notice, he may do so by serving appellees personally, or their attorney of record and the clerk of the court below; but if he adopts the second method, and seeks service through an official notice, resident appellees must be served in person, and nonresidents by publication notice, and service on the attorneys of record of appellees is insufficient.

3.   The court therefore has no jurisdiction, and the appeal is dismissed.

Note.—Reported in 100 N. E. 874. See, also, under (1) 2 Cyc. 865; (2) 2 Cyc. 868; (3) 2 Cyc. 873.

MOORE-MANSFIELD CONSTRUCTION COMPANY *v.* MARION, BLUFFTON AND EASTERN TRACTION COMPANY ET AL.

[No. 7,998.   Filed March 4, 1913.]

1.   APPEAL.—*Review.*—*Answer in Abatement.*—*Sufficiency.*—*Failure to Point Out Defect.*—An answer in abatement which appears to state sufficient facts will be deemed on appeal to be sufficient to withstand a demurrer, where appellant fails to point out any specific defect therein. p. 551.

2.   DISMISSAL.—*Right to Dismiss.*—*Common-Law Rule.*—*Statutes.*— The rule prevailing in common-law jurisdictions, that the plaintiff in an action at law has a right to dismiss his action at any time before verdict, but that complainant in a suit in equity does not possess a similar right, is not applicable in this State, since under §249 Burns 1908, §249 R. S. 1881, providing that there shall be but one form of action denominated a civil action, and abolishing all distinctions in pleading and practice between actions at law and suits in equity, the provisions of §338 Burns 1908, §333 R. S. 1881, that a plaintiff may dismiss his action at any time before the jury retires, or, when the trial is by the court, at any time before the finding of the court is announced, must be held to apply

Moore-Mansfield, etc., Co. v. Marion, etc., Co.—52 Ind. App. 548.

to a civil action, regardless of whether the relief sought is legal or equitable. pp. 553, 554.

3. ACTIONS.—*Actions at Law.—Suits in Equity.—Effect of Statute Abolishing Distinctions.*—Section 249 Burns 1908, §249 R. S. 1881, providing that there shall be but one form of action, denominated a civil action, and abolishing all distinctions in pleading and practice between actions at law and suits in equity, neither abridges the power of courts to grant equitable relief nor changes the rules of law or principles of equity as applied in determining the substantial rights of the parties, though in some instances it changes the form of procedure by which the remedy is obtained. p. 554.

4. COURTS.—*Judicial Duties.—Master Commissioner.—Report.*— The report of a master commissioner is not a finding of the court, since a master commissioner is not a court, and judicial duties, which a court alone can exercise, cannot be conferred on him. p. 555.

5. DISMISSAL.—*Right to Dismiss.—Report of Master Commissioner as Affecting Right.*—The right of plaintiff to dismiss his action, under §338 Burns 1908, §333 R. S. 1881, providing that plaintiff may dismiss at any time before the finding of the court is announced, is not affected by the fact that prior to asking the dismissal, the report of the master commissioner, to whom the case had been referred, had been prepared and copies submitted to the parties. p. 555.

6. DISMISSAL.—*Wrongful Dismissal.—Effect.*—Where a court has jurisdiction of the subject-matter and of the parties to the action, an order of dismissal wrongfully entered is not ineffective, but merely erroneous, and is binding on the parties unless reversed on appeal or set aside in a direct proceeding brought for that purpose. p. 555.

7. DISMISSAL.—*Collateral Attack.*—An order of dismissal, even if erroneous, is not subject to collateral attack. p. 555.

8. DISMISSAL.—*Voluntary Dismissal.—Effect as to Set-off.—Rights of Defendant.*—A set-off is not affected by the dismissal of the cause of action stated in the complaint, but defendant may proceed to final judgment on the issues tendered by such set-off, although the court, in determining the questions thus presented, would have no right to consider any issues formed on the complaint. p. 555.

9. APPEAL.—*Review.—Assumption That Trial Court Will Err.*— The court on appeal has no right to assume that a trial court, in passing on a matter, will consider questions not presented by the pleadings then on file. p. 556.

10. ABATEMENT.—*Another Action Pending.—Evidence.—Sufficiency.* —An answer in abatement on the ground that another action is

pending is not sustained by evidence showing that a former action was commenced on the same cause of action, where it is also apparent that such former action was dismissed and was not pending when the latest action was filed. p. 556.

11. PLEADING.—*Pleas to Jurisdiction.—Requisites.*—An answer denying the jurisdiction of the court is a dilatory plea and must be certain and definite and must anticipate and exclude all such supposable facts as would, if alleged on the opposite side, defeat the plea, since nothing can be supplied by intendment. p. 557.

12. VENUE.—*Joinder of Several Defendants.—Answer in Abatement.—Sufficiency.*—Under §315 Burns 1908, §312 R. S. 1881, authorizing an action against two or more defendants, jointly liable, in the county where either resides, jurisdiction is not acquired by a defendant against whom plaintiff has a cause of action, in an action brought in a county of which he is not a resident, by joining him as a codefendant with a person residing where the action is brought, but against whom plaintiff has no cause of action, so that an answer showing that jurisdiction of a defendant could not have been acquired by the service of summons in the county where the action was brought, and that the other defendant, who resided in such county, was not in any way indebted to plaintiff on the cause of action stated in the complaint, stated facts sufficient to abate the action. p. 558.

13. PLEADING.—*Demurrer.—Admissions.*—For the purpose of testing the sufficiency of a pleading, a demurrer admits the truth of its averments. p. 558.

14. PLEADING.—*Answer in Abatement.—Joinder of Matter in Abatement With Matter in Bar.—Waiver of Grounds of Abatement.*—A plea in abatement must precede a plea in bar, and where matter in abatement is joined in the same paragraph with matter in bar, the matter in abatement is waived and may be stricken out on motion. p. 558.

From Huntington Circuit Court; *Samuel E. Cook,* Judge.

Action by Moore-Mansfield Construction Company against the Marion, Bluffton and Eastern Traction Company and another. From a judgment for defendants, the plaintiff appeals. *Reversed.*

Wm. A. Ketcham and *Lesh & Lesh,* for appellants.

Abram Simmons and *Frank C. Dailey,* for appellees.

LAIRY, J.—Appellant filed its complaint in the Huntington Circuit Court, by which it sought to recover from appellees a large sum of money alleged to be due it on various

claims arising out of the construction of an electric interurban railway. Each appellee filed a separate answer in
abatement to which a separate demurrer by appellant was
addressed and overruled. The issues were closed by a reply
in general denial to each paragraph of the answer in abatement. A trial resulted in a judgment in favor of appellees
on such answers. The answer in abatement by the Bluffton
and Marion Construction Company is in two paragraphs,
the first of which is similar in its essential averments to the
one paragraph of answer filed by the other appellee.

1. Each of these paragraphs appears to the court to
state facts sufficient to constitute a cause for the
abatement of the action, and as appellant has not called
our attention to any specific defect they will be deemed
sufficient to withstand a demurrer.

It is claimed on behalf of appellant that the evidence is
not sufficient to sustain these paragraphs, and that the
result of this appeal depends on a decision of the question
thus presented. This question must be determined from a
consideration of the evidence in connection with the answers
in support of which it was admitted. These answers aver,
in substance, that prior to the commencement of this action
appellant brought an action in the Circuit Court of Huntington County, Indiana, against the two appellees in this
action alleging the same cause of action against them as is
set out in the complaint filed in this case. It is further
alleged that the parties to the action previously filed are
the same as the parties to this action, and that the same is
still pending in said court and is undetermined. The evidence adduced at the trial consisted entirely of records and
documents, being the pleadings and other papers filed in the
former case and the order-book entries made therein. It
seems to be conceded by appellant that the complaint filed
in the action referred to in appellees' answers in abatement
states the same cause of action stated by the complaint in
the case at bar, the only difference being that the complaint

in the former action stated facts on which a mechanic's lien was asserted, and that it asked a foreclosure of such lien. It is also conceded by appellant that since the decision of the Supreme Court of this State in the case of *Indianapolis, etc., Traction Co.* v. *Brennan* (1910), 174 Ind. 1, 87 N. E. 215, 90 N. E. 65, 90 N. E. 68, 91 N. E. 503, 30 L. R. A. (N. S.) 85, the complaint in question does not state facts sufficient to show a lien in favor of appellant or to entitle it to a foreclosure; and that it states only a cause of action for damages for breach of contract, work and labor done and materials furnished; and that, so considered, the issues tendered by the complaint in the action previously filed are identical with those tendered by the complaint in this action.

The evidence also shows that the plaintiff in the former action, on August 30, 1909, dismissed its action against the defendants, in vacation, and that at the next term the court, over the objections of the defendants, entered a judgment dismissing plaintiff's cause of action as set out in its complaint without prejudice, and awarding to defendants their costs. It thus appears that the issues joined on the complaint and the answers thereto were withdrawn from the consideration of the court before the commencement of this action, and that no cause of action, based on the issue presented by the complaint, was pending at the time this action was commenced.

Appellees state that appellant had no right to dismiss its complaint as it did, at the time and under the circumstances disclosed by the record introduced in evidence. The evidence shows that issues were formed in the former action by defendants' filing an answer in eight paragraphs, the first of which was a general denial and the last of which was a set-off, and by a general denial to the affirmative paragraphs of answer and to the set-off. The case was then referred to a master commissioner to take testimony and report his findings to the court. At the time this reference was made, the court and the attorneys were treating the case as one for foreclosure of a subcontractor's lien. After the court had made the order dismissing plaintiff's cause of action as stated in its complaint, the commissioner to whom the case had been referred filed his report, with the court's finding on all the issues made by the pleadings. Plaintiff unsuccessfully objected to the filing of this report, and afterward moved to strike it from the files, which objection was overruled. Afterward plaintiff filed exceptions to the report of the master commissioner, and, so far as the evidence in this case shows, the exceptions so filed were pending at the time the answers in abatement were filed in this case.

We will first consider the right of plaintiff to dismiss the cause of action stated in the complaint. Under the common-law practice, a plaintiff in an action at law 2. had a right to dismiss his action at any time before verdict, but in a suit in equity the complainant did not possess a similar right, the privilege being granted or withheld by the chancellor. A dismissal was allowed in cases where it would work no hardship or injustice to the defendant, but the right was denied where, in the opinion of the chancellor, the defendant would be injured by the termination of the suit, or where the dismissal would be inequitable. This rule still seems to prevail in states where the common-law pleading and practice are adhered to, and where it has not been changed by statute. *Electrical Accumulator Co.* v. *Brush Electric Co.* (1890), 44 Fed. 602; *Chicago, etc., R. Co.* v. *Union Rolling-Mill Co.* (1884), 109 U. S. 702, 713, 3 Sup. Ct. 594, 27 L. Ed. 1081; *Watt* v. *Crawford* (1845), 11 Paige 470.

In jurisdictions where the common law prevails, it has been held that no dismissal will be allowed in equity after an order of reference has been made. *Pullman's Palace-Car*

Co. v. *Central Transp. Co.* (1891), 49 Fed. 261; *Briscoe* v. *Brett* (1814), 2 Ves. & B. 377; *Wyatt* v. *Sweet* (1882), 48 Mich. 539, 12 N. W. 692, 13 N. W. 525.

By an application of this rule and on the authorities cited in its support, appellees insist that appellant in the former action had no right to dismiss the cause of action stated in the complaint, and that for this reason we must regard it as still pending. This position cannot be maintained.

Under the provisions of our code there is no dis-
3. tinction in pleading and practice between actions at law and suits in equity. §249 Burns 1908, §249 R. S. 1881. This statute does not abridge the power of the court to grant equitable relief, neither does it change the rules of law or the principles of equity as applied in determining the substantial rights of parties, but in some instances it does change the form of procedure by which the remedy is obtained. *Emerick* v. *Miller* (1902), 159 Ind. 317, 64 N. E. 28; *Terre Haute, etc., R. Co.* v. *State, ex rel.* (1902), 159 Ind. 438, 65 N. E. 401.

The section of our code heretofore cited provides that there shall be but one form of action for the enforcement or protection of private rights, and the redress of
2. private wrongs, which is denominated a civil action.

A statute providing for the dismissal of actions, enacted after the adoption of the code, must be held to apply to a civil action, regardless of whether the relief sought is legal or equitable. Section 338 Burns 1908, §333 R. S. 1881, provides that an action may be dismissed by the plaintiff, without prejudice before the jury retires; or, when the trial is by the court, at any time before the finding of the court is announced. The next succeeding section provides for a dismissal in vacation. The distinction contended for by appellees has never been recognized in this State, and the provisions of the statute have been frequently invoked in the dismissal of actions which prior to the enactment of the code were of exclusive equitable jurisdiction. *Beard* v.

Becker (1880), 69 Ind. 498; *Burns* v. *Reigelsberger* (1880), 70 Ind. 522.

The report of the commissioner was not the finding of the court. A master commissioner is not a court, and
4. judicial duties which courts alone can exercise cannot be conferred on him. *Terre Haute, etc., R. Co.* v. *State, ex rel., supra; Shoultz* v. *McPheeters* (1881), 79 Ind. 373.

At the time of the dismissal of the cause of action stated in the complaint in the former action the commissioner had prepared his report, and, at the request of coun-
5. sel, had furnished to them copies of such report, but it had not yet been filed. The court under such circumstances properly ordered a dismissal on the motion of . plaintiff. *Crafton* v. *Mitchell* (1893), 134 Ind. 320, 33 N. E. 1032; *Mitchell* v. *Friedley* (1890), 126 Ind. 545, 26 N. E. 391.

There is another and more cogent reason why the
6. order of dismissal, entered in the former action, is binding on the parties. The court had jurisdiction of the subject-matter and of the parties to the action,
7. and the question was properly before the court for decision. It had the power to decide and might decide right or wrong. Under such circumstances, an order of dismissal wrongfully entered would not have been ineffective but merely erroneous. It would have been binding on the parties unless reversed on appeal or set aside in a direct proceeding brought for that purpose. It could not be collaterally attacked. 14 Cyc. 421; *County of Northampton* v. *Geisinger* (1885), 1 Lehigh Val. Law Rep. (Pa.) 113.

If the eighth paragraph of answer filed by defendants in the former suit is to be treated as a set-off, it would not be affected by the dismissal of the cause of ac-
8. tion stated in the complaint. The defendants would have the right to proceed to final judgment on the

issues tendered by the set-off, and to recover thereon any amount shown to be due them from the plaintiff under the issues so formed, but the court would have no right, in determining the questions presented by the set-off and the answers thereto, to consider or determine any issues formed on the complaint. The fact that the master commissioner ignored the dismissal of the cause of action stated in the complaint, and filed a report covering all of the issues originally presented by the pleadings does not in any manner affect the duties of the court in this respect, and

9. we have no right to assume that the court in passing on such report, will consider any question not presented by the pleadings then on file.

The evidence shows without dispute that a former suit was commenced on the same cause of action stated in the complaint in this case, but we think that it is equally

10. apparent from the evidence that the cause of action so begun was dismissed before the complaint in this case was filed, and that it was not then pending and undecided. The evidence is not sufficient to sustain the first paragraph of answer in abatement as filed by each defendant, and a new trial must be granted for this reason.

Neither the allegations of the complaint nor those of the set-off are of such a character as to justify the court in construing either as an equitable action for an accounting. *Field* v. *Brown* (1896), 146 Ind. 293, 45 N. E. 464.

Inasmuch as this case will probably be retried, it becomes important for us to determine the sufficiency of the second paragraph of answer in abatement filed by defendant Bluffton & Marion Construction Company. From the averments of this answer it appears that this defendant is a corporation organized under the laws of the State of Indiana, and that its home office and place of business is in Bluffton, Wells county, Indiana, and other facts averred showing that no service of summons could be legally had on this defendant in Huntington county, Indiana, and that no such service was in fact made.

It seems to be conceded by appellant that the averments of the answer are sufficient to show that the Circuit Court of Huntington county did not and could not obtain jurisdiction over the person of this defendant by the service of process in Huntington county, but it is contended that the averments are not sufficient to show that such court did not obtain jurisdiction in some other manner. Our attention is called to §315 Burns 1908, §312 R. S. 1881, which, so far as applicable, reads as follows: "Where there are several defendants, residing in different counties, the action may be brought in any county where either defendant resides, and a separate summons may be issued to any other county where the other defendants may be found." It is suggested that the venue of the action was properly laid in Huntington county as to the defendant traction company, and that if the defendant filing this answer was joined as a codefendant in such action, the Circuit Court of Huntington county might have obtained jurisdiction of the person of such codefendant by causing a summons to be issued and served on it in Wells county, or in any other county of the State where such service could be legally made. An

11. answer denying the jurisdiction of the court is a dilatory plea and is not regarded with favor. It must be certain and definite, and nothing in its favor can be supplied by intendment. Such a plea must anticipate and exclude all such supposable facts as would if alleged on the opposite side defeat the plea. *Rush* v. *Foose Mfg. Co.* (1898), 20 Ind. App. 515, 51 N. E. 143; *Brown* v. *Underhill* (1892), 4 Ind. App. 77, 30 N. E. 430; *Needham* v. *Wright* (1895), 140 Ind. 190, 39 N. E. 510; *State* v. *Comer* (1902), 157 Ind. 611, 62 N. E. 452.

Defendant construction company by its separate answer has endeavored to aver facts showing that the trial court

did not obtain jurisdiction over its person in the man-
12. ner suggested by appellant.   In addition to the facts
heretofore stated the answer avers "that its codefendant, the Marion, Bluffton and Eastern Traction
Company is not indebted to the said plaintiff for any of
the causes of action stated in the complaint or in any paragraph thereof, or for any item of indebtedness stated in
said complaint or in any paragraph thereof, and that no
contract either express or implied was ever entered into between the plaintiff and the defendant, the Marion, Bluffton
and Eastern Traction Company, by which said defendant,
the Marion, Bluffton and Eastern Traction Company became indebted to said plaintiff for the cause of action
stated in said complaint or in any paragraph of said
complaint or for any item of indebtedness stated in said
complaint or any paragraph thereof."

The demurrer to this answer admits the truth of
13. the averments quoted for the purpose of testing the
sufficiency of the pleading.   If these averments are
true, they show that the defendant traction company was
not liable on the cause of action stated in the complaint, and
a fortiori that the two corporations who were joined as defendants were not liable to the plaintiff on a joint cause of
action.   Under our practice, a plea in abatement
14. must precede a plea in bar, and it is well settled that
where matter in abatement is joined in the same paragraph with matter in bar, the matter in abatement is waived
and may be stricken out on motion.   *Smith* v. *Pedigo*
(1896), 145 Ind. 361, 422, 33 N. E. 777, 44 N. E. 363, 19
L. R. A. 433, 32 L. R. A. 838.

We cannot, however, agree with appellant's contention
that the averments which we have quoted from the answer
go to the merits of the case, and should be regarded
12. as matter in bar.   These facts if established by the
evidence would not defeat or tend to defeat the plaintiff's cause of action against the party filing this answer.

A judgment in favor of the defendant construction company on this answer would not even determine that the plaintiff had no cause of action against the defendant traction company so as to be binding between such parties; but it would determine as between the plaintiff and the defendant construction company that the two defendants were not jointly liable. If the defendant construction company was solely liable, it could not be compelled to defend this action on the merits in Huntington county, because it had been joined as a codefendant with another corporation with which it was not jointly liable; and this is true even though the venue as to its codefendant was properly laid in Huntington county, and a summons was properly issued and served on the construction company in another county.

Under the provisions of our statute, a plaintiff may bring an action against two or more persons jointly liable in the county where either resides, and the court may obtain jurisdiction over the persons of the defendants residing in other counties by the issue and service of summons on them in the counties in which they reside; but this does not authorize a plaintiff having a cause of action against a nonresident of the county in which the action is brought to join him as a codefendant with a resident of such county against whom he has no cause of action. If he does so the court does not obtain jurisdiction of the person of such nonresident, because a summons may have been issued and served on him in the county of his residence. A person cannot thus be compelled to defend, in a county other than that of his residence, a case, upon its merits, in which he is solely liable, and such a state of facts, if properly pleaded in abatement and proved, is sufficient to abate the action as to such defendant.

The question here considered has not, to our knowledge, been decided by either the Supreme Court or the Appellate Court of this State. As different forms of practice prevail in the various states, the decisions of other courts of last resort cannot be considered as directly in point, but the propositions on which our conclusion is based seem to be supported by abundant authority· from other states. *Barry v. Wachosky* (1899), 57 Neb. 534, 77 N. W. 1080; *Penney v. Bryant* (1903), 70 Neb. 127, 96 N. W. 1033; *Hamilton* v. *DuPre* (1900), 111 Ga. 819, 35 S. E. 684; *Adams* v. *Williams* (1906), 125 Ga. 430, 54 S. E. 99; *Atchison, etc., R. Co.* v. *Waddell Bros.* (1905), 38 Tex. Civ. App. 434, 86 S. W. 655.

The judgment is reversed, with directions to grant a new trial.

NOTE.—Reported in 101 N. E. 15. See, also, under (2) 14 Cyc. 402; (3) 1 Cyc. 736; (10) 1 Cyc. 24; (11) 31 Cyc. 168. For a discussion of what constitutes a "final submission" of a cause so as to preclude a voluntary dismissal, see 4 Ann. Cas. 510.

DIXON *v.* THOMPSON ET AL.

[No. 7,553. Filed May 28, 1912. Rehearing denied March 4, 1913.]

1. TAXATION.—*Tax Sales.*—*Validity.*—To convey title, a tax sale must be in accordance with the statute, and if any essential act has been omitted, or has been improperly done, the sale is ineffectual and insufficient to convey title to the purchaser. p. 563.

2. TAXATION.—*Tax Sales.*—*Place of Sale.*—*Validity.*—Under §10355 Burns 1908, Acts 1891 p. 199, §184, providing for posting copies of the delinquent list, and also notice that so much of such delinquent lands and lots as may be necessary to discharge the taxes. etc., will be sold at public auction at the courthouse door, etc., and §10380 Burns 1908, Acts 1891 p. 191, §206, providing the form of tax deed, the failure to conduct a tax sale at the courthouse door renders such sale invalid and the tax deed will not convey a good and sufficient title. p. 564.

3. TAXATION.—*Tax Sales.*—*Invalid Sales.*—*Rights of Purchaser.*— Under the provisions of §§10388, 10394 Burns 1908, Acts 1901 p. 366, §§1, 3, where a conveyance of land for taxes is invalid, the lien for taxes, which the State had prior to the sale, is transferred to the purchaser at such sale and he becomes subrogated to all of the rights of the State therein, and such right of lien remains a charge against the land until the taxes, interest and penalty, are actually repaid to him, or until such time as the lien grows into an absolute title. p. 564.

4. TAXATION.—*Tax Sales.—Invalid Sales.—Priority of Lien Over Lien for Street Improvement.—Estoppel.*—Although by §8714 Burns 1908, Acts 1905 p. 219, §109, relating to special assessments for street improvements, it is provided that liens for such special assessments shall have precedence over all liens except taxes, where a purchaser of a lot at a tax sale, holding a tax deed regular on its face, and having knowledge of irregularities in conducting the sale which rendered same invalid, remained silent after notice of the adoption of a resolution for the improvement of the street on which such lot abuts, and did not disclose that he was not the absolute owner of such lot until after the improvement was made and suit was brought to foreclose the assessment lien, he thereby waived the superiority of the lien for taxes, and is estopped from setting up the defect in his title to defeat the lien for such assessment. p. 565, 567.

5. SUBROGATION.—*Equitable Rights.*—The right of subrogation is an equitable right, and one who asserts such right must act fairly and equitably before the courts will decree in his favor. p. 566.

From Howard Circuit Court; *Lex J. Kirkpatrick*, Judge.

Action by Walter J. Dixon against George M. Thompson and another. From a judgment for defendants, the plaintiff appeals. *Reversed.*

Harness, Moon & Voorhis, for appellant.

Blacklidge, Wolf & Barnes, John E. Osborn and *Horace C. Skillman*, for appellees.

IBACH, J.—The city of Kokomo caused one of its streets to be improved by the construction of a sidewalk thereon. For a part of the cost of the improvement an assessment was spread against the lots involved in this suit, which appeared on the records in the names of appellees Thompson and Osborn. These assessments were not paid, and appellant brought suit against them to recover the amount thereof.

It appears from the record that appellees Thompson and Osborn purchased the lots at a sale for delinquent taxes, and were holding them under tax deeds at the time suit was brought by appellant. The other appellees are junior lien holders, who acquired sewer assessment liens subse-

quent to the lien obtained by appellant by construction of
the sidewalk. These parties were defaulted, and their interests are not involved in this appeal. The sufficiency of
the complaint was not questioned in the court below, neither
is it raised here. Issues were joined by the filing of a general denial and a cross-complaint.

In their cross-complaint appellees aver a number of defects in the sale of the lots for taxes, disclaim having title
to the lots under the tax deeds issued on these sales, and seek
to enforce their tax liens, insisting that they could not be
deprived of their statutory lien for the taxes so paid and
interest, whenever it was made to appear that the conveyance to them availed nothing, for the reason that the tax
sale had been improperly conducted. At the trial they introduced evidence tending to prove but one of the defects
alleged, namely, that the sales to them were defective because they were not held at the courthouse door, as the law
requires, but instead were held in the office of the county
treasurer.

The cause was tried by the court, which found for appellees on their cross-complaint that appellant had no lien
on the lots as against appellees, and that their lien was a
first lien for all the money they had expended, together
with 20 per cent interest. The decree provided for a sale
and for distributing the funds recovered from the sale first
to appellees Thompson and Osborn, and the remainder, if
any, to appellant. No errors are raised and argued here
except that the decision is contrary to law and is not sustained by sufficient evidence.

The first tax sale at which the two lots in question were
sold to appellees was held on February 10, 1902, and the
deed issued to them on February 5, 1906. Taxes for subsequent years were not paid, and they were again sold to
appellees on February 8, 1904, and a second deed issued
September 2, 1907. At the time of the first sale by the
county treasurer the same lots were sold by the city treas-

urer to appellees for delinquent city taxes, and a deed given therefor on February 6, 1906. These deeds were all duly recorded in the recorder's office, and were regularly transferred on the transfer records in the auditor's office. So we find nothing on the face of the proceedings, nor in the recitals in the deeds, which would indicate any irregularities in any of such sales. Yet it is averred in the cross-complaint, and the evidence supports the averment, that the sales were wholly illegal and irregular, in that they were made in the county treasurer's office in the courthouse, and not at the courthouse door, as required by statute. See §§10355, 10380 Burns 1908, Acts 1891 p. 199, §§184, 206.

The manner of conducting a delinquent tax sale to
1. make the same effective to convey title must be in accordance with the statute, and each step required from the first publication notice to the delivery of the deed must be taken. If any material and essential act required to be done has been omitted, or has been improperly done, the entire sale must be held ineffectual and insufficient to convey title to the purchaser. *Gavin* v. *Shuman* (1864), 23 Ind. 32; *Mattox* v. *Stevens* (1895), 140 Ind. 282, 39 N. E. 460; *Green* v. *McGrew* (1905), 35 Ind. App. 104, 72 N. E. 1049, 73 N. E. 832, 111 Am. St. 149.

Again, it is provided by statute that "if any conveyance for taxes shall prove to be invalid and ineffectual to convey title because the description is insufficient, or for any other cause than the first two enumerated in the preceding section, the lien which the state has on such lands shall be transferred to and vested in the grantee * * * who shall be entitled to recover from the owner of such land * * * the amount of such taxes, interest and penalty legally due thereon at the time of such sale, with interest as in this act hereinafter provided, and all taxes subsequently paid and such lands shall be bound for the final payment thereof." §10388 Burns 1908, Acts 1901 p. 366. It is further provided that "if any conveyance made by the county auditor pursuant to a sale made for the nonpayment of taxes, under this or any former tax law, shall prove to be invalid and ineffectual to convey title for any other cause than such as are enumerated in the section immediately preceding the last section, the lien which the state had on such land for state, county, township and all lawful purposes, shall remain in full force and shall be transferred by such deed to the grantee and vested in him, * * * who shall be entitled to recover from the owner of such lands the owner of any life estate, or any other person first personally liable for the payment of such taxes, the amount of such legal taxes * * * and also the amount of all subsequent taxes paid, with like interest and such claim shall be a lien upon such lands, and the same shall be bound for the final payment thereof.'' §10394 Burns 1908, Acts 1901 p. 366.

In the consideration of a somewhat similar case,
2. this court has announced the rule to be that where title to land does not pass by virtue of the auditor's
3. deed, the purchaser, having acquired the lien of the State through the sale, should be granted the compensation provided by the statute for the money expended at the sale. *Green* v. *McGrew, supra.* The first question then is, Did title to the lots pass to appellees under and by virtue of these sales, or do they simply hold a lien on such lands for taxes paid? Construing the statute first mentioned strictly, as we must, we are disposed to hold that because of the failure on the part of the public officers to conduct the tax sale at the particular place provided by law, the sale was invalid, and the deed would not convey a good and sufficient title to appellees. See 37 Cyc. 1336, and cases cited under note 78. Likewise construing the remaining two sections set out above, we hold that the lien for taxes, which the State had prior to the sale, was transferred by such sale to appellees, and that they became subrogated to all the rights of the State therein. It seems that the legislature by the enactment of the section last above quoted intended to re-

move any and all doubt from the minds of all bidders at delinquent tax sales as to their right to maintain a lien at all times on the property purchased for any sums paid for taxes. They thereby made it plain that whatever lien the State had the purchaser would have, and in case title failed, the lien for the money paid was not lost. This assurance and confidence bestowed has always enabled the State to recover promptly and without delay its portion of the taxes for the support of the common government. If we were to hold otherwise, doubt and uncertainty would at once arise in such matters and the State would be seriously handicapped in the receipt of the funds justly due it. No such result could have been intended by the legislature. For the reasons given we hold the tax sales illegal, and that the purchasers did not acquire title thereby. But their rights of lien for the amount of taxes paid remained a charge against the lots until the taxes, interest and penalty were actually repaid to them as provided by law, or until such time that the lien would grow into an absolute title.

The question then remains, Is the lien of appellees paramount to that of appellant? To this we must answer affirmatively (*Ellison* v. *Branstrator* [1910], 45 Ind.

4. App. 307, 88 N. E. 963, 89 N. E. 513), unless it can be said that they are estopped from making such claim, or that by their own conduct they have waived the right to have their lien so declared.

The deeds from the auditor to appellees show *prima facie* title in them, and nothing appears from any record from the beginning of the tax sale to the recording of the several deeds to indicate that there was irregularity in such sales, or that appellees thereby acquired anything less than absolute title to the lots. It is shown by the record that on April 15, 1908, the board of public works of the city of Kokomo adopted a declaratory resolution for the construction of the sidewalk along and in front of this property. It is admitted by appellees that the averments of the complaint as relating to the construction of the sidewalk are true, and this includes the admission that notice of such resolution was obtained on appellees as the owners of the real estate, to the effect that said property would be assessed to pay for the improvement. That was the time for appellees to make it known that they were not claiming title to the land, because of a defect in the sale. To this defect they were parties, as the records show they attended the sale in person and knew of the character of such sale. Yet, being fully informed of all these conditions, and being fully informed of the fact that the special improvement was to be made and the property was to be assessed for it and would be sold to make the assessment if not paid, they failed to reveal their true interest. In our judgment, the notice provided for by statute, and which they admittedly received, was such as fully to protect their interest if objection was timely made. It was their duty, before the expense of improvement had been incurred, to speak and make known their claim that the records disclosing title in them were erroneous, and that they were simply holders of a lien for taxes paid, title having failed. As they did not do this, but remained silent until the improvement was made and the value of the property enhanced thereby, and for more than a year thereafter, and did not speak until appellant brought suit to foreclose his lien, they must then be held under the facts of this particular case, as against appellant to have acquiesced in the apparent record title shown in them, and to have waived their rights to insist upon a lien superior to the claim and lien of appellant, and by their conduct to have estopped themselves from attacking his claim. The

5. right of subrogation is recognized to be an equitable right, and the person who asserts such a right will be required to act fairly and equitably before the courts will decree in his favor. The law is not so unjust as to permit a party acting in good faith and relying on the facts disclosed by all the records of all these proceedings

as speaking the truth that appellees were the owners of the property, to be subjected to a claim for a lien asserted by them after the time when it became their duty to speak and no longer remain silent.

Appellees consented to the holding of the sale in the treasurer's office, accepted title under those circumstances, paid no attention to the fact that the city and appellant

4. were relying on the record disclosing title in them.

Since appellant improved the lots in good faith without any notice that appellees were not the legal owners thereof, he cannot now be held to suffer, being without fault, and at the same time appellees be permitted to profit, and allow their own lack of diligence in failing to make known a latent interest to work a benefit to themselves to the injury and detriment of appellant. We therefore hold that as against appellant they cannot assert a prior lien.

We are mindful of the provisions of the statute relating to special assessment liens, wherein it is provided that the lien of the same "shall have precedence over all liens except taxes" (§8714 Burns 1908, Acts 1905 p. 219, §109), and were it not for the conduct of appellees in this case we would hold their tax lien superior to the lien for improvement assessments, but by reason of their having by their own affirmative conduct waived this right of superiority, the sidewalk assessment became a lien on the lots in the name of Thompson and Osborn superior to their tax title to the same extent as if they had purchased them from a former owner, and had received and placed of record a warranty deed therefor.

We do not intend to hold that appellees could not assert the State's lien for taxes successfully were their title attacked for invalidity by some person other than themselves, or that they could not ordinarily, by a proper proceeding, themselves raise the question of defect of title, and have a lien declared in their favor, but what we do decide is, that, under the facts of the present case, appellees have no right themselves to set up a defect in their title, it having been attacked by no one else, in order to defeat appellant's lien.

The judgment is reversed, with directions to the trial court to find for appellant in accordance with the prayer of his complaint.

Hottel, C. J., Lairy, Felt and Adams, JJ., concur. Myers, J., not participating.

NOTE.—Reported in 98 N. E. 788. See, also, under (1) 37 Cyc. 1468; (2) 37 Cyc. 1336; (3) 37 Cyc. 1531; (4) 37 Cyc. 1534; (5) 37 Cyc. 371. As to who may purchase and enforce a tax title, see 75 Am. St. 229.

HOLTHOUSE *v.* POLING.

[No. 7,702.   Filed November 20, 1912.   Rehearing denied March 4, 1913.]

1. PRINCIPAL AND AGENT.—*Bills and Notes.—Equitable Defenses.*— In an action by an agent against his principal on a note for money borrowed from the agent and invested by the principal in the business which the agent was conducting for him, the principal may, by cross-complaint, present an equitable defense and require the agent to give an account of his trust. p. 570.

2. PRINCIPAL AND AGENT.—*Actions.—Waiver of Tort.—Action on Implied Contract.*—A principal may waive the tort of his agent based on his failure to account, and sue him as on an implied contract for the money due. p. 570.

3. PRINCIPAL AND AGENT.—*Accounting by Agent.*—Where an agent has been intrusted with his principal's money to be expended for a definite purpose, he may be required to account in equity, and in making such accounting he has the burden of showing that his trust duties have been performed, and the manner of such performance. p. 571.

4. PRINCIPAL AND AGENT.—*Accounting by Agent.—Evidence.—Sufficiency.*—Where, on the question of whether an agent, intrusted with the management of a store, had accounted for the property and funds which came into his hands, it was shown that although the system of bookkeeping was careless, both the principal and the agent knew the condition of the business, and the agent testified that he had accounted for and turned over to the principal all moneys he received, except his salary, there was some evidence from which it may be said that such agent had accounted for the money coming into his hands. p. 571.

5. APPEAL.—*Review.*—*Findings.*—*Evidence.*—Where there is some evidence to sustain the finding of the trial court, the evidence will not be weighed on appeal. p. 572.

6. APPEAL.—*Questions Reviewable.*—*Excessive Amount of Recovery.*—*Manner of Saving Question.*—An assignment, as ground for a new trial, that the assessment of the amount of the recovery is erroneous, being too large, correctly saves the question, and a motion to modify the judgment is not necessary. p. 573.

7. APPEAL.—*Review.*—*Findings.*—*Evidence.*—In the absence of evidence to the contrary, the court on appeal cannot say that the amount of attorney's fees allowed by the trial court, based on the testimony of a practicing attorney, is either against the evidence or in conflict therewith. p. 573.

From Jay Circuit Court; *John F. LaFollette,* Judge.

Action by John W. Poling against Peter Holthouse. From a judgment for plaintiff, the defendant appeals. *Affirmed.*

John M. Smith and *Peterson & Moran,* for appellant.

Clark J. Lutz and *Emerson McGriff,* for appellee.

IBACH, J.—This was an action in the ordinary form, brought by appellee against appellant on a note for $600, interest and attorney's fees, executed by appellant to appellee. Appellant filed an answer in five paragraphs: a general denial, a plea of payment, a plea of want of consideration, two paragraphs of set-off, and a cross-complaint. Demurrers to each paragraph of answer except the first were overruled. The issues were then formed by filing replies to the several paragraphs of answer, and an answer to the cross-complaint. A trial by the court resulted in a finding and judgment against appellant and in favor of appellee in the sum of $1,103. Appellant's motion for a new trial having been overruled, and his exception saved, he has appealed to this court from the judgment below, assigning and arguing error of the court in overruling his motion for new trial. The causes assigned for new trial were that the finding of the court was not sustained by sufficient evidence and was contrary to law, and that the assessment of the amount of recovery was too large.

It is contended by appellant that a partnership existed between appellant and appellee in the conduct of a store at Redkey, Indiana; that each was to share alike in the losses and net profits of the business; that since appellant has traced a sum of money into the hands of appellee belonging to the partnership, it became appellee's duty to show what became of the money, when that issue was presented by the cross-complaint, and failing to do so, he could not recover on the note.

Appellee, however, contends that the evidence does not disclose a partnership between the parties, and, therefore, if appellee did retain funds in his possession which he failed to account for to appellant, the amount thereof could not be set up in a counterclaim against the note, because a tort cannot be set up as a counterclaim to a contract. Appellee also contends that even if there was a duty on him to make an accounting, the evidence shows this duty sufficiently complied with.

Whether the evidence disclosed a partnership between appellant and appellee in the conduct of the store, is not a controlling question in this appeal, for the fact still

1. remains that the relationship which did exist between them was one of trust and confidence, and the position of appellee devolved on him trust duties and obligations similar to those of a partner. Appellee at least stood as the agent of appellant in the use of his money to purchase goods for him, to pay the bills for the same, and, after paying his own salary and the expense of the store, to account to appellant for the profits. So that when appellee brought this action on his note, the proceeds of which were used in discounting current bills of the store, appellant could in the same action present an equitable defense and require him to give an account of his trust, and this was the evident purpose of the cross-complaint. By the filing of his an-

2. swers in set-off and cross-complaint appellant waived any tortious conduct on appellee's part, and sued him

as on an implied contract to return or pay over to appellant all money due him from the profits of the store. This he had a legal right to do. *Cooper* v. *Helsaback* (1838), 5 Blackf. 14; *Furry* v. *O'Connor* (1891), 1 Ind. App. 573; *Rittenhause* v. *Knoop* (1894), 9 Ind. App. 126.

The rule is well established, that where an agent has been intrusted with his principal's money to be expended for a definite purpose, the former may be required to ac-
3. count in equity, and in the making of such accounting the burden is on him to show that his trust duties have been performed and the manner of performing them. *Young* v. *Powell* (1885), 87 Mo. 128; *Carder* v. *Primm* (1892), 52 Mo. App. 102; *Marvin* v. *Brooks* (1883), 94 N. Y. 71, 81; *Thatcher* v. *Hayes* (1884), 54 Mich. 184, 19 N. W. 946. This appellee attempted to do, and the main
4. question involved in this appeal is whether he has accounted for the property and funds which came into his hands while managing the Redkey store. Summarizing the evidence, we find him chargeable with

Original stock of goods..................	$6,000.00
Cash received from sale of goods.........	120,188.27
Cash sent appellee by appellant...........	2,100.00
Cash from loan (note sued on)...........	600.00
Total charges......................	128,888.27
Credit for money deposited in bank and paid out for indebtedness..............	$109,349.67
Cash paid for expenses.................	12,187.46
Total thus accounted for...........	121,537.13
Total receipts	128,888.27
Balance receipts.................	7,351.14

There is also an explanation on the part of appellee which tends at least to account for this balance, and he shows specifically what was done with all of it save a few hundred dollars. Appellee says he invoiced the store each year, that appellant was present, and both knew the store "wasn't doing any good.'' He deposited in the bank in the name of Holthouse & Co. all moneys collected, and paid the running expenses out of daily sales. Some of the bills for goods he paid in cash and not by check. He charged himself with cash sales each evening, he put the money in the safe and often paid out of the fund so charged many minor expenses, and a book which contained a large number of these items was kept in the store, but had been lost after he had left the store. In other words, he testified that he accounted for and turned over to appellant all moneys he received, except his salary. The method of keeping the books of the store, and the manner in which its financial affairs were conducted, were, to say the least, very careless, and yet appellant himself, who had twenty-five years experience in the same line of business, was largely to blame for this condition. Besides, the evidence shows that before the store in question was opened, appellee had worked for appellant five years, and that he had managed the Redkey store for nine years, during all of which time appellant had absolute confidence in him and trusted him fully, and, so far as the evidence shows, made no objection to any of his conduct while acting as manager of the store. It is not to be wondered at that appellee is now unable to show in detail the manner in which all the money apparently coming into his hands has been disposed of, and it is a matter of common knowledge that under such conditions as stated above, it would be almost impossible that each item of expense could be kept clearly in mind and be disclosed specifically after so many years.

The trial court heard all the evidence, saw appellee on the witness stand, and observed his demeanor, and must have believed him when he testified that he had not taken any money out of the store except his salary. This

5. is some evidence from which it may be said that he accounted for the money which came into his hands, and where there is some evidence to sustain the finding this court will not weigh the evidence on appeal.

It was also assigned as a ground for a new trial

6. that the assessment of the amount of recovery is erroneous, being too large.   This correctly saved the question, and no motion to modify the judgment was necessary.   To prove the amount of attorneys' fees, ap-

7. pellee called Frank B. Jaqua, a practicing attorney of the Jay county bar, who testified as to what would be a reasonable attorneys' fee for the collection of a note of the amount sued on, where the attorneys rendered services such as were rendered by the attorneys in this case, and this was all the evidence on this point.   In the absence of any evidence to the contrary, we cannot say that the amount of attorneys' fees allowed by the trial court, based on this evidence, is either against the evidence or in conflict therewith.   The court did not err in overruling appellant's motion for a new trial.

It having been shown to the court that appellant has died since the submission of this appeal, the judgment is affirmed as of the date of submission.

NOTE.—Reported in 99 N. E. 810.   See, also, under (1) 1 Cyc. 737; 31 Cyc. 1609; (2) 31 Cyc. 1608; (3) 31 Cyc. 1609, 1649; (4) 31 Cyc. 1667; (5, 7) 3 Cyc. 360; (6) 29 Cyc. 954.   As to the waiving generally of tort for the seeking of relief in assumpsit, see 17 Am. Dec. 242.   As to waiving tort by principal where aggrieved by fraud of agent, see 134 Am. St. 194.

KNAPP *v.* BEACH.

[No. 7,807.   Filed March 5, 1913.]

1. CONTRACTS.—*Construction.*—*Surplusage.*—In construing a contract for the sale of corn, where it appears that the memorandum was written on a blank form providing for the advancement of a money loan on an agreement for the sale of grain, and no money loan was in fact made, the part of the memorandum referring to such loan will be disregarded, as being mere surplusage.   p. 575.

2. FRAUD, STATUTE OF.—*Contracts.*—*Signatures.*—The statute of frauds, §7469 Burns 1908, §4910 R. S. 1881, under which a contract, for the sale of goods worth more than $50, in the absence of part payment or partial delivery, must be in writing, etc., is satis-

fied, and the contract is enforceable, if it is signed alone by the party sued. p. 575.

3. CONTRACTS.—*Signatures.—Acceptance of Contract.—Effect.*—A contract, though signed by one party only, may become mutual and binding on both, if it is accepted and acted upon by the party not signing. p. 576.

4. CONTRACTS.—*Acceptance.—Action.—Mutuality.*—The bringing of an action on a contract, signed alone by the party to be charged, is in itself a sufficient acceptance to make the contract mutual. p. 576.

5. CONTRACTS. — *Executory Contracts. — Consideration. — Mutual Promises.*—Where a contract is executory on both sides, consisting of promises by each party to do something, the mutual promises of the parties are a sufficient consideration, each for the other, to render either party liable for a failure to carry out his part. p. 576.

6. FRAUDS, STATUTE OF.—*Contract of Sale.—Consideration.*—It is not necessary under the statute of frauds, §7464 Burns 1908, §4905 R. S. 1881, that the memorandum of a contract of sale should state the consideration. p. 576.

7. APPEAL.—*Review.—Evidence.—Verdict.*—A verdict for plaintiff is supported by sufficient evidence, where there was evidence to support the complaint in all particulars. p. 577.

From Clinton Circuit Court; *Joseph Combs*, Judge.

Action by John R. Beach against Wilson M. Knapp. From a judgment for plaintiff, the defendant appeals. *Affirmed.*

Joseph Claybaugh, for appellant.
Joseph P. Gray, for appellee.

IBACH, C. J.—The complaint asked for damages for breach of a contract, entered into by plaintiff and defendant, whereby plaintiff purchased and defendant sold and agreed to deliver to plaintiff 1,200 bushels of corn. A memorandum of the contract in the following words was attached to the complaint:

"Cambria, Ind. Aug. 6, 1909.
In consideration of the sum of .... dollars, to me in hand paid, the receipt whereof is hereby acknowledged, I hereby agree to sell and deliver unto J. R. Beach at his elevator, Cambria, Indiana, 1,200 Bushels of 72 lbs. No. 3. Yel. Corn. Said Grain to be delivered

by me in November, 1909, and to be in sound and merchantable condition, for which I am to receive payment at the rate of 40 c. per bushel after deducting all indebtedness, which may be due and owing by me to said J. R. Beach, that said grain is now on the land of W. M. Knapp in Clinton county, Ind., that the same is mine and is unincumbered by any mortgage or lien, and I hereby make this statement in order to procure the above named sum, and that I received a copy of this agreement.

W. M. Knapp.''

Appellant contends that the above written instrument is not on its face a complete and enforceable contract, because there is a lack of consideration and because it is unilateral.

The above memorandum appears to have been written on a blank form providing for the advancement of a money loan on an agreement for the sale of grain. No money loan was made in this case, and the court will disregard, as mere surplusage, the part of the memorandum referring to such loan. Disregarding the surplusage, there appears an agreement by appellant to sell to appellee at his elevator in Cambria, Indiana, "1,200 bushels of 72 lbs. of No. 3 yellow corn,'' to be delivered in November, 1909, in sound and merchantable condition, for which he was to receive 40 cents a bushel, after deducting any indebtedness owing by him to appellee.

1.

The only point of importance presented by the appeal is as to the mutuality of the contract. This was a contract for the sale of goods worth more than $50, and as there was no part payment, nor partial delivery, the contract, under the statute of frauds, must be in writing and signed by the party to be charged, or his authorized agent, before it can be enforced. §7469 Burns 1908, §4910 R. S. 1881. The general rule is that the statute is satisfied and the plaintiff may enforce the contract if the writing is signed alone by the party sued, the defendant in the action, and is not signed by the plaintiff. 29 Am. and Eng. Ency. Law (2d ed.) 858; *Dennis Simmons Lumber Co.*

2.

v. *Corey* (1906), 140 N. C. 462, 53 S. E. 300, 6 L. R. A. (N. S.) 468; *Bailey* v. *Leishman* (1907), 32 Utah 123, 89 Pac. 78, 13 Ann. Cas. 1117 and note; *Ullsperger* v. *Meyer* (1905), 217 Ill. 262, 75 N. E. 482, 2 L. R. A. (N. S.) 221, 3 Ann. Cas. 1032 and note; *Smith* v. *Smith* (1846), 8 Blackf. 208; *Newby* v. *Rogers* (1872), 40 Ind. 9.

Especially is it true that a contract signed by one 3. party only may become mutual and binding on both if the contract is accepted and acted on by the party not signing. *Munson* v. *Wray* (1845), 7 Blackf. 403; *Alcorn* v. *Morgan* (1881), 77 Ind. 184; *Chicago, etc., R. Co.* v. *Derkes* (1885), 103 Ind. 520, 3 N. E. 239.

The complaint avers that plaintiff contracted to 4. sell the aforesaid corn to his customers, and in consequence of defendant's failure to deliver the corn to him he was unable to carry out his contracts with his customers, and was thereby damaged. This shows that appellee accepted the contract and acted on it. Many of the authorities above cited hold that merely bringing an action on the contract is a sufficient acceptance to make it mutual.

Where a contract is executory on both sides, consisting of promises by each party to do something, the mutual promises of the parties, are a sufficient consideration, each 5. for the other, to render either party liable for a failure to carry out his part. In order to make a written executory contract for the sale of goods binding, it is not necessary for any money to pass from the purchaser to the seller until the seller has performed his part of the contract. But the present contract states what the consideration for the corn shall be, namely, the price of 40 cents per bushel to be paid to the seller. Furthermore, it is not necessary under our statute of frauds 6. that the memorandum of a contract of sale should state the consideration. §7464 Burns 1908, §4905 R. S. 1881.

The court did not err in overruling the demurrer to the complaint. There was evidence to support the com-

7. plaint in all particulars, therefore the verdict was supported by the evidence.

Judgment affirmed.

NOTE.—Reported in 101 N. E. 37. See, also, under (1) 9 Cyc. 585; (2) 20 Cyc. 272; (3, 4) 9 Cyc. 300; (5) 9 Cyc. 323; (6) 20 Cyc. 262, 269; (7) 3 Cyc. 348. As to the necessity that the memorandum be signed by the person to be charged, see 47 Am. Rep. 533. As to the sufficiency of the signature by one party only to a memorandum required by the statute of frauds, see 3 Ann. Cas. 1036; 13 Ann. Cas. 1121; Ann. Cas. 1912 C 416.

NEWSOM *v.* CHICAGO AND EASTERN ILLINOIS RAILROAD COMPANY.

[No. 7,838. Filed March 5, 1913.]

1. APPEAL. — *Record.* — *Evidence.* — *Questions Not Considered.* — Where the evidence is not in the record on appeal, the objection that the verdict is contrary to law, and to the evidence, cannot be considered. p. 578.

2. APPEAL.—*Record.—Bill of Exceptions.—Instructions.*—No question is presented on appeal as to the instructions, where such instructions are not brought into the record by a bill of exceptions, as provided by §660 Burns 1908, §629 R. S. 1881, or are not made a part of the record in one of the methods provided in other statutory provisions relating thereto. (§§558, 559, 560 Burns 1908, §§533, 534, 535 R. S. 1881; §561 Burns 1908, Acts 1907 p. 652; §691 Burns 1908, §650 R. S. 1881.) p. 578.

3. APPEAL. — *Record.* — *Instructions.* — Instructions that are not authenticated by the signature of the judge are not properly in the record under the provisions of §561 Burns 1908, Acts 1907 p. 652. p. 580.

4. APPEAL.—*Record.—Instructions.*—Where the record fails to disclose an order of court that the instructions be made a part of the record, they are not properly in the record under the provisions of §691 Burns 1908, §650 R. S. 1881. p. 580.

From Sullivan Circuit Court; *Charles E. Henderson,* Judge.

Action by Ray Q. Newsom against the Chicago and Eastern Illinois Railroad Company. From a judgment for defendant, the plaintiff appeals. *Affirmed.*

John A. Riddle and *Henry Bordenet*, for appellant.
Lamb, Beasley, Douthitt & Crawford, for appellee.

SHEA, J.—This action was brought by appellant against appellee to recover damages for his wrongful expulsion from one of appellee's passenger trains, and alleged unlawful arrest and imprisonment. The complaint was in two paragraphs, to each of which a demurrer was overruled. Answer in general denial. Trial, finding and judgment for appellee. Appellant's motion for a new trial was overruled, and this ruling is the only error assigned.

The reasons for a new trial are: (1) The verdict of the jury is contrary to law. (2) The verdict of the jury is contrary to the evidence. (3) The verdict of the jury is contrary to the law and the evidence. (4) The court erred in giving to the jury "of its own motion" instructions Nos. 10 and 14, and in refusing to give appellant's instructions Nos. 12 and 13. The evidence not being in the record, the first three reasons, if they were technically correct, which is doubtful, cannot be considered by this court.

It is earnestly argued by appellee that no assignment of error is attached to the record in conformity with Rule 4 of this court. While the manner of incorporating what purports to be an assignment of errors in the record is subject to criticism, we do not decide its sufficiency in this case. The other reasons in support of appellant's motion for a new trial go to the alleged error of the court in giving and refusing to give certain instructions.

It is very earnestly insisted by appellee that the instructions are not properly in the record, therefore no question is presented. On this point we direct attention to the record. On pages 19-21 of the record are to be found twelve instructions signed by attorneys for appellee, with marginal notes on each page as follows: "Instructions tendered by defendant," and on page 23 a marginal note: "Filing of instructions tendered by defendant." At the bottom of page 23 is a request by plaintiff that the court give certain instructions numbered 1 to 14, and that he indicate before the argument in said cause such instructions as will be given, by writing opposite each of them the words, "Given", "given as modified by the court", or "Refused." On pages 24-28, inclusive, are found fourteen instructions, marginal notes on each page, as follows: "Instructions tendered by plaintiff;" No. 1, "Given"; No. 2, "Refused"; No. 3, "Given"; Nos. 4, 5, 6, 7 and 8, "Refused"; No. 9, "Given"; Nos. 10, 11, 12, 13 and 14, "Refused", none of which marginal notes are signed by the judge, nor does the judge's signature appear at the end of the instructions. Beginning on page 28, up to and including page 42, are seventeen instructions, with the following marginal notes on each page: "Instructions given by Court of its own motion." At the close of the instructions the following entry is made: "Dated and signed this 25th day of March, 1910. Charles E. Henderson, Judge. Filed Mar. 25, 1910. Arthur E. DeBaun, Clerk." On April 20, 1910, the motion for a new trial was filed by appellant's attorneys. Afterward, as it appears in the record, but without date, the following entry is made: "And Plaintiff excepts to giving of instructions Numbers 10 and 14 given by the Court of its own motion separately and severally, and for refusing to give instructions numbers 12 & 13 requested by the plaintiff." It will be observed that the instructions are not brought into the record by a bill of exceptions as provided by §660 Burns 1908, §629 R. S. 1881. They are not made a part of the record in accordance with the provisions of §§558, 559, 560 Burns 1908, §§533, 534, 535 R. S. 1881. See *Petrie* v. *Ludwig* (1908), 41 Ind. App. 310, 83 N. E. 770; *Malott* v. *Hawkins* (1902), 159 Ind. 127, 138, 63 N. E. 308;

Oglebay v. *Tippecanoe Loan, etc., Co.* (1908), 41 Ind. App.
481, 82 N. E. 494. They are not properly in the
3. record under the provisions of §561 Burns 1908, Acts
1907 p. 652, because they are not authenticated by
the signature of the judge, as required by the provisions of
this section. *Strong* v. *Ross* (1905), 36 Ind. App. 174, 75
N. E. 291; *Cleveland, etc., R. Co.* v. *Powers* (1909), 173 Ind.
105, 88 N. E. 1073, 89 N. E. 485; *Fowler* v. *Fort Wayne, etc.,
Traction Co.* (1910), 45 Ind. App. 441, 91 N. E. 47; *Wiseman* v. *Gouldsberry* (1910), 45 Ind. App. 677, 91 N. E. 616;
Indianapolis, etc., R. Co. v. *Ragan* (1909), 171 Ind. 569, 86
N. E. 966; *Hotmire* v. *O'Brien* (1909), 44 Ind. App. 694, 90
N. E. 33; *Delaware, etc., Tel. Co.* v. *Fiske* (1907), 40 Ind.
App. 348, 81 N. E. 1110; *Supreme Tent, etc.,* v. *Ethridge*
(1909), 43 Ind. App. 475, 87 N. E. 1049; *Inland Steel Co.* v.
Smith (1907), 168 Ind. 245, 80 N. E. 538. They are
4. not properly in the record under the provisions of
§691 Burns 1908, §650 R. S. 1881, because the record
fails to disclose an order of court that the instructions be
made a part of the record. *Tell City Canning Co.* v. *Wilbur*
(1910), 46 Ind. App. 550, 93 N. E. 174; *Close* v. *Pittsburgh,
etc., R. Co.* (1898), 150 Ind. 560, 50 N. E. 560; *Russ* v. *Russ*
(1895), 142 Ind. 471, 474, 41 N. E. 941; *Town of Fredericks-
burg* v. *Wilcoxen* (1902), 158 Ind. 359, 63 N. E. 566; *Board,
etc.,* v. *Gibson* (1902), 158 Ind. 471, 63 N. E. 982; *Pennsylvania Co.* v. *Ebaugh* (1899), 152 Ind. 531, 53 N. E. 763.

It is very doubtful if proper exceptions were taken and
saved as to the giving of any instructions by the court on its
own motion, or the refusal to give those tendered by appellant, but it is unnecessary to decide that question.

It follows that the judgment of the lower court must be
affirmed.

NOTE.—Reported in 101 N. E. 26. See, also, under (1) 3 Cyc.
166; (2) 3 Cyc. 28, 170; (3, 4) 3 Cyc. Anno. 28—New.

SEIGMUND *v.* TYNER ET AL.

[No. 8,352. Filed March 5, 1913.]

1. APPEAL.—*Briefs.*—*Waiver of Error.*—Questions as to alleged errors in the admission and exclusion of testimony are waived by appellant's failure to discuss them in his brief, or to cite authority in support thereof. p. 583.

2. APPEAL.—*Review.*—*Objection to Evidence.*—*Waiver.*—Questions as to alleged error in the admission and exclusion of testimony are waived by a failure to state specific objections. p. 583.

3. LIMITATION OF ACTIONS.—*Accrual of Cause of Action.*—*Injury to Property.*—*Statutes.*—An action for injury by the overflow of real property is barred by the six years' statute of limitations, §294 Burns 1908, §292 R. S. 1881, where the acts which produced the overflow occurred more than six years before the bringing of the action, although the injuries are alleged to have been suffered within such six year period. p. 584.

4. APPEAL.—*Review.*—*Harmless Error.*—*Rulings on Demurrers to Answers Pleading Statute of Limitations.*—Where a cause of action was barred by the six years' statute of limitations, §294 Burns 1908, §292 R. S. 1881, which was pleaded, the action of the court in overruling demurrers to paragraphs of answer pleading the other statutes of limitations was harmless. p. 584.

5. WATERS AND WATERCOURSES.—*Drainage of Surface Water.*—*Answer Showing Easement by Prescription.*—*Sufficiency.*—In an action for injury to land by the drainage of surface water thereon, an answer showing an open, notorious, exclusive and adverse possession and use of the drains complained of for thirty years, with the right to flow water through the same across plaintiff's land during all that time, is sufficient as an answer showing an easement by prescription. p. 585.

6. WATERS AND WATERCOURSES.—*Drainage of Surface Water.*—*Rights of Purchaser With Notice.*—In an action for damages in overflowing plaintiff's land, the fact that defendant's drains were constructed and in use by and with the consent of all the owners of the lands affected, long before plaintiff purchased his real estate, and that he purchased with full knowledge of such fact and of defendant's easement or right to flow water across such land, constitutes a good defense. p. 585.

7. WATERS AND WATERCOURSES.—*Overflowing Land.*—*Actions.*—*Evidence.*—*Sufficiency.*—In an action for damages in overflowing plaintiff's land, evidence showing that from time immemorial water collected in small, well-defined, branch streams on defend-

ant's land and was carried over a portion of plaintiff's land and emptied into an ancient natural watercourse flowing through said land, that defendant placed certain tile ditches which empty into said branch streams on his land, and that no more water was emptied into said branch streams and carried over plaintiff's land into said watercourse than formerly resulted from the natural drainage of the land, is sufficient to support a finding and judgment for defendant. p. 586.

From Wabash Circuit Court; *A. H. Plummer*, Judge.

Action by Christopher H. Seigmund against John S. Tyner and others. From a judgment for defendants, the plaintiff appeals. *Affirmed.*

D. F. Brooks, for appellant.

Warren G. Sayre and *Nelson G. Hunter*, for appellees.

FELT, P. J.—This suit was brought by appellant against appellees, to recover damages for collecting water on their real estate and casting it on the land of appellant, and to enjoin the continued use of certain drains.

The complaint alleges, in substance, that appellant was, and had been for more than five years previous to the commencement of this suit, the owner of the southwest quarter of a certain section of land in Wabash county, and that appellees were the owners of real estate in said section, lying to the north and east of his said real estate; that appellees constructed many tile drains on their lands, by means of which they collected water on said lands and cast it upon the land of appellant in unusual and large quantities, thereby washing away the soil, overflowing said lands, and damaging crops thereon; that by collecting water, as aforesaid, and throwing it upon appellant's land, the grass and crops on his land have been damaged in the sum of $1,000, as shown by bill of particulars, which is as follows:

"Exhibit A.

Overflowing 10 acres of grass years 1906,-7,-8,-9.-$200.00
Washing away of soil over-flowing land by percolation,   500.00"

To this complaint appellees filed answer in six paragraphs, the first of which is a general denial. The substance of the second is that for more than thirty years appellees and their grantors have been in open, notorious, exclusive and adverse possession of the drains complained of in appellant's complaint, with the right to flow water through the same onto appellant's land. The third; fourth and fifth paragraphs set up respectively the six, fifteen, and twenty years' statute of limitations.

Appellant demurred separately and severally to each of said paragraphs of answer except the first, on the ground that neither paragraph states facts sufficient to constitute a defense to the cause of action stated in his complaint. Each of said demurrers was overruled, and appellant duly excepted. Appellant replied by general denial to each of said paragraphs of answer except the first. Errors are assigned on the overruling of the demurrer to each of said several paragraphs of answer, and the overruling of appellant's motion for a new trial.

1. The motion for a new trial alleges that the decision of the court is contrary to law and is not sustained by sufficient evidence; also a number of errors in the admission and exclusion of certain testimony, but

2. these questions are waived by failure of appellant to discuss them in his brief or to cite authority in support thereof; also for the reason that appellant has stated no specific objections to the admission of any of such testimony. Furthermore, in the discussion of the motion for a new trial, appellant confines himself exclusively to the assignment that the decision of the court is not sustained by sufficient evidence.

The undisputed facts show that appellant's real estate is bounded on the north by a highway known as Dova Pike; that about fifteen or twenty rods south of said highway and running practically parallel with the same, there is a small creek known as Ross Run which crosses appellant's land, and going west therefrom empties into Wabash river; that said stream is an ancient and natural watercourse, and is much lower than the land in that vicinity; that the lands of appellees, on which the ditches complained of are situate, lie north and northeast of appellant's land and north of Ross Run; that said highway is from six to ten feet higher than the ordinary level of said creek; that the land to the north and east of appellant's land slopes toward the creek; that the water which falls on said lands has always passed over the same and through well-defined channels, or small branch streams, which cross said highway and empty into said Ross Run; that the ditches complained of are tile drains on appellees' lands, which empty into said open ditches, or natural channels of water, on the land of appellees, and do not pass over or upon appellant's land; that prior to the building of such turnpike, wooden culverts were built across the road through which said natural drains carried the water across appellant's land to Ross Run; that said turnpike was built about thirty years ago by public authority, and stone culverts were built in the place of the old wooden culverts, and have been in continuous use since that time for the purposes aforesaid.

Appellant's suit is to recover damages for injuries
3. to his property alleged to have occurred in the years
    1906, 1907, 1908 and 1909. By the third clause of
    §294 Burns 1908, §292 R. S. 1881, injuries to prop-
4. erty are barred by the six years' statute of limitations.
Appellant's cause of action arose, if at all, at the time the damage occurred for which the action is brought, and such right of action is barred by the six years' statute of limitations. The rulings on the other paragraphs of answer pleading the other statutes could not therefore harm appellant in any view of their sufficiency or application. *Sherlock* v. *Louisville, etc., R. Co.* (1888), 115 Ind. 22, 38, 17 N. E. 171; *Kelly* v. *Pittsburgh, etc., R. Co.* (1902), 28 Ind.

App. 457, 463, 63 N. E. 233, 91 Am. St. 134; *Pickett v. Toledo, etc., R. Co.* (1892), 131 Ind. 562, 31 N. E. 200; *Southern Ind. R. Co.* v. *Brown* (1903), 30 Ind. App. 684, 66 N. E. 915; *Porter* v. *Midland R. Co.* (1890), 125 Ind. 476, 478, 25 N. E. 556; *City of Lebanon* v. *Twiford* (1895), 13 Ind. App. 384, 386, 41 N. E. 844.

The court did not err in overruling the separate demurrers to each of the several paragraphs of answer setting up respectively the six, fifteen and twenty years' statute of limitations.

The second paragraph of answer is sufficient, for it shows an open, notorious, exclusive and adverse possession and use of the drains complained of for thirty years, with

5. the right to flow water through the same across appellant's land during all that time. Proof of such facts would show an easement by prescription. *McCardle* v. *Barricklow* (1879), 68 Ind. 356; *Parish* v. *Kaspare* (1887), 109 Ind. 586, 10 N. E. 109; *Davis* v. *Cleveland, etc., R. Co.* (1894), 140 Ind. 468, 470, 39 N. E. 495; *Cleveland, etc., R. Co.* v. *Huddleston* (1899), 21 Ind. App. 621, 628, 52 N. E. 1008, 69 Am. St. 385; *Connor* v. *Woodfill* (1890), 126 Ind. 85, 87, 25 N. E. 876, 22 Am. St. 568; *Pyott* v. *State* (1908), 170 Ind. 118, 121, 83 N. E. 737.

Appellant has pointed out no objection to the sixth paragraph of answer. Its averments show that said drains were constructed and in use by and with the consent of

6. all the owners of said lands long before appellant purchased his real estate; that he purchased with full knowledge of the same and of appellee's easement, or right to flow water across his said lands. Under the authorities the answer states a good defense to appellant's complaint. *Ross* v. *Thompson* (1881), 78 Ind. 90; *Parish* v. *Kaspare, supra; Joseph* v. *Wild* (1896), 146 Ind. 249, 253, 45 N. E. 467; *McAllister* v. *Henderson* (1893), 134 Ind. 453, 34 N. E. 221.

Appellant insists that the evidence is not sufficient to support the judgment and that his motion for a new trial should be sustained. The evidence, practically without dispute, shows that Ross Run is an ancient and natural watercourse, and that the water from appellees' lands naturally flows toward it, and has from time immemorial collected in small, well-defined branch streams, made by the action of the water, and through them reached and emptied into Ross Run, after crossing the highway under said culverts. No new channel has been made on or across appellant's land, and the water from appellees' lands now, as formerly, passes through natural channels across appellant's lands to Ross. Run. Certain tile ditches have been constructed on the lands of appellees and empty into said branch streams on the lands of appellees. Appellant claims that these tile drains collect more water and precipitate it in shorter time than resulted from the natural drainage before the tile ditches were constructed. There is evidence tending to prove that before the tile drains were constructed, Ross Run carried a greater volume of water than it has since the tile drains have been in operation; that some of the tile ditches on appellees' lands drain a pond, that was the source of Ross Run, into another channel and away from appellant's lands.

There was ample evidence from which the court could find that no more water came into said channels and reached Ross Run through appellant's lands since the tile drains complained of were constructed than formerly resulted from the natural drainage of the land, and that the construction and operation of said tile drains on the lands of appellees have not materially changed the volume or flow of water across appellant's lands, nor in anyway damaged him. Such a finding shows no liability. *Wharton* v. *Stevens* (1891), 84 Iowa 107, 50 N. W. 562, 15 L. R. A. 630, 635, 35 Am. St. 296.

There is evidence supporting the finding and judgment of the trial court, and no error is shown harmful to appellant. Judgment affirmed.

NOTE.—Reported in 101 N. E. 20. See, also, under (1) 3 Cyc. 388; (2) 38 Cyc. 1393; (3) 25 Cyc. 1142, 1145; (4) 31 Cyc. 858; (5) 40 Cyc. 649, 653; (6) 40 Cyc. 649; (7) 40 Cyc. 653. As to waiver of appeal, expressly or as implied from acts or omissions, see 13 Am. Dec. 546. As to prescriptive title to water, see 93 Am. St. 712. As to right of, and liability for injuring others' property by flowage, see 57 Am. Dec. 684. On the question of the right to drain surface water into watercourse, see 24 L. R. A. (N. S.) 908.

BARBER ASPHALT PAVING COMPANY *v*: CITY OF INDIANAPOLIS.

[No. 7,786.   Filed March 5, 1913.]

1. MUNICIPAL CORPORATIONS.—*Public Improvements.—Contracts.— Guaranties of Work and Stipulations for Repairs.*—Where a contract for street improvement provided that the work should be done in such substantial manner that no repairs would be required for a period of nine years, that if such repairs became necessary the contractor would make good any damage to the work or any defect in the workmanship, materials, or condition of the work, which made such repairs necessary, that he would keep the work 'in good repair during that time, and make all repairs as directed, etc., that the guaranty should cover all repairs growing out of the imperfection or unsuitability of materials or composition, too great or too little moisture, defects in workmanship, extremes of heat or cold and other effects of climate, holes or cracks in the pavement, etc.; and that at the end of the guaranty period the pavement should be in good condition, present a surface so true and even that it would in no way be an obstruction to travel, and have such drainage that water could stand in no place to a greater depth than a quarter of an inch, such provisions are more than a guaranty against defects resulting from improper workmanship or unsuitable materials, and amount to a guaranty that the workmanship and materials which entered into the work were of such character that the street would withstand all the usual and necessary uses of travel for a period of nine years. pp. 593, 595.

2. CONTRACTS.—*Pleading.—Breach of Warranty.*—A breach of warranty, pleaded as a cause of action or defense, must, to be good

upon demurrer, aver the character and extent of the warranty, and the nature and particulars of the breach. p. 595.

3. MUNICIPAL CORPORATIONS—*Public Improvements.—Contracts.— Guaranties of Work and Stipulations for Repairs.—Breach.— Complaint.*—Where a street paving contract required that all repairs resulting from causes incident to the use of the street for public travel should be made by the contractor, a complaint, in an action to recover the cost of repairs made by the city, alleging that the wearing surface commenced to roll and wave and in many places the vehicles using said pavement in the ordinary course of travel cut through the wearing surface and the concrete into the sub-grade of the street, that the pavement became deteriorated and so badly worn that it could not be satisfactorily patched, and that in order to put it in good repair as contemplated in the contract, etc., it was necessary entirely to reconstruct and relay all the portion of the wearing surface above the concrete base, and in some places to repair the concrete base, shows that the defects were the result of breaches of defendant's guaranty contained in the contract sued on, and was sufficient. p. 598.

4. MUNICIPAL CORPORATIONS.—*Public Improvements.—Contracts.— Guaranties of Work and Stipulations for Repairs.—Breach.—Evidence.—Sufficiency.*—In an action by a city against a contractor for the cost of street repairs rendered necessary within the guaranty period, although there was evidence that such repairs were made necessary by the loss of lateral support due to the delay of a street car company in paving its portion of the street after the excavation therefor had been made, the decision for plaintiff was sustained by sufficient evidence and cannot be said to be contrary to law, where there was evidence that the repairs were made necessary by the use of defective material and improper lateral support by the contractor and which tended to support all the material averments of the complaint. p. 599.

5. MUNICIPAL CORPORATIONS—*Public Improvements.—Contracts.— Guaranties of Work and Stipulations for Repairs.—Notice to Repair.*—Under a contract for street paving in which the work was warranted for a certain period, and by which the character and extent of the repairs were left to the board of public works, and the repairs were to be made to its satisfaction, where the notice to repair was given pursuant to a resolution and order of the board, and gave complete information of the action of such board, the fact that such notice required the complete resurfacing of the street, which was unnecessary, will not relieve the contractor from liability for the cost of repairs made by the city on his failure to make them. p. 602.

6. MUNICIPAL CORPORATIONS.—*Public Improvements.*—*Contracts.*—*Guaranties of Work and Stipulations for Repairs.*—*Retention of Guaranty Fund After Judgment for Repairs Made.*—Where by a contract for street paving, the contractor warranted the work and agreed to make such repairs as should become necessary, and the city was authorized to retain a portion of the contract price as a repair guaranty fund, a recovery by the city of the cost of resurfacing a portion of the street does not prevent it from holding the balance of the fund as a guaranty for the repair of other portions of the street until the end of the guaranty period. p. 602.

From Superior Court of Marion County (77,834); *John L. McMaster,* Judge.

Action by the City of Indianapolis against the Barber Asphalt Paving Company. From a judgment for plaintiff, the defendant appeals. *Affirmed.*

Morris M. Townley, David B. Gaun and *George H. Peake,* for appellant.

Joseph B. Kealing, Merle N. A. Walker and *Newton J. McGuire,* for appellee.

HOTTEL, J.—On October 23, 1905, appellee, City of Indianapolis, through its board of public works, adopted a preliminary resolution for the improvement of a part of one of its streets known as West Michigan street. Other preliminary and necessary steps were taken by such board leading up to the confirmation of the original resolution for such improvement. The notice required in such cases, inviting bids for the proposed improvement, was given, and the contract therefor was awarded appellant, May 21, 1906.

Pursuant to such award, appellant and appellee on May 23, 1906, entered into a written contract, whereby appellant, for approximately $58,000, agreed to improve said street with Trinidad Pitch Lake Asphalt according to the plans and specifications adopted by said board of public works. Appellant completed said improvement, and procured an acceptance thereof by said board of public works. About six months later defects, ruts and holes appeared in a portion of that part of the street so improved, and the condition thereof was such that said board of public works, by a resolution to that effect, ordered a resurfacing of said part of said street, and other repairs thereon, and that notice of the action of such board be given to appellant. After receiving such notice, appellant failed and refused to make such repairs, whereupon they were made by appellee.

This is an action by appellee to recover on its said contract for such repairs. The complaint sets out in detail the various steps taken by the board of works in connection with said improvement leading up to the letting of the contract to appellant, and avers the execution of said contract, a copy of which, together with a copy of the plans and specifications, is filed with and made part of such complaint.

It then avers the completion of the work within the time provided by the contract, the acceptance thereof by such board of public works, the adoption of the preliminary assessment roll on April 12, 1907, and the adoption of the final assessment roll on May 6, 1907, and that within about six months after such completion and acceptance of said improvement, it became so out of repair and in such condition that appellee, by its board of public works, determined that a resurfacing of the street was necessary, and served notice on appellant to make such repairs; that appellant failed and refused to make such repairs or any part thereof; that appellee resurfaced the part of the street in question at a cost to it of $10,763.83. Facts showing that appellant is entitled to a credit on account of material furnished appellee, and on account of certain bonds held and sold by appellee under said contract, are averred, and judgment asked for a balance still due of $865.51. A demurrer to this complaint for want of facts was overruled and exceptions saved by appellant.

Appellant filed a cross-complaint in two paragraphs, by the first of which it is sought to recover the sum of $5,811.60, with interest, for asphalt sold by appellant to appellee, and by the second paragraph it sought to recover the sum of

$4,086.72, on an implied contract to pay for certain bonds of appellants, wrongfully converted by the appellee. These items were the same as those set out in the complaint and admitted to be proper credits against the total cost of repairs made by appellee.

Appellant filed an answer to the complaint in two paragraphs, the first being a general denial. The second paragraph of answer admits the execution of the contract sued on, and sets out in detail the character of the improvement required to be made thereunder, the materials used therein and the manner of construction. The substance and effect of these averments in brief are that the asphalt surface required by such contract is of a semi-fluid nature, with a tendency to spread in warm weather, and requires a lateral support to prevent its displacement; that the binder course under such asphalt surface is porous in character, and readily admits the infiltration of water where the conditions are favorable, and that such infiltration tends to disintegrate and break up the pavement. It is then averred that the street to be improved under said contract was occupied by he Indianapolis Traction and Terminal Company; that un-ler its franchise with the city it was the duty of such trac-ion company to improve its portion of said street lying be-ween its rails and for eighteen inches on the outside thereof, d to proceed with such improvement at the same time ap-llant was proceeding with its improvement; that appellant ished its portion of the improvement in 1906; that the raction company excavated the portion of street to be im-roved by it in the fall of 1906, and abandoned the work of nstruction, leaving the excavation in the center of said treet until the summer or fall of 1907; that appellee took o steps to compel the traction company to proceed with id improvement; that the absence of the pavement which hould have been put in by the street-car company made it ecessary for appellant to construct a temporary lateral upport for the improvement made by it; that for this pur-

pose appellant placed oak headers along the edge of its
pavement and adjacent to the excavation made by the street-
car company; that afterwards the street-car company, without appellant's knowledge, removed said headers, leaving
the edge of the pavement adjacent to said excavation unpro-
tected during the following winter and summer; that such
excavation was full of water, which permeated appellant's
pavement and caused it to become thoroughly watersoaked,
with the result that the defects appeared therein which made
necessary the repairs made by appellee on said improvement,
for which the recovery herein is sought; that by reason of the
foregoing facts appellant is not liable under its provision
of guarantee for said repairs.

Appellee filed a reply in denial to the special paragraph
of answer. The cause was tried by the court without a jury.
The court rendered judgment for appellee on its complaint
in the sum of $2,000, and for appellant on its first paragraph
of cross-complaint in the sum of $6,291.05, and on the second
paragraph of cross-complaint in the sum of $4,236.89. It
was adjudged that the $2,000 recoverable by appellee should
be deducted from the $4,236.89 recoverable by appellant on
its second paragraph of cross-complaint, and that the balance
of such sum recoverable by appellant on its second paragraph of cross-complaint, namely the sum of $2,236.89
should be retained by appellant and invested in municipal
bonds to be held by appellee as collateral to secure the faithful performance of the remaining portion of appellant's
warranty obligations. A motion for a new trial was overruled and exceptions properly saved by appellant.

Appellant moved to modify the judgment by striking out
that portion thereof which authorized appellee to retain the
said sum of $2,236.89, and to invest the same in bonds, etc.
The errors assigned and relied on are as follows: (1) The
overruling of appellant's demurrer to the complaint. (2)
The overruling of appellant's motion for new trial. (3)
The overruling of appellant's motion to modify the judg-

ment. In support of its contention that the trial court erred in its ruling on the demurrer to the complaint, appellant insists, in effect, that the provision in the contract for the improvement of the street in question, which obligated appellant to repair for a period of nine years, was in the nature of a warranty, by which appellant agreed to warrant the pavement for said period against defects resulting from improper workmanship or imperfect or unsuitable materials, and that appellant, by said contract, was not obligated to make general repairs for said period; that such being the effect of the contract, the burden was on appellant to allege and prove the specific facts constituting the breach of warranty relied on, and that the complaint in this case contains no such averments.

1. An intelligent presentation of the question thus presented requires us to set out the guaranty provisions of the contract sued on. They are as follows:

"Guarantee: The work shall be done in such a substantial manner that no repairs will be required for a period of nine years in the case of asphalt, * * * pavements. * * * Should repairs become necessary, however, during any such period, then the contractor will be required to make good any damage to the work or any defect in the workmanship, materials or condition of the work which may have occurred during said period, and which made such repairs necessary. * * * Said contractor shall keep such work in good repair during the time of the guarantee period and shall make all repairs at such time as directed by the Board of Public Works or the city engineer. It shall be the duty of said contractor to notify the Board of Public Works in writing at least thirty days prior to the expiration of the said guarantee period to inspect the work, and unless the contractor shall furnish such notice, the obligation to maintain the said work in proper condition shall continue in force until such notice shall have been furnished and for thirty days thereafter, and until such time as the contractor shall place said work in proper condition, if notified so to do within the thirty days' period. It is understood and agreed that this guarantee shall cover all repairs growing out of the imperfection or unsuitability of materials or composition, too great or too little moisture, all defects in workmanship, extremes of heat or cold and all other effects of climate, and shall cover all other excessive deteriorations more specifically described as follows: In case of asphalt, * * * pavements, any holes or cracks in the same, and any defects resulting from the decomposition of the wearing surface or foundation. The pavement, at the expiration of the guarantee period, shall be in good condition, present a surface so true and even that it will in no way be an obstruction to travel, and have drainage so perfect that water may collect in no place to a depth of more than one quarter of an inch. * * *

'*Guarantee Repair Fund.*'

* * * The party of the first part hereby consents that the City shall retain, in street improvement bonds of said city, issued on account of said improvement, a sum equal to twenty (20) cents per square yard of pavement herein contracted for, which sum shall be and constitute a Repair Guarantee Fund, in the hands of the City, for the purpose of securing the repair and maintenance of said pavement by said party of the first part, to the satisfaction of the Board of Public Works of said city for a period of nine years from the date of the final estimate on said work, and that said pavement shall be so left at the expiration of said period. Should the improvement bonds issued on account of this improvement be insufficient to make the deposit herein provided for, the party of the first part shall deposit such other City of Indianapolis Improvement Bonds, in lieu thereof, as shall be satisfactory to the City Comptroller. It is hereby agreed that the face value of the bonds to be deposited shall at no time during the guaranty period, be decreased by the contractor to an amount less than twenty cents for each square yard of pavement contracted for. In the event the pavement during the guarantee period is being maintained and kept in repair by the contractor to the satisfaction of said Board of Public Works, then the contractor shall be permitted to receive and receipt, from time to time, for all maturing interest coupons, and at the end of such guarantee period, the bonds deposited, with all unpaid coupons, shall thereupon be delivered and turned over to said first party or assigns: *Provided, however,* That the contractor shall first receive

NOVEMBER TERM, 1912.   595

Barber Asphalt Pav. Co. v. City of Indianapolis—52 Ind. App. 587.

from said Board of Public Works a certificate that the said pavement is in good repair and condition to the satisfaction of said Board, but not otherwise. In the event the pavement during the guarantee period is not in good condition and repair to the satisfaction of said Board, then said Board shall retain all bonds and coupons (principal and interest) until said pavement is so put in repair; and if the first party shall refuse or neglect to put the same in repair, to the satisfaction of said Board, on proper written notice from them—said notice to be at least ten days—said Board may cause the same to be done and collect all maturing bonds and coupons, and with the proceeds thereof pay for such repairs provided the amount so collected be sufficient, if not, said Board may sell all or a part of the bonds and coupons deposited to guarantee said pavement, and apply the proceeds to the making of said repairs, or such an amount thereof as it may deem necessary, retaining the remainder of said sum, if any, in said Repair Guarantee Fund for use in future repairs. Should the cost of such repairs made by the order of the Board of Public Works exceed the amount collected on bonds retained as above, the party of the first part shall be held responsible to the City of Indianapolis for the amount of such excess and such excess shall be collected by suit from the contractor. The contractor failing to make a satisfactory deposit on bonds, as required in this contract, will be permitted to deposit cash, in the sum of twenty cents for each square yard laid, subject to all restrictions and conditions named above as to the bond guarantee.'
* * * ''

"It is a well settled principle that a breach of warranty pleaded as a cause of action or defense must, to be good upon demurrer, aver the character and extent of the

2. warranty, and the nature and particulars of the breach." *Shirk* v. *Mitchell* (1894), 137 Ind. 185, 188, 36 N. E. 850, and authorities cited.

The serious question in this case is not, therefore, whether the principle of law contended for by appellant is correct, but whether it should be applied to a pleading of the

1. character here involved, and, if applied, whether the averments of the complaint substantially comply with its requirements.

Appellant relies on the case of *Shank* v. *Smith* (1901), 157 Ind. 401, 61 N. E. 932, 55 L. R. A. 564, in support of its contention that the provision of the contract in suit for the repairs of the street in question must be construed as a warranty rather than as an obligation on the part of appellant to make general repairs.

Appellant further insists in support of this contention that it is to be presumed that appellee and appellant when they entered into the contract for the improvement of the street in question intended to enter into a valid rather than invalid contract, and that if that construction of the contract be adopted which would obligate the contractor to make general repairs it would be equivalent to holding that the contract was invalid when executed, because the contract by its terms provided that the cost of the improvement was payable by special assessments, and appellee had no power to levy such special assessments for street repairs as distinguished from improvements, and that a "special assessment contract which included the making of general repairs would have been unenforceable."

As supporting this contention appellant relies on the following cases: *Shank* v. *Smith, supra; Portland* v. *Bituminous Pav. Co.* (1898), 33 Or. 307, 52 Pac. 28, 44 L. R. A. 527, 72 Am. St. 713; *Boyd* v. *City of Milwaukee* (1896), 92 Wis. 456, 66 N. W. 603; *Brown* v. *Jenks* (1893), 98 Cal. 10, 32 Pac. 701; *Alameda Macadamizing Co.* v. *Pringle* (1900), 130 Cal. 226, 62 Pac. 394, 52 L. R. A. 264, 80 Am. St. 124: *Excelsior Pav. Co.* v. *Leach* (1893), 34 Pac. (Cal.) 116; *McAllister* v. *City of Tacoma* (1894), 9 Wash. 272, 37 Pac. 447; *Verdin* v. *City of St. Louis* (1895), 131 Mo. 26, 33 S. W. 480, 36 S. W. 52; I Page & Jones, Taxation by Assessment §516; *Young* v. *City of Tacoma* (1903), 31 Wash. 153, 71 Pac. 742; *City Council, etc.,* v. *Barnett* (1907), 149 Ala. 119, 43 South. 92; *Barfield* v. *Gleason* (1901), 111 Ky. 491, 63 S. W. 964; *City of Louisville* v. *Selvage* (1889), 106 Ky. 730, 51 S. W. 447, 52 S. W. 809; *Gosnell* v. *City of Louis-*

ville (1898), 104 Ky. 201, 46 S. W. 722; *State, ex rel.,* v. *District Court, etc.* (1900), 80 Minn. 293, 83 N. W. 183; *People, ex rel.,* v. *Maher* (1890), 9 N. Y. Supp. 94, 56 Hun 81; *Fehler* v. *Gosnell* (1896), 99 Ky. 380, 35 S. W. 1125; *City of Kansas City* v. *Hanson* (1898), 8 Kan. App. 290, 55 Pac. 513; *Scranton City* v. *Sturges* (1902), 202 Pa. St. 182, 51 Atl. 764; *Bradshaw* v. *City of Jamestown* (1908), 109 N. Y. Supp. 618, 125 App. Div. 86.

While there seems to be some difference in the wording of the repair provisions of the contract construed in the case of *Shank* v. *Smith, supra,* and the wording of the one here involved, yet, the provision there in question and construed by the court was so nearly identical with this that we would feel bound by that construction. In so far as that decision holds that the provision should not be construed as an obligation to make general repairs, it is supported by authority. *People, ex rel.,* v. *Featherstonhaugh* (1902), 172 N. Y. 112, 64 N. E. 802, 60 L. R. A. 768; *McGlynn* v. *City of Toledo* (1901), 22 Ohio C. C. 34, affirmed *Toledo* v. *McGlynn* (1902), 67 Ohio St. 498, 67 N. E. 1103; *Lindsey* v. *Brawner* (1906), 29 Ky. Law Rep. 1236, 97 S. W. 1; *Barber Asphalt Pav. Co.* v. *City of Louisville* (1906), 123 Ky. 687, 97 S. W. 31, 9 L. R. A. (N. S.), 156 with notes; *Owensboro City R. Co.* v. *Barber Asphalt Pav. Co.* (1908), 107 S. W. (Ky.) 244, 14 L. R. A. (N. S.), 1217.

Assuming then that the provision in the contract in suit was one of guaranty or warranty, and not one to repair generally, Are the averments of the complaint sufficient?

The complaint in question sets out the entire contract, including the guaranty, and therefore meets the requirements of the rule before announced, which requires the pleading to allege the nature and extent of the warranty, so that the only question to be determined is whether the averments are sufficient to show a breach of such warranty.

The provision here involved, even though construed as a guaranty, was more than a guaranty against defects resulting from improper workmanship or unsuitable materials. It was, in effect, a guaranty that the materials and the workmanship which entered into the construction of such street were of such a character that they would withstand any and all the usual and necessary uses of travel to which such street might be subjected for a period of nine years, and at the end thereof would be "in good condition and present a surface so true and even that it would be in no way an obstruction to travel, and have a drainage so perfect that water would collect in no place to a depth of more than one quarter of an inch." This provision contemplated that all holes and defects of every kind or character appearing in said street within said guaranty period, resulting from any and all proper use and travel of said street, should be repaired and made good by appellant. The guaranty is in effect a covenant obligating the appellant to make, within the period designated, any and all repairs resulting from any and all causes incident to the use of the street for public travel, and covers all repairs except those resulting from fire, flood or other act of God or some extraneous cause in noway connected with the usual and proper use of such street for travel.

This being the effect and scope of the guaranty here involved, whether the burden was on appellee to allege in his complaint and prove on the trial a negative, viz.:

3. that the defects in the street, which necessitated the repairs sued for, were not the result of causes extraneous to and independent of its use for travel, or whether this was a defense to be set up and proved by appellant, may, we think, be open to serious question, but in view of the averments of this complaint we need not and do not decide this question.

The averments of this complaint in this respect are, that after the completion of said work under said contract, and after the acceptance thereof by said board, the wearing surface of said street pavement between Blake street on the east and the White river on the west, being about twelve street squares, "commenced to roll and wave *and in many places the vehicles using said pavement in the ordinary course of travel* on said *public street cut through the wearing surface and the concrete into the sub-grade of said street* (our italics) ; that said pavement deteriorated so badly that by the early spring of the year 1908, the same was almost entirely worn cut and was in such condition that it could not satisfactorily be patched and that in order to put said pavement * * * into good condition and repair as contemplated and required in said contract and said plans and specifications for the construction of said pavement and fit and suitable to be used by the traveling public, it became and was necessary entirely to reconstruct and relay all the portion of the wearing surface above the concrete base of said pavement and in some places to repair and construct portions and reconstruct portions of said concrete base."

We think it affirmatively appears from these averments that the part of the pavement resurfaced by appellee, for which this recovery is sought, was in such condition before it was resurfaced that it would not and did not withstand the ordinary travel thereon, and that the defects which made such resurfacing necessary were such as were contemplated by the guaranty provision in appellant's contract. The character of the averments are such that the only reasonable inference deducible therefrom is that the defects, which necessitated the repairs sued for, were the result of breaches of appellant's guaranty contained in the contract sued on and set out and made part of the complaint.

The complaint in the respect indicated is clearly sufficient under the recent holding of the Supreme Court in the case of *Domestic Block Coal Co.* v. *De Armey* (1913), 179 Ind. ——, 100 N. E. 675, 102 N. E. 99. ·

This same question is presented in another form in the discussion of the assigned error presented by the
4. motion for a new trial. The grounds of this motion are that (1) the decision of the court was contrary

to law, and (2) the decision of the court is not sustained by sufficient evidence.

It will appear from the averments of appellant's answer before set out, that it proceeds on the theory that the defects in the street in question, which necessitated the repairs made thereon, were the result of the acts and conduct of the street-car company, and that such repairs were not made necessary on account of any defect in the material or workmanship in the original construction of the paving material. Appellant, in its discussion of the ruling on the motion for a new trial, insists that on the issue presented by this answer the decision of the court is not sustained by sufficient evidence and is contrary to law.

There is considerable evidence which supports appellant's contention that the defects in the street in question, which made necessary the repairs for which appellee seeks a recovery, were due to, and the result of, the character of the lateral support placed along the edge of the part of the street improved by appellant, and adjacent to that part of the street excavated by the street-car company, and to the after removal of such support by the street-car company, thereby leaving appellant's improved part of the street without lateral support and exposed to the infiltration of water collected in the excavated part of said street. The evidence, however, does not disclose that appellee, by reason of its contract with appellant, or by reason of the franchise which it granted the street-car company, was under any legal obligation to appellant to see that the street-car company proceeded with its work along with appellant, and that it furnished the lateral support necessary to keep the part of the street improved by appellant in proper condition and repair.

The terminal traction company could not be required to pave its tracks except on an order of the board of public works. The proof does not show that any such order had been made when appellant contracted with appellee. Appellant contracted with appellee with reference to the cordition and occupancy of the street in question as it existed at the time of entering into the contract. It knew that the street-car company occupied the part of the street covered by its tracks, and that, under its franchise, it was obligated to improve its part of such street when required to do so by the board of public works of said city.

The evidence discloses that appellant and the street-car company begun their improvement about the same time; that after the street-car company had excavated its part of said street preparatory to such improvement, it and appellant entered into some agreement, pursuant to the terms of which the street-car company furnished, and appellant placed in position, oak headers as a temporary lateral support for appellant's improved part of said street, to serve until the street-car company put in the permanent improvement necessary for such support. Under these facts, it is questionable whether, under the law, in a suit of this character by the city, appellant should be relieved from making the repairs involved, but the evidence in this case makes unnecessary the decision of this question.

The repairs on the part of the street in question, for which a recovery is sought, cost appellee $10,763.83, more than $5,000 of which sum was represented by material furnished by appellant and represented by the judgment which it recovered on its first paragraph of cross-complaint. Appellee recovered on its complaint only $2,000.

There was some evidence tending to show, or from which the court might reasonably infer, that a part of the repairs in question were made necessary both on account of defective material and improper lateral support put in by appellant. There was some evidence tending to support all the material averments of the complaint, and this is enough to prevent a reversal on the ground of the insufficiency of the evidence. For the reasons indicated we cannot say that the decision is contrary to law.

Some question is made because the notice served on ap-

pellant was a notice to repair by completely resurfacing the
street, and it is claimed that the evidence shows that
5. such resurfacing was not necessary. This objection is
not tenable. By the terms of appellant's contract
the character and extent of the repairs were left to the board
of public works, and the repairs were to be made to its satisfaction.

The complaint alleges and the proof shows that the notice
was given after, and pursuant to, a resolution and order of
such board; that such notice gave appellant complete information of the action of such board in the premises, and
that after receiving such notice appellant wholly failed and
refused to make such repairs or any part thereof.

Lastly, it is insisted that the court erred in overruling
appellant's motion to modify the judgment. As before indicated this motion was to strike out that part of
6. the judgment rendered on the second paragraph of
cross-complaint, which adjudged that the $2,000 re-
covered by appellee should be deducted therefrom, and that
the balance—$2,236.89—should be retained by appellee and
invested in municipal bonds, and held ''as collateral to secure the faithful performance of the remaining portion of
appellant's.warranty obligations.''

It is insisted that the court had no right to order the city
to reinvest said funds and retain the same as collateral, etc.

Appellant would have some reason and ground for its
contention if the repairs or resurfacing, for which a recovery is sought in this action, covered the entire part of the
street covered by the contract for improvement, but such is
not the case. Only a portion of that part of the street
covered by the improvement contract is here involved. The
guaranty period had several years yet to run, and the part
of the street not involved in this action might get out of repair and defective, requiring additional expenditure
therefor.

It is insisted by appellant that the guaranty is a single,

Michigan, etc., R. Co. *v.* Farrell—52 Ind. App. 603.

entire and inseparable obligation, and that the present judgment bars any future action to enforce it. Authorities are cited to support this contention, but we can find nothing·in any of the cases cited that would furnish any justification for our holding that the guaranty in this case does not apply to that part of the street improved which was in no way involved in this litigation. We think this part of the judgment entirely proper, and within both the spirit and letter of the provision of the guaranty here involved.

Judgment affirmed.

NOTE.—Reported in 101 N. E. 31. See, also, under (1, 3, 4, 6) 28 Cyc. 1056; (2) 9 Cyc. 728, 732; (5) 28 Cyc. Anno. 1056—New. As to parol evidence to show warranty outside of written contract, see 5 Am. St. 197.

MICHIGAN CENTRAL RAILROAD COMPANY *v.* FARRELL.

[No. 7,754. Filed November 26, 1912. Rehearing denied March 5, 1913.]

1. RAILROADS.—*Injuries to Animals on Tracks.—Complaint.—Sufficiency.*—A complaint in an action against a railroad company for killing plaintiff's horses, alleging that at the time the defendant owned, operated and controlled a certain line of railroad over which it ran locomotives and cars for the transportation of passengers and freight, that plaintiff's horses, without plaintiff's fault or negligence, entered in and strayed upon defendant's right of way and tracks and that defendant, by its servants and employes, then and there ran one of its locomotives against said horses, etc., sufficiently shows that defendant was operating its locomotive by its agents while in the line of their duty or employment. p. 605.

2. RAILROADS.—*Injuries to Animals on Tracks.—Complaint.—Sufficiency.*—A complaint to recover for stock killed by being struck by a train, alleging that plaintiff's horses, without any fault or negligence on the part of plaintiff, entered in and strayed upon the right of way and tracks of defendant at a point where the right of way and track were not sufficiently fenced, and were struck and killed by defendant's train, is not open to the objection that it fails to show that the killing was without plaintiff's fault. pp. 607, 608.

3. RAILROADS.—*Injuries to Animals on Tracks.—Violation of Statutory Duty.—Contributory Negligence.—Complaint.*—Where liability of a railroad company for injury to animals is predicated on the violation of its statutory duty to fence properly its right of way, the complaint need not aver that plaintiff was without fault. p. 607.

4. APPEAL.— *Review.— Issues.— Evidence.— Instructions.*— Where the evidence has not been brought into the record, if the instructions objected to can be said to be proper and applicable to any evidence that might have been introduced under the issues, no available error is presented. p. 608.

5. APPEAL.— *Review.— Presumptions.— Evidence.— Instructions.*— Where the evidence in an action against a railroad company for killing horses on its track is not in the record on appeal, the court will presume that the evidence of the killing of the horses was without conflict, so that an instruction authorizing a recovery without requiring a finding that the horses were killed by a train will not be held erroneous. p. 608.

6. RAILROADS.—*Injuries to Animals on Tracks.—Complaint.—Instructions.*—Where, in an action against a railroad company for killing horses on the track, the complaint alleged that defendant failed properly to maintain its fences, an instruction which in effect stated that the law imposed on defendant the duty of erecting a fence of the kind and character required by statute and to maintain the same in proper condition of repair, was within the issues. pp. 609, 610.

7. RAILROADS.—*Fencing Tracks.—Statutory Duty.*—The duty imposed by statute on railroad companies to erect and maintain fences is a continuing one, which required them not only to erect fences in the first instance, but to maintain them in proper condition. p. 610.

From Lake Superior Court; *Virgil S. Reiter*, Judge.

Action by John J. Farrell against the Michigan Central Railroad Company. From a judgment for plaintiff, the defendant appeals. *Affirmed.*

J. G. Ibach and *L. V. Cravens,* for appellant.
McAleer Bros., for appellee.

HOTTEL, J.—This is an appeal from a judgment for $300 obtained by appellee in the Lake Superior Court.

The complaint is in two paragraphs, each of which charges appellant with negligently running over and killing two of appellee's horses, which had entered on its right of way at a point where it is alleged appellant had negligently failed to maintain a sufficient fence.

The first paragraph proceeds on the theory that appellant had negligently allowed its fence at the point where the horses entered on its right of way "to become broken down, old, worn out, and out of repair and down." The second paragraph differs from the first in that it proceeds on the theory that appellant had negligently failed to fence its track "properly * * * and in fact had no fence at all or any guard or protection of any character to prevent stock or said horses from entering in or on the right of way," etc. To each of these paragraphs a demurrer was filed and overruled and exceptions saved. A general denial was the only answer. A motion for new trial was overruled. The rulings on said demurrers and the motion for a new trial present the errors assigned and relied on.

It is urged against the sufficiency of each paragraph of the complaint that it is not alleged (1) "that the servants and employes of the appellant at the time of the alleged injury to plaintiff's horses were operating appellant's train in the line of their duty or employment," and (2) that the running of appellant's train against appellee's horses was without any fault or neglect on the part of appellee.

The averments of the first paragraph of complaint, against which said objections are urged, are, in substance, as follows: On July 12, 1907, defendants owned, operated 1. and controlled a certain line of railroad and railroad tracks running through the town of Gary, Lake county, Indiana, and on said day ran locomotives and cars over said railroad tracks and on its right of way for the transportation of passengers and freight; that on July 12, 1907, this plaintiff was the owner of two horses, of the value of $300 each, which said horses, on the above-mentioned date, without any fault or negligence on the part of plaintiff, entered in and strayed upon the right of way and tracks belonging to said defendant, and were struck by one of defendant's trains; that said defendant by its servants and employes did then and there run one of its locomotives upon and against said horses, striking said horses, then and there wounding and injuring said horses, so that they then and there died as a result of said injury. It is averred that said horses entered on said track at a point where it was not sufficiently fenced, etc.

The second paragraph of said complaint avers on this subject that the defendant "on the 12th day of July, 1907, owned and operated and controlled certain railroad tracks, right of way and trains of cars running through the town of Gary, Lake county, Indiana; that on said day the defendant by their servants, agents, and employes were then and there running locomotives and cars over said tracks and right of way for the transportation of passengers and freight; that on said day aforesaid the plaintiff was the owner of two horses of the value of $300 each, which said horses on the above mentioned date without any fault or negligence on the part of plaintiff strayed upon the tracks or right of way of said defendants in the town of Gary, Lake county, Indiana, and were struck by a locomotive belonging to said defendants and running upon said defendant's tracks and conducted by the servants, agents and employes of said defendants in their behalf and were so injured by being struck that they then and there died as a result; * * * that the said right of way and tracks and engines operated on said tracks belonged to said defendant and were controlled, operated and managed by the agents, servants and employes of the defendants on said day and for six months prior thereto; * * * that at the point where the horses so entered upon defendant's said right of way, said right of way was not properly or securely fenced, * * * and in fact at said point * * * there was no fence of any kind or character," etc.

The above allegations sufficiently show that appellant was

operating its locomotives by its agents, etc. In support of this conclusion see *Baltimore, etc., R. Co.* v. *Dickey* (1909), 43 Ind. App. 509, 511, 87 N. E. 1047; *Cleveland, etc., R. Co.* v. *VanNatta* (1909), 44 Ind. App. 608, 612, 87 N. E. 999, 88 N. E. 716, and authorities cited; *Chicago, etc., R. Co.* v. *Stepp* (1909), 44 Ind. App. 353, 88 N. E. 343; *Indianapolis Union K. Co.* v. *Waddington* (1907), 169 Ind. 448, 457, 458, 82 N. E. 1030; *Southern R. Co.* v. *Elliott* (1908), 170 Ind. 273, 82 N. E. 1051; *Indianapolis St. R. Co.* v. *Schmidt* (1904), 163 Ind. 360, 71 N. E. 201; *Indianapolis St. R. Co.* v. *Ray* (1906), 167 Ind. 236, 78 N. E. 978.

In support of the second objection above indicated, it is insisted by appellant that the averments simply show that the horses entered on the right of way of appel-

2. lant without the fault of appellee, but fail to show that the killing was without appellee's fault. Taking the averment in its entirety we do not think that it is open to the objection made. It should be stated, however,

3. in this connection that where liability is predicated on the violation of a statute which provides a civil remedy for damages resulting from such violation, as in this case, that the authorities hold that it is not necessary that the complaint in such case should aver that the plaintiff was without fault. It has been decided in cases where liability was predicated on the statute here involved, that this averment was unnecessary. *Toledo, etc., R. Co.* v. *Cory* (1872), 39 Ind. 218; *Louisville, etc., R. Co.* v. *Whitesell* (1879), 68 Ind. 297; *Welty* v. *Indianapolis, etc., R. Co.* (1886), 105 Ind. 55, 4 N. E. 410; *Chicago, etc., R. Co.* v. *Brannegan* (1892), 5 Ind. App. 540, 32 N. E. 790; *Terre Haute, etc., R. Co.* v. *Schaefer* (1892), 5 Ind. App. 86, 88, 31 N. E. 557; *Fort Wayne, etc., R. Co.* v. *Woodward* (1887), 112 Ind. 118, 120, 13 N. E. 260. There are some cases, however, which by inference or by express language indicate a different holding. These cases fail to distinguish between statutes which impose a criminal liability only for the violation of a duty im-

posed and those which expressly provide a civil remedy in
damages for such violation. But, for the purposes of
2. this case it is not important what the rule is with reference to such an averment in the complaint, because
if it be granted that such an averment is necessary, and that
the words "without fault or negligence on the part of appellee" modifies and limits only the averment that the horses
went upon the track of appellant, we think it would be sufficient to show that appellee was not guilty of contributory
negligence, for the reason that it is clear that each paragraph
of the complaint proceeds on the theory that the proximate
cause of the injury to the stock was appellant's failure to
maintain and keep a fence along its right of way sufficient to
turn said stock, and it was only necessary that appellee
should aver facts showing that he in no way contributed to
the negligence which he alleged to be the proximate cause of
the injury to such stock. *Salem-Bedford Stone Co.* v.
O'Brien (1895), 12 Ind. App. 217, 40 N. E. 430; *Louisville,
etc., R. Co.* v. *Hendricks* (1891), 128 Ind. 462, 28 N. E. 58.

In support of the alleged error in the ruling of the court
on the motion for a new trial, it is insisted that the court
erred in giving instructions Nos. 2 and 3. It is ques-
4. tionable whether the exceptions to these instructions
were properly saved, but in any event appellant has
failed to bring up the evidence in the case and in such case
if the instructions objected to can be said to be proper and
applicable to any evidence that might have been introduced
under the issues, no available error is presented. *Mankin*
v. *Pennsylvania Co.* (1902), 160 Ind. 447, 454, 67 N. E. 229;
Ferris v. *State* (1901), 156 Ind. 224, 230, 59 N. E. 475;
South Bend, etc., Plow Co. v. *Geidie* (1900), 24 Ind. App.
673, 675, 57 N. E. 562, and cases cited.

The second instruction is as follows: "If you find from
the evidence that the horses in question got upon the
5. defendant's railroad right of way and from thence
got upon said railroad track at a point where the

company was by law bound to erect a fence and maintain it, and you further find from the evidence that the road had been in operation for six months or more prior to the accident, and that the fence where the horses got upon the track was through the negligence and carelessness of the company insufficient to prevent the said horses from getting upon the tracks, and that the horses did in fact get upon the track by reason of the insufficiency of said fence and were killed without any fault or negligence on the part of the plaintiff, then your finding should be for the plaintiff.'' It is insisted that this instruction authorized the jury to find for appellee, even though it failed to find that the horses were run over and killed by one of appellant's trains.

In view of the principle of law above announced, this court, in the absence of the evidence, will indulge the presumption that the evidence on the subject of the manner of the killing of said stock was without conflict, and that it was admitted, or, at least, not contradicted, by appellant that its trains did in fact run over and kill the stock, in which case the instruction would have been proper, or, at least, not harmful.

The third instruction objected to is as follows: ''You are further instructed that railroad companies are not required to keep such a guard on their road as to see a

6. breach in their fence and to repair it the instant it occurs; still they are required under the law to keep such a force as will discover breaches and openings in their fences and to close them within a reasonable time. If they neglect to so do within a reasonable time it is a neglect of duty which will render them liable for injury to stock if it comes onto the road through such openings or broken fences, providing the owner or persons having the stock in charge is guilty of no negligence which contributes to the injury.'' It is insisted that this instruction is outside the issues and could not be said to be applicable to any phase of the case.

It is urged that there is no provision of the law that requires a railroad company to keep any force of men for the purpose of discovering and repairing breaches or openings in the fences along its right of way.   While it is true that there is no statutory provision that expressly requires a force of men to be employed by the railroad for such purpose, the section of statute under which liability exists in this case imposed on such company the duty of erecting and maintaining fences along its right of way sufficient to

7.   turn stock.   This duty is a continuing one, and required the company not only to erect in the first instance a fence sufficient for such purpose, but required it to keep and maintain the fence in such condition.   It

6.   follows, as an incident to this duty imposed, that such company must of necessity employ men to discharge the duty, and, under the averment of the complaint that the company had failed in its duty in this regard and had neglected to maintain and keep its fence in such condition that it would turn stock, evidence might have been introduced to which the instruction would have been applicable. There can be no question that it was not only the right, but it was the duty of the court, under the issues tendered, to tell the jury that the law did impose upon appellant the duty of erecting a fence of the kind and character required by the statute, and that the duty did not end with the erection of the fence, but that it was a continuing one, and required the company, after the erection of the fence, to look after and maintain the same in such condition of repair that it would meet the purpose and the conditions of the statute involved.   We think this was the effect of the instruction given, and that there might have been evidence introduced under the issues to which the instructions as given may have been proper and applicable.

We cannot, in any event, in the absence of the evidence, say that the instruction was not applicable to some phase of the evidence which may have been properly admitted under the issues, or that it was prejudicial to appellant.

We find no available error presented by the record. The judgment is therefore affirmed.

Ibach, J., not participating.

NOTE. Reported in 99 N. E. 1026. See, also, under (1) 33 Cyc. 1207; (2) 33 Cyc. 1257, 1266; (3) 33 Cyc. 1266; (4) 3 Cyc. 169, 304; (5) 3 Cyc. 303; (6) 33 Cyc. 1312; (7) 33 Cyc. 1201. As to railway company's statutory duty to maintain fences and cattle-guards, see 21 Am. St. 289. On the question of the measure of care of railroad company to maintain fence once constructed, see 11 L. R. A. (N. S.) 228. As to the duty of a railroad company to keep cattle-guards in condition, see 36 L. R. A. (N. S.) 997. For a discussion of the care required of a railroad in keeping a right of way fence in repair, see 11 Ann. Cas. 430.

HUBBARD *v.* RANJE ET AL.

[No. 7,574. Filed April 26, 1912. Rehearing denied June 28, 1912. Transfer denied March 6, 1913.]

1. EVIDENCE.—*Admissions.*—*Admissibility.*—Where a woman signed and gave her son a mortgage to be delivered to the mortgagee to indemnify him against loss by reason of a certain contract of her son on which the mortgagee was his bondsman, and the mortgagee suffered loss by reason of bonding the son on other contracts, but not on the bond contemplated by the mortgagor, the exclusion of offered testimony of the mortgagee, in a foreclosure suit, that at the time of delivering the mortgage the son stated that the note and mortgage were executed and delivered for the purpose of indemnifying mortgagee for any loss he might sustain as surety for the son on building bonds to be thereafter executed, was proper, in the absence of evidence that the son was authorized to speak for his mother in that respect. pp. 614, 617.

2. APPEAL.—*Presentation of Questions Below.*—*Objections to Evidence.*—Objections to offered evidence must state the particular grounds relied on to be available on appeal, unless the evidence appears on its face to be incompetent. p. 615.

3. EVIDENCE.—*Admissibility.*—*Res Gestae.*—The testimony of the mortgagor that, at the time of signing the mortgage, her son told her it was a bond of indemnity upon a certain building contract, but that he said nothing about other contracts, was admis-

sible in an action to foreclose, as being a part of the *res gestae* of the transaction. p. 615.

4. PRINCIPAL AND AGENT.—*Authority of Agent.—Reliance on Authority.*—While a third party may rely on the apparent authority of an agent, such apparent authority must rest on facts or circumstances warranting such reliance; and where a mortgagor delivered a note and mortgage to her son to be by him delivered to the mortgagee, such fact at most constituted the son a special agent to deliver the instruments in the form and with the effect they possessed when they left her possession, and did not warrant a reliance on his authority to bind her by statements to the mortgagee giving to such instruments a different effect. p. 615.

5. MORTGAGES.—*Foreclosure.—Evidence.—Burden of Proof.*—In an action to foreclose a mortgage, while plaintiff may show that the mortgage, although in form definite in amount, was in fact an indemnity against contingent loss, he has the burden of proving such fact by competent evidence, and the instrument, unaided by parol evidence, would be insufficient to establish the claim to indemnity. p. 616.

6. APPEAL.—*Review.—Exclusion of Evidence.*—Where, in a foreclosure suit, plaintiff offered testimony to show certain losses, without preceding the offer by showing that the mortgage was in fact given to secure such losses, and the record discloses no statement that the offered evidence would be followed by testimony showing that such losses were in fact secured by said mortgage, such offered testimony was properly excluded. p. 617.

7. APPEAL.—*Review.—Presumptions.*—The trial court is presumed to have acted advisedly and correctly in the exclusion of testimony, where the record fails to show preliminary proof necessary to make it competent, or an offer to make such proof. p. 617.

From Boone Circuit Court; *W. H. Parr*, Judge.

Action by Walter J. Hubbard against Ida M. Ranje and others. From a judgment for defendants, the plaintiff appeals. *Affirmed.*

Charles B. Clarke, Walter C. Clarke and *A. J. Shelby*, for appellant.

Sheridan & Gruber and *Means & Buenting*, for appellee.

FELT, C. J.—Suit on a promissory note given by appellee Ida M. Ranje to appellant for $2,500, and for foreclosure of a real estate mortgage given to secure the same. The complaint was in two paragraphs. The first was in the usual form for the foreclosure of a mortgage, and the second, in addition to the allegations of the first, averred in substance that the mortgage, while in form to secure the payment of the note therein described, was in fact given to appellant by said appellee to indemnify the former and save him from loss on account of his liability on certain builder's bonds which he was about to execute as surety for Henry Ranje, son of said appellee, at the request of the latter; that appellant had previously gone on such bonds as surety for said Henry Ranje, and said appellee had secured him from loss on account thereof by mortgages on her property; that she was about to depart for Europe, and to induce appellant to continue to act as surety for her said son on bonds to be thereafter executed during her absence, said appellee executed the note and mortgage in suit, and caused the same to be delivered to appellant; that it was the intent and purpose of said appellee to indemnify appellant against loss as surety on such bonds as he might thereafter execute as surety for her son; that appellant relied on said mortgage as indemnity against loss as such surety, and thereafter became surety on builder's bonds for the son, of said appellee, and by reason thereof has been compelled to pay as such surety the sum of $3,053.35, to his damage in that sum; that no part of said amount has been paid to him, and the same is due and unpaid.

Appellee Ranje answered by general denial; failure of consideration; payment, and by a paragraph alleging, in substance, that she executed the note and mortgage sued on to indemnify appellant for any loss he might sustain by reason of a certain contract of her said son with one Gausepohl, on which appellant was his bondsman, and not otherwise; that she had full confidence in her said son, and relied on him in all particulars; that she had for years signed papers as indemnity to appellant; that said Gausepohl contract was executed on or about April 17, 1905, and appellant has not been required to pay, and has not paid anything on account thereof; that she signed said mortgage and others previously executed to appellant at the request of her said son. Appellant replied by general denial to said appellee's affirmative answers.

The only error assigned is the overruling of the motion for a new trial. The new trial was asked for alleged error in the admission and exclusion of certain evidence. Henry Ranje was shown to be out of the jurisdiction of the court, and his testimony was not obtained.

Evidence was introduced by appellant showing that the note and mortgage in suit were executed on June 1, 1905,

1. by said appellee in her home, before one Beerman, a notary public, not in appellant's employment, and in the presence of her son Henry and other members of her family; that she gave said instruments to her said son, and the same were thereafter delivered to appellant by him on or about June 1, 1905. Appellant while on the stand as a witness in his own behalf was asked to state what was said at the time, in connection with the act of so delivering the mortgage. To this question said appellee objected, on the ground that she was not bound by any statements that were made by appellant in her absence, because the same were selfserving declarations. Appellant offered to prove, in answer to the question, that Henry Ranje brought the note and mortgage to him at his office, and, at the time they were delivered, stated that his mother (appellee) was going to Europe to be gone some time, and had executed the note and mortgage to indemnify appellant for any loss he might sustain as surety for him on building bonds to be thereafter executed during his mother's absence abroad, and that his mother had delivered them to him to be by him delivered to appellant, for the purpose of so securing him as such bondsman. The court sustained appellee's objection, and appellant duly excepted.

In determining the admissiblity of evidence, it is always necessary to keep in mind (1) the issues and (2) the grounds

of the objection. When an objection is made to
2. offered evidence, the particular grounds of the objection must be stated to be available. General objections
present no question unless the evidence appears on its face to
be incompetent. *Heap* v. *Parrish* (1885), 104 Ind. 36, 3 N.
E. 549; *McCullough* v. *Davis* (1886), 108 Ind. 292, 9 N. E.
276; *Bundy* v. *Cunningham* (1886), 107 Ind. 360, 8 N.
E. 174.

Appellant insists that this testimony was competent on the
theory that it was a part of the *res gestae*, and that Henry
Ranje was the agent of his mother for the delivery of
3. the note and mortgage to appellant. The theory is
correct, but the question turns on the sufficiency of
the showing of agency. Both appellant, and Mrs. Ranje, so
far as disclosed by the record, were doing gratuitous acts
beneficial to Henry Ranje. The record shows, however, that
appellant wrote the mortgage and delivered it either to
Henry Ranje or the attorney who took the acknowledgment.
Mrs. Ranje testified that her son told her it was a bond of
indemnity on the Gausepohl job; that he said nothing about
other jobs, and she received nothing for signing the instrument; that she delivered the mortgage to her son, and did
not know what he was to do with it; that appellant suffered
no loss on the Gausepohl job. The conversation at the time
the note and mortgage were signed was admissible as a part
of the *res gestae* of the transaction. *Creighton* v. *Hoppis*
(1885), 99 Ind. 369; *Mitchell* v. *Colglazier* (1886), 106 Ind.
464, 7 N. E. 199; *Porter* v. *Waltz* (1886), 108 Ind. 40, 46, 8
N. E. 705; *Gaar, Scott & Co.* v. *Shaffer* (1894), 139 Ind. 191,
38 N. E. 811.

But the right of appellant to give in evidence the alleged
statements of Henry Ranje when the latter delivered the
mortgage to him depends upon the authority of said
4. Ranje to speak for his mother on the subject indicated
by the offered testimony. True, a third party may
rely on the apparent authority of the agent, but such ap-

parent authority must rest on facts or circumstances warranting such reliance.

Agency may be implied from circumstances and conduct.
In this case the one fact mainly relied on to show that Henry
Ranje was the agent of his mother is the delivery by her to
him of the note and mortgage after she had signed them.
The authority so implied cannot exceed the necessary and
legitimate effect of the facts from which it is inferred. At
most it only constituted him her special agent, with authority to deliver the instruments to the payee in the form and
with the effect they possessed when they left her possession.
Mechem, Agency §274; Story, Agency §87; *Robinson* v.
Bank of Winslow (1908), 42 Ind. App. 350, 353, 85 N. E.
793; *Ford* v. *Postal Tel. Cable Co.* (1899), 124 Ala. 400, 27
South. 409, 410; *McAlpin* v. *Cassidy* (1856), 17 Tex. 449,
462. In Story, Agency §87, it is said: "In short, an implied agency is never construed to extend beyond the obvious
purposes for which it is apparently created." The implied
authority to deliver the note and mortgage would not include
the power to change the meaning and effect of such written
instruments. *Robinson & Co.* v. *Nipp* (1898), 20 Ind. App.
156, 163, 50 N. E. 408.

The mortgage left the hands of appellant ready for execution, and was returned to him by the son in the same form
after it was signed and acknowledged. Appellant
5. wrote and accepted, and appellee Ranje signed and
acknowledged, the mortgage in a form that did not
evidence the real purpose of its execution nor disclose the
true character of the transaction. In this respect each was
equally careless, but the burden was on appellant to establish by competent evidence his right to recover. The instruments unaided by parol testimony were insufficient to establish his claim to indemnity. The law will permit proof to
show that notwithstanding the mortgage was in form to secure a note definite in amount, it was in fact an indemnity
against contingent loss. 16 Am. and Eng. Ency. Law (2d

ed.) 183; *First Nat. Bank* v. *Henry* (1900), 156 Ind. 1, 12, 58 N. E. 1057; *Mayor* v. *Grottendick* (1879), 68 Ind. 1.

But appellant in order to bind appellee Ranje by statements, changing the meaning and effect of the instru-
1. ment, must first show that the one alleged to speak as her agent had authority so to do. 1 Elliott, Evidence §252; Gillett, Indirect and Collat. Ev. §33.

Appellant also offered testimony for the purpose of showing loss on jobs other than the Gausepohl job, but such testimony was preceded by no proof showing that the
6. mortgage in suit was in fact given to secure such losses, and the record discloses no statement from appellant that the offered evidence would be followed by testimony showing that such losses were in fact secured by said mortgage. In this situation the court committed no error in excluding the offered testimony.

Other questions were asked by appellant on examination in chief, which could only be proper, if at all, on rebuttal. The record discloses no prejudicial error on account thereof.

Appellant suggests a theory which, if supported by necessary preliminary proof, would make certain excluded testimony competent, but the record fails to show such
7. proof, or offer of proof. The trial court is presumed to have acted advisedly and correctly.

No available error having been pointed out by appellant, the judgment is affirmed.

DISSENTING OPINION.

ADAMS, J.—As stated in the majority opinion, both appellant and appellee Ida M. Ranje were rendering a gratuitous service to Henry Ranje. The mortgage in question was written by appellant, and given to a notary, not in the employ of appellant, who took the acknowledgment of Ida M. Ranje, in the presence of her son Henry. She gave the mortgage and note to her son, who delivered it to appellant. She knew that she was not executing the mortgage to secure the payment of the note for $2,500, but to indemnify appellant against loss on account of becoming surety for her son in his contracting business. The extent of her indemnity obligation I do not think pertinent to the present inquiry. She knew that it was necessary, after signing and acknowledging, to deliver the note and mortgage to appellant. If she did not wish to do so herself, she knew that some one must deliver the same for her, in order to make the instrument effective. She must be presumed to have known that delivery was a necessary part of the execution of the mortgage, and she entrusted that part of its execution to her son. I think it clearly appears that under such conditions Henry Ranje was the agent of his mother in delivering the indemnity mortgage, and it follows that his statements made to appellant at the time of delivery were a part of the *res gestae,* and binding on his principal.

I believe the trial court erred in rejecting the testimony offered, and for the error in overruling the motion for a new trial, the judgment should be reversed.

Ibach, P. J., concurs.

NOTE.—Reported in 98 N. E. 314, 317. See, also, under (1) 16 Cyc. 1005, 1028; (2) 38 Cyc. 1378; (3) 16 Cyc. 1148; (4) 31 Cyc. 1331; (5) 27 Cyc. 1613; (6) 38 Cyc. 1329; (7) 3 Cyc. 300. As to admissibility of parol evidence to affect written terms of a mortgage, see 56 Am. St. 667; 11 Am. St. 844. As to principal's not being bound by agent's act outside the scope of his authority, see 6 Am. St. 87.

PATTERSON *v.* SOUTHERN RAILWAY COMPANY OF INDIANA ET AL.

[No. 7,656. Filed October 15, 1912. Rehearing denied January 31, 1913. Transfer denied March 6, 1913.]

1. TRIAL.—*Directed Verdict.*—The trial court may direct a verdict for defendant only where the evidence most favorable to the plaintiff, together with all reasonable and legitimate inferences that a jury might draw therefrom, is clearly insufficient to establish one or more facts essential to plaintiff's right of action. p. 620.

2. MASTER AND SERVANT.—*Places of Work.*—*Tools and Appliances.*—*Duty of Master.*—*Delegation of Duty.*—The master's duty of providing a reasonably safe place for the servant to work, and safe tools and appliances with which to work, is a continuing one and cannot be delegated by him to an employe so as to avoid responsibility for its violation. p. 623.

3. MASTER AND SERVANT.—*Negligence.*—*Vice Principal.*—An employe, regardless of his rank or grade, who is authorized to perform a duty which is clearly the master's duty, is to that extent a vice principal and his act is the act of the master, and, in determining the master's liability for his negligence, the controlling inquiry is whether his act or omission involved a duty owing by the master to the injured servant. p. 623.

4. MASTER AND SERVANT.—*Injury to Servants.*—*Negligence.*—*Fellow Servants.*—Where workmen, in the construction of a bridge, erect a scaffold on their own initiative and for their own convenience, and the order of the foreman directing the building of same was merely an executive detail of the work, the foreman is a fellow servant for whose negligence in such construction the master is not liable. p. 624.

5. MASTER AND SERVANT.—*Injury to Servants.*—*Fellow Servants.*—*Jury Question.*—In an action by a servant for personal injuries sustained by the falling of a temporary scaffold erected on the side of a railroad fill, on which ties were being prepared to use in the construction of a railroad bridge, where there was evidence that during the three years that plaintiff was employed by defendant as a bridge carpenter such platforms were always constructed under the direction of the foreman, that it was usual and customary, in erecting such platforms on the side of a fill, to make secure the ends of the stringer ties next to the track to keep the structure from tipping, and that plaintiff believed the platform was thus made secure when he went upon it, the court was not warranted in directing a verdict for defendant, but the question of whether such evidence warranted the conclusion that the erection of such platforms was a part of defendant's general plan of operation under similar conditions, so as to render the negligence of the foreman in directing the construction of the platform that of a vice principal should have gone to the jury under proper instructions of the court. p. 625.

From Pike Circuit Court; *John L. Bretz,* Judge.

Action by John W. Patterson against the Southern Railway Company of Indiana and another. From a judgment for defendants, the plaintiff appeals. *Reversed.*

R. W. Armstrong, for appellant.

Alex P. Humphrey, Edward P. Humphrey, John D. Welman and *Thomas Duncan,* for appellees.

ADAMS, P. J.—This action was brought by appellant against appellees, to recover damages for personal injuries sustained by appellant while in the service of appellee Southern Railway Company, and was based on a common-law right.

At the conclusion of appellant's evidence the court directed the jury to return separate verdicts in favor of each defendant. Verdicts were accordingly returned, and judgment rendered thereon.

The only error assigned is that the court erred in overruling appellant's motion for a new trial, and the only error relied on for reversal is that the court erred in giving the peremptory instruction. Whether or not this was error depends on the evidence given in the cause on behalf on plaintiff.

It is a settled rule in this State that the right of the court to direct a verdict for a defendant can only be upheld

1. where, after a consideration of all the evidence most favorable to the plaintiff, together with all the reasonable and legitimate inferences which the jury might have drawn therefrom, it can be said that the evidence is clearly insufficient to establish one or more facts essential to plaintiff's right of action. *Gregory* v. *Cleveland, etc., R. Co.* (1887), 112 Ind. 385, 388, 14 N. E. 228; *Wolfe* v. *McMillan* (1888), 117 Ind. 587, 593, 20 N. E. 509; *Diezi* v. *G. H. Hammond Co.* (1901), 156 Ind. 583, 588, 60 N. E. 353; *Davis* v. *Mercer Lumber Co.* (1905), 164 Ind. 413, 425, 73 N. E. 899.

The facts disclosed by the evidence show that appellant was a bridge carpenter, and, as such, had been in the service of the Southern Railway Company for three years, and during the entire time of his employment was under appellee Teaford, who was foreman of the bridge gang. Teaford

had been in the employ of the railway company as foreman
and bridge carpenter for twenty years. Appellant's duties
were general, doing whatever he was directed to do. In
February, 1909, the railway company was repairing a certain bridge, by redecking the same, which was done by placing new stringers and ties thereon. The company had delivered on the right of way, at or near the bridge, sawed
timbers of proper size and quality, which were to be dressed
by the carpenters and placed in the structure. About
twenty men were employed in this work, who were under
the general direction of Teaford. Immediately east of the
bridge was a fill of six or eight feet, about thirteen feet
wide at the top, and on which there was a rock ballast of
twenty inches.

On the day of appellant's injury he was working at the
north side of the track, ninety or one hundred feet east of
the point where he was injured. Teaford directed two of
the men to build a scaffold, on which bridge ties were to be
dressed and made ready for use, and was present while the
same was being built. Such platforms were always constructed under the direction of the foreman. This particular scaffold was erected on the south side of the track
by placing two bridge ties one on top of the other on the
side of the fill parallel with the track. Two ties were then
laid from the top of the foundation ties, the north ends
resting on the shoulder of the fill and the south ends extending over the foundation ties three or four feet. These
ties or stringers were four or five feet apart, and on them
were placed twelve or thirteen other ties, to be dressed and
prepared for use. These ties completely covered the stringer ties. Two men working at the north end of the scaffold
marked the ties, and after marking turned them back to the
south to two other men, who sawed the ties as indicated by
the marks. When properly sawed, the ties were turned
over to the south to the adz men, who worked at the south
end of the scaffold. The foundation ties as well as the

stringers and the ties in course of preparation for use, were all eleven feet in length. Appellant was one of the two adz men, who worked at the south end of the scaffold. He did not see how far the stringers projected over the foundation ties at the time he went on the scaffold, and did not see how the stringers were placed on the foundation ties, on account of the ties, placed thereon for dressing, completely covering the stringers. Appellant had been working at the south end of the scaffold about twenty-five minutes, when the same by reason of increased weight, tipped, throwing him down the embankment, and resulting in injuries for which this action is brought. The stringer ties were not anchored at the north end or supported at the south end, except by the foundation ties.

At the time appellant went on the scaffold he believed that the stringer ties had been anchored or made secure at the north end. During all the time of his service with appellee, appellant had never seen a platform erected at a similar place that was not fastened to the ground. It was usual and customary in constructing a platform at a place of this kind to make secure the ends next to the tracks, to prevent tipping. Before appellant went on the scaffold, the bridge foreman, Teaford, said to him: "Get your adz, and go to adzing; the scaffold is ready." He then walked to the west on the north side of the track, secured his adz, which was lying almost north of the scaffold, crossed over the track, and commenced work. The scaffold was an improvised structure, which required about twenty minutes in building, and was designed as a place where ties placed thereon could be dressed, and would not be in use for more than two hours.

The only question presented and argued by appellant in his brief pertains to the status of Teaford. Was he the representative of the master and a vice principal in the erection of the scaffold, or was he a fellow servant with appellant, engaged in the same general undertaking? Was he discharging a duty which the master owed to the servant, or was he performing a duty which the servant owed to the master? These questions are generally not free from doubt. The difficulty is not in applying the law when the relation is definitely shown, but in applying the law to the conceded facts in determining the relation.

We think no good purpose would be served by an extended review of the decided cases, and by adding to the confusion which already exists in the texts and decisions relative to who are and who are not fellow servants. This seeming confusion clearly arises from the extent and variety of the facts on which rules have been declared and applied, and it is not surprising that no certain and definite test can be applied in all cases. Out of the confusion, however, some general principles may be gathered which are fundamental in the determination of all cases presenting the fellow servant question.

It is recognized that the primary duty of providing a reasonably safe place for the servant to work, and safe tools and appliances with which to work is on the

2. master, and this duty is a continuing one, which the master cannot delegate to an employe and escape responsibility. If this duty is so delegated, the em-

3. ploye, no matter what his rank or grade may be, becomes a vice principal and not a fellow servant, and his act is the act of the master. *Dill* v. *Marmon* (1905), 164 Ind. 507, 512, 73 N. E. 67, 69 L. R. A. 163; *Thacker* v. *Chicago, etc., R. Co.* (1902), 159 Ind. 82, 64 N. E. 605, 59 L. R. A. 792; *Federal Cement Tile Co.* v. *Korff* (1912), 50 Ind. App. 608, 97 N. E. 185; *Standard Oil Co.* v. *Bowker* (1895), 141 Ind. 12, 18, 40 N. E. 128; *Indiana, etc., R. Co.* v. *Snyder* (1895), 140 Ind. 647, 655, 39 N. E. 912; *Louisville, etc., R. Co.* v. *Berkey* (1894), 136 Ind. 181, 190, 35 N. E. 3; *Indiana Car Co.* v. *Parker* (1885), 100 Ind. 181, 191, and cases cited.

In 3 Elliott, Railroads §1317, it is said: "The term

'vice principal' is generally used to denote an employe to whom the employer has entrusted the performance of a duty which the law requires the employer himself to perform. We think that a superior agent or vice principal is an employe who is entrusted generally with the performance of the master's duties, or is entrusted with the performance of some of the master's duties, although he may not be entrusted with all the duties of the employer. We believe that were the duty 'which the law imposes on the employer is entrusted to an employe, the employe is a vice principal as to that duty, although the matter to which it relates may not be in the strict sense a general one.'' This definition is quoted and approved in *Cleveland, etc., R. Co.* v. *Foland* (1910), 174 Ind. 411, 416, 91 N. E. 594, 92 N. E. 185. It is also quoted, but questioned, in *Peirce* v. *Oliver* (1897), 18 Ind. App. 87, 97, 47 N. E. 485. But whatever difference of opinion may exist as to the definition of vice principal, all authorities agree that an employe authorized to perform a duty which is clearly the master's duty is, to that extent, a vice principal, and the controlling inquiry must be whether an act or omission resulting in an injury involved a duty owing by the master to the injured servant. *Justice* v. *Pennsylvania Co.* (1892), 130 Ind. 321, 30 N. E. 303; *Thacker* v. *Chicago, etc., R. Co., supra,* and cases cited.

In the case under consideration, the general order of the master was to repair the bridge by redecking it, and to that end, as far as appears, the master furnished
4.   materials of approved quality, and delivered the same on the right of way at or near the bridge. If the scaffold was constructed on the initiative of the workmen, and to suit their own convenience, and if the order of the foreman directing the building of the same was but mere executive detail of the work, then, under well-established rules, Teaford was a fellow servant for whose negligence the master would not be liable. *Cleveland, etc., R. Co.* v. *Foland, supra; Indianapolis Traction, etc., Co.* v.

Kinney (1909), 171 Ind. 612, 622, 85 N. E. 954, 23 L. R. A.
(N. S.) 711; *Haskell & Barker Car Co.* v. *Przezdziankowski*
(1908), 170 Ind. 1, 10, 83 N. E. 626, 14 L. R. A. (N. S.)
972, 127 Am. St. 352; *Indianapolis St. R. Co.* v. *Kane*
(1907), 169 Ind. 25, 30, 80 N. E. 841, 81 N. E. 721; *Dill* v.
Marmon, supra, 515; *Southern Ind. R. Co.* v. *Harrell*
(1904), 161 Ind. 689, 700, 68 N. E. 262, 63 L. R. A. 460;
Southern Ind. R. Co. v. *Martin* (1903), 160 Ind. 280, 287,
66 N. E. 886.

If, however, by taking the evidence most favorable to appellant and indulging every reasonable and legitimate inference which a jury might draw therefrom, it cannot
5. be said as a matter of law that appellant and Teaford were fellow servants, then the court erred in
giving the peremptory instruction, and in withdrawing the
case from the jury. Appellant testified, as we have seen,
that for three years prior to his injury he was employed by
the railroad company as a bridge carpenter; that during
the time of his service these platforms were always constructed under the direction of the foreman, and that it
was usual and customary in the building of a platform
on the side of a fill to make secure the ends of the stringer
ties next to the track to keep the structure from tipping.
He also testified that he had never seen a platform at such
a place that was not so secured, and that he believed it was
thus made secure when he went on it.

There was, therefore, some evidence before the jury that
platforms of the kind and character, and used for the same
purpose, as the one in this case, were used in appellee's
bridge work, where timbers were to be prepared on the
side of an embankment. And if it was customary, as the
evidence indicates, to erect such platforms at such places
in the prosecution of appellee's work, then the erection of
the platform in this case was not a mere executive detail
of the work, but was a part of appellee's general plan of

operation under similar conditions. The rule would then apply that the master is bound to provide the servant a reasonably safe place in which to work, and if this primary duty was delegated in this case to Teaford, the foreman, the act of Teaford was the act of the master. Whether the evidence was strong enough to warrant such a conclusion was not a matter for the determination of the court, but should have gone to the jury, under proper instructions by the court.

For error in giving the peremptory instruction, the judgment is reversed and the cause remanded, with instructions to the trial court to sustain appellant's motion for a new trial.

NOTE.—Reported in 99 N. E. 491. See, also, under (1) 38 Cyc. 1576; (2) 26 Cyc. 1104; (3) 26 Cyc. 1318; (4) 26 Cyc. 1329; (5) 26 Cyc. 1474. As to court's invading jury's province by instructing on matters of fact, see 14 Am. St. 36. As to master's duty to provide safe appliances and places for servant, see 33 Am. St. 766. As to master's delegation of duty see note to *Brazil Block Coal Co.* v. *Gibson* (Ind.), 98 Am. St. 300. As to fellow-servant rule and who are vice principals, see 75 Am. St. 584. For vice principalship considered with reference to rank of superior servant, see 51 L. R. A. 513. On the question of vice principalship as determined with reference to character of act causing injury, see 54 L. R. A. 37. On the duty of a master to furnish safe appliances as affected by fact that defective appliances are prepared by fellow servants, see 4 L. R. A. (N. S.) 220. As to the liability of a master for injuries to a servant caused by the fall of scaffolding, see 18 Ann. Cas. 611; Ann. Cas. 1913 B 1123.

SWAIN *v.* HUNT ET AL.

[No. 7,729. Filed October 31, 1912. Rehearing denied March 6, 1913.]

1. HUSBAND AND WIFE.—*Actions.*—*Parties.*—Where, in an action against a husband and wife on a note executed by the wife before her marriage, judgment was had against the wife, but no finding or judgment was rendered against the husband, the husband is neither a necessary nor proper party in an action on such judgment, brought after a divorce had been granted. p. 627.

2. FRAUD.—*Complaint.—Allegations.—Bringing Action in Wrong County.*—A complaint in an action to set aside a judgment, on the ground that the original action was fraudulently brought in the wrong county, is insufficient in the absence of averments of acts or conduct constituting fraud. p. 628.

3. VENUE.—*Action Brought in Wrong County.—Waiver of Objection.*—Where an action is brought in the wrong county, and defendant is lawfully served with notice of the pendency of the action, the question of jurisdiction is waived by permitting a default to be taken, under §348 Burns 1908, §343 R. S. 1881, providing that an objection that the action is brought in the wrong county shall be deemed waived, if not taken by answer or demurrer. p. 628.

From Hamilton Circuit Court; *Dan Waugh*, Judge.

Action by Hannah M. Swain against Charles L. Hunt and another. From a judgment for defendants, the plaintiff appeals. *Affirmed.*

Joseph A. Roberts and *Walter L. Carey*, for appellant.
John F. Neal, C. M. Gentry and *E. E. Cloe*, for appellees.

ADAMS, P. J.—The only error relied on for reversal in this action is predicated on the sustaining of appellees' demurrer to appellant's complaint.

It is shown by the complaint that on December 16, 1886, Gideon Hunt, as guardian of appellees, who were then minors, recovered a judgment in the Hamilton Circuit Court against appellant on a promissory note executed to said guardian by appellant, under the name of H. M. White. Before the maturity of the note, and before suit was brought thereon, appellant became the wife of Luther Swain, who was made a codefendant in the action, but against whom no finding or judgment was made or rendered. Soon after the rendition of the judgment, appellant and Luther Swain were divorced, and appellant became a resident of Marion county, Indiana. On December 8, 1906, appellees, then of full age, brought suit on the judgment against appellant in the Hamilton Circuit Court, to which action Luther Swain was made a party defendant.

Summons for appellant was issued by the clerk directed to the sheriff of Marion county, and was served by reading and by copy. On December 22, 1906, the court found that each defendant had been duly served with process, appellant was defaulted, and judgment rendered against her on default, and in favor of Luther Swain for his costs.

This action was brought by appellant against appellees on December 17, 1908, to set aside said judgment, on the ground that the court rendering the same had no jurisdiction over her person.

It is contended by appellant that the judgment sought to be set aside is void; that the Hamilton Circuit Court did not have jurisdiction over the person of appellant, and that Luther Swain was made a party defendant to the action for the fraudulent purpose of giving the Hamilton Circuit Court jurisdiction to hear and determine the cause.

It is clear that Luther Swain was neither a proper nor a necessary party defendant, and that the action was brought in the wrong county; but it cannot be said that the 2. bringing of an action in the wrong county is fraudulent, without any averment as to the acts or conduct constituting the fraud. All actions brought in the Hamilton Circuit Court are brought for the purpose of vesting jurisdiction in that court.

Appellant asserts that a defendant sued in the wrong county does not waive the question of jurisdiction over his person by failing to appear and raise the question by 3. demurrer or answer, and in support cites, among other cases, *Dobbins* v. *McNamara* (1887), 113 Ind. 54, 14 N. E. 887, 3 Am. St. 626, and *Cavanaugh* v. *Smith* (1882), 84 Ind. 380. These cases are not in point, and only hold that where a judgment is rendered on default against a defendant on whom there was no service of process, and over whose person the court acquired no jurisdiction, such judgment may be set aside in a direct proceeding, whether the defendant had a good defense or not.

In the case at bar, appellant was lawfully served with notice of the pendency of the action, and suffered a default to be taken. Under the plain terms of the statute, this constituted a waiver of jurisdiction. The proviso of §348 Burns 1908, §343 R. S. 1881, reads as follows: "Provided, however, That the objection that the action was brought in the wrong county, if not taken by answer or demurrer, shall be deemed to have been waived." The subject-matter of the action was clearly within the ordinary jurisdiction of the Hamilton Circuit Court, and although the action should have been brought against appellant in Marion county, the jurisdiction of the Hamilton Circuit Court over the person of appellant was waived by failure to raise the question by answer or demurrer. *Eel River R. Co.* v. *State, ex rel.* (1896), 143 Ind. 231, 234, 42 N. E. 617; *Chicago, etc., R. Co.* v. *Marshall* (1906), 38 Ind. App. 217, 222, 75 N. E. 973; *Globe Accident Ins. Co.* v. *Reid* (1898), 19 Ind. App. 203, 219, 47 N. E. 947, 49 N. E. 291.

It would be a harsh rule that would permit appellant in this case to disregard the summons of the Hamilton Circuit Court, suffer a judgment to be taken against her on default, wait until the original judgment became barred by the statute of limitations; and then set aside the judgment rendered on the original judgment.

The demurrer to the complaint was properly sustained, and the judgment is affirmed.

NOTE.—Reported in 99 N. E. 529. See, also, under (1) 21 Cyc. 1550; (2) 23 Cyc. 1041; (3) 40 Cyc. 111. As to what law governs a wife's capacity to sue or be sued, see 85 Am. St. 577.

NATIONAL BISCUIT COMPANY v. WILSON.

[No. 7,730.   Filed November 21, 1912.   Rehearing denied January
23, 1913.   Transfer denied March 6, 1913.]

1. MASTER AND SERVANT.—*Injury to Servant.—Complaint.—Proof.*
—To entitle a servant to judgment in an action against the
master for personal injuries, the complaint must allege, and he
must prove. some act of negligence by defendant which resulted
in the injury.   p. 631.

2. APPEAL. — *Review.* — *Answers to Interrogatories.* — *Motion for
Judgment.—Evidence Not in Record.*—Where the evidence is not
in the record on appeal, the court will not reverse the trial court
for overruling a motion for judgment on the answers to interrogatories notwithstanding the general verdict, unless the conflict
between such answers and the general verdict is such that it
could not be removed by any evidence legitimately admissible
under the issues, and will presume that such evidence was before
the jury.   p. 633.

3. MASTER AND SERVANT.—*Injury to Servant.—Elevator Accident.
—Elevator Not in Control of Master.—Liability.*—Where a servant is employed to hoist flour by an elevator to the upper story
of a building leased in part by his employer, and is injured by
reason of defects in such elevator, even though the employer
under his lease has no control over the elevator, the rule that
the master is bound to furnish a reasonably safe place for the
servant to work. and reasonably safe appliances and machinery,
applies, and such employer is liable, if, by the exercise of ordinary care the elevator would have been known to be dangerous.
p. 633.

4. TRIAL.—*Answers to Interrogatories.—Conclusions of Law.*—Interrogatories to the jury asking whether defendant had a right to
alter and repair the elevator on which plaintiff was injured, or to
inspect it, were improper and the answers involved conclusions
of law.   p. 638.

From Marion Circuit Court (12,099); *Charles Remster,*
Judge.

Action by Melvin L. Wilson against the National Biscuit
Company.   From a judgment for plaintiff, the defendant
appeals.   *Affirmed.*

John B. Elam, James W. Fesler and *Harvey J. Elam,* for
appellant.

Bailey & Young and *Wymond J. Beckett,* for appellee.

IBACH, J.—This was an action for damages on account of personal injuries alleged to have been caused by the negligence of appellant. The case was tried and appealed once before. *National Biscuit Co.* v. *Wilson* (1907), 169 Ind. 442, 82 N. E. 916. The issues in the present trial were formed by an amended complaint in two paragraphs and an answer in general denial, the cause was tried by a jury, and a verdict for $1,500 returned for the plaintiff, and in connection with the verdict sixty-three interrogatories were answered. The defendant moved for judgment in its favor on the interrogatories and answers thereto, but the court entered judgment on the general verdict. The error relied on for reversal is in overruling the motion for judgment in favor of defendant on the interrogatories and answers.

To entitle plaintiff to judgment in the present case, he must charge in his complaint some act of negligence on the part of defendant that resulted in injury to him, and 1. must prove that act of negligence. Therefore in considering the error assigned, we must consider the charge of negligence in the complaint, and we deem it sufficient for the purposes of this opinion to set out the charge of the third paragraph of complaint, the substance of which is that the defendant owned, operated and managed an elevator and hoist in said building, which was wholly under the control and inspection and supervision of the defendant. Then follows a description of certain alleged defects in the elevator, and the charge, "that defendant was negligently using said elevator and said gear in said weakened and worn condition. That said worn condition of said gear wheel and said cogs was well known to the defendant, National Biscuit Company, and that said elevator with said gear wheel and cogs in said condition was dangerous, was also well known to said defendant the National Biscuit Company, in ample time to have repaired said gear wheel or to have replaced the same with a new wheel long before the happening of the accident." It is further charged that the elevator fell and caused the injury ''by reason of the defendant's negligence in using said elevator with said cogs and said gear wheel in said weakened and defective condition as aforesaid, and failing to properly inspect said cogs and gear wheel and in failing to repair or replace the same.'' The gist of the charge is that defendant was negligent in using the elevator with weakened and defective cogwheels, and in failing to repair the same. Appellant contends that the answers to interrogatories show that it was under no duty to repair the elevator.

From the answers to interrogatories, which tend to sustain the general verdict, it appears that plaintiff was injured while employed by defendant on October 16, 1900; that he was engaged in hoisting sacks of flour from the first floor of a building, a part of which was occupied by defendant as tenant, to an upper story thereof, by means of a freight elevator which was operated by a man riding on it with a load. This elevator was built for a freight elevator and used as such, and persons doing business in the building and employes of different occupants thereof sometimes rode on it to get from one floor to another. Plaintiff was injured by said elevator falling while he was upon it as operator, and while he was hoisting a load of flour by means of it. It was in plaintiff's power to start and stop the elevator at his pleasure, and the elevator was caused to break at the particular moment when it did break by a weak point in the gear wheel.

Appellant contends that the following facts, appearing from answers to interrogatories, are in conflict with the general verdict. The building and elevator were owned by the Hitz Baking Company, which carried an insurance policy insuring against accidents by reason of said elevator, and had an elevator inspector in its employ who inspected it from time to time to discover defects. The Hitz Baking Company carried on business in parts of the same building where the elevator was used, and used it in its business.

One of the upper floors of the building was occupied by a cold storage company, which used the elevator to reach its rooms and carry articles to and from them. The Hitz Baking Company employed engineers to take care of the boilers and other machinery in the basement of the building, and employed Jesse Hitz to take charge of the elevator, and Jesse Hitz was in a better position to know of certain dangers arising from the operation of the elevator than was plaintiff. The engineers of the baking company also gave some attention to the elevator, and the Hitz Baking Company paid for such repairs as were made on the elevator from time to time. Interrogatories Nos. 59, 60, and 61, and the answers thereto follow in full. "59. Did the National Biscuit Company have the right to make any alterations or repairs on the elevator? No. 60. Did the National Biscuit Company have any right to take the elevator to pieces and inspect it? No. 61. Did the Hitz Baking Company undertake to furnish elevator service to its tenant the National Biscuit Company. Yes."

Where, as in the present case, the evidence is not brought before this court, in reviewing a motion for judgment on answers to interrogatories, notwithstanding the gen-

2. eral verdict, the court will not reverse the lower court's decision unless such answers are in such irreconcilable conflict with the general verdict that the conflict could not be removed by any evidence legitimately admissible under the issues, for in the absence of the evidence the court will treat the case as if such evidence had been before the jury. *Evansville, etc., Traction Co.* v. *Spiegel* (1912), 49 Ind. App. 412, 94 N. E. 718, 97 N. E. 949.

Appellant's contention is that these answers to interrogatories show that the facts make a case wherein the effort is to hold a defendant liable for the condition

3. of premises in no way under its control, and that the present case falls within the rule that a tenant who merely rents rooms in a building and does not rent the ele-

vator is under no obligation to keep it in repair, and that
the duty to inspect and repair the elevator in this case rested
on the lessor, namely the Hitz Baking Company, for whose
acts this defendant was not responsible. Appellee urges
that where a master knows of a defective and dangerous
condition in the machinery with which his servant is required to work, he is liable for any injury to the servant
by reason thereof, without any regard to the question
whether he is lessor or lessee, or without any regard to
whose duty it was to repair as between lessor and lessee;
that it was the duty therefore of appellant to inspect the
elevator, and whether it did this itself or through the
agency of the Hitz Baking Company made no difference, for
if done by the Hitz Baking Company, this company was, as
between appellant and appellee, the agent adopted by appellant for that purpose; that appellant could not delegate
the duty while acting as master to keep the elevator, the
safety device and the hoisting machinery, on and with
which plaintiff was required to work, in a reasonably safe
condition for him to work upon, and that where a master
either uses, occupies or controls the premises where his servant is placed at work, it becomes his duty to make the place
reasonably safe for such servant. The case of *Channon* v.
Sanford Co. (1898), 70 Conn. 573, 40 Atl. 462, 41 L. R. A.
200, 66 Am. St. 133, is authority for the statement that it
is the duty of the master to use reasonable care to make
the place reasonably safe where his servant works, if the
master uses, occupies or controls the premises.

The case of *De Maries* v. *Jameson* (1906), 98 Minn. 453,
108 N. W. 830, was an action to recover for injuries sustained by the plaintiff while in the employ of the defendants
as a teamster, by the breaking of a guide rope, which was a
part of a block and tackle he was using by direction of the
defendants in unloading hay at the barn of a customer. The
court said: "Where a party directs, without further instruction, his employe to deliver goods upon the premises

of another, he is not responsible for the safety of the premises or appliances of his customers. Such cases are within the general rule that a master is not liable to his employe who is injured by using appliances which the master neither owns nor controls. The ownership or control of an appliance by the master is not, however, in all cases, the test of his liability for injury resulting to his employe by its use. As between the servant and master all appliances, owned or in possession of another, of such a character and use as to impose the duty of inspection, which the master directs or authorizes his servant to use in the business of the master stand upon the same footing as those that actually belong to him. If the master is not in a position to safeguard his servants by an inspection of such appliances, he must refrain from giving them orders to use them, whereby their safety will be imperiled. 1 Labatt, Master and Servant, §171." Similar reasoning is followed in the case of *Harding* v. *Railway Transfer Co.* (1900), 80 Minn. 504, 83 N. W. 395.

The reported case most similar to the present which we have been able to find is that of *Frolich* v. *Cranker* (1901), 21 Ohio C. C. 615, 618. There the defendant rented the third floor of a building, the landlord occupying and using the basement. By the lease contract the defendant had access to and used, along with the building, a freight elevator for his own purposes and those of his employes, and for the purpose of taking foods up to the third floor. The elevator was operated by means of an engine which was situated in the basement, it being propelled by water, and the machinery and that particular portion of the cable which broke were in the basement, that part of the building which was retained by the landlord and not leased to the tenant. The plaintiff, a drayman for the defendant, brought to the building a load of glass for the defendant, and put it into the elevator for the purpose of taking it to the third floor, he and another employe, who was assisting him, riding on

the elevator, the other employe operating the elevator, and
the plaintiff was injured by the fall of the elevator caused
by the cable breaking in the basement. We quote from
the opinion: ''The chief complaint of the plaintiff in error
is, that under the undisputed facts in the case, the defendant
below was not liable to Cranker as his employer, for the
reason, that under the contract of lease by which he had
possession of the third floor, he, Frolich, had no control over
the elevator or machinery, that the elevator and machinery
were operated by Smith & Co., and that the engine was in
that part of the building over which Frolich had no control.
* * * It is urged by the plaintiff in error in this case,
that Frolich was not in possession of this elevator or of
this machinery; that he had no control over it, and that
therefore he is not liable if there was any defect in the
cable. * * * We think that under the testimony in
the record the jury were warranted in finding that Frolich.
either by himself or his manager, Blair, authorized and permitted the use of this elevator by the men when conveying
goods from the bottom to the third floor, * * * and
that his manager, Blair, directed the men to use and operate it in performing these duties; and it may be presumed
that they did so find. * * * This duty [to furnish reasonably safe machinery and a reasonably safe place to work]
being imposed upon Frolich, were the jury warranted in
finding that he failed in the performance of it? Mr. Frolich admits that he did not examine or inspect this cable.
His defense here rests upon the ground that the elevator
was not in his possession or under his control. It seems to us
that an employer cannot avoid the duty of furnishing a safe
place and safe machinery to his employes by permitting or
requiring them to use machinery or appliance that are or
may be to some extent in the possession of or under the
control of others. The employe may have no knowledge of
the contractual relations that exist between the employer
and the persons from whom he leases the premises. In

this case all that Cranker knew was that his employer was using the third floor; that he had the use of this elevator; that he was using it, and that Cranker, according to his testimony, was required to use it in the performance of his duty in conveying goods to the third floor and was ordered by Blair, the foreman, to ride on the elevator when performing this duty, and Mr. Frolich could not avoid this duty and responsibility by the claim that he did not lease the elevator; he could not close his eyes to the condition of the elevator or refuse to inspect it, or neglect to inspect it, or to make any examination of it, for the reason that he only leased the third floor and simply had the use of the elevator. It was his duty, before requiring or permitting the men to use this elevator, to inspect and examine the machinery, to ascertain by a personal examination, or through agents, what the condition of the machinery was, and if he either knew, or by the exercise of ordinary care might have known, of the defective condition of the elevator, he would be liable for injuries resulting therefrom.''

The reasoning of the court in the case just quoted from seems to us almost entirely applicable to the present case. Appellant has cited cases to the effect that where a portion of a building is leased to a tenant, and an elevator is used merely as a means of access thereto, and is under the control of the landlord, the landlord is liable for injuries to persons riding on the elevator. But this is not a case where the elevator was used merely as a means of access to the premises of appellant. Here appellee, an employe of appellant, was employed by appellant to hoist flour to the upper story of a building by means of the elevator, and the circumstances bring the case clearly within the rule that the master is bound to furnish reasonably safe appliances and machinery with which his servant is to work, and a reasonably safe place in which to work. It makes no difference that appellant was not the owner of the elevator, nor even whether or not it had absolutely leased the elevator. It appears from the answers that appellant had sufficient control over the elevator that it could direct appellee to use it and operate it as a machine with which to work, and such being the case, it owed to him the master's duty of inspection.

As to interrogatories Nos. 59 and 60, we believe the

4. answers involve conclusions of law, and that such interrogatories were not proper. But granting that appellant had no right in itself to inspect the elevator, still the facts fall within the rule announced by *Frolich* v. *Cranker, supra,* and it could not escape its master's liability to the employe for setting him to work with and on a dangerous machine, which in the exercise of ordinary care would have been known to be dangerous, simply because under the contract, license or other arrangement by which it was enabled to use the machine, it had not the right personally to inspect. Suppose, for example, that appellant had no right whatever to direct appellee to hoist the flour by means of the elevator, but was a trespasser when it directed him to use it. In such a case we must admit that it would have no right to inspect, or even to use, but having taken control of the elevator, and made it its machine, so far as appellee was concerned, and set him to operate it, it must furnish him a machine as reasonably safe as if it was the absolute owner. As between appellant and appellee, appellant having set appellee to work with the elevator, is clearly liable to him for the injuries sustained by the defect proved.

Judgment affirmed.

NOTE.—Reported in 99 N. E. 819. See, also, under (1) 26 Cyc. 1386, 1415; (2) 3 Cyc. 173, 313; (3) 26 Cyc. 1109; (4) 26 Cyc. 1912. As to liability of master to servant injured by elevator, see 56 Am. St. 806. For a discussion of the duty of a master to furnish safe appliances as applicable to a servant sent to work on the premises of a third person, see Ann. Cas. 1913 B 796.

NOVEMBER TERM, 1912.   639

Baltimore, etc., R. Co. v. Cincinnati, etc., R. Co.—52 Ind. App. 639.

BALTIMORE AND OHIO SOUTHWESTERN RAILROAD
COMPANY *v.* THE CINCINNATI, LAWRENCEBURG
AND AURORA ELECTRIC STREET
RAILROAD COMPANY.

[No. 7,750. Filed November 26, 1912. Rehearing denied
March 6, 1913.]

1. CONTRACTS.—*Actions.*—*Consideration.*—As a general rule, the
promise contained in a contract, in order to support an action,
must have been made upon a valuable consideration. p. 643.

2. CONTRACTS.—*Valuable Consideration.*—A valuable consideration,
necessary to support a contract, must consist of the forbearance
or acquisition of some legal right, and, unless it is the forbearance or acquisition of a legal right, there is no consideration,
even though the parties may believe otherwise. p. 643.

3. RAILROADS.—*Street Railroads.*—*Crossing Agreement Between
Steam and Street Railroads.*—*Consideration.*—The consent of a
steam railroad company to cross its tracks at grade on a certain
street, does not constitute a sufficient consideration for the
promise of a street railroad company to pay for, keep and maintain a watchman at such crossing, if the same should be required, since the steam railroad company could be required
to maintain a watchman regardless of whether the street
railroad crossed its tracks, and the street railroad company, in
obtaining such consent, acquired no right to which it was not
already legally entitled. p. 643.

4. RAILROADS.—*Street Railroads.*—*Additional Burden on Streets.*—
Right to Cross Tracks of Steam Road.—The use of city streets
by a street railway company, with the consent of the common
council, does not constitute an additional burden, and it may,
subject to no other conditions than those to which the general
public is subject, use the street and cross the track of a steam
road without the latter's consent. p. 644.

5. RAILROADS.—*Use of Streets.*—*Street Railroads.*—It will be assumed that a steam railroad constructed its track across a street
with the understanding that a street or interurban railroad
might thereafter be lawfully located on such street and across
its track at such point. p. 645.

6. RAILROADS.—*Street Railroads.*—*Right to Cross Tracks of Steam
Road.*—*Priority in Use of Crossing.*—A street railroad company
and a steam railroad company are on equal terms in the use of a
street except that, on due notice, the steam road has the priority
in the use of the crossing, where its tracks are crossed by those
of a street car company. p. 645.

7. RAILROADS.—*Street Railroads.*—*Crossing Agreement Between Steam and Street Railroads.*—Where a street railway company desires to lay its tracks across those of a steam road, the character of the crossing, and of the materials, appliances and equipment to be used in its construction and maintenance, are the proper subjects of contract, since both companies are chargeable with certain duties relative to the safety of the street occasioned by such crossing, and the rights and duties of each with reference thereto, as between themselves, may be specifically defined by contract. p. 645.

From Dearborn Circuit Court; *George E. Downey,* Judge.

Action by the Baltimore & Ohio Southwestern Railroad Company against the Cincinnati, Lawrenceburg & Aurora Electric Street Railroad Company. From a judgment for defendant, the plaintiff appeals. *Affirmed.*

Edward Barton, R. S. Alcorn and *McMullen & McMullens,* for appellant.

Shutts & Davies and *M. J. Givan,* for appellee.

MYERS, J.—Appellant brought this action against appellee, to collect a sum of money alleged to be due it by the terms of a certain written contract. The complaint was in one paragraph, to which a demurrer for want of facts was sustained, and this ruling is assigned as error.

From the complaint it appears that both appellant and appellee were Indiana corporations, the former owning and operating a line of railroad through the city of Lawrenceburg for the carriage of freight and passengers for hire, and the latter owning and operating a street railroad through said city for the carriage of passengers for hire. On March 21, 1900, these companies entered into a written contract, made a part of the complaint by exhibit, which, omitting the formal parts, reads as follows:

"WITNESSETH:
    Whereas, the said party of the second part desires to cross at grade the right of way and track or tracks of the party of the first part for the purpose of constructing and operating an electric railroad at Walnut Street in the City of Lawrenceburg and at George

Street in the City of Aurora, both in the State of Indiana; and

Whereas, the parties have mutually agreed that said party of the second part may construct, maintain and operate its electric railroad over and across the right of way, railroad and track of the party of the first part at the points named, to-wit: Walnut Street in the City of Lawrenceburg and George Street in the City of Aurora, and State of Indiana, upon the terms and conditions hereinafter set forth:

Now, Therefore, It is agreed between the parties,

1. The party of the first part grants to the party of the second part the right to cross at grade, construct, maintain and operate an electric street railroad over and across the right of way, railroad and track of the party of the first part at Walnut Street in the City of Lawrenceburg, also at George Street in the City of Aurora, State of Indiana, upon the conditions and terms hereinafter set forth.

2. The party of the second part, in consideration of the grant of the right to cross at grade the right of way, railroad and track of the party of the first part above mentioned, covenants and agrees that it will, at its own sole cost and expense, construct and forever afterwards maintain the crossing, frogs, fixtures and appliances necessary for the safe and proper crossing of the said right of way, railroad and track of the party of the first part at Walnut Street in the city of Lawrenceburg, and for the safe and proper crossing of the said right of way; railroad and track of the party of the first part at George Street in the City of Aurora, in the State of Indiana, all of which said work crossing, frogs, fixtures and appliances, and the manner of construction and maintenance of the same, shall be done to the satisfaction of the party of the first part.

3. Said party of the second part further covenants and agrees that it will bring its cars to a full stop on each side upon approaching either of said crossings over the said right of way, railroad and track of the party of the first part at Walnut Street in the City of Lawrenceburg, and at George Street in the City of Aurora, and will in each case upon approaching said railroad track with its cars send a conductor ahead of such car, whose duty it shall be to observe the approach of trains at said crossings, or either of them and direct

the movement of said electric cars so that the same
shall not collide or be struck by the engines or cars of
the party of the first part being operated over said
line of railroad, it being the distinct understanding and
agreement of the parties that the said party of the first
part shall have precedence in the operation of its trains
over said crossings, and that the party of the second
part, in the operation of its electric cars, shall only
attempt to cross the line of said railroad at a time when
the same may be done with safety.

4.   The said party of the second part further covenants and agrees that whenever it shall be necessary for
the safety of said crossings, or either of them, or whenever the said party of the first part shall be required by
any law or ordinance of either of the said Cities of Lawrenceburg or Aurora, or the State of Indiana, to keep
or maintain any crossing watchman or watchmen at said
crossing of Walnut Street, Lawrenceburg, or George
Street, Aurora, or either of them, then the party of the
second part hereby covenants and agrees to pay for,
keep and maintain such watchman or watchmen.

5.   The provisions of this contract shall extend to
and be binding upon the parties and both of them, their
successors, assigns and legal representatives, and the
provisions of this contract shall govern and control the
operation of said crossings so long as the same shall be
used for the purposes provided by this contract.''

An ordinance of said city, passed and approved December
13, 1906, and continually thereafter in force, requiring appellant to keep a watchman at the crossing of its track on
Walnut street, was made a part of the complaint, as was
also an itemized statement of the money paid by appellant
for the services of a watchman at said crossing from December, 1906, up to and including February, 1910.   Other facts
are alleged, but the question here for decision is apparent
from the facts stated.   The objection to the complaint is
that it fails to disclose a consideration for appellee's agreement to pay for the services of a watchman.

The fourth specification of the contract is the only one
concerning the subject of pay for a watchman's services,
and appellee's promise in this respect, as we read the instru-

1. ment in question, must be supported by a valuable consideration. In 1 Beach, Contracts §5, it is said: "The general rule is that in order to support an action, the promise must have been made upon a legal consideration moving from the promisee to the promisor."

The same author (1 Beach, Contracts §147) says:

2. "A 'valuable consideration' consists either in some right, interest, profit, or benefit accruing to the one party, or some extension of time of payment, detriment, loss, or responsibility given, suffered, or undertaken by the other." In 1 Page, Contracts §274, it is said: "A valuable consideration is some legal right acquired by the promisor in consideration of his promise, or foreborne by the promisee in consideration of such promise." And again (1 Page, Contracts §301): "While the parties to a contract may make such terms and select such consideration as they choose, the consideration selected must be the forbearance or acquisition of some legal right. If they select something which is not a legal right, the acquisition or forbearance of it constitutes no consideration, though the parties may believe otherwise."

3. The contract before us recites, in effect, that appellee in the construction, maintenance and operation of its road desired to cross appellant's track in Walnut street in the city of Lawrenceburg, and that appellant consented thereto on certain terms and conditions, among which was the promise of appellee to pay for, keep and maintain a watchman at Walnut street crossing. Or, in other words, the consideration for appellee's promise was the consent of appellant to cross at grade its track on Walnut street.

If appellee acquired some legal right, or any legal possibility of benefit by its promise, a sufficient consideration would be shown, but the mere consent or withdrawal of an objection by appellant to the doing of that which appellee had a legal right to do, is not a consideration sufficient to support a promise. This is so on the theory that the promisor gets nothing in return for his promise but that to which he is legally entitled. *Beaver* v. *Fulp* (1894), 136 Ind. 595, 36 N. E. 418; *Reynolds* v. *Nugent* (1865), 25 Ind. 328; *Shortle* v. *Terre Haute, etc., R. Co.* (1892), 131 Ind. 338, 30 N. E. 1084; 1 Beach, Contracts §157; 9 Cyc. 347; *Horton* v. *Erie R. Co.* (1901), 72 N. Y. Supp. 1018, 65 App. Div. 587; *Brooklyn, etc., R. Co.* v. *Brooklyn City R. Co.* (1861), 33 Barb. (N. Y.) 420; *New York, etc., R. Co.* v. *Forty-Second Street, etc., R. Co.* (1867), 50 Barb. 309; *Market St. R. Co.* v. *Central R. Co.* (1877), 51 Cal. 583; *Highland Ave., etc., R. Co.* v. *Birmingham Union R. Co.* (1890), 93 Ala. 505, 9 South. 568.

What then was the legal right or benefit gained by appellee through its promise to pay for the services of a watchman, or right forborne by appellant in consideration of such promise? The city of Lawrenceburg, by legislative enactment, had the power to require appellant to maintain a watchman at its railroad crossing over Walnut street. §8655 Burns 1908, subd. 49, Acts 1905 p. 219. This power was not enhanced, limited or affected by the fact that appellant gave its consent for appellee to construct, maintain and operate its road in the street across appellant's track.

At the time of making the contract in question, and ever since that time, it was, and still is, the settled law of this State that the use of city streets by a street railway company with the consent of the common council does not constitute an additional burden. After affirming this doctrine in the case of *Chicago, etc., Terminal R. Co.* v. *Whiting, etc., St. R. Co.* (1894), 139 Ind. 297, 38 N. E. 604, 26 L. R. A. 337, 47 Am. St. 264, the court said on page 304: "So long, therefore, as it is the settled law of this State that a street railway is not an additional burden to that of the easement which the general public has in the street, and that the street railway company's right to use

the street is founded on that easement, that long it must
be held that the right of such street railway to cross over the
tracks of a steam railway laid on such street is subject to
no conditions other than those to which the general public is
subject in traveling over such streets.'' While such company's cars may be propelled by electricity, its right to
use the street and cross the track of a railway company without the consent and against its will is no longer an open
question. *Pittsburgh, etc. R. Co.* v. *Muncie, etc., Traction
Co.* (1910), 174 Ind. 167, 91 N. E. 600, and cases cited;
Michigan Cent. R. Co. v. *Hammond, etc., Electric R. Co.*
(1908), 42 Ind. App. 66, 83 N. E. 650; *Pittsburgh, etc., R.
Co.* v. *Browning* (1904), 34 Ind. App. 90, 71 N. E. 227;
Evansville, etc., Traction Co. v. *Evansville Belt R. Co.*
(1909), 44 Ind. App. 155, 87 N. E. 21.

When appellant constructed its road across Walnut street,
it must be assumed that it did so with the understanding
"that a street or interurban railroad might there-

5. after be lawfully located upon said highway and
across the track at that point.'' *South East, etc., R.
Co.* v. *Evansville, etc., R. Co.* (1907), 169 Ind. 339, 82 N.
E. 765, 13 L. R. A. (N. S.) 916, 14 Ann. Cas. 214. Hence
priority in the location of tracks has nothing to do

6. with the right to cross, for the reason that both companies in the use of the street are on equal terms, except that the steam road has the right of way on giving due
notice of its purpose so to do. *Evansville, etc., R. Co.* v.
Berndt (1909), 172 Ind. 697, 88 N. E. 612. But the

7. kind and character of the crossing, materials, appliances and equipment to be used in its construction
or maintenance, are the proper subjects of contract. *Evansville, etc., Traction Co.* v. *Evansville Belt R. Co., supra.*
This is so, for the reason that the companies owning such
intersecting lines are charged with certain duties relative
to the safety of the street from defects occasioned by such
crossing, and the rights and duties of each with reference

thereto, as between themselves, may be specifically defined by contract.

In the case last cited the court, in speaking of a contract in some respects similar to the one before us, held that it was not void for want of consideration. But it must be kept in mind that the court then was considering the right of the companies owning such intersecting lines, and charged with the highest duty to guard and protect their passengers and servants operating their cars and trains, as well as their property, from the increased hazard of such crossing, and not the public generally intending to cross the tracks, which it is the purpose of the ordinance to protect by requiring a watchman. These considerations lead us to conclude that the complaint in this case does not state facts sufficient to constitute a cause of action.

The judgment is therefore affirmed.

NOTE.—Reported in 99 N. E. 1018. See, also, under (1) 9 Cyc. 309; (2) 9 Cyc. 311; (4) 33 Cyc. 242; 36 Cyc. 1419; (5) 33 Cyc. 240, 242; (6) 33 Cyc. 240; (7) 33 Cyc. 243. As to failure of consideration as a defense in an action on contract, see 13 Am. Dec. 378. As to moral obligation as consideration to uphold an express promise, see 39 Am. St. 735. As to street railways as additional servitude, see note to *Mordhurst* v. *Ft. Wayne, etc., Co.* (Ind.) 106 Am. St. 242.

THE CLEVELAND, CINCINNATI, CHICAGO AND ST. LOUIS RAILWAY COMPANY ET AL. *v.* CLARK, ADMINISTRATOR.

[No. 7,711. Filed November 1, 1912. Rehearing denied January 31, 1913. Transfer denied March 6, 1913.]

1. APPEAL.—*Review.—Complaint.—Evidence.—Sufficiency.*— Where two persons were injured in the same accident, and two separate actions were filed to recover damages, and both actions were appealed, the determination, in the one appeal, of the sufficiency of the complaint, and of the evidence to show that defendants' negligence was the proximate cause of the injury, is conclusive in the other appeal, where the complaint and evidence are practically the same in each case. p. 649.

Cleveland, etc., R. Co. *v.* Clark—52 Ind. App. 646.

2. RAILROADS.—*Crossing Accidents.—Evidence.—Sufficiency.*—In an action to recover for the death of plaintiff's decedent as the result of a railroad crossing accident, evidence tending to show that she was thrown out of her buggy, and showing that before the accident decedent was strong and healthy and did all her own work, that after the accident, and up to the time of her death, she complained of pains in her side and back almost continuously, that she became greatly emaciated and was able to do but very little work, that she was internally injured and that her death was directly caused by peritonitis caused by such internal injuries, sufficiently supports a finding that decedent was injured by the collision with the train and that such injuries were the cause of her death, notwithstanding there was other evidence to show that almost immediately after the accident decedent was on her feet and running down the road, and that she got out of the buggy before it was struck. p. 649.

3. APPEAL.—*Review.—Harmless Error.—Instructions.—Mistake in Use of Word.*—Where a mistake in the use of words in an instruction is so obvious that the jury could not have been misled, the error will be deemed immaterial. p. 650.

4. APPEAL.—*Review.—Refusal of Instructions.*—The refusal of requested instructions is not ground for reversal, where, so far as they were proper, they were covered by other instructions given. p. 651.

5. RAILROADS.—*Crossing Accidents.—Evidence.—Admissibility.*—In an action for the death of plaintiff's decedent in a collision with a train caused by the defective condition of the crossing, evidence as to the condition of the crossing after the accident was admissible, where it was shown that the condition was the same before the accident. p. 651.

6. RAILROADS.—*Crossing Accident.—Evidence.—Admissibility.—Notice of Defect.*—In an action for the death of plaintiff's decedent in a collision with a train caused by the defective condition of the crossing, testimony of a witness that, shortly before the accident, his horse had caught its foot between the rail and a plank of the crossing, as it was alleged that decedent's horse had done, was proper as showing constructive notice to the railroad company of the character of the crossing. p. 651.

7. APPEAL.—*Review.—Harmless Error.—Admission of Evidence.*—In an action against a railroad company and a construction company for the death of plaintiff's decedent who was struck by a construction train at a crossing, error, if any, in admitting evidence as to the defective condition of the crossing could not have harmed the defendant construction company, where, under the pleadings, it was not charged with any responsibility for the condition of such crossing. p. 651.

8. WITNESSES.—*Cross-Examination.*—*Matter Not Brought Out on Direct Examination.*—A question, on the cross-examination of a witness, as to a matter not brought out on direct examination is properly refused. p. 652.

9 EVIDENCE.— *Declarations of Existing Pain.—Admissibility.*— Where, in an action to recover for a wrongful death, one of the issues involved the extent of decedent's injuries from the accident, declarations of the decedent, made the day after the accident, that her shoulder was hurt and that she suffered pain, were admissible as declarations of present existing pain to show the extent of her injuries. p. 652.

10. APPEAL.—*Review.—Misconduct of Counsel.*—Where, in an action against several defendants, the court overruled a motion to withdraw the submission of the cause to the jury because of the statement of plaintiff's counsel in argument that defendants desired that liability should be fixed on one of them that was insolvent, but instructed the jury that it should consider only the evidence in the case, and not what the attorneys say outside the evidence, defendants received all the relief to which they were entitled, since in view of the circumstances and the evidence in the case, the statement did not warrant the withdrawal of the submission. p. 653.

From Clay Circuit Court; *John M. Rawley,* Judge.

Action by James M. Clark, administrator of the estate of Selma Clark, deceased, against The Cleveland, Cincinnati, Chicago and St. Louis Railway Company and others. From a judgment for plaintiff, the defendants appeal. *Affirmed.*

Louis D. Leveque, A. J. Kelly, A. W. Knight, George A. Knight, L. J. Hackney, and *Sullivan & Knight,* for appellants.

S. M. McGregor and *S. A. Hays,* for appellee.

IBACH, J.—This was an action to recover damages from appellants on account of the death of Selma Clark, appellee's decedent, alleged to have been the result of injuries caused by appellants' negligence on November 1, 1906.

Cleveland, etc., R. Co. v. Clark (1912), 51 Ind. App. 392, 97 N. E. 822, is a companion case to this, being an action for damages caused by the negligent killing of Maggie Clark in the same accident. The women were sisters-in-law, and were riding in a buggy which was struck by a construction train at the crossing of a public highway with appellant railway company's tracks. Selma Clark was driving. Maggie Clark was very severely crushed about the limbs, and died in a few days. Selma Clark, it is alleged, received injuries which caused her death on April 24, 1908. The complaint in this case, except that it sets out the facts of the occurrence more in detail, is almost an exact copy of the second paragraph of the complaint in the other case. The actionable negligence averred is practically the same. The former complaint was held by this court to be good as against all the defendants. The evidence tending to show that appellant railway company was negligent in maintaining a defective highway crossing, and that appellant Wabash Constructon Company was negligent in the operation of its construction train, and that such negligence on the part of these appellants was the proximate cause of the collision between the train and the buggy, is likewise practically the same as that considered in the former case, and we have nothing to add to what was said in the former opinion concerning this evidence. The sufficiency of the com-

1. plaint in the present case, and the sufficiency of the evidence in the present case to show negligence on the part of appellants which was the proximate cause of the collision, were conclusively determined against appellants' contentions by the opinion in the former case.

It is urged that the evidence in the case at bar is not sufficient to prove that appellee's decedent was injured at all by the collision, or that, if injured, her injuries caused

2. her death. Many witnesses, including members of her family, and neighbors who saw her frequently, testified that before the accident she was strong and healthy, and did all her own work, including her washing and ironing; that after the accident, up to the time of her death, she complained of pains in her side and back almost continuously; that she became greatly emaciated, and was able to do but very little work, scarcely her cooking. Mrs. Strachn

testifies that the morning after the accident decedent said
that she was hurt down her left shoulder and side, and witness looked and saw that her shoulder was discolored. Dr.
Siner, her physician, who was called to attend her the night
of the accident because of her nervousness, and who attended her frequently up to her death, testified that in his
opinion she was injured internally by the accident, and that
her death was caused directly by peritonitis caused by these
internal injuries. It is true that decedent was seen running down the road almost immediately after the accident,
and appellants introduced evidence tending to show that
decedent got out of the buggy before it was struck, but the
jury, in answer to interrogatories, stated that it believed
she was thrown out, and there was evidence tending to support such a finding. Kate Hardesty, who saw her immediately
after the collision, testified that there was dirt on her black
coat, as if she had been down. We think that the evidence
that she received injuries in the collision which caused her
death is sufficient to sustain the verdict on this point.

The objections made to instructions are, in substance,
those made to the instructions given in the Maggie Clark
case. Instructions Nos. 8, 9, 12 and 14 given at plaintiff's
request, were given in that case, and the same objections
here urged to them were considered on the appeal to this
court. Instruction No. 15 in the present case is the same as
instruction No. 15 set out in the opinion in the former case,
with the omission of the word "wrongful," which occurs
twice in the instruction there set out, and the objections
made to it are there answered. There was no error in giving instructions Nos. 2½ and 10, when they are considered
in connection with all the other instructions given.

Instruction No. 7, as it appears in the transcript, contains
a clause which reads, "and if such negligence results in
injury to a person who was rightfully using the high-
3.   way without *of such* and in the exercise of due care for
his own protection." Appellants urge that such an in-

struction is meaningless and unintelligible to the jury. Appellee gives an explanation which we think the true one, that the present reading is merely a clerical error in copying, and that the instruction as read to the jury contained the words "without fault," instead of "without of such." But if it had been given as copied in the record there would be no reversible error, for where a mistake in the use of words in an instruction is so obvious that the jury could not have been misled, the error will be deemed immaterial. *Anderson* v. *Anderson* (1891), 128 Ind. 254, 27 N. E. 724; *Pittsburgh, etc., R. Co.* v. *Carlson* (1899), 24 Ind. App. 559, 56 N. E. 251.

Instructions Nos. 9, 10, 11, 17, 22 and 31, which the court refused to give on the motion of appellant Wabash Construction Company, were covered, so far as proper,

4. by other instructions given. The same is true of instruction No. 12, which the court refused to give on motion of appellant railway company.

The objection to the evidence of the witness Kattman,

5. man, as to the condition of the boards at the crossing on the main track, that he was testifying to a time after the accident, was not well taken, for it was shown that conditions were the same before the accident. The witness Muir's testimony that his horse had caught its

6. foot between the rail and a plank at the crossing, as it was alleged decedent's horse had done, was proper as showing constructive notice to appellant railway company of the character of the crossing, the witness having fixed the time when his horse's foot was caught as shortly before the accident, the same fall. But if there had been

7. error in the admission of the testimony of these witnesses, appellant Wabash Construction Company, which is the only one of appellants which argues this point here, could not take advantage of the error. Such error would be harmless as to the Wabash Construction Company, for such testimony could under the pleadings in no way

fasten liability on this defendant, which was not charged with any responsibility for the condition of the crossing on the main track.

It was not error to refuse to permit Dr. Siner, upon cross-examination, to answer the question, "Did Selma Clark ever tell you on any occasion when you were waiting on her
8. that somebody at the crossing hollered out to her that the track was clear, hurry up?" No matter was called out on direct examination which would make this question proper on cross-examination.

Witness Barbara Strachn testified to seeing Selma Clark the morning after the accident, and that she was nervous and trembling. Then, in answer to the question.
9. "What did she say upon your inquiry?" the witness testified, "Well, I went to her, and it was natural for me to ask her how she felt, and she answered me and told me that she felt awfully bad, and I said, 'Where are you hurt?' and she said, 'Down this shoulder [the left] and down this side [the left].' This shoulder [the left] and part of her arm seemed to be discolored, I looked at it and it was discolored all over her left shoulder and she was very nervous." Appellants objected to this answer on the ground of self-serving declarations. The witness further testified, without objection, that Mrs. Clark was holding her side when she was trembling, and said her side was hurting her. We do not think appellants' objection was well taken. One of the issues in the case was the extent of decedent's injuries from the accident. The witness was testifying as to what decedent said of present, existing pain. Decedent's declarations and complaints at the time were competent to show the extent of her suffering. *Cleveland, etc., R. Co.* v. *Carey* (1904), 33 Ind. App. 275, 71 N. E. 244; *Indianapolis St. R. Co.* v. *Schmidt* (1904), 163 Ind. 360, 71 N. E. 201; *Indianapolis St. R. Co.* v. *Haverstick* (1905), 35 Ind. App. 281, 74 N. E. 34; *Southern Ind. R. Co.* v. *Davis* (1904), 32 Ind. App. 569, 69 N. E. 550.

One of appellee's counsel, while addressing the jury, said: "They [defendants] want the liability fixed on the Guilfoil Company, and that would be all right as far as they

10. are concerned, but it might make a difference to the plaintiff when he comes to collect his judgment and finds the Guilfoil Company to be insolvent, when he would be unable to collect his judgment." Objection was made by appellants' counsel to this language, and they moved the court to withdraw the submission of the cause to the jury and discharge the jury because of this remark. The court overruled this motion, and instructed the jury as follows: "You will consider only the evidence in the case, and not what the attorneys say outside the evidence." Thus the remark was withdrawn from the consideration of the jury by the court's instruction, if, in fact, it was improper and outside the evidence. In view of the circumstances, and considering the evidence given at the trial, the language of counsel was not a ground for withdrawal of the submission to the jury, and appellants received all the relief to which they were entitled. *Malott* v. *Central Trust Co.* (1907), 168 Ind. 428, 79 N. E. 369; *Southern Ind. R. Co.* v. *Fine* (1904), 163 Ind. 617, 72 N. E. 589· *Blume* v. *State* (1900), 154 Ind. 343, 56 N. E. 771.

Judgment affirmed.

NOTE.—Reported in 99 N. E. 777. See, also, under (1) 11 Cyc. 745; (2) 33 Cyc. 1090; (3) 38 Cyc. 1595; (4) 38 Cyc. 1711; (5) 33 Cyc. 1077; (6) 33 Cyc. 1076; (7) 38 Cyc. 1411; (8) 40 Cyc. 2500; (9) 16 Cyc. 1164; (10) 38 Cyc. 1502. As to mode of curing error in respect of counsel's misconduct in the course of argument, see 9 Am. St. 569. As to liability for negligence when the unsafe condition of one's premises or utility has caused injury to another, see 14 Am. St. 435. As to the admissibility in evidence of exclamations and expressions of pain in actions involving bodily injuries, see 15 Ann. Cas. 799.

GASKILL v. BARNETT.

[No. 7,867.   Filed March 6, 1913.]

1. WATERS AND WATERCOURSES.—*Natural Watercourse.*—A natural watercourse is a channel, cut through the turf by the erosion of running water, with well defined banks and bottom, through which water flows, and has flowed immemorially, not necessarily all the time, but ordinarily, and permanently for substantial periods of each year. p. 658.

2. WATERS AND WATERCOURSES.—*Surface Waters.*—The rules relating to watercourses are not applicable to surface currents that do not follow a designated and known channel. p. 658.

3 WATERS AND WATERCOURSES.—*Natural Watercourse.*—*Drainage of Surface Water.*—*Artificial Channels.*—The same line of discharge of water in times of heavy rains or melting snows, from a pond created by the natural assembling of surface water, does not constitute a natural watercourse, and neither does an artificial channel, constructed solely for the purpose of expediting surface drainage, which is employed but occasionally and temporarily in carrying away an excess of surface water caused by heavy rains or melting snows. p. 658.

4. WATERS AND WATERCOURSES.—*Surface Waters.*—Surface water is a common enemy which every proprietor may fight and ward off his premises by dams, embankments or other available means constructed or used on his own property. p. 659.

5. WATERS AND WATERCOURSES.—*Natural Watercourse.*—*Artificial Drains.*—While it is the law that a natural watercourse, which is lost in a swamp or lake and emerges therefrom at a lower level in a well defined channel, does not cease to be a watercourse because it passes through such swamp or lake, the rule is not applicable to a drain which leads into and emerges from a pond, so as to render one who closes the same liable for the obstruction of a natural watercourse, although in addition to surface drainage it carries the water from springs located above such pond, where it is shown that such pond was closed by the natural elevation of the land and had no connection with such springs, nor with a natural channel and bayou to the south, and that prior to the construction of such drain water stood in such pond until evaporated. p. 659.

6. WATERS AND WATERCOURSES.—*Surface Waters.*—*Obstruction.*—Where, in an action for the obstruction of a drain, it is shown that the former owner of defendant's land opened a channel from a basin on his land to connect with a gulley a short distance south of his north line, and that the owner north of such

line made a ditch down to the line to connect with such basin, and that each owner from time to time cleaned out the channel on his land, such facts, in the absence of some agreement at the time the channel was made, do not establish an easement by which the plaintiff may flow water through the channel on defendant's land, but merely show a permissive use. p. 659.

7. EASEMENTS.—*Easements by Prescription.*—A mere permissive use is insufficient to establish a prescriptive right to an easement, but, to be sufficient, the use must be shown to be adverse, under a claim of right, continuous and uninterrupted for twenty years. p. 660.

8. WATERS AND WATERCOURSES.—*Drainage of Surface Water.—Easement.—Extent of Right.*—Even if one has acquired an easement to flow water from a pond through a ditch on his land into a channel on the land of an adjoining owner, such right will not authorize him to wrongfully accumulate additional water and turn it through such ditch onto the lands of such adjoining owner. p. 660.

From Greene Circuit Court; *Charles E. Henderson,* Judge.

Action by John A. Gaskill against Clarence C. Barnett. From a judgment for defendant, the plaintiff appeals. *Affirmed.*

W. L. Slinkard, for appellant.

Cyrus E. Davis and *Fred E. Dyer,* for appellee.

FELT, P. J.—Appellant filed suit against appellee in two paragraphs of complaint. The first paragraph is for damages alleged to have been caused by appellee's construction of a dam across a natural watercourse, and for a mandatory injunction to compel the removal of said obstruction. The second paragraph seeks damages for the obstruction of an easement, and also to quiet title thereto. Issues were joined by a general denial, and the cause was tried by the court. On request the court made a special finding of facts and stated its conclusions of law thereon, to which appellant duly excepted. The only error assigned is that the court erred in its conclusions of law.

The substance of the finding of facts is as follows: That plaintiff and defendant are the owners of adjoining farm lands in Greene county, Indiana; that the lands of plaintiff lie north and east of those of defendant, and there is a public highway running north and south on the west side of said lands; that all of said real estate was formerly owned by James Foster; that he is the remote grantor of defendant, and the immediate grantor of plaintiff; that there is a spring on the farm adjoining that of plaintiff on the north; that leading southwest from said spring there is a depression in the ground, with well-defined banks through which the water from said spring runs, the year round, until it reaches another spring on plaintiff's land; that at a point "about 21 rods north of the line dividing the lands of the plaintiff and the defendant, the water coming from said springs and surface water spread out and made a pond at times covering as much as two acres and would extend westward and overflow a highway running north and south, until the building of a certain free gravel road along said highway, after which the embankment made by the free gravel road prevented the water from crossing the said road, and the said pond stood there until evaporated;" that said basin or pond extends below the line dividing the lands of plaintiff and defendant about 75 feet on the land of the latter; that defendant purchased his land from one Maxwell, who in 1897 dug a ditch with well-defined banks, from the point where the water came from plaintiff's land onto that of defendant, and continued the same in a southeasterly direction for a considerable distance to a bayou, and from thence the water continued on to White river through a natural channel; that the water so carried was surface water, except in wet seasons the water from said springs was intermingled with the surface water; that said depression was closed by the elevation of the ground so as to form a basin, and in rainy seasons was a pond of water; that from the point where said depression crosses the line between the lands of said parties, plaintiff constructed a ditch north across said basin on his lands for a distance of about 20 rods; that he

also made a roadway on his land just north of said dividing
line, and constructed a bridge thereon across said ditch;
that the ditches aforesaid on each of said tracts of land were
kept open by the respective owners thereof until June 24,
1908, when defendant constructed on his own land a dam
across said ditch to the height of about three feet, and thereby filled the ditch and shut off the flow of said surface water
and the spring water when mingled therewith, as aforesaid,
and backed the same onto the lands of plaintiff, to his damage in the sum of $50; that when defendant purchased his
said lands said ditches were open, visible and connected, and
carried off the surface water, and the spring water when
mingled therewith; that water from said springs, except
when mingled with surface water as aforesaid, did not at
any time reach the point where the water spread out and
formed the aforesaid pond; that the water from said springs
was and is insufficient, unaided by surface water, to make
a flowing stream reaching down to said basin; that the
water which reached the line dividing the lands of plaintiff
and defendant was surface water; that said low land, or
basin, on plaintiff's land was cleared in 1893, and since that
time has been cultivated and crops raised thereon in reasonably dry seasons; that plaintiff has made and kept open a
deep furrow in the lowest part of said basin, down to his
south line, which has greatly facilitated the flow of water
out of said basin, and cast the same on defendant's lands in
larger quantities than would have resulted from the natural
drainage of the land without such furrow; that there are no
banks or shores of any stream or current through said basin,
other than the furrow aforesaid, which made a ditch varying
in depth from six inches to two feet; that said ditch carries
no water except in times of heavy rain; that for three years
last past plaintiff has maintained on his land a private
driveway, and used it largely for the purpose of hauling
gravel from a pit on his land to the highway on the west

thereof; that the wagons have worn trenches in the ground through which water has run into said ditch or furrow across said depression, that formerly spread out over the land without flowing into said basin; that said gutters have collected, and emptied into said furrow or ditch, and from there onto defendant's land, water in greater quantities than that which came from the natural drainage of the land; that plaintiff at various times, when said gutters in said roadway were obstructed used shovels and opened them up so as to drain the water therefrom into said cross furrow or ditch, from which it passed to defendant's land; that the deepest portion of said basin is on defendant's land, and the natural drainage of the land, north, east and west thereof, has from time immemorial been into said basin; that from a point about 21 rods south of said dividing line there is a natural gulley or channel leading to said bayou, and thence to White river.

A natural watercourse is a channel, cut through the turf by the erosion of running water, with well-defined banks and bottom, through which water flows, and has

1. flowed immemorially, not necessarily all the time, but ordinarily, and permanently for substantial periods of each year. *New Jersey, etc., R. Co.* v. *Tutt* (1907), 168 Ind. 205, 211, 80 N. E. 420. Surface currents that

2. do not follow a designated and known channel are not governed by the rules relating to watercourses.

The same line of discharge of water in times of heavy rains or melting snows, from a pond created by the natural assembling of surface water, does not constitute a

3. natural watercourse. Neither does an artificial channel, constructed solely for the purpose of expediting surface drainage, which is employed but occasionally and temporarily in carrying away an excess of surface water, caused by heavy rains or melting snows, constitute a natural watercourse, but must be deemed a surface water drain. *New Jersey, etc., R. Co.* v. *Tutt, supra*, 211, 212; *Cleveland,*

etc., R. Co. v. *Huddleston* (1899), 21 Ind. App. 621, 625, 52
N. E. 1008, 69 Am. St. 385.

Surface water is a common enemy which every proprietor
may 'fight and ward off from his premises by dams, embankments or other available means constructed or used
4. on his own property. *New Jersey, etc., R. Co.* v.
Tutt, supra, 212; *Benthall* v. *Seifert* (1881), 77 Ind.
302, 304; *Shelbyville, etc., Turnpike Co.* v. *Green* (1885), 99
Ind. 205, 215.

The facts found by the court show conclusively that there
was no ancient and natural watercourse on appellant's land
for more than 20 rods above the dividing line afore-
5. said, and for more than that distance south of that
line on the lands of appellee. The basin or pond
above described is shown to be closed at both its north and
south termini by the natural elevation of the land, and to
have no connection with the springs above, or with said natural channel and bayou south thereof; that before any artificial drains were constructed, water stood in said basin until it
evaporated or was absorbed by the earth. It is the law, as
claimed by appellant, that a natural watercourse which is
lost in a swamp or lake and emerges therefrom at a lower
level in a well-defined channel does not cease to be a watercourse because it passes through such swamp or lake.
Mitchell v. *Bain* (1895), 142 Ind. 604, 42 N. E. 230. But
the facts found in this case do not bring the drain in question within the rule so declared, but, on the other hand, show
that there is no natural watercourse which either enters or
emerges from the basin or depression above described, and
that prior to the construction of the gravel road on the west
of said lands the excess of water from said basin drained to
the west across the road.

But appellant contends that the facts show that he has
acquired an easement by which he has the right to
6. flow water through the artificial channel obstructed
by appellee. The facts found do not show any agree-

ment or arrangement of any kind between the owners of the two tracts of land at the time said artificial channel was made. All that appears is that the former owner of appellee's land opened a channel from said basin on his land to connect with a natural gulley or channel about 21 rods south of his north line, and that the owner of the land north of said dividing line made a furrow or ditch down to the line, and that each owner from time to time cleaned out such channel on his farm. At most the proprietor of the land north of the dividing line had only a permissive use of the drain south of the line for a few years.

To acquire a prescriptive right to an easement, something more must be shown than a mere permissive use. In the absence of an agreement, or grant of the easement,

7. where the right is claimed to have been acquired by user, the use which will establish such prescriptive right must be shown to be adverse, under a claim of right, continuous and uninterrupted for twenty years. Such use for such time is in law equivalent to a grant. *Parish* v. *Kaspare* (1887), 109 Ind. 586, 10 N. E. 109; *Nowlin* v. *Whipple* (1889), 120 Ind. 596, 598, 22 N. E. 669, 6 L. R. A. 159; *Connor* v. *Woodfill* (1890), 126 Ind. 85, 25 N. E. 876, 22 Am. St. 568; *Null* v. *Williamson* (1906), 166 Ind. 537, 547, 78 N. E. 76; *Gascho* v. *Lennert* (1912), 176 Ind. 677, 97 N. E. 6.

The facts found do not show any prescriptive right authorizing appellant to collect water by artificial drainage and cast it on the land of appellee in a manner that accelerates the flow and increases the quantity of the water that is thus brought upon his land.

Furthermore, the facts found show that subsequent to the opening of said drain across said pond, appellant opened a roadway, along his south line, and by means of gutters

8. worn in the road conveyed a large amount of water into the ditch and onto appellee's land that otherwise would not have drained into such channel. If it were con-

ceded that he had acquired the right to flow water from said pond through the ditch he constructed on his land and empty the same into the channel on appellee's land, such right would not authorize him to wrongfully accumulate additional water and pour it upon appellee's land, and by so doing he has placed himself in a situation that to grant him the relief prayed would enable him to profit by his own wrong. This the courts will not do. *McAllister* v. *Henderson* (1893), 134 Ind. 453, 34 N. E. 221.

The trial court did not err in its conclusions of law, and the judgment is therefore affirmed.

NOTE.—Reported in 101 N. E. 40. See, also, under (1, 5) 40 Cyc. 553; (2) 40 Cyc. 640; (3) 40 Cyc. 554; (4) 40 Cyc. 642; (6, 8) 40 Cyc. 649; (7) 14 Cyc. 1151. As to right of landowner to diminish or accelerate flowage to or from lands of his neighbor, see 85 Am. St. 708. As to surface waters and the right of lower proprietor to obstruct flow, see 16 Am. St. 710. As to the distinguishing character of watercourse, see 1 L. R. A. (N. S.) 756. For watercourse as distinguished from surface water, see 25 L. R. A. 527. As to the acquisition by an artificial stream of the character of a natural watercourse, see 14 Ann. Cas. 909.

THE PITTSBURGH, CINCINNATI, CHICAGO AND ST. LOUIS RAILWAY COMPANY *v.* COTTMAN.

[No. 7,858.   Filed March 6, 1913.]

1. NEGLIGENCE.—*Contributory Negligence.—Complaint.—Sufficiency.*
—A complaint which states facts sufficient to show negligence on the part of defendant and that such negligence resulted in the injury complained of, is sufficient on demurrer, unless other facts pleaded show affirmatively, as a matter of law, that plaintiff was guilty of contributory negligence. pp. 664, 665.

2. RAILROADS. — *Crossing Accidents.* — *Contributory Negligence.* — *Complaint.—Sufficiency.*—A complaint, in an action against a railroad company for injuries sustained by being struck by a train at a crossing, is not insufficient on the theory that plaintiff's contributory negligence may be inferred from his failure to allege an excuse for his failure to observe the approach of the train, since under §362 Burns 1908, Acts 1899 p. 58, plaintiff is not required to allege or prove that he was free from contributory negligence. p. 664.

3. PLEADING.—*Presumptions Against Pleader.—Application of Rule.*
—The rule, that a plaintiff is presumed to have stated his case
as strongly in his favor as the facts warrant, applies only to
such facts as are necessary to his cause of action, and does not
apply to facts which tend to disclose a defense. p. 665.

4. TRIAL.—*Instructions.—Contributory Negligence.*—In an action
for personal injuries where contributory negligence is a defense,
an instruction which tells the jury that the burden is on defendant to prove contributory negligence, that such proof may be
made under the general denial, and that in order to render such
defense available it must be proved by a fair preponderance of
all the evidence in the case, is not open to the objection that
would lead the jury to believe that contributory negligence could
be proved only by the evidence produced by defendant. p. 665.

5. APPEAL.—*Review.—Instructions.—Refusal.—Matter Covered by
Other Instructions.*—In an action for personal injuries, where,
on the subject of contributory negligence, the jury was instructed
that such defense must be proved by a fair preponderance of all
the evidence in the case, the refusal of a requested instruction
stating that if evidence of contributory negligence appeared from
the testimony of plaintiff it would be available to defendant on
such question, was not error, although such instruction could
properly have been given. p. 666.

6. TRIAL.—*Instructions.—Refusal.*—It is error to refuse requested
instructions that state the law correctly, if they are not fully
covered by the instructions given. p. 666.

7. RAILROADS.—*Crossing Accidents.—Instructions.—Refusal.*— An
instruction, in an action for injuries sustained in a railroad crossing accident, stating that if a person is struck by a train at a
crossing, the law deems the fault *prima facie* his own, etc., was
properly refused, since the burden of proving contributory negligence is on defendant. p. 667.

8. APPEAL.—*Review.—Verdict.—Evidence.—Sufficiency.*—The court
on appeal cannot weigh conflicting evidence, and where there is
some evidence tending to support the verdict, although a strong
preponderance seems to be in favor of appellant, the verdict will
not be disturbed on the ground of insufficient evidence. p. 668.

9. RAILROADS.—*Crossing Accidents.—Contributory Negligence.—
Jury Question.*—Where, in an action for injuries sustained in a
railroad crossing accident, plaintiff testified that the crossing
watchman touched him and told him to go on across the track
and that he was thus led to believe that no train was approaching and that it was safe to cross, and that he thereupon started
to cross the track, the question of whether he was guilty of contributory negligence was one of fact for the jury, and its finding
in his favor is conclusive on appeal, although the evidence in the

record tends strongly to show that he was guilty of contributory negligence. pp. 669, 670.

10. APPEAL.—*Review.—Verdict.—Evidence.—Sufficiency.* — On appeal, in determining whether the verdict is supported by the evidence, the court can consider only the evidence which tends to sustain the verdict, and must ignore all evidence to the contrary. p. 670.

11. RAILROADS.—*Crossings.—Care Required in Crossing.—Reliance on Signals of Watchman.*—A signal or direction given by the watchman at a railroad crossing directing a traveler on the highway to cross, is an affirmative assurance that there is no danger, and relieves the traveler from exercising the high degree of diligence and caution that otherwise would be required in approaching a crossing. p. 670.

12. TRIAL. — *Evidence. — Weight and Sufficiency. — Credibility of Witnesses.—Province of Jury.—Motion for New Trial.—Duty of Trial Court.*—While a question of fact, where the evidence is conflicting, should be submitted to the jury, and the weight of the evidence and the credibility of the witnesses are questions to be passed on by the jury in arriving at a verdict, it is the duty of the trial court, after verdict, on a motion for new trial on the ground that the evidence is insufficient to sustain the verdict, to weigh the evidence and consider the credibility of the witnesses in determining whether the jury has arrived at a correct result. p. 670.

13. APPEAL.—*Review.—Presumptions.—Weight and Sufficiency of Evidence.—Credibility of Witnesses.*—On appeal, it will be presumed that the trial court, in passing on a motion for new trial on the ground that the evidence is insufficient, has considered the credibility of the witnesses and has weighed their testimony, and that in overruling the motion it was satisfied with the result. p. 671.

From Wayne Circuit Court; *Henry C. Fox*, Judge.

Action by Earl Cottman against The Pittsburgh, Cincinnati, Chicago and St. Louis Railway Company. From a judgment for plaintiff, the defendant appeals. *Affirmed.*

John L. Rupe, for appellant.
Robbins & Robbins, for appellee.

LAIRY, J.—Appellee was injured at a street and railway crossing, by one of appellant's locomotives, for which injury he recovered a judgment in the Wayne Circuit Court. This appeal is prosecuted to reverse the judgment on the following grounds: (1) The trial court erred in overruling appellant's demurrer to the complaint;   (2) the court erred in overruling appellant's motion for a new trial.

The complaint was in one paragraph, and charged two acts of negligence against defendant.   The first is that it was operating a train on its tracks within the corporate limits of the city of Richmond at a rate of speed in excess of that provided by ordinance; and second, that a watchman employed by defendant negligently directed the plaintiff to cross the tracks at a time when a train was approaching the crossing and in dangerous proximity thereto.

The complaint states facts sufficient to show negligence on the part of the defendant and that the negligence charged resulted in the injury of which plaintiff complains.

1.   It is therefore sufficient, unless the other facts stated in the complaint are sufficient to show affirmatively, as a matter of law, that the plaintiff was guilty of contributory negligence.

The complaint shows that appellee was attempting to cross the railroad track of appellant on foot at the time he was injured.   It is averred that plaintiff's view toward

2.   the west was obstructed, for a part of the distance as he approached the track, by the watchman's shanty which stood in the street seven or eight feet from the track. It is argued on behalf of appellant that as the complaint contains no other allegation showing any other excuse for plaintiff's failure to observe the approach of the train, the court must presume, as against the pleader, that no other excuse existed, and that plaintiff, as he approached, had an unobstructed view toward the west at all times after he was within seven or eight feet of the track.   By statute, the plaintiff in cases such as this is relieved of alleging or proving that he was free from contributory negligence.   A failure to observe the approach of a train at a crossing may be contributory negligence, and facts tending to show an excuse for such failure are facts tending to rebut contribu-

tory negligence. It is, therefore, unnecessary for the plaintiff to aver any fact showing an excuse for his failure to observe the approach of the train at a crossing, although the rule was otherwise before the enactment of the statute changing the burden of proof as to contributory negligence in actions for personal injuries. The rule that a

3. plaintiff is presumed to have stated his case as strongly in his favor as the facts warrant applies only to such facts as are necessary to constitute his cause of action, and does not apply to facts which tend to disclose a defense. *Cleveland, etc., R. Co.* v. *Clark* (1912), 51 Ind. App. 392, 97 N. E. 822; *Cole* v. *Searfoss* (1912), 49 Ind. App. 334, 97 N. E. 345.

The complaint does not aver facts which affirmatively show as a matter of law that plaintiff was guilty of contributory negligence, and it cannot therefore be held

1. insufficient on the ground that it discloses a defense. *Evansville, etc., R. Co.* v. *Berndt* (1909), 172 Ind. 697, 88 N. E. 612.

Appellant objects to instruction No. 10 given by the court, on the ground that it was so worded as to mislead the jury into the belief that contributory negligence of the

4. plaintiff could be proved only by evidence produced by the defendant. The part of the instruction of which complaint is made reads as follows: "If contributory negligence is relied upon as a defense, the burden of proving the same rests upon the defendant. The proof, however, may be made under the general denial, which is the only answer the defendant has filed in this case; and in order to render this defense available it must be proved by a fair preponderance of all the evidence in the case." We do not think that this instruction is open to the objection urged against it. The jury was thereby expressly told that contributory negligence, to be available must be proved by a fair preponderance of all the evidence in the case. This was equivalent to saying to the jury that in determining on

which side the preponderance of the evidence lay on that question it should consider all the evidence in the case; and that would include the evidence produced by the plaintiff as well as that introduced on behalf of the defendant. *Newcastle Bridge Co.* v. *Doty* (1907), 168 Ind. 259, 79 N. E. 485; *Pittsburgh, etc., R. Co.* v. *Collins* (1907), 168 Ind. 467, 80 N. E. 415. Appellant tendered an instruction

5. by which he requested the court to charge the jury specifically to the effect that contributory negligence might appear from the testimony of the plaintiff as well as that of the defendant, and that evidence so appearing was available to the defendant on this question. The instruction thus tendered correctly states the law, and should have been given, unless it is covered by instruction No. 10, given by the court. The instruction given told the jury that it should consider all of the evidence in the case in passing on the question of contributory negligence, and the instruction tendered and refused stated the same proposition in different form. It is true that the instruction tendered is a little more specific in calling attention to the evidence of the plaintiff as a part of the evidence in the case, and we see no reason why it should not have been given in connection with instruction No. 10, but we think that a jury of intelligence would correctly understand and apply the instruction given. If we are right in this, the court did not err in refusing to give the instruction tendered.

Appellant, at the proper time requested the court to give certain instructions, among which was one numbered three, which was intended to advise the jury as to the law

6. of contributory negligence as applied to the conduct of a traveler on a highway in approaching a railway crossing. The instructions given by the court on this subject were not as full and specific as appellant had a right to ask, and if this instruction properly stated the law in this particular it would have been error for the court to refuse to give it. *Newcastle Bridge Co.* v. *Doty, supra;*

Keller v. *Reynolds* (1895), 12 Ind. App. 383, 40 N. E. 76, 40 N. E. 280; *McAfee* v. *Montgomery* (1898), 21 Ind. App. 196, 51 N. E. 957.

Instruction No. 3, tendered by appellant, was in most respects a correct statement of the law as applicable to the facts of this case, but is erroneous in at least one 7. particular, and for that reason the court properly refused to give it. The language which condemns the instruction is as follows: "If a person is struck by a train at a crossing, the law says the fault is *prima facie* his own; and these rules of law are firmly established, and unless a party claiming damages proves to the satisfaction of the jury that he has complied with them, there can be no recovery." This may have been the law in this State prior to the enactment of the statute changing the burden of proof upon the question of contributory negligence in cases such as this; but in the light of such a statute, the mere statement of the proposition is sufficient to demonstrate its fallacy.

The only other question discussed by counsel for appellant is the sufficiency of the evidence to sustain the verdict. The evidence shows that appellee was a boy almost thirteen years of age at the time of the accident which caused his injury. Between 1 o'clock and 2 o'clock in the afternoon of a September day, appellee was standing on the east side of Sixteenth street, in the city of Richmond, Indiana, at a point about eighteen feet south of the south rail of appellant's railroad tracks, which intersected Sixteenth street practically at right angles. There was a sidewalk along the east side of Sixteenth street, and the shanty of the crossing watchman stood in the street just west of this sidewalk, and seven or eight feet south of the track. The point where appellee was standing immediately before the accident was a short distance south of the watchman's shanty, and there were no other obstructions of any character to interfere with his view of appellant's tracks toward the west. Appellee left the point where he was standing and ran north along the sidewalk to appellant's south track, where he came in contact with a locomotive which had approached from the west. The facts, so far as stated, are established by the undisputed evidence; but there is some conflict in the testimony as to the speed of the train and as to the occurrences immediately preceding the accident. There is some evidence tending to show that the train was moving at a rate of speed in excess of the rate provided by ordinance, but this evidence is not of a convincing or satisfactory character. The plaintiff testified that the train was running very fast, much faster than a streetcar; but on cross-examination he testified that he did not see it till it struck him, and that he judged of the speed by the force with which he was struck. On reëxamination he stated that he saw the train in motion immediately before he was struck. The only other witness who testified in favor of plaintiff as to speed of the train was a man in charge of a team of mules a short distance from the crossing. He stated that he heard the train coming, and that he looked up and saw it just as plaintiff was struck, and that he thought the train was running about twelve miles an hour, but on cross-examination he said, "Well I couldn't explain how fast the train was running because I did not see it until it was right at the crossing, and then the train came to a standstill as soon as it struck the boy; therefore I could not give any definite answer about what speed they were making." The engineer in charge of the locomotive testified that the train stopped so that a switch one square west of Sixteenth street could be closed and that at the time of the accident the train was running from four to six miles an hour, and that it would have been impossible for the train to have attained a greater rate of speed in the distance it had moved after it was put in motion. The engineer is corroborated, as to the speed of the train, by three other members of the train crew and by Harry McBride, a disinterested witness. On this question the strong preponder-

8. ance of the evidence seems to be in favor of appellant, but there is some evidence tending to support the verdict, and under the well-settled rule governing courts of appeal we are not permitted to weigh conflicting evidence.

The evidence in the record also tends strongly to show that appellee was guilty of contributory negligence. The uncontradicted evidence shows that he had an unob-

9. structed view of the track toward the west from the place where he was standing, and that he ran north a distance of eighteen feet, to the track where he was injured, without observing the approach of the train, and that the only object that could have obstructed his view for any part of that distance was the shanty of the watchman, which was six feet square. As an excuse for this conduct, the plaintiff testified that the watchman, who was standing beside him, touched him and told him to go on across the track. He states that, from this, he thought that no train was approaching and that it was safe to cross, and that this is the reason he did not look for a train; that he took him at his word and started to run across, and that he was on the track when he was struck. Plaintiff further stated that before he started to cross he was standing with his back toward the west, and for that reason did not see the train approaching. This evidence of plaintiff was contradicted by that of the watchman, the engineer and Herbert Williams a disinterested witness. They all testified that the watchman was standing in the street in front of the shanty, and that he called to appellee when he saw him running toward the track, and that he tried to catch him, but that he was too late, and that appellee ran against the side of the locomotive and was injured. The watchman also testified that he did not say anything to appellee about crossing the track.

The jury found that appellee was free from fault contributing to his injury. In determining whether the verdict in this respect is supported by the evidence, this court ·10. can consider only the evidence which tends to sustain it, and must ignore all evidence to the contrary. *Keys* v. *McDowell* (1913), 54 Ind. App. —, 100 N. E. 385.

If the facts disclosed by the uncorroborated testimony of the plaintiff are true, then the question as to 9. whether or not plaintiff was guilty of contributory negligence was one of fact for the jury.

A signal or direction given by the watchman at a railroad crossing directing a traveler on the highway to cross, is an affirmative assurance that there is no danger. 11. A person acting under such an assurance is not required to exercise the high degree of diligence and caution that would be otherwise required of him in approaching a crossing. *Lake Erie, etc., R. Co.* v. *Fike* (1905), 35 Ind. App. 554, 74 N. E. 636; *Alabama, etc., R. Co.* v. *Anderson* (1895), 109 Ala. 299, 19 South. 516.

If the jury believed the testimony of plaintiff, and further believed that, in view of the assurance of safety given by the watchman, he used such care as was reasonable in a person of his age and experience, it was justified in finding that he was free from contributory negligence.

Where there is a conflict in the evidence it is the duty of the court to submit the question of fact to the jury, and the weight of the evidence and the credibility of the 12. witnesses are questions to be passed on by the jury in arriving at the verdict. After a verdict is returned and a motion for a new trial is filed on the ground that the evidence is insufficient to sustain the verdict, the trial court is called on to weigh the evidence, and to consider the credibility of the witnesses in determining whether or not the jury by its verdict has reached a correct result. In considering the evidence the trial court is not governed by the same rules that confront this court on appeal. The trial court has an opportunity to look into the faces of the witnesses and to observe their conduct and demeanor while testifying, and its ability to judge of their credibility is equal, if not superior, to that of the jury. The duty, with its corresponding responsibility, which the law thus imposes on the trial court is one which it cannot escape, or shift to any other tribunal. The jury is in a sense responsible for the verdict, but the court is responsible for any judgment that may be pronounced thereon. If a court permits a verdict to stand which is not supported by evidence, or which is clearly against the greater weight of the evidence, the responsibility rests on the judge, and cannot be shifted to the jury. If there is a total want of evidence as to some fact essential to the verdict, this court on appeal may correct the error, but this court is powerless to grant relief where the evidence is in conflict. The responsibility rests entirely upon the judge of the trial court to grant relief in cases where the evidence is conflicting, and clearly preponderates against the verdict returned by the jury.

We have referred at length to the evidence in this case, for the purpose of emphasizing our remarks on the duties of the trial judge in respect to weighing the evidence and considering the credibility of the witnesses in ruling on the motion for a new trial where the sufficiency of the evidence to sustain the verdict is assigned as a cause. We know that the judges of the trial courts are thoroughly conscientious in the discharge of their duties, and that they have no disposition to shirk a single responsibility resting on them; but, from a consideration of the evidence in the case at bar, and in many others of a similar character, we are led to believe that trial courts, in considering the sufficiency of the evidence to sustain the verdict, when it is presented by a motion for a new trial, frequently apply the rule which governs courts of appeal, instead of the correct rule as heretofore stated.

If, as contended by appellant, the verdict in this case is

against the overwhelming preponderance of the evidence,
it should have been set aside and a new trial granted,
13. but the trial judge alone had power to determine that
question. He was in a position to consider the credibility of the witnesses and to weigh their testimony and
he is presumed to have done so and to have been satisfied
with the result. If he made a mistake is this respect, this
court is without power to correct it.

Judgment affirmed.

NOTE.—Reported in 101 N. E. 22. See, also, under (1) 29 Cyc.
575; (2) 33 Cyc 1060; (3) 31 Cyc. 78; (4) 29 Cyc. 644; (5) 38
Cyc. 1711; (6) 38 Cyc. 1718; (7) 33 Cyc. 1138; (8) 3 Cyc. 348;
(9) 33 Cyc. 1111. 1127; (10) 3 Cyc. 348; (11) 33 Cyc. 1035; (12)
29 Cyc. 1007; (13) 3 Cyc. 318. As to contributory negligence as
question for jury, see 8 Am. St. 849. As to burden of proof and
where it rests generally, see 28 Am. Rep. 563. As to duty on railroad company to keep flagman at highway crossing to warn pedestrians and vehicle drivers of approaching trains, see 100 Am. Dec.
412. On the duty of one crossing a railroad track as affected by
flagman's signal to proceed, see 15 L. R. A. (N. S.) 803. As to the
conduct of a flagman or absence from his post as affecting liability
for injury at crossing, see 41 L. R. A. (N. S.) 355. For a discussion
of the duty to stop, look and listen at a railroad crossing where a
flagman is stationed, see 10 Ann. Cas. 418; 13 Ann. Cas. 854.

DOWNEY v. THE NATIONAL EXCHANGE BANK.

[No. 7,300. Filed November 14, 1911. Rehearing denied March 28,
1912. Transfer denied March 6, 1913.]

1. BANKS AND BANKING. — *Deposit of Check for Collection.—
Agency.—Liability.*—Where a check is deposited with a bank for
collection, a privity of contract exists between the depositor and
each bank through which the check passes, whereby a duty is
imposed to use reasonable care and diligence in its collection and
renders that bank, whose negligence or misconduct results in the
loss of the debt, liable to the depositor. p. 676.

2. BANKS AND BANKING.—*Deposit of Check.—Character of Deposit.*
—The question of whether a check deposited by the payee in a
bank other than the one on which it is drawn amounts to a sale
of the check, or merely constitutes a deposit of same for collection, must be determined from the facts and circumstances attending the transaction. p. 677.

3. BANKS AND BANKING. — *Deposit of Check for Collection.— Agency.*—Where a check is indorsed for collection, or where there is a definite understanding that such is the purpose of the parties, or where the memorandum of deposit shows that it is deposited as a check, it remains the property of the depositor and the bank holds it as his agent for collection. p. 677.

4. BANKS AND BANKING.—*Deposit of Check.—Deposit as Cash.*— Where there is a definite agreement that a check is deposited as cash, the title passes to the bank and it has a right to control its collection and receive the proceeds. p. 677.

5. BANKS AND BANKING.—*Deposit of Check.—Character of Deposit.—Presumptions.*—Where a check, bearing an indorsement not indicating that it was indorsed for collection, is passed to the credit of the depositor as cash, and nothing further appears, the presumption arises that the transaction constitutes a sale of the check to the bank, but such presumption may be rebutted by facts or circumstances showing a contrary intention. p. 678.

6. BANKS AND BANKING.—*Deposit of Check.—Character of Deposit.—Duty to Depositor.*—Where the transaction of depositing a check amounts to a sale thereof to the bank, a bank to which it is subsequently passed for collection is not the agent of such depositor and owes him no duty in respect to its collection. p. 679.

7. BANKS AND BANKING.—*Deposit of Check.—Return of Check to Depositor.—Effect.*—Where a check which has been deposited as cash and sent out for collection is returned to the bank in which it was deposited, and is by such bank charged to the account of the depositor, and is turned over to him and accepted by him, the transaction amounts to a resale of the check to such depositor. p. 680.

8. APPEAL.—*Review.—Ruling on Motion for New Trial.*—A finding will not be reversed on alleged error in overruling the motion for new trial, based on the ground that the evidence is insufficient and that the finding is contrary to law, and that the court failed to find facts supported by the evidence, where there is not a total want of evidence to support the findings, and it is not shown that any material fact, supported by undisputed evidence, has been omitted from the finding. p. 680.

9. APPEAL.—*Review.—Presumptions.—Failure to Find Fact.*—A failure to find a fact is a finding against the party having the burden of the issues to which such fact is relevant. p. 680.

10. APPEAL.—*Review.—Harmless Error.—Unsupported Finding of Fact.*—Even though a finding of fact is wholly unsupported by the evidence, it is not cause for reversal, where such fact was wholly immaterial to the decision of the case. p. 680.

From Madison Circuit Court; *John F. McClure*, Judge.

Action by Jacob F. Downey against The National Exchange Bank. From a judgment for defendant, the plaintiff appeals. *Affirmed.*

John H. Kiplinger, John D. Megee and *Austin Retherford,* for appellant.

William A. Kittinger and *William S. Diven,* for appellee.

LAIRY, C. J.—Appellant brought this action for the proceeds of a check. After all the pleadings were in, the issues thus formed were tried by the court without the intervention of a jury. The court made a special finding of facts and rendered conclusions of law thereon in favor of appellee, and judgment was rendered against appellant.

The facts set out in the special finding, so far as material to a decision of this case, are, in substance, as follows: John W. Jones executed his individual check in the sum of $1,225, drawn on the Citizens Bank of Anderson, Indiana, and made payable to Jacob F. Downey, appellant herein, and dated June 12, 1905. Appellant came into possession of said check and deposited it in the Bank of Arlington, Indiana, receiving credit therefor. The Arlington bank forwarded it to the Capital National Bank, at Indianapolis, Indiana, for collection, and received credit therefor, and said Capital National Bank forwarded it to the National Exchange Bank, of Anderson, Indiana, and charged it to said bank, appellee herein. The check came into the hands of appellee on the morning of June 16, 1905.

There are several banks in Anderson, Indiana, and by an arrangement among them, about 10 o'clock each morning there is a meeting composed of a clerk from each bank, at which time the checks held by each bank, drawn on any other of said banks and cashed the day before, or coming for collection to each of said other banks, are taken by said clerks and summed up, the checks drawn on each delivered to the clerk so representing it, and the difference in the amounts of the checks settled later in the day. The checks on each bank are then taken by the representative there-from and turned over to the proper officer or cashier there-of, to be passed on, honored if proper, or if not proper, to be returned to the bank which held them on the same day.

Prior to June 16, 1905, and after said check had been signed by said John W. Jones, said John W. Jones had stopped payment on said check, and ordered said Citizens Bank not to pay it. On June 16, 1905, the clerks of said banks of Anderson, Indiana, met and exchanged checks, and summed up the amounts thereof, appellee bank turned over to the clerk representing the Citizens Bank said check drawn by said John W. Jones for $1,225, and the same was included in the amounts cast up by said clerks, and later in the day the differences in said amounts were settled by said banks. The officers of said Citizens Bank on said June 16, 1905, which was Friday, in examining the large number of checks drawn on it and turned over to it by the clerk of appellee bank, as aforesaid, by inadvertence and mistake overlooked the check drawn by John W. Jones for $1,225, and it reached the bookkeeper without being noticed, and was not discovered until late on Saturday. On Monday, June 19, 1905, said Citizens Bank of Anderson returned said check to the National Exchange Bank, at the time representing to said appellee that the check had been received by inadvertence and mistake, and that payment thereof had been stopped by said John W. Jones, and that the Citizens Bank had no right to and no intention of paying it; thereupon requesting appellee bank to correct said mistake, receive back the check and give the Citizens Bank of Anderson credit for said amount in its settlement, which was done.

Appellee thereupon returned said check to the Capital National Bank, of Indianapolis, as not paid, and the Capital National Bank received the same and credited the amount thereof to appellee. The Capital National Bank thereupon returned the check as unpaid to said Bank of Arlington from which it had received the same, and the

Bank of Arlington received the check and credited the Capital National Bank therewith. The Bank of Arlington thereupon returned the check to appellant as unpaid, and appellant received and accepted the same, and gave the Bank of Arlington credit for the amount thereof. Appellant has ever since had and still retains possession of the check. He has demanded of appellee the payment of said check, and said demand has been refused.

Appellant excepted to the conclusions of law and also filed a motion for a new trial, which motion was overruled by the court. The errors assigned for reversal are that the court erred in its conclusions of law and also erred in overruling appellant's motion for a new trial.

Appellant's theory of his right to recover against appellee is that the check drawn in his favor by John W. Jones was placed in the Bank of Arlington for collection and that when said check was transmitted to the Capital National Bank of Indianapolis, and by that bank transmitted to the National Exchange Bank of Anderson, each of the banks named held the check for collection as agents of appellant. If under the facts disclosed by the special finding, each of the banks named became successively the agent of appellant, then a privity of contract existed between appellant and each one of the banks named, whereby a duty arose to use reasonable care and diligence in the collection of said check, and if any of said banks were guilty of negligence or misconduct resulting in the loss of the debt it would be liable to appellant. *First Nat. Bank* v. *First Nat. Bank* (1881), 76 Ind. 561, 40 Am. Rep. 261.

1.

It is the theory of appellee that the facts found by the court disclose that the check was not placed in the bank at Arlington for collection, as claimed by appellant, but that the transaction which occurred amounted to a sale of the check by appellant to said bank; that the title to the check passed to the bank at the time of said endorsement and the bank's indebtedness to appellant was increased by the amount of the credit which he received at the time; that thereafter the bank at Arlington, being the owner of the check, had the sole right to control its collection, and that the banks to which it was subsequently transmitted were either owners of the check by purchase or held it for collection as agents of the Bank of Arlington; and that in either event such banks were not agents of appellant. If the facts disclosed by the special finding show that appellant was not the owner of the check at the time it was paid to the appellee, then appellee was not his agent and owed him no duty, for the reason that there was no privity of contract between them.

When a check, which is indorsed by the payee and placed in a bank other than the one on which it is drawn, the question as to whether the transaction constitutes a sale
2. of the check, or whether it amounts to a deposit of the check for collection, depends on the facts and circumstances attending the transaction. Where the indorsement shows that it is indorsed for collection, or where
3. there is a definite understanding that such is the purpose of the parties, there is no question that the title to the paper does not pass, or where the check is deposited as a check and the memorandum of deposit so shows, there can be no question that the relation of debtor and creditor does not arise and that the check remains the property of the depositor and the bank holds it as his agent for collection. *First Nat. Bank* v. *Greenville Nat. Bank* (1892), 84 Tex. 40, 19 S. W. 334; *Bailie* v. *Augusta Sav. Bank* (1895), 95 Ga. 277, 21 S. E. 717, 51 Am. St. 74. It is also quite clear that where there is a definite agreement at the time of such
4. deposit that the check is deposited as cash, the title passes to the bank. In such a case the depositor of such check, if he indorses it, becomes liable on his indorsement, and the bank becomes indebted to him for the amount credited to his account, and such bank has a right to control the collection of such check and receive the proceeds.

Where, however, there is no specific agreement or understanding at the time a check is deposited as to how it is to be treated, and the bank gives the depositor credit for the check as so much cash, the question arises whether the title passes to the bank or whether it remains in the depositor and the bank holds it for collection. On this question the authorities are not without conflict.

According to the weight of authority, where it appears that a check, bearing an indorsement not indicating that it was indorsed for collection, is passed to the credit of the depositor as cash, and nothing further appears, the presumption arises that the transaction constitutes a sale of the check to the bank. This presumption, however, is not conclusive and may be rebutted by facts or circumstances showing a contrary intention. *Hoffman* v. *First Nat. Bank* (1884), 46 N. J. L. 604; *In re State Bank* (1894), 56 Minn. 119, 57 N. W. 336, 45 Am. St. 454; *Fourth Nat. Bank* v. *Mayer* (1892), 89 Ga. 108, 14 S. E. 891; *Williams* v. *Cox* (1896), 97 Tenn. 555, 37 S. W. 282; *Metropolitan Nat. Bank* v. *Loyd* (1882), 90 N. Y. 530; *First Nat. Bank* v. *Dickson* (1889), 6 Dak. 301, 50 N. W. 124; *Ayres* v. *Farmers', etc., Bank* (1883), 79 Mo. 421, 49 Am. Rep. 235; *American Trust, etc., Bank* v. *Gueder & Paeschke Mfg. Co.* (1894), 150 Ill. 336, 37 N. E. 227; *Wasson* v. *Lamb* (1889), 120 Ind. 514, 22 N. E. 729, 6 L. R. A. 191, 16 Am. St. 342. There are a few cases which hold that where a check is indorsed to a bank and credited to the depositor as cash, the title thereto *prima facie*, remains in the depositor, and the bank holds such check for collection, and that to show title in the bank, facts and circumstances must appear indicating such an intention. *Balbach* v. *Frelingheysen* (1883), 15 Fed. 675; *National Gold Bank, etc., Co.* v. *McDonald* (1875), 51 Cal. 64, 21 Am. Rep. 697; *National Commercial Bank* v. *Miller & Co.* (1884), 77 Ala. 168, 54 Am. Rep. 50. The decided weight of authority, however, is in favor of the doctrine as first announced. This rule has been adopted and applied by the Supreme Court of this State in the case of *Wasson* v. *Lamb*, *supra*, where the court states the rule in the following language: "Ordinarily, whenever a deposit is made the amount and date thereof are entered by the cashier or teller in the bank-book or pass-book of the depositor, and such entries when made by the proper officer bind the bank as admissions. In some cases it has been held that they become conclusive upon the bank like an account stated, when the bank-book is balanced. 1 Morse, Banks and Banking (3d ed.) §291. The settled rule is, where checks, drafts, or other evidences of debt are received in good faith as deposits, if the bank credits them as so much money, the title to the checks or drafts is immediately transferred to the bank, and it becomes legally liable to the depositor as for so much money deposited. *Cragie* v. *Hadley* [1885], 99 N. Y. 131 [1 N. E. 537, 52 Am. Rep. 9]; *Metropolitan Nat. Bank* v. *Loyd* [1882], 90 N. Y. 530. So, where a bank credits a depositor with the amount of a check drawn upon it by another customer, and there is no want of good faith on the part of the depositor, the act of crediting is equivalent to a payment in money. 'Nor can the bank recall or repudiate the payment, because, upon an examination of the accounts of the drawer, it is ascertained that he was without funds to meet the check, though when the payment was made, the officer making it labored under the mistake that there were funds sufficient.' *City Nat. Bank, etc.*, v. *Burns* [1880], 68 Ala. 267 [44 Am. Rep. 138]; *Bolton* v. *Richard* [1795], 6 Term 139; *Oddie* v. *National City Bank* [1871], 45 N. Y. 735, 6 Am. Rep. 160.''

The special finding shows that appellant deposited the check in the Bank of Arlington, and received credit therefor. The transaction thus shown, *prima facie*, constituted a sale of the check, and the title thereto immediately passed to the bank. Appellee was not therefore the agent of appellant at the time the money was paid to it on said check, and the money so received was not the property of appellant, and appellee owed no duty in re-

spect thereto which would give rise to a cause of action in
his favor. When the check was returned to the Bank

7. of Arlington, and was by it turned over to appellant,
and was by him accepted and charged to his account
by the bank, this constituted a resale of the check to appellant.

From what has been said it is apparent that the court committed no error in its conclusions of law on the facts found.

The court did not err in overruling appellant's motion for
a new trial. The causes for a new trial assigned below and
relied on here are, (1) the special finding is not sus-

8. tained by sufficient evidence, (2) the finding is contrary to law and is not sustained by sufficient evidence, and (3) the court failed to find facts supported by
the evidence. Appellant does not contend that there is a
total want of evidence to support the findings that we have
treated as material to a decision of this case, and he has not
called the attention of the court to any material fact which
is supported by undisputed evidence, and which the court
has not embodied in its finding. A failure to find a

9. fact is a finding against the party having the burden
of the issues to which such fact is relevant, and this
court cannot reverse such finding where the evidence is conflicting. Appellant contends that there is a total want of
evidence to sustain certain findings of the court in reference
to the illegal character of the consideration for which the
check was given. We have treated this finding as

10. wholly immaterial to the decision of this case. The
finding, being immaterial, did not harm appellant,
and he cannot, therefore, complain even though it is wholly
unsupported by the evidence.

Finding no reversible error, the judgment is in all things
affirmed.

NOTE.—Reported in 96 N. E. 403. See, also, under (1) 5 Cyc.
493, 509; (2, 3, 4, 6) 5 Cyc. 493; (5) 5 Cyc. 494; (7) 5 Cyc. 499;

Marion, etc., Construction Co. *v.* Claycomb—52 Ind. App. 681.

(8) 3 Cyc. 360; (9) 38 Cyc. 1985; (10) 38 Cyc. 1967. As to bank checks and whether they operate to assign the fund, see 19 Am. St. 609. As to liability of bank acting in capacity of collecting agent, see 77 Am. St. 613.

MARION COUNTY CONSTRUCTION COMPANY *v.* CLAYCOMB ET AL.

[No. 7,649. Filed June 4, 1912. Rehearing denied January 28, 1913. Transfer denied March 6, 1913.]

1. TRIAL.—*Verdict.—Special Findings.*—Under §573 Burns 1908, §547 R. S. 1881, the special finding of facts controls the general verdict only when inconsistent therewith, and the general verdict must stand where the special finding can be reconciled with it under any state of facts provable under the issues. p. 683.

2. NEGLIGENCE.—*Breach of Legal Duty.*—Negligence arises on the breach of a legal duty to use care, and where there is no duty there can be no negligence. p. 684.

3. MUNICIPAL CORPORATIONS. — *Streets. — Excavations. — Duty to Guard.*—It is the duty of one who causes an excavation to be made in a public street to guard the same, and to use reasonable care to protect persons lawfully using such street from injury on account of such excavation. p. 684.

4. NEGLIGENCE.—*Actionable Negligence.*—An action for negligence will not lie against a defendant, unless he was owing some duty to the injured person at the time and place where the injury occurred, and which he omitted to perform. p. 685.

5. NEGLIGENCE.—*Delegation of Legal Duty.—Joint Tort-Feasors.*—While one, personally bound to perform a duty, cannot relieve himself from such obligation by a contract for its performance by another, and cannot interpose such contract as a defense, such rule does not apply as between joint tort-feasors. p. 686.

6. MUNICIPAL CORPORATIONS.—*Streets.—Excavation by Water Company in Connection With Work of Sewer Construction Company. —Negligence.—Verdict.—Answers to Interrogatories.*—Where, in an action for injuries sustained in falling into an excavation in a street made by a water company in connection with the work of sewer construction in charge of a construction company, it was shown that the construction company in undertaking the construction of the sewer undertook to use all due precaution for the safety of persons and property, and where, under the issues, it was competent to show that in its contract with the city the construction company undertook to protect the mains and service

pipes of the water company, it will be presumed that such fact was shown, so that interrogatories showing that the excavation was made by the water company for the purpose of closing a water pipe laid across the street where the sewer was being constructed, and was made pursuant to a contract with the construction company wherein the latter agreed to place lights and danger signals at such excavation, and that it failed to do so, are not in conflict with the general verdict against the construction company on the theory that its agreement with the water company was not binding on it. p. 686.

From Clark Circuit Court; *Harry C. Montgomery*, Judge.

Action by Clara Belle Claycomb against the Marion County Construction Company and others. From a judgment for plaintiff, the defendant, Marion County Construction Company, appeals. *Affirmed.*

Robert W. McBride, for appellant.

Charles D. Kelso and *George H. Voigt*, for appellees.

ADAMS, P. J.—Action by appellee Clara Belle Claycomb against appellant, appellee The New Albany Waterworks and the City of New Albany, to recover damages for personal injuries occasioned by the negligence of defendants in failing to guard an excavation in one of the public streets of New Albany, into which appellee fell and was injured. Before verdict the action was dismissed as to the City of New Albany.

It is charged in the complaint that at the time of the happening of the grievances complained of, The New Albany Waterworks was the owner of and engaged in operating a system of waterworks in the city of New Albany, and in supplying said city and its inhabitants with water; that a part of its system of mains and pipes was located in State street, one of the public streets of said city, and near the point where plaintiff was injured; that defendant the Marion County Construction Company, under a contract with the city of New Albany was at the time engaged in the construction of a general system of public storm and sanitary sewers in said city, and in the performance of its work excavated trenches in said State street near the point where plaintiff was injured; that this excavation intersected a service pipe of the water company, and, for the purpose of enabling defendant construction company to pursue its work, defendants dug a large hole in said street at a place used by the public, in order that they might cut off the water from such service pipe, to prevent the tearing up of the pipe by the construction company and flooding its trenches; that this hole became filled with water, and was negligently left by defendants uncovered and unguarded, and without any signal lights or barriers to warn the public of its existence and of the danger caused thereby; that defendants knew that this hole had been made in the street, and that it was unguarded, but that plaintiff had no knowledge of its existence; that the excavation was made in pursuance to the terms of a contract between defendant construction company and the city; that on the night of July 22, 1905, plaintiff, without fault on her part, and while exercising due care, when walking along said street, stepped into said excavation, and was thereby severely and permanently injured. Each defendant answered the complaint by general denial. Trial by jury; finding and verdict against appellant in favor of appellee Claycomb in the sum of $1,700, and in favor of appellee The New Albany Waterworks for costs. With its general verdict the jury returned answers to fifty interrogatories. Appellant's motion for judgment in its favor on the answers to the interrogatories, notwithstanding the general verdict, was overruled, and this constitutes the only error relied on for reversal.

It is a matter of statutory enactment that the special finding of facts controls the general verdict only when inconsistent therewith. §573 Burns 1908, §547 R. S. 1881.

1. Where the general verdict and special findings can be reconciled with each other under any state of facts provable under the issues, the general verdict will stand. *Consolidated Stone Co.* v. *Summit* (1899), 152 Ind. 297, 304,

684   APPELLATE COURT OF INDIANA,

Marion, etc., Construction Co. v. Claycomb—52 Ind. App. 681.

53 N. E. 225; *Louisville, etc., R. Co.* v. *Summers* (1892), 131 Ind. 241, 243, 30 N. E. 873; *Shoner* v. *Pennsylvania Co.* (1892), 130 Ind. 170, 181, 28 N. E. 616, 29 N. E. 775; *Ohio, etc., R. Co.* v. *Trowbridge* (1890), 126 Ind. 391, 398, 26 N. E. 64; *Evansville, etc., R. Co.* v. *Marohn* (1893), 6 Ind. App. 646, 653, 34 N. E. 27; *Indianapolis Union R. Co.* v. *Neubacher* (1896), 16 Ind. App. 21, 64, 43 N. E. 576, 44 N. E. 669; *Southern R. Co.* v. *Utz* (1913), 52 Ind. App. 270, 98 N. E. 375.

Negligence arises on the breach of a legal duty to use care, and where there is no duty there can be no negligence.

2. *Barrett* v. *Cleveland, etc., R. Co.* (1911), 48 Ind. App. 668, 96 N. E. 490; *Brooks* v. *Pittsburgh, etc., R. Co.* (1902), 158 Ind. 62, 68, 62 N. E. 694. It is the duty of a party who causes an excavation to be made in a public

3. street to guard the same, and to use reasonable care to protect from injury, on account of such excavation, persons lawfully using such street. *Indianapolis St. R. Co.* v. *James* (1905), 35 Ind. App. 543, 74 N. E. 536.

The jury, by special interrogatories twenty-five to thirty-two, inclusive, which are the only interrogatories set out in appellant's brief, found that the construction company at the time of and prior to plaintiff's injury was engaged in constructing a sewer under State street; that the excavation into which plaintiff fell was made for the purpose of closing a water pipe laid across the street where the sewer was being constructed; that the excavation was made by the employes of the water company, under a prior agreement between the construction company and the water company; that the workmen of the water company, under the direction of the superintendent of said company, made the excavation for the construction company, pursuant to said agreement; that the construction company in said agreement undertook to place lights as danger signals at excavations made by the employes of the water company wherever necessary; that the construction company did not place lights at the excavations while constructing said sewer, and no light was placed at the excavation into which plaintiff fell.

The single proposition urged by appellant and relied on for reversal is that the New Albany Waterworks was legally bound to make and guard the excavation into which plaintiff fell; that the alleged agreement on the part of appellant to guard, as found by the jury, was without consideration, was a mere *nudum pactum*, was void, and imposed no legal obligation, contractual or otherwise, on appellant.

An action for negligence will not lie against a defendant, unless the defendant was owing some duty to the injured person at the time and place where the injury occurred, and which duty the defendant omitted to perform. *Faris* v. *Hoberg* (1893), 134 Ind. 269, 274, 33 N. E. 1028, 39 Am. St. 261; *Daugherty* v. *Herzog* (1896), 145 Ind. 255, 256, 44 N. E. 457, 32 L. R. A. 837, 57 Am. St. 204; *Evansville, etc., R. Co.* v. *Griffin* (1885), 100 Ind. 221, 222, 50 Am. Rep. 783.

The theory of appellant is that whatever franchise rights were granted by the city of New Albany to the water company to use the streets for the purpose of laying its mains and service pipes were subordinate to the right of the city to construct sewers in the same streets; that the franchise necessarily carried with it an implied reservation by the city thereafter to construct sewers and subject to an implied duty on the part of the water company to make any and all changes in the location of its mains and service pipes that might be found necessary to permit the construction of such sewers; that this implied duty was a continuing obligation running through the life of the franchise, from which the water company could not relieve itself by contract with third persons, and that it carried with it the duty of making excavations in streets which might be found necessary to prevent interference by its mains and pipes with the construction of such sewers.

It is true that one who is personally bound to perform a

686   APPELLATE COURT OF INDIANA,

Marion, etc., Construction Co. r. Claycomb—52 Ind. App. 681.

duty cannot relieve himself from the burden of such obligation by any contract which he may make for its

5. performance by another person, and that the one on whom the obligation originally rests cannot successfully interpose the defense that he has entered into a contract with another by which the latter undertook to perform the duty, but this principle applies to persons injured by some neglect of duty, and does not obtain as between joint tort-feasors.

In this case it was competent under the issues to show, and as a matter of fact it was shown, that appellant not only undertook to construct the sewer according to speci-

6. fications, but to employ all necessary day and night watchmen, to erect and place all necessary barricades and lights, and to use all due precaution for the safety of persons and property.

It was competent to show, and it must be presumed that it was shown, that appellant in its contract with the city undertook to protect the mains and service pipes of the water company. No authority has been cited, and we assume that none can be found, holding that under such conditions appellant could not lawfully contract with the water company to do this work, and agree to guard all excavations made by said company in so doing, and be bound by such agreement.

The jury specially found that the unguarded excavation in the street was made by the water company pursuant to a contract with appellant, wherein the latter agreed to place lights and danger signals at such excavation, and failed to do so. The answers to interrogatories are not in conflict with the general verdict, but clearly support the general verdict.

Judgment affirmed.

NOTE.—Reported in 98 N. E. 744. See, also, under (1) 38 Cyc. 1929; (2, 4) 29 Cyc. 419; (3) 29 Cyc. 471; (5) 22 Cyc. 86; (6) 38 Cyc. 1927. As to when municipalities are not liable for injuries arising from negligence of contractors, see 54 Am. Rep. 90.

COOLEY *v.* KELLEY.

[No. 7,761. Filed December 8, 1911. Rehearing denied May 31, 1912. Transfer denied March 6, 1913.]

1. PLEADING.—*Complaint.—Ruling on Demurrer.—Effect as to Subsequent Rulings.—Trial.*—A ruling on demurrer, holding a complaint good, is not binding on a trial court so as to require its subsequent rulings to be in harmony therewith, irrespective of its correctness. p. 693.

2. APPEAL.—*Record.—Findings.—Opinion of Trial Court.*—Where the record on appeal fails to disclose a request that the trial court render special findings, the opinion delivered by the trial court in announcing its decision, although carried into the record, will be regarded merely as a general finding. p. 693.

3. APPEAL.—*Review.—Findings.—Motion for Venire de Novo.*—Overruling a motion for a *venire de novo* is not error where the finding is general, since the motion reaches only matters of form, and can only be sustained when the finding is so defective and uncertain that no judgment can be rendered thereon. p. 693.

4. APPEAL.—*Review.—Findings.—Motion for Judgment Notwithstanding Findings.*—Error cannot be predicated on the overruling of a motion for judgment notwithstanding the findings of the court, where under the circumstances, the alleged findings amount to but a general one. p. 694.

5. APPEAL.—*Review.—Ruling on Motion to Modify Judgment.*—Where a motion to modify a judgment questions the validity of the judgment, and not its form, the same is properly overruled. p. 694.

6. APPEAL.—*Review.—Harmless Error.—Admission of Pleading as Evidence.*—Where plaintiff offered in evidence a special answer, pleaded by defendant in addition to the general denial and specifically admitting the facts averred in the complaint, the error, if any, in its admission is not available to plaintiff on appeal. p. 694.

7. JUDGMENTS.—*Foreign Judgments.—Admissibility in Evidence.*—A certified copy of the proceedings of a probate court of another state disposing of property within its jurisdiction, is admissible in evidence in this State. p. 694.

8. JUDGMENT.—*Foreign Judgments.—Conclusiveness.*—Under Art. 4, §1, of the Federal Constitution, providing that full faith and credit shall be given in each state to the public records and judicial proceedings of every other state, a judgment rendered by a court of one state, having jurisdiction of the parties and the subject-matter, is as conclusive in every other state as in the one in which it was rendered. p. 694.

9. NEW TRIAL—*Grounds*—*Statutes.*—Causes assigned for a new trial, but which are not included in the statute enumerating the causes for which a new trial will be granted, are not available. p. 695.

10. JUDGMENTS.—*Foreign Judgments.*—*Collateral Attack.*—Where the judgment of a probate court of another state terminating a testamentary trust, was made pursuant to statutory provisions of such state giving probate courts full power to hear and determine all matters relating to the manner in which a trustee has executed his trust, and requiring trustees to render accounts to the probate court, etc., such judgment cannot be collaterally questioned in this State, unless want of jurisdiction appears on the face of the pleadings. p. 695.

11. TRUSTS.—*Trustee and Cestui Que Trust.*—*Judgments.*—*Conclusiveness.*—A *cestui que trust* is privy to his trustee, and an order made or judgment rendered affecting the *res* of the trust is binding on the *cestui* without notice, where the trustee is in court and the court has jurisdiction of the subject-matter. p. 696.

12. EVIDENCE.—*Common Law of Other States.*—Where one claims the benefit of the common law of another state, as modified by legislation and judicial construction, he must plead and prove the same, otherwise the law of this state will furnish the rule of decision. p. 697.

13. TRUSTS.—*Power of Trustees.*—*Execution of Power.*—The right of surviving trustees of a testamentary trust to terminate the trust is not dependent on any order of court, where, under the terms of the will, they have authority to exercise the discretionary power therein conferred of terminating the same. p. 697.

14. TRUSTS.—*Trustees.*—*Power Coupled with Interest.*—*Survival of Power.*—Where a will bequeathed certain property to trustees to pay the income to a named beneficiary, and gave them discretionary power to pay over the principal and terminate the trust, if in their opinion, it would be to the best interest of the *cestui que trust*, the power conferred was not a naked power, but was a power coupled with an interest, since the trustees held the legal title to the *res* of the trust, and on the death of one of the trustees, such power survives and may be executed by those remaining. p. 698.

15. TRUSTS.—*Power of Trustees.*—*Survival of Power.*—*Intention of Donor.*—The intention of the donor as to the survival of the power conferred in creating a trust will be followed, when such intention can be reasonably ascertained from the instrument, but no construction will be indulged which would result in any serious impairment of the donor's intention, or leave the trust imperfectly executed. p. 700.

16. TRUSTS.—*Power of Trustees.*—*Survival of Power.*—*Intention of Donor.*—The presumption that every power coupled with an interest was given *ex officio*, and meant to survive, will not be excluded on the ground that the power conferred is one of special trust and confidence in the trustees as individuals, so as to defeat, on the death of one of the trustees named in a testamentary trust, the survival of the power to terminate the trust when, in their judgment, such termination would be to the best interest of the *cestui que trust*, unless the clear and apt language of the instrument imports a contrary intention. p. 701.

From Vigo Circuit Court; *Joshua Jump*, Special Judge.

Action by Winifred Harper Cooley against Frank A. Kelley individually, and as executor of the last will of Thomas W. Harper, deceased. From a judgment for defendant, the plaintiff appeals. *Affirmed.*

C. A. Royse, for appellant.

Frank A. Kelley and *Foley, Royse & O'Mara*, for appellee.

ADAMS, J.—This action was brought by appellant against appellee individually, and as executor of the last will of Thomas W. Harper, to establish a trust in certain personal property held by appellee, and to follow and recover the trust fund. The question presented by the record being essentially one of law, it is necessary, for a proper understanding of the same, to set out the undisputed facts, as they appear in the amended complaint and the third paragraph of answer.

The complaint shows that appellant is a daughter and only child of Thomas W. Harper, and a grand-daughter of William H. Harper, who died testate at Lima, Ohio, on April —, 1901, leaving surviving him four children, viz: William H. Harper, Jr., Thomas W. Harper (father of appellant), Vinnie Annat and Mary Syfers. The will of William H. Harper was duly proved in the Probate Court of Allen County, Ohio, on April 24, 1901. By its terms the will provided for the payment of the testator's debts, and made certain specific bequests. The balance of his property was devised and bequeathed to his four children above named, share and share alike, subject to the provision that all his real estate be appraised and sold, providing the manner in which it should be sold, and distributed according to the terms of item six of said will, which is as follows:

"I direct that the share of each of my children in my personal property and the proceeds of my real estate be paid to them in money or kind as soon as possible under the provisions of this will, except that one half of the share of my son Thomas W. Harper in the property described in items four and five hereof remain in the hands of my executor and my son-in-laws, R. K. Syfers and William Annat, whom I hereby appoint trustees for that purpose, until the death of my son, Thomas W. Harper. Said trustees to invest said sum and pay to my said son Thomas, yearly the income therefor. But I direct that if at any time in the opinion of my said trustees it would be for the best interests of my said son Thomas to pay him the whole or a part of said sum, they are hereby empowered to do so. If at the death of my said son Thomas, any part of said trust remain in the hands of my said trustees, they shall pay the same to any child or children of said Thomas surviving him, or to their legal representatives; if my said son Thomas at his decease leave no surviving child or grand-child, such remaining sum shall be paid to my surviving children or their legal representatives, share and share alike."

William H. Harper, Jr., was named as executor of the will, and after qualifying and making final settlement was duly discharged.

The three trustees named in item six received as a trust, for the purpose set out in said item, the sum of $7,230.09, invested the same, and paid the income thereof from time to time to Thomas W. Harper. On January 15, 1908, Rufus K. Syfers, one of the trustees named, died, and thereafter William H. Harper, Jr., and William Annat, as surviving trustees, concluded that a termination of said trust would be for the best interests of said Thomas W. Harper. On February 8, 1908, the surviving trustees delivered to said Thomas W. Harper certain notes, mortgages and cash, aggregating in value the sum of $7,230.09, and received from said Thomas a receipt therefor. On March 4, 1908, Thomas W. Harper, being then a resident òf the city of Terre Haute, Indiana, died, testate, and his will was duly proved in the Circuit Court of Vigo County, Indiana, and admitted to probate on March 10, 1908. By said will the testator devised and bequeathed all his property to Ella Harper, who was his second wife and childless. Thomas W. Harper failed to make any provision for his daughter, the appellant, but recited in his will that he made such disposition of his property, for the reason, among other reasons, that his daughter, Winifred Harper Cooley, might, in a certain contingency, receive a portion of the property left by the will of his father. The will of Thomas W. Harper was dated December 11, 1903, and long before the principal fund of the trust estate was delivered to him. By the will of said Thomas, appellee, Frank A. Kelley, was appointed executor of the same, qualified as such executor on March 10, and took possession of all the personal property and estate of said Thomas W. Harper.

A demurrer to the complaint was overruled, and appellee answered in three paragraphs. The first was in denial. The third paragraph included the averments of the second, and admitted the facts averred in the complaint, but alleged that after the death of Rufus K. Syfers, on January 15, 1908, the two surviving trustees continued to administer said trust, and on February 3, 1908, filed in the Probate Court of Allen County, Ohio, their report and petition, averring that, in their opinion, a termination of the trust created by the will of William H. Harper would be for the best interests of Thomas W. Harper, asking for an order to turn over to said Thomas the balance of the trust funds in their hands, and that on producing the receipt of said Thomas for the same they be discharged as such trustees, and said trust ended; that on the filing of said final report the probate court entered an order authorizing said trustees to turn over said trust estate to said Thomas W. Harper, and they did so in obedience to said order; that the court approved their final report, which showed that they had turned over said trust property, and released and discharged said trustees.

It is also averred in the third paragraph of answer that at the time the will of William H. Harper was executed, Thomas W. Harper was unmarried, and a man of intemperate habits, which was known to William H. Harper, and his purpose and intention was to preserve to his said son the benefit of a part of the property bequeathed to him; that prior to the time said trustees turned over the property to Thomas W. Harper, he had married, and was living in a quiet and respectable manner, and was able and competent to take charge of his own property at the time the same was turned over to him by the trustees; that on the death of Thomas W. Harper, the appellee, as executor of his will, took possession of the notes and securities in question as a part of the personal estate of said Thomas W. Harper. This paragraph of answer also sets out certain statutes and laws of the State of Ohio in force at and since the date of the probate of the will of William H. Harper.

A demurrer was sustained to the second paragraph of answer and overruled to the third. The cause was put at issue by a reply in denial to the third paragraph of answer, and submitted to the court for trial, which resulted in a finding for appellee.

Upon the hearing, appellant offered in evidence the third paragraph of appellee's answer, and by the testimony of appellee showed the amount of money, and the nature and amount of the securities held by him as executor. Appellee offered in evidence a transcript of the proceedings of the Probate Court of Allen County, Ohio, with reference to the trust in question, including the final report of the surviving trustees, the approval thereof by the court, and the discharge of the trustees. Appellee also offered in evidence the will of Thomas W. Harper, his marriage certificate, and certain sections of the Ohio statutes, relating to probate matters and the jurisdiction of the probate court. No other evidence was heard.

The finding of the court was in the form of a written opinion, which has been carried into the record on appeal. It is unnecessary to set out this opinion, for reasons which will hereinafter appear.

The errors assigned and relied upon for reversal are as follows: (1) Overruling the demurrer to the third paragraph of answer; (2) overruling the motion for a new trial; (3) overruling the motion for a *venire de novo*; (4) overruling the motion for judgment, notwithstanding the finding of the court; (5) overruling the motion to modify the judgment. The last three specifications of error present the same matters, and are preliminary to the important questions involved in this appeal.

It is urged by appellant that the complaint having been held good, and the written opinion of the court being based on the theory that the complaint was not good, this

1. constitutes error. There is no merit in this contention.

The ruling on demurrer is not binding on the court, and does not require subsequent rulings to be in harmony. *Newman* v. *Perrill* (1880), 73 Ind. 153, 156; *Stewart* v. *Terre Haute, etc., R. Co.* (1885), 103 Ind. 44, 47, 2 N. E. 208.

The record does not show any request for a special finding in this case, and under well-established rules the opinion of the court delivered in announcing its decision, al-

2. though carried into the record on appeal, cannot be regarded as anything more than a general finding.

Hinshaw v. *Security Trust Co.* (1911), 48 Ind. App. 351, 93 N. E. 567, 569; *Bass* v. *Citizens Trust Co.* (1904), 32 Ind. App. 583, 584, 70 N. E. 400; *Northcutt* v. *Buckles* (1878), 60 Ind. 577, 579. The finding being a general one for

3. appellee, who was defendant below, it follows that there was no error in overruling the motion for a

venire de novo. This motion reaches only matters of form,

and can only be sustained when the finding is so defective and uncertain that no judgment can be rendered thereon. *Zink* v. *Dick* (1891), 1 Ind. App. 269, 274, 27 N. E. 622; *Case* v. *Ellis* (1894), 9 Ind. App. 274, 275, 36 N. E. 666.

The motion for judgment notwithstanding the finding was based on the written opinion of the court, and as we have seen this opinion must be disregarded and the find-
4. ing treated as a general one, there was no error in overruling the motion. The motion to modify the judgment was on the same ground, and as the motion questioned
5. the validity of the judgment, and not its form, the same was properly overruled. *Stone* v. *Stone* (1902), 158 Ind. 628, 630, 64 N. E. 86.

The overruling of the demurrer to the third paragraph of answer and the motion for a new trial, separately assigned as error, present substantially the same questions for re-
6. view. Appellant sought to establish her right to recover by offering in evidence the third paragraph of answer, which specifically admitted the facts averred in the complaint, with certain matters of defense added. Whether the facts admitted in the third paragraph of answer can be considered as proof supporting the complaint, when the general denial was pleaded, is not before us. The proof was offered by appellant and received by the court. If erroneous, the error is not availale to appellant, and as the finding was for appellee, he was not harmed.

All matters of defense were admitted in evidence without objection, except the certified copy of the proceedings of the Probate Court of Allen County, Ohio, relating to
7. this trust. There was no error in receiving this proof. It is provided by Art. 4, §1, of the Federal Constitution that "full faith and credit shall be given in each state to the public records and judicial proceed-
8. ings of every other state." This section requires that where a court of one state, having jurisdiction of the parties and the subject-matter, renders judgment, such judg-

ment is as conclusive in the other states of the Union as in the state where the same was rendered. *Old Wayne, etc., Assn.* v. *McDonough* (1905), 164 Ind. 321, 330, 73 N. E. 703; *American Mut. Life Ins. Co.* v. *Mason* (1902), 159 Ind. 15, 16, 64 N. E. 525.

Causes for a new trial numbered four, five, six, seven, eight and nine relate directly or indirectly to the alleged error of the court in reconsidering the sufficiency of
9. the amended complaint. The statute enumerates the causes for which a new trial will be granted, and none of the causes as numbered above is included in the statute, and cannot be considered on appeal. *Over* v. *Dehne* (1906), 38 Ind. App. 427, 431, 75 N. E. 664, 76 N. E. 883.

Two questions arising on the motion for a new trial remain for consideration: (1) Had the Probate Court of Allen County, Ohio, jurisdiction to make the order directing the surviving trustees to turn over the trust fund? (2) Did the surviving trustees have the right to execute the power contained in item six of the will of William H. Harper, Sr.?

As we have seen, appellee set out various statutes of the State of Ohio, and made proof thereof on the trial. From this proof it appears by §6330 Bates' Ann. Stat.
10. (Ohio), that the probate court "shall have full power to hear and determine all matters relative to the manner in which the trustee has executed his said trust, and as to the correctness of his accounts rendered as aforesaid." By §5985 Bates' Ann. Stat. (Ohio), it is provided that when two or more trustees are appointed by will to execute a trust, and one or more of them die, decline, resign or remove, the survivors or remaining trustee or trustees may execute the trust, unless the terms of the will express a contrary intention. By §6187 Bates' Ann. Stat. (Ohio), it appears that when an account is settled in the absence of any person adversely interested, and without actual notice to him, the account may be opened on his final exceptions to the same at any time within eight months thereafter. By §6328 Bates'

Ann. Stat. (Ohio), it is provided that any trustee appointed by any last will to execute a trust, created by such will, shall as often as once every two years render an account of the execution of said trust to the probate court of the county in which he was appointed, in the manner provided by law for the settlement of accounts of executors and administrators. It is not contended by appellant that the Probate Court of Allen County, Ohio, had no jurisdiction to determine all' matters relating to the execution of the trust, but she insists that such probate court had no jurisdiction to approve the settlement made or to discharge the trustees. It is shown by the record that the surviving trustees filed their final report, and asked for an order to turn over to Thomas W. Harper the trust funds in their hands, and that they be discharged on producing his receipt for the same. Notice was given by publication, as required by law, and at the time set for the hearing of the report and petition the court made the following entry and order: "And the court, upon the examination of said account, and the final receipt of said testamentary ward, finds said account to be in all respects correct, and the same is therefore approved and confirmed and ordered recorded. And as provided by said will of William H. Harper, said trustees elect to terminate said trust, the said account is approved as final, and said trustees relieved and discharged from said trust." The power to hear and determine probate matters, as provided by the Ohio statute, constitutes jurisdiction, and unless want of jurisdiction appears on the face of the proceedings, a judgment cannot be collaterally questioned. *Baltimore, etc., R. Co.* v. *Freeze* (1907), 169 Ind. 370, 375, 82 N. E. 761.

As to notice, the general rule is that a *cestui que trust* is privy to his trustee, and an order made or judgment rendered affecting the *res* of the trust is binding on the

11. *cestui* where the trustee is in court, and where the court has jurisdiction of the subject-matter. *Robertson* v. *Van Cleave* (1891), 129 Ind. 217, 220, 26 N. E. 899, 29

N. E. 781, 15 L. R. A. 68; *Hoard* v. *Bradbury* (1901), 156 Ind. 30, 33, 59 N. E. 31.

There was no proof of the laws of Ohio offered other than that introduced by appellee. It has been held that where a party in this jurisdiction claims the benefit of the common law of another state, as modified by legislation and judicial construction, he must plead and prove the same as any other facts not judicially known by the courts of this State. In the absence of such proof, our own laws will furnish the rule of decision. *Buchanan* v. *Hubbard* (1889), 119 Ind. 187, 190, 21 N. E. 538; *Bierhaus* v. *Western Union Tel. Co.* (1893), 8 Ind. App. 246, 263, 34 N. E. 581.

12.

If the surviving trustees were authorized to exercise the discretionary power conferred by item six of the will of William H. Harper, we do not think it important to determine whether the Probate Court of Allen County, Ohio, had jurisdiction to settle and close the trust or not. If the surviving trustees had such right, granted by the terms of the will, an order of the probate court could not enlarge the right. The exercise of the power was made dependent on the opinion of the trustees that a termination of the trust would be for the best interests of Thomas W. Harper. No order of court was required or contemplated. Indeed, such an order would imply a substitution of the opinion of the court for the opinion of the trustees, to whom was committed the duty of determining this question. And it will be noted that the court did not make any finding in the matter, but only approved the account, reciting that as the trustees had, pursuant to the will, elected to terminate the trust, the account was approved as final and the trustees discharged.

13.

The important question is whether the discretionary power given to the trustees named in item six of the will of William H. Harper, on the death of one of the trustees, passed to the survivors. This question considered alone is not free from doubt under the authorities. By the Ohio statute offered in evidence, it is clear that a trust created by will may be executed by surviving trustees, unless a contrary intention is expressed in the testament. But we are not now dealing with the execution of the trust. We are concerned with the exercise of the power. The record in this case does not disclose any law of Ohio authorizing a discretionary power incident to a trust to be exercised by surviving trustees, and we must look elsewhere for authority

It is obvious that the trustees in this case held the legal title to the *res* of the trust (2 Perry, Trusts §475); and therefore the power conferred on them was not a naked
14. power, but one properly denominated "a power coupled with an interest." *Rowe* v. *Beckett* (1868), 30 Ind. 154, 159, 95 Am. Dec. 676. This expression was early defined by Chief Justice Marshall, in *Hunt* v. *Rousmanier* (1823), 8 Wheat. *174, *203, 5 L. Ed. 589, as follows: "The power must be engrafted on an estate in the thing. The words themselves would seem to import this meaning. 'A power coupled with an interest' is a power which accompanies, or is connected with, an interest. The power and the interest are united in the same person."

The United States Supreme Court, in the case of *Lorings* v. *Marsh* (1867), 6 Wall. 337, 354, 18 L. Ed. 802, said: "Inasmuch as the trustees are invested with the legal estate in order to enable them to discharge the various trusts declared, it is well settled that the power conferred is a power coupled with an interest, which survives, on the death of one of them, and may be executed by the survivor. * * * It is not necessary that the trustees should have a personal interest in the trust; it is in the possession of the legal estate, or a right *virtute officii* in the subject over which the power is to be exercised, that makes an interest, which, when coupled with the power, the latter survives."

The same court in the case of *Peter* v. *Beverly* (1836), 10 Pet. *532, *564, 9 L. Ed. 522, said: "The general principle of the common law, as laid down by Lord Coke [Co. Litt.

112b], and sanctioned by many judicial decisions, is that when the power given to several persons is a mere naked power to sell, not coupled with an interest, it must be executed by all, and does not survive; but when the power is coupled with an interest, it may be executed by the survivor." See, also, *In re Wilkin* (1905), 183 N. Y. 104, 75 N. E. 1105; *Sells* v. *Delgado* (1904), 186 Mass. 25, 28, 70 N. E. 1036; *Stanwood* v. *Stanwood* (1901), 179 Mass. 223, 60 N. E. 584; 22 Am. and Eng. Ency. Law 1101; 2 Perry, Trusts §505; Lewin, Trusts (9th ed.) 689; *Hadley* v. *Hadley* (1897), 147 Ind. 423, 46 N. E. 823.

The last case cited has been pressed on our attention by both appellant and appellee in support of their several contentions. In that case, at page 428, the court said: "If the authority be committed to trustees, the presumption is that, as the power was coupled with an interest, it was meant to survive. If a power be a joint one coupled with an interest, it will survive if one of the donees of the power die. But where it is a mere naked authority it will not survive. So if the authority be to two or more in an official capacity *ratione officii* it will survive if one die. But if it be to them *nominatim* or they are clothed with a special confidence of a personal nature, it will not survive. 2 Wash. Real Prop. (5th ed.) 553. For if the act to be done requires an exercise of the judgment and discretion of the several persons named as trustees, it can only be exercised by them all. 2 Wash. Real Prop. 554."

It will be noted that the rule last above declared relates only to cases where the donee has but a simple, naked power, and has reference to the facts in that particular case. These facts are that one Hadley, devised to his wife certain real estate for life, and at her death three persons, named in the will, were authorized to take charge as trustees, and devote the same, if thought practicable, to the erection and maintenance of a charitable institution. But it was provided that if the erection of such institution was not, in the judgment of the trustees, deemed practicable, the lands were to be sold and the proceeds divided among his heirs. After the execution of the will, and before the death of Hadley, one of the trustees died, which fact was known to the testator. The court held the power conferred to be a simple naked power, and one that did not survive. This holding is clearly right, for the reason that no interest whatever passed by the will to the trustees. The first duty of the trustees, under the will, was to pass on the practicability of the erection of the institution, which, if determined in the negative, ended their connection with the estate.

In the case before us, the *res* of the trust was personal property. All of the trustees named survived the testator, and held the legal title to the trust fund. The exercise of the discretionary power provided for was an incident to and connected with the trust.

The cases are collected and the principles are stated in 2 Washburn, Real Property (5th ed.) 554, from which the learned author draws the following conclusions: "The rule to be gathered from what is above said may be again stated, that where there are several joint-trustees, and one of them dies, the survivors take and are authorized to act by virtue of their survivorship, in the same way as one of two joint-tenants of a legal estate takes by survivorship, unless it is a power only, and one not coupled with an interest; because, as an almost invariable rule, two or more trustees hold as joint-tenants, and not as tenants in common. If it is such a power, it ceases with the death of either of the trustees. A power is considered as coupled with an interest where the trustees have a right to the possession of the legal estate, or have a right in the subject over which the power is to be executed."

It would unduly extend this opinion to make further quotations from the settled law relating to trusts and 15. powers. All the authorities agree, however, that the intention of the donor as to the survival of the power will be followed, whenever from the instrument creating the power the purpose can be reasonably ascertained. No construction is to be indulged which would result in any serious impairment of the donor's intention, or leave the trust imperfectly executed.

It will appear from even a casual reading of the will of William H. Harper that his primary intention was to treat his unfortunate son the same as his other children, and put him in possession of his full inheritance as soon as his conduct and manner of life seemed to warrant it. As to the time when this should be done, if at all, his trustees were to determine; but the welfare of Thomas was the object of the father's solicitude, and knowing, as he did, the uncertainties of life, we cannot believe that he contemplated or intended that his benevolent purpose should be defeated by the death of one of his trustees.

From the manifest intention of the testator, as well as from the weight of authority, we think the surviving trustees were fully warranted in exercising the power, and terminating the trust.

Judgment affirmed.

ON PETITION FOR REHEARING.

ADAMS, P. J.—In her petition for rehearing, appellant, while not disputing the general rule that a power coupled with an interest will survive, insists that the power given by section six of the will of William H. Harper to his trustees was one of special trust and confidence in them as individuals, and not a power committed to them by virtue of their office.

The case of *Dillard* v. *Dillard* (1899), 97 Va. 434, 34 S. E. 60, is pressed on our attention, and is in point, assuming that the above construction of the will is true. In that
16. case it is held that a power conferred on three trustees, without words of survivorship, and involving personal confidence, was one that could only be exercised

conjointly, and that on the death of one of the trustees the authority would be determined.

In support of this proposition, the case of *Cole* v. *Wade* (1807), 16 Ves., Jr., *27, with others, is cited, and is in point. In that case, the Master of Rolls said: "I conceive, that, wherever a power is of a kind that indicates a personal confidence, it must *prima facie*, be understood to be confined to the individual, to whom it is given; and will not except by express words pass to others, to whom by legal transmission the same character may happen to belong." This case was determined by the High Court of Chancery in 1807, and almost a century later, the same court (*In re Smith* [1903], 73 L. J. 74) overruled *Cole* v. *Wade, supra*, and held that the general principle would be applicable if it had been followed and adopted by the later cases. The court further said: "The principle, however, is open to the criticism that it is expressed in loose and general terms. All, or nearly all, powers necessitate, the personal confidence of the testator in the donees thereof, and it is very difficult to draw the line—for example, powers of leasing, and selling and investing, powers of maintenance and advancement of children, all require the exercise of discretion, but the principle could hardly be applied to them. I find it impossible to formulate any rule by which the court can say that certain powers are, and others are not, of such a nature that they must necessarily be given only to individuals known to the testator. There is no standard of measurement, but the more or the less becomes a mere matter of conjecture, affording no basis for judicial determination." The court reviews a number of cases and concludes: "Every power given to trustees, which enables them to deal with or affect the trust property is *prima facie* given to them *ex officio* as an incident of their office, and passes with the office to the holders or holder thereof for the time being. Whether a power is so given *ex officio* or not depends in each case on the construction of the document giving it; but the mere fact that the power is one requiring the exercise of a very

Cooley *v.* Kelley—52 Ind. App. 687.

wide personal discretion is not enough to exclude the *prima facie* presumption, and little regard is now paid to such minute differences as those between 'my trustees,' 'my trustees, A and B,' and 'A and B my trustees.' The testator's reliance on the individuals to the exclusion of the holders of the office for the time being must be expressed in clear and apt language.''

Hadley v. *Hadley* (1897), 147 Ind. 423, 46 N. E. 823, the only Indiana case wherein the question of powers has been considered, followed the rule laid down by Washburn, that where the power is coupled with an interest the presumption is that it was meant to survive. It also appears from the latest expression of the High Court of Chancery that the rule of presumption in cases of this kind has now been changed in England, and that where a power is given to trustees, it is *prima facie* by virtue of their office. To overcome such presumption requires the use of clear and apt language in the instrument creating the trust and conferring the power. No such language is used in the will of William H. Harper. As the donees of the power hold the same *ex officio*, and no words are used importing a contrary intention, the power was one that would survive, and could be lawfully exercised in this case by the two surviving trustees.

Rehearing denied.

NOTE.—Reported in 96 N. E. 638, 98 N. E. 653. See, also, under (1) 31 Cyc. 350; (2) 3 Cyc. 181; 38 Cyc. 1976; (3, 4) 38 Cyc. 1990; (5) 23 Cyc. 866, 868; (6) 3 Cyc. 244; (7) 23 Cyc. 1545; (8) 23 Cyc. 1546; (9) 29 Cyc. 759; (10) 23 Cyc. 1546; (11) 23 Cyc. 1246; (12) 16 Cyc. 1084; (13) 40 Cyc. 1809; (14, 15, 16) 40 Cyc. 1834. As to the effect of judgments of sister-state courts, see 2 Am. Dec. 42; 103 Am. St. 304. As to what are collateral attacks upon judgments, see 23 Am. St. 104. As to the effect to be given a power coupled with an interest, see 110 Am. St. 860.

THE CLEVELAND, CINCINNATI, CHICAGO AND ST. LOUIS RAILWAY COMPANY *v.* WHEELER.

[No. 6,990. Filed November 15, 1910. Rehearing denied February
14, 1911. Transfer denied December 19, 1912.]

From Putnam Circuit Court; *John M. Rawley*, Judge.

Action by Alonzo Wheeler against The Cleveland, Cincinnati, Chicago & St. Louis Railway Company. From a judgment for plaintiff, the defendant appeals. *Affirmed.*

Frank L. Littleton and *Enloe & Pattison*, for appellant.

Wilson S. Doan, Charles J. Orbison and *Silas A. Hays*, for appellee.

ROBY, J.—Action by appellee for damages on account of the occupation by appellant, with fills, tracks and other railroad structures, of a strip of land alleged to be a highway on which appellant's real estate abuts. In the first paragraph of complaint it is averred that such strip of land was a public highway, and in the second that appellee had a right of way over the same. Appellee had judgment for $900. The assignments of error are that the court erred in overruling the demurrer to each paragraph of the complaint and in overruling the motion for a new trial. There is, as stated by appellant's counsel, practically no dispute as to the facts. They contend that the case of the *Baltimore, etc., R. Co. v. City of Seymour* (1900), 154 Ind. 17, 55 N. E. 953, is "on all fours with" and decisive of the case at bar. For appellee it is stated that the parallelism between this case and the case of *Pittsburgh, etc., R. Co. v. Town of Crown Point* (1898), 150 Ind. 536, 50 N. E. 741, is so marked and the cases are so similar that nothing short of the reversal of the law as therein declared would be possible in event that the judgment herein is not affirmed.

In *Baltimore, etc., R. Co. v. City of Seymour, supra*, it was shown that the railroad right of way extended forty feet each side of the center of the track, that a side-track had been constructed fifteen feet from the main track, and that during many years persons who had freight to send or receive had come with teams upon the right of way to load and unload freight cars placed upon the siding, and that persons not having business with the company also drove over that part of the right of way. On these facts it was held that a mere permissive use was shown, concurrent with that of the owner and not indicative of a prescriptive right. The facts considered in *Pittsburgh, etc., R. Co. v. Town of Crown Point, supra*, were that the town was proposing to pave a strip of land over which persons approaching the company's depot had passed for many years. Such strip formed a continuation of and connected two streets in said town. The right of way was fifty feet each side of the track, except for the distance of 1,125 feet, where it broadened to 150 feet on each side, the depot being there located. The strip in dispute was within the extra 100 feet, and furnished a way to the depot. Emphasis was laid in the opinion on the marked character of the route, on the fact that the public authorities had improved it, that it was traveled by the public as well as by the company's employes and those having business at the depot, that the way was necessary as an outlet to residences and business houses built on the streets thereby connected, and that a livery stable was for many years maintained having its outlet on the way in dispute, and that no objection had been made to the public use of the same.

The two causes were differentiated in *Baltimore, etc., R. Co.* v. *City of Seymour, supra,* as follows: "The facts in this case differ essentially from those in *Pittsburgh, etc., R. Co.* v. *Town of Crown Point* [1898], 150 Ind. 536 [50 N. E. 741]. There, it was found that a portion of the station grounds, on the opposite side of the depot from the tracks, of the width of thirty feet, had been marked out, ditched, graded and worked by the town authorities for thirty years, and throughout that time the public's possession of the ground as a street had been open, notorious, continuous, adverse and exclusive.

The determination of this appeal depends on whether the facts exhibited bring it within the one authority or the other. The facts briefly stated are that on May 7, 1869, appellant acquired a right of way ninety-nine feet wide by condemnation. On October 29, 1870, it purchased a strip south of the right of way, seventy-five feet wide and 1,000 feet long, and a strip of equal length twenty-five feet wide on the north side thereof. The deed therefor reserved the right to put in a crossing at the west end of said strip. On December 8, 1894, appellee platted "Wheelers addition", lying north of the west end of said twenty-five-foot strip. The plat shows a twenty-five-foot strip between the lots and the strip, which it is now claimed is itself a street. The west end of said strip extends to the quarter section line north and south, along which there is a highway.

It was shown that the railroad depot was constructed east of the quarter line and was also used as a country store; that there was a crossing made over the railroad track east of the depot and the strip was used as other highways since 1870. Houses were built with reference to it and work done on it by public authority. This is an incomplete summary of facts, but is sufficient to show that the case comes within the authority of *Pittsburgh, etc., R. Co.* v. *Town of Crown Point, supra,* and kindred cases cited.

Various minor questions are mooted, but the judgment is in accord with the proof, and is not therefore subject to reversal.

The judgment is affirmed.

MILLER *v.* THE BANK OF ADVANCE.

[No. 7,763. Filed December 20, 1912.]

From Boone Circuit Court; *James V. Kent,* Special Judge.

Action between Matthew G. Miller and The Bank of Advance, and from an adverse judgment, Miller appeals. *Affirmed.*

B. F. Ratcliff and *B. S. Higgins,* for appellant.
Terhune & Adney, for appellee.

ADAMS, J.—This appeal was, by agreement of the parties, submitted on the record and briefs filed in *Miller* v. *Farmers State Bank* (1912), 52 Ind. App. 5, 100 N. E. 119. Following that case, the judgment in this case is affirmed.

MILLER *v.* HOGSHIRE.

[No. 7,764. Filed December 20, 1912.]

From Boone Circuit Court; *James V. Kent,* Special Judge.

Action between Matthew G. Miller and George Hogshire, and from an adverse judgment, Miller appeals. *Affirmed.*

B. F. Ratcliff, for appellant.
Terhune & Adney, for appellee.

ADAMS, J.—This appeal was, by agreement of the parties, submitted on the record and briefs filed in *Miller* v. *Farmers State Bank* (1912), 52 Ind. App. 5, 100 N. E. 119. Following that case, the judgment in this case is affirmed.

MILLER *v.* MELLETTE.

[No. 7,765. Filed December 20, 1912.]

From Boone Circuit Judge; *James V. Kent*, Special Judge.

Action by James T. Mellette against Matthew G. Miller. From a judgment for plaintiff, the defendant appeals. *Affirmed.*

B. F. Ratcliff, for appellant.

Terhune & Adney, for appellee.

ADAMS, J.—This appeal was, by agreement of the parties, submitted upon the record and briefs filed in *Farmers State Bank v. Miller* (1912), 52 Ind. App. 5, 100 N. E. 119. Following that case, the judgment in the case at bar is affirmed.

INDEX

[NOTE.—The citation *Moore-Mansfield, etc., Co. v. Marion, etc., Traction Co.*, 548, 556 (10), indicates that the case begins on page 548, the point cited is on page 556, and that such point is numbered 10 in the margin.—REPORTER.]

ABATEMENT—

Answer in, see PLEADING 23; VENUE 2.

An answer in, which appears to state sufficient facts will be deemed on appeal to be sufficient to withstand a demurrer, where appellant fails to point out any specific defect therein, see APPEAL 83.

Another Action Pending.—Evidence.—Sufficiency.—An answer in abatement on the ground that another action is pending is not sustained by evidence showing that a former action was commenced on the same cause of action, where it is also apparent that such former action was dismissed and was not pending when the latest action was filed.
Moore-Mansfield, etc., Co. v. Marion, etc., Traction Co., 548, 556 (10).

ABUTTING OWNERS—

A property owner, who, by some affirmative wrongful act, causes the defective condition of a street, is liable to the city or town for any amount which it may be required to pay·as damages on account of such defect, see MUNICIPAL CORPORATIONS 10.

ACCEPTANCE—

See SALES 2.

Of a proposal, to constitute a contract, must be as broad as the proposal itself, and exactly meet its terms, see CONTRACTS 3.

ACCOUNT—

Books, see EVIDENCE 5.

ACTION—

Accrual of cause of, see LIMITATION OF ACTIONS 1-3.
Concealment of cause of, see LIMITATION OF ACTIONS 4-9.

ACTIONS—

See CONTRACTS 4-7; MASTER AND SERVANT 43-49; PRINCIPAL AND AGENT 1; WATERS AND WATERCOURSES 11.

Actions at Law.—Suits in Equity.—Effect of Statute Abolishing Distinctions.—Section 249 Burns 1908, §249 R. S. 1881, providing that there shall be but one form of action, denominated a civil action, and abolishing all distinctions in pleading and practice between actions at law and suits in equity, neither abridges the power of courts to grant equitable relief nor changes the rules of law or principles of equity as applied in determining the substantial rights of the parties, though in some instances it changes the form of procedure by which the remedy is obtained.
Moore-Mansfield, etc., Co. v. Marion, etc., Traction Co., 548, 554 (3).

ADMISSIONS—

See PLEADING 24-26.

Testimony of a party given in another action, is admissible as, see EVIDENCE 1.

AFFIRMANCE—

See APPEAL 123, 143-147.

AGENT—

See PRINCIPAL AND AGENT.

ALLOWANCE—

Statutory, see WILLS 3-5.

ANIMALS—

Injury to, on tracks, see RAILROADS 38-41.

ANSWER—

See PLEADING, 21-23.

ANSWERS TO INTERROGATORIES—

See TRIAL 21-24, 29-40

APPEAL.

I. APPELLATE JURISDICTION, 1.
II. DECISIONS REVIEWABLE, 2-10.
III. PARTIES, 11-15.
IV. REQUISITES OF TRANSFER.
    (a) TIME, 16-18.
    (b) NOTICE, 19-22.
V. RECORD AND PROCEEDINGS NOT IN RECORD, 23-29.
VI. ASSIGNMENT OF ERRORS, 30-36.
VII. BRIEFS, 37-46.
VIII. REVIEW,
    (a) AS TO EVIDENCE, 47-64.
    (b) AS TO INSTRUCTIONS, 65-82.

    (c) AS TO PLEADING, 83.
    (d) PRESUMPTIONS, 84-92.
    (e) VERDICT, ANSWERS TO INTERROGATORIES, FINDINGS AND RULINGS ON MOTIONS, 93-116.
    (f) HARMLESS ERROR, 117-139.
IX. DETERMINATION AND DISPOSITION OF CAUSE,
    (a) DECISIONS IN GENERAL, 140-142.
    (b) AFFIRMANCE, 143-147.
    (c) REVERSAL, 148, 149.

See PLEADING 10-15.

I. APPELLATE JURISDICTION.

1. *Void Appeal.—Substitution of Parties.—*Where an appeal was void for want of jurisdiction, because of the death of a party to the judgment before the appeal was filed, an order substituting his administrator as an appellee is also void.

Thompson v. *Newsom,* 444, 447 (4).

II. DECISIONS REVIEWABLE.

2. *Invited Error.—*Invited error cannot be taken advantage of on appeal. *Pittsburgh, etc., R. Co.* v. *Johnson,* 457, 477 (11).

3. *Review.—Assumption That Trial Court Will Err.—*The court on appeal has no right to assume that a trial court, in passing on a matter, will consider questions not presented by the pleadings then on file.

Moore-Mansfield, etc., Co. v. *Marion, etc., Traction Co.,* 548, 556 (9).

APPEAL—Continued.

4. *Presentation of Questions Below.—Objections to Evidence.*—Objections to offered evidence must state the particular grounds relied on to be available on appeal, unless the evidence appears on its face to be incompetent.   *Hubbard* v. *Ranje*, 611, 615 (2).

5. *Review.—Discretion of Lower Court.—Order of Proof.*—The action of a trial court in permitting the introduction of evidence out of the usual order is a matter within its sound discretion, and will not be interfered with on appeal, unless it is made to appear affirmatively that there has been an abuse of such discretion which prevented the complaining party from having a fair trial.
            Modern Woodmen v. *Jones*, 149, 151 (3).

6. *Presentation of Questions for Review.—Errors Occurring During Trial.*—No question is presented on appeal by assignment that the trial court erred in overruling a motion to dismiss the action for want of certain proof, and that it erred in sustaining certain objections to questions asked a witness, since errors occurring during the trial, to be available, must be saved by assigning them as causes for a new trial.   *Davis* v. *Bryant*, 343, 344 (1).

7. *Questions Presented for Review.—Exceptions to Conclusions of Law.*—Where there is a special finding in which the facts have been fully and correctly found within the issues, and on which the trial court has stated its conclusions of law, to which the appellant has duly excepted, such exceptions will present the same question as the overruling of a demurrer to the complaint.
            Town of Cicero v. *Lake Erie, etc., R. Co.*, 298, 308 (4).

8. *Questions Reviewable.—Excessive Amount of Recovery.—Manner of Saving Question.*—An assignment, as ground for a new trial, that the assessment of the amount of the recovery is erroneous, being too large, correctly saves the question, and a motion to modify the judgment is not necessary.
            Holthouse v. *Poling*, 508, 573 (6).

9. *Questions Reviewable.—Evidence.—Bill of Exceptions.*—Where it is not shown that the bill of exceptions containing the long-hand transcript of the evidence was presented within time, and the filing thereof, after being signed, does not appear by a record entry independent of the bill itself, or by the clerk's certificate, the evidence is not in the record and questions arising thereon cannot be considered.
            Ladoga Can. Co. v. *Corydon Can. Co.*, 23, 28 (7).

10. *Review.—Misconduct of Counsel.*—Where, in an action against several defendants, the court overruled a motion to withdraw the submission of the cause to the jury because of the statement of plaintiff's counsel in argument that defendants desired that liability should be fixed on one of them that was insolvent, but instructed the jury that it should consider only the evidence in the case, and not what the attorneys say outside the evidence, defendants received all the relief to which they were entitled, since in view of the circumstances and the evidence in the case, the statement did not warrant the withdrawal of the submission.
            Cleveland, etc., R. Co. v. *Clark*, 646, 653 (10)

III. PARTIES

11. *Vacation Appeal.*—In a vacation appeal, all those against whom a judgment has been rendered, either *in rem* or *personam*, or who, in any manner are bound or affected thereby, must be made coappellants.   *Masoari* v. *Hert*, 345, 347 (3).

APPEAL—Continued.

12. *Jurisdiction.—Notice.*—Notice to all necessary parties is essential to jurisdiction of an appeal, and unless such notice is given, or there is an appearance, a submission may be set aside and the appeal dismissed. *Thompson v. Newsom, 444, 445 (1).*

13. *Judgment.*—Although the only question involved in an appeal is one of costs adjudged against appellant, and by the judgment appellant's codefendant recovered her costs, such codefendant is a necessary party to the appeal, since any order changing the judgment of the lower court must affect her interest. *Mascari v. Hert, 345, 348 (4).*

14. *Dismissal.*—Where a party to the judgment below, in so far as the record discloses, is not a party to the appeal, and has not been served with notice as required by §674 Burns 1908, Acts 1899 p. 5, providing that, in case of appeal by a part of several coparties, notice of the appeal must be served on all the coparties not appealing, the appeal cannot be entertained for want of jurisdiction. *Mascari v. Hert, 345, 347 (2), 348 (2).*

15. *Jurisdiction.—Death.*—The court cannot acquire jurisdiction of an appeal prosecuted against parties who have died after the rendition of the judgment appealed from, and before the filing of the appeal, but under §677 Burns 1908, §636 R. S. 1881, in such case the proper method of appealing is to serve notice of the appeal on the persons against whom the action might have been revived, if death had occurred before judgment. *Thompson v. Newsom, 444, 446 (3).*

IV. REQUISITES OF TRANSFER.

(A) TIME.

16. *Vacation Appeal.*—Where judgment was rendered on the eighteenth judicial day of the October term, 1909, and a motion to modify was filed on the twenty-second judicial day of such term, and overruled on the nineteenth judicial day of the January term, 1910, and the precipe bears date of January 31, the certificate to the transcript is dated February 14 and the record on appeal was filed October 20, 1910, the appeal must be regarded as a vacation appeal. *Mascari v. Hert, 345, 347 (1).*

17. *Term-time Appeal.—Bond.—Approval of Surety.—Waiver.*—The requirement that, to perfect a term-time appeal under §679 Burns 1908, §638 R. S. 1881, the sureties on the bond must be named and approved by the court during the term at which the final judgment is rendered, is not waived by appellee's failure to object to the order fixing the penalty without naming the sureties. *Price v. Huddleston* (1905), 36 Ind. App. 450, and *Yanthis v. Kemp* (1907), 40 Ind. App. 649, overruled. *Penn, etc., Plate Glass Co. v. Poling, 492, 494 (2).*

18. *Term-time Appeal.—Bond.—Approval of Surety.*—The failure to name and approve sureties on an appeal bond during the term at which the final judgment was rendered, is an omission of a necessary step to be taken in order to perfect a term-time appeal, under §679 Burns 1908, §638 R. S. 1881, providing that when an appeal is taken during the term at which the judgment is rendered, it shall operate as a stay of all further proceedings on the judgment, upon an appeal bond being filed by appellant, with such penalty and surety as the court shall approve, and within such time as it shall direct, and requires a dismissal of the appeal unless it has been perfected as a vacation appeal. *Penn, etc., Plate Glass Co. v. Poling, 492, 493 (1).*

APPEAL—Continued..

the name of the administrator for that of the decedent, the court will not permit such amendment to be thereafter made.
Thompson v. *Newsom*, 444, 447 (5).

VII. Briefs.

37. *Record.—Sufficiency.*—Where the transcript and briefs substantially comply with the rules of court, they are sufficient to prevent a dismissal of the appeal.   *Camp* v. *Camp*, 250, 252 (2).

38. *Review.—Insufficient Briefs.*—On appeal from a judgment for plaintiff in replevin, the court cannot determine if proof of a demand was necessary where appellant's brief does not contain any of the evidence in the case.   *Davis* v. *Bryant*, 343, 344 (3).

39. *Rules of Court.—Force and Effect.*—The rule of the Supreme and Appellate Courts requiring appellant's brief to contain a statement of the errors relied on for reversal, has the force and effect of law, binding alike on litigant and the Court.
Griffith v. *Felts*, 268, 269 (2).

40. *Omission of Error Relied on for Reversal.—Affirmance.*—Where appellant's brief does not contain a statement of the errors relied on for reversal, and does not inform the court, except by inference, that any assignment of errors is in the record, the judgment must be affirmed.   *Griffith* v. *Felts*, 268, 269 (1).

41. *Objection to Instructions.—Waiver.*—Alleged error in the giving of instructions is waived by appellant's failure to discuss them.   *Heston* v. *Dougan*, 40, 50 (8).

42. *Waiver of Error.*—Questions as to alleged errors in the admission and exclusion of testimony are waived by appellant's failure to discuss them in his brief, or to cite authority in support thereof.   *Scigmund* v. *Tyner*, 581, 583 (1).

43. *Ruling on Demurrer.—Waiver.*—Error alleged in the overruling of a demurrer is waived by appellant's failure to set out in its brief a copy of such demurrer, or to state its substance or the grounds thereof.   *Modern Woodmen* v. *Jones*, 149, 150 (1).

44. *Ruling on Motion for New Trial.—Waiver of Error.*—An assignment of error in overruling a motion for a new trial, based on the insufficiency of the evidence, will not be considered, where neither the motion nor any of its grounds are set out in appellant's brief, and no statement of the evidence is contained therein.   *Davis* v. *Bryant*, 343, 344 (4).

45. *Sufficiency.—Statement of Substance of Pleadings.*—Where appellant makes a good faith effort to set out the substance of each of the pleadings and gives a reference to the page and lines of the record where the entire pleading is found, so that the court can know by reference to the brief alone the real question attempted to be raised as to the sufficiency of such pleadings, the brief is sufficient to require a consideration of such question.
Nave v. *Powell*, 496, 498 (1).

46. *Questions Reviewable.—Motion for New Trial.*—Where appellant's brief contains neither a copy of the motion for a new trial, nor its substance, and does not disclose that such motion was filed, that it was overruled, or that an exception was taken, there is a total failure to comply with the rule requiring appellant's brief to contain a concise statement of so much of the record as fully presents every error and exception relied on, with reference to the

APPEAL—Continued.

pages and lines of the transcript, so that an assignment of error in overruling such motion cannot be considered.

Cleveland, etc., R. Co. v. *Beard*, 105, 106 (2).

VIII. REVIEW.

(A) AS TO EVIDENCE.

47. *Verdict.*—A verdict for plaintiff is supported by sufficient evidence, where there was evidence to support the complaint in all particulars. *Knapp* v. *Beach*, 573, 577 (7).

48. *Verdict.—Conclusiveness.*—Where the evidence is conflicting, the jury's finding in the general verdict will not be disturbed on appeal, if there is any evidence tending to support each material issue. *Mortimer* v. *Daub*, 30, 35 (3).

49. *Verdict.—Conclusiveness.*—Where the evidence is of such a character that opposite inferences may reasonably be drawn therefrom, a finding by the jury of a fact, sustained by either of such inferences, is supported by evidence and will not be disturbed on appeal. *Paul* v. *Snyder*, 291, 294 (2).

50. *Verdict.*—The verdict for plaintiff in a negligence case will not be disturbed on the evidence, on appeal, where such evidence is conflicting on the question of defendant's negligence, and does not show contributory negligence as a matter of law.

Cleveland, etc., R. Co. v. *Van Laningham*, 156, 169 (15).

51. *Refusal to Direct Verdict.*—Where there was some evidence to support each material averment of the complaint, it was proper to refuse to direct a verdict for defendant.

Modern Woodmen v. *Jones*, 149, 151 (4).

52. *Findings.*—Where there is some evidence to justify a finding of the trial court, such finding is sustained by sufficient evidence.

Fuller v. *Fuller*, 488, 490 (3).

53. *Findings.*—On appeal the court will not weigh conflicting evidence consisting of oral testimony, but will consider only that which is favorable to the finding in determining the sufficiency of the evidence to support same. *Fuller* v. *Fuller*, 488, 490 (2).

54. *Record.—Questions Not Considered.*—Where the evidence is not in the record on appeal, the objection that the verdict is contrary to law, and to the evidence, cannot be considered.

Newsom v. *Chicago, etc., R. Co.*, 577, 578 (1).

55. *Issues.—Instructions.*—Where the evidence has not been brought into the record, if the instructions objected to can be said to be proper and applicable to any evidence that might have been introduced under the issues, no available error is presented.

Michigan, etc., R. Co. v. *Farrell*, 603, 608 (4).

56. *Exclusion of Evidence.*—Where, in a foreclosure suit, plaintiff offered testimony to show certain losses, without preceding the offer by showing that the mortgage was in fact given to secure such losses, and the record discloses no statement that the offered evidence would be followed by testimony showing that such losses were in fact secured by said mortgage, such offered testimony was properly excluded. *Hubbard* v. *Ranje*, 611, 617 (6).

57. *Damages.*—Where, in an action for damages, the evidence shows injuries to the person of appellee, which, though slight, are not capable of being definitely ascertained, a verdict for $100 will not be set aside on the ground that the damages are excessive.

Craig v. *Zent*, 10, 22 (4).

APPEAL—Continued.

58. *Exceptions to Conclusions of Law.*—Technical objections as to
the sufficiency of appellants' exceptions to conclusions of law will
not be considered, where the evidence fails to prove the same
essential facts omitted from the findings, thereby showing that the
motion for a new trial should have been sustained.
                    Town of Cicero v. *Lake Erie, etc., R. Co.*, 298, 314 (16).

59. *Weight and Sufficiency.*—Although the evidence is conflicting on
some of the material issues, the decision of the trial court will not
be disturbed, if there is evidence tending to support every fact
essential thereto, since the court on appeal will not weigh conflicting evidence.   *Grubb* v. *Brendel*, 531, 536 (7).

60. *Weight of Evidence.*—*Statutes.*—Where the evidence on which
the finding of the trial court rests consists in whole or in part of
oral testimony, §698 Burns 1908, Acts 1903 p. 338, providing that
in causes not triable by jury, the court on appeal shall weigh the
evidence, etc., does not apply, even though the cause was not
triable by jury.   *Fuller* v. *Fuller*, 488, 489 (1).

61. *Objections to Evidence.*—*Availability.*—Objections to evidence,
which do not state the grounds on which they are based, are
unavailing on appeal.   *Fuller* v. *Fuller*, 488, 491 (7).

62. *Objection to Evidence.*—*Waiver.*—Questions as to alleged error
in the admission and exclusion of testimony are waived by a
failure to state specific objections.
                                        Seigmund v. *Tyner*, 581, 583 (2).

63. *Objection to Evidence.*—Although appellant saved exceptions to
the admission of certain evidence, and to the refusal to admit certain evidence, where no specific objection is pointed out, and none
is disclosed by the record, no error can be predicated thereon.
                Terre Haute, etc., Traction Co. v. *Maberry*, 114, 123 (10).

64. *Complaint.*—*Sufficiency.*—Where two persons were injured in
the same accident, and two separate actions were filed to recover
damages, and both actions were appealed, the determination, in
the one appeal, of the sufficiency of the complaint, and of the evidence to show that defendants' negligence was the proximate
cause of the injury, is conclusive in the other appeal, where the
complaint and evidence are practically the same in each case.
                          Cleveland, etc., R. Co. v. *Clark*, 646, 649 (1).

(B)   As to Instructions.

65. *Invading Province of Jury.*—*Refusal.*—An instruction which
invades the province of the jury is properly refused.
                          Lake Shore, etc., R. Co. v. *Myers*, 59, 71 (13).

66. *Assumption of Facts.*—An instruction assuming a fact about
which the evidence is undisputed is not erroneous.
                Terre Haute, etc., Traction Co. v. *Maberry*, 114, 121 (5).

67. *Consideration as a Whole.*—Instructions given in a case should
be considered as a whole, and a separate instruction will not be
held erroneous for the omission of a point covered by other instructions. *Terre Haute, etc., Traction Co.* v. *Maberry*, 114, 123 (9).

68. *Consideration as a Whole.*—On appeal instructions will be considered as a whole, and if, when so considered, they fairly state
the law, an inaccuracy in a particular instruction will not cause a
reversal.   *Southern R. Co.* v. *Friedley*, 192, 196 (6).

69. *Record.*—Where the record fails to disclose an order of court
that the instructions be made a part of the record, they are not

APPEAL—Continued.

properly in the record under the provisions of §691 Burns 1908, §650 R. S. 1881. *Newsom v. Chicago, etc., R. Co.,* 577, 580 (4).

70. *Record.*—Instructions that are not authenticated by the signature of the judge are not properly in the record under the provisions of §561 Burns 1908, Acts 1907 p. 652.

Newsom v. Chicago, etc., R. Co., 577, 580 (3).

71. *Refusal.*—The refusal of requested instructions, that were covered by others given, was not error.

Vandalia Coal Co. v. Heverkamp, 397, 403 (6).

72. *Refusal of Instructions.*—The refusal of instructions, that are covered in their essential features by the instructions given, is not error. *Indianapolis Southern R. Co. v. Emmerson,* 403, 416 (11).

73. *Refusal of Instructions.—Inapplicability to Issues.*—A requested instruction, not shown to be applicable to the issues, was properly refused. *Mortimer v. Daub,* 30, 38 (9).

74. *Refusal.*—The refusal of requested instructions that are covered by instructions given, or are inapplicable to the issues and the evidence, is not error. *Espenlaub v. Hedderick,* 139, 142 (7).

75. *Refusal.*—The refusal of requested instructions is not error, where they are fully covered by others given, or where they are not applicable to the evidence. *Barton v. Barton,* 537, 541 (5).

76. *Refusal of Instructions.*—The refusal of requested instructions is not ground for reversal, where, so far as they were proper, they were covered by other instructions given.

Cleveland, etc., R. Co. v. Clark, 646, 651 (4).

77. *Refusal.*—The refusal of tendered instructions is not error, where the law applicable to the issues was correctly and fully stated in the instructions given.

Angola R., etc., Co. v. Butz, 420, 431 (15).

78. *Refusal of Instructions.—Burden of Proof.*—An instruction which in substance stated that plaintiff, to recover, must prove each paragraph of his complaint by a preponderance of the evidence, was properly refused. *Mortimer v. Daub,* 30, 38 (8).

79. *Refusal of Instructions Covered by Others Given.*—The refusal of requested instructions is not error, where the essential elements of such refused instructions were completely covered and better stated in the instructions that were given.

Mortimer v. Daub, 30, 39 (10).

80. *Refusal.—Matter Covered by Other Instructions.*—In an action for personal injuries, where, on the subject of contributory negligence, the jury was instructed that such defense must be proved by a fair preponderance of all the evidence in the case, the refusal of a requested instruction stating that if evidence of contributory negligence appeared from the testimony of plaintiff it would be available to defendant on such question, was not error, although such instruction could properly have been given.

Pittsburgh, etc., R. Co. v. Cottman, 661, 666 (5).

81. *Defect Cured by Other Instructions.*—An instruction, that if plaintiff has proved both paragraphs of the complaint, the jury should find generally for plaintiff, is not objectionable for the omission of any reference to a preponderance of the evidence, where the jury was fully advised on that subject in other instructions given. *Southern R. Co. v. Friedley,* 192, 196 (5).

82. Instructions in an action against a street car company, which attempted only to define certain duties of those in charge of

APPEAL—Continued.

street cars, in the management thereof, for the breach of which
there may be a liability against the company, but not purporting
to state the entire law of the case, were not objectionable on the
ground of ignoring the question of contributory negligence, where
other instructions were given which covered that question, since
the instructions must be considered as a whole.

Mortimer v. *Daub*, 30, 36 (5).

(C)   As TO PLEADINGS.

83. *Answer in Abatement.—Sufficiency.—Failure to Point Out Defect.*—An answer in abatement which appears to state sufficient
facts will be deemed on appeal to be sufficient to withstand a
demurrer, where appellant fails to point out any specific defect
therein.

Moore-Mansfield, etc., Co. v. *Marion, etc., Traction Co.*, 548, 551 (1),

(D)   PRESUMPTIONS.

84. *Failure to Find Fact.*—A failure to find a fact is a finding
against the party having the burden of the issues to which such
fact is relevant. *Downey* v. *National Exchange Bank*, 672, 680 (9).

85. The trial court is presumed to have acted advisedly and correctly in the exclusion of testimony, where the record fails to
show preliminary proof necessary to make it competent, or an
offer to make such proof.   *Hubbard* v. *Ranje*, 611, 617 (7).

86. *Judgment.—Burden of Showing Error.*—On appeal every presumption is indulged in favor of the correctness of the judgment
of the trial court, and the burden is on appellant to show error,
and to point out the same substantially in the manner required
by the rules.   *Cleveland, etc., R. Co.* v. *Beard*, 105, 107 (3).

87. *Weight and Sufficiency of Evidence.—Credibility of Witnesses.*
—On appeal, it will be presumed that the trial court, in passing
on a motion for new trial on the ground that the evidence is insufficient, has considered the credibility of the witnesses and has
weighed their testimony, and that in overruling the motion it was
satisfied with the result.

Pittsburgh, etc., R. Co. v. *Cottman*, 661, 671 (13),

88. *Findings.—Evidence.*—On appeal all presumptions will be indulged in favor of the finding of the trial court, and if there is
any evidence in the record to support the judgment, the same
must be upheld.   *Miller* v. *Farmers State Bank*, 5, 7 (2).

89. *Verdict.—Special Findings.*—Every reasonable presumption will
be indulged in favor of a general verdict, but nothing will be pre
sumed in aid of the special findings of the jury.

Ladoga Can. Co. v. *Corydon Can. Co.*, 23, 27 (2)

90. *Verdict.—Answers to Interrogatories.*—On appeal all reasonable
presumptions are indulged in support of the general verdict and
against the answers to interrogatories, and if the general verdict,
thus aided, is not in irreconcilable conflict with such answers, it
must stand.   *Sanitary Can Co.* v. *McKinney*, 379, 383 (3),

91. *Verdict.—Answers to Interrogatories.*—Every presumption is
indulged in favor of the general verdict as against the answers to
interrogatories, and it is only when the conflict between them and
the general verdict is irreconcilable on any theory, or on any
supposable state of facts provable under the issues, that such
answers will control.

Indianapolis Southern R. Co. v. *Emmerson*, 403, 417 (14).

APPEAL—Continued.

92. *Evidence.—Instructions.*—Where the evidence in an action against a railroad company for killing horses on its track is not in the record on appeal, the court will presume that the evidence of the killing of the horses was without conflict, so that an instruction authorizing a recovery without requiring a finding that the horses were killed by a train will not be held erroneous.
Michigan, etc., R. Co. v. *Farrell,* 603, 608 (5).

(E) VERDICT, ANSWERS TO INTERROGATORIES, FINDINGS AND RULINGS ON MOTIONS.

93. *Refusal to Direct Verdict.*—The refusal to direct a verdict for defendant was not error, where there was evidence tending to support a verdict for plaintiff.
Indianapolis Outfitting Co. v. *Cheyne Electric Co.,* 153, 156 (4).

94. *Verdict.—Evidence.*—In determining the sufficiency of the evidence to support a verdict, the court will not weigh the evidence, but will consider only that most favorable to appellee.
Vandalia Coal Co. v. *Haverkamp,* 397, 402 (4).

95. *Verdict.—Evidence.—Sufficiency.*—Where there is some evidence on each fact essential to its support, a verdict will not be set aside on the ground of insufficient evidence.
Indianapolis Southern R. Co. v. *Emmerson,* 408, 418 (15)

96. *Verdict.—Evidence.—Sufficiency.*—The court on appeal cannot weigh conflicting evidence, and where there is some evidence tending to support the verdict, although a strong preponderance seems to be in favor of appellant, the verdict will not be disturbed on the ground of insufficient evidence.
Pittsburgh, etc., R. Co. v. *Cottman,* 661, 668 (8).

97. *Verdict.—Evidence.—Sufficiency.*—On appeal, in determining whether the verdict is supported by the evidence, the court can consider only the evidence which tends to sustain the verdict, and must ignore all evidence to the contrary.
Pittsburgh, etc., R. Co. v. *Cottman,* 661, 670 (10).

98. *Conflicting Evidence.—Verdict.—Conclusiveness.*—The verdict of a jury on a question of fact, where the evidence is conflicting or is of such character that reasonable minds might draw opposite inferences therefrom, will not be disturbed on appeal.
Espenlaub v. *Hedderick,* 139, 142 (6).

99. *Verdict.—Answers to Interrogatories.*—In considering a motion for judgment on answers to interrogatories notwithstanding the general verdict, all evidence admissible under the issues will be treated as actually in the record, and the court will indulge every reasonable presumption in favor of the general verdict and reconcile such answers therewith, if possible on any reasonable theory within the issues.
Osborn v. *Adams Brick Co.,* 175, 188 (16).

100. *Verdict.—Answers to Interrogatories.*—A general verdict will not be set aside on appeal on answers to interrogatories that are not in irreconcilable conflict therewith.
Lake Shore, etc., R. Co. v. *Myers,* 59, 66 (7).

101. *Verdict.—Answers to Interrogatories.*—In determining the correctness of the trial court's ruling on a motion for judgment on answers to interrogatories, only the pleadings, the general verdict, and the interrogatories and answers, will be considered.
Indianapolis Southern R. Co. v. *Emmerson,* 408, 417 (13).

APPEAL—Continued.

102. *Verdict.—Answers to Interrogatories.—Motion for Judgment on Answers.*—In determining whether the trial court in overruling a motion for judgment on the answers to interrogatories notwithstanding the general verdict, the investigation is confined to the complaint. the interrogatories and the answers thereto, and the general verdict.
Columbia Creosoting Co. v. *Beard*, 260, 262 (1).

103. *Verdict.—Answers to Interrogatories.—Conclusions.—Ruling on Motion for Judgment.*—The objection that some of the findings included in the answers to interrogatories are statements of conclusions, and not facts, does not affect the question presented by the motion for judgment on such answers, where the general verdict includes a finding of facts covering practically the same proposition.
Angola R., etc., Co. v. *Butz*, 420, 428 (8).

104. *Verdict.—Answers to Interrogatories.*—The antagonism between the general verdict and the answers to interrogatories must be apparent on the face of the record and beyond the possibility of being removed by any evidence within the issues, before the court is authorized to direct a judgment on such answers.
Sanitary Can Co. v. *McKinney*, 379, 383 (4).

105. *Judgment on Answers to Interrogatories.—Disposition of Cause.*—Where, on appeal, the facts are complicated and close questions of law are involved, and reversible error is found in the action of the trial court in rendering judgment *non obstante verdicto*, a new trial will be ordered rather than judgment on the general verdict.
Osborn v. *Adams Brick Co.*, 175, 189 (18), 190 (18).

106. *Ruling on Motion for Judgment on Answers to Interrogatories.*—In determining questions presented by an assignment of errors in overruling a motion for judgment on the answers to interrogatories notwithstanding the general verdict, only the general verdict, the complaint and answer, and the interrogatories and the answers thereto, will be considered.
Southern R. Co. v. *Utz*, 270, 272 (1).

107. *Ruling on Motion for Judgment on Answers to Interrogatories.—Evidence.—Instructions.—Consideration.*—In considering the question presented on appeal by the ruling of the trial court on a motion for judgment on the answers to interrogatories notwithstanding the general verdict, the court will look neither to the evidence nor to the instructions given.
Southern R. Co. v. *Utz*, 270, 275 (4).

108. *Answers to Interrogatories.—Motion for Judgment.—Evidence Not in Record.*—Where the evidence is not in the record on appeal, the court will not reverse the trial court for overruling a motion for judgment on the answers to interrogatories notwithstanding the general verdict, unless the conflict between such answers and the general verdict is such that it could not be removed by any evidence legitimately admissible under the issues, and will presume that such evidence was before the jury.
National Biscuit Co. v. *Wilson*, 630, 633 (2).

108a. *Questions Presented for Review.—Motion for New Trial.—Grounds.—Special Verdict.*—No question is raised on appeal by the grounds of a motion for a new trial, that the special verdict is not sustained by sufficient evidence, and is contrary to law.
Indianapolis Southern R. Co. v. *Emmerson*, 403, 419 (16).

108b. *Objection to Form of Judgment.—Presenting Question for Review.—Motion for New Trial.*—Questions arising on the form of

APPEAL—Continued.

a judgment are not presented by a motion for a new trial, on the ground that the decision is not sustained by sufficient evidence, except in cases where the facts are specially found and an error in the finding is carried into the judgment, but such questions are saved by objection and exception made at the time the judgment is rendered, or by a motion to modify or correct.
Kreitlein v. *Ferger*, 199, 209 (8), 210 (8).

109. *Ruling on Motion to Modify Judgment.*—Where a motion to modify a judgment questions the validity of the judgment, and not its form, the same is properly overruled.
Cooley v. *Kelley*, 687, 694 (5).

110. *Ruling on Motion for New Trial.*—A finding will not be reversed on alleged error in overruling the motion for new trial, based on the ground that the evidence is insufficient and that the finding is contrary to law, and that the court failed to find facts supported by the evidence, where there is not a total want of evidence to support the findings, and it is not shown that any material fact, supported by undisputed evidence, has been omitted from the finding.
Downey v. *National Exchange Bank*, 672, 680 (8).

111. *Findings.—Evidence.*—Where there is some evidence to sustain the finding of the trial court, the evidence will not be weighed on appeal. *Holthouse* v. *Poling*, 568, 572 (5).

112. *Findings.—Evidence.*—In the absence of evidence to the contrary, the court on appeal cannot say that the amount of attorney's fees allowed by the trial court, based on the testimony of a practicing attorney, is either against the evidence or in conflict therewith. *Holthouse* v. *Poling*, 568, 573 (7).

113. *Findings.—Motion for Judgment Notwithstanding Findings.*—Error cannot be predicated on the overruling of a motion for judgment notwithstanding the findings of the court, where under the circumstances, the alleged findings amount to but a general one. *Cooley* v. *Kelley*, 687, 694 (4).

114. *Findings.—Motion for Venire de Novo.*—Overruling a motion for a *venire de novo* is not error where the finding is general, since the motion reaches only matters of form, and can only be sustained when the finding is so defective and uncertain that no judgment can be rendered thereon. *Cooley* v. *Kelley*, 687, 693 (3).

115. *Record.—Findings.—Opinion of Trial Court.*—Where the record on appeal fails to disclose a request that the trial court render special findings, the opinion delivered by the trial court in announcing its decision, although carried into the record, will be regarded merely as a general finding.
Cooley v. *Kelley*, 687, 693 (2).

116. *Special Findings.—Conclusions of Law.*—Although a complaint, attacked for the first time on appeal, is found sufficient, the question of whether the facts provable thereunder have been so fully and correctly found as to sustain the conclusions and support the judgment of the trial court must be determined on the exceptions to the conclusions of law.
Town of Cicero v. *Lake Erie, etc., R. Co.*, 298, 308 (7).

(F) HARMLESS ERROR.

117. *Evidence.*—The erroneous admission of evidence which in no way affected the result of the case, was harmless.
Lake Shore, etc., R. Co. v. *Myers*, 59, 75 (16).

APPEAL—Continued.

118. *Admission of Evidence.*—Error, if any, in the admission of evidence which was not of a character to harm appellant, will not work a reversal. *Angola R., etc., Co.* v. *Butz,* 420, 431 (16).

119. *Admission of Testimony.*—Error, if any, in the admission of testimony, is not cause for a reversal, where the findings and judgment of the trial court show that such testimony was disregarded. *Pittsburgh, etc., R. Co.* v. *Johnson,* 457, 477 (12).

120. *Admission of Evidence.*—In an action against a railroad company and a construction company for the death of plaintiff's decedent who was struck by a construction train at a crossing, error, if any, in admitting evidence as to the defective condition of the crossing could not have harmed the defendant construction company, where, under the pleadings, it was not charged with any responsibility for the condition of such crossing.
Cleveland, etc., R. Co. v. *Clark,* 646, 651 (7).

121. *Admission of Pleading as Evidence.*—Where plaintiff offered in evidence a special answer, pleaded by defendant in addition to the general denial and specifically admitting the facts averred in the complaint, the error, if any, in its admission is not available to plaintiff on appeal. *Cooley* v. *Kelley,* 687, 694 (6).

122. *Exclusion of Evidence.*—Error, if any, in the exclusion of evidence, is harmless, where the record discloses that substantially the same facts were proved in another way.
Koehler v. *Harmon,* 315, 318 (3).

123. *Exclusion of Evidence.—Affirmance.*—Where it appears that the trial court reached a correct result which would not have been affected by the admission of evidence which was excluded, the error, if any, is not cause for reversal.
Griffith v. *Felts,* 268, 270 (3).

124. *Unsupported Finding of Fact.*—Even though a finding of fact is wholly unsupported by the evidence, it is not cause for reversal, where such fact was wholly immaterial to the decision of the case. *Downey* v. *National Exchange Bank,* 672, 680 (10).

125. *Instructions.*—A judgment will not be reversed for error in an instruction, where, by answers to interrogatories, it is shown that appellant was not harmed.
Angola R., etc., Co. v. *Butz,* 420, 431 (14).

126. *Instructions.*—Error, if any, in omitting the element of contributory negligence from instructions, given in an action for damages for personal injuries, was harmless, where it was not contended at the trial that plaintiff was guilty of contributory negligence, and the evidence does not indicate that he was at any time at fault. *Mortimer* v. *Daub,* 30, 37 (6).

127. *Refusal of Instructions.*—Reversible error cannot be predicated on the refusal of a requested instruction that was fully and properly covered by instructions given.
Ohlwine v. *Pfaffman,* 357, 362 (3).

128. *Instructions.—Refusal.*—The refusal of requested instructions is not reversible error, where the instructions given were applicable to the issues and fully and fairly stated the law.
Cleveland, etc., R. Co. v. *Nichols,* 349, 355 (7).

129. *Instructions.—Mistake in Use of Word.*—Where a mistake in the use of words in an instruction is so obvious that the jury could not have been misled, the error will be deemed immaterial.
Cleveland, etc., R. Co. v. *Clark,* 646, 650 (3).

APPEAL—Continued.

130. *Instructions.*—An instruction that although a common carrier of passengers does not insure the safety of its passengers the law will not tolerate any negligence on the part of the carrier, though inaccurate in failing to limit the negligence to that charged in the complaint, is harmless where the omission was covered by other instructions given.

Southern R. Co. v. Adams, 322, 331 (10).

131. *Instructions.*—*Damages.*—In an action on a fire policy, which stipulated that the company would not be liable in the event of loss for an amount greater than three-fourths of the actual cash value of the property covered by the items of the policy at the time of the loss, error in an instruction which did not accurately state the rule for the measurement of damages, was harmless, where the damages assessed were in a sum less than the amount of the aggregate three-fourths of the value of the items, as shown by the evidence, together with interest on the sum that would be properly chargeable against defendant.

Northern Assurance Co. v. Carpenter, 432, 434 (1).

132. *Amount of Recovery.*—While error in the amount of recovery, whether too large or too small, is a statutory cause for new trial, appellant cannot avail himself thereof, where the verdict against him was for $400 less than it should have been, as shown by the evidence, since it is manifest that he was not harmed thereby.

Croan v. Myers, 143, 148 (6).

133. *Overruling Demurrer to Answer.*—Overruling a demurrer to a paragraph of answer, even if erroneous, is harmless, where the finding is for plaintiff on the complaint.

Pittsburgh, etc., R. Co. v. Johnson, 457, 466 (2).

134. *Ruling on Demurrer.*—Overruling a demurrer to an answer is harmless where the facts alleged are provable under the general denial. *Campbell v. Maryland Casualty Co.*, 228, 231 (2).

135. *Ruling on Demurrer.*—Overruling a demurrer to a bad paragraph of answer is harmless, where the matters averred therein are provable under the general denial.

Heston v. Dougan, 40, 45 (2).

136. *Ruling on Demurrer.*—Error, if any, in overruling appellant's demurrer to a paragraph of answer, was harmless, where the finding was in appellant's favor.

Ladoga Can. Co. v. Corydon Can. Co., 23, 28 (6).

137. *Rulings on Demurrers to Answers Pleading Statute of Limitations.*—Where a cause of action was barred by the six years' statute of limitations, §294 Burns 1908, §292 R. S. 1881, which was pleaded, the action of the court in overruling demurrers to paragraphs of answer pleading the other statutes of limitations was harmless. *Siegmund v. Tyner*, 581, 584 (4).

138. *Misconduct of Counsel.*—*Refusal to Set Aside Submission of Cause.*—Where counsel indulged in improper remarks in argument, and the court instructed the jury to disregard them, the refusal of the court to set aside the submission of the cause will not work a reversal, where there is nothing in the record to overcome the presumption that the instructions were heeded, or indicating that appellants were thereby prevented from having a fair trial. *Southern R. Co. v. Adams*, 322, 329 (6).

139. *Ruling on Motion to Dismiss.*—Where an action was brought before a justice of the peace to recover $200 for material fur-

APPEAL—Continued.

nished and labor performed at the special instance and request of defendant, and, on appeal to the superior court, plaintiff filed an additional paragraph of complaint to recover the same amount on the theory of an express contract, error in overruling defendant's motion to dismiss the action, on the ground that the court had not jurisdiction of the subject-matter, was harmless, where, after such ruling the plaintiff dismissed such additional paragraph and proceeded to trial on the original complaint.
Indianapolis Outfitting Co. v. *Cheyne Electric Co.*, 153, 154 (1).

IX. DETERMINATION AND DISPOSITION OF CAUSE.

(A) DECISIONS IN GENERAL.

140. *Exceptions to Conclusions of Law.—Admissions.*—An exception to the conclusions of law concedes, for the purpose of the exception, that the facts are fully and correctly found.
State, ex rel., v. *Jackson,* 254, 260 (9).

141. *Error in Form of Judgment.—Disposition of Cause.*—In an action on a judgment with relief and without exemption, error in rendering judgment with benefit of exemption and, without relief, will not operate as a cause for reversal on appeal, but the judgment will be ordered cured by a modification.
Krettlein v. *Ferger,* 199, 211 (9).

142. *Theory of Action.*—Where the assignee of a contract, granting the right to maintain a gas main on the right of way of a railroad company, sued to enjoin the company from removing such main, and the company defended on the theory that the contract was not assignable and that plaintiff obtained no rights by virtue of such assignment, it will be held to such theory on appeal, and cannot adopt the theory that plaintiff has no rights because the evidence fails to show that the stipulated rental was paid.
Lake Erie, etc., R. Co. v. *Marott,* 332, 341 (6).

(B) AFFIRMANCE.

143. Where there is ample evidence to support the verdict, and no prejudicial error is shown by the record, the judgment must be affirmed.
Barton v. *Barton,* 537, 542 (6).

144. A judgment will be affirmed, where it appears that the case was fully and fairly presented to the jury and that substantial justice has been accomplished.
Heston v. *Dougan,* 40, 52 (12).

145. *Burden of Showing Error.*—Appellant must show prejudicial error, to obtain relief on appeal, since a judgment will be affirmed where the only errors disclosed by the record were harmless.
Lake Shore, etc., R. Co. v. *Myers,* 59, 74 (15).

146. *Harmless Error.*—A judgment will not be reversed on account of an error which did not prejudice the substantial rights of the party complaining.
Indianapolis Outfitting Co. v. *Cheyne Electric Co.*, 153, 155 (2).

147. *Verdict.—Evidence.*—The fact that the evidence may be weak, or unsatisfactory, will not authorize a reversal, if there is some evidence to support the verdict in every material respect.
Vandalia Coal Co. v. *Haverkamp,* 397, 402 (5).

(C) REVERSAL.

148. *Error Warranting Reversal.*—A judgment will be reversed for error only when it is shown to have been prejudicial to the complaining party.
Croan v. *Myers,* 143, 148 (7).

APPEAL—Continued.

149. *Scope.*—On reversing a judgment and ordering further proceedings, the court will not anticipate and decide questions not presented by the record, and which may never arise.

Southern R. Co. v. *Town of French Lick*, 447, 456 (13).

APPELLATE COURT—

See Courts 1, 3.

APPLICATION—

Conditions in, see Bonds 2.

APPROPRIATION—

Of railroad property for street, see Injunction 4-6.
Subsequent, for street, see Eminent Domain 2-4.

ARGUMENT OF COUNSEL—

Objections to, should be directed to the objectionable part and not to the whole statement, see Trial 3.

ARREST OF JUGMENT—

Complaint sufficient on motion in, see Pleading 10.

ASSIGNMENT OF ERRORS—

See Appeal 30-36.

ASSUMPTION—

The court on appeal has no right to assume that a trial court will consider question not presented by the pleadings then on file, see Appeal 3.

ASSUMPTION OF RISK—

See Master and Servant 11, 34-42.

AUTHORITY—

Of agent, see Principal and Agent 8-14.

BANKRUPTCY—

Certificate of discharge in, see Evidence 13.
Defense of discharge in, see Judgment 6.

1. *Provable Debts.—Judgment.*—A judgment is a provable debt under §63a (1) of the bankruptcy act of 1898 as amended in 1903. (1 Fed. Stat. Annot. 679.)

Kreitlein v. *Ferger*, 199, 205 (3).

2. *Discharge.—Debts Affected.*—Under the provisions of the bankruptcy act of 1898, as amended in 1903, a discharge in bankruptcy does not operate as a discharge of all the debts of the bankrupt. but releases him from all provable debts, except as therein otherwise specially provided. *Kreitlein* v. *Ferger*, 199, 204 (2).

3. *Debts Discharged.—Notice.*—Under the bankruptcy act of 1898, as amended in 1908, providing that debts not duly scheduled in time for proof and allowance, with the name of the creditor, if known to the bankrupt, are not affected by a discharge in bank-

BANKRUPTCY—Continued.

ruptcy, unless the creditor had actual knowledge of the proceeding in bankruptcy, and providing that, in his list of creditors, the bankrupt shall show the residence of each creditor, if known, a debt was not discharged by a bankruptcy proceeding, where the schedule of the debt gave only the initial, instead of the full Christian name, of the creditor, and gave his residence as Indianapolis, without any street or number, and such creditor received no actual notice of the proceedings.

Kreitlein v. *Ferger*, 199, 205 (4), 206 (4).

BANKS AND BANKING—

1. *Deposit of Check.—Character of Deposit.—Duty to Depositor.—*Where the transaction of depositing a check amounts to a sale thereof to the bank, a bank to which it is subsequently passed for collection is not the agent of such depositor and owes no duty in respect to its collection.

Downey v. *National Exchange Bank*, 672, 679 (6).

2. *Deposit of Check.—Return of Check to Depositor.—Effect.—*Where a check which has been deposited as cash and sent out for collection is returned to the bank in which it was deposited, and is by such bank charged to the account of the depositor, and is turned over to him and accepted by him, the transaction amounts to a resale of the check to such depositor.

Downey v. *National Exchange Bank*, 672, 680 (7).

3. *Deposit of Check.—Character of Deposit.—Presumption.—*Where a check, bearing an indorsement not indicating that it was indorsed for collection, is passed to the credit of the depositor as cash, and nothing further appears, the presumption arises that the transaction constitutes a sale of the check to the bank, but such presumption may be rebutted by facts or circumstances showing a contrary intention.

Downey v. *National Exchange Bank*, 672, 678 (5).

4. *Deposit of Check.—Deposit as Cash.—*Where there is a definite agreement that a check is deposited as cash, the title passes to the bank and it has a right to control its collection and receive the proceeds.   *Downey* v. *National Exchange Bank*, 672, 677 (4).

5. *Deposit of Check for Collection.—Agency.—*Where a check is indorsed for collection, or where there is a definite understanding that such is the purpose of the parties, or where the memorandum of deposit shows that it is deposited as a check, it remains the property of the depositor and the bank holds it as his agent for collection.   *Downey* v. *National Exchange Bank*, 672, 677 (3).

6. *Deposit of Check.—Character of Deposit.—*The question of whether a check deposited by the payee in a bank other than the one on which it is drawn amounts to a sale of the check, or merely constitutes a deposit of same for collection, must be determined from the facts and circumstances attending the transaction.

Downey v. *National Exchange Bank*, 672, 677 (2).

7. *Deposit of Check for Collection.—Agency.—Liability.—*Where a check is deposited with a bank for collection, a privity of contract exists between the depositor and each bank through which the check passes, whereby a duty is imposed to use reasonable care and diligence in its collection and renders that bank, whose negligence or misconduct results in the loss of the debt, liable to the depositor.   *Downey* v. *National Exchange Bank*, 672, 676 (1).

BILL OF EXCEPTIONS—

See EXCEPTIONS, BILL OF.

BILL OF PARTICULARS—

See CONTRACTS 7; PLEADING 17.

BILLS AND NOTES—

See PRINCIPAL AND AGENT 2, 13, 14.

1. *Action.—Defenses.*—Where a husband upon lending money took a note payable to his wife, the wife's delivery of the note to defendant after the death of the husband, pursuant to the husband's request, is no defense to an action thereon, in the absence of averments showing a gift, or that it was delivered pursuant to an agreement based on a sufficient consideration.

Croan v. *Myers,* 143, 146 (3).

2. *Action.—Answer.—Sufficiency.*—In an action on an ordinary promissory note, appearing on its face to be complete, an answer admitting its execution but alleging that an oral agreement was made at the time, whereby the note was not to be paid in the event an enterprise, in furtherance of which it was executed, should terminate unsuccessfully, and that such enterprise had failed, is insufficient in the absence of a showing that fraud or mistake entered into the transaction.

Croan v. *Myers,* 143, 144 (1).

3. *Note Executed by Agent.—Evidence.*—In an action on a promissory note to which defendant's name had been signed by his son, where there was evidence that defendant had given his son general authority to use his name on notes, the introduction of the note in evidence was not erroneous.

Miller v. *Farmers State Bank,* 5, 11 (6).

4. *Note Payable to Wife for Money Loaned by Husband.—Consideration.—Presumptions.*—Where a husband upon lending his money, took a note payable to his wife, it will be presumed, in the absence of any averment to the contrary, that the note was so made on a sufficient consideration.

Croan v. *Myers,* 143, 147 (4).

BOARD OF COMMISSIONERS—

Is a perpetual body not affected by changes in its membership, see LIMITATION OF ACTIONS 7.

BONDS—

Sureties on, must be named and approved by the court during the term at which the final judgment is rendered, see APPEAL 17.

1. *Fidelity Bonds.—Liability.—Estoppel.—Failure to Return Premium.*—A surety company is not estopped, by failure to return premium, from setting up the defense of forfeiture of a bond securing an employer against embezzlement by his sales manager, occasioned by the employer's breach of conditions binding him to require such manager to furnish daily reports, monthly statements, etc., where the bond was valid and in force when issued.

Marion, etc., Bed Co. v. *Empire State Surety Co.,* 480, 484 (2).

2. *Fidelity Bonds.—Conditions in Application.—Breach.—Effect.*—Where a bond to secure an employer against embezzlement by a sales manager, was issued by a surety company on such employ-

BONDS—Continued.

er's representation in the application that daily reports and monthly statements would be required of such manager, and that a representative would check up his accounts, such representations were conditions precedent, a breach of which would prevent a recovery on the bond, in the absence of a waiver thereof by the surety.

Marion, etc., Bed Co. v. Empire State Surety Co., 480, 484 (1).

3. *Fidelity Bonds.—Breach of Conditions.—Forfeiture.—Waiver.—* The right of a surety company to declare the forfeiture of a bond, executed to secure an employer against embezzlement by his employe, because of the employer's breach of conditions binding him to require the employe to furnish daily reports, monthly statements, etc., is not waived by the company's request for the prosecution of the defaulting employe, in the absence of a showing that it knew of such breaches by the employer prior to the time of requesting the prosecution of such employe.

Marion, etc., Bed Co. v. Empire State Surety Co., 480, 487 (3).

BREACH—

See BONDS 2.

Of contract, see DAMAGES 1; MUNICIPAL CORPORATIONS 21, 22; WILLS 1.

Of contract to bequeath or devise, see LIMITATION OF ACTIONS 2, 3.

Negligence arises on the, of a legal duty to use care, see NEGLIGENCE 5.

Of warranty, see CONTRACTS 15.

BRIEFS—

See APPEAL 32, 33, 37-46.

BURDEN OF PROOF—

See DEEDS 4; MORTGAGES; RAILROADS 1; TRIAL 19.

One who alleges and relies on concealment to avoid the statute of limitations has the burden of proving same, see LIMITATION OF ACTIONS 4.

BY-LAWS—

See INSURANCE 11-13, 18.

CARRIERS—

1. *Passengers.—Contract Relation.—*The law implies a contract between passenger and carrier, that the latter shall carry the passenger safely, so far as human foresight, reasonably exercised, can guard against disaster.

Indianapolis Southern R. Co. v. Emmerson, 403, 409 (1).

2. *Duty.—Injury to Passengers.—Liability.—*A carrier is required to exercise the highest degree of care to secure the safety of passengers, and is responsible for the slightest neglect which is the proximate cause of injury to a passenger who is himself without fault. *Indianapolis Southern R. Co. v. Emmerson*, 403, 409 (2).

3. *Injury to Passengers.—Derailment of Train.—Particular Defects.—Proof.—*Where a passenger, in an action for injuries caused by the derailment of a train, alleged a number of defects

CARRIERS—Continued.

as cause for the derailment, proof that the derailment was occasioned by any one or more of the causes alleged would warrant a finding for plaintiff. *Southern R. Co.* v. *Adams*, 322, 328 (4).

4. *Injury to Passengers.—Derailment of Train.—Instructions.—Refusal.*—Where, in a passenger's action for injuries caused by the derailment of a train, plaintiff alleged that the derailment was caused by defective axles, defective tracks and excessive speed, a requested instruction that to be entitled to recover the plaintiff must prove that the derailment was the result of the three causes combined was properly refused. *Southern R. Co.* v. *Adams*, 322, 330 (8).

5. *Injury to Passengers.—Derailment of Train—Complaint.—Allegation of Particular Defects.—Proof.*—Where the complaint, in a passenger's action for injuries caused by the derailment of a train, alleges the particular defects that caused the derailment, the carrier is relieved from the burden of disproving or meeting any other negligence in regard to the derailment than that alleged, nor can the plaintiff prove any other causes than those alleged. *Southern R. Co.* v. *Adams*, 322, 327 (2).

6. *Injury to Passengers.—Derailment of Train.—Negligence.—Presumptions.*—In a passenger's action for injuries caused by the derailment of a train, proof of the relation of carrier and passenger, and a derailment resulting in injury to the passenger, creates a presumption of negligence on the part of the carrier, entitling plaintiff to recover, unless it is removed by evidence, and plaintiff is not deprived of such presumption by the fact that he has alleged specific acts of negligence as causing the derailment. *Southern R. Co.* v. *Adams*, 322, 330 (7).

7. *Injury to Passengers.—Negligence.—Derailment of Train.—Res Ipsa Loquitur.—Complaint.*—Where the complaint, in an action against a railroad company for personal injuries, clearly shows that the relation of carrier and passenger existed, and that the plaintiff was injured by the derailment of the train, the rule of *res ipsa loquitur* applies, notwithstanding several causes are alleged to have produced the derailment. *Southern R. Co.* v. *Adams*, 322, 326 (1).

8. *Injury to Passengers.—Verdict.—Answers to Interrogatories.—Construction.*—In an action by a railway mail clerk for personal injuries sustained while transferring mail from one of defendant's trains to another, affirmative answers to interrogatories propounded to the jury asking whether the fact that plaintiff was a railway mail clerk was sole reason for plaintiff being on the train and on the platform, and answers to other questions showing that he had paid nothing to ride, are not equivalent to a finding that plaintiff was not a passenger. *Southern R. Co.* v. *Utz*, 270, 275 (5).

9. *Injury to Passengers.—Evidence.—Admissibility.—Contributory Negligence.*—In a passenger's action for injuries in being thrown from a train by the sudden jerking of the train while plaintiff was standing near the door preparatory to alighting at a station, evidence in relation to plaintiff's experience in riding on trains, and her information as to the length of time the train stopped at the station, was admissible as affecting the question of whether she was guilty of negligence contributing to her injury. *Indianapolis Southern R. Co.* v. *Emmerson*, 403, 419 (17).

CARRIERS—Continued.

10. *Injury to Passengers.—Negligence.—Instructions.*—An instruction, in a passenger's action for injuries, that if defendant was guilty of other negligence than that charged, there can be no recovery, was properly refused, since its effect was that, even though defendant was guilty of the negligence charged, and it was the proximate cause of the injury, plaintiff could not recover if the jury found that defendant was also guilty of other negligence.   *Indianapolis Southern R. Co.* v. *Emmerson,* 403, 415 (8).

11. *Injury to Passengers.—Presumption of Negligence.—Instructions.*—In a passenger's action for injuries, an instruction that if a carrier provides perfect machinery, cars and roadbed, and the servants in charge of same are negligent, there is a breach of duty, and a presumption of negligence arises in favor of the passenger injured without fault by the negligent operation of the train, the same as it would in case the injury flowed from defective track, cars, or machinery, is not open to the objection that it tells the jury that defendant's negligence will be presumed from the injury regardless of the circumstances under which it was received.   *Indianapolis Southern R. Co.* v. *Emmerson,* 403, 413 (6).

12. *Injury to Passengers.—Presumption of Negligence.—Instructions.—Reference to Complaint.*—An instruction, in a passenger's action for personal injuries from being thrown from a train, that if, plaintiff has proved by a fair preponderance of the evidence that she was a passenger on defendant's train, "and that she was jerked or thrown therefrom and injured as charged in her complaint, without any fault on her part," such facts would raise a presumption of negligence on the part of defendant, and that defendant would have the burden of proving that the injury could not have been avoided by the highest practical care and diligence, in order to rebut such presumption, did not tell the jury that proof of the injury alone would create a presumption of negligence, but stated as an express condition that the injury must be shown to have occurred in the manner charged in the complaint, and without fault on plaintiff's part, and therefore was not erroneous.   *Indianapolis Southern R. Co.* v. *Emmerson,* 403, 411 (5).

13. *Injury to Passengers.—Complaint.—Sufficiency.*—Where the complaint, in an action for injury to a passenger by the derailment of a train, charged negligence in three respects, namely, defective track, defective axles and excessive speed, and further alleged that thereby and on account of the negligent and careless manner in which the train was run and managed, it was derailed and plaintiff was thereby injured, sufficiently charged that the derailment was caused by the negligence of defendant and that such negligence was the proximate cause of the injury.
    Southern R. Co. v. *Adams,* 322, 328 (3).

14. *Injury to Passengers.—Complaint.*—In a passenger's action for injuries caused by being thrown from a train while standing near the door of the car preparatory to alighting, a complaint alleging that after defendant's agents had called the station, and at a time when, according to usage and custom, passengers were making preparation to leave the train at said station, defendant's agents, well knowing such custom and that passengers were preparing to leave the train, and that they were likely to be standing in the aisles, "negligently, unnecessarily and suddenly increased the speed of said train and unnecessarily and negligently jerked said coach," etc., whereby plaintiff was thrown and injured, sufficiently charges negligence so as to withstand a demurrer, in the

CARRIERS—Continued.

absence of specific averments that overcome the effect of those constituting such charge.
Indianapolis Southern R. Co. v. *Emmerson*, 403, 410 (4).

15. *Injury to Passengers.—Railway Mail Clerk.—Complaint.—Verdict.—Answers to Interrogatories.*—In an action by a railway mail clerk for injuries sustained while transferring mail from one of defendant's trains to another, the averments in the complaint that plaintiff was being carried on defendant's train in the character of a postal clerk in the service of the United States, in charge of United States mail, under a contract between defendant and the United States, were sufficient, under §4000 R. S. U. S. making it the duty of railroad companies carrying mail to carry without extra charge the person in charge thereof, to show the relation of passenger and carrier, so that a general verdict for plaintiff was equivalent to a finding that he was a passenger at the time of his injury and answers to interrogatories, showing that plaintiff was on the train solely because of his position as a railway mail clerk, are consistent, rather than inconsistent, with such verdict.　　　　　*Southern R. Co.* v. *Utz*, 270, 277 (7).

16. *Injury to Passengers.—Contributory Negligence.—Children.—Instructions.*—Where, in a passenger's action defended on the ground that plaintiff contributed to her injury by leaving her seat before the train had stopped, there was evidence that plaintiff was sixteen years of age and had comparatively no experience in riding on trains, that the brakeman had twice announced the station, that the train had slowed down, and that plaintiff, believing that it was nearing the station, and with information that it stopped but a few seconds, left her seat and walked to the door through which the brakeman had passed when, by a sudden jerk of the train, she was thrown and injured, an instruction that recovery could not be defeated on the ground of contributory negligence, if considering her age and experience and all the surrounding circumstances, plaintiff acted as a reasonably prudent person, similarly situated, would have acted, was proper and applicable to the evidence.
Indianapolis Southern R. Co. v. *Emmerson*, 403, 413 (7).

CASES—

OVERRULED:

Price v. *Huddleston* (1905), 36 Ind. App. 450, see *Penn, etc., Plate Glass Co.* v. *Poling*, 492, 494 (2).

South Bend, etc., Plow Co. v. *Cissne* (1905), 35 Ind. App. 373, see *I. F. Force Handle Co.* v. *Hisey*, 235, 242 (3).

Yanthis v. *Kemp* (1907), 40 Ind. App. 649, see *Penn, etc., Plate Glass Co.* v. *Poling*, 492, 494 (2).

CESTUI QUE TRUST—

See TRUSTS 10, 11.

CHATTEL MORTGAGES—

1. *Location of Property.—Residence of Mortgagor.*—The presence of chattels in a county other than that of the residence of the mortgagor does not warrant the assumption that the mortgagor resides in such county.　　*Fife* v. *Ohio Investment Co.*, 108, 113 (6).

2. *Record.—Failure to Record in County Where Mortgagor Resides.—Effect.*—The failure of the mortgagee of chattels to record

CHATTEL MORTGAGES—Continued.

the mortgage in the county where the mortgagor resided at the time of its execution, as required by §7472 Burns 1908, Acts 1897 p. 240, renders such mortgage void as against the right of possession of one holding by virtue of a prior valid mortgage.

Fife v. *Ohio Investment Co.*, 108, 112 (3), 113 (3).

3. *Removal of Property.—Consent of Mortgagee.—Effect.*—The removal of mortgaged chattels to another county without the consent of the mortgagee, does not invalidate the mortgage, since §2299 Burns 1908, Acts 1905 p. 584, §406, making it a penal offense to remove mortgaged property from the county in which the mortgagor resides without the written consent of the mortgagee, in so far as it relates to the personal rights of the parties, is for the protection of the mortgagee, but does not affect the validity of the mortgage. *Fife* v. *Ohio Investment Co.*, 108, 113 (5).

4. *Priority.—Estoppel.*—Where the mortgagor of chattels removed the goods to another county without the consent of the mortgagee, the mere fact that the mortgagee acquiesced in the keeping of the goods in the county to which they had been removed, and made collections from the mortgagor while the property was in such county, and, on failure of the mortgagor to make a payment, suggested that he borrow the money to make such payment, and received part of the money which the mortgagor borrowed, does not estop the mortgagee from questioning the validity of a second mortgage executed for the money borrowed pursuant to such suggestion and recorded in the county to which the property had been removed. *Fife* v. *Ohio Investment Co.*, 108, 111 (1).

5. *Application of Proceeds of Second Mortgage to Payment of Debt Secured by First Mortgage.—Subrogation.*—Where the mortgagor of chattels removed the goods to another county without the consent of the mortgagee, and the mortgagee thereafter acquiesced in such removal and the keeping of the property in the county to which it had been removed, and, on failure of the mortgagor to make a payment, suggested that he borrow the money to make such payment, and the mortgagor thereupon borrowed $84 for which he executed a mortgage on the goods in the county to which they had been removed, and applied $33 of such borrowed money to the payment of the first debt, leaving $80 remaining unpaid, of which the sum of $51.90 was still unpaid when the holder of the second mortgage brought suit to recover the mortgaged property, such facts were insufficient to entitle the second mortgagee to subrogation under the first mortgage.

Fife v. *Ohio Investment Co.*, 108, 111 (2).

CHECKS—

Deposit of, see BANKS AND BANKING 1-7.

CHILD—

See CARRIERS 16; RAILROADS 42.

Injury to, see RAILROADS 46.

Verdict awarding plaintiff $3,000 for the death of his son, seven and one-half years old, is not excessive, see DEATH 1.

Cannot recover damages for injuries for loss of time, loss of wages, or decreased earning power during minority, since his wages during said time belong to his parents, see INFANTS 3.

COLLATERAL ATTACK—

An order of dismissal, even if erroneous, is not subject to, see DISMISSAL 1.

Judgment of a probate court of another state, cannot be collaterally questioned in this State, unless want of jurisdiction appears on the face of the pleadings, see JUDGMENT 9.

COMMON LAW—

Of other states, see EVIDENCE 7.

Rule at, as to dismissal of actions not applicable in this State, see DISMISSAL 5.

The right to return a warranted article and rescind the contract does not exist at, see SALES 4.

COMPLAINT—

See PLEADING 6-20.

CONCLUSION—

Of law, see TRIAL 24, 27, 28.

CONFIDENTIAL RELATIONS—

Of physician and patient, see TRIAL 18.

CONSIDERATION—

See CONTRACTS 5, 9, 10; DEEDS 3; PRINCIPAL AND SURETY 1.

It is not necessary under the statute of frauds that the memorandum of a contract of sale should state the, see FRAUDS, STATUTE OF 1.

CONSTRUCTION—

See PLEADING 5.

Of complaint, see MASTER AND SERVANT 2.

Of contracts, see CONTRACTS 13, 14, 17; INSURANCE 7.

Of constitution, by-laws and other writings of fraternal order, see INSURANCE 12.

CONTRACTS—

See FRAUDS, STATUTE OF 1, 2; MUNICIPAL CORPORATIONS 19-23.

Act involving violation of, see INJUNCTION 7.

Breach of, see DAMAGES 1; SALES 1, 3.

Breach of, to bequeath or devise, see LIMITATION OF ACTIONS 2, 3.

Construction of insurance, see INSURANCE 7.

Enforceable, see SPECIFIC PERFORMANCE 1, 2.

Parol, of insurance are valid and enforceable, see INSURANCE 1.

To bequeath or devise, see WILLS 1, 2.

The law implies a, between passenger and carrier, see CARRIERS 1.

1. *Elements.—Meeting of Minds.—*To constitute a contract, there must be a meeting of the minds of the parties on one and the same thing. *Miller* v. *Sharp*, 11, 16 (2).

CONTRACTS—Continued.

2. *Contract Partly in Writing.—Parol Contract.*—A contract that is partly in writing and partly in parol will be treated as a parol contract. *Brotherhood, etc., v. Corder,* 214, 218 (4).

3. *Acceptance.—Scope.*—The acceptance of a proposal, to constitute a contract, must be as broad as the proposal itself, and exactly meet its terms. *Miller v. Sharp,* 11, 17 (4).

4. *Acceptance.—Action.—Mutuality.*—The bringing of an action on a contract, signed alone by the party to be charged, is in itself a sufficient acceptance to make the contract mutual.
Knapp v. Beach, 573, 576 (4).

5. *Actions.—Consideration.*—As a general rule, the promise contained in a contract, in order to support an action, must have been made upon a valuable consideration.
Baltimore, etc., R. Co. v. Cincinnati, etc., St. R. Co., 639, 643 (1).

6. *Action.—Contract Partly in Writing.—Parol Contract.*—Where a written contract is relied on, the entire contract must be in writing, since a contract, partly in writing and partly in parol, is deemed in law a parol contract. *Miller v. Sharp,* 11, 13 (1).

7. *Action.—Complaint.—Sufficiency.—Bill of Particulars.*—Where, in an action on a building contract, each paragraph of complaint stated facts sufficient to constitute a cause of action on the contract, plaintiff's failure to file a bill of particulars of items claimed as extras in each paragraph, does not render the complaint demurrable. *Tishbein v. Paine,* 441, 443 (3).

8. *Signatures. — Acceptance of Contract. — Effect. —* A contract, though signed by one party only, may become mutual and binding on both, if it is accepted and acted upon by the party not signing.
Knapp v. Beach, 573, 576 (3).

9. *Valuable Consideration.*—A valuable consideration, necessary to support a contract, must consist of the forbearance or acquisition of some legal right, and, unless it is the forbearance or acquisition of a legal right, there is no consideration, even though the parties may believe otherwise.
Baltimore, etc., R. Co. v. Cincinnati, etc., St. R. Co., 639, 643 (2).

10. *Executory Contracts. — Consideration. — Mutual Promises. —* Where a contract is executory on both sides, consisting of promises by each party to do something, the mutual promises of the parties are a sufficient consideration, each for the other, to render either party liable for a failure to carry out his part.
Knapp v. Beach, 573, 576 (5).

11. *Written Agreements.—Nature.—Determination.*—In determining the nature of a written agreement, the courts will look to the engagements of the parties as therein set out, rather than to the designation of the instrument.
Lake Erie, etc., R. Co. v. Marott, 332, 338 (3).

12. *Contracts Partly in Writing.—Action.—Complaint.—Sufficiency.*—A contract, partly in writing and partly in parol, rests entirely in parol, and a complaint thereon is not rendered insufficient by failure to set out therein the portion of the contract that is written, or to make the same an exhibit thereto.
Tishbein v. Paine, 441, 443 (2).

13. *Construction.*—The true meaning of any contract is to be ascertained from a consideration of all its provisions in their entirety, and not from a literal or technical construction of any isolated or special clause. *Nave v. Powell,* 496, 508 (8).

CONTRACTS—Continued.

14. *Construction.—Surplusage.*—In construing a contract for the sale of corn, where it appears that the memorandum was written on a blank form providing for the advancement of a money loan on an agreement for the sale of grain, and no money loan was in fact made, the part of the memorandum referring to such loan will be disregarded, as being mere surplusage.
Knapp v. Beach, 573, 575 (1).

15. *Pleading.—Breach of Warranty.*—A breach of warranty, pleaded as a cause of action or defense, must, to be good upon demurrer, aver the character and extent of the warranty, and the nature and particulars of the breach.
Barber Asphalt Pav. Co. v. City of Indianapolis, 587, 595 (2).

16. *Grant of Right to Lay Gas Main.—Assignability.*—An agreement by a railroad company specifically providing that for a definite consideration, the company grants to a named company the right to lay and maintain a gas main along and across its right of way for a certain number of years, subject to certain supervisory control by the chief engineer of the railroad company, though designated both as an agreement and a license, constitutes an assignable agreement in the absence of an express covenant against assignment. *Lake Erie, etc., R. Co. v. Marott,* 332, 338 (4).

17. *Grant of Right to Lay Gas Main.—Covenant Against Assignment.—Construction.*—Where a contract granting the right to lay a gas main along the right of way of a railroad company, provided that it should not be assigned without the written consent of the railroad company, an assignment by a receiver of the grantee passed to the assignee all rights of the grantee under such contract, since such covenants are not favored, and do not operate against an assignment by operation of law, but will be held to be directed only against a voluntary assignment by the grantee. *Lake Erie, etc., R. Co. v. Marott,* 332, 339 (5).

CONTRIBUTORY NEGLIGENCE—

See CARRIERS 9, 16; MASTER AND SERVANT 20, 26-29; NEGLIGENCE 12-18; RAILROADS 13-23, 27-29, 38; TRIAL 20.

CORPORATIONS—

Assessed value of, see EVIDENCE 16.

COUNTY BOARD OF REVIEW—

Record of, is admissible as affording some evidence of value of shares of stock in corporation, see EVIDENCE 16.

COURTS—

Appellate, may search their own record of former appeal, see APPEAL 23; *Studabaker v. Faylor,* 171, 173 (3).

1. *Appellate Court.—Powers.—New Trial.*—The Appellate Court has the power to order a new trial, and it is its duty to do so, where it appears that the ends of justice will be best subserved thereby. *Osborn v. Adams Brick Co.,* 175, 190 (19).

2. *Judicial Duties.—Master Commissioner.—Report*—The report of a master commissioner is not a finding of the court, since a master commissioner is not a court, and judicial duties, which a court alone can exercise, cannot be conferred on him.
Moore-Mansfield, etc., Co. v. Marion, etc., Traction Co., 548, 555 (4).

COURTS—Continued.

3. *Appellate Court. — Jurisdiction. — Constitutional Questions.* — Where appellant's petition for the vacation of a street proceeds on the theory that appellant is the only one having any special interest in that part of the street to be vacated, the Appellate Court has jurisdiction, since a decision does not involve the question of the taking of property without compensation, in which any one is specially interested, and no constitutional question is presented. *Southern R. Co. v. Town of French Lick*, 447, 456 (12).

CROSS-EXAMINATION—

See WITNESSES 1, 2.

CROSSINGS—

Accident on, see RAILROADS 1-29.

Care in approaching, see RAILROADS 2, 3.

Highway, see RAILROADS 33.

Signals on, see RAILROADS 30-32.

Street, see RAILROADS 34.

A railroad company is primarily liable for injuries resulting from its failure to keep its, in proper condition, see MUNICIPAL CORPORATIONS 11.

DAMAGES—

See APPEAL 57, 131; DEATH 3; INFANTS 3; MASTER AND SERVANT 5, 6; MUNICIPAL CORPORATIONS 2; WATERS AND WATERCOURSES 8.

Action for, see FRAUD 2.

Measure of, see SALES 1.

1. *Breach of Contract.—Nominal Damages.*—Where there has been a breach of a contract by one of the parties, the other is at least entitled to recover nominal damages.
   Ladoga Can. Co. v. Corydon Can. Co., 23, 28 (5).

2. *Excessive Damages.*—Damages assessed by a jury will not be considered excessive unless they are such as to induce the belief that the jury in awarding them acted from prejudice, passion, partiality or corruption.
   Terre Haute, etc., Traction Co. v. Maberry, 114, 123 (12).

DEATH—

Of parties after rendition of judgment how affects jurisdiction on appeal, see APPEAL 15.

1. *Death of Child.—Damages.—Excessive Damages.*—A verdict awarding plaintiff $3,000 for the death of his son, seven and one-half years old, in a collision with an interurban car, is not excessive. *Terre Haute, etc., Traction Co. v. Maberry*, 114, 123 (11).

2. *Death of Child.—Measure of Damages.—Instructions.*—An instruction, in an action by a father for the wrongful death of his child, that the measure of plaintiff's damages would be the reasonable value of the child's services from the date of its death until it would have become twenty-one years of age less the reasonable expense of providing it with the ordinary necessaries of life during that time, is not objectionable as leading the jury to conclude that the father was obliged to furnish only the bare necessities of life, since the word "ordinary" must have been

DEATH—Continued.

understood by the jury as synonymous with "usual" or "customary." *Terre Haute, etc., Traction Co.* v. *Maberry*, 114, 123 (8).

3. *Damages.—Excessive Damages.*—In an action for death against a railroad company, where decedent was sixty-two years old, able-bodied, living with and supporting his wife and daughter, and had a life expectancy of thirteen and one-half years, a verdict for $5,200 will not be held excessive, where there is no showing that the jury adopted an improper method of calculating the damages, or was misled by sympathy, or influenced by unfair means. *Cleveland, etc., R. Co.* v. *Van Laningham*, 156, 170 (16).

4. *Action.—Limitation.—Statutes.*—Under §285 Burns 1908, Acts 1889 p. 405, providing that when the death of one is caused by the wrongful act or omission of another, the personal representatives of the former may maintain an action therefor against the latter, if the former might have maintained an action, had he or she lived, against the latter for an injury for the same act or omission, and providing that such action shall be commenced within two years, death is the foundation of the right given by the statute, and an action for death under such statute is not affected by the fact that the right of action for the injury in favor of decedent was barred before his death, but is governed by the rule of limitation therein contained. *German, etc., Trust Co.* v. *Lafayette Box, etc., Co.*, 211 213 (1).

DECLARATIONS—

Of existing pain, see EVIDENCE 8.

DEDICATION—

To public use, see EMINENT DOMAIN 1.

DEFECTS—

Allegation of particular, see CARRIERS 5.

Where a passenger in an action for injuries caused by the derailment of a train, alleged a number of defects as cause for the derailment, proof that the derailment was occasioned by any one or more of the causes alleged would warrant a finding for plaintiff, see CARRIERS 3.

DEEDS—

1. *Operation.— Presumptions.— Evidence.— Mortgage.—* The presumption is that a deed, absolute on its face, is what it purports to be, and, unless the evidence proves it to be a mortgage, it will operate as a conveyance of the fee. *Grubb* v. *Brendel*, 531, 536 (4).

2. *Action to Declare Deed a Mortgage.—Evidence.—Debt.*—In an action to have a deed declared a mortgage, the absence of any written evidence of a debt due defendant from plaintiff, is a circumstance tending to support the theory of a sale. *Grubb* v. *Brendel*, 531, 536 (5).

3. *Action to Declare Deed a Mortgage.—Evidence.—Consideration.*—In determining whether a deed, absolute on its face is in fact a mortgage, the adequacy of consideration supports the theory of a sale, and inadequacy supports that of a loan with security. *Grubb* v. *Brendel*, 531, 536 (6).

DEEDS—Continued.

4. *Action to Declare Deed a Mortgage.—Evidence.—Burden of Proof.*—In an action to have a deed declared to be a mortgage, the burden of proving that the deed, and a contract executed at the same time, evidenced a loan with security, rather than a purchase of the land by defendant and an option to sell to plaintiff, rests on plaintiff. *Grubb* v. *Brendel*, 531, 536 (3).

DEMAND—

On appeal from a judgment for plaintiff in replevin, the court cannot determine if proof of a demand was necessary where appellant's brief does not contain any of the evidence in the case, see APPEAL 38.

DEMURRER—

See PLEADING 24-27.

DESCENT AND DISTRIBUTION—

1. *Right to Inherit.—Vested Rights.*—An heir has no vested right to inherit the property of the ancestor.
   Cropper v. *Glidewell*, 52, 56 (2).

2. *Subsequent Wife.—Lease of Lands.—Right to Rents Accruing After Death of Subsequent Wife.*—Where a surviving second wife, whose husband had no children by her, but who had a child by a former wife, leased for a year land which descended to her under §3017 Burns 1908 and §2644 Burns 1894, §§2486, 2487 R. S. 1881, and died before the expiration of the term, the rents accruing after her death belonged to such child, since the wife had no power to incumber the estate so as to defeat or impair the inheritance vested by law in such child.
   Cropper v. *Glidewell*, 52, 57 (4).

3. *Surviving Subsequent Wife.—Rights of Children of Intestate.*—Under §2644 Burns 1894, §2487 R. S. 1881, providing that on the death of a husband, leaving a second or subsequent wife by whom he had no children, but leaving children alive by a previous wife, the land which descends to such wife, shall, at her death, descend to his children, the interest of such wife in such lands is a fee simple, which, on her death is cast upon the children of the intestate as the enforced heirs of such wife, and the right to take as such enforced heir is one that cannot be defeated by any act of such wife. *Cropper* v. *Glidewell*, 52, 54 (1).

4. *Surviving Subsequent Wife.—Rights of Children of Intestate.—Statutes.—Repeal.*—Section 3017 Burns 1908, §2486 R. S. 1881, providing that on the death of a husband, intestate, leaving a widow and one child only, his real estate descends one-half to each, and §2644 Burns 1894, §2487 R. S. 1881, providing that, if he die leaving a widow who was his second or subsequent wife, by whom he had no children, but leaving children alive by a previous wife, the land which descends to such widow shall, at her death, descend to such children, are modified by Acts 1899 p. 131, §2, to the extent of providing that a childless subsequent wife takes only a life estate in the share descending to her and that the fee vests at once in the children of the former marriage, but the latter statute is not in conflict with §2644 Burns 1894, §2487 R. S. 1881, making the children of a former marriage the enforced heirs of a childless subsequent wife, in so far as such provision applies to an estate which descended to such childless subsequent wife prior to the taking effect of said act of 1899.
   Cropper v. *Glidewell*, 52, 56 (3).

DISCHARGE—

Under the provisions of the bankruptcy act of 1898, as amended in 1903, a discharge in bankruptcy does not operate as a discharge of all debts of the bankrupt, but releases him from all provable debts, except as therein otherwise specially provided, see BANKRUPTCY 2.

DISCRETION OF COURT—

As to introduction of evidence is within the, see TRIAL 2.

Order of admission of evidence within the sound, see APPEAL 5.

DISMISSAL—

When appeal must be dismissed, see APPEAL 10.

When appeal cannot be entertained for want of jurisdiction, see APPEAL 14.

1. *Collateral Attack.*—An order of dismissal, even if erroneous, is not subject to collateral attack.
   Moore-Mansfield, etc., Co. v. Marion, etc., Traction Co., 548, 555 (7).

2. *Voluntary Dismissal.—Effect as to Set-off.—Rights of Defendant.*—A set-off is not affected by the dismissal of the cause of action stated in the complaint, but defendant may proceed to final judgment on the issues tendered by such set-off, although the court, in determining the questions thus presented, would have no right to consider any issues formed on the complaint.
   Moore-Mansfield, etc., Co. v. Marion, etc., Traction Co., 548, 555 (8).

3. *Wrongful Dismissal.—Effect.*—Where a court has jurisdiction of the subject-matter and of the parties to the action, an order of dismissal wrongfully entered is not ineffective, but merely erroneous, and is binding on the parties unless reversed on appeal or set aside in a direct proceeding brought for that purpose.
   Moore-Mansfield, etc., Co. v. Marion, etc., Traction Co., 548, 555 (6).

4. *Right to Dismiss.—Report of Master Commissioner as Affecting Right.*—The right of plaintiff to dismiss his action, under §338 Burns 1908, §333 R. S. 1881, providing that plaintiff may dismiss at any time before the finding of the court is announced, is not affected by the fact that prior to asking the dismissal, the report of the master commissioner, to whom the case had been referred, had been prepared and copies submitted to the parties.
   Moore-Mansfield, etc., Co. v. Marion, etc., Traction Co., 548, 555 (5).

5. *Right to Dismiss.—Common-Law Rule.—Statutes.*—The rule prevailing in common-law jurisdictions, that the plaintiff in an action at law has a right to dismiss his action at any time before verdict, but that complainant in a suit in equity does not possess a similar right, is not applicable in this State, since under §249 Burns 1908, §249 R. S. 1881, providing that there shall be but one form of action denominated a civil action, and abolishing all distinctions in pleading and practice between actions at law and suits in equity, the provisions of §338 Burns 1908, §333 R. S. 1881, that a plaintiff may dismiss his action at any time before the jury retires, or, when the trial is by the court, at any time before the finding of the court is announced, must be held to apply to a civil action, regardless of whether the relief sought is legal or equitable.
   Moore-Mansfield, etc., Co. v. Marion, etc., Traction Co., 548, 553 (2), 554 (2).

DRAINS—

Artificial, see WATERS AND WATERCOURSES 6.

DUES—

Nonpayment of, see INSURANCE 14.

DUPLICITY—

The question of, is raised by a motion to require that the causes be separated and stated in separate paragraphs, see PLEADING 19.

"DUTY"—

See WORDS AND PHRASES.

"DYNAMO"—

See WORDS AND PHRASES.

EASEMENTS—

See WATERS AND WATERCOURSES 1, 2.

Easements by Prescription.—A mere permissive use is insufficient to establish a prescriptive right to an easement, but, to be sufficient, the use must be shown to be adverse, under a claim of right, continuous and uninterrupted for twenty years.

Gaskill v. Barnett, 654, 660 (7).

ELECTRICITY—

Generation of Electricity.—"Manufacturing Establishment".—Factory Act.—A plant for the generation of electricity is a manufacturing establishment, as contemplated by the provisions of the factory act, §§8021, 8029 Burns 1908, Acts 1899 p. 231, §§1, 9.

Angola R., etc., Co. v. Butz, 420, 424 (4).

ELEVATOR—

Accident, see MASTER AND SERVANT 16.

EMINENT DOMAIN—

1. *Railroads.—Right of Way.—Dedication to Public Use.*—Land held by a railroad corporation for a right of way, when in actual use as such, is dedicated to a public use.

Town of Cicero v. Lake Erie, etc., R. Co., 298, 310 (12).

2. *Railroads.—Right of Way.—Subsequent Appropriation for Street.*—Under general statutory authority to lay out and establish streets, a street may be laid out through railroad grounds, unless the use for railroad purposes would thereby be destroyed or materially impaired.

Town of Cicero v. Lake Erie, etc., R. Co., 298, 313 (14).

3. *Railroads.—Right of Way.—Subsequent Appropriation for Street.*—Although §§8700, 8759 Burns 1908, Acts 1905 p. 219, §§97, 265, providing that towns may appropriate or condemn, for the public use, any property, real or personal, and may open, change, lay out or vacate any street, etc., including proposed street or alley crossings of railways or other rights of way, are general in their terms, and do not specifically authorize the taking of a longitudinal strip of a railroad's right of way for other public purposes, it cannot be held as a matter of law that a town cannot by proper proceedings acquire such a strip for highway purposes, and its right to do

EMINENT DOMAIN—Continued.

so will be upheld in the absence of proof that it had not acquired the right in any of the ways recognized by the law.

Town of Cicero v. *Lake Erie, etc., R. Co.,* 298, 313 (15).

4. *Land Appropriated to Public Use.—Subsequent Appropriation.* —Where land is once appropriated to an important public use, it cannot again be devoted to another public use wholly inconsistent with the former, and which must necessarily supersede or destroy such former use, unless it is shown that the right to the second appropriation is authorized by an act of the legislature, either expressly or by necessary implication; but, where the two uses may co-exist, and the second does not destroy or seriously impair the use for which the first appropriation was made, the second appropriation may be had under a general statute authorizing the condemnation of ground for public purposes.

Town of Cicero v. *Lake Erie, etc., R. Co.,* 298, 310 (13).

EMPLOYER'S LIABILITY INSURANCE—

See INSURANCE 4-6.

EQUITY—

See JURY 3; SUBROGATION.

Effect of statute abolishing suits of law and suits in, see ACTIONS.

ESTOPPEL—

See BONDS 1; CHATTEL MORTGAGES 4; TAXATION 4.

EVIDENCE—

See APPEAL 33, 87, 88, 92, 94-98, 107, 108, 111, 112, 147; BILLS AND NOTES 3; CARRIERS 9; DEEDS 1-4; INSURANCE 15; JUDGMENT 1, 4, 7, 10; MASTER AND SERVANT 6, 20; MUNICIPAL CORPORATIONS 17; PRINCIPAL AND AGENT 4, 7, 8, 12, 14; RAILROADS 5-8, 45, 47, 48; VENDOR AND PURCHASER; WILLS 2; WITNESSES 2.

Admission of, see APPEAL 117-121.

Exclusion of, see APPEAL 122, 123; WATERS AND WATERCOURSES 7, 11.

Parol, see TRUSTS 4, 5.

Reception of, see TRIAL 1. 2.

Review as to, see APPEAL 47-64.

When, not in the record, see APPEAL 9.

Insufficiency of, to sustain answer in abatement, see ABATEMENT.

Necessary to maintain an action in replevin, see REPLEVIN 2.

Order of admission of, within discretion of trial court, see APPEAL 5.

Objections to offered, must state the particular grounds relied on to be available on appeal unless the evidence on its face appears to be incompetent, see APPEAL 4.

Sufficiency of the, cannot be considered on appeal, unless it shall affirmatively appear over the signature of the trial judge, that the bill of exceptions contains all the evidence, see APPEAL 25.

1. *Admissions.—Testimony in Another Action.*—Testimony of a party, given in another action, is admissible as an admission.

Fuller v. *Fuller* 488, 491 (6).

EVIDENCE—Continued.

2. *Admissibility.—Res Gestae.*—The testimony of the mortgagor that, at the time of signing the mortgage, her son told her it was a bond of indemnity upon a certain building contract, but that he said nothing about other contracts, was admissible in an action to foreclose, as being a part of the *res gestae* of the transaction.
Hubbard v. *Ranje*, 611, 615 (3).

3. *Admissions.—Admissibility.*—Where a woman signed and gave her son a mortgage to be delivered to the mortgagee to indemnify him against loss by reason of a certain contract of her son on which the mortgagee was his bondsman, and the mortgagee suffered loss by reason of bonding the son on other contracts, but not on the bond contemplated by the mortgagor, the exclusion of offered testimony of the mortgagee, in a foreclosure suit, that at the time of delivering the mortgage the son stated that the note and mortgage were executed and delivered for the purpose of indemnifying mortgagee for any loss he might sustain as surety for the son on building bonds to be thereafter executed, was proper, in the absence of evidence that the son was authorized to speak for his mother in that respect.
Hubbard v. *Ranje*, 611, 614 (1), 617 (1).

4. *Judicial Notice.—Noise of Approaching Train.*—The court may take judicial notice of the fact that an approaching train will make some noise.   *Cleveland, etc., R. Co.* v. *Nichols*, 349, 353 (3).

5. *Account Books.—Ledger.*—In an action to recover for material furnished and labor performed, a ledger kept by plaintiff's bookkeeper in the regular course of plaintiff's business, the entries in which were made from memoranda furnished by the employes who sent out the material and by the men who did the work, was admissible as affording some proof of the account, although such bookkeeper had no personal knowledge of the amount of material furnished or the amount of labor performed at the time such entries were made by him.
Indianapolis Outfitting Co. v. *Cheyne Electric Co.*, 153, 155 (3).

6. *Conclusion of Witness.*—Where, while testifying as a witness with reference to the execution of a lease, which he claimed he had been induced to sign through the representations of plaintiff, on whom he relied, that the lease was merely a copy of a lost contract, defendant was asked if plaintiff advised him about business affairs, such question was not objectionable as calling for a conclusion, since, under the circumstances, the answer called for was the result of observations and dealings with plaintiff that were peculiarly within the knowledge of the witness.
Heston v. *Dougan*, 40, 48 (7).

7. *Common Law of Other States.*—Where one claims the benefit of the common law of another state, as modified by legislation and judicial construction, he must plead and prove the same, otherwise the law of this State will furnish the rule of decision.
Cooley v. *Kelley*, 687, 697 (12).

8. *Declarations of Existing Pain.—Admissibility.*—Where, in an action to recover for a wrongful death, one of the issues involved the extent of decedent's injuries from the accident, declarations of the decedent, made the day after the accident, that her shoulder was hurt and that she suffered pain, were admissible as declarations of present existing pain to show the extent of her injuries.
Cleveland, etc., R. Co. v. *Clark*, 646, 652 (9).

EVIDENCE—Continued.

9. *Judicial Notice.—Matters of Common Knowledge.—Matters of Science.*—Courts take judicial notice of such matters of common knowledge and science as are known to all men of ordinary understanding and intelligence, and they judicially know that a dynamo is used for generating electricity and not merely for the purpose of transmitting or storing the same.
Angola R., etc., Co. v. *Butz,* 420, 424 (3).

10. *Presumptions.—Performance of Official Duty.*—The law presumes the acts of public officers to be legal and regular, and until the contrary is made to appear, they are presumed to have done their duty according to law.
Town of Cicero v. *Lake Erie, etc., R. Co.,* 298, 309 (10).

11. *Presumptions.—Regularity of Corporate Acts.*—It will be presumed that the officers of a corporation, in preparing a statement of the value of all its tangible property and of the shares of stock, as required by §10233 Burns 1908, Acts 1903 p. 49, made a true statement. *Ohlwine* v. *Pfaffman,* 357, 368 (9).

12. *Parol Evidence.—Variation of Terms of Written Instrument.*— In the absence of a showing of fraud or mistake, parol evidence is not admissible to annul or substantially vary the terms of a written instrument. *Croan* v. *Myers,* 143, 145 (2).

13. *Discharge in Bankruptcy.*—A certificate of discharge in bankruptcy is evidence of the jurisdiction of the court, the regularity of the proceedings in the bankruptcy case, and the fact that such order of discharge was made therein.
Kreitlein v. *Ferger,* 199, 203 (1).

14. *Self-disserving Statements of Party.—Nature.*—Self-disserving statements by defendant admitting his liability on notes to which his name was signed by his son, and his son's authority to thus sign his name, made by defendant when it was incumbent on him to speak the truth, are not in the nature of impeaching evidence, for which a foundation must be laid, but, in addition to being evidence that the admissions were made, constitute evidence of the facts admitted. *Miller* v. *Farmers State Bank,* 5, 10 (4).

15. *Wrongful Acts.—Intention.—Presumptions.*—The rule that every person is presumed to intend the natural and probable consequences of his wrongful or unlawful acts applies in civil as well as in criminal cases, and such intent may be shown by direct evidence, or may be inferred from conduct showing a reckless disregard of consequences and a willingness to inflict injury by purposely and voluntarily doing an act with knowledge that some one is unconsciously or unavoidably in a situation to be injured thereby. *Terre Haute, etc., Traction Co.* v. *Maberry,* 114, 120 (4).

16. *Value.—Assessed Value of Corporation.—Record of County Board of Review.*—Under §§10233, 10234 Burns 1908, Acts 1903 p. 49, requiring corporations to make out and deliver to the assessor a sworn statement showing the value of all tangible property, and the market value, or if no market value, the actual value of the shares of stock, and providing that such statement shall be laid before the county board of review, it will be presumed, in the absence of a showing to the contrary, that the board of review in fixing the assessment has regarded such statement as true and correct and has fixed the true cash value of the property in accordance with the facts thereby shown, so that the record of such board showing the assessed value of corporate stock, unless made too remotely, is admissible as affording some evidence of its value. *Ohlwine* v. *Pfaffman,* 357, 365 (8).

EXCEPTIONS—

To conclusions of law, see PLEADING 12.

To conclusions of law present the same question as the overruling of a demurrer to the complaint, see APPEAL 7.

To conclusions of law concede, for the purpose of the exception, that the facts are fully and correctly found, see APPEAL 140.

EXCEPTIONS, BILL OF—

Containing the evidence should contain the words: "And this was all the evidence given in said cause," see APPEAL 24.

EXCESSIVE DAMAGES—

See DAMAGES 2; DEATH 1, 3.

EXECUTION—

Action to Enjoin Enforcement.—Irregularity in Rendition of Judgment.—Cross-Complaint.—In an action to enjoin the enforcement of an execution on the ground that no judgment had been rendered, or, that if rendered, the record entry thereof had not been signed, a cross-complaint seeking to cure irregularity in the rendition of such judgment by having the same read in open court and signed by the court *nunc pro tunc*, is a proper pleading and germane to the subject-matter of the complaint.
Pittsburgh, etc., R. Co. v. *Johnson*, 457, 465 (1).

FELLOW SERVANTS—

See MASTER AND SERVANT 30-33.

FENCES—

The duty imposed by statute on railroad companies to erect and maintain, is a continuing one, see RAILROADS 35.

FINDINGS—

Special, see TRIAL 25-27, 36.

FIRE INSURANCE—

See INSURANCE 7-10.

FOREIGN JUDGMENTS—

See JUDGMENTS 7-9.

FORFEITURES—

See BONDS 3.

Presumption against, see INSURANCE 8.

FRAUD—

1. *Complaint.—Allegations.—Bringing Action in Wrong County.*— A complaint in an action to set aside a judgment, on the ground that the original action was fraudulently brought in the wrong county, is insufficient in the absence of averments of acts or conduct constituting fraud. *Swain* v. *Hunt*, 626, 628 (2).

2. *Action for Damages.—Waiver of Fraud.—Ratification of Contract.—Effect.*—The retention of property by a party who has suffered loss through another's fraud does not preclude him from maintaining an action for damages, nor does an express waiver of

FRAUD—Continued.

the fraud and explicit ratification of the contract, unless of such a character as to imply a release from the consequences of such fraud. *Ohlwine* v. *Pfaffman*, 357, 361 (1).

3. *Action.—Issues.—Instructions.*—In an action to recover damages for fraud perpetrated on plaintiff in the exchange of corporate stock for plaintiff's land, where the complaint alleged that T. and the other defendant conspired to induce plaintiff to believe that T. owned the stock exchanged, that the other would retain his stock and control the business with plaintiff, and that T. in fact owned no stock, but that the stock exchanged was a part of the stock owned by the other defendant, the question of the ownership of the stock was material, so that an instruction stating that it was wholly immaterial who was the owner of such stock, provided plaintiff acquired a good title to same, was properly refused. *Ohlwine* v. *Pfaffman*, 357, 362 (5).

4. *Remedies.*—A person who has been induced by fraud to enter into a contract, may either repudiate the contract *in toto*, return or offer to return whatever of value he has received under it, and recover the property he has parted with, or its value; or he may affirm the contract, keep what property or advantage he has obtained under it, and recover the damages he has sustained by reason of such fraud. *Ohlwine* v. *Pfaffman*, 357, 362 (2).

5. *Statements of Value.—Representations by Vendor.—Reliance.*—Representations of value by a vendor, who has, or assumes to have, special knowledge of the value of property sold, made as a basis of a contract between the parties, and with knowledge that the vendee is ignorant of the value and is relying on such representations, are binding on the vendor.
Ohlwine v. *Pfaffman*, 357, 364 (7).

6. *Statements of Value.—Opinion.*—Statements by defendants that they had paid par for their stock in a corporation, made to induce plaintiff to exchange land therefor, were representations as to material, existing facts, and not the mere expression of opinions as to value, and constitute actionable fraud, if they were false and were relied upon by plaintiff to his damage.
Ohlwine v. *Pfaffman*, 357, 364 (6).

7. *Waiver.—Acts Constituting.*—The fact that plaintiff, in an action for damages resulting through fraud, had instituted a former suit to rescind the contract and to obtain a reconveyance of the land, which was thereafter dismissed by him at his own costs, and that he thereafter retained the stock he had received for the land, and continued to act as a director of the corporation, was not inconsistent with his right to affirm the contract and rely on his action for damages. *Ohlwine* v. *Pfaffman*, 357, 362 (4).

FRAUDS, STATUTE OF—

1. *Contract of Sale.—Consideration.*—It is not necessary under the statute of frauds, §7464 Burns 1908, §4005 R. S. 1881, that the memorandum of a contract of sale should state the consideration.
Knapp v. *Beach*, 573, 576 (6).

2. *Contracts.—Signatures.*—The statute of frauds, §7469 Burns 1908, §4910 R. S. 1881, under which a contract, for the sale of goods worth more than $50, in the absence of part payment or partial delivery, must be in writing, etc., is satisfied, and the contract is enforceable, if it is signed alone by the party sued.
Knapp v. *Beach*, 573, 575 (2).

GAS—

Grant of right to lay, main, see CONTRACTS 16, 17.

GUARANTY—

Of work and stipulations for repairs, see MUNICIPAL CORPORATIONS 19-23.

HARMLESS ERROR—

See APPEAL 117-139, 146; RAILROADS 10, 11.

HIGHWAYS—

Injury to persons on, see RAILROADS 47.

The rights of a person on a public highway are equal to those of a railroad company whose tracks are situate thereon, except as to the latter's right of priority when both need to use the highway at the same time, see RAILROADS 33.

HUSBAND AND WIFE—

When a husband upon lending his money, took a note payable to his wife, it will be presumed, in the absence of any averment to the contrary that the note was so made on a sufficient consideration, see BILLS AND NOTES 4.

A power of attorney executed by, directly authorizing the attorney in fact to convey the property to "any one of us," etc., and not containing any power to convey joint property, is several and is not revoked by the death of the wife, see PRINCIPAL AND AGENT 5.

*Actions.—Parties.—*Where, in an action against a husband and wife on a note executed by the wife before her marriage, judgment was had against the wife, but no finding or judgment was rendered against the husband, the husband is neither a necessary nor proper party in an action on such judgment, brought after a divorce had been granted.   *Swain* v. *Hunt,* 626, 627 (1).

IMPROVEMENTS—

Public, see MUNICIPAL CORPORATIONS 19-23.

INDEMNITY INSURANCE—

See INSURANCE 4.

INFANTS—

See LIMITATION OF ACTIONS 12.

1. *Capacity to Contract.—Presumptions.—*A person dealing with an infant is bound to know his incapacity to contract.
     Weidenhammer v. *McAdams,* 98, 103 (6).

2. *Powers.—Authorization or Ratification of Acts.—*A minor cannot authorize any one to act as his agent nor can he acquiesce in or ratify the acts of any person so as to make them his own.
     Weidenhammer v. *McAdams,* 98, 103 (3).

8. *Personal Injuries.—Recovery by Child.—Damages.—*A minor, having a widowed mother, cannot, in an action against his employer for injuries, recover for loss of time, loss of wages, or decreased earning power during minority, since his wages during such time belong to his mother.
     Sanitary Can Co. v. *McKinney,* 379, 388 (10).

INJUNCTION—

1. *Nature of Remedy.*—Injunction is a form of proceeding in which the relief sought is negative in character, that is, it is to prevent the commission of some threatened act involving the violation of a contract or duty.   *Lake Erie, etc., R. Co.* v. *Marott*, 332, 337 (2).

2. *Closing Passway.—Right to Relief.*—An action to enjoin the closing of a passway cannot be maintained where it does not appear from the complaint that plaintiff has any right therein that is about to be invaded.   *Park* v. *Morgan*, 478, 479 (2).

3. *Closing Passway.—Complaint.—Sufficiency.*—A complaint to enjoin defendant from closing a passway, from which it is apparent that no prescriptive right exists in the easement claimed, and which alleges that defendant, with the consent of his son, who was then the owner of the land now owned by plaintiff, opened the passway in lieu of another which had been purchased by a remote grantor, and had since kept the same open as a passway from the land now owned by plaintiff to the public highway, but that defendant is now threatening to and will close same unless restrained from doing so, does not show a right of action in favor of plaintiff.   *Park* v. *Morgan*, 478 (1).

4. *Actions to Enjoin Municipal Corporations.—Appropriation of Railroad Property for Street.—Complaint.—Proof.*—In an action by a railroad company to enjoin a town from appropriating a portion of the right of way for a street, plaintiff must allege and prove facts showing that the town and its officers were acting without warrant of law.
   Town of Cicero v. *Lake Erie, etc., R. Co.*, 298, 309 (9).

5. *Action to Enjoin.—Municipal Corporations.—Appropriation of Railroad Property for Street.—Complaint.—Sufficiency.—Initial Attack on Appeal.*—In an action by a railroad company to enjoin a town and its officers from laying out a street over railroad property, a complaint alleging the acquisition of the property for railroad purposes, and the use thereof for over twenty years, that the town acquired a strip along the railroad property and began the construction of a street thereon and that it intended to and would construct such street over a portion of the railroad right of way, etc., is sufficient when attacked for the first time on appeal.   *Town of Cicero* v. *Lake Erie, etc., R. Co.*, 298, 308 (6).

6. *Actions Against Municipal Corporations. — Appropriation of Railroad Property for Street.—Special Findings.—Sufficiency.*—In an action by a railroad company to enjoin a town from appropriating a portion of its right of way for a street, a special finding of facts which fails to show that the town or its officers acted wrongfully or unlawfully or that the proceeding was not pursuant to some legal procedure authorizing such action, even if sufficient to exclude the theory of a street by dedication or prescription, is not sufficient to sustain a judgment for permanent injunction, but such omission amounts to an affirmance that the acts of defendant were lawful.
   Town of Cicero v. *Lake Erie, etc., R. Co.*, 298, 309 (11).

7. *Act Involving Violation of Contract.—Complaint.—Sufficiency.—Exhibit.*—In an action by the assignee of a contract, granting the right to lay and maintain a gas main along the right of way of a railroad company, to enjoin the company from removing the main, the complaint was not demurrable on the ground that it contained an insufficient statement of the contract and that the defect was not cured by making the contract an exhibit thereto, since the contract was the foundation of plaintiff's right and was

INJUNCTION—Continued.

properly incorporated into the complaint by attaching thereto and filing therewith a copy as an exhibit, as provided by §368 Burns 1908, §362 R. S. 1881, requiring, where a pleading is founded on a written instrument, that the original, or a copy thereof, must be filed with such pleading.

Lake Erie, etc., R. Co. v. *Marott*, 332, 337 (1).

INSTRUCTIONS—

See TRIAL 6-20.

Review as to, see APPEAL 65-82.

INSURANCE—

1. *Parol Contracts.*—A parol contract of insurance is valid and enforceable.   *Brotherhood, etc.,* v. *Corder*, 214, 219 (6).

2. *Action on Parol Contract.—Complaint.—Testing Sufficiency.*— Although some writings are set out and made part of a complaint in an action against an insurance company, drawn on the theory of a parol contract, such fact does not require the sufficiency of the pleading to be tested by the rules applicable where the action is based on a certificate or policy actually issued.

Brotherhood, etc., v. *Corder*, 214, 218 (3).

3. *Action on Policy.—Proof.—General Denial.*—Where, in an action on an employer's liability policy, it is essential to a recovery by plaintiff that he allege and prove payment of a judgment against him in favor of the employe, it may be shown under the general denial that such payment was not in good faith and that the money claimed to have been paid was advanced by the agents and attorneys of the employe and had since been returned to them.   *Campbell* v. *Maryland Casualty Co.*, 228, 231 (1).

4. *Employer's Liability Insurance.—Indemnity Contract.—Proof.*— In an action on an employer's liability policy, if the contract is one to indemnify against loss, plaintiff must show a damage before he can recover.   *Campbell* v. *Maryland Casualty Co.*, 228, 231 (3).

5. *Employer's Liability Insurance.—Insurance Against Liability.— Right of Action.*—Where an employer's liability policy is a contract to protect the assured against liability merely, an action may be brought and recovery had thereon as soon as the liability is legally imposed, regardless of whether any actual loss or damage has been suffered.

Campbell v. *Maryland Casualty Co.*, 228, 231 (4).

6. *Employer's Liability Insurance.—Construction of Policy.—Insurance Against Liability.*—Where an employer's liability policy stated that the company agreed to indemnify the assured against loss from liability for damages on account of bodily injuries to an employe caused by the negligence of the assured, and provided that no action should lie against the company unless brought by the assured himself to reimburse him for loss actually sustained and paid by him in satisfaction of a judgment after trial of the issue, the language indicates an intention to indemnify against loss only; but, when construed in connection with a rider providing that the policy should "only cover losses sustained by and liabilities for any claims against the assured as a result of the risk specified in the contract," the policy insured against liability as well as against loss and the employer could recover thereon without showing an actual loss.

Campbell v. *Maryland Casualty Co.*, 228, 232 (5).

INSURANCE—Continued.

7. *Fire Insurance.—Construction of Contract.*—A fire insurance policy will not be interpreted with the strictness which ordinarily obtains in written instruments, since the insured has no part in drawing the contract.
Northern Assurance Co. v. *Carpenter*, 432, 437 (4).

8. *Fire Insurance.—Actions.—Presumptions.—Presumption Against Forfeiture.*—Every presumption is indulged in favor of the good faith of the parties to fire policy, and inconsistencies on its face will be resolved in favor of the actual contract, and against forfeiture.
Northern Assurance Co. v. *Carpenter*, 432, 436 (2).

9. *Fire Insurance.—Inconsistent Provisions.—Waiver.—Fraud.*—Where the insurer receives pay for a valid and binding policy, and the insurer believes that he has such a policy, the law will not impute to the insurer a fraudulent intent not to deliver that kind of a policy, but will hold that conditions therein inconsistent with the risk were either waived or overlooked, and that the insurer is estopped from setting up a breach thereof.
Northern Assurance Co. v. *Carpenter*, 432, 440 (5).

10. *Fire Insurance.—Provisions of Policy.—Waiver.*—Where the insuring clause of a fire policy stated that for the consideration named the company insures the owner of the property described against loss by fire for a definite term, and the policy contained defeasance clauses inconsistent therewith and providing that before the policy shall take effect the insured shall make an inventory, and requiring him to keep books of account, etc., the provisions of such clauses were waived and the risk attached at once, where the company delivered the policy and accepted and retained the full premium, without calling the attention of the insured to such clauses or making any inquiry as to an inventory, or as to his method of doing business.
Northern Assurance Co. v. *Carpenter*, 432, 436 (3), 439 (3).

11. *Fraternal Insurance.—By-Laws.—Waiver.*—A fraternal insurance organization may waive compliance with a by-law or regulation made for its benefit, and it may ratify the action of a local lodge in waiving compliance with any such by-law or regulation.
Brotherhood, etc., v. *Corder*, 214, 225 (0).

12. *Fraternal Insurance.—By-laws.—Construction.*—Where the object of a fraternal order is not the seeking of profit, but the protection of its members and their beneficiaries by means of indemnity, its constitution, by-laws and other writings are to be liberally construed to promote the benevolent objects of the organization.
Brotherhood, etc., v. *Corder*, 214, 224 (8).

13. *Fraternal Insurance.—Parol Contract.—Complaint.—By-Laws.*—In an action against a fraternal insurance company, where the complaint was on the theory of a parol contract of insurance, it was not essential to the sufficiency of the complaint that copies of the constitution and by-laws be set out therein.
Brotherhood, etc., v. *Corder*, 214, 219 (5).

14. *Fraternal Insurance.—Defense.—Nonpayment of Dues.—Conditions Precedent.*—A fraternal insurance company may not defend an action on a certificate issued by it on the ground that a payment of dues was made too late, and at the same time retain the amount of such payment, but, to defend on such ground, it should show that it had refused to accept such payment, or had offered to return it and had kept the tender good by bringing the amount into court.
Modern Woodmen v. *Jones*, 149, 152 (6).

INSURANCE—Continued.

15. *Fraternal Insurance.—Evidence.—Direction of Verdict.*—In an action on a fraternal benefit certificate, uncontradicted documentary evidence as to the issuance of the certificate, the payment of dues and the death of the member made a *prima facie* case for plaintiff, notwithstanding evidence showing an offer to return the last payment of dues where defendant failed to keep the tender good, and, in the absence of any other evidence, an instruction to return a verdict for plaintiff was not erroneous.
Modern Woodmen v. Jones, 149, 152 (7).

16. *Fraternal Insurance.—Medical Examiner. — Powers.* — Where the authority of the grand medical examiner of an insurance order, under its constitution and by-laws, extended to the determination of the physical qualifications of the applicant, and to the ascertainment that the application complies generally with the prescribed forms, rules and laws of the order, he had no authority to deny an applicant a beneficiary certificate because he was not initiated within a certain time after medical examination, as prescribed by the laws of the order.
Brotherhood, etc., v. Corder, 214, 226 (10).

17. *Fraternal Insurance. — Parol Contract. — Complaint. — Sufficiency.*—A complaint against a fraternal order, stating that decedent applied to a local lodge for a beneficiary certificate, naming plaintiff, his sister, as beneficiary, that the application was accepted and approved, that he paid his fees, became a member and performed all the conditions required of him to entitle him to a certificate, that defendant agreed to insure his life for a specified sum to be paid to plaintiff on decedent's death, and that he was assessed as a member until his death, but that a certificate was never issued and that defendant refused to issue it, etc., sufficiently states a cause of action on the theory of a parol contract of insurance.
Brotherhood, etc., v. Corder, 214, 216 (2), 218 (2), 219 (2).

18. *Fraternal Insurance.—By-laws.—Conditions Precedent.—Waiver.*—Where the by-laws of a fraternal insurance society make an application for a beneficiary certificate a condition precedent to initiation in a local lodge, and provide that the same shall be in possession of the lodge at the time of the initiation, that before initiation a committee of the local lodge must pass on the qualification of the applicant and recommend him for membership, and that the local physician must make the required medical examination and report thereon before initiation, and that if the applicant has met the conditions and is initiated within the prescribed time, he is entitled to a beneficiary certificate, subject only to the approval of the grand medical examiner, the action of a local lodge in initiating a member after the expiration of the time prescribed in the by-laws, and the failure of the grand lodge to reject him as a member of the lodge, was a waiver of the objection that he was not initiated within the prescribed time following his medical examination.
Brotherhood, etc., v. Corder, 214, 224 (7), 225 (7).

INTERURBAN RAILROADS—

See RAILROADS 42-48.

INVITED ERROR—

Cannot be taken advantage of on appeal, see APPEAL 2.

JUDGES—

1. *Judge Pro Tem.—Appointment.—Objections.—Waiver.—Appeal.* —Where a judge has been called, or an attorney appointed as judge, to try a cause, and no objection is made at the time, or to his sitting in the cause when he assumes to act, all objections thereto will be deemed waived on appeal, and the same rule applies as to the appointment of a judge *pro tem.*

Jordan v. *Indianapolis Coal Co.*, 542, 545 (5).

2. *Judge Pro Tem.—Appointment.—Validity.—Judge De Facto.—* Where the regular judge appointed a judge *pro tem.* to preside over the court during his illness, and the court has jurisdiction of the subject-matter of the action and of the person of the defendant, and the judge so appointed took the oath and assumed the duties of a judge *pro tem.*, he was a judge *de facto*, if not *de jure*, notwithstanding the failure of the regular judge to sign the order of appointment.

Jordan v. *Indianapolis Coal Co.*, 542, 544 (3), 545 (3).

JUDGMENT—

See PARTITION 1; TRIAL 31, 35.

Binding effect of, see TRUSTS 10.

Rendition of, see EXECUTION.

On answers to interrogatories, see APPEAL 105-108.

Is a provable debt under bankruptcy act, see BANKRUPTCY 1; *Kreitlein* v. *Ferger*, 199, 205 (3).

Error in form of, will be ordered cured by a modification, see APPEAL 141.

On appeal every presumption is indulged in favor of the correctness of the judgment of the trial court, see APPEAL 86.

The fact that the jury's answers to interrogatories are not consistent with the evidence, or with each other, furnishes no ground for sustaining a motion for judgment thereon, see TRIAL 23.

1. *Nunc Pro Tunc Entries.—Evidence.—*As a general rule a *nunc pro tunc* entry cannot be made on oral testimony alone.

Pittsburgh, etc., R. Co. v. *Johnson*, 457, 476 (10).

2. *Record.—Pleadings.—*The pleadings filed in a cause are a part of the record, though not required to be copied at length into the order-book entries.   *Mitten* v. *Caswell-Runyan Co.*, 521, 525 (1).

3. *Rendition During Pendency of Motion for New Trial.—Validity.* —A judgment is not void because it is rendered while a motion for a new trial is pending, but such pending motion merely operates to suspend the effect and enforcement of the judgment.

Pittsburgh, etc., R. Co. v. *Johnson*, 457, 469 (6).

4. *Rendition.—Evidence.—Sufficiency.—*In an action to enjoin the enforcement of an execution, wherein defendant secured a *nunc pro tunc* reading and signing of the judgment, special findings that a judgment was rendered and entered, and that the only irregularity consisted of a failure to read and sign the entry in open court, are sufficiently supported by the evidence, where, besides the testimony of witnesses to the effect that the judgment had been rendered and entered in the order book, there was some record and documentary evidence to support every material part of each and all the findings made by the court.

Pittsburgh, etc., R. Co. v. *Johnson*, 457, 471 (9).

5. *Action on Judgment.—Review.—Form of Judgment.—Failure to Object.—*Although it was improper, in an action on a judgment

JUDGMENT—Continued.

with relief and without exemption, to render a judgment with benefit of exemption and without relief, the judgment will not be reversed, where appellant failed to make objections or take exception to the form of the judgment, and made no motion to modify same. *Kreitlein* v. *Ferger* 199, 209 (7).

6. *Action on Judgment.—Defense.—Discharge in Bankruptcy.— Proof.—Burden.*—In an action on a prior judgment, where defendant pleaded a discharge in bankruptcy, he had the burden of proving that the debt which he listed in his schedule of creditors in the bankruptcy proceeding was the debt of the plaintiff on which the action is brought, so that a judgment for plaintiff will not be disturbed on the ground that the decision is not sustained by sufficient evidence, or that it is contrary to law, where there was no proof in any way identifying the judgment sued on and the debt listed in the bankruptcy proceedings as being one and the same debt. *Kreitlein* v. *Ferger*, 199, 208 (6).

7. *Foreign Judgments.—Admissibility in Evidence.*—A certified copy of the proceedings of a probate court of another state disposing of property within its jurisdiction, is admissible in evidence in this State. *Cooley* v. *Kelley*, 687, 694 (7).

8. *Foreign Judgments.—Conclusiveness.*—Under Art. 4, §1, of the Federal Constitution, providing that full faith and credit shall be given in each state to the public records and judicial proceedings of every other state, a judgment rendered by a court of one state, having jurisdiction of the parties and the subject matter, is as conclusive in every other state as in the one in which it was rendered. *Cooley* v. *Kelley*, 687, 694 (8).

9. *Foreign Judgments.—Collateral Attack.*—Where the judgment of a probate court of another state terminating a testamentary trust, was made pursuant to statutory provisions of such state giving probate courts full power to hear and determine all matters relating to the manner in which a trustee has executed his trust, and requiring trustees to render accounts to the probate court, etc., such judgment cannot be collaterally questioned in this State, unless want of jurisdiction appears on the face of the pleadings. *Cooley* v. *Kelley*, 687, 695 (10).

10. *Res Judicata.—Parol Evidence.*—Parol evidence is not admissible to determine what was in fact adjudicated in a former action, where the pleadings in such action are definite and unambiguous. *Mitten* v. *Caswell-Runyan Co.*, 521, 528 (4), 530 (4).

11. *Res Judicata.—Issues.—Pleading.*—What was in issue in a former action must generally be determined by the pleadings therein, and everything which might have been adjudged under such issues will be presumed to have been adjudicated.
Mitten v. *Caswell-Runyan Co.*, 521, 527 (3).

12. *Res Judicata.*—A judgment determines all material issues involved between the parties to the action and all matters which might have been properly litigated and settled within the issues tendered or made by the pleadings, and is *res judicata* in a subsequent action, though the form of the two actions is not the same. *Mitten* v. *Caswell-Runyan Co.*, 521, 525 (2).

13. *Failure to Read and Sign.—Reading and Signing Nunc Pro Tunc.—Effect.*—Where the only irregularity in the rendition of a judgment consisted of the failure to read and sign the order book entry of same, as required by §1450 Burns 1908, Acts 1885 p. 124, the *nunc pro tunc* reading and signing thereof, as authorized by

JUDGMENT—Continued.

§1451 Burns 1908, §1331 R. S. 1881, gave to it regularity authorizing its enforcement by execution as of the date of its rendition.
Pittsburgh, etc., R. Co. v. *Johnson*, 457, 470 (8).

14. *Validity.—Failure to Read and Sign.*—While the rendition of a judgment by the trial court, its entry on the order book by the clerk, and its final approval and authentication by the judge's signature, after it has been read in open court, are separate, independent acts essential to support an execution issued on such judgment, the failure of the court to cause the order book entry to be read in open court, and to sign same, as required by §1450 Burns 1908, Acts 1885 p. 124, will not render the judgment void. *Pittsburgh, etc., R. Co.* v. *Johnson*, 457, 467 (4).

15. *Failure to Read and Sign.—Findings.—Conclusions of Law.— Nunc Pro Tunc Proceedings.*—Where, in an action to enjoin the enforcement of an execution, the special findings show that the judgment on which the execution issued had been rendered, and that it had been properly entered by the clerk, but had not been read and signed, a conclusion of law stated thereon that such judgment and record entry "should be and the same now is read and signed in open court *nunc pro tunc*, and said judgment may now be enforced by proper writ," is not open to the objection that it is a *nunc pro tunc* rendition of the judgment.
Pittsburgh, etc., R. Co. v. *Johnson*, 457, 469 (7).

JUDICIAL NOTICE—

See EVIDENCE 4, 9.

JURISDICTION—

See PLEADING 22.

Of Appellate Court, see COURTS 3.

Appeal void for want of, see APPEAL 1.

Notice to all necessary parties is essential to, of an appeal, see APPEAL 12.

JURY—

See QUESTIONS FOR JURY.

Right of trial by, see LANDLORD AND TENANT 3.

An instruction which invades the province of the, is properly refused, see APPEAL 65.

Instructions are properly refused which if given would invade the province of the, see TRIAL 8.

1. *Right to Trial by Jury.—Refusal.*—Where a cause is triable by jury, the court's refusal to permit it to be so tried is error.
Camp v. *Camp*, 250, 252 (3).

2. *Right to Trial by Jury.—Determination.—Issues.*—Whether an equitable issue is raised so as to prevent the trial of a cause by jury, must be determined from the substantial and material facts averred in the pleadings. *Heston* v. *Dougan*, 40, 47 (5).

3. *Right to Trial by Jury.—Equity.—Trusts.*—Under §418 Burns 1908, §409 R. S. 1881, providing how causes shall be tried, where the complaint in an administrator's action disclosed that plaintiff's decedent was the mother of defendant's decedent, and that

JURY—Continued.

the mother and son lived for many years in relations of the greatest trust and confidence, during which time the son marketed the products of the mother's land for her benefit, and deposited and loaned out the proceeds in his own name in trust for her, by reason of which the son's estate was indebted to the mother's estate in a certain sum, the refusal of the trial court to submit the entire cause to a jury was not erroneous.

Camp v. Camp, 250, 252 (4), 254 (4).

KNOWLEDGE—

Matters of common, see EVIDENCE 9.

LANDLORD AND TENANT—

1. *Action for Possession.—Defenses.—Pleading.—General Denial.—* In an action by a landlord against the tenant for possession, all defenses, legal and equitable, are admissible under the general denial. Heston v. Dougan, 40, 47 (6).

2. *Action for Possession.—Pleading.—Reply.—*The procedure and pleading in the circuit court, in an action by a landlord against the tenant for possession, follow the procedure in civil cases before justices, and by §1752 Burns 1908, §1463 R. S. 1881, in civil cases before a justice, a replication is unnecessary, so that the action of the circuit court in striking out plaintiff's reply to a paragraph of answer, in such a proceeding, is not error. Heston v. Dougan, 40, 46 (3).

3. *Action for Possession.—Answer Denying Relation of Landlord and Tenant.—Trial.—Right to Trial by Jury.—*In an action by a landlord against the tenant for possession, the defendant's answer averring that the relation of landlord and tenant never existed, that defendant was the owner of the land, and that the paper relied on by plaintiff as a lease was signed by defendant in reliance on the representations of plaintiff that it was a copy of a lost contract, and in which defendant asked for no affirmative relief, tendered issues provable under the general denial and amounted merely to an argumentative denial, so that the pleadings presented an ordinary action in ejectment, triable by jury. Heston v. Dougan, 40, 46 (4), 47 (4).

4. *Action for Possession.—Denial of Landlord's Title.—Answer.—Sufficiency.—*In an action for the possession of land alleged to be held by defendant as the lessee of plaintiff, an answer alleging title in defendant, denying that the relationship of landlord and tenant existed, and alleging that defendant's signature to the paper relied on by plaintiff as a lease was procured through the misrepresentation and fraud of plaintiff, is not demurrable on the theory that a tenant may not controvert the landlord's title during the existence of the tenancy, since that rule only applies where the relation of landlord and tenant exists and does not control where the existence of such relation is denied. Heston v. Dougan, 40, 45 (1).

5. *Action for Possession. — Instructions. — Issues. —* Where, in a landlord's action for possession, defendant alleged that the relation of landlord and tenant never existed and that he had been induced to sign the lease through the representation of plaintiff that it was merely a copy of a contract relating to a conveyance of the land that defendant had made to plaintiff to secure a debt, an instruction that if defendant and his wife executed a deed to plaintiff solely to secure a debt owing to plaintiff, such deed,

LANDLORD AND TENANT—Continued.

though absolute on its face, would be a mortgage and defendant would be entitled to possession of the property mentioned, and that such fact should be considered with all the other evidence relative to that issue in determining whether defendant knowingly executed the lease, was within the issues and a proper instruction on that branch of the case.

Heston v. *Dougan*, 40, 50 (10).

LAST CLEAR CHANCE—

See RAILROADS 12, 24.

LEASES—

See PARTITION 2.

LIABILITY—

See MUNICIPAL CORPORATIONS 12-15, 18.
Of carrier to passengers, see CARRIERS 2.

LIMITATION OF ACTIONS—

See DEATH 4.

1. *Accrual of Cause of Action.—Injury to Property.—Statutes.—* An action for injury by the overflow of real property is barred by the six years' statute of limitations, §294 Burns 1908, §292 R. R. 1881, where the acts which produced the overflow occurred more than six years before the bringing of the action, although the injuries are alleged to have been suffered within such six year period. *Seigmund* v. *Tyner*, 581, 584 (3).

2. *Accrual of Cause of Action.—Breach of Contract to Bequeath or Devise.—*Where a person fully performs his contract to perform services and to board and care for another during his lifetime, in consideration of the other's promise to will all his property to him, and the other party fails to leave such a will in force at his death, the breach occurs immediately prior to his death, at which time the cause of action accrues and the statute of limitations begins to run. *Paul* v. *Snyder*, 291, 295 (4).

3. *Accrual of Cause of Action.—Breach of Contract to Bequeath or Devise.—*Where a party who has agreed to will all his property to another, in consideration of the other's services in running his farm and providing him board and care during life, prevents performance on such person's part by so mistreating him that he is compelled to abandon his efforts to perform, the contract is terminated at the time of such abandonment and thereupon the statute of limitations begins to run against the right of action for the value of services rendered under the contract. *Paul* v. *Snyder*, 291, 296 (5).

4. *Concealment of Cause of Action.—Burden of Proof.—*One who alleges and relies on concealment to avoid the statute of limitations has the burden of proving same. *State, ex rel.,* v. *Jackson*, 254, 259 (6).

5. *Concealment of Cause of Action.—Entries on Public Records.—* Entries on public records, that may tend to mislead, cannot of themselves constitute a concealment of a cause of action, where, on investigation, such records reveal facts showing that such cause of action does exist. *State, ex rel.,* v. *Jackson*, 254, 259 (5).

LIMITATION OF ACTIONS—Continued.

6. *Concealment of Cause of Action.—Special Findings.*—Special findings, to be sufficient to avoid the statute of limitations on the ground of concealment, should show such concealment as an ultimate fact, or it must appear therefrom as a necessary inference from the facts found.   *State, ex rel.,* v. *Jackson,* 254, 259 (7).

7. *Concealment of Cause of Action.—Knowledge of Existence of Cause of Action.—Board of County Commissioners.*—Where a board of county commissioners had knowledge of the existence of an indebtedness to the county, the subsequent change in the personnel of the board could not affect the question of knowledge thereof by the board, since such board is a perpetual body not affected by changes in its membership.
State, ex rel., v. *Jackson,* 254, 259 (4).

8. *Concealment of Cause of Action.*—To constitute concealment of a cause of action so as to prevent the running of the statute of limitations, some trick or artifice must be employed to prevent inquiry or elude investigation, or which is calculated to mislead and hinder the party who has the cause of action from obtaining information, by the use of ordinary diligence, that a right of action exists, and the acts relied on must be of an affirmative character and fraudulent.   *State, ex rel.,* v. *Jackson,* 254, 258 (2).

9. *Concealment of Cause of Action.—Entries on Public Records.—Special Findings.—Sufficiency.*—In an action by the state on relation of the board of county commissioners against a former official and the sureties on his bond to recover money wrongfully appropriated, special findings, showing that an entry had been made by the board of commissioners authorizing the dismissal of a former action for the recovery of such money, stating that it had been compromised and settled, and showing its dismissal, and findings showing that nothing had ever been paid pursuant to such compromise, and that the persons constituting the board of commissioners at the time of the latter action had no knowledge of the indebtedness until shortly before bringing the action, were insufficient to show a concealment of the cause of action so as to avoid the statute of limitations pleaded by such sureties.
State, ex rel., v. *Jackson,* 254, 259 (3), 260 (3).

10. *Mortgage Debt.—Part Payment by Adult Tenant in Common.—Effect on Infant Tenant in Common.*—An adult heir, who is a tenant in common of real estate with a minor heir, is not by virtue of the relation of co-tenancy the implied agent of the minor and cannot, by making part payments on the ancestor's mortgage debt, toll the statute of limitations against such minor.
Weidenhammer v. *McAdams,* 98, 104 (7).

11. *Part Payment by One of Several Joint Debtors.—Effect.*—A part payment by one of several joint debtors can serve only to suspend the running of the statute of limitations as against the party making the payment, by himself or duly authorized agent.
Weidenhammer v. *McAdams,* 98, 101 (1).

12. *Part Payment of Debt.—Implication.—Infants.*—Part payment takes a debt out of the statute of limitations by virtue of the legal implication that such part payment is a new promise to pay the residue of the debt, but such implied promise does not operate to bind an infant, since he cannot toll the statute even by an express promise.   *Weidenhammer* v. *McAdams,* 98, 103 (4).

MACHINERY—

As to the guarding of, see MASTER AND SERVANT 13.

Unguarded, see MASTER AND SERVANT 29, 49.

"MANUFACTURING ESTABLISHMENT"—

See WORDS AND PHRASES.

MASTER AND SERVANT.

I. THE RELATION, 1-4.

II. SERVICES AND COMPENSATION, 5-7.

III. MASTER'S LIABILITY TO SERVANT.
    (a) NATURE AND EXTENT IN GEN-
      ERAL, 8-12.
    (b) WORKS, WAYS AND MACHIN-
      ERY, 13-23.

(c) WARNING AND INSTRUCTING
    SERVANTS, 24, 25.

(d) CONTRIBUTORY NEGLIGENCE,
    26-29.

(e) FELLOW SERVANTS, 30-33.

(f) ASSUMPTION OF RISK, 34-42.

IV. ACTIONS, 43-49.

I. THE RELATION.

1. *Injury to Servant.—Existence of Relation.—Complaint.*—The statement in a complaint for injuries to a servant, that plaintiff was in the employ of defendant as a common laborer, fixes the relation of master and servant, and sufficiently shows the existence of the legal duty owing to plaintiff by defendant to use ordinary care to furnish him a reasonably safe place in which to work, and reasonably safe appliances with which to work. *South Bend, etc., Plow Co.* v. *Cissne* (1905), 35 Ind. App. 373, is overruled. *I. F. Force Handle Co.* v. *Hisey*, 235, 242 (3).

2. *Injury to Servant.—Complaint.—Construction.*—A complaint alleging that plaintiff was employed in defendant's shale bank or pit as a common laborer or shoveler, that defendant's shot-firer was discharged by defendant, and that defendant, knowing that the pit was unsafe, wrongfully and negligently ordered and directed plaintiff to go into such dangerous place and blast and loosen such shale and continue loading cars, does not show that plaintiff was employed as, or accepted the position of shot-firer, but that he was merely transferred temporarily from his employment as a shoveler to that of a shot-firer.
Osborn v. *Adams Brick Co.*, 175, 182 (5).

3. *Injury to Servant.—Complaint.—Sufficiency.*—In a servant's action for personal injuries, a complaint alleging that plaintiff was employed as a common laborer in and about defendant's factory, and that while so employed, and while he was engaged in his duties as such common laborer, and while he was so standing in the yards of said defendant, he was injured through the negligence of defendant, is not insufficient on the ground that it does not show that plaintiff at the time of his injury was acting in the line of his duty as an employe of defendant, or that defendant owed him any duty, since the word "duties" refers to any work which his employment required him to perform as common labor, and the word "so," in the allegation that the injury occurred while he was "so" standing in the yards, refers back to the statement that he was engaged in his duties.
I. F. Force Handle Co. v. *Hisey*, 235, 239 (1).

4. *Injury to Servant.—Place of Work.—Duty of Master.—Complaint.—Necessary Allegations.*—Where the relation of master and servant exists, the law imposes on the master the general duty to furnish the servant a reasonably safe place in which to perform his work, so that a complaint in a servant's action for

MASTER AND SERVANT—Continued.

personal injuries, showing that the relation of master and servant existed at the time of the injury and that the servant was performing the work which he was employed to do, need not specifically aver that the material duty was owing to him; but the allegation of facts showing the existence of such duty is necessary where the complaint discloses that the servant's employment required him to do a particular work in a particular place, and that at the time of the injury he was not in such place, but in a different one where the performance of the particular work could not have called him.

> *I. F. Force Handle Co.* v. *Hisey*, 235, 240 (2).

II. Services and Compensation.

5. *Injury to Servant.—Instructions.—Damages.*—Where, in an employe's action for damages, there was evidence that was not competent on the question of the amount of damages, an instruction, that in determining the amount of damages, "every particular and phase of the injury may enter into consideration in estimating such damages," was erroneous.

> *Sanitary Can Co.* v. *McKinney*, 379, 387 (9).

6. *Injury to Servant.—Instructions.—Evidence.—Damages.*—In an action by an employe for personal injuries, where there was evidence that plaintiff was living at home with a widowed mother, who had six children, that plaintiff began working at the age of fourteen, and that two of his sisters were working in defendant's factory, an instruction that the amount of damages should be determined "from all the facts and circumstances in the case as shown by the evidence," was erroneous, since such evidence was not competent on the question of damages.

> *Sanitary Can Co.* v. *McKinney*, 379, 386 (8).

7. *Injury to Servant.—Proximate Cause.—Furnishing Employes Beer.*—The act of defendant's superintendent in furnishing beer on his own account to defendant's employes as a reward for accomplishing an unusual amount of work, was not the proximate cause of injury to an employe who was crushed by an electric motor operated by an incompetent and intoxicated person, who was not the regular motorman, but was in control thereof at the request of the regular motorman, without the knowledge or acquiescence of defendant, or any of its officers or agents, and such regular motorman was not intoxicated and had not partaken of the beer.   *Columbia Creosoting Co.* v. *Beard*, 260, 266 (7).

III. Master's Liability to Servant.

(A) Nature and Extent in General.

8. *Injury to Servant.—Work Outside Regular Employment.—Liability.*—Where a servant employed to do certain work, was injured while performing work which he voluntarily undertook to perform without direction, request or acquiescence of the employer, and which was not included in the service which he was employed to perform, recovery for such injury is precluded.

> *Columbia Creosoting Co.* v. *Beard*, 260, 265 (5).

9. *Negligence.—Vice Principal.*—An employe, regardless of his rank or grade, who is authorized to perform a duty which is clearly the master's duty, is to that extent a vice principal and his act is the act of the master, and, in determining the master's

MASTER AND SERVANT—Continued.

liability for his negligence, the controlling inquiry is whether his act or omission involved a duty owing by the master to the injured servant. *Patterson* v. *Southern R. Co.*, 618, 623 (3).

10. *Places of Work.—Tools and Appliances.—Duty of Master.—Delegation of Duty.*—The master's duty of providing a reasonably safe place for the servant to work, and safe tools and appliances with which to work, is a continuing one and cannot be delegated by him to an employe so as to avoid responsibility for its violation. *Patterson* v. *Southern R. Co.*, 618, 623 (2).

11. *Injury to Servant.—Complaint.—Violation of Statutory Duty.—Assumption of Risk.*—The doctrine of assumption of risk does not apply in a servant's action for personal injuries, where the complaint alleges facts showing the master's violation of a statutory duty, and in such case it is unnecessary to allege facts showing that the risk was not assumed. *Koehler* v. *Harmon*, 315, 318 (2).

12. *Injury to Servant.—Violation of Statutory Duty.—Negligence.—Complaint.—Sufficiency.*—A complaint for the death of an employe, alleging that the death was caused by the employer's omission, in violation of statute, to guard a dangerous belt, sufficiently charges negligence without averring such failure to be a negligent failure, since the failure to discharge a duty imposed by statute is negligence *per se*. *Angola R., etc., Co.* v. *Butz*, 420, 425 (5).

(B) WORKS, WAYS AND MACHINERY.

13. *Injury to Servant. — Guarding Machinery. — Sufficiency of Guards.—Question for Jury.*—Since §8029 Burns 1908, Acts 1899 p. 231, providing for the guarding of dangerous machinery, does not describe the manner in which dangerous machinery shall be guarded or what shall be deemed a proper guard, the question of whether the statutory requirement has been complied with is, in each case, one of fact to be determind by the jury from the character of the machine and the nature of the peril. *Sanitary Can Co.* v. *McKinney*, 379, 385 (6).

14. *Injury to Servant.—Failure to Comply with Factory Act.—Complaint.—Sufficiency.*—A complaint, in an action for the death of a servant who was caught in an unguarded belt, alleging that defendant furnished electricity to various customers, and that, as a part of the machinery in its plant, it had boilers, dynamos and engines, sufficiently shows that defendant was engaged in the generation of electricity, so as to be within the provisions of §8029 Burns 1908, Acts 1899 p. 231, for the guarding of certain dangerous machinery. *Angola R., etc., Co.* v. *Butz*, 420, 423 (1).

15. *Injury to Servant.—Verdict.—Answers to Interrogatories.*—In an action for the death of a servant, whose arm was caught by an unguarded belt while he was attempting to adjust the idler, the general verdict for plaintiff is not overcome by answers to interrogatories showing that he was attempting to do the work with the means provided, and in the usual way, but that the place where he was attempting to adjust such idler was more dangerous than other places where he could have done the same work. *Angola, R., etc., Co.* v. *Butz*, 420, 430 (11).

16. *Injury to Servant.—Elevator Accident.—Elevator Not in Control of Master.—Liability.*—Where a servant is employed to hoist flour by an elevator to the upper story of a building leased in part by his employer, and is injured by reason of defects in such

MASTER AND SERVANT—Continued.

elevator, even though the employer under his lease has no control
over the elevator, the rule that the master is bound to furnish
a reasonably safe place for the servant to work, and reasonably
safe appliances and machinery, applies, and such employer is
liable, if, by the exercise of ordinary care the elevator would
have been known to be dangerous.
				National Biscuit Co. v. *Wilson,* 630, 633 (3).

17. *Injury to Servant.—Verdict.—Answers to Interrogatories.—*
Where the complaint in a servant's action for personal injuries
is on the theory that plaintiff was employed by defendant as a
common laborer, and that he was ordered by defendant to perform temporarily the duties of a shot-firer in defendant's shale
pit, in the performance of which duties he was injured, a general verdict for plaintiff is not overcome by answers to interrogatories showing that plaintiff was given the position of, and proceeded to discharge the duties of, shot-firer in the place of a
shot-firer who had been discharged, since such answers do not
conclusively show that plaintiff was employed to take the position in any other sense or to any further extent than that charged
in the complaint.		*Osborn* v. *Adams Brick Co.,* 175, 187 (15).

18. *Injury to Servant.—Verdict.—Answers to Interrogatories.—*In
a servant's action for injuries to his hand by being caught in the
unguarded cogs of a machine, a verdict for plaintiff is not overcome by answers to interrogatories showing that such cogs were
covered by a box, which plaintiff had removed, that such removal
was necessary in doing the work that he was doing at the time
of the injury, and that if he had not removed it, he could not
have received the injury, since the general verdict amounted to a
finding that such box was not a proper guard.
				Sanitary Can Co. v. *McKinney,* 379, 384 (5), 385 (5).

19. *Injury to Servant.—Complaint.—Verdict.—Answers to Interrogatories.—*In an action for the death of a servant by being
crushed by an electric motor, allegations of the complaint to the
effect that the device for controlling the motor was defective and
that defendant placed an incompetent person in charge of the motor, cannot be reconciled with facts specially found showing that
the accident was not caused by defects in the motor, that a competent motorman was employed by defendant to operate such motor, but that defendant's switchman, without the direction or
knowledge of defendant, or of any person representing it, undertook to and was operating such motor at the time of the accident.
				Columbia Creosoting Co. v. *Beard,* 260, 265 (4).

20. *Injury to Servant.—Unguarded Saw.—Contributory Negligence.
—Evidence.—Verdict.—*In a servant's action for injury to his
hand by coming in contact with an unguarded saw while he was
attempting to remove a piece of wood that had lodged in the
saw-table, where there was evidence showing that plaintiff could
have stopped the saw by going around the table and using a
lever provided for that purpose, while other evidence showed that
if he had attempted to do so he would thereby have exposed
himself to other serious dangers, and that in attempting to remove the wood without stopping the saw plaintiff was pursuing
the usual course, the question of whether he used due care was
one of fact for the jury and its verdict thereon will not be disturbed.		*Espenlaub* v. *Hedderick,* 139, 142 (5).

21. *Injury to Servant.—Verdict.—Answers to Interrogatories.—*In
an action by a servant for injuries sustained by the breaking of

MASTER AND SERVANT—Continued.

a defective link in a chain used by defendant in moving a car, the general verdict for plaintiff amounted to a finding that the defect would have been apparent to one making a reasonably careful inspection of the chain, and one with knowledge of which defendant was chargeable, and answers to interrogatories showing that the link was defective because of imperfect weld, that a slight darkness in it at one point of the weld was the only thing to indicate any imperfections in the link or to distinguish its appearance from any other link in the chain, are not inconsistent with such general verdict, since it cannot be said therefrom that an inspection would have been useless, nor that the defect was a hidden one which defendant could not have discovered by the exercise of proper care, nor that the accident was inevitable and one which defendant could not anticipate.

I. F. Force Handle Co. v. *Hisey*, 235, 243 (5).

22. *Injury to Servant.—Verdict.—Answers to Interrogatories.—* Where the complaint, in a servant's action for personal injuries, alleged that plaintiff was a common laborer employed in defendant's shale pit, that defendant discharged its shot-firer for refusing to obey defendant's order to have the men work in the pit while it was in a dangerous condition, and that defendant, knowing that the pit was unsafe, wrongfully and negligently directed plaintiff to perform the duties of shot-firer, with knowledge that plaintiff was inexperienced and did not know and appreciate the danger, answers to interrogatories showing that the shot-firer was discharged because of unsatisfactory work, though excluding the idea that he was discharged because he refused to obey orders as alleged in the complaint, do not negative the facts found by the general verdict, that defendant knew and plaintiff did not know the hidden dangers incident to the new duties to which plaintiff was assigned. *Osborn* v. *Adams Brick Co.*, 175, 189 (17).

23. *Injury to Servant.—Verdict.—Answers to Interrogatories.—* Where the allegations of the complaint in a servant's action for personal injuries showed that plaintiff was employed as a common laborer and while working as such was called upon by de-defendant to perform temporarily the duties of shot-firer in defendant's shale pit, that it was a dangerous place in which to work, but appeared to plaintiff to be safe, that the danger was such that without long experience it was impossible for a person of ordinary prudence and foresight to discern it, that plaintiff had no experience and did not know or appreciate the danger, all of which defendant knew, and that defendant wrongfully and negligently ordered plaintiff to proceed to blast and loosen shale and to load cars in said dangerous place, and that in performing such work plaintiff was injured, a verdict for plaintiff is a finding that such allegations are true, so that a recovery by plaintiff is authorized unless the answers to interrogatories are in irreconcilable conflict therewith. *Osborn* v. *Adams Brick Co.*, 175, 185 (13).

(C) WARNING AND INSTRUCTING SERVANTS.

24. *Inexperienced Servant.—Duty to Warn and Instruct.—*Where the master requires a dangerous service at the hands of an inexperienced servant, it is the duty of the master to warn him and to give him such instructions as will enable him to avoid injury, unless both the danger and the means of avoiding it are apparent. *Osborn* v. *Adams Brick Co.*, 175, 183 (6).

25. *Injury to Servant.—Work Outside Scope of Employment.— Duty to Warn and Instruct.—*Where defendant, knowing of the

MASTER AND SERVANT—Continued.

dangerous condition of its shale pit, and knowing that plaintiff was a common laborer and did not understand and appreciate such danger, ordered him, in an emergency, to take the place of shot-firer in such pit, and plaintiff was injured within a few minutes after beginning such duties, the defendant's failure to warn and instruct plaintiff as to the dangers was inexcusable.

Osborn v. Adams Brick Co., 175, 186 (14).

(D)   CONTRIBUTORY NEGLIGENCE.

26.   *Injury to Servant.*—Contributory negligence is not necessarily established against an employe by showing that he continued to use defective machinery after he knew it was out of repair.

Angola R., etc., Co. v. Butz, 420, 429 (9).

27.   *Injury to Servant.*—*Jury Question.*—In an action for the death of a stationary engineer, whose arm was caught by an unguarded belt while he was attempting to adjust the idler, where it was shown that he was attempting to do the work by the means provided and in the usual way, but that the place where he was attempting to adjust the idler was more dangerous than other places where he could have done the same work, the question of his contributory negligence was for the jury.

Angola R., etc., Co. v. Butz, 420, 429 (10).

28.   *Injury to Servant. — Verdict. — Conclusiveness. — Motion for Judgment on Answers to Interrogatories.*—Where an employe was injured by his hand being caught in the cogs of a machine, the question of whether he was guilty of contributory negligence in attempting to remove certain receptacles while the machine was running, was determined in his favor by the general verdict, and cannot be considered under a motion for judgment on answers to interrogatories which presents the question as to whether such answers, which showed that the cogs were guarded by a box and that the injury could not have happened if plaintiff had not removed the box, were in conflict with the general verdict.

Sanitary Can Co. v. McKinney, 379, 385 (7).

29.   *Injury to Servant.*—*Unguarded Machinery.*—*Complaint.*—In a servant's action for personal injuries, the allegations of the complaint that the injury was caused by defendants' negligence in failing to guard the saw, that by reason of a defect in the saw-table a piece of wood became lodged near the saw, and that, while attempting to remove it, plaintiff's hand was caught in the saw and injured, but which neither show the distance of plaintiff's hand from the saw when he took hold of the wood, nor that he placed his hand in dangerous proximity to the saw, do not show affirmatively as a matter of law that plaintiff was guilty of contributory negligence.   *Espenlaub v. Hedderick*, 139, 141 (1).

(E)   FELLOW SERVANTS.

30.   *Injury to Servant.*—*Complaint.*—*Negligence of Fellow Servant.*—A complaint, from which it affirmatively appears that the injury was the proximate result of the negligence of a fellow servant, is bad and there can be no recovery thereon, but the rule does not apply where the negligence of the master, combined with the negligence of the fellow servant, was the proximate cause of the injury. *Vandalia Coal Co. v. Haverkamp*, 397, 400 (2).

31.   *Injury to Servants.*—*Negligence.*—Where workmen, in the construction of a bridge, erect a scaffold on their own initiative and

INDEX. 763

MASTER AND SERVANT—Continued.

for their own convenience, and the order of the foreman directing the building of same was merely an executive detail of the work, the foreman is a fellow servant for whose negligence in such construction the master is not liable.

Patterson v. Southern R. Co., 618, 624 (4).

32. *Injury to Servant.—Incompetent Fellow Servants.—Verdict.—Answers to Interrogatories.*—No recovery can be had against the master for injury to a servant, on the theory of the master's negligence in employing an incompetent fellow servant, where the injury resulted from the act of an intoxicated, inexperienced and incompetent servant in starting an electric motor backward instead of forward, and the special findings show that such incompetent servant was not employed to operate the motor and was not placed in charge thereof by defendant, or anyone representing defendant, but that he took charge of same at the request of defendant's regular and competent motorman, without the knowledge or consent of defendant or any person representing it.

Columbia Creosoting Co. v. Beard, 260, 266 (6).

33. *Injury to Servants.—Jury Question.*—In an action by a servant for personal injuries sustained by the falling of a temporary scaffold erected on the side of a railroad fill, on which ties were being prepared to use in the construction of a railroad bridge, where there was evidence that during the three years that plaintiff was employed by defendant as a bridge carpenter such platforms were always constructed under the direction of the foreman, that it was usual and customary, in erecting such platforms on the side of a fill, to make secure the ends of the stringer ties next to the track to keep the structure from tipping, and that plaintiff believed the platform was thus made secure when he went upon it, the court was not warranted in directing a verdict for defendant, but the question of whether such evidence warranted the conclusion that the erection of such platforms was a part of defendant's general plan of operation under similar conditions, so as to render the negligence of the foreman in directing the construction of the platform that of a vice principal should have gone to the jury under proper instructions of the court.

Patterson v. Southern R. Co., 618, 625 (5).

(F) ASSUMPTION OF RISK.

34. The risks assumed by an employe in any case are those ordinarily incident to the particular work covered by the contract of hiring. *Osborn v. Adams Brick Co.*, 175, 184 (10).

35. *Employment to Make Dangerous Place Safe.*—One employed to do the work of making a dangerous place safe, assumes the risks ordinarily incident to such employment.

Osborn v. Adams Brick Co., 175, 184 (9).

36. *Hazardous Employment.*—One who enters upon an employment which is from its nature necessarily hazardous, assumes the usual and ordinary risks and perils of such service.

Osborn v. Adams Brick Co., 175, 184 (8).

37. *Injury to Servant.—Violation of Statutory Duty.*—The doctrine of assumed risk has no application when the death or injury of an employe is caused by the employer's failure to safeguard machinery as required by statute.

Angola R., etc., Co. v. Butz, 420, 425 (6).

38. *Work Outside Scope of Employment.*—The servant's implied assumption of risk, which is a part of the contract of hiring, is

MASTER AND SERVANT—Continued.

confined to the particular work or class of work for which he is
employed, and if he is ordered temporarily to do other work, involving different or greater dangers than those incident to the
work within the scope of his employment, he does not, by obeying
such orders, necessarily assume the risk incident thereto.

Osborn v. *Adams Brick Co.*, 175, 183 (7).

39. *Injury to Servant.—Negligence of Master.—Instructions.*—An
instruction, that while a servant assumes the ordinary risks incident to his master's business, in which he is engaged, he does not
assume those risks occasioned by the master's negligence, unless
such risks were occasioned by defects of which the servant had
knowledge, or of which he is chargeable with knowledge, is cor-
rect.   *I. F. Force Handle Co.* v. *Hisey*, 235, 246 (7).

40. *Right of Servant to Rely on Master Providing Safe Place to
Work.—Employment to Make Dangerous Place Safe.*—A servant
may ordinarily assume that the master has provided him a safe
place in which to work, and rely on that assumption, except as to
defects and dangers which he may ascertain by ordinary care for
his own safety; and while one who undertakes to make a dangerous place safe may not presume that the master has already done
the work he is employed to do, he does not assume all possible
risks, but only those incident to such employment.

Osborn v. *Adams Brick Co.*, 175, 184 (11).

41. *Injury to Servant.—Instructions.*—Where the complaint, in a
servant's action for personal injuries, alleged facts sufficient to
constitute a cause of action and showing nonassumption of risk,
an instruction that if plaintiff has proved the material allegations
thereof by a preponderance of the evidence, he is entitled to a
verdict, provided the evidence does not show that he was guilty of
contributory negligence, was not erroneous on the ground that it
omitted the question of assumption of risk by plaintiff, and especially where the jury was fully informed on that subject by other
instructions.   *I. F. Force Handle Co.* v. *Hisey*, 235, 246 (6).

42. *Injury to Servant.—Work Outside Scope of Employment.*—
Where a complaint against the master for personal injuries proceeds on the theory that plaintiff was employed as a common
laborer and while working as such was called upon by defendant
to perform temporarily the duties of shot-firer after the discharge
of defendant's regular shot-firer, and alleges that plaintiff was
assigned to such new duties after the regular shot-firer had reported to defendant that conditions in the place of work were unsafe and had refused to send the men back to work in such place
unless he was first permitted to make the place safe, the rule as
to assumption of risk, governing where one is employed to make
a dangerous place safe, is not applicable.

Osborn v. *Adams Brick Co.*, 175, 185 (12).

IV. ACTIONS.

43. *Injury to Servant.—Complaint.—Proof.*—To entitle a servant
to judgment in an action against the master for personal injuries, the complaint must allege, and he must prove, some act of
negligence by defendant which resulted in the injury.

National Biscuit Co. v. *Wilson*, 630, 631 (1).

44. *Injury to Servant.—Complaint.—Allegations.—"Duty."*—In an
action for the death of a stationary engineer, whose arm was
caught by an unguarded belt, the allegation of the complaint, that

MASTER AND SERVANT—Continued.

it was a part of decedent's duty to adjust such belt, is not the statement of a conclusion, but is the allegation of an ultimate fact. *Angola R., etc., Co.* v. *Butz,* 420, 426 (7).

45. *Injury to Servant.—Complaint.—Sufficiency.—Initial Attack on Appeal.*—A complaint for injuries to an employe, which was sufficient to bar another action for the same injury, was good as against an objection, first made on appeal, that it did not state facts sufficient to constitute a cause of action, although its averments do not clearly show how the machine was constructed or operated, nor the manner in which plaintiff received his injury.

Sanitary Can Co. v. *McKinney,* 379, 283 (2).

46. *Injury to Servant.—Complaint.—Theory.*—Where the complaint, in a servant's action for personal injuries, although alleging in general terms that defendant directed plaintiff to go to work on a certain machine, without giving proper instructions as to the use and operation thereof, averred that the gearing and cogs were not guarded, and that the injury was caused solely by the failure and neglect of defendant to guard same, the failure to guard such gearing and cogs must be deemed to be the theory on which the right to recover is predicated.

Sanitary Can Co. v. *McKinney,* 379, 382 (1).

47. *Injury to Servant.—Complaint.—Proximate Cause.*—A complaint, in an action by a coal miner for personal injuries, alleging that defendant failed to furnish him a reasonably safe place in which to work, and failed to perform its statutory duty of sprinkling the roadways and entries of its mine, so that the air therein became charged with dust, that the same could have been sprinkled and the dust allayed without interfering in the operation of the mine, that the concussion and fire, resulting from illegal shots fired by other miners, acted on the air in the roadways and entries so as to produce a dust explosion in which plaintiff was injured, and that such explosion could not have occurred if defendant had sprinkled the dust and if such illegal shots had not been fired, shows that the combined negligence of the defendant and the miners was the proximate cause of the injury, and was sufficient to withstand a demurrer.

Vandalia Coal Co. v. *Haverkamp,* 307, 309 (1).

48. *Injury to Servant.—Knowledge of Defect.—Instructions.*—Where the complaint in a servant's action for personal injuries, caused by the breaking of a chain, charged that the chain was defective and also that it was not sufficient to stand the strain to which it was put and for which it was used, and the law governing the necessity of showing knowledge of the danger on the master's part was sufficiently stated to the jury, an instruction that if plaintiff has proved by a preponderance of the evidence either of such allegations, and if under the evidence he is otherwise entitled to recover, and was not guilty of contributory negligence and had not assumed the risk, he has made a case, is not open to the objection that the element of knowledge or means of knowledge on defendant's part is ignored.

I. F. Force Handle Co. v. *Hiscy,* 235, 247 (8).

49. *Injury to Servant.—Unguarded Machinery.—Complaint.—Sufficiency.*—A complaint, in a servant's action for personal injuries, alleging that a lathe used in defendant's shops, and which plaintiff was employed to operate, was of dangerous character, that the same could have been guarded, without impairing its usefulness, so as to protect the eyes and face of the operator from

MASTER AND SERVANT—Continued.

injury, that on the day of the injury the dog-plate on said lathe
had been removed and plaintiff was directed to use a face-plate
thereon instead, that said lathe was thereby rendered unsafe and
dangerous, that defendant furnished a defective file to be used in
connection with the work on said lathe, and negligently
failed to guard said lathe, and that while operating said
lathe the file was, by reason of its defective condition and
the absence of a guard on said lathe, hurled against plaintiff's
face, causing the injury complained of, sufficiently states a cause
of action within the provisions of §8029 Burns 1908, Acts 1899 p.
231, requiring certain machinery to be guarded.
　　　　　　　　　　　Koehler v. *Harmon,* 315, 316 (1).

MASTER COMMISSIONER—

The report of a, is not a finding of the court, see COURTS 2.

MEASURE OF DAMAGES—

In an action by a father for the wrongful death of his child, see
DEATH 2.

MEDICAL EXAMINER—

Powers of, see INSURANCE 16.

MISCONDUCT—

Of counsel, relief from, see APPEAL 10.
Of counsel, see APPEAL 138.

MISTAKE—

In the use of words in an instruction so obvious that the jury could
not have been misled, the error will be deemed immaterial, see
APPEAL 129.

MORTGAGES—

Action to declare deed a mortgage, see DEEDS 2-4.

Foreclosure.—Evidence.—Burden of Proof.—In an action to foreclose a mortgage, while plaintiff may show that the mortgage, although in form definite in amount, was in fact an indemnity
against contingent loss, he has the burden of proving such fact by
competent evidence, and the instrument, unaided by parol evidence, would be insufficient to establish the claim to indemnity.
　　　　　　　　　　　Hubbard v. *Ranje,* 611, 616 (5).

MUNICIPAL CORPORATIONS—

See INJUNCTION 4-6.

1. *Streets.—Duty to Light.—Liability for Failure.*—The lighting of
streets by a municipality is merely the exercise of a governmental
function, and negligence cannot be imputed for a failure to exercise such power.
　　　　City of Bloomington v. *Chicago, etc., R. Co.,* 510, 520 (7).

2. *Streets.—Vacation.—Damages.*—A person claiming damages by
reason of the vacation or obstruction of a street must show that
he has suffered, or will suffer, an injury different in kind, and not
simply in degree, from that suffered by the community in general.
　　　　Southern R. Co. v. *Town of French Lick,* 447, 456 (11).

MUNICIPAL CORPORATIONS—Continued.

3. *Streets.—Vacation.—Procedure.—*To be entitled to the rights and privileges given by §§8910, 8916 Burns 1908, Acts 1907 p. 617, §§3, 9, providing for the vacation of streets, and the method of procedure, the parties must bring themselves within the provisions of the statute.
Southern R. Co. v. Town of French Lick, 447, 452 (1).

4. *Streets.—Vacation.—Procedure.—Demurrer to Petition.—*Filing a demurrer to a petition for the vacation of a street is a permissible means of objecting to its sufficiency, and is not inconsistent with the provisions of §§8910, 8916 Burns 1908, Acts 1907 p. 617, §§3, 9, providing for the vacation of streets and the method of procedure, since, if the petition is insufficient under the statute, no remonstrance is necessary, and, if it is sufficient, the right to file a remonstrance within the specified time is not thereby lost.
Southern R. Co. v. Town of French Lick, 447, 453 (4).

5. *Streets.—Vacation.—Petition.—Sufficiency.—*A petition for the vacation of a street, alleging that the petitioner is the owner of all the ground on both sides of that part of the street to be vacated, and that other streets particularly described "afford proper ingress and egress to the citizens of said town and the residents of said street," sufficiently complies with the requirement of §8910 Burns 1908, Acts 1907 p. 617, §3, requiring such petition to state the names of the persons "particularly interested" in the vacation of the street "who shall be affected thereby."
Southern R. Co. v. Town of French Lick, 447, 453 (6), 454 (6).

6. *Streets.—Vacation.—Persons Entitled to Object.—Statutes.—*While §§8910, 8916 Burns 1908, Acts 1907 p. 617, §§3, 9, providing for the vacation of streets and the method of procedure, do not limit the right to object to the vacation of a street to those persons who own property abutting on that part of the street to be vacated, persons, who have sufficient or "specially suited" means of ingress or egress, have no more than a general interest common to all the citizens, and are not required to be named in the petition. *Southern R. Co. v. Town of French Lick,* 447, 455 (10).

7. *Streets.—Vacation.—Remonstrance.—Time for Filing.—*Under §8910 Burns 1908, Acts 1907 p. 617, §3, providing that notice of the filing and pendency of a petition for the vacation of a street "shall be given as in this act provided," and if no objection within such time be made in writing, the court shall grant the prayer of such petition, construed with §8916 Burns 1908, Acts 1907 p. 617, §9, providing for the giving of such notice by publication for ten days by two successive weekly publications which shall state the time and place when and where the petition shall be heard, where the notice was first published on November 29 and stated that the hearing would be had on December 10, a remonstrance filed on December 10 was filed in time.
Southern R. Co. v. Town of French Lick, 447, 452 (2).

8. *Streets.—Excavations.—Duty to Guard.—*It is the duty of one who causes an excavation to be made in a public street to guard the same, and to use reasonable care to protect persons lawfully using such street from injury on account of such excavation.
Marion, etc., Construction Co. v. Claycomb, 681, 684 (3).

9. *Streets.—Excavation by Water Company in Connection With Work of Sewer Construction Company.—Negligence.—Verdict.—Answers to Interrogatories.—*Where, in an action for injuries sustained in falling into an excavation in a street made by a water

MUNICIPAL CORPORATIONS—Continued.

company in connection with the work of sewer construction in charge of a construction company, it was shown that the construction company in undertaking the construction of the sewer undertook to use all due precaution for the safety of persons and property, and where, under the issues, it was competent to show that in its contract with the city the construction company undertook to protect the mains and service pipes of the water company, it will be presumed that such fact was shown, so that interrogatories showing that the excavation was made by the water company for the purpose of closing a water pipe laid across the street where the sewer was being constructed, and was made pursuant to a contract with the construction company wherein the latter agreed to place lights and danger signals at such excavation, and that it failed to do so, are not in conflict with the general verdict against the construction company on the theory that its agreement with the water company was not binding on it. *Marion, etc., Construction Co. v. Claycomb*, 681, 686 (6).

10. *Defective Streets.—Liability of Abutting Owners.*—A property owner, who, by some affirmative wrongful act, causes the defective condition of a street, is liable to the city or town for any amount which it may be required to pay as damages on account of such defect. *City of Bloomington v. Chicago, etc., R. Co.*, 510, 515 (2).

11. *Defective Streets.—Railroad Crossings.—Liability of Railroad Company.—Statutes.*—Under §5250 et seq. Burns 1908, Acts 1895 p. 233, requiring railroad companies to properly grade and plank their roads at all street crossings, so as to afford security for life and property at such crossings, providing for the collection of penalties for failure so to do, and also providing that the municipality may, on their failure so to do, have the work done at the expense of such railroads, it is the primary duty of a railroad company so to construct and maintain all street crossings as to make them reasonably safe for travel, and a railroad company is primarily liable for injuries resulting from its failure to perform such duty. *City of Bloomington v. Chicago, etc., R. Co.*, 510, 515 (3).

12. *Defective Streets.—Railroad Crossings.—Liability.*—One, who is injured by a defective street caused by the failure of a railroad company to properly repair such street at the intersection of its tracks therewith, may bring an action against the railroad company, or he may bring it against the city, since, as between the city and the public, the city stands as a guarantor that the company will not be negligent, and, it is therefore primarily liable for such negligence; and where the city has been obliged to pay, the company is primarily liable to it for such damages, together with the costs and expenses fairly incurred. *City of Bloomington v. Chicago, etc., R. Co.*, 510, 517 (4), 518 (4).

13. *Care of Sidewalks.—Notice of Defects.—Liability.*—It is the duty of a municipal corporation to keep its sidewalks in a reasonably safe condition for the use of the public, and it is liable for all defects therein of which it had actual knowledge, or which were so obvious, or had existed for such a length of time, that its officers would be apprised of them, if they were diligent in the performance of their duty. *City of Indianapolis v. Ray*, 388, 391 (2).

14. *Defective Sidewalk.—Notice of Defect by City Fireman.—Liability.*—Knowledge of the defective condition of a sidewalk by a

MUNICIPAL CORPORATIONS—Continued.

member of the city fire department, will not of itself constitute notice to the city of such defect.

City of Indianapolis v. Ray, 388, 396 (5).

15. *Defective Sidewalks.—Liability.*—In the absence of actual notice, municipal corporations are only liable for such defects in sidewalks as are apparent, or are suggested by appearances, or are disclosed by a test in the nature of the ordinary use of such walks. *City of Indianapolis v. Ray*, 388, 395 (4).

16. *Defective Sidewalks.—Injury to Pedestrian.—Complaint.*—In an action against a municipal corporation for personal injuries caused by a defective sidewalk, a paragraph of complaint alleging facts showing that the sidewalk had been unsafe for a number of years, that defendant, by the exercise of proper care and diligence, could have known of such unsafe condition and could have made the same safe before the injury, that, for a period of two years before the injury, employes of defendant inspected the basement of a building adjacent to such sidewalk, and, if such inspections had been made with proper care, the defect could have been discovered, and that plaintiff had no knowledge of such defective condition, and could not have discovered it in the exercise of ordinary care, shows a violation of a duty owing to plaintiff and is sufficient to withstand a demurrer.

City of Indianapolis v. Ray, 388, 390 (1).

17. *Defective Sidewalks.—Injury to Pedestrian.—Notice of Defect.—Evidence.*—In an action for injuries in falling through a defective sidewalk, evidence that the defect could not be discovered from any outward appearance of the walk, that the walk broke and allowed plaintiff to fall at the given point, because the foundation thereunder had been washed out, that the sand and gravel composing the foundation had gradually washed into the basement of an adjacent building, through an opening where a waterpipe penetrated the basement wall, that some years prior to the injury a similar defect in the walk had been caused by the giving way of the basement wall, and that for two years prior to plaintiff's injury a member of the city fire department entered such basement at various times to direct the removal of paper and rubbish, was insufficient to show that the city had either actual or constructive notice of the defect which caused the injury.

City of Indianapolis v. Ray, 388, 392 (3).

18. *Streets and Public Ways.—Defects.—Liability.*—Cities have complete jurisdiction over all streets and public ways within their respective limits, under §§8655, 8960-8966 Burns 1908, Acts 1905 p. 219, §§53, 266-271, and consequently are liable for failure to keep such public highways in reasonably safe condition for travel.

City of Bloomington v. Chicago, etc., R. Co., 510, 515 (1).

19. *Public Improvements.—Contracts.—Guaranties of Work and Stipulations for Repairs.—Retention of Guaranty Fund After Judgment for Repairs Made.*—Where by a contract for street paving, the contractor warranted the work and agreed to make such repairs as should become necessary, and the city was authorized to retain a portion of the contract price as a repair guaranty fund, a recovery by the city of the cost of resurfacing a portion of the street does not prevent it from holding the balance of the fund as a guaranty for the repair of other portions of the street until the end of the guaranty period.

Barber Asphalt Pav. Co. v. City of Indianapolis, 587, 602 (6).

MUNICIPAL CORPORATIONS—Continued.

20. *Public Improvements.—Contracts.—Guaranties of Work and Stipulations for Repairs.—Notice to Repair.*—Under a contract for street paving in which the work was warranted for a certain period, and by which the character and extent of the repairs were left to the board of public works, and the repairs were to be made to its satisfaction, where the notice to repair was given pursuant to a resolution and order of the board, and gave complete information of the action of such board, the fact that such notice required the complete resurfacing of the street, which was unnecessary, will not relieve the contractor from liability for the cost of repairs made by the city on his failure to make them.
Barber Asphalt Pav. Co. v. *City of Indianapolis,* 587, 602 (5).

21. *Public Improvements.—Contracts.—Guaranties of Work and Stipulations for Repairs.—Breach.—Evidence.—Sufficiency.*—In an action by a city against a contractor for the cost of street repairs rendered necessary within the guaranty period, although there was evidence that such repairs were made necessary by the loss of lateral support due to the delay of a street car company in paving its portion of the street after the excavation therefor had been made, the decision for plaintiff was sustained by sufficient evidence and cannot be said to be contrary to law, where there was evidence that the repairs were made necessary by the use of defective material and improper lateral support by the contractor and which tended to support all the material averments of the complaint.
Barber Asphalt Pav. Co. v. *City of Indianapolis,* 587, 599 (4).

22. *Public Improvements.—Contracts.—Guaranties of Work and Stipulations for Repairs.—Breach.—Complaint.*—Where a street paving contract required that all repairs resulting from causes incident to the use of the street for public travel should be made by the contractor, a complaint, in an action to recover the cost of repairs made by the city, alleging that the wearing surface commenced to roll and wave and in many places the vehicles using said pavement in the ordinary course of travel cut through the wearing surface and the concrete into the sub-grade of the street, that the pavement became deteriorated and so badly worn that it could not be satisfactorily patched, and that in order to put it in good repair as contemplated in the contract, etc., it was necessary entirely to reconstruct and relay all the portion of the wearing surface above the concrete base, and in some places to repair the concrete base, shows that the defects were the result of breaches of defendant's guaranty contained in the contract sued on, and was sufficient.
Barber Asphalt Pav. Co. v. *City of Indianapolis,* 587, 598 (3).

23. *Public Improvements.—Contracts.—Guaranties of Work and Stipulations for Repairs.*—Where a contract for street improvement provided that the work should be done in such substantial manner that no repairs would be required for a period of nine years, that if such repairs became necessary the contractor would make good any damage to the work or any defect in the workmanship, materials, or condition of the work, which made such repairs necessary, that he would keep the work in good repair during that time, and make all repairs as directed, etc., that the guaranty should cover all repairs growing out of the imperfection or unsuitability of materials or composition, too great or too little moisture, defects in workmanship, extremes of heat or cold and other effects of climate, holes or cracks in the pavement, etc.;

MUNICIPAL CORPORATIONS—Continued.

and that at the end of the guaranty period the pavement should be in good condition, present a surface so true and even that it would in no way be an obstruction to travel, and have such drainage that water could stand in no place to a greater depth than a quarter of an inch, such provisions are more than a guaranty against defects resulting from improper workmanship or unsuitable materials, and amount to a guaranty that the workmanship and materials which entered into the work were of such character that the street would withstand all the usual and necessary uses of travel for a period of nine years.

Barber Asphalt Pav. Co. v. *City of Indianapolis,* 587, 593 (1), 595 (1).

24. *Action for Personal Injuries.—Defective Railroad Crossing.— Judgment.—Res Judicata.—Matters Directly in Issue.*—In an action by a pedestrian against a city for injuries caused by the defective condition of a railroad street crossing, where the railroad company, after notice, failed to appear and defend, the only matters adjudicated, so far as the right of the railroad company is concerned, were such as were essential to support the verdict, namely, the existence of the defect, the liability of the city to plaintiff, and the amount of damages which the city was required to pay; so that in an action by the city against the railroad company to recover the amount of the judgment rendered against it, the company was not prevented from showing that it was under no duty to repair the defect, and that the injury was not caused by any negligence on its part.

City of Bloomington v. *Chicago, etc., R. Co.,* 510, 519 (6).

NAMES—

Initials.—The initial of a given name alone and unexplained is not recognized as a name. *Kreitlein* v. *Ferger,* 190, 206 (5).

NEGLIGENCE—

See CARRIERS 6, 7, 10-12; MASTER AND SERVANT 9, 12, 30, 31; MUNICIPAL CORPORATIONS 9; TRIAL 14.

Sufficient charge of, see RAILROADS 43.

It is, *per se* for a railroad company to operate its cars in violation of a statute or municipal ordinance regulating the speed thereof, see RAILROADS 49.

1. *Questions of Law or Fact.—Different Inferences.*—Negligence is not a matter of law, where different inferences may be drawn from the facts. *Cleveland, etc., R. Co.* v. *Rumsey,* 371, 376 (5).

2. *Proximate Cause.*—There may be several elements combining to make up the proximate cause of an injury.

Vandalia Coal Co. v. *Haverkamp,* 397, 401 (3).

3. *Proximate Cause.—Efficient Cause.*—The proximate cause of an injury is not necessarily the immediate cause, but must be the efficient cause, which is the cause that sets in motion the chain of circumstances leading up to the injury.

Columbia Creosoting Co. v. *Beard,* 260, 267 (8).

4. *Delegation of Legal Duty.—Joint Tort-Feasors.*—While one, personally bound to perform a duty, cannot relieve himself from such obligation by a contract for its performance by another, and cannot interpose such contract as a defense, such rule does not apply as between joint tort-feasors.

Marion, etc., Construction Co. v. *Claycomb,* 681, 686 (5).

INDEX.

NEGLIGENCE—Continued.

5. *Breach of Legal Duty.*—Negligence arises on the breach of a legal duty to use care, and where there is no duty there can be no negligence. *Marion, etc., Construction Co. v. Claycomb*, 681, 684 (2).

6. *Acts Constituting Negligence.—Operation of Train.*—The sudden or violent motion or jerking of a train may be negligence.
Indianapolis Southern R. Co. v. Emmerson, 403, 410 (3).

7. *Actionable Negligence.*—An action for negligence will not lie against a defendant, unless he was owing some duty to the injured person at the time and place where the injury occurred, and which he omitted to perform.
Marion, etc., Construction Co. v. Claycomb, 681, 685 (4).

8. *Complaint.—Charges of Several Acts of Negligence.*—A complaint for personal injuries is not objectionable for charging several acts of negligence in one paragraph, unless it counts upon the combined effects of two or more of the alleged negligent acts.
Lake Shore, etc., R. Co. v. Myers, 59, 62 (1).

9. *Complaint.—Charges of Several Acts of Negligence.—Proof.*—Where several acts of negligence are charged in the same paragraph of complaint, proof that any one of such acts was the proximate cause of the injury is sufficient to sustain the action.
Lake Shore, etc., R. Co. v. Myers, 59, 62 (2).

10. *Complaint.—General Charge of Negligence.—Sufficiency.*—Objection that the charge of negligence, in a complaint for personal injuries, is not specific, can only be taken by a motion to make the complaint more specific, and, in the absence of such motion, a complaint stating the injury and alleging that it was caused as a consequence and solely by reason of defendant's negligence, sufficiently charges actionable negligence.
Terre Haute, etc., Traction Co. v. Maberry, 114, 118 (2).

11. *Complaint.—Allegations.—Legal Duty.*—In a negligence case, the complaint to be sufficient, must show that there was a legal duty, owing by defendant to the person injured, which was violated by a want of care on the part of the wrongdoer proportionate to the duty imposed on him by law.
Rossiter v. Lake Shore, etc., R. Co., 88, 92 (1).

12. *Complaint.—Allegations.—Presumptions of Contributory Negligence.*—Contributory negligence of plaintiff will not be presumed from allegations of the complaint tending to disclose such defense. *Espenlaub v. Hedderick*, 139, 141 (3).

13. *Complaint.— Demurrer.— Contributory Negligence.— Presumptions.*—On demurrer to a complaint in a negligence case, it will be considered that plaintiff used due care, unless all reasonable inferences drawn from the facts alleged show that he was guilty of negligence as a matter of law.
Cleveland, etc., R. Co. v. Van Laningham, 156, 163 (3).

14. *Contributory Negligence.—Complaint.—Sufficiency.*—A complaint in a negligence case need not negative contributory negligence on the part of plaintiff, and will be held sufficient in this respect, unless facts are specifically averred therein disclosing the defense of contributory negligence.
Espenlaub v. Hedderick, 139, 141 (2).

15. *Contributory Negligence.—Complaint.—Sufficiency.*—A complaint which states facts sufficient to show negligence on the part of defendant and that such negligence resulted in the injury complained of, is sufficient on demurrer, unless other facts pleaded

NEGLIGENCE—Continued.

show affirmatively, as a matter of law, that plaintiff was guilty of contributory negligence.

Pittsburgh, etc., R. Co. v. *Cottman,* 661, 664 (1), 665 (1).

16. *Complaint.—Contributory Negligence.—Jury Question.*—Where, in an action for personal injuries, the averments of the complaint do not show contributory negligence as a matter of law, it is for the jury to determine from the evidence whether plaintiff used due care to prevent the injury.

Lake Shore, etc., R. Co. v. *Myers,* 59, 63 (4).

17. *Contributory Negligence.—Jury Question.*—Where the facts are of a character to be reasonably subjected to more than one inference or conclusion, the ultimate fact of contributory negligence, or due care, should be determined by the jury.

Cleveland, etc., R. Co. v. *Nichols,* 349, 354 (5).

18. *Contributory Negligence.—Jury Question.*—A court is not justified in declaring as a matter of law that a party was guilty of contributory negligence, simply because the facts relating to his conduct are undisputed and seem to indicate a want of due care, but if different inferences may reasonably be drawn from such facts, the question is for the jury. *Craig* v. *Zent,* 19, 20 (1).

NEW TRIAL—

Ground for a motion for a, see APPEAL 35.

Errors occurring during the trial, to be available, must be saved by assigning them as causes for a, see APPEAL 6; *Davis* v. *Bryant,* 343, 344 (1).

An assignment, as ground for, that the assessment of the amount of the recovery is erroneous, being too large, correctly saves the question, see APPEAL 8; *Holthouse* v. *Poling,* 568, 573 (6).

The Appellate Court has the power to order a, and it is its duty to do so, where it appears that the ends of justice will be best subserved thereby, see COURTS 1.

Ruling on motion for, will not be considered on appeal, where neither the motion nor any of its grounds are set out in appellant's brief, and no statement of the evidence is contained therein, see APPEAL 44.

A judgment is not void because it is rendered while a motion for a, is pending, but such pending motion merely operates to suspend the effect and enforcement of the judgment, see JUDGMENT 3.

1. *Grounds.—Statutes.*—Causes assigned for a new trial, but which are not included in the statute enumerating the causes for which a new trial will be granted, are not available.

Cooley v. *Kelley,* 687, 695 (9).

2. *Rights of Parties.*—The party against whom a general verdict has been rendered, on proper motion, has the right to have the trial court pass on the verdict before judgment thereon is rendered against him. *Osborn* v. *Adams Brick Co.,* 175, 190 (20).

3. *Misconduct of Juror.*—The fact that a juror, who had instituted an action which was compromised and dismissed before issues were formed on being asked on his *voir dire* if he had ever had any litigation, answered "no," was not ground for a new trial, since the question was not calculated to call to his mind a case which was only filed and dismissed.

Ohlwine v. *Pfaffman,* 357, 369 (10).

NEW TRIAL—Continued.

4. *As of Right.*—Where two or more substantive causes of action proceed to judgment in the same case, and a new trial as of right is authorized by §1110 Burns 1908, §1054 R. S. 1881, as to one or more of such causes, but not as to others, a new trial as of right must be denied. *Grubb* v. *Brendel*, 531, 534 (2).

5. *As of Right.*—*Action for Money Judgment.*—A complaint alleging that a deed executed by plaintiff was in fact a mortgage, and seeking the recovery of a money judgment for the difference between the actual value of the land and the debt secured by the alleged mortgage, states a cause of action that is not within the provisions of the statute (§1110 Burns 1908, §1054 R. S. 1881) authorizing a new trial as of right. *Grubb* v. *Brendel*, 531, 534 (1).

NOTICE—

See APPEAL 19-22; BANKRUPTCY 8.

NUNC PRO TUNC—

Entry cannot be made on oral testimony alone, see JUDGMENT 1.

The right to have a bill of exceptions signed, on account that the presentation within the time allowed was defeated by the absence of the judge from the State, depends on the diligence shown by the party seeking such signature, see APPEAL 27.

OBJECTIONS—

To questions asked of witnesses, to be available, should be interposed before the answer is made, see TRIAL 1.

OFFER—

See SALES 2.

OVERRULED CASES—

See CASES.

PAROL—

Contract, see CONTRACTS 2, 6.

Contracts of insurance are valid, see INSURANCE 1.

Evidence, see TRUSTS 4, 5.

A trust in personal property may be created by, see TRUSTS 1; *Camp* v. *Camp*, 250, 253 (5).

PARTIES—

See APPEAL 11-15; HUSBAND AND WIFE.

A demurrer for want of facts presents no question concerning a defect of, see PLEADING 27.

Substitution of administrator of a party as an appellee where an appeal was void for want of jurisdiction, is also void, see APPEAL 1.

PARTITION—

1. *Judgments.*—*Conclusiveness.*—A judgment in a partition proceeding is conclusive between the parties, and exempt from collateral attack, as to all matters within the issues. *Heritage* v. *Heritage*, 76, 79 (1).

PARTITION—Continued.

2. *Adverse Claim.—Lease.*—Where the lands of the ancestor were apportioned among his heirs by a proceeding in partition, each heir became the implied warrantor of the title of every other as to the portion allotted to each, so that one of the heirs cannot thereafter assert that he has a right, under a lease executed by the ancestor, but which was not set up in any pleading in the partition proceeding, to hold possession of any of the land allotted to one of the other heirs. *Heritage* v. *Heritage*, 76, 88 (3).

3. *Implied Warranty.*—The law annexes an implied warranty in all compulsory partitions, between tenants in common, of land derived by inheritance, extending to defects which existed in the title of the common ancestor, whereby each partitioner is made the warrantor of every other to the extent of the portion allotted to him, and cannot, therefore, be permitted to assert an adverse interest or title for the purpose of ousting another party to the same partition from his allotted portion.
Heritage v. *Heritage*, 76, 86 (2).

PAYMENTS—

See TENANCY IN COMMON 3.

Of money to authorized agent, see PRINCIPAL AND AGENT 15.

PASSENGERS—
See CARRIERS 1.

Injury to, see CARRIERS 2-16.

PERSONS—
Duty towards, on tracks, see RAILROADS 42.

Injury to, on tracks, see RAILROADS 36, 37.

PETITION—
For the vacation of a street, see MUNICIPAL CORPORATIONS 5.

PLEADING.

I. FORM AND ALLEGATIONS. 1-5.	III. PLEA OR ANSWER AND CROSS-COMPLAINT, 21-23.
II. COMPLAINT, 6-20.	IV. DEMURRER, 24-27.

Review as to, see APPEAL 83.

What was in issue in a former action must generally be determined by the, see JUDGMENT 11.

Filed in a case is a part of the record, though not required to be copied at length into the order-book entries, see JUDGMENT 2.

A breach of warranty, pleaded as a cause of action or defense, must to be good upon demurrer, aver the character and extent of the warranty, and the nature and particulars of the breach, see CONTRACTS 15.

I. FORM AND ALLEGATIONS.

1. *Presumptions.*—It is always presumed that a party's pleading is as strong in his favor as the facts will warrant.
Croan v. *Myers*, 143, 147 (5).

2. *Presumptions Against Pleading.*—Presumptions against a pleading relate only to the facts necessary to constitute a cause of action, and not to facts tending to disclose an affirmative defense.
Espenlaub v. *Hedderick*, 139, 142 (4).

PLEADING—Continued.

3. *Special Statutory Procedure.*—While, in all special statutory enactments, the procedure prescribed by the statute must be followed, the practice authorized by the civil code may be followed, where it is not inconsistent with the procedure so prescribed.
Southern R. Co. v. Town of French Lick, 447, 452 (3).

4. *Presumptions Against Pleader.*—*Application of Rule.*—The rule, that a plaintiff is presumed to have stated his case as strongly in his favor as the facts warrant, applies only to such facts as are necessary to his cause of action, and does not apply to facts which tend to disclose a defense.
Pittsburgh, etc., R. Co. v. Cottman, 661, 665 (3).

5. *Statement of Cause of Action.*—*Requisites.*—*Construction.*—A pleading is required to state facts constituting the cause of action in plain and concise language, in such manner as to enable a person of common understanding to know what is intended, and, in construing the same, the words used will be taken in their plain, ordinary and usual meaning, unless they have some peculiar and technical significance.
Southern R. Co. v. Town of French Lick, 447 454 (8).

II. COMPLAINT.

See CARRIERS 5, 7, 12-15; MASTER AND SERVANT 1-4, 11, 12, 14, 19, 29, 30, 43-49; MUNICIPAL CORPORATIONS 16, 22; NEGLIGENCE 8-16; RAILROADS 22-26, 37-41, 43; TRUSTS 3, 6; WATERS AND WATERCOURSES 10.

Charging several acts of negligence in one paragraph, see NEGLIGENCE 8, 9.

Sufficiency of, against fraternal order, see INSURANCE 17.

Sufficiency of, when attacked for the first time on appeal, see INJUNCTION 5.

Sufficiency of, in an action against an insurance company, drawn on the theory of a parol contract, see INSURANCE 2.

The incorporation of the whole complaint in an instruction to the jury, while not to be commended is not ground for reversal, see TRIAL 13.

A contract, partly in writing and partly in parol, rests entirely in parol and a complaint thereon is not rendered insufficient by failure to set out therein the portion of the contract that is written, see CONTRACTS 12.

Averments sufficiently showing the existence of the legal duty owing to plaintiff by defendant to use ordinary care to furnish him a reasonably safe place to work and reasonably safe appliances with which to work, see MASTER AND SERVANT 1.

In an action to set aside a judgment on the ground that the original action was fraudulently brought in the wrong county, is insufficient in the absence of averments of acts or conduct constituting fraud, see FRAUD 1.

In an action by a railroad company to enjoin a town from appropriating a portion of the right of way for a street, plaintiff must allege and prove facts showing that the town and its officers were acting without warrant of law, see INJUNCTION 4.

In an action against a fraternal insurance company, where the complaint was on the theory of a parol contract of insurance, it

PLEADING—Continued.

was not essential to the sufficiency of the complaint that copies of the constitution and by-laws be set out therein, see INSURANCE 13.

6. *Demurrer.*—A complaint is sufficient to withstand a demurrer, if it states facts sufficient to entitle plaintiff to some relief.
Tishbein v. Paine, 441, 443 (4).

7. *Demurrer.—Inferences.*—Where a complaint is tested by demurrer, no inferences or intendments are indulged in favor of its sufficiency. *Town of Cicero v. Lake Erie, etc., R. Co.,* 208, 307 (1).

8. *Theory.*—The theory of an action must be determined from the general character and tenor of the leading and controlling averments of the complaint. *Southern R. Co. v. Friedley,* 192, 195 (1).

9. *Determination of Theory.*—The theory of a complaint must be determined from its general scope and tenor, and not from fragmentary statements, detached parts or conclusions, and that theory which is most apparent and clearly outlined by the leading averments of the pleading will be adopted.
Osborn v. Adams Brick Co., 175, 182 (4).

10. *Sufficiency.—Motion in Arrest of Judgment.—Appeal.*—Where an omission or defect in a complaint is one that may be supplied by proof, and the facts alleged will bar another action for the same cause, the complaint will be held sufficient on motion in arrest of judgment, or when first tested by assignment of error on appeal. *Town of Cicero v. Lake Erie, etc., R. Co.,* 298, 308 (3).

11. *Sufficiency.—Initial Attack After Judgment.*—Where a complaint is tested for the first time after judgment, all inferences and intendments are indulged in favor of the pleading, and if there is not a total failure to aver some essential fact, and it is sufficient to bar another action for the same cause, it will be held sufficient to support the judgment.
Town of Cicero v. Lake Erie, etc., R. Co., 208, 307 (2).

12. *Sufficiency.—Initial Attack on Appeal.—Exceptions to Conclusions of Law.*—Where the sufficiency of a complaint is attacked for the first time on appeal, and appellant's exceptions to the conclusions of law raise the same questions as are raised by the assignment challenging the complaint, the sufficiency will be tested by the rule applicable after verdict.
Town of Cicero v. Lake Erie, etc., R. Co., 298, 308 (5).

13. *Sufficiency.—Initial Attack on Appeal.*—A complaint is good as against attack made for the first time on appeal, if it is sufficient to bar another action on the same state of facts.
Cleveland, etc., R. Co. v. Rumsey, 371, 372 (1).

14. *Sufficiency.—Initial Attack on Appeal.*—A complaint is good as against an attack made for the first time by assignment of errors on appeal, if it contains facts sufficient to bar another action for the same cause. *Jordan v. Indianapolis Coal Co.,* 542, 543 (1).

15. *Sufficiency.—Objections on Appeal.*—A complaint, in an action for the wrongful appropriation of a highway, alleging that the ground appropriated was a highway and dedicated to the public for that purpose, and used by the public as a highway for more than thirty years, with the permission, consent, acquiescence and donation of defendant, was, in the absence of a motion to make more specific, sufficient, on the theory of dedication, to bar another action, and is good as against an attack made for the first time on appeal. *Cleveland, etc., R. Co. v. Beard,* 105, 106 (1).

PLEADING—Continued.

16. *Ruling on Demurrer.—Effect as to Subsequent Rulings.—Trial.* —A ruling on demurrer, holding a complaint good, is not binding on a trial court so as to require its subsequent rulings to be in harmony therewith, irrespective of its correctness.

Cooley v. Kelley, 687, 693 (1).

17. *Bill of Particulars.—Objections on Appeal.*—The objection that a bill of particulars filed with a complaint is not properly referred to or identified by the complaint cannot be successfully presented for the first time on appeal.

Jordan v. Indianapolis Coal Co., 542, 544 (2).

18. *Sufficiency.—Defects Curable by Motion to Make Specific.— Demurrer.*—A complaint is not demurrable for defects that may be reached by a motion to make more specific, and will be held good if it states facts entitling plaintiff to any relief.

Barton v. Barton, 319, 321 (1).

19. *Duplicity.—Remedy.*—Where each paragraph of complaint contains two separate and distinct causes of action, that may be properly joined, the defect cannot be reached by a demurrer for want of facts, but the remedy is by a motion to require that the causes be separated and stated in separate paragraphs.

Tishbein v. Paine, 441, 442 (1).

20. *Sufficiency.*—A complaint alleging facts from which it may readily be determined that defendant was the agent of plaintiff in buying and selling real estate, that on account of moneys advanced by plaintiff, interest collected, and profits derived from the sale of real estate, defendant became indebted to plaintiff, that defendant, as attorney in fact for plaintiff, wrongfully and without any consideration, conveyed certain real estate to his wife for the purpose and with the intent to cheat and defraud plaintiff, and which demands an accounting and the setting aside of such conveyance, is sufficient to withstand a demurrer.

Barton v. Barton, 319, 321 (2).

III. PLEA OR ANSWER AND CROSS-COMPLAINT.

See BILLS AND NOTES 2.

Showing easement by prescription, see WATERS AND WATERCOURSES 2.

21. *Complaint.—General Denial.*—The general denial puts in issue every material allegation of the complaint.

Fuller v. Fuller, 488, 490 (4).

22. *Pleas to Jurisdiction.—Requisites.*—An answer denying the jurisdiction of the court is a dilatory plea and must be certain and definite and must anticipate and exclude all such supposable facts as would, if alleged on the opposite side, defeat the plea, since nothing can be supplied by intendment.

Moore-Mansfield, etc., Co. v. Marion, etc., Traction Co., 548, 557 (11).

23. *Answer in Abatement.—Joinder of Matter in Abatement With Matter in Bar.—Waiver of Grounds of Abatement.*—A plea in abatement must precede a plea in bar, and where matter in abatement is joined in the same paragraph with matter in bar, the matter in abatement is waived and may be stricken out on motion.

Moore-Mansfield, etc., Co. v. Marion, etc., Traction Co., 548, 558 (14).

PLEADING—Continued.

IV. DEMURRER.

See *ante* 6, 7, 16, 18.

Ruling on, see APPEAL 133-137.

Ruling on, waived by failure to set out in brief a copy of such demurrer, or to state its substance or the grounds thereof, see APPEAL 43.

Filing a, to a petition for the vacation of a street is a permissible means of objecting to its sufficiency, see MUNICIPAL CORPORATIONS 4.

On, to a complaint in a negligence case, it will be considered that plaintiff used due care, unless all reasonable inferences drawn from the facts alleged show that he was guilty of negligence as a matter of law, see NEGLIGENCE 13.

24. *Admissions.*—For the purposes of a demurrer to a pleading, the facts alleged are to be taken as true.
Southern R. Co. v. Town of French Lick, 447, 454 (9).

25. *Admissions.*—For the purpose of testing the sufficiency of a pleading, a demurrer admits the truth of its averments.
Moore-Mansfield, etc., Co. v. Marion, etc., Traction Co., 548, 558 (13).

26. *Admissions.*—On demurrer to a complaint, all the material facts that are well pleaded must be taken as true for the purposes of the demurrer.
Cleveland, etc., R. Co. v. Van Laningham, 156, 163 (1).

27. *Questions Raised.*—*Defect of Parties.*—Under the code, a demurrer for want of facts presents no question concerning a defect of parties plaintiff or defendant.
Southern R. Co. v. Town of French Lick, 447, 453 (5).

POLICY—

Construction of employer's liability policy, see INSURANCE 6.

PRESCRIPTION—

Easements by, see EASEMENTS.

PRESUMPTIONS—

See APPEAL 84-92; BANKS AND BANKING 3; BILLS AND NOTES 4; CARRIERS 6; DEEDS 1; EVIDENCE 10, 11, 15; INFANTS 1; INSURANCE 8; NEGLIGENCE 13; PLEADING 1, 2, 4; TENANCY IN COMMON 3; TRIAL 32, 37.

PRINCIPAL AND AGENT—

A minor cannot authorize any one to act as his agent, nor can he acquiesce in or ratify the acts of any person so as to make them his own, see INFANTS 2.

Where a check is indorsed for collection, or where the memorandum of deposit shows that it is deposited as a check, it remains the property of the depositor and the bank holds it as his agent for collection, see BANKS AND BANKING 5.

1. *Actions.*—*Waiver of Tort.*—*Action on Implied Contract.*—A principal may waive the tort of his agent based on his failure to account, and sue him as on an implied contract for the money due. *Holthouse v. Poling*, 568, 570 (2).

2. *Bills and Notes.*—*Equitable Defenses.*—In an action by an agent against his principal on a note for money borrowed from

PRINCIPAL AND AGENT—Continued.

the agent and invested by the principal in the business which the agent was conducting for him, the principal may, by cross-complaint, present an equitable defense and require the agent to give an account of his trust.   *Holthouse* v. *Poling*, 568, 570 (1).

3. *Declarations of Agent.—Res Gestae.*—In an action against defendant on a note to which his name had been signed by his son, since deceased, evidence of declarations made by the son at the time of the execution of the note, but in defendant's absence, relative to his authority to sign his father's name, was admissible as part of the *res gestae*, when properly limited in its effect so as not to bind defendant on the question of such authority.
                       Miller v. *Farmers State Bank*, 5, 10 (5).

4. *Existence of Relation.—Evidence.—Instructions.*—In an action for money loaned, where it was alleged that defendant borrowed the money through an agent, evidence that the alleged agent received a check from plaintiff and deposited same to defendant's credit, and was constantly loaning money for defendant, and performed other and similar acts for defendant, an instruction by which the question of whether he was the defendant's agent in the making of such loan was left wholly to the jury, after a consideration of all the facts shown, was proper.
                       Barton v. *Barton*, 537, 541 (3).

5. *Husband and Wife.—Power of Attorney.—Construction.—Death of Wife.—Revocation.*—A power of attorney executed by a husband and wife directly authorizing the attorney in fact to convey the property to "any one of us," etc., and not containing any power to convey joint property, is several and is not revoked by the death of the wife.   *Barton* v. *Barton*, 537, 539 (1).

6. *Accounting by Agent.*—Where an agent has been intrusted with his principal's money to be expended for a definite purpose, he may be required to account in equity, and in making such accounting he has the burden of showing that his trust duties have been performed, and the manner of such performance.
                       Holthouse v. *Poling*, 568, 571 (3).

7. *Accounting by Agent.—Evidence.—Sufficiency.*—Where, on the question of whether an agent, intrusted with the management of a store, had accounted for the property and funds which came into his hands, it was shown that although the system of book-keeping was careless, both the principal and the agent knew the condition of the business, and the agent testified that he had accounted for and turned over to the principal all moneys he received, except his salary, there was some evidence from which it may be said that such agent had accounted for the money coming into his hands.   *Holthouse* v. *Poling*, 568, 571 (4).

8. *Authority of Agent.—Evidence.—Verdict.*—A verdict for plaintiff, in an action for the price of a car of crushed stone, is sustained by sufficient evidence, where the evidence shows that a landscape gardener employed by defendant, after a conversation with defendant on the subject, ordered the stone from plaintiff, and that the car was billed to defendant and used in the improvement of a driveway on his premises.
                       Jordan v. *Indianapolis Coal Co.*, 542, 545 (6).

9. *Authority of Agent.—Apparent Authority.*—Where the acts of a principal are such as to justify innocent third persons, who have relied thereon, in believing that the agent is authorized to do that which he does, although the agent in fact had no such authority,

PRINCIPAL AND AGENT—Continued.

the principal is bound thereby, under the rule that where one of two innocent persons must suffer because of the betrayal of a trust reposed in a third, the person most at fault must bear the loss. *Wagner* v. *McCool*, 124, 134 (3).

10. *Authority of Agent.—Reliance on Authority.*—While a third party may rely on the apparent authority of an agent, such apparent authority must rest on facts or circumstances warranting such reliance; and where a mortgagor delivered a note and mortgage to her son to be by him delivered to the mortgagee, such fact at most constituted the son a special agent to deliver the instruments in the form and with the effect they possessed when they left her possession, and did not warrant a reliance on his authority to bind her by statements to the mortgagee giving to such instruments a different effect. *Hubbard* v. *Ranje*, 611, 615 (4).

11. *Authority of Agent.—Evidence.—Letter Written by Agent.*—A letter written by an attorney, who had negotiated a loan for defendant, informing plaintiffs that he could not accept payment of the principal at a semi-annual interest date, that under the contract, from which he quoted, such payment could be made only at an anniversary date, and asking plaintiffs to remit the amount of the interest payment, though not constituting evidence establishing the agency of such attorney, is important as tending to show that he had possession of the papers connected with the loan and was assuming to act in the matter of the collection of the note in question previous to the time of its payment. *Wagner* v. *McCool*, 124, 133 (2).

12. *Authority of Agent.—Evidence.—Sufficiency.*—In an action to quiet plaintiff's title to real estate held by defendant under a deed conveying the land as security for a loan made to plaintiffs, and to compel a reconveyance, where plaintiffs had repaid the loan to an attorney by whom such loan had been made for defendant, evidence showing that interest payments had been made to such attorney and credited on the note by defendant, that on plaintiffs offering to repay the loan at a semi-annual interest date such attorney informed them that he could not accept payment except at an anniversary date, that shortly before the next anniversary date, defendant, at the request of such attorney and to enable him to "look something up," left with him the papers connected with such loan, that when plaintiffs went to the office of such attorney to repay the loan, the attorney was not in, and, on being called by telephone, directed plaintiffs to leave a check for the amount and said that he would send them the papers to which they were entitled, and that plaintiffs then left a check for the amount at the office of such attorney, who cashed the same and disappeared, was sufficient to justify a finding that such attorney was at no time acting as the agent of plaintiffs, but was the agent of the defendant. *Wagner* v. *McCool*, 124, 127 (1), 135 (1).

13. *Execution of Notes.—Authority of Agent.—Determination.*—In an action against defendant as surety on a promissory note, where it was claimed by plaintiff that defendant's name was signed by defendant's son, pursuant to a general authority, the question of such general authority was a question of fact to be determined from a preponderance of all the evidence. *Miller* v. *Farmers State Bank*, 5, 7 (1).

PRINCIPAL AND AGENT—Continued.

14. *Execution of Notes.—Authority of Agent.—Evidence.—Sufficiency.*—In an action on a note, on the theory that defendant's
name was signed as surety by his son pursuant to a general
authority, evidence that defendant and his son transacted business in partnership for many years, that they owned a farm as
tenants in common which the son later occupied in the business of
buying and selling live stock and in which business he often had
use for large sums of money, that the son was a man of standing
in the community, that the personal relation of defendant with
his son was most cordial, together with positive testimony that
eight or nine years before the execution of the note sued on,
defendant had given his son authority to use his name as surety
on notes, and that notes thus signed by the son at different times
thereafter, were, after the son's death, recognized by defendant
as binding obligations on himself, was sufficient to show a general authority in the son to sign defendant's name so as to render
him liable as surety on the note sued on, notwithstanding defendant's denial of having given authority to sign that particular note.
                    Miller v. Farmers State Bank, 5, 8 (3).

15. *Power of Attorney.—Payment of Money to Authorized Agent.—
Recovery.*—One who pays money to an agent authorized to receive
it is entitled to his credit without tracing the fund through the
hands of the agent and into those of his principal, so that where
an agent, authorized by a power of attorney to borrow money on
"the note, notes, mortgage or mortgages" of the principal, borrowed money on his promise to give the note of the principal
therefor, a recovery may be had by the lender against the principal, although no note was ever executed.
                    Barton v. Barton, 537, 540 (2).

16. *Power of Attorney.—Recovery of Money Paid to Agent.—Instructions.*—In an action to recover money alleged to have been
loaned to defendant through his agent, an instruction that if the
jury determined from all the evidence that a power of attorney
from defendant to such agent was in force during the time of the
business dealings between plaintiff and such agent, and that such
agent borrowed the money under the authority therein granted,
defendant would be liable, was not erroneous.
                    Barton v. Barton, 537, 541 (4).

PRINCIPAL AND SURETY—

Sureties on the bond must be named and approved by the court, in
term-time appeal, during the term at which the final judgment is
rendered, see APPEAL 17.

1. *Creation of Contract.—Consideration.*—Where a note is signed
by a surety at the time of its execution by the principal, the
surety's undertaking will be deemed to be a part of the original
transaction supported by the consideration moving to the principal but if his undertaking is entered into at a time subsequent to
the execution by the principal, it is a new contract, and not binding on the surety, unless supported by a new consideration.
                    Ailes v. Miller, 280, 282 (1).

2. *Creation of Contract.—Ratification.*—Where, on borrowing
money, the maker of the note told the payee that his father would
become surety thereon, and subsequently to the death of the
maker, the payee presented the note to maker's father, who signed
same, saying that if the son had signed it for him it would have
been all right, and that he would sign it then just the same as if

PRINCIPAL AND SURETY—Continued.

the son were living, the acts of the father constituted a ratification of the agreement made by his son as of the date when the agreement was made, and rendered him liable as surety.

Alles v. Miller, 280, 282 (2).

8. *Judgment.—Res Judicata.*—Where, in an action by a building contractor to recover on the countract, defendant filed a cross-complaint to recover on the contractor's bond and recovered judgment thereon, such judgment was the measure of the contractor's liability, and is conclusive in a subsequent action on such bond as to the liability of the sureties.

Mitten v. Caswell-Runyan Co., 521, 530 (5).

PRIVILEGED COMMUNICATIONS—

Waiver of, see WITNESSES 3-5.

Persons entitled to waive privilege, see WITNESSES 5.

"PROPER"—

See WORDS AND PHRASES.

PROPERTY—

Location of, see CHATTEL MORTGAGES 1.

Injury to, see LIMITATION OF ACTIONS 1; WATERS AND WATERCOURSES 10.

Transactions concerning common, see TENANCY IN COMMON 1.

PROXIMATE CAUSE—

See MASTER AND SERVANT 7, 47; NEGLIGENCE 2, 3.

QUESTIONS FOR JURY—

See MASTER AND SERVANT 27, 33; NEGLIGENCE 16-18; RAILROADS 15, 17, 18.

The question of whether the statutory requirement as to the guarding of machinery is one of fact to be determined by the jury from the character of the machine and the nature of the peril, see MASTER AND SERVANT 13.

RAILROADS—

See EMINENT DOMAIN 1-3.

1. *Crossing Accident.—Action.—Burden of Proof.*—In an action to recover for the death of plaintiff's decedent in a railroad crossing accident, plaintiff has the burden of showing negligence as charged, and the burden of showing contributory negligence by the decedent is on defendant.

Cleveland, etc., R. Co. v. Van Laningham, 156, 169 (14).

2. *Crossing Accidents.—Care in Approaching Crossings.*—A person approaching a railroad crossing must use ordinary care to avoid injury, and whether ordinary care was used in a given case must be determined from a consideration of the situation of the party at the time, his surroundings, and the apparent danger.

Cleveland, etc., R. Co. v. Nichols, 349, 354 (4).

3. *Crossing Accident.—Care by Persons Approaching Crossings.*— A person approaching a railroad crossing is required to use only ordinary care to avoid injury, and while he is required to use

RAILROADS—Continued.

every reasonable precaution and to look and listen for an approaching train, he has a right to rely on the railroad company
performing its duty and is not bound to anticipate that it will
fail to give proper warning of the approach of its train.

Cleveland, etc., R. Co. v. *Van Laningham,* 156, 164 (7).

4. *Crossing Accident.—Verdict.—Answers to Interrogatories.—*
Where the complaint, for injuries received at a railroad crossing,
alleged that before driving onto the tracks plaintiff stopped his
horse and looked and listened and that he continued to look and
listen as he drove onto the tracks, but neither saw nor heard a
train approaching, and that when plaintiff's vehicle was upon
defendant's tracks, plaintiff was struck by defendant's train,
which was being negligently operated at a dangerous rate of
speed, and which approached without. the sounding of whistle or
ringing of bell, answers to interrogatories showing that plaintiff
knew the crossing was dangerous, that plaintiff's hearing and
sight were good, that he drove his horse under full control upon
the north track, and before his horse had entered on the track
farthest south, he saw the train approaching on such south track
at a rapid rate of speed, and that he did not see the train in
time to have stopped the horse and avoid the collision, are not in
irreconcilable conflict with a verdict for plaintiff, as showing contributory negligence, since, under the issues, evidence was admissible showing a state of facts on which it could not be said that
plaintiff was guilty of contributory negligence in crossing in front
of the train he saw approaching.

Cleveland, etc., R. Co. v. *Rumsey,* 371, 374 (3), 376 (3).

5. *Crossing Accidents. — Evidence. — Verdict. — Conclusiveness. —*
Where, in an action against a railroad company to recover for
the death of plaintiff's decedent in a crossing accident, defended
on the ground of contributory negligence, appellant's negligence
and decedent's care were, under the evidence, controverted questions of fact, a verdict for plaintiff cannot be disturbed on the
ground of insufficient evidence.

Cleveland, etc., R. Co. v. *Nichols,* 349, 356 (8).

6. *Crossing Accidents.—Evidence.—Admissibility.—*In an action for
the death of plaintiff's decedent in a collision with a train
caused by the defective condition of the crossing, evidence as to
the condition of the crossing after the accident was admissible,
where it was shown that the condition was the same before the
accident.   *Cleveland, etc., R. Co.* v. *Clark,* 646, 651 (5).

7. *Crossing Accident.—Evidence.—Admissibility.—Notice of Defect.—*In an action for the death of plaintiff's decedent in a collision with a train caused by the defective condition of the crossing, testimony of a witness that, shortly before the accident, his
horse had caught its foot between the rail and a plank of the
crossing, as it was alleged that decedent's horse had done, was
proper as showing constructive notice to the railroad company of
the character of the crossing.

Cleveland, etc., R. Co. v. *Clark,* 646, 651 (6).

8. *Crossing Accidents.—Evidence.—Sufficiency.—*In an action to
recover for the death of plaintiff's decedent as the result of a railroad crossing accident, evidence tending to show that she was
thrown out of her buggy, and showing that before the accident decedent was strong and healthy and did all her own work. that after the accident, and up to the time of her death, she complained
of pains in her side and back almost continuously, that she became

RAILROADS—Continued.

greatly emaciated and was able to do very little work, that she was internally injured and that her death was directly caused by peritonitis caused by such internal injuries, sufficiently supports a finding that decedent was injured by the collision with the train and that such injuries were the cause of her death, notwithstanding there was other evidence to show that almost immediately after the accident decedent was on her feet and running down the road, and that she got out of the buggy before it was struck. *Cleveland, etc., R. Co.* v. *Clark,* 646, 649 (2).

9. *Crossing Accidents.—Instructions.—Refusal.*—An instruction, in an action for injuries sustained in a railroad crossing accident, stating that if a person is struck by a train at a crossing, the law deems the fault *prima facie* his own, etc., was properly refused, since the burden of proving contributory negligence is on defendant. *Pittsburgh, etc., R. Co.* v. *Cottman,* 661, 667 (7).

10. *Crossing Accident.—Instructions.—Harmless Error.*—An instruction in an action against a railroad company for injuries incurred in a crossing accident, stating that the whistle on defendant's engine should have been sounded when the train was within eighty rods of the crossing, though technically incorrect, was harmless where the jury found that the whistle was not sounded at all. *Lake Shore, etc., R. Co.* v. *Myers,* 59, 71 (12).

11. *Crossing Accident.—Instructions.—Harmless Error.*—In an action against a railroad company for injuries received in a crossing accident, an instruction submitting to the jury the question of whether ordinary care on the part of defendant required the presence of a watchman at the crossing, and an instruction on defendant's liability with reference to lighting the crossing, if erroneous, were harmless, where the jury by its answers to interrogatories, found that defendant's failure to sound the whistle or ring the bell as the train approached the crossing was the proximate cause of plaintiff's injury.
Lake Shore, etc., R. Co. v. *Myers,* 59, 73 (14).

12. *Crossing Accident.—Instructions.—Last Clear Chance.*—In an action against a railroad company for the death of plaintiff's decedent in a crossing accident, where there was evidence that the engineer saw the decedent when he was some distance from the railroad, that decedent then disappeared behind an embankment which prevented decedent from seeing the train and hid him from the engineer's view, and that the engineer next saw the horse appear about fifteen feet from the track, an instruction that where a person traveling on a highway, and a train are each approaching a crossing under circumstances indicating if neither stops a collision is likely, the engineer, if he has signalled the approach of the train, has a right to presume that such person will stop and to proceed with the train until he sees that such person does not stop, and if, after making such discovery in time to stop the train and avoid a collision, his failure to do so will render the company liable for the resulting injury, was a proper instruction and applicable to the evidence, even under the view that the engineer was not bound to use the last clear chance to avoid accident until he saw the horse emerging from behind the embankment. *Cleveland, etc., R. Co.* v. *Van Laningham,* 156, 167 (10), 168 (10).

Vol. 52—50

RAILROADS—Continued.

13. *Crossing Accident.—Contributory Negligence.*—It is not necessarily contributory negligence in every case to cross a track in front of a locomotive which one sees approaching rapidly.
Cleveland, etc., R. Co. v. *Rumsey*, 371, 376 (7).

14. *Crossing Accident.—Contributory Negligence.—Reliance on Railroad's Performance of Duty.*—A person approaching a crossing is not bound to anticipate and act on the theory that the railroad company will be negligent, but he may assume that it will obey the law. *Cleveland, etc., R. Co.* v. *Rumsey*, 371, 376 (6).

15. *Crossing Accidents.—Contributory Negligence.—Jury Question.*—Where decedent failed to stop his horse after he had reached a point within five feet of defendant's tracks, and from there look in both directions before attempting to cross, it is for the jury to determine from the evidence, under proper instructions, whether he was guilty of contributory negligence.
Cleveland, etc., R. Co. v. *Nichols*, 349, 354 (6).

16. *Crossing Accident.—Contributory Negligence.—Failure to Look and Listen.*—One, who, on approaching a railroad track fails to look and listen for an approaching train, is guilty of negligence as a matter of law.
Cleveland, etc., R. Co. v. *Van Laningham*, 156, 164 (5).

17. *Crossing Accident.—Contributory Negligence.—Jury Question. —Looking and Listening.*—Where a person, on approaching a railroad crossing, looked and listened in good faith, the question of whether he looked and listened enough is for the jury.
Cleveland, etc., R. Co. v. *Van Laningham*, 156, 164 (6).

18. *Crossing Accidents.—Contributory Negligence.—Jury Question.* —Where, in an action for injuries sustained in a railroad crossing accident, plaintiff testified that the crossing watchman touched him and told him to go on across the track and that he was thus led to believe that no train was approaching and that it was safe to cross, and that he thereupon started to cross the track, the question of whether he was guilty of contributory negligence was one of fact for the jury, and its finding in his favor is conclusive on appeal, although the evidence in the record tends strongly to show that he was guilty of contributory negligence. *Pittsburgh, etc., R. Co.* v. *Cottman*, 661, 669 (9), 670 (9).

19. *Crossing Accident.—Care Required by Person in Perilous Position.—Contributory Negligence.*—The law does not hold a person, who, without fault on his part, is placed in a position of imminent peril, to the same rule of deliberation and care that governs one who is not in such peril and has time and opportunity more accurately to determine his line of conduct, so that where plaintiff, after waiting for a west-bound train to pass on defendant's south track, saw another west-bound train approaching while he was crossing the track, and after he had advanced far enough to see an east-bound train on the north track, was in a position of peril from which there was no escape except by continuing across the north track or retreating across the south track, it cannot be said as a matter of law that he was guilty of contributory negligence, but the question was one for determination by the jury.
Lake Shore, etc., R. Co. v. *Myers*, 59, 69 (9).

20. *Crossing Accident.—Contributory Negligence.—Verdict.—Answers to Interrogatories.*—In an action against a railroad company to recover for the death of plaintiff's decedent in a crossing accident, answers to interrogatories showing decedent was familiar

RAILROADS—Continued. ·

with the crossing, that he stopped, looked and listened before approaching the same, that from where he stopped to a point within five feet of the track he could not have seen the approaching train, that when decedent arrived at the point in the highway where he could see the train he could not stop his horse in time to avoid injury, and had not space enough in which to turn the horse around, and that the whistle was not sounded until the engineer saw decedent crossing the track, do not show that decedent failed to use ordinary care and are not in conflict with the general verdict for plaintiff.

Cleveland, etc., R. Co. v. Van Laningham, 156, 166 (9).

21. *Crossing Accident.—Contributory Negligence.—Verdict.—Answers to Interrogatories.—*Where, in an action for injuries sustained in a railroad crossing accident, the jury's answers to interrogatories show that plaintiff looked and listened before attempting to cross the tracks, that he heard no sound or signal of a train from the west on the north track, but saw a train approaching from the east on the south track, the speed of which he could not determine, that his line of vision was cut off and that as he approached the north track he heard a signal which confused him and caused him to halt, and that his position on the south track was one of danger, it cannot be said that plaintiff was negligent as a matter of law in attempting to cross the north track, since he was not bound to wait until absolutely certain that no train was approaching on the north track, but to use ordinary care in attempting to cross, and such answers are not in irreconcilable conflict with the finding in the general verdict for plaintiff, that he was in the exercise of ordinary care.

Lake Shore, etc., R. Co. v. Myers, 59, 65 (6).

22. *Crossing Accidents.—Contributory Negligence.—Complaint.—Sufficiency.—*A complaint, in an action against a railroad company for injuries sustained by being struck by a train at a crossing, is not insufficient on the theory that plaintiff's contributory negligence may be inferred from his failure to allege an excuse for his failure to observe the approach of the train, since under §362 Burns 1908, Acts 1899 p. 58, plaintiff is not required to allege or prove that he was free from contributory negligence.

Pittsburgh, etc., R. Co. v. Cottman, 661, 664 (2).

23. *Crossing Accident.— Contributory Negligence.— Complaint.—*Where, in an action for the death of plaintiff's decedent, in a railroad crossing accident, the conclusions to be drawn from the allegations of the complaint, with reference to decedent's conduct in approaching the crossing, lead to no other legitimate inference than that decedent was guilty of contributory negligence, the existence of such contributory negligence will be determined as a matter of law, but if the allegations are such as might properly cause reasonable men to differ as to the existence of such negligence on the part of decedent, the question is for the jury.

Cleveland, etc., R. Co. v. Van Laningham, 156, 163 (2).

24. *Crossing Accident.—Issues.—Last Clear Chance.—Complaint.—*A complaint, in an action for the death of plaintiff's decedent in a crossing accident, averring that the servants of defendant carelessly and negligently caused the train to strike decedent, while knowing that he did not and could not know of the approach of such train, is sufficient to bring into the case the doctrine of last clear chance.

Cleveland, etc., R. Co. v. Van Laningham, 156, 167 (11).

RAILROADS—Continued. ·

25. *Crossing Accident.—Complaint.—Sufficiency.*—In an action
against a railroad company for injuries received in a crossing
accident, a complaint averring that defendant maintained double
tracks across a street that was used by many people, that such
crossing was dangerous and was so recognized by defendant, that
on the evening of the injury, plaintiff was waiting to cross as
soon as defendant's west-bound train had passed, that such train
was closely followed by another train on the same track, that
plaintiff attempted to cross when said train had passed and was
struck by an east-bound train which approached without notice
or warning, and charging negligence in failing to light the crossing, in failing to maintain a flagman thereat, in running the west-
bound trains in such close proximity to each other as to divert
plaintiff's attention from the danger of the east-bound train, in
failing to give warning or signal of the approach of the east-
bound train, and in running said train at a dangerous rate of
speed, sufficiently averred actionable negligence warranting a
recovery in the absence of contributory fault on the part of
plaintiff.   *Lake Shore, etc., R. Co.* v. *Myers,* 59, 63 (3).

26. *Crossing Accidents.—Complaint.—Sufficiency.*—A complaint to
recover for the death of plaintiff's decedent in a crossing accident, alleging that as decedent approached the crossing he had an
unobstructed view for half a mile to the east, and that, when
fifty feet from the crossing, he looked to the east and saw no
train approaching, that the view to the west was obstructed by
freight cars on defendant's tracks, and that decedent was thereby
required to keep a close watch to the west until he was upon
defendant's right of way to ascertain if a train were approaching
from that direction, and that on ascertaining that no train was
approaching from the west, he attempted to cross, that the crossing was defective and was dangerous to cross without going
slowly, that while he was on the crossing a train approached from
the east at the rate of sixty miles per hour and without ringing a
bell, in violation of city ordinances regulating the operation of
trains through the city, and, though he made every effort to get
out of its way, he was struck by such train and killed, sufficiently
states a cause of action.
                    Cleveland, etc., R. Co. v. *Nichols,* 349, 351 (1).

27. *Crossing Accident.—Contributory Negligence.—Complaint.*—A
complaint for personal injuries in a crossing accident, alleging
that plaintiff approached the crossing with care and caution, and
that before driving onto the tracks he stopped his horse and
looked in both directions and listened for approaching trains,
that he continued to look and listen as he drove onto the tracks,
but neither saw nor heard a train approaching, that when plaintiff's vehicle was upon defendant's track, plaintiff was struck by
defendant's train which was negligently run at a high and dangerous rate of speed and without giving any signal of its approach to the crossing, is not open to the objection that it affirmatively shows that plaintiff was guilty of contributory negligence.
                    Cleveland, etc., R. Co. v. *Rumsey,* 371, 373 (2).

28. *Crossing Accidents.—Complaint.—Contributory Negligence.*—
Where the complaint, in an action against a railroad company,
alleged that decedent, as he approached a crossing, was obliged to
keep a close watch to the west, on account of obstructions, and
that, relying on a previous look to the east which gave him a
clear view for a distance of one-half mile and disclosed no ap-

RAILROADS—Continued.

proaching train, he traveled the last fifty feet of the approach without looking to the east, that the crossing was defective, making progress over the track slow, and that while he was on the crossing a train from the east approached the crossing without warning, and at an unlawful rate of speed, and killed decedent, it cannot be said, as a matter of law, that decedent was guilty of contributory negligence.

Cleveland, etc., R. Co. v. Nichols, 349, 352 (2).

29. *Crossing Accident.—Contributory Negligence.—Complaint.—*A complaint to recover for the death of plaintiff's decedent in a railroad crossing accident, alleging that decedent was sixty years old and had good hearing and eyesight, that when about 100 feet from the crossing he stopped and looked and listened for an approaching train, and, neither seeing nor hearing any, he proceeded toward the crossing, that, from the point where he stopped to a point five feet from the tracks, he could not see an approaching train because of obstructions which defendant negligently permitted to exist, that defendant negligently failed to give any signal or warning of the train's approach to the crossing by sounding the whistle or ringing the bell, and that the train was negligently run at a high rate of speed over said crossing, thereby causing the death, does not show contributory negligence as a matter of law and is sufficient to withstand a demurrer.

Cleveland, etc., R. Co. v. Van Laningham, 156, 164 (4), 165 (4).

30. *Crossings.—Signals.—Duty.—*It is the duty of a railroad company, independently of statute or ordinance, to give reasonable and timely warning of the approach of its trains to a public highway crossing. *Lake Shore, etc., R. Co. v. Myers,* 59, 64 (5).

31. *Crossings.—Signals.—Statutory Provision.—*Section 5431 Burns 1908 §4020 R. S. 1881, requiring the sounding of the whistle and the ringing of the bell on the approach of a train to a crossing, applies to crossings in an incorporated town, in the absence of an ordinance of the town prescribing different regulations.

Lake Shore, etc., R. Co. v. Myers, 59, 70 (11), 71 (11).

32. *Crossings.—Care Required in Crossing.—Reliance on Signals of Watchman.—*A signal or direction given by the watchman at a railroad crossing directing a traveler on the highway to cross, is an affirmative assurance that there is no danger, and relieves the traveler from exercising the high degree of diligence and caution that otherwise would be required in approaching a crossing.

Pittsburgh, etc., R. Co. v. Cottman, 661, 670 (11).

33. *Highway Crossings.—Rights of Persons on Highway.—*The rights of a person on a public highway are equal to those of a railroad company whose tracks are situate thereon, except as to the latter's right of priority when both need to use the highway at the same time. *Lake Shore, etc., R. Co. v. Myers,* 59, 70 (10).

34. *Street Crossings.—Approaches.—Duty to Maintain.—*The approaches of a street to a railroad crossing constitute a part of such crossing, and the company is bound to maintain such portion of the street as well as that which crosses the tracks.

City of Bloomington v. Chicago, etc., R. Co., 510, 518 (5).

35. *Fencing Tracks.—Statutory Duty.—*The duty imposed by statute on railroad companies to erect and maintain fences is a continuing one, which required them not only to erect fences in the first instance, but to maintain them in proper condition.

Michigan, etc., R. Co. v. Farrell, 603, 610 (7).

RAILROADS—Continued.

36. *Injury to Persons on Tracks.—Negligence.—Violation of Ordinance.*—The violation of a city ordinance regulating the speed of trains, is negligence rendering the railroad company liable for injuries caused thereby to a person who was lawfully upon its tracks.   *Rossiter* v. *Lake Shore, etc., R. Co.*, 88, 92 (3).

37. *Injury to Persons on Tracks.—Complaint.—Sufficiency.—Allegations as to Place of Injury.*—In an action against a railroad company for the death of plaintiff's decedent caused by the negligent operation of defendant's train in violation of a city ordinance, a complaint charging that defendant was operating trains on its tracks in the city at the time of the injury, that it had four separate railroad tracks on its right of way within the city limits, that it had a railroad bridge within the city limits, that the right of way and the four tracks at such bridge and for a number of rods to the east thereof are curved sharply, that while decedent was necessarily on defendant's right of way, defendant negligently operated its train around said curve and over the curved track through the limits of the city, sufficiently shows that the place where decedent was killed was within the city limits.
                       Rossiter v. *Lake Shore, etc., R. Co.*, 88, 97 (6).

38. *Injuries to Animals on Tracks.—Violation of Statutory Duty.—Contributory Negligence.—Complaint.*—Where liability of a railroad company for injury to animals is predicated on the violation of its statutory duty to fence properly its right of way, the complaint need not aver that plaintiff was without fault.
                       Michigan, etc., R. Co. v. *Farrell*, 603, 607 (3).

39. *Injuries to Animals on Tracks.—Complaint.—Instructions.*—Where, in an action against a railroad company for killing horses on the track, the complaint alleged that defendant failed properly to maintain its fences, an instruction which in effect stated that the law imposed on defendant the duty of erecting a fence of the kind and character required by statute and to maintain the same in proper condition of repair, was within the issues.
                       Michigan, etc., R. Co. v. *Farrell*, 603, 609 (6), 610 (6).

40. *Injuries to Animals on Tracks.—Complaint.—Sufficiency.*—A complaint to recover for stock killed by being struck by a train, alleging that plaintiff's horses, without any fault or negligence on the part of plaintiff, entered in and strayed upon the right of way and tracks of defendant at a point where the right of way and track were not sufficiently fenced, and were struck and killed by defendant's train, is not open to the objection that it fails to show that the killing was without plaintiff's fault.
                       Michigan, etc., R. Co. v. *Farrell*, 603, 607 (2), 608 (2).

41. *Injuries to Animals on Tracks.—Complaint.—Sufficiency.*—A complaint in an action against a railroad company for killing plaintiff's horses, alleging that at the time the defendant owned, operated and controlled a certain line of railroad over which it ran locomotives and cars for the transportation of passengers and freight, that plaintiff's horses, without plaintiff's fault or negligence, entered in and strayed upon defendant's right of way and tracks and that defendant, by its servants and employes, then and there ran one of its locomotives against said horses, etc., sufficiently shows that defendant was operating its locomotive by its agents while in the line of their duty or employment.
                       Michigan, etc., R. Co. v. *Farrell*, 603, 605 (1).

42. *Interurban.—Duty Toward Persons on Tracks.—Children.*—Where a person is seen walking on the track, or where there is

RAILROADS—Continued.

nothing to prevent the motorman from seeing one in that position, especially a child, and such person is unmindful of the approach of the car, the motorman is bound to use every reasonable care and means at command to warn him, and, if necessary to avoid a collision, to stop the car.

Terre Haute, etc., Traction Co. v. *Maberry*, 114, 122 (7).

43. *Interurban.—Crossing Accident.—Complaint.—Charge of Negligence.—Sufficiency.—*A complaint, in an action against an interurban railroad company for the death of plaintiff's child in a crossing accident, charging that the motorman negligently failed to sound the gong with which the car was equipped, which could have been heard by a person approaching the crossing when the car was a quarter of a mile away, and negligently ran said car against said child, thereby causing the injury, sufficiently charged negligence to withstand a demurrer.

Terre Haute, etc., Traction Co. v. *Maberry*, 114, 118 (1).

44. *Interurban.—Injury to Persons on Highway.—Duty to Stop Car.—Instructions.—*In an action for injuries caused by the collision of an interurban car with plaintiff's team, which had become frightened by the approach of such car, an instruction that while those in charge of a car being operated on and through a public street are not required to immediately stop the car on seeing a team manifesting fright, it is the duty of such person to be constantly on the alert and if he discovers a person so situated that injury must follow unless the car is stopped, it is his duty to make all reasonable efforts to stop such car, and his failure to do so will render the company liable for the resulting damage, is correct and stated the rule with reference to the duty to stop as favorably to appellant as the authorities warrant.

Mortimer v. *Daub*, 30, 36 (4).

45. *Interurban.—Crossing Accident.—Wilful Injury.—Evidence.—*In an action against an interurban railroad company for the death of plaintiff's child, evidence showing that the motorman saw the child approaching the crossing when the car was about a quarter of a mile away, and watched it continuously until within about fifty or one hundred feet of the place where the injury occurred, before sounding the whistle or making any effort to stop the car, and that he knew the child's attention was diverted from the approaching car, and that the car was going at a speed sufficient to drive it 150 to 200 feet beyond the point where it struck the boy, was, in the absence of any reason for the motorman's failure to sound the whistle or gong in time to attract the child's attention before reaching the point of danger, or for his failure to stop the car sooner, sufficient to justify a finding that the motorman's conduct was wilful.

Terre Haute, etc., Traction Co. v. *Maberry*, 114, 119 (3).

46. *Interurban.—Crossing Accident.—Injury to Child.—Instructions.—*In an action for the death of plaintiff's child by being struck by an interurban car, where the motorman saw the child approaching the track and watched it continuously from the time the car was a quarter of a mile away until within fifty or one hundred feet from the place where the injury occurred without signalling the approach of the car or attempting to stop it, an instruction that "the presumption that a person seen on an interurban car track or approaching the track will leave it or not enter upon it before the car reaches him, cannot be indulged in where a child of tender years is seen on the track or is seen

RAILROADS—Continued.

approaching it apparently unconscious of the approaching car," is not objectionable as being mandatory in telling the jury not to consider any presumption that the child would not come on the track in front of the car.

Terre Haute, etc., Traction Co. v. Maberry, 114, 122 (6).

47. *Interurban.—Injury to Persons on Highway.—Instructions.—Issues.—Evidence.—*In an action for injuries in a collision with an interurban car, where the complaint alleged that plaintiff's team became frightened through the negligent operation of the car, and that the car ran against the team, and there was some evidence that the car was running in excess of the speed allowed by ordinance, that as it approached it made unusual and loud noise, frightening the team, that the motorman was signalled to stop the car when 300 feet away, and that the speed was not slackened until the team was struck, an instruction which told the jury that when the operator of the car sees another in danger of peril from which he cannot extricate himself by the exercise or reasonable care and prudence, it is the highest duty of the operator to so act as not to increase such peril, and, if he does so act as to increase the peril, with full knowledge of the facts, it is negligence rendering the company liable for the injuries caused thereby, was not objectionable, as injecting the doctrine of "last clear chance," and was warranted by the issues and evidence.

Mortimer v. Daub, 30, 37 (7).

48. *Interurban.—Injury to Persons on Highway.—Evidence.—Sufficiency.—*In an action for injuries sustained in a collision with an interurban car, where the complaint charged that the car was being operated "at an excessive, negligent and careless rate of speed of about thirty miles an hour," thereby causing unusual, excessive and unnecessary noises which frightened plaintiff's team and caused it to turn upon the track in front of said car, whereby plaintiff was injured, evidence showing that there was at the time a city ordinance in force prohibiting the running of cars at a higher rate of speed than ten miles per hour, and that, as the car approached, it was running at twenty-five or thirty miles an hour and made a loud noise and raised considerable dust, was sufficient to justify the jury in finding that the car was operated in excess of the speed allowed by ordinance, and that the team was frightened by the unusual noise and high rate of speed, and was sufficient to charge defendant with liability although there was some evidence tending to show that at the time of the collision the car had slowed down and was not running to exceed eight or ten miles an hour. *Mortimer v. Daub*, 30, 34 (1).

49. *Operation.—Excessive Speed.—Negligence Per Se.—*It is negligence *per se* for a railroad company to operate its cars in violation of a statute or municipal ordinance regulating the speed thereof, making the company liable for injury proximately caused thereby to one who is himself without fault.

Mortimer v. Daub, 30, 35 (2).

50. *Use of Streets.—Street Railroads.—*It will be assumed that a steam railroad constructed its track across a street with the understanding that a street or interurban railroad might thereafter be lawfully located on such street and across its track at such point.

Baltimore, etc., R. Co. v. Cincinnati, etc., St. R. Co., 639, 645 (5).

51. *Injury to Trespassers.—Care Required.—*A railroad company owes no duty to a trespasser upon its tracks unless he is ob-

RAILROADS—Continued.

served to be in a perilous position, in which event it at once becomes the duty of those operating the train to do all that persons of ordinary care and caution would do under like circumstances to save him from injury.

Rossiter v. Lake Shore, etc., R. Co., 88, 92 (2).

52. *Right of Way.—Trespassers.—Rights of Adjoining Landowner.*—The general rule that between stations and public crossings the track of a railroad company belongs to it exclusively, and that all persons who walk or drive thereon are trespassers, is limited in its operation with respect to the right of the owner of the fee to enter thereon when such entry is indispensable to the proper enjoyment of the adjoining land, and with respect to such owner's statutory right to a private crossing.

Rossiter v. Lake Shore, etc., R. Co., 88, 96 (5).

53. *Right of Way.—Rights of Owner of Fee.—Injury to Person on Tracks in Service of Owner of Fee.—Liability.*—Where a railroad company holds only an easement, the landowner has certain rights to the use of the right of way which entitle him to enter thereon when such entry is indispensable in the proper use and occupation of the fee in the adjoining land, so that where the complaint, in an action against a railroad company for the death of a surveyor, alleged that it was necessary for the landowner, in the survey of his lands adjoining the right of way, to take measurements along, across, upon and over defendant's right of way, and that while upon defendant's track in the performance of the work of taking such measurements for the landowner, plaintiff's decedent was killed, it cannot be said, as a matter of law that such use of the tracks was an interference with the superior rights of the railroad company so as to render decedent a trespasser, but the question is one of fact to be determined from the circumstances of the case.

Rossiter v. Lake Shore, etc., R. Co., 88, 93 (4).

54. *Street Railroads.—Right to Cross Tracks of Steam Road.—Priority in Use of Crossing.*—A street railroad company and a steam railroad company are on equal terms in the use of a street except that, on due notice, the steam road has the priority in the use of the crossing, where its tracks are crossed by those of a street car company.

Baltimore, etc., R. Co. v. Cincinnati, etc., St. R. Co., 639, 645 (6).

55. *Street Railroads.—Additional Burden on Streets.—Right to Cross Tracks of Steam Road.*—The use of city streets by a street railway company, with the consent of the common council, does not constitute an additional burden, and it may, subject to no other conditions than those to which the general public is subject, use the street and cross the track of a steam road without the latter's consent.

Baltimore, etc., R. Co. v. Cincinnati, etc., St. R. Co., 639, 644 (4).

56. *Street Railroads.—Crossing Agreement Between Steam and Street Railroads.*—Where a street railway company desires to lay its tracks across those of a steam road, the character of the crossing, and of the materials, appliances and equipment to be used in its construction and maintenance are the proper subjects of contract, since both companies are chargeable with certain duties relative to the safety of the street occasioned by such crossing, and the rights and duties of each with reference thereto, as between themselves, may be specifically defined by contract.

Baltimore, etc., R. Co. v. Cincinnati, etc., St. R. Co., 639, 645 (7).

RAILROADS—Continued.

57. *Street Railroads.—Crossing Agreement Between Steam and Street Railroads.—Consideration.*—The consent of a steam railroad company to cross its tracks at grade on a certain street, does not constitute a sufficient consideration for the promise of a street railroad company to pay for, keep and maintain a watchman at such crossing, if the same should be required, since the steam railroad company could be required to maintain a watchman regardless of whether the street railroad crossed its tracks, and the street railroad company, in obtaining such consent, acquired no right to which it was not already legally entitled.

Baltimore, etc., R. Co. v. *Cincinnati, etc., St. R. Co.,* 639, 643 (3).

RATIFICATION—

Of contract, see PRINCIPAL AND SURETY 2.

REMONSTRANCE—

Time for filing, against vacation of street, see MUNICIPAL CORPORATIONS 7.

REPLEVIN—

1. *Action.—Necessity for Demand.*—Where the possession of goods sought to be replevied was wrongfully obtained, no demand is necessary before bringing the action.

Davis v. *Bryant,* 343, 344 (2).

2. *Proof Essential to Maintain Action.*—To maintain an action in replevin, the plaintiff must show that he has a right to the possession of the property he seeks to recover.

Fife v. *Ohio Investment Co.,* 108, 113 (4).

REPRESENTATIONS—

By vendor, when binding on him, see FRAUD 5.

RES GESTAE—

See EVIDENCE 2; PRINCIPAL AND AGENT 3.

RES IPSA LOQUITUR—

See CARRIERS 7.

RES JUDICATA—

See JUDGMENT 10-12; MUNICIPAL CORPORATIONS 24; PRINCIPAL AND SURETY 3.

RESCISSION—

See SALES 4, 9.

RESIDENCE—

Of mortgagor, see CHATTEL MORTGAGES 1, 2.

REVERSAL—

See APPEAL 148, 149.

REVIEW—

Errors occurring during the trial to be available on, must be saved by assigning them as causes for a new trial, see APPEAL 6; *Davis* v. *Bryant,* 343, 344 (1).

RIGHT OF WAY—

See EMINENT DOMAIN 1-3; RAILROADS 52, 53.

RULES—

Of the Supreme and Appellate Courts have the force and effect of law, see APPEAL 39.

SALES—

1. *Breach of Contract.—Measure of Damages.*—The measure of damages for the seller's failure to deliver goods contracted for, is the difference between the market price and the contract price at the place of delivery on the date of the default.
Ladoga Can. Co. v. Corydon Can. Co., 23, 27 (3).

2. *Contracts.—Offer.—Acceptance.*—Where defendant, by letter to plaintiffs, indicated a desire to sell his corn, both old and new, and asked for prices on both, and plaintiffs replied by stating that they understood that he wanted to sell both the new and old corn, stating the prices that they could give for each kind, based on the day's bid, and requesting an acceptance by return mail, and defendant, instead of accepting by return mail, replied the following day that he would sell the corn on the home farm at the price offered, but that as to the old corn he would like a little more, no valid contract of sale was thereby created, since defendant's acceptance, not being in accordance with the offer, was at most only a partial acceptance of plaintiff's proposition, and not binding upon either party.
Miller v. Sharp, 11, 16 (3), 18 (3).

3. *Breach of Contract.—Verdict.—Answers to Interrogatories.*—In an action against a seller for breach of a contract to deliver 5,000 cases of tomatoes as soon as packed, answers to interrogatories showing that defendant had the 5,000 cases ready for delivery before September 28, that no delivery had been made, except of sample, that on October 10 the market price was higher than the contract price, but failing to show the market price at any other time, are not in conflict with a general verdict awarding plaintiff nominal damages only, since, indulging all presumptions in favor of the general verdict, it means that defendant did not comply with the contract to deliver the tomatoes as soon as packed, and that at the time of the default the market price was no higher than the contract price.
Ladoga Can. Co. v. Corydon Can. Co., 23, 27 (4).

4. *Rescission.—Common-Law Rule.*—The right to return a warranted article and rescind the contract does not exist at common law, except in cases of fraud or where there is a special contract to that effect, and the purchaser is limited in his remedy to a recovery of damages for the breach of warranty.
Nave v. Powell, 496, 504 (2).

5. *Warranty.—Construction Against Warrantor.*—The rule, that an express warranty should be construed most strongly against the party in whose interest the contract was prepared, applies only where there is ambiguity or uncertainty in ascertaining the intent of the parties. *Nave v. Powell, 496, 506 (5).*

6. *Warranty.—Construction.—Intention of Parties.*—In construing an express warranty, the object to be attained is the intention of the parties, and such intention must be ascertained, if possible, by the language used, and not by reading into it words that import an understanding wholly unintended and unexpressed

SALES—Continued.

when the contract was written, but suggested by some apparent hardship in the enforcement thereof. *Nave v. Powell*, 496, 506 (6).

7. *Warranty.—Construction.—Exclusiveness of Remedy.*—A contract of sale, in which the seller of a horse contracted that "in the event the above named stallion, in perfect health with proper usage * * * does not get with foal 50 per cent * * * then on return * * * in good health and condition I agree to furnish another," etc., and which stated that should the stallion thereafter become injured or disabled through accident or disease, the warranty should be null and void and of no effect and all obligations of the seller considered fulfilled and ended, and that the contract contained all the agreements of warranty connected with such sale, construed in its entirety, limits the buyer's remedy for a breach of the warranty, and an action for damages for such breach will not lie.

Nave v. Powell, 496, 506 (7), 508 (7).

8. *Warranty.—Breach.—Limitation of Remedy.*—In a contract of sale, the parties may provide all and entire the remedies contemplated and agreed upon to be applied in the event of a breach of the warranty, in which case they are bound thereby and limited to the remedy, or remedies, so provided.

Nave v. Powell, 496, 505 (4).

9. *Warranty.—Return of Property and Rescission of Contract.—Exclusiveness of Remedy.*—Contracts of sale containing provisions for the return of the property and a rescission of the contract, or for the substitution of other property for that which fails to comply with the warranty, are not treated as exclusive in the remedy provided, unless such intention is clearly expressed by the language and terms of the warranty.

Nave v. Powell, 496, 505 (3).

SET-OFF—

Not affected by the dismissal of the cause of action stated in the complaint, but defendant may proceed to final judgment on the issues tendered by such set-off, see DISMISSAL 2.

SIDEWALKS—

Care of, see MUNICIPAL CORPORATIONS 13-17.

SIGNALS—

On crossings, see RAILROADS 30-32.

STATUTES—

See APPEAL 60; DEATH 4; MUNICIPAL CORPORATIONS 6.

SPECIFIC PERFORMANCE—

1. *Contracts Enforceable.*—Courts of equity will decree the specific performance of a contract only when it is for an adequate consideration, and is in writing, certain and definite in all its provisions, fair and mutual in its terms, and is capable of being performed. *Cline v. Strong*, 286, 287 (1).

2. *Contracts Enforceable.*—In suits for specific performance, the equitable doctrine is that the enforcement must be mutual, and before a vendee is entitled to specific performance, the vendor must likewise be able to compel the acceptance of a deed and the payment of the stipulated consideration.

Cline v. Strong, 286, 290 (3).

SPECIFIC PERFORMANCE—Continued.

3. *Contract for Sale of Real Estate.—Sufficiency.—Right to Enforce.*—A letter from a real estate agency stating that it has, from the owner of certain real estate, an agreement to accept a certain sum for same, if taken on or before a certain date, that it was obtained after an offer made by the addressee, and that the agency would be glad to hold the offer open for the addressee's account until the date specified, together with the addressee's written acceptance, and the agency's receipt for one dollar as earnest money, does not constitute a contract capable of being specifically enforced in a court of equity, since it is uncertain as to terms and time of payment and assumption of liens, and is susceptible of being construed as merely an option.
Cline v. *Strong*, 286, 288 (2).

STREET RAILROADS—

See RAILROADS 50, 54-57.

STREETS—

Defective, see MUNICIPAL CORPORATIONS 10-12.
Duty to light, see MUNICIPAL CORPORATIONS 1.
Excavations of, see MUNICIPAL CORPORATIONS 8, 9.
Use of, see RAILROADS 50.
Vacation of, see MUNICIPAL CORPORATIONS 2-7.

SUBROGATION—

See CHATTEL MORTGAGES 5.
Equitable Rights.—The right of subrogation is an equitable right, and one who asserts such right must act fairly and equitably before the courts will decree in his favor.
Dixon v. *Thompson*, 560, 566 (5).

SURETY—

See PRINCIPAL AND SURETY.

SURFACE WATERS—

See WATERS AND WATERCOURSES 1-3, 12-14.
Drainage of, see WATERS AND WATERCOURSES 2, 3, 5.

TAXATION—

1. *Tax Sales.—Validity.*—To convey title, a tax sale must be in accordance with the statute, and if any essential act has been omitted, or has been improperly done, the sale is ineffectual and insufficient to convey title to the purchaser.
Dixon v. *Thompson*, 560, 563 (1).
2. *Tax Sales.—Place of Sale.—Validity.*—Under §10355 Burns 1908, Acts 1891 p. 199, §184, providing for posting copies of the delinquent list, and also notice that so much of such delinquent lands and lots as may be necessary to discharge the taxes, etc., will be sold at public auction at the courthouse door, etc., and §10380 Burns 1908, Acts 1891 p. 191, §206, providing the form of tax deed, the failure to conduct a tax sale at the courthouse door renders such sale invalid and the tax deed will not convey a good and sufficient title.
Dixon v. *Thompson*, 560, 564 (2).
3. *Tax Sales.—Invalid Sales.—Rights of Purchaser.*—Under the provisions of §§10388, 10394 Burns 1908, Acts 1901 p. 366, §§1, 3,

TAXATION—Continued.

where a conveyance of land for taxes is invalid, the lien for taxes, which the State had prior to the sale, is transferred to the purchaser at such sale and he becomes subrogated to all of the rights of the State therein, and such right of lien remains a charge against the land until the taxes, interest and penalty, are actually repaid to him, or until such time as the lien grows into an absolute title. *Dixon* v. *Thompson*, 560, 564 (3).

4. *Tax Sales.—Invalid Sales.—Priority of Lien Over Lien for Street Improvement.—Estoppel.*—Although by §8714 Burns 1908, Acts 1905 p. 219, §109, relating to special assessments for street improvements, it is provided that liens for such special assessments shall have precedence over all liens except taxes, where a purchaser of a lot at a tax sale, holding a tax deed regular on its face, and having knowledge of irregularities in conducting the sale which rendered same invalid, remained silent after notice of the adoption of a resolution for the improvement of the street on which such lot abuts, and did not disclose that he was not the absolute owner of such lot until after the improvement was made and suit was brought to foreclose the assessment lien, he thereby waived the superiority of the lien for taxes, and is estopped from setting up the defect in his title to defeat the lien for such assessment *Dixon* v. *Thompson*, 560, 565 (4), 567 (4)

TAX SALES—

Invalid, see TAXATION 3, 4.
Validity of, see TAXATION 1, 2.

TENANCY IN COMMON—

1. *Transactions Concerning Common Property.*—One who deals with a tenant in common, in regard to the common property, does so at his peril. *Weidenhammer* v. *McAdams*, 98, 103 (5).

2. *Nature of Interests.*—The interests of tenants in common are several, and not joint, and ordinarily neither tenant can bind the estate or person of the other by any act in relation to the common property, not previously authorized or subsequently ratified. *Weidenhammer* v. *McAdams*, 98, 102 (2).

3. *Incumbrances.—Payments.—Presumptions.*—Where a mortgage existing on land held by a father and son as tenants in common as heirs of the mother, bound the mortgagors personally to pay the mortgage debt, and the father had joined the mother in the execution of such mortgage, it will be presumed that payments made by him, after the vesting of the tenancy in common, were made in fulfillment of such personal agreement to pay, rather than to relieve the common estate of the burden of the mortgage lien. *Weidenhammer* v. *McAdams*, 98, 104 (8).

TRIAL.

I. RECEPTION OF EVIDENCE, 1, 2.
II. ARGUMENT AND CONDUCT OF COUNSEL, 3.
III. DIRECTION OF VERDICT, 4, 5.
IV. INSTRUCTIONS, 6-20.
V. ANSWERS TO INTERROGATORIES, 21-24.

VI. SPECIAL FINDINGS AND CONCLUSIONS OF LAW, 25-28.
VII. VERDICT, 29-41.
VIII. WAIVER AND CORRECTION OF IRREGULARITIES AND ERRORS, 42.

Errors occurring during, to be available, must be saved by assigning them as causes for a new trial, see APPEAL 6; *Davis* v. *Bryant*, 343, 344 (1).

TRIAL—Continued.

I. Reception of Evidence.

1. *Reception of Evidence.—Objections.—Time.—*Where a question asked a witness is of such character as to indicate that its answer will divulge matter that is incompetent, an objection to be available, should be interposed before the answer is made.
Craig v. *Zent,* 19, 22 (3).

2. *Reception of Evidence.—Discretion of Court.—*Where, in an action on an insurance certificate, plaintiff rested her case without having shown that proofs of death had been made as provided for in the certificate, the action of the court in permitting plaintiff to reopen the case and introduce such proof and other evidence, after defendant had asked for a peremptory instruction, was a matter within the discretion of the trial court, and not erroneous.
Modern Woodmen v. *Jones,* 149, 150 (2), 151 (2).

II. Argument and Conduct of Counsel.

3. *Argument. — Statement of Counsel. — Objection. — Motion. —*Where a party objects to a statement made by counsel in argument, a part of which is proper and warranted by evidence, he should direct his motion to the objectionable part and not to the whole statement.
Southern R. Co. v. *Adams,* 322, 329 (5).

III. Direction of Verdict.

4. *Direction of Verdict for Plaintiff.—When Authorized.—*Where the evidence to support the material averments of the complaint is documentary and clearly makes out a case for plaintiff, and is susceptible of no other inference, and there is no evidence to contradict it or to establish a defense, an instruction to find for the plaintiff is proper.
Modern Woodmen v. *Jones,* 149, 151 (5).

5. *Directed Verdict.—*The trial court may direct a verdict for defendant only where the evidence most favorable to the plaintiff, together with all reasonable and legitimate inferences that a jury might draw therefrom, is clearly insufficient to establish one or more facts essential to plaintiff's right of action.
Patterson v. *Southern R. Co.,* 618, 620 (1).

IV. Instructions.

See Appeal 33, 55, 65-82, 92, 107, 125-131; Carriers 4, 10-12, 16; Death 2; Fraud 3; Landlord and Tenant 5; Master and Servant 5, 6, 39, 41, 48; Principal and Agent 4, 16; Railroads 9-12, 39, 44, 46, 47; Waters and Watercourses 8.

Refusal of, see Appeal 71-80.

No question is presented on appeal as to where such instructions are not brought into the record by a bill of exceptions, see Appeal 29.

6. *Construction.—*Instructions should all be construed together and not separately.
I. F. Force Handle Co. v. *Hisey,* 235, 247 (9).

7. *Repetition of Principles.—*It is not necessary that the rules or principles contained in instructions should be repeated in different language.
Mortimer v. *Daub,* 30, 39 (11).

8. *Invading Province of Jury.—*Instructions are properly refused, which, if given, would invade the province of the jury.
Heston v. *Dougan,* 40, 51 (11).

TRIAL—Continued.

9. *Refusal.*—The refusal of requested instructions on questions fully covered by the instructions given, is proper.
Cleveland, etc., R. Co. v. Van Laningham, 156, 169 (13).

10. *Refusal of Instructions.*—The refusal of requested instructions that are covered by other instructions given is not error.
Southern R. Co. v. Adams, 322, 330 (9).

11. *Refusal.*—It is error to refuse requested instructions that state the law correctly, if they are not fully covered by the instructions given. *Pittsburgh, etc., R. Co. v. Cottman*, 661, 666 (6).

12. *Incomplete General Instruction.*—A general instruction when incomplete, but correct as far as it goes, may be completed by other instructions. *Angola, R., etc., Co. v. Butz*, 420, 430 (13).

13. *Incorporating Complaint.*—The incorporation of the whole complaint in an instruction to the jury, while not to be commended, is not ground for reversal.
Angola R., etc., Co. v. Butz, 420, 430 (12).

14. *Negligence.*—Instructions on the question of negligence should apply only to the negligence charged in the complaint, where the acts charged are definite and specific.
Cleveland, etc., R. Co. v. Van Laningham, 156, 169 (12).

15. *Refusal.*—An instruction open to criticism on account of being inaccurate, ambiguous, uncertain or misleading, may be properly refused, even when its giving might not constitute reversible error. *Indianapolis Southern R. Co. v. Emmerson*, 403, 415 (9).

16. *Conflicting Evidence.—Assumption of Facts.—Refusal.*—A requested instruction stating that the evidence shows certain facts, where the evidence as to such facts is conflicting, invades the province of the jury and is properly refused.
Indianapolis Southern R. Co. v. Emmerson, 403, 415 (10).

17. *Assumption of Facts.*—An instruction in a personal injury action, that if the jury finds for plaintiff, it becomes its duty to assess his damages at such sum as the evidence relating thereto shows him to be entitled, not exceeding the sum of $15,000, and that the elements of damage which the jury may consider consist of all the effects of the injury complained of, if any, as shown by the evidence relating thereto, is not objectionable as assuming the truth of facts in issue, or that certain facts have been proved.
I. F. Force Handle Co. v. Hisey, 235, 248 (10).

18. *Confidential Relation of Physician and Patient.*—In an action for personal injuries, an instruction is not objectionable which states that the law recognizes the relation of physician and patient as confidential, and that a physician is not competent to testify to matters communicated to him by the patient in the course of his professional services, if the privilege is claimed by the patient, and that plaintiff's failure to call such physician as a witness should not influence the verdict.
Mortimer v. Daub, 30, 39 (12).

19. *Burden of Proof.*—Instructions informing the jury that the burden is on plaintiff to establish the material allegations of his complaint, and that plaintiff cannot recover if the evidence is evenly balanced on any proposition which he is bound to show by a preponderance of the evidence, telling the jury that the burden is on defendant to prove the material allegations of his affirmative answer, and that if he has not done so he must fail, and stating what is meant by the preponderance of the evidence, correctly state the law. *Heston v. Dougan*, 40, 50 (9).

TRIAL—Continued.

20. *Contributory Negligence.*—In an action for personal injuries where contributory negligence is a defense, an instruction which tells the jury that the burden is on defendant to prove contributory negligence, that such proof may be made under the general denial, and that in order to render such defense available it must be proved by a fair preponderance of all the evidence in the case, is not open to the objection that would lead the jury to believe that contributory negligence could be proved only by the evidence produced by defendant.
Pittsburgh, etc., R. Co. v. *Cottman,* 661, 665 (4).

V. Answers to Interrogatories.

See *post* 29-40.

See Appeal 90, 91, 99-108; Carriers 8, 15; Master and Servant 15, 17-19, 21-23, 32; Municipal Corporations 9; Railroads 4, 20, 21; Sales 3; Waters and Watercourses 9.

Motion for judgment on, see Master and Servant 28.

21. *Interrogatories to Jury.*—*Interrogatories Calling for Conclusions.*—Interrogatories to the jury calling for legal conclusions are objectionable. *Southern R. Co.* v. *Utz,* 270, 277 (6).

22. *Contradictory Answers.*—*Effect.*—Where the answers to interrogatories returned by the jury are contradictory, they nullify each other and are rendered ineffective.
Lake Shore, etc., R. Co. v. *Myers,* 59, 68 (8).

23. *Motion for Judgment.*—*Grounds.*—The fact that the jury's answers to interrogatories are not consistent with the evidence, or with each other, furnishes no ground for sustaining a motion for judgment thereon.
Indianapolis Southern R. Co. v. *Emmerson,* 403, 416 (12).

24. *Conclusions of Law.*—Interrogatories to the jury asking whether defendant had a right to alter and repair the elevator on which plaintiff was injured, or to inspect it, were improper and the answers involved conclusions of law.
National Biscuit Co. v. *Wilson,* 630, 638 (4).

VI. Special Findings and Conclusions of Law.

See Appeal 52, 53, 88, 89, 111-116; Injunction 6; Limitation of Actions 6, 9.

25. *Special Findings.*—*Failure to Find Material Fact.*—*Effect.*— The failure to find a material fact, of which the burden of proof is on the plaintiff, is equivalent to a finding against plaintiff as to such fact. *Town of Cicero* v. *Lake Erie, etc., R. Co.,* 298, 309 (8).

26. *Special Findings.*—*Failure to Find Material Fact.*—*Effect.*— Where a special finding of facts is made, the failure to find a material fact is the equivalent of finding such fact against the party having the burden of proving the same.
State, ex rel., v. *Jackson,* 254, 260 (8).

27. *Special Findings.*—*Conclusions of Law.*—In an action to enjoin the enforcement of an execution, where the special findings show that a judgment had been rendered, but that the order book entry had not been read in open court and signed, a conclusion of law that such judgment is valid, but that no execution may issue thereon until the record is read and signed in open

TRIAL—Continued.

court, is not inconsistent with a conclusion that the enforcement
of the existing execution should be enjoined.
Pittsburgh, etc., R. Co. v. *Johnson,* 457, 468 (5).

28. *Conclusions of Law.—Conformity to Issues.*—The conclusions
of law announced by the trial court are not improper, where they
are within the issues tendered by a cross-complaint and the
answer thereto, although they may be outside the issues tendered
by the complaint. *Pittsburgh, etc., R. Co.* v. *Johnson,* 457, 467 (3).

VII. VERDICT.

See APPEAL 47-51, 89-91, 93-104, 147; CARRIERS 8, 15; INSURANCE
15; MASTER AND SERVANT 15, 17-19, 20-23, 28, 32; MUNICIPAL
CORPORATIONS 9; PRINCIPAL AND AGENT 8; RAILROADS 4, 5, 20, 21;
SALES 3; WATERS AND WATERCOURSES 9.

Refusal to direct, see APPEAL 51.

29. *Answers to Interrogatories.—Inconsistent Answers.*—A general
verdict is not overcome by answers to interrogatories which are
in themselves inconsistent and contradictory.
Southern R. Co. v. *Utz,* 270, 279 (8).

30. *Answers to Interrogatories.*—A general verdict must stand,
unless the answers to interrogatories are in such irreconcilable
conflict with it, as to be beyond the possibility of removal by any
evidence legitimately admissible under the issues.
Cleveland, etc., R. Co. v. *Rumsey,* 371, 375 (4).

31. *Answers to Interrogatories.—Judgment.*—To authorize a judgment on the facts found by answers to interrogatories, such facts
must be sufficient to overcome any evidence legitimately admissible under the issues. *Osborn* v. *Adams Brick Co.,* 175, 182 (3).

32. *Answers to Interrogatories.—Presumptions.*—Every reasonable
presumption is indulged in favor of the general verdict, and nothing is presumed in favor of the answers to the interrogatories.
Osborn v. *Adams Brick Co.,* 175, 182 (2).

33. *Answers to Interrogatories.—Control of General Verdict.*—
Where the jury's answers to interrogatories are in irreconcilable
conflict with any fact or facts of the complaint, essential to recovery, the general verdict must yield to the facts found by such
answers. *Columbia Creosoting Co.* v. *Beard,* 260, 263 (3).

34. *Answers to Interrogatories.*—A general verdict is overcome by
answers to interrogatories only when they exclude every reasonable hypothesis consistent with the verdict which might have
been proven under the issues.
Cleveland, etc., R. Co. v. *Van Laningham,* 156, 166 (8).

35. *Answers to Interrogatories.—Motion for Judgment.*—A motion
for judgment on the answers to interrogatories can only be sustained where the facts thereby found are in irreconcilable conflict with the general verdict.
Osborn v. *Adams Brick Co.,* 175, 182 (1).

36. *Special Findings.*—Under §573 Burns 1908, §547 R. S. 1881, the
special finding of facts controls the general verdict only when
inconsistent therewith, and the general verdict must stand where
the special finding can be reconciled with it under any state of
facts provable under the issues.
Marion, etc., Construction Co. v. *Claycomb,* 681, 683 (1).

TRIAL—Continued.

37. *Answers to Interrogatories.—Presumptions.*—To support a general verdict for plaintiff, as against the facts found by the answers to interrogatories, every intendment and presumption that plaintiff has proved the allegations of his complaint constituting a cause of action will be indulged.
Columbia Creosoting Co. v. *Beard,* 200, 262 (2).

38. *Answers to Interrogatories.*—A general verdict will not be set aside on the answers to interrogatories, unless there is an apparent conflict between it and such answers that cannot be reconciled on any theory, or on any supposable state of facts provable under the issues, whether actually proved or not.
Southern R. Co. v. *Utz,* 270, 279 (9).

39. *Answers to Interrogatories.*—A general verdict will stand, as against the jury's answers to interrogatories, where the facts specially found are not inconsistent therewith, or where the verdict and the special findings can be reconciled with each other under any state of facts provable under the issues.
Ladoga Can. Co. v. *Corydon Can. Co.,* 23, 26 (1).

40. *Answers to Interrogatories.*—On a motion for judgment on answers to interrogatories notwithstanding the general verdict, all reasonable intendments are taken in favor of the general verdict, and no intendments are made in favor of the moving party, and, in order to grant such motion, the special findings must be in such conflict with the general verdict that the two cannot be reconciled. *I. F. Force Handle Co.* v. *Hisey,* 235, 242 (4).

41. *Effect.*—A general verdict for plaintiff is a finding that every material averment of the complaint was proved.
Southern R. Co. v. *Utz,* 270, 272 (2).

VIII. WAIVER AND CORRECTION OF IRREGULARITIES AND ERRORS.

42. *Evidence.—Weight and Sufficiency.—Credibility of Witnesses. —Province of Jury.—Motion for New Trial.—Duty of Trial Court.*—While a question of fact, where the evidence is conflicting, should be submitted to the jury, and the weight of the evidence and the credibility of the witnesses are questions to be passed on by the jury in arriving at a verdict, it is the duty of the trial court, after verdict, on a motion for new trial on the ground that the evidence is insufficient to sustain the verdict, to weigh the evidence and consider the credibility of the witnesses in determining whether the jury has arrived at a correct result.
Pittsburgh, etc., R. Co. v. *Cottman,* 661, 670 (12).

TRUSTS—

1. *Creation.—Creation by Parol.*—A trust in personal property may be created by parol. *Camp* v. *Camp,* 250, 253 (5).

2. *Creation.—Wills.—Construction.*—A bequest of a note for the express purpose of building a New Jerusalem Hall and Library on the lot devised by testator to his brother, with direction that the note be paid out of the first moneys derived from the estate does not create a trust in personalty.
General Convention, etc., v. *Smith,* 136, 137 (2).

3. *Creation.—Wills.—Complaint.—Sufficiency.*—A complaint alleging that a bequest of a note for $2,000 had been made by a testator for the purpose of erecting a New Jerusalem Hall and Library for the benefit of plaintiffs on a lot devised by the testator to his brother, and that such brother used the proceeds of the note

TRUSTS—Continued.

in erecting a hall and library on such lot, which was used by plaintiffs for about twenty years, but not averring that it was testator's intention that the title to the property should ever pass to plaintiffs, or that testator's brother ever promised him to convey such title to plaintiffs, and not showing that the alleged trust was to continue for any definite or indefinite period of time, is insufficient on demurrer, since, if any trust is shown to have been created, it is not shown that the same has not been fully terminated.   *General Convention, etc.*, v. *Smith*, 136, 138 (3).

4. *Establishment.—Parol Evidence.*—The rule that a trust in an absolute legacy may be shown by parol applies only in case of actual or constructive fraud.
                                 General Convention, etc., v. *Smith*, 136, 138 (4).

5. *Establishment.—Parol Evidence.*—Where money is intrusted in parol to one person to be invested in real estate for the benefit of another, a volunteer, such volunteer cannot, in the absence of fraud, enforce such trust.
                                 General Convention, etc., v. *Smith*, 136, 139 (5).

6. *Establishment.—Complaint.—Sufficiency.*—A complaint to declare a trust in relation to real estate is insufficient under §4012 Burns 1908, §2969 R. S. 1881, where no writing, on which the action should be founded, is filed with or made a part thereof.
                                 General Convention, etc., v. *Smith*, 136, 137 (1).

7. *Power of Trustees.—Execution of Power.*—The right of surviving trustees of a testamentary trust to terminate the trust is not dependent on any order of court, where, under the terms of the will, they have authority to exercise the discretionary power therein conferred of terminating the same.
                                 Cooley v. *Kelley*, 687, 697 (13).

8. *Power of Trustees.—Survival of Power.—Intention of Donor.*—The intention of the donor as to the survival of the power conferred in creating a trust will be followed. when such intention can be reasonably ascertained from the instrument, but no construction will be indulged which would result in any serious impairment of the donor's intention, or leave the trust imperfectly executed. ·   *Cooley* v. *Kelley*, 687, 700 (15).

9. *Power of Trustees.—Survival of Power.—Intention of Donor.*—The presumption that every power coupled with an interest was given *ex officio*, and meant to survive, will not be excluded on the ground that the power conferred is one of special trust and confidence in the trustees as individuals, so as to defeat, on the death of one of the trustees named in a testamentary trust, the survival of the power to terminate the trust when, in their judgment, such termination would be to the best interest of the *cestui que trust*, unless the clear and apt language of the instrument imports a contrary intention.   *Cooley* v. *Kelley*, 687, 701 (16).

10. *Trustee and Cestui Que Trust.—Judgments.—Conclusiveness.*—A *cestui que trust* is privy to his trustee, and an order made or judgment rendered affecting the *res* of the trust is binding on the *cestui* without notice, where the trustee is in court and the court has jurisdiction of the subject-matter.
                                 Cooley v. *Kelley*, 687, 696 (11).

11. *Trustees.—Power Coupled with Interest.—Survival of Power.*—Where a will bequeathed certain property to trustees to pay the income to a named beneficiary, and gave them discretionary power to pay over the principal and terminate the trust if in

TRUSTS—Continued.

their opinion, it would be to the best interest of the *cestui que trust*, the power conferred was not a naked power, but was a power coupled with an interest, since the trustees held the legal title to the *res* of the trust, and on the death of one of the trustees, such power survives and may be executed by those remaining. *Cooley* v. *Kelley*, 687, 698 (14).

VACATION—

Appeal, when regarded as such, see APPEAL 16.

In a, appeal, all those against whom a judgment has been rendered, either in *rem* or *personam*, or who, in any manner are bound or affected thereby, must be made coappellants, see APPEAL 11.

VENDOR AND PURCHASER—

Vendor's Lien.—Issues.—Evidence.—In an action to enforce a vendor's lien, the plaintiff, under the issues formed by the general denial, must prove that the vendee is still indebted for some part of the purchase price. *Fuller* v. *Fuller*, 488, 490 (5).

VENIRE DE NOVO—

Overruling a motion for a, is not error where the finding is general, since the motion reaches only matters of form, and can only be sustained when the finding is so defective and uncertain that no judgment can be rendered thereon, see APPEAL 114.

VESTED RIGHTS—

An heir has no, to inherit the property of the ancestor, see DESCENT AND DISTRIBUTION 1.

VENUE—

1. *Action Brought in Wrong County.—Waiver of Objection.*— Where an action is brought in the wrong county, and defendant is lawfully served with notice of the pendency of the action, the question of jurisdiction is waived by permitting a default to be taken, under §348 Burns 1908, §343 R. S. 1881, providing that an objection that the action is brought in the wrong county shall be deemed waived, if not taken by answer or demurrer.
   Swain v. *Hunt*, 626, 628 (3).

2. *Joinder of Several Defendants.—Answer in Abatement.—Sufficiency.*—Under §315 Burns 1908, §312 R. S. 1881, authorizing an action against two or more defendants, jointly liable in the county where either resides, jurisdiction is not acquired by a defendant against whom plaintiff has a cause of action, in an action brought in a county of which he is not a resident, by joining him as a codefendant with a person residing where the action is brought, but against whom plaintiff has no cause of action, so that an answer showing that jurisdiction of a defendant could not have been acquired by the service of summons in the county where the action was brought, and that the other defendant, who resided in such county, was not in any way indebted to plaintiff on the cause of action stated in the complaint, stated facts sufficient to abate the action.
   Moore-Mansfield, etc., Co. v. *Marion, etc., Traction Co.*, 548, 558 (12).

VICE PRINCIPAL—

See MASTER AND SERVANT 9.

WAIVER—

See Appeal 30-32, 41-44, 62; Bonds 3; Fraud 2; Insurance 9-11, 18; Judges 1; Venue 1.

Of tort, see Principal and Agent 1.

Of ground of abatement, see Pleading 23.

Of privilege, see Witnesses 3-5.

WARRANTY—

See Sales 5-9.

Breach of, see Contracts 15.

Implied, see Partition 3.

WATERS AND WATERCOURSES—

1. *Drainage of Surface Water.—Easement.—Extent of Right.—* Even if one has acquired an easement to flow water from a pond through a ditch on his land into a channel on the land of an adjoining owner, such right will not authorize him to wrongfully accumulate additional water and turn it through such ditch onto the lands of such adjoining owner.
Gaskill v. *Barnett*, 654, 660 (8).

2. *Drainage of Surface Water.—Answer Showing Easement by Prescription.—Sufficiency.—* In an action for injury to land by the drainage of surface water thereon, an answer showing an open, notorious, exclusive and adverse possession and use of the drains complained of for thirty years, with the right to flow water through the same across plaintiff's land during all that time, is sufficient as an answer showing an easement by prescription.
Seigmund v. *Tyner*, 581, 585 (5).

3. *Drainage of Surface Water.—Rights of Purchaser With Notice.* —In an action for damages in overflowing plaintiff's land, the fact that defendant's drains were constructed and in use by and with the consent of all the owners of the lands affected, long before plaintiff purchased his real estate, and that he purchased with full knowledge of such fact and of defendant's easement or right to flow water across such land, constitutes a good defense.
Seigmund v. *Tyner*, 581, 585 (6).

4. *Natural Watercourse.—* A natural watercourse is a channel, cut through the turf by the erosion of running water, with well defined banks and bottom, through which water flows, and has flowed immemorially, not necessarily all the time, but ordinarily, and permanently for substantial periods of each year.
Gaskill v. *Barnett*, 654, 658 (1).

5. *Natural Watercourse.—Drainage of Surface Water.—Artificial Channels.—* The same line of discharge of water in times of heavy rains or melting snows, from a pond created by the natural assembling of surface water, does not constitute a natural watercourse, and neither does an artificial channel, constructed solely for the purpose of expediting surface drainage, which is employed but occasionally and temporarily in carrying away an excess of surface water caused by heavy rains or melting snows.
Gaskill v. *Barnett*, 654, 658 (3).

6. *Natural Watercourse.—Artificial Drains.—* While it is the law that a natural watercourse, which is lost in a swamp or lake and emerges therefrom at a lower level in a well defined channel, does not cease to be a watercourse because it passes through such swamp or lake, the rule is not applicable to a drain which leads

WATERS AND WATERCOURSES—Continued.

into and emerges from a pond, so as to render one who closes the same liable for the obstruction of a natural watercourse, although in addition to surface drainage it carries the water from springs located above such pond, where it is shown that such pond was closed by the natural elevation of the land and had no connection with such springs, nor with a natural channel and bayou to the south, and that prior to the construction of such drain water stood in such pond until evaporated.
Gaskill v. *Barnett*, 654, 659 (5).

7. *Obstruction.—Permanent Injury to Land.—Trial.—Exclusion of Evidence.*—In the trial of an action on the theory of permanent injury to land caused by the obstruction of a natural watercourse, testimony in support of any other theory was properly excluded. *Southern R. Co.* v. *Friedley*, 192, 196 (3).

8. *Obstruction.—Permanent Injury to Land.—Damages.—Instructions.*—Where an action was based on the theory of a permanent injury to land by the obstruction of a natural watercourse, instructions, that the measure of damages was the depreciation in the rental value of the land, were properly refused.
Southern R. Co. v. *Friedley*, 192, 196 (4).

9. *Obstruction.—Permanent Injury to Land.—Verdict.—Answers to Interrogatories.*—In an action based on the theory of permanent injury to land caused by the obstruction of a natural watercourse, where there was evidence that defendants had placed piles so as to deflect the stream and cut plaintiff's bank, and had allowed the bed to become partially filled with stone and debris, thereby casting the water onto plaintiff's land and causing the same to cut, wash away, and cave in, answers to interrogatories showing that a large portion of the damage to plaintiff's property was caused by natural overflow, and that part of it was done by cutting, are not in irreconcilable conflict with a general verdict for plaintiff. *Southern R. Co.* v. *Friedley*, 192, 197 (7).

10. *Obstruction.—Injury to Property.—Complaint.—Sufficiency.*—A complaint in substance alleging that by the wrongful acts and negligence of defendants in obstructing a natural watercourse, excavations were washed in plaintiff's land, crops growing thereon were destroyed, the soil was washed away, the fertility of the land was destroyed, and that the stream was changed from its natural channel onto plaintiff's land, shows a complete loss or destruction of a part of plaintiff's land, and was sufficient on the theory of a permanent injury.
Southern R. Co. v. *Friedley*, 192, 195 (2).

11. *Overflowing Land.—Actions.—Evidence.—Sufficiency.*—In an action for damages in overflowing plaintiff's land, evidence showing that from time immemorial water collected in small, well-defined, branch streams on defendant's land and was carried over a portion of plaintiff's land and emptied into an ancient natural watercourse flowing through said land, that defendant placed certain tile ditches which empty into said branch streams on his land, and that no more water was emptied into said branch streams and carried over plaintiff's land into said watercourse than formerly resulted from the natural drainage of the land, is sufficient to support a finding and judgment for defendant.
Seigmund v. *Tyner*, 581, 586 (7).

12. *Surface Waters.*—The rules relating to watercourses are not applicable to surface currents that do not follow a designated and known channel. *Gaskill* v. *Barnett*, 654, 658 (2).

WATERS AND WATERCOURSES—Continued.

13. *Surface Waters.*—Surface water is a common enemy which every proprietor may fight and ward off his premises by dams, embankments or other available means constructed or used on his own property. .   *Gaskill* v. *Barnett*, 654, 659 (4).

14. *Surface Waters.—Obstruction.*—Where, in an action for the obstruction of a drain, it is shown that the former owner of defendant's land opened a channel from a basin on his land to connect with a gulley a short distance south of his north line, and that the owner north of such line made a ditch down to the line to connect with such basin, and that each owner from time to time cleaned out the channel on his land, such facts, in the absence of some agreement at the time the channel was made, do not establish an easement by which the plaintiff may flow water through the channel on defendant's land, but merely show a permissive use.   *Gaskill* v. *Barnett*, 654, 659 (6).

WIDOWS—

Election by, see WILLS 3, 4.

WIFE—

Right of rents accruing after death of subsequent, see DESCENT AND DISTRIBUTION 2.

Rights of children of intestate on death of surviving subsequent, see DESCENT AND DISTRIBUTION 3, 4.

WILLS—

See TRUSTS 2, 3.

1. *Contracts to Bequeath or Devise.—Breach.—Remedy.*—Where a person has fully performed his contract to perform services and board and care for another during his lifetime, in consideration of the other's promise to will all his property to him, he may, upon the failure of the other party to leave such a will in force at his death, recover as damages for such breach the reasonable value of the services rendered under such contract.
.   *Paul* v. *Snyder*, 291, 295 (3).

2. *Contracts to Bequeath or Devise.—Evidence.—Sufficiency.*—Evidence showing that shortly after plaintiff moved onto the farm of decedent, he and the decedent went together to a justice of the peace, where a will was prepared by decedent by which he devised and bequeathed to plaintiff and his heirs all his real and personal property, and that at that time decedent said he wanted plaintiff and his heirs to have his property, that he loved plaintiff and his children and wanted them to have his farm, and that he wanted plaintiff to come and run it until he died and take care of him in his old age, was sufficient to warrant the jury in drawing an inference that the will was made in consideration of an agreement on the part of plaintiff to move on decedent's farm and run it so long as decedent lived, and to take care of him in his old age.   *Paul* v. *Snyder*, 291, 293 (1).

3. *Election by Widow.—Statutory Allowance.—Intention of Testator.*—The intention of a testator, that a specific testamentary provision for his widow shall be in lieu of her rights under the statute, need not be declared in so many words, but may be deduced or implied, when the enforcement of the widow's claim under the law would be plainly inconsistent with the will.
                    Manning v. *Wilson*, 1, 4 (2).

WILLS—Continued.

4. *Election by Widow.—Effect.—Right to Statutory Allowance.—* Where a husband has made specific testamentary provision for his widow, more valuable or more acceptable than that which the law gives her, and has disposed of the remainder of his estate in such a manner as to evince a clear intention to limit the interest of his widow to the provision so made for her, and she elects to take under the will, she will be bound by such election and can not claim the $500 allowance provided by §2786 Burns 1908, §2269 R. S. 1881. *Manning v. Wilson,* 1, 3 (1).

5. *Intention of Testator.—Provision for Widow.—Statutory Allowance.—* Whether a testator intended that a specific testamentary provision for his widow should be in lieu of her rights under the statute, so that an election to take under the will would deprive her of the $500 allowance provided by §2786 Burns 1908, §2269 R. S. 1881, must be gathered from the testament itself, and the fact that the estate is solvent, and that land devised to testator's children had been sold prior to the widow's action to recover such statutory allowance, cannot be considered.
Manning v. Wilson, 1, 5 (3).

WITNESSES—

Credibility of, see APPEAL 87.

1. *Cross-Examination.—Matter Not Brought Out on Direct Examination.—* A question, on the cross-examination of a witness, as to a matter not brought out on direct examination is properly refused. *Cleveland, etc., R. Co. v. Clark,* 646, 652 (8).

2. *Examination.—Cross-Examination.—Evidence.—* While ordinarily a statement against the interest of a party, made in his absence, is not admissible as evidence against him, where, in an action for damages, defendant's attorney elicited from plaintiff on cross-examination part of a conversation had between such attorney and plaintiff, relative to the damage to certain articles, exclusive of plaintiff's horse, it was proper on the redirect examination to show what was further said in relation to the same subject, although it was also thereby shown that defendant's attorney had told plaintiff he ought to have $100 for the damage to his horse. *Craig v. Zent,* 19, 20 (2).

3. *Communications to Physician.—Waiver of Privilege.—* The privilege conferred by §520 Burns 1908, §497 R. S. 1881, on communications by a patient to his physician, may be waived by the patient, or by those who stand in his place, or are authorized to represent him. *Studabaker v. Faylor,* 171, 172 (1).

4. *Competency.—Privileged Communications.—Communications to Physicians.—Waiver of Privilege.—Failure to Object.—* The privilege conferred by §520 Burns 1908, §497 R. S. 1881, on communications by a patient to his physician, is waived where the witness has been permitted without objection to testify at a former trial as to matters learned in such communications.
Studabaker v. Faylor, 171, 172 (2).

5. *Privileged Communications.—Communications to Physician.—Waiver.—Persons Entitled to Waive Privilege.—* The right to waive the privilege of confidential communications after the death of the patient, in litigation affecting the estate, is lodged in those who represent and stand in the place of decedent, and the waiver may be express, or implied from the conduct of such persons in standing by and permitting the testimony to be given without objection. *Studabaker v. Faylor,* 171, 174 (4).

WORDS AND PHRASES—

"Duty" when not the statement of a conclusion, see MASTER AND SERVANT 44; *Angola R., etc., Co.* v. *Butz,* 420, 428 (7).

"*Dynamo.*"—A dynamo is a machine for generating or converting mechanical energy into electricity.

Angola R., etc., Co. v. *Butz,* 420, 424 (2).

A plant for the generation of electricity is a "manufacturing establishment," as contemplated by the factory act, see ELECTRICITY; *Angola R., etc., Co.,* v. *Butz,* 420, 424 (4).

"*Proper.*"—The word "proper" is a usual word in pleadings to show ordinary and sufficient means of ingress to and egress from property.   *Southern R. Co.* v. *Town of French Lick,* 447, 454 (7).

WRITTEN INSTRUMENTS—

In the absence of a showing of fraud or mistake, parol evidence is not admissible to annul or substantially vary the terms of a written instrument, see EVIDENCE 12.

Lightning Source UK Ltd.
Milton Keynes UK
UKHW012135170119
335727UK00008B/254/P